Mass units

pounds × 16	= ounces
ounces × 0.0625	= pounds
ounces × 28.35	= grams
grams × 0.0353	= ounces
pounds × 0.454	= kilograms
kilograms × 2.205	= pounds
short tons × 2000	= pounds
pounds × 0.0005	= short tons
long tons (metric tons) × 1000	= kilograms
kilograms × 0.001	= long tons (metric tons)
short tons × 0.907	= metric tons
metric tons × 1.10	= short tons
milligrams × 0.001	= grams
grams × 1000	= milligrams
micrograms × 0.000001	= grams
grams × 1,000,000	= micrograms
nannograms × 0.000000001	= grams
grams × 1,000,000,000	= nannograms

Energy units

horsepower × 745.7 = watts
Btu × 0.293 — watt-hours
kilowatt-hours × 3416 = Btu

One quad is one quadrillion Btu or 10^{15} Btu.
One pound of coal yields 13,000 Btu when burned.
One kilogram of coal yields 28,600 Btu when burned.
One metric ton of coal yields 28.6 million Btu when burned.
One pound of coal burned in a 40%-efficient electric power plant
　　yields 1.52 kilowatt-hours of electrical energy.
One barrel of oil yields 5.5 million Btu when burned.
One billion barrels of oil yields 5.5 Quads when burned.
One ton of oil = approximately 300 gallons
　　　　　　　 = approximately 7 barrels
One cubic foot of natural gas yields 1,032 Btu when burned.

Units used in water resources

million acre-feet × 1.23	= cubic kilometers
cubic kilometers × 0.813	= million acre-feet
million acre-feet per year × 0.893	= billion gallons per day
billion gallons per day × 1.12	= million acre-feet per year

Concentration units

milligrams/liter	= parts per million (ppm)
grams/liter × 1000	= parts per million (ppm)
ppm × 0.001	= grams/liter
micrograms/liter (μg/l)	= parts per billion (ppb)
grams/liter × 1,000,000	= parts per billion (ppb)
ppb × 0.000001	= grams/liter
nannograms/liter (ng/l)	= parts per trillion (ppt)
grams/liter × 1,000,000,000	= parts per trillion (ppt)
ppt × 0.000000001	= grams/liter

THE GLOBAL ENVIRONMENT
Securing a Sustainable Future

Penelope ReVelle
Essex Community College and
The Johns Hopkins University

Charles ReVelle
The Johns Hopkins University

JONES AND BARTLETT PUBLISHERS

BOSTON   LONDON

This book is printed on recycled, acid-free paper.

Editorial, Sales, and Customer Service Offices:

Jones and Bartlett Publishers, Inc.
One Exeter Plaza
Boston, MA 02116

Jones and Bartlett Publishers International
PO Box 1498
London W6 7RS
England

Library of Congress Cataloging-in-Publication-Data
ReVelle, Penelope.
    The global environment: securing a sustainable future / Penelope ReVelle.
Charles ReVelle.
        p.   cm.
    Includes bibliographical references and index.
    ISBN 0-86720-321-8
    1. Pollution—Environmental aspects.   2. Environmental protection.
3. Human ecology.   4. Natural resources—Management.   5. Economic
development.   I. ReVelle, Charles.   II. Title.
TD174.R52   1992
363.7—dc20   92-9879
                                                                                CIP

Cover: **Elephants march beneath a rainbow in Kenya's Masai Mara Reserve.** Heavy poaching of elephants for ivory has led to the listing of African elephants as an endangered species. In 1989, a ban prohibiting the importation of ivory was passed at the meeting of the Convention on the Trade in Endangered Species (CITES). The ban led to a virtual collapse of the international ivory trade.

    The survival of the elephants is, however, by no means assured. Growing human populations encroach on the large land area needed by elephant herds, while some poaching for meat and illegally traded ivory still goes on. In some ways the elephant is a victim of greed—the greed of poachers and of those who stand to profit greatly from the sale of elephant ivory—and the trade ban addresses this problem. But in other ways the elephant is a victim of human poverty and human population growth. These are the problems we must work to solve if we hope to have elephants in our global future. (*Photo:* W. Perry Conway/Tom Stack & Associates)

Printed in the United States of America
96 95 94 93   10 9 8 7 6 5 4 3 2

To parents and children,
to memory and to hope

Contents in Brief

Contents

v

Towards a Sustainable Society

Preface

We have been writing about the environment now for over 20 years. In that time we have seen significant changes in the way people view the study of environmental issues. Our first book was an encyclopedic treatment of environmental topics and concepts, *Sourcebook on the Environment*. We soon recognized that a case-by-case approach to describing environmental problems was not a fully adequate way to address the issues society had to face. As a result, the next book we wrote emphasized the interrelatedness of environmental issues. We searched for and identified root causes of environmental problems. As an example, one such root cause is the way in which society depends on fossil fuel energy. Obtaining and using fossil fuels causes water pollution, air pollution, loss of species and, as a consequence of acid rain, loss of soil fertility. These root causes of environmental problems were described in *The Environment: Issues and Choices for Society*, editions 1, 2, and 3.

As we researched the material for *The Environment: Issues and Choices for Society,* we became acutely aware of the fact that there are often two sides to environmental issues. Social factors, political differences, and moral dilemmas are common components of decisions about environmental problems. Sometimes, scientists don't even agree on the underlying scientific basis for decisions. To reflect this conflict in environmental decision making, we introduced controversy boxes. The boxes juxtapose the conflicting views of real people in real situations. The opposing views are drawn from congressional hearings, books, journals and newspapers. The boxes highlight the different and sometimes contradictory views which are so characteristic of decision making in the real world.

The third edition of *The Environment: Issues and Choices for Society* recognized another truth about environmental problems: they are, in many cases, not confined to individual countries, but are global in nature—and so must their solutions be also.

In developing this present book, *The Global Environment: Securing a Sustainable Future,* we have come to two further conclusions. First, based on the courses we teach both at The Johns Hopkins University and Essex Community College, the amount of material included in many environmental textbooks is now far beyond what can be comfortably accommodated in a one-semester course. A professor can and does, of course, pick and choose among the chapters and topics in such a book, but this method may leave some topics unmentioned and results in a feeling of not having adequately surveyed the field. How much better, we thought, to condense the material in *The Environment: Issues and Choices for Society,* third edition, even as we added all the new ideas and issues that have surfaced since it was written. We have created a new book—shorter, comprehensive, and one that fits well into a one-semester course. In this new book, carefully chosen references point the way to more in-depth study of any particular topic.

Secondly, and more important, it is clear that the field of environmental studies has matured. The past practice of describing and responding to environmental problems as they occur is no longer sufficient. Perched atop the mountain of knowledge that has been accumulated in these endeavors, humans can now see that they must plan their present and future relationship with the environment. Further, such plans must include a recognition of our dependence on the environment and the limits to the environment's ability to sustain us. In short, we must, as a condition of our species' long-term survival, develop into a sustainable society—one that interacts with, but does no lasting harm to, its environment.

A plan for our relationship with our environment has not yet been agreed upon, although many of the components it must include have emerged. Clearly, it is beyond the expertise of any few people or politicians to devise a workable plan. Instead, it will require the combined knowledge and cooperation of people from all countries of the world and all walks of life. For these reasons we have, first, invited 26 people, who have demonstrated through their actions their sincere concern for the environment, to contribute their best idea on how we can evolve into a sustainable society. Secondly, we have synthesized current thinking about the principles on which a sustainable society might be based.

Our contributors hail from a variety of countries, backgrounds and professions. To a person, they responded enthusiastically to our request for their thoughts on sustainable societies. We feel we have tapped a deep well of thought and expertise on how to construct sustainable societies. Their ideas are contained in the series of essays distributed throughout the text. From these ideas and from our own research grew the last chapter: Principles for

a Sustainable Society, and the Conclusion: Towards a Sustainable Society, which consist of clear, practical suggestions for achieving sustainability.

Though we feel we have gathered together many ideas, humans are a creative lot. We know that more ideas are waiting to be born, and we know that those who use this text are especially motivated and qualified to expand the spectrum of suggestions provided here. Please feel free to write to us to share your ideas on achieving a sustainable society.

NEW IN *THE GLOBAL ENVIRONMENT: SECURING A SUSTAINABLE FUTURE*

The twenty chapters in this book are organized into six parts: Ecology, the Background; Human Population Issues; Land and Wildlife Resources; Energy Resources and Recycling; Air and Water Resources; and Sustainable Global Societies. New to this book are full chapters on solid waste and recycling, acid rain, global climate change, and principles for sustainable societies.

Many timely issues are discussed. Examples are: the development of an environmental consciousness worldwide; wetland policies; the spotted owl and old-growth forest issues; worldwide unmet need for contraception; AIDS and population growth; ALAR; locusts and screwworm plagues in Africa; sustainable agriculture; agroforestry and polycropping; biodiversity as a resource; debt-for-nature swaps; chemical prospecting in the rainforest; the Chernobyl disaster; new solar and wind energy schemes; "Green" products; eruption of Mount Pinatubo; migratory bird losses; ozone treaty agreements; salmon losses in the Pacific Northwest; the Aral Sea; the *Exxon Valdez* spill; oil pollution; and the Persian Gulf War.

We have included all the features that made *The Environment: Issues and Choices for Society,* third edition, valuable: Controversies (including new ones), references and annotated further readings, chapter summaries, questions for thought and discussion, extensive illustrations, and part opening essays that tie together the various parts of the book. In addition, each chapter has one or more new essays on the topic, "Towards a Sustainable Society."

INSTRUCTIONAL PACKAGE

We have prepared an instructional package that contains a variety of materials intended to help organize and enrich environmental courses. Components of the instructional package include:

- Instructor's Resource Manual
- Test Bank
- Transparency Masters
- Student Study Guide
- Videos

Further information on the instructional package is available by contacting the publisher.

ACKNOWLEDGMENTS

Many people influenced this book and made it possible. We are indebted to our good friend and agent John Riina, who recognized new possibilities in our ideas and prose. John steered us with a gentle hand toward creation of a new and better shape for our text and has always been available for advice and counsel. The many suggestions and guidance of our editor, Joe Burns, have also been especially valuable to us.

A number of people graciously took time from their own busy schedules to answer questions and clarify points. We would like to thank Dr. Faith Campbell of Natural Resources Defense Council; Lisa Hearns, Jim Titus and John Lishman of the Environmental Protection Agency; Peter Johnson at the U.S. Census Bureau; Debra Little from the International Boundary and Water Commission; J. R. Herman at NASA–Goddard Space Flight Center; Shayam Thapa, Family Health International; and, once again, Renaldo Reyes, at the U.N. Photo Library, for his generous help in finding illustrations for this book.

Our major sources for the controversy boxes were articles we found in scientific journals and in the popular press. In this area, two people contributed particularly. Peter and Linda Rottmann called our attention to the fire at Baxter Park and the sharp debate in the Bangor *Daily News*. It was an archetype of a problem without an answer.

We are deeply grateful for the time and effort all of the essay contributors spent in answering the question, "How can we best move towards a sustainable society?" Clearly, this is a question to which they had all already devoted much time and thought. On such people and such efforts depends the long-term survival of the human species.

We would also like to thank the following professors who have reviewed this book and its previous incarnation, *The Environment: Issues and Choices for Society,* and contributed greatly to their quality:

Ruth Allen, American University;
Richard Andren, Montgomery Community College;
David Appenbrink, Chicago State University;
David Ashley, Missouri Western State College;
Bill Baker, Rockland Community College;
William Battin, State University of New York, Binghamton;
James Beddard, New Hampshire College;
Bruce Bennett, Community College of Rhode Island;
Robert Bertin, Miami University;
Charles Biernbaum, College of Charleston;
Thomas Bilbs, Mobile College;
Richard Bonalewicz, Gannon University;
Arthur C. Borror, University of New Hampshire;
George Carey, Stonehill College;
Don Collins, Montana State University;
Arthur Driscoll, Westfield State College;
N. DuBowsky, Westchester Community College;
F. F. Flint, Randolph-Macon College;
David Gates, University of Michigan, Ann Arbor;
Harry Gershenowitz, Glassboro State College;
Joseph Gould, Georgia Institute of Technology;
James H. Grosklags, Northern Illinois University;

Ted L. Hanes, California State University at Fullerton;

Karen Harding, Ft. Steilacoom Community College;

Jay Hatch, University of Minnesota;

Tom Hellier, University of Texas, Arlington;

Clyde W. Hibbs, Ball State University;

Harry L. Holloway, University of North Dakota;

Clyde Houseknecht, Wilkes College;

Jerry Howell, Morehead State University;

David I. Johnson, Michigan State University;

Eric Karlin, Ramapo College;

Terry Keiser, Ohio Northern University;

Michael Kelley, United States Military Academy;

Phyllis Kingsburg, Drake University;

Paul Knuth, Edinboro University;

Kipp Kruse, Eastern Illinois University;

Greg Lindsey, Indiana University;

Edward Lukacevic, Cuyahoga Community College;

Daniel Mark, William Jewell College;

R. J. McCloskey, Boise State University;

Earl McCoy, University of South Florida;

Edward McLean, Clemson University;

John Meyers, Middlesex Community College;

John Mikulski, Oakton Community College;

Joseph Moore, University of California, Northridge;

Kenneth Moore, Seattle Pacific University;

Steven Mueller, Brainard Community College;

Norton Nickerson, Tufts University;

John Pawling, Temple University;

Robert Pearson, Northern Illinois University;

John Peck, St. Cloud State University;

John Pigage, Waubonsee Community College;

G. Puttick, Harvard University;

Dominic Roberti, St. Joseph's College;

David Robinson, Albany State College;

C. Lee Rockett, Bowling Green State University;

Diane Schulman, Erie Community College;

Donald Scoby, North Dakota State University;

A. J. Slavin, Trent University;

Barbara Smigel, Clark County Community College;

Sherilyn Smith, Skidmore College;

Edwin R. Squiers, Taylor University;

George E. Stanton, Columbus College;

Harold Stevenson, McNeese State University;

Ellis Sykes, Albany State College;

James Taylor, University of Alabama;

Susanna Tak-Yung Tong, University of California, Los Angeles;

Margaret Trussell, California State University at Chico;

Linda L. Wallace, Research Division, Yellowstone National Park;

Irvine Wei, Northeastern University;

Donald Winslow, Indiana University;

Dennis Woodland, Andrews University.

The New Pioneers: Towards a Sustainable Global Society

Awareness of the environment of the earth, of its species and of the place of humanity in that environment reaches back a very long way in time. Likewise, concern for the environment is not a momentary enthusiasm only, but a commitment made by many peoples in many places. To some people the watershed of modern-day environmental concern in the United States was the first Earth Day, celebrated in 1970, a spontaneous upwelling of resolve to improve the environment. The benchmark of world environmental concern, on the other hand, is for many the 1972 U.N.-sponsored World Environment Conference in Stockholm, Sweden. Our engagement with the environment and actions to preserve parts of it are, however, much older. In India there is an ancient tradition of forest communities, or ashrams, dedicated to living in harmony with the environment. From this tradition grew the modern Indian environmental, or Chipko, movement. Many poets have celebrated the healing and restoring qualities of the natural, as opposed to the human-made, environment. The eighth-century Chinese poet Li Po wrote, "There is another heaven and earth beyond the world of men."★

Nonetheless, while our appreciation of the natural environment and efforts at environmental protection reach far back in time, early steps to preserve the environment were fragmentary and piecemeal responses to a sequence of serious problems. A recounting of the history of environmental awareness in the United States and in the world underscores the point that we have not had—in fact, still lack—an agreed-upon plan for protecting and restoring the environment.

The discussion that follows emphasizes the flowering of environmental consciousness in the United States. In many ways the modern environmental movement did have its beginnings in America. We also describe, however, a number of other ways in which aspects of environmental consciousness showed up in other countries and other cultures.

★ Li Po, quoted in Yi-Fu Tuan, *Man and Nature,* Commission on College Geography resource paper # 10 (Washington, D.C.: Association of American Geographers, 1971).

A BRIEF HISTORY OF THE ENVIRONMENTAL MOVEMENT

Environmental awareness in America goes back much further than the first Earth Day in 1970. In fact, if we acknowledge that North American culture did not begin with European settlement, awareness goes back to the Native Americans who lived on these lands for 20,000 years before European settlers arrived. The recorded speeches of Indian chiefs show us a people who considered themselves as one with nature.

Chief Seattle of the Dwamish said in 1854, "All things are connected, like the blood which unites one family. . . . Man did not weave the web of life; he is merely a strand in it. Whatever he does to the web, he does to himself." Chief Luther Standing Bear explained at the turn of the century, "Only to the white man was nature a wilderness—to us it was tame."

Standing Bear's point is crucial. European settlers did think of their environment as a wilderness that needed to be tamed and beaten back. This attitude led to America's first environmental awakening and the world's first institutionalized response to a major environmental problem.

The First Awakening: Loss of Forests and Wilderness

As a young country, America had no cathedrals, no long history of culture, or tradition of art. But it did have something almost eradicated from much of the European continent. America had a magnificent wilderness—vast prairies, mountains and waterfalls, and primeval forests—that its citizens felt was the equal in splendor, if not in kind, of the buildings and monuments of the Old World. Yet by the early 1800s these natural wonders were being threatened by human settlement. Farmers were turning over more and more of the vast prairies to grow crops; the northeastern forests were disappearing under the onslaught of ship builders and loggers; the communities of grasses and wildflowers in the high meadows of the West were being grazed to extinction by sheep.

In 1827 the artist George Catlin, concerned about the disappearance of the wilderness that he so loved to paint, called for preservation of part of the American prairie in a "nation's park." John Muir, who founded the conservation group that later became the Sierra Club, wrote and lobbied tirelessly for the preservation of the West's mountain wildernesses.

"There is no daylight in towns," he wrote, "and the weary public ought to know that there is light here. . . . Come all who need rest and light, bending and breaking with overwork, leave your profits and losses and metallic dividends and come."

Yet Muir also noted sadly, ". . . it appears that all the destructible beauty of this remote Yosemite is doomed to perish like that of its neighbors, and our tame law-loving citizens plant and water their garden daisies without concern, wholly unconscious of loss."★

By the 1870s people were concerned enough about the vanishing beauty represented by the American wilderness that Congress began to set aside some of the nation's natural wonders. Yellowstone was the first of the National Parks, established in 1872, and Yosemite the second in 1890 (see Figures I-1 and I-2).

As forests across the nation fell to the settlers' and the lumbermen's axes, concern grew that our supply of timber would disappear altogether. Forest preserves were first set aside in 1892, in response to these fears. Later, in 1905, during Teddy Roosevelt's term of office, governance of these forests was transferred to the Bureau of Forestry, which soon became the U.S. Forest Service, which it still is today. The preserves themselves became known as the National Forests. Interestingly, Britain's William the Conqueror, when he took power in 1066 A.D., also established a series of forest preserves, the Royal Forests, one of which, New Forest, survives to this day.

The formal American tradition of preserving wild land for the use of the public began early, perhaps as early as anywhere on the globe. Yel-

★ R. Engberg, (Ed.), *John Muir Summering in the Sierra* (Madison, Wis.: University of Wisconsin Press, 1984).

FIGURE I-1 Half Dome in Yosemite National Park.
(*Photo:* National Park Service, U.S. Department of the Interior)

lowstone, when it was created in 1872, was not only the first national park in the United States; it was the first national park in the world. In 1885, Canada created a preserve in a spectacular region in the Canadian Rockies. It became Banff National Park, the first of Canada's national parks, in 1887. New Zealand established a national park, Ruawori, that same year, beginning a tradition that is sustained to this day. Today New Zealand ranks first in the world in the proportion (8%) of its total area set aside in national parks. The United States and Canada, however, rank first and second in the world in total area set aside in national parks.

The European experience with national parks was different, however. Large tracts of unused public land did not exist. Forest preserves to maintain a stable timber supply in Germany date from at least the first half of the nineteenth century. German practice influenced U.S. thinking in this regard. National park systems did not appear in most European countries until after World War II, although India, a British colony at the time, established a national park at Kaziranga in Assam in 1908. The national park concept did not penetrate England itself until 1949, when legislation established such a system. Norway's first national park was designated in 1967.

Even though the national park was late to flower in Europe, the former USSR created a preservation concept of its own. During the nineteenth-century reign of the Alexanders, when the nation of Russia was extending its territory across Asia, powerful

FIGURE I-2 Cloud Forest, Alto Madidi, in the Andean Foothills of Bolivia. Many developing countries now face the problem that the United States faced 100 years ago—how to protect remaining wilderness areas from human populations intent on farming, grazing, or mining the land. This forest in Bolivia was recently surveyed by a team of scientists requested to help the Bolivian government decide which areas were most valuable and most in need of protection. Alto Madidi was judged one of the most diverse forests ever studied. (*Photo:* Ted Parker/Conservation International)

barons caused the creation of *zapovedniks,* preserves meant to protect a dominant species of an area. Today the zapovedniks protect whole ecosystems as well as natural phenomena such as waterfalls and canyons.

The 1970s saw the rapid creation of national parks in the nations of Central Africa, so that now such nations as Botswana, Zambia, Uganda, and Kenya are among the leaders in the world in proportion of land area designated as parks. By the early 1970s some Latin American countries—notably Costa Rica—had also begun to establish national parks.

The Second Awakening: Loss of Animal Species

North America was once a land with seemingly inexhaustible supplies of fish and birds and mammals. In 1614 John Smith wrote:

> *You shall scarce find any bay, shallow shore or cove of sand, where you may not rake many clams or lobsters or both at your pleasure, and in many places load your boat if you please, nor isles where you find not fruits, birds, crabs and mussels, or all of them. . . . He is a very bad fisher that cannot kill in one day with his hook and line one, two, three hundred cods.* ★

But by the late 1800s it was clear that some of the supplies of species in America were not at all inexhaustible. By 1884 there was only one herd of 300 buffalo on the plains that had once supported millions. In 1914 the last passenger pigeon, lone representative of flocks that once darkened the sky overhead, died in the Cincinnati Zoo (see Figure I-3).

The nation's response to the threatened losses of these and other species was to set aside refuges for wild species. These areas of land were called wildlife refuges. For some animals, such as the buffalo, such action came in time. Today there are once again enough buffalo to allow hunting. For other species, such as the passenger pigeon, the idea of refuges came too late.

The three traditions of protection of wilderness, of species, and of resources such as timber were evidence of the maturing environmental sense of the immigrant Americans. Most of them had finally come to the same conclusions that the Native Americans had long held: Wilderness is not the enemy, and it is worth preserving.

★ Captain John Smith, *New England's Trials,* 1614.

FIGURE I-3 Passenger Pigeons. Long before the last passenger pigeon died, it was clear that their numbers were declining every year. Yet, despite many efforts to save it, the passenger pigeon became extinct. At some unrecognized moment a crucial point was passed, the opportunity to save this species lost forever. This etching of the 1870s depicts hunters in northern Louisiana shooting for sport at a migrating flock of passenger pigeons. (*Source:* S. Bennett, *Illustrated Sporting and Dramatic News*, London, July 3, 1875, p. 332)

The Third Awakening: Pollution of Drinking Water

All this time, human populations were growing. Methods of disposing of waste, such as dumping it in a nearby stream or lake, that might have worked for a sparsely populated country no longer worked for a more densely populated one. In the middle to late 1800s, disposing of human wastes in nearby bodies of water precipitated a third environmental emergency: waterborne epidemics of disease.

Actually, the notion that water can carry disease first occurred to the ancient Greeks. The physician Hippocrates advised that polluted water be boiled or filtered before being consumed. Despite Hippocrates' early recommendations, however, only 150 years ago most people were still unaware that human diseases could be spread by water. For this reason, many communities dumped their raw sewage into the same lake or river that they or other communities used for drinking water.

Typhoid and Asiatic **cholera** are two diseases spread by water polluted with human wastes. These diseases attack and infect the intestinal tract of humans. Bowel discharges of infected individuals contain the **pathogens** (disease-producing microorganisms) that spread the diseases. If these bowel discharges enter a water source, there is a high probability that new infections will occur among those who drink the water. As a consequence of the dumping of raw sewage and the drinking of untreated water, a number of large-scale waterborne epidemics occurred in the United States and in Europe in the latter half of the nineteenth century.

One epidemic in particular was destined to spur the movement toward treated water supplies. It was 1892, and the city of Hamburg in Germany was struck by an epidemic of cholera. Located on the Elbe River in Germany are the adjoining cities of Altona and Hamburg. Although they had a common boundary, the cholera epidemic that occurred in the fall of 1892 was unequally distributed through the region. Hamburg experienced a case rate seven times more intense than did Altona. The crucial difference between the two cities was in their water supplies. Whereas Hamburg drew its water from the Elbe at a site upstream from the cities, Altona took its water from the river downstream from the cities. Hamburg treated its water not at all before distribution, but Altona, whose supply was polluted by the sewage of both cities, filtered its water through sand beds prior to distribution. These facts suggested strongly that sand filtration was an effective method of water purification. The fact that cholera did occur in Altona but to a lesser extent is attributed to the population that lived in Altona but worked in Hamburg.

By 1910, courts in the United States were ordering water supply companies to provide their contracting cities with pure water, using such techniques as chlorination and sand filtration. Requirements for treatment of water supplies in Europe appeared in roughly this same period.

Though the developed world gradually made the transition to safe drinking water and to cautious disposal of wastes, water sanitation in the developing world remained dismal. It was only in 1948 that the newly founded World Health Organization (WHO) at its charter meeting in Geneva decided, at the urging of an American environmental engineer, to expand its objectives. Dr. Abel Wolman, a professor from The Johns Hopkins University and delegate to the charter assembly, convinced his fellow delegates that health included environmental health. He argued persuasively that the scope of WHO's mission should be broadened from a focus on maternal and child health and communicable diseases to the protection of the environment through the provision of safe drinking water and the sanitary disposal of human excreta. The charter added this new objective to the mission of the World Health Organization. Although sanitation has become a goal of WHO, progress at achieving this goal has proved elusive, as we describe in Chapter 19.

The Fourth Awakening: Adulteration and Contamination of Food

Recognition of a fourth environmental problem began in the early 1900s in America with the consumer and public health movements. "Muckrakers," as certain newspaper writers were known, looked for sensational stories to catch the public's attention. Among other stories, they uncovered the widespread adulteration of foods with poisonous dyes and other fillers. Red candy was found colored with mercury compounds. Coconut candy was extended with ground bone. The sanitary conditions in stockyards and slaughterhouses were shown to be appalling.

In response to public outcry, the U.S. government began to establish agencies to oversee the safety of the public food supply, functions now carried out by the Food and Drug Administration, the Environmental Protection Agency, and the Department of Agriculture. Allotting to the government the responsibility for ensuring the safety of the food supply laid the foundation for later government regulation of the use of pesticides in agriculture.

In many developing countries today serious problems still exist with contamination of food supplies. It is especially difficult for understaffed bureaucracies to regulate pesticide use by farmers who may not understand, or even be able to read, warning labels on pesticide containers. This problem is covered in more detail in Chapter 8.

The Fifth Awakening: Erosion Leading to the Creation of Deserts

The next crisis to spring upon the American consciousness had, in fact, been predicted almost 70 years previously. In 1864 George Perkins Marsh had noted in his book *Man and Nature: The Earth as Transformed by Human Action* that human actions were capable of turning forested land into desert. Marsh was a lawyer, a Congressman, an industrialist, ambassador to Italy and Turkey—and an unusually observant human being. He noted on his extensive trips in Europe that the pattern of human settlement was to turn forest to farmland or pasture and then, as fertile soil eroded away in wind and rain, to barren, infertile land, even desert. He recounted how this sequence of events had already occurred in the Fertile Crescent of ancient Persia and in southern France.

In the 1930s Marsh's fear that a large portion of the United States might suffer the same fate as lands in other parts of the world became a reality. A series of droughts, combined with farming techniques that encouraged erosion, turned the American Midwest into a dust bowl (see Figure I-4). The response to this fifth environmental crisis was the establishment of the Soil Conservation Service. The Service is still in existence, educating farmers and doing research on methods to prevent soil erosion.

The recognition that serious soil erosion could result from farming occurred in other countries as well. In the last quarter of the sixteenth century, one Chinese observer noted that population growth was forcing some farmers into the hill country of South China. The result of farming these sloped lands was devastating soil erosion on the hills and flooding in the valleys.

Although the effects of cutting away vegetation are well known, such activities continue worldwide, especially in the tropical forests of South America and Southeast Asia and on the hills of North Africa. The gradual failure of the land in countries like Ethiopia proceeds parallel to the dust-

FIGURE I-4 Dust Storm, Cimarron County, Oklahoma, 1936. A farmer and his two small children run for the shelter of their dugout during a dust storm in this famous photo by Arthur Rothstein. In the 1930s the Midwest suffered a series of severe dust storms caused by winds blowing soil off fields during dry weather. So many dust storms hit the southern Great Plains that the area became known as the "Dust Bowl."

bowl conditions that struck the United States in the 1930s.

The Sixth Awakening: Air Pollution

In 1948 America had its first air pollution episode, which was clearly the beginning of its sixth envi-ronmental crisis. This first air pollution emergency occurred in the small Pennsylvania town of Donora. During the last week of October 1948, a heavy smog settled over the area surrounding Donora. Meteorologists described it as a **temperature in-version,** a stable weather condition that allows the accumulation of air pollutants in the layer of air next to the earth. As the Public Health Service re-counted in 1949, at first the residents of Donora were not alarmed by the smog:

Smogs of short duration are not unusual and except for discomfort due to irritation and nuisance of the dirt and poor visibility, no unusual significance is attached to such occurrences.

This particular smog encompassed the Donora area on the morning of Wednesday, October 27. It was even then of sufficient density to evoke comments by the residents. It was reported that streamers of carbon appeared to hang motionless in the air and that visibility was so poor that even natives of the area became lost.

The smog continued through Thursday, but still no more attention was attracted than that of conversational comment.

On Friday, however, a marked increase in illness began to take place in the area. By Friday evening the physicians' telephone exchange was flooded with calls for medical aid, and the doctors were making calls unceasingly to care for their patients. Many persons were sent to nearby hospitals, and the Donora Fire Department, the local chapter of the American Red Cross, and other organizations were asked to help with the many ill persons.

There was, nevertheless, no general alarm about the smog's effects even then. On Friday evening the annual Donora Hallowe'en parade was well attended, and on Saturday afternoon a football game between Donora and Monongahela high schools was played on the gridiron of Donora High School before a large crowd.

The first death during the smog had already occurred, however, early Saturday morning—at 2 A.M., to be precise. More followed in quick succession during the day and by nightfall word of these deaths was racing through the town. By 11:30 that night 17 persons were dead. Two more were to follow on Sunday, and still another who fell ill during the smog was to die a week later on November 8.

On Sunday afternoon rain came to clear away the smog. But hundreds were still ill, and the rest of the residents were still stunned by the number of deaths that had taken place during the preceding 36 hours. That night the town council held a meeting to consider action, and followed with another on Monday night. By this time emergency aid was on its way to do whatever possible for the stricken town. ★

Of course, the Donora tragedy was not the first air pollution incident to occur in the world. Air pollution has existed since industrialization began. The first episode to be well studied took place in 1930 in the Muse Valley in Belgium and caused the deaths of 63 people. In 1952 in London a severe fog combined with air pollutants lasted five days. The effects of the air pollutants killed an estimated 4,000 people, mostly the elderly and people with respiratory or cardiac diseases. New York City had air pollution episodes in 1953, 1962, 1963, and 1966.

In London, rules forbidding the use of coal for home heating have prevented a recurrence of the deadly fog. In the United States and in Europe, a series of regulations designed to decrease the release of air pollutants from industry have served to clean up the air to some extent, although all of the industrialized countries still battle the air pollutants generated by automobiles. Even so, the focus of the air pollution crisis has clearly shifted to the developing countries. As these countries gain the economic benefits of industrialization and the mobility of motor vehicle transport, they also fall heir to air pollution episodes resembling those that racked the industrialized countries into the 1960s.

The Seventh Awakening: Synthetic Pesticides

In the early 1940s the seeds for America's next crisis were sown. The synthetic pesticide DDT, introduced near the end of World War II, was hailed as a near miracle because it killed lice and fleas, thus helping to prevent disease among the Allied soldiers. In this respect DDT probably made a significant contribution to winning the war. After the war the pesticide seemed no less miraculous. DDT was used to kill insects on all kinds of crops, and it killed the mosquitoes that carried malaria. DDT and related pesticides soon came into widespread use, worldwide.

Not until the publication of Rachel Carson's *Silent Spring* in the late 1950s was the public made

★ From "Air Pollution in Donora, PA," Public Health Bulletin No. 306, U.S. Public Health Service, 1949.

FIGURE I-5 Pesticide Contamination. In the developing world, many people are still unaware of the hazards of using pesticides. After the day's work is over, this Indonesian farmer will allow the water buffalo to cool off in the nearby canal, possibly contaminated with pesticides. (*Photo:* UN Photo Library)

aware of the looming crisis of pesticides contamination of the environment. DDT (and pesticides like it) is not easily broken down in the environment. Instead, it remains in the soil or blows around the world on dust particles, even to such remote places as Antarctica. Worse, it accumulates in the fatty tissues of birds and animals and people. Carson envisioned a silent spring, where no birds sang, and warned of the danger of indiscriminate use of pesticides.

Her fears were partly confirmed when it was shown in the late 1960s that the loss of a number of species of birds of prey was imminent, a result of the buildup of DDT in their bodies. This buildup caused them to lay eggs with shells so thin that they cracked when the parents tried to incubate them. DDT was outlawed in 1972 because of its effects on birds, and in the years since then, other pesticides have been withdrawn from the market because of their effects on the environment or on human health (see Figure I-5).

In her prediction of the effect that indiscriminate use of pesticides would have, Carson echoed the words of Chief Seattle: "[The natural world] is built of a series of interrelationships between living things, and between living things and their environment. You can't just step in with some brute force and change one thing without changing a good many others."★

LOOKING BACK, LOOKING FORWARD

By the 1960s then, environmental awareness had come to include not just a concern for wilderness, or wild species, or human health, or soil. Instead, a realization was dawning that all parts of the environment were connected, that harm to one part of the web could reverberate through the whole system, yielding effects where none were anticipated.

Water pollution, air pollution, pesticides pollution, loss of good cropland to erosion—why did this new set of crises surface in this century in America and in the world? One part of the answer must be laid at the door of the unfettered use of new technology. Some of the chemicals, such as

★ C. B. Gartner, *Rachel Carson* (New York: Fredrick Ungar, 1983).

pesticides, released into the environment were simply too new on the face of the Earth for the environment to absorb them without harm.

But a serious and more intractable part of the answer to the question of why air, water, and land pollution issues surfaced slowly over the first 50 years of this century lies in the growth of the human populations. Once there were so few people living in the Americas, in Asia, Europe, and Africa that they could count on wilderness to dilute the effects of their living. If the land was played out or the game all killed, the people could move on. Now there is nowhere else to go. Once sewage or mining wastes could be dumped into the nearest stream or lake or ocean. But now other people are drinking that water, or fishing in it, or using the beaches that border it.

The realization that there are limits to the resources of air, water and arable land constitutes hard-won knowledge. And the realization that human populations cannot continue to grow without disastrous consequences to the planet is still not widely understood.

TODAY'S GLOBAL ENVIRONMENTAL PROBLEMS

This brief history would not be complete without mention of the "modern" environmental problems with which we live today. Global warming, ozone depletion, acid rain, the energy policy crisis—these are all issues we hear about almost every day. But such problems cannot simply be lumped into a discussion of the history of environmental awareness of a single country. The reason is that they are qualitatively different kinds of problems. They are problems that cannot be dealt with by any one nation acting alone. They are global problems, and their solution requires a recognition of that fact.

Acid rain stems from the long-distance transport of air pollutants, often across national boundaries, before they finally wash out of the atmosphere. Pollutants from U.S. power plants cause acid rain in Canada. Acid rain originating in Germany is destroying Scandinavian forests.

The chlorofluorocarbons released from spray cans and refrigeration units all over the world rise into the stratosphere and destroy the earth's protective ozone layer. The effect is especially severe over the Antarctic—where, surely, refrigeration chemicals are in little use.

The major portion of the carbon dioxide released into the atmosphere from the burning of fossil fuels comes from the industrialized countries of the developed world. But the global temperature rises that may result could affect all regions of the world, developed and undeveloped alike.

Oil resources are maldistributed. Two-thirds of these resources are in the Middle East. Two-thirds of the demand is in the United States, Western Europe, and Japan. This maldistribution will require global cooperation or will result in international turmoil.

The global nature of these most pressing environmental concerns inspired the title for this book and the theme that runs through its pages. Unless we can learn to think in terms of global problems, there is little chance that we will be able to generate solutions.

THE SUSTAINABLE SOCIETY

The history of growing environmental awareness seems to be one of staggered and isolated reactions to a series of difficult problems. Perhaps there is an excuse for our lurching along from crisis to crisis, not solving problems until they have forced themselves upon us. We did not really know enough about our environment and how it worked to formulate a policy, a plan for how humans could fit into the system without destroying it. We were, for the largest portion of human history, not even aware that we could destroy it. But this is no longer true, and no longer an excuse.

We are now finally in a position in which we begin to have hope of dealing with the environment in a coordinated and unified manner. Our responses need not go on indefinitely being clumsy and late. We are a species capable of planning for the sustained support of the earth's environment (see Figure I-6). We are a species capable of creating a

FIGURE I-6 The Ozone Layer. Looking like an exclamation point against the infinite blue of the sky, a balloon carrying equipment to gather information on the state of the earth's ozone layer is sent aloft by the crew at NASA's Wallops Flight Center.

In 1990, 93 nations signed an agreement to phase out the use of certain ozone-destroying chemicals by the year 2000. The treaty is hailed as a model for international cooperation—it contains provisions for economic help to developing countries to enable them to meet the treaty's goals. (*Photo:* NASA)

sustainable society, a society which draws on but does not diminish the environment that nurtures us.

In Chapter 20 we summarize the principles on which a sustainable human society could be based. However, although these principles can be stated succinctly, putting them into action is no easy task. Moreover, the global nature of environmental problems demands that these principles, and solutions to environmental problems in general, be implemented by representatives of all of earth's human societies. This is why we have invited people from many countries and many walks of life to present to you their best ideas for establishing sustainable societies.

Throughout this text you will find insightful essays from environmental scientists and planners and volunteers, giving their thoughts on how we can plan for the future, how we can create a sustainable society. It is no exaggeration to say that such planning is an endeavor that may be crucial to the continued survival of human beings on this earth. It is an endeavor in which the peoples of the world can finally join hands.

Part One

Ecology: The Background

Ecologists at Work. (*Bottom right*) Theodore Parker, of Conservation International's RAP, or Rapid Assessment Team. (*Photo:* Ted Wolf, Conservation International) (*Top right*) Richard Bierregaard of the Smithsonian Institution, at work in the Brazilian jungle. (*Photo:* Courtesy of R. Bierregaard). (*Left*) Members of The Nature Conservancy team that explored what is now the Maya Biosphere Reserve in Guatemala. Based on the team's results, the Guatemalan Congress created the 3.5-million-acre reserve. (*Photo:* Brian Houseal, © The Nature Conservancy)

*T*he world's tropical forests are disappearing at an alarming rate—over 100,000 kilometers per year. Along with the forests, we lose some of the millions of species that live there. According to Harvard biologist E. O. Wilson, somewhere between 4,000 and 6,000 species are lost each year due to deforestation, most of them in the tropical forests, most of them before they have even been described and named.

Several groups of ecologists are currently in a race against time to explore the most threatened tropical forests. They hope to establish some sort of priorities for setting aside the richest areas before they are gone forever. These ecologists explore small sections of larger forested areas in order to identify birds, trees, mammals, insects, and reptiles. Those areas with the greatest number of species per area or the largest number of species found nowhere else in the world are ranked high on the list of areas to be protected, if possible. Most of the new species being discovered are plants and insects, but even previously unknown birds are being found.

Many subjects contribute to the understanding of environmental issues. Biology, law, sociology, mathematics, anthropology, and physics are only some of the subjects useful in understanding environmental problems. Like the problem of disappearing tropical forests, however, most environmental problems have an underpinning of ecological principles. For this reason, the discipline most closely tied to environmental studies is probably ecology.

The word **ecology** is made up of the Greek words *oikos,* house, and *logos,* to study. Thus, ecology means, roughly, the study of where organisms live, or their environment. Perhaps a better way to put it is that ecology is concerned with the relationship between organisms and their environment. Many ecological terms are used in environmental studies. The photo montage that opens this part shows some of the ecologists involved in rapid surveys of the tropical forest environment.

The purpose of the ecology chapters in this part is to explain the ecological principles that you will need in order to understand environmental problems. In the first chapter we examine the parts of natural ecosystems: both the living organisms and the nonliving parts that make up these systems. In the second chapter, various global habitats, both land habitats (called *biomes*) and water environments, are described and characterized.

The third chapter deals with ecosystem dynamics. The environment is a dynamic system in which many materials cycle and energy is con-tinuously used and transferred from one com-partment to another. The final chapter in this part introduces the concepts of population dynamics, necessary for the understanding of the growth of various populations, including the human population.

Species, Communities, Ecosystems, Evolution, and Competition

PEREGRINE FALCONS AND THE DEFINITION OF A SPECIES

Birds belonging to the species called peregrine falcons are spectacular hunters. Sailing with wings outspread, peregrines search for the smaller birds that are their prey. When a falcon spots something that looks as if it would make a meal, it plunges downward at speeds over 200 mi/hr (320 km/hr) and snatches its unsuspecting dinner in mid-air.

Since the early 1960s there has been no natural population of peregrine falcons east of the Mississippi. The birds fell victim to poisons in their ecosystem, most likely DDT. But DDT, which was first used in this country in 1945, is now banned, and levels in the environment seem to be decreasing. For this reason, ornithologist Tom Cade, then a professor of ornithology at Cornell University, thought it was a good time to try to restore the Eastern peregrine falcon population. He bred the birds in captivity and then trained them to live successfully in the wild areas in which they were once found (see Figure 1-1).

During the course of this project, Cade and the U.S. Fish and Wildlife Service came into conflict over the definition of a species. Cade breeds his falcons from European peregrine falcons as well as from native North American birds. Because the European birds live in fairly populous areas, Cade feels that European falcons have characteristics that would be valuable to falcons attempting to settle along the populous eastern coast of the United States. The U.S. Fish and Wildlife Service was uneasy about allowing the result of this cross-breeding, which might be called a foreign species, to be established in this country because an executive order prohibits the introduction of "exotic species" into the United States. Many scientists came to Cade's defense by pointing out that all the different birds Cade used are simply subspecies of peregrine falcons. Who was right?

What Is a Species?

An animal **species** is most often defined in terms of reproduction. That is, a species consists of a group of individuals that can successfully breed

FIGURE 1-1 Young Peregrine Falcons Waiting to Be Fed. Ornithologist Tom Cady is now chairman of The World Center for Birds of Prey, in Boise, Idaho. The center breeds peregrine falcons for eventual release in the wild, as well as endangered raptors from around the world, such as Mauritius kestrels. One hundred of these extremely rare birds have been released on their home island of Mauritius. (*Photo:* The Peregrine Fund, Inc.)

with one another; that share ties of common parentage; and that therefore possess a common **pool of genes,** or hereditary material. In most cases it is possible to tell species apart on the basis of their different appearance or behavior or physiological makeup. However, these differences in themselves do not define species. If two apparently similar groups of organisms cannot interbreed successfully when given the opportunity, the two groups make up two separate species. Similarly, if two different-seeming groups of organisms are capable of interbreeding, there can be a flow of genes between them, and they are thus members of the same species, no matter how different they are in appearance.

We should keep in mind that by defining species, scientists are attempting to describe part of the natural world in an orderly way, and the natural world does not always fit neatly into scientific categories. Thus, there are exceptions to these rules for defining species. Remmert (1980) pointed out that two species that have developed in different parts of the world, but with similar requirements for food, climate, living space, and so on, can sometimes interbreed if they eventually meet in natural surroundings. This has been noted in several species of birds, fish, and insects.

In a similar way, plants cannot always be classified into species on the basis of whether they can interbreed. Plants as a group have more diverse reproductive methods and genetic systems than animals do.

What, then, is a species? If we remember that the definition of a species is not based on hard and fast rules, we can say that as a general rule, a species is a group of organisms that can breed successfully, that share ties of parentage, and that therefore possess a common pool of hereditary material.

Populations and Subspecies

A **population** is all the individuals of a given species that live together in the same location—for example, the 50 or so birds that make up the entire population of peregrine falcons west of the Rockies. One or more populations of a particular kind of plant or animal make up a species.

In general, even though they all belong to the same species, the members of a particular population resemble each other more closely than they resemble members of other populations. The reasons are that pairing is more likely to occur between individuals within a population than between those from different populations, and that members of a population are all subject to similar environmental influences upon their direction of evolution.

In some cases, geographic conditions in which various populations of a species live are very different, or the barriers to travel between the localities are great. For example, populations of the same species may live on different islands or in different rivers or on opposite sides of mountain ranges. The populations may then be found to have some very different genetic characteristics (although not

FIGURE 1-2 Kenyan Cheetahs. Sometimes a population of organisms all are descended from a relatively small number of individuals. For instance, cheetahs were apparently close to extinction several times in the past. Today's cheetah populations are descended from, and thus share the genes of, relatively few ancestors. In fact, cheetahs are more genetically uniform than strains of laboratory mice that have been intentionally bred to ensure that individuals possess as many of the same genes as possible! Breeding success with captive cheetahs has been very poor—fertility is low and there is high infant mortality. These are both effects common in genetically homogeneous populations. Zoos and other wildlife institutions interested in breeding endangered species are now aware that they must try to obtain partners from as diverse sources as possible in their breeding programs. (*Photo:* Grant Heilman Inc.)

enough differences to prevent successful interbreeding if given the opportunity). Populations of a species that are unlikely to breed because of geographic factors and that show genetic differences are sometimes defined as **subspecies** or **races.** Because Cade's peregrine falcons seem to breed successfully (although he did use some complicated artificial insemination techniques), it has been argued that they are all members of one species—or at worst, subspecies—and that the executive order does not apply. The Fish and Wildlife Service appeared to be unconvinced by this argument but agreed to allow an exception to the executive order so that the peregrine falcons could be released.

(Can members of a species be *too* much alike? See Figure 1-2.)

COMMUNITIES AND ECOSYSTEMS

Communities

Definition. Within a given environment, organisms are not grouped randomly; rather, populations of organisms characteristic of that particular type of environment are organized into a **community.** This community includes all the living organisms, both plant and animal (including microorganisms), interacting in that particular environment. The term *community* can be applied to a relatively small number of organisms, such as those that make up a small pond community, or it can be used to describe a much larger number, such as would be found in the forest communities into which Cade reintroduces his peregrine falcons. These large forest communities include populations of small bird species that are the prey of the peregrine falcons, as well as populations of many other species of large and small animals and populations of various species of trees and other plants.

Functions. The degree to which organisms in a community interact with one another varies. In some environments, such as the African Serengeti grasslands, interactions are so important that the various species could probably not survive without one another. In the grasslands, zebra graze when the grass is tall, exposing some of the sheath portion of the grass, which is the food for wildebeest. Wildebeest crop the grass further, allowing small herbs, which are the food of Thompson's gazelles, to grow.

In a similar way, the presence of the grazing animals helps to maintain the grass itself. Grazing encourages continued growth of the grasses, while lack of grazing may allow forest species to grow up and take over.

In other communities, notably those in harsh or fluctuating environments such as floodplains or the Arctic, there seems to be less of this type of species interaction. The animals in floodplains are mostly transients; they leave the community during a flood and return when conditions improve for them.

They therefore act less to shape or maintain the environment than do the grazing species on the Serengeti plains.

Habitats and Niches

Before we go any further, two useful ecological terms need to be defined. One is habitat; the other is niche.

The physical surroundings in which an organism lives are called its **habitat.** This is where you would go to find that particular organism. For example, the habitat of bloodworms, or chironimids, is the mud at the bottom of lakes, while the habitat of deer mice is temperate-zone woodlots. These habitats consist, of course, of a variety of physical factors, such as temperature, soil type, and moisture, but they also contain many other animals as well as plants. Thus, an organism's habitat includes living as well as nonliving elements (see Figure 1-3).

Peregrine falcons prefer to build their nest, or eyrie, on a narrow ledge or a steep cliff. This habitat provides protection for the baby falcons from predators such as owls or raccoons. In at least one case, a skyscraper seems to fill a peregrine's habitat requirements. Scarlet, one of the peregrines released by Tom Cade, chose to roost on a 35-story building in Baltimore, to the delight of its inhabitants (see Figure 1-4).

The term **niche** is somewhat more difficult to define, in part because different people use it in different ways. It can refer to an organism's particular habitat. But it can also mean the organism's ecological function—that is, what the organism does, such as what time of day or night it is active, how much sunlight it requires, what parasites it is host to, and in what ways it acts as a **predator★** (eats other organisms) or **prey** (is eaten by other organisms). The niche thus corresponds to an organism's way of life.

It is a general rule that two species cannot occupy the same niche forever. Competition between the species should cause a change in some aspect

---

★ Predators are generally larger than the organisms they eat, while parasites are smaller than their host organisms.

FIGURE 1-4 Reintroducing the Peregrine Falcon. A mother falcon feeds her young in their nest on the window ledge of a skyscraper in downtown Baltimore. Over 300 pairs of peregrine falcons have been successfully reintroduced into the wild since ornithologist Tom Cady began his work in the early 1970s. Several pairs of falcons have successfully nested on the ledges of tall buildings in cities. The skyscrapers apparently provide a habitat similar to the cliffs on which the birds nest in the wild. (*Photo:* David Thorndill)

FIGURE 1-3 Australian Koalas. The habitat for koalas, mammals that raise their young in the mother's pouch, is the eucalyptus or gum forests of Australia. The koala's diet consists almost exclusively of the shoots and leaves of certain species of eucalyptus trees, and the koalas sleep in the trees at night. Without its eucalyptus forest habitat the koala is unlikely to survive. Some 80% of the original habitat has been destroyed to make way for homes, farms, and tourist services. This loss of habitat, along with an outbreak of disease among the koalas, has raised grave fears about the survival of the species. (*Photo:* Australian Tourist Bureau)

of the lifestyle of one of them, force one to move somewhere else, or eliminate one of them. Sometimes two species are found who do live in the same habitat and eat the same food. However, closer examination often proves that their niche is not the same because some other factor, such as predators or parasites, prevents either of the species alone from using all the available habitat or eating all that type of food.

A major problem that can arise when a new species is introduced into an area is that it may occupy the same niche as a native species. Competition between the new and native species may result in elimination of the native species.

Ecosystems

In ecological terms, *community* refers to a system of living organisms. This living system and the nonliving, or **abiotic,** components of the environment plus the ecological processes that take place there make up an **ecosystem** (see Figure 1-5). The nonliving parts of an ecosystem include such things as soil, amount of rainfall, and sunlight.

FIGURE 1-5 A Diagrammatic Representation of the Relationship of Population, Community, and Ecosystem. The populations (circles) of the various species living together in a specified location make up a community. Together with the nonliving features of the area (rectangles) and the ecological processes (arrows) that take place there, they make up an ecosystem. Many ecological processes take place in an ecosystem, such as energy flow and the cycling of water. Only a few are shown in the diagram. (All these processes are discussed in Chapter 3.)

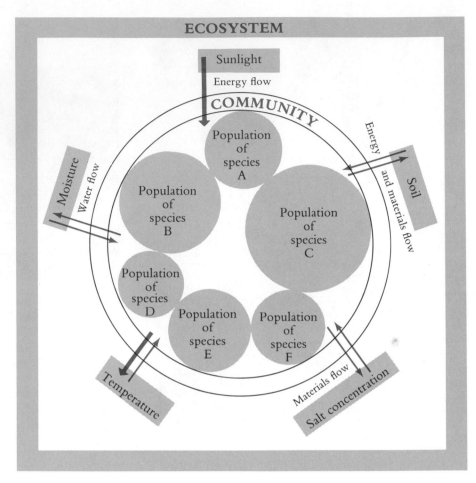

Because of the interactions among the organisms in an ecosystem, we might say that an ecosystem adds up to more than the sum of its parts. That is, the system itself has certain ecological properties in addition to the characteristics of the individuals or species making up the community. These properties include the flow of materials or energy through ecosystems; such processes are the subject of Chapter 3.

Some systems are not self-sufficient but depend on neighboring communities for such inputs as organic food materials; an example might be a small stream ecosystem. Others are large and complete enough to require little more than energy from the sun to function as a unit. Examples of ecosystems include a meadow, a stream, a forest, a lake, or any other clearly defined part of the landscape. (See Figure 1-6.)

ABIOTIC FACTORS IN ECOSYSTEMS

The abiotic factors in an environment influence the kind and numbers of organisms found there. Often when we speak of pollution we are concerned about substances or procedures that change these nonliving factors in an ecosystem and, in turn, affect the community of organisms living there. For instance, later we discuss pollutants that can change patterns of rainfall, increase or decrease environmental temperature, affect the oxygen or salt content of water,

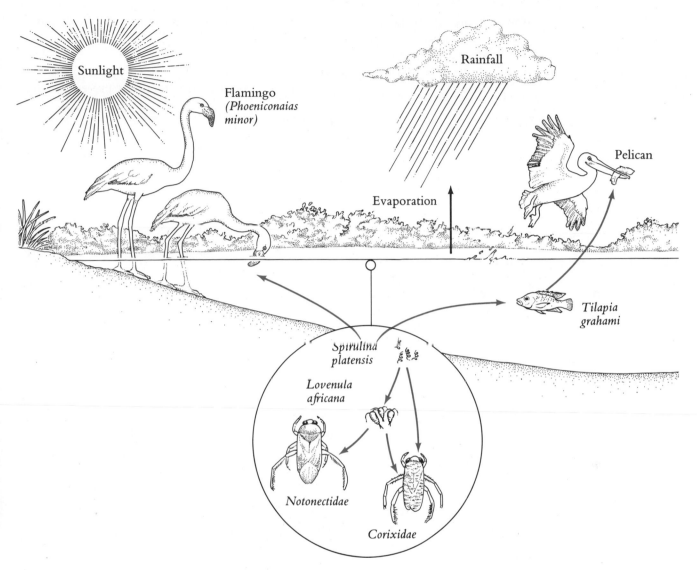

FIGURE 1-6 A Simple Ecosystem: Lake Nakuru, Kenya. Conditions are such that few species can live here. The living community in Lake Nakuru consists of populations of various species that can withstand the high concentration of sodium carbonate and the low concentration of hydrogen ions (pH 10.5). The main species found are blue-green algae (*Spirulina platensis*); flamingos (*Phoeniconaias minor*) and fish (*Tilapia grahami*), both of which eat the algae; and fish-eating birds such as pelicans and cormorants. Some of the important nonliving components of this ecosystem, in addition to sodium carbonate, are sunlight and rainfall. In more hospitable environments, such as the eastern deciduous forest ecosystem, many more species are found. (*Source:* Adapted from H. Remmert, *Ecology* [New York: Springer-Verlag, 1980])

or change the concentration of inorganic plant nutrients in water. For this reason, we now examine more closely the important abiotic components of ecosystems and briefly consider how they affect the living community.

Light

Sunlight is one of the principal nonliving factors in an ecosystem because green plants use sunlight to produce organic material. This process is called **photosynthesis.** In addition to sunlight, photosynthesis requires water and carbon dioxide. The organic products of photosynthesis include a variety of sugars. Carbon dioxide is a chemical compound that can be described as "low energy," while sugars have a great deal of energy stored in their chemical bonds. Thus, in the process of photosynthesis the energy from sunlight is turned into, or stored as, chemical energy.

In addition to organic materials, oxygen is produced during photosynthesis. Plants themselves use some of this oxygen, but they generally produce more than they need. All animal life, including human life, depends on this excess oxygen for respiration. We also depend on the sugars produced during photosynthesis for food, whether we eat the plants directly or whether we eat animals that eat plants.

The process of photosynthesis can be summarized as follows:

$$\text{Carbon dioxide} + \text{water} \xrightarrow[\text{sunlight}]{\text{green plants}} \text{organic material (sugars)} + \text{oxygen}$$

Or, using chemical formulas, photosynthesis can be written as the following equation:

$$6CO_2 + 6H_2O \xrightarrow[\substack{\text{green plants} \\ \text{(chlorophyll, enzymes)}}]{\substack{\text{energy from} \\ \text{sunlight}}} C_6H_{12}O_6 + 6O_2$$

However, this equation is only a summary. Photosynthesis actually consists of many separate re-

actions facilitated by a number of different **enzymes** (biological catalysts). A variety of organic materials are formed, here represented by the formula $C_6H_{12}O_6$.

In most ecosystems, sunlight is present in sufficient amounts. Only in the depths of the ocean or of inland lakes or in caves does the lack of sunlight limit growth in an ecosystem. How the energy captured in photosynthesis is transferred within ecosystems is discussed in Chapter 3.

Moisture

The amount of moisture in environments varies widely, from desert areas to lakes and oceans. All forms of life on earth require water to live, and the abundance and quality of water are major factors in determining what kinds of communities will develop in a given environment. In land environments the amount of available moisture is a function of precipitation, humidity, and the evaporation rate. In water environments the types of communities may also depend on the availability of water; however, in this case the availability of water means changes in water levels—that is, changes with the tides. Availability of water can also refer to differences in salt content, which affects the rate at which water enters or leaves organisms. In Chapter 2 we examine the different kinds of water environments and the specific communities that inhabit them. In this section we will look at the properties of water itself that have directly influenced the development of life as we know it.

Water and Temperature. Water is unusual in that a relatively large amount of heat is needed to change its temperature or to change solid water (ice) to a liquid or liquid water to a gas (water vapor). For these reasons, temperature changes in water tend to occur slowly, and changes in water temperature occur more slowly than changes in air temperature. This is important for organisms living in water, since it gives them more time to adjust to temperature changes.

Water reaches its greatest density at 3.94°C. That is, a given volume of water (for example, a 1-cm cube) weighs more at 3.94°C than at any other temperature. Its density decreases as the temperature decreases below this point. If you keep in mind that ice forms at 0°C, you can see that a given volume of ice at 0°C is lighter than the same volume of water at 3.94°C. This is why ice floats on cold water. This is an important property because it prevents lakes from freezing solid. The ice layer floats on top of the lake and insulates the water beneath it, allowing many aquatic creatures to survive during winter in the water below the ice.

Warm water, being less dense than cold water, also floats on cold water. This is important in managing reservoirs (see page 391) and also in determining the effects of pollutants on lakes, such as the phosphorus in detergents (Chapter 18).

Water as a Solvent. Water is the most common solvent in nature. The amount and kinds of nutrients dissolved in water affect the growth of organisms. In a similar way, pollutants dissolved in water, even those that are only slightly soluble, affect organisms in land or water environments. For instance, **acid rain** is formed when sulfur oxides, produced by burning fossil fuels, dissolve in rain. Acid rain has reduced forest growth in Scandinavian countries and has caused entire populations of sport fish to disappear from some lakes in the Adirondack Mountains of New York State. (See Chapter 16 for more on acid rain.)

Salinity

Salt waters, such as the oceans, generally contain about 3.5% salt, or 35 parts of salt for every 1,000 parts of water. (Terms such as parts per thousand, parts per million, and parts per billion are explained inside the back cover of this book.) Some inland lakes and seas can have even higher salt concentrations, for example, Great Salt Lake in Utah or Lake Nakuru in Kenya (Figure 1-6). In contrast, fresh waters average 0.05% salt, or 0.5 parts per thousand. Most of the salt in the oceans is sodium chloride, but many other salts are present.

The salt content of water is one of the major factors determining what organisms will be found there. Freshwater organisms, both plant and animal, have a salt concentration in their body fluids and inside their cells higher than that of the water in which they live. Because substances tend to move from areas of higher concentration to areas of lower concentration, salts tend to leave these organisms. Freshwater organisms have developed mechanisms or structural parts to cope with this situation. In addition, freshwater organisms have evolved so that they contain lower salt concentrations in their bodies than organisms found in salt water.

Some saltwater organisms (for example, marine algae and many marine invertebrates) have a salt concentration in their bodies or cells almost identical to that of ocean water. However, many marine organisms have body fluids with a lower salt concentration than the water in which they live. For these organisms, water tends to leave their cells or bodies and salts tend to enter. Their regulatory mechanisms must solve a different problem from that of freshwater organisms. Bony fish, for instance, have developed ways of excreting salt and retaining water. The main point is that the two environments, salt water and fresh water, provide different conditions for organisms to adapt to and thus are inhabited by different kinds of organisms.

In addition to salt and fresh waters, there are brackish waters, with intermediate salt concentrations. Such waters occur wherever salt and fresh waters meet—in estuaries, for instance, or where salt water intrudes on fresh groundwaters. Certain organisms are adapted, for all or part of their life cycles, to various intermediate salt concentrations.

Land-dwelling animals and plants tend to lose water to the atmosphere. In this respect they resemble many marine species because during their evolution they have also had to develop mechanisms to conserve water.

The kinds of water communities that develop in salt and fresh water are examined more closely in Chapter 2.

Temperature

Temperature has a profound effect on the growth and well-being of organisms. The biochemical reactions necessary for life are dependent on temperature. In general, chemical reactions speed up two to four times for a 10°C rise in temperature.

Nonetheless, it is not possible to make sweeping generalizations about the effects of environmental temperature on the distribution of organisms because organisms have developed so many and varied mechanisms to deal with temperature changes.

Warm-blooded organisms, such as humans, are able to maintain a constant body temperature independent of the temperature of their environment. They are called **endothermic** or **homeothermic** organisms. Body warmth is a by-product of internal biochemical reactions that produce energy for the organism. In a cold environment, warm-blooded animals can retain this body warmth by insulation (blubber, feathers, fur, clothing). In a warm environment, the heat is lost by processes usually involving the evaporation of water (humans sweating from the skin, dogs panting and allowing their tongues to hang out). During very cold weather, when animals have difficulty finding enough food to burn to keep their body temperatures at a high level, some of them hibernate. During this time, their rate of energy use falls, so their body temperature falls as well.

The temperature of so-called cold-blooded (**ectothermic**) animals, as well as of plants and microorganisms, varies with that of the environment. However, even in this group of organisms there are a variety of mechanisms to adjust body temperature. Most of these mechanisms would be classified as *behavioral* methods of regulation. For example, bees can warm their hive by beating their wings. This is such an effective method that bees can live and reproduce in arctic regions. Many insects, snakes, and lizards warm themselves in the sun, taking up a position broadside to the sun's rays during the cool morning hours. Mosquito larvae develop quickly in the uppermost layers of ponds, where the sun's rays warm the water. When temperatures rise, many organisms take refuge in holes or burrows or under rocks. This helps them escape a lethal rise in body temperature or, in the case of desert organisms, prevents excessive use of precious water for cooling. During freezing weather, ectothermic animals and plants may produce antifreeze substances in their cells to prevent them from freezing. Many animals produce glycerol, while plants produce sugars such as hamamelose.

Photosynthesis does not depend on temperature as strongly as other reactions do because it is not just a biochemical reaction but also involves **photochemical** (light-driven) reactions. Thus, photosynthesis is almost as effective in producing organic material in cold as in warm climates.

Most of the observations we can make about temperature and its effects on organisms are on a large scale. For instance, fewer types of organisms seem able to adapt to conditions in the Arctic, where temperatures are far below the biological optimum. Even this seemingly obvious principle is complicated by the observation that besides the severity of temperature, the variability of conditions is also important. That is, fewer types of organisms are found where temperatures vary widely from day to night or season to season than where temperatures are more constant. However, one thing we can say with confidence is that organisms, during the course of their evolution, have developed mechanisms to deal with temperature as it is found in their environment, whether that is warm or cold, constant or fluctuating. Human actions that change these temperatures can have devastating effects on ecosystems. For example, in Denmark the brown weevil (*Hylobius abieties*) normally takes three years to develop. When the forest is **clear cut** (all trees cut, regardless of size or species), the sun warms the ground more than before and the weevil matures in two years. For this reason, the weevil does much greater damage to forests where clear cutting is allowed. In Chapter 18 we discuss the effects of **thermal pollution:** the addition of excess heat to water environments.

Oxygen Supply. Both plants and animals use oxygen in the process of respiration, whereby they obtain energy for growth and metabolism. Respiration consists of a series of biochemical reactions in which an energy-containing organic material, such as the sugar glucose, is broken down by biological catalysts called enzymes. The energy released is used to drive other reactions in the cell. If oxygen is available, the material is fully broken down to carbon dioxide, water, and energy. The summary of these reactions resembles photosynthesis in reverse:

$$\text{Oxygen} + \underset{\text{(glucose)}}{\text{organic material}} \xrightarrow{\text{enzymes}} \text{carbon dioxide} + \text{water} + \text{energy}$$

Using chemical formulas, respiration can be summarized as:

$$6O_2 + C_6H_{12}O_6 \longrightarrow 6CO_2 + 6H_2O + \text{energy}$$

In land environments, oxygen is rarely in short supply. (Exceptions would be in some soils or on high mountaintops.) In water, on the other hand, the supply of oxygen may easily be a problem. The concentration of oxygen in water depends on the rate at which the gas diffuses into water, as well as on the rates at which it is produced by the plants living there and used by the plants and animals in the water.

In some lakes the supply of plant nutrients allows the growth of masses of algae, which die, sink to the bottom, and are decomposed by bacteria. This last process can use up all the oxygen in the water. Other desirable organisms cannot live in this oxygen-poor water. The addition of sewage to natural water environments results in the loss of much of the oxygen present. These effects are discussed more fully in Chapter 18.

Fire

Fire can also be considered an abiotic factor that influences the types of communities in an ecosystem. Some environments are subject to regular natural cycles of fire. In southeastern pine forests of the United States, in the grassy savannahs of Africa, and the steppe regions of the U.S.S.R., periodic fires are a natural event.

In grasslands, periodic fires kill tree seedlings, while grasses, whose major energy stores and growth centers are underground, quickly sprout up after the fire. In this way, fire prevents the transition of grasslands to forests in certain areas.

Trees in forests where fires are regular may have thick bark that enables them to survive fires. The cones of some pines, such as the Jack pine (*Pinus banksiana*), release seeds best when heated to a certain temperature. In this way, the seeds are sown at times when other plants that might compete for

living space have been eliminated from the area. In fact, in the pine-spruce forests in northern Europe, fire actually allows pines to grow. There are certain areas in these forests where the spruce have grown up in dense stands, crowding out the pines, which do not compete well for living space. Although the spruce are easily damaged by fire, once they form a dense stand it is difficult for fire to spread because the short spruce needles pack tightly on the ground and are resistant to fire. However, where pine and spruce are mixed, the forest floor accumulates loose piles of litter shed by the pines. Periodic fires in the mixed pine-spruce forest injure the spruce and allow pines to flourish.

In several cases, it has been shown that the vegetation growing up after a fire has more nutrients, such as phosphorus, potassium, calcium, and magnesium. Animals feeding on this vegetation may be better nourished. When humans prevent these natural fires, they are really causing changes in ecosystems that have come to depend on fire for periodic renewal.

Fire has now become an accepted part of forest management, although the public has been slow to accept this idea. (See Controversy 1-1.)

Soils

The type of soil found in an area is very important to humans because soils vary widely in their ability to support crops. The most useful soils from this point of view are the grassland and temperate forest soils. Other types, such as desert soil or the soil in tropical rain forests, are not as generally suited for raising crops. However, scientists looking at the effect of soil type on the kinds and distribution of organisms in an area have concluded that while soil type can have some effects on communities, the communities themselves have a profound effect on the type of soil in an area. To understand this it is necessary to realize that soil is not an entirely abiotic component of ecosystems but rather is a mixture of living and nonliving materials.

The nonliving part of soil is the finely divided particles produced by the action of weathering on the parent material of the earth's surface. Combined with this is organic material: organisms and their products, which grow, die, and become mixed in.

Controversy 1-1

The Baxter Fire, the Yellowstone Fire—Would You Let Them Burn?

Just think if you can, but don't strain yourself, do-gooder, of all the comfortable homes that could have been built with that wasted lumber.

E. D. Chasse, *Bangor Daily News,* July 27, 1977

If you could look at the park as something besides a giant woodlot you might not be so concerned about the burn. This beautiful park has burned many times in the past, and it will burn in the future.

Melvin Ames, *Bangor Daily News,* August 19, 1977

Fire can play two important functions in the forest ecosystem. First, light surface fires clear away dead underbrush, which, if it were to accumulate, could cause massive and intense forest fires. In this century, our very success in preventing forest fires has led to conditions in many forests that have led to terribly severe fires, such as the Yellowstone Park fire in 1988.

Prescribed burning has been used by professional foresters in some forests to prevent such buildups. Prescribed burning is undertaken with caution; days chosen are moist and windless; all forest uses are curtailed.

The second function of fire is replacement or renewal of forest stock. Fire may act as nature's instrument of forest renewal and has acted in this fashion for hundreds and thousands of years without the aid of the forester.

Knowledge of the role of fire will increasingly be put to use in "managing" forests, but it is not yet clear precisely how the knowledge will enter into future decisions.

In the summer of 1977, a massive fire occurred in Baxter State Park in Maine. The fire was started by lightning; its intensity was fed by downed timber. Let us, for a moment, reenact the scene: Prime recreation land is being destroyed,

but the wilderness is renewing itself. Will you let the fire burn?

The story began many decades ago when the will of Percival Baxter, former Governor of Maine, was opened by his lawyers. To the people of Maine, Baxter bequeathed a 200,000-acre (81,000 hectares) forested tract with 46 mountain peaks and ridges. The jewel of the tract was towering Mount Katahdin. This mountain, at 5,240 feet (1,600 m), is the northernmost point of the Appalachian Trail, the wilderness footpath that runs from Georgia to Maine. Governor Baxter's will instructed that the land is

> forever to be held by the State of Maine in trust for public park, public forest, public recreational purposes, and scientific forestry, the same also forever shall be held in its natural wild state and except for a small area forever shall be held as a sanctuary for wild beasts and birds.

If we dig a trench vertically down into a particular kind of soil, along the sides of the trench we can see several layers, or horizons. The arrangement of these horizons is called the **soil profile** (Figure 1-7). This profile differs for soils found in various biomes.

The top layer, or A horizon, varies in depth from less than an inch (2.5 cm) in tropical rain forests to several feet in some grasslands. This layer, often called **topsoil,** contains plant roots, fungi, microorganisms, and a wide variety of soil insects and other burrowing animals. Also found here are

Over the years, the park had been developed, so that by 1977 it included an automobile road and seven campgrounds. The camps had space for trailers and tents, as well as bunkhouses and shelters. Because of the popularity of the park, reservations were suggested for those who needed to be sure of space. When the fire struck in Baxter Park in 1977, it was a foregone conclusion that the park authority would fight it. The battle, however, was exceedingly difficult because of the rough terrain and the presence of numerous downed trees. The trees were in the aftermath of a fierce winter storm that had struck the southwest slope of Mt. Katahdin in 1974. Wind and ice had combined to snap tall trees in two, leaving a pileup of dead logs on the slopes. The Great Northern Paper Company had been allowed into the park to harvest the blowdown for use as pulpwood in the hopes of lessening the risk of fire, but the harvest had never been completed.

Legal action had been taken by the Baxter Park Defense Fund, and a judge's order brought the harvest to a halt in August 1976. While the judge did not forbid the removal of the downed trees, he directed that the heavy equipment being used had to be removed from the park. The heavy equipment was cutting into the forest floor, leaving gouge marks that might be used as roads or that could reroute streams into the depressions. Increased erosion from scarred areas would be likely as well. The equipment was removed by the paper company and the harvest of the blowdown came to an abrupt end. The following summer, when lightning ignited the blaze, much of the tangle of deadwood still lay on the ground.

In the heat of the blaze, the Baxter Defense Fund, which had prevented removal of the blowdown, let it be known that it planned once again to go to court. The group's aim, as before, was to force out the heavy pieces of equipment that were scarring the slopes of the park and crisscrossing the mountain streams in an effort to create the fire line. Although public reaction to the threatened suit was intense, the Defense Fund would have gone ahead with the legal action had the group not seen that the fire was in fact being brought under control faster than court action could be taken.

Although the fire was out, the controversy raged on. Letters and editorials in the newspapers of Maine insulted the environmentalists. Letters also appeared expressing sympathy for the concerns of the Baxter Defense Fund. The quotations that began this discussion were from such letters.

Eventually the controversy, too, appeared to go out, only to be reignited in the summer of 1988 when a raging fire broke out in Yellowstone National Park. Park managers intended to allow the blaze to burn itself out, only protecting vital park buildings. However, public outcry was enormous at the thought of the trees being lost and the animals that might be endangered. Political pressure eventually forced park officials to fight the fire on all fronts. Moreover, as a result of the negative publicity the park service received, it may well decide to fight park fires in all cases, whether or not officials feel the fires would serve a useful purpose.

How do you feel about fires in public recreational areas? If the fires rage again, would you let them burn?

dead and decaying parts of plants and animals. In land ecosystems, this is where the chief turnover of organic matter occurs. Here all the unused organic materials are recycled and broken down, first to humus and eventually to inorganic materials. **Humus** is an organic substance that is broken down relatively slowly. It is not a plant food; however, it helps retain water in soil and to keep soil loose, or friable. These are important qualities for soil fertility.

Inorganic substances, formed from decomposition in the topsoil, filter down into the second soil layer, or **subsoil.** Finally, we come to the third layer, or **parent material,** on which the process of soil formation began.

Soil Formation. Many soil scientists believe that the type of soil that eventually forms in an area is dependent only on the climate of the region. Although plant and animal materials and the parent rock contribute the substances from which soil is formed, climate determines the process of soil development. In strong support of this theory is the fact that world climate maps (Figure 2-2) closely match maps of world soil types (Figure 2-3). According to this theory, the rock from which the soil is originally derived is not important except in early stages of soil formation, when it has an effect on the type of vegetation that arises.

Exceptions do occur where climatic conditions are extreme, such as in the desert. Here, small differences in the mineral composition of soils can make a large difference in the type of community that develops.

Soil Types. Temperature and precipitation are the two climatic factors of greatest importance in soil formation. As an example of how climate affects soil type, consider hot, humid climates. The warm temperatures and moisture speed the processes of decay. Organic material rapidly decomposes to inorganic materials and is absorbed by a mat of plant roots on or close to the surface. Heavy rainfall causes soluble materials to leach rapidly out of the topsoil layers. You would expect the result to be a topsoil having little organic material and not much in the way of soluble plant nutrients either. This is exactly what is found in hot, humid tropical rain forests. Some of these soils are so poor in humus and minerals that they are almost white (Figure 1-8). Materials such as silica are rapidly leached out of tropical soils by the heavy rains, leaving high concentrations of aluminum, magnesium, and iron oxides in the soil. In some areas, when tropical rain forests are cut down and the soil is laid bare, the iron enrichment of certain soil layers can cause the formation of **laterite.** The result is a soil so hard that it has been cut up for use as building blocks.

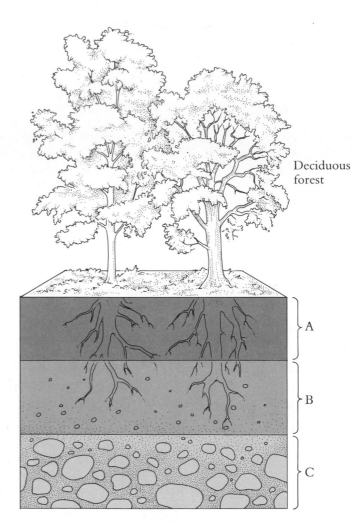

Deciduous forest

A

B

C

FIGURE 1-7 Soil Profiles. This is how soil would appear on the sides of a trench cut into the ground. The upper layer, or A horizon, is topsoil and contains plant and animal debris, which is being turned into humus by soil microorganisms. In the B horizon, most of the organic material has been changed into its inorganic components. The third, or C, horizon is parent material—that is, soil characteristic of the rock from which it was formed. Climate and vegetation act on parent rock material over the ages to form the soil characteristic of a given era.

Some of these blocks have lasted for 400 to 500 years in Southeast Asian temples. Obviously such soils can no longer be cultivated.

Desert soils, in contrast, tend to be coarse and high in salts or lime, since little water is available to leach them out. Further, evaporation draws salts

FIGURE 1-8 Eroded Land in Bolivia. After the forest has been cut down, the little fertility that remains in the soil is quickly depleted by crops or eroded away by heavy rains. Land allowed to degrade to this extent will not regain fertility on any human time scale. (*Photo:* P. Almasy, UNEP)

up to the surface where they can form a crust, called **hardpan** or **caliche.**

Grassland soil is typically black and rich in finely divided, organic humus. Plant nutrients such as calcium, magnesium, and potassium are abundant. Such soils are valuable for agriculture. Temperate-soil forests have less humus, and nutrients tend to leach out more easily, but these soils, too, can be successfully farmed if fertilizers and lime are added.

Abiotic Factors Working Together

Undoubtedly, many other abiotic components of ecosystems could be mentioned. However, those factors already discussed are generally agreed to be the most important ones.

Although they are discussed separately, it is important to note that abiotic factors act together.

Temperature, for instance, almost always acts in combination with moisture and wind. To predict how particular temperatures will affect the kinds of organisms found in a given environment, we need to know about these other factors as well. Likewise, the development of soil type involves the interaction of climate, the organisms that grow up in a given area, and the breakdown of parent rock.

DIVERSITY IN ECOSYSTEMS

When ecologists speak of **diversity,** they are referring to two features of an ecosystem. The first is the number of species in a given area compared to the number of individuals. In other words, it is a way of measuring variety. Sometimes this is called

---
Towards a Sustainable Society

Developing an Environmental Agenda
by William C. Clark

William C. Clark is currently a senior research associate at Harvard University's Kennedy School of Government and editor of Environment *magazine. He has directed*

studies on sustainable development at the International Institute for Applied Systems Analysis in Austria and is a member of the U.S. National Academy of Sciences Committee on Global Change. In 1983, Clark received a MacArthur Award.

At the individual level, people have begun to respond to increased awareness of global environmental change by altering their values, beliefs, and actions. Changes in individual behavior are surely necessary but are not enough. It is as a global species that we are transforming the planet. It is only as a

global species—pooling our knowledge, coordinating our actions, and sharing what the planet has to offer—that we have any prospects for managing the planet's transformation along pathways of sustainable development. Self-conscious, intelligent management of the earth is one of the great challenges facing humanity as it approaches the twenty-first century.

We have entered an era characterized by syndromes of global change that stem from the interdependence between human development and the environment. As we attempt to move from merely causing these syndromes to

---

the *species richness* of an ecosystem. The second feature is *dominance*. This term measures relative numbers of individuals present in each species. Two ecosystems may have the same number of species present, but in one there may be approximately equal numbers of individuals of each species while in the second most of the individuals may be of the same species. The first ecosystem is then considered to have greater diversity.

One reason why diversity is an important measurement is that human interference with a natural ecosystem often results in reduced diversity. Fewer kinds of species are found in a polluted ecosystem than in a similar ecosystem that is not polluted. Measurements of diversity in a given area over time can be an indication of the effects of pollution.

Reasons for Diversity. The more diverse the environmental conditions, the more different niches are possible and, assuming a long enough time has passed for evolutionary changes to have taken place, the more species are found. It should be emphasized, though, that there are basic biological processes common to all organisms. These processes work best at certain optimum temperatures, light intensities, and so forth. The farther conditions are from these optima, the less easily organisms can adapt to the conditions. For this reason, the farther conditions are from biological optima, the fewer species are found. To put it another way, fewer species are able to use the available niches in harsh climates. Thus, fewer species are found in arctic regions, on icy mountaintops, and in deserts than

managing them consciously, two central questions must be addressed: What kind of planet do we want? What kind of planet can we get?

What kind of planet we want is ultimately a question of values. How much species diversity should be maintained in the world? Should the size or the growth rate of the human population be curtailed to protect the global environment? How much climatic change is acceptable? How much poverty? Should the deep ocean be considered an option for hazardous-waste disposal? Science can illuminate such questions, but our ultimate choices are a matter of will, not truth.

Determining what kind of planet we can get involves an assessment of what we already know about the relationships of humans and their environment, as well as

a commitment to the sort of scientific research and social learning that will fill in the gaps in our knowledge.

Discussions of what is desirable and what is feasible must finally lead to agendas for action—on both the national and the international level. On a national level, the most immediate need is for mechanisms to debate and agree upon environmental goals. It is both shortsighted and reckless that we have, as a country, no clear understanding of the choices before us, much less of the way we should go. Without a well-articulated set of goals for a sustainable society, we are destined to react to events but never direct them.

On an international level, a large and rapidly growing number of governmental bodies, governmental agencies, and multilateral organizations are scrambling to

play some part in the management of planet earth. Pluralism has much to recommend it. But are we not nearing a point of diminishing returns where too many meetings, too many declarations, and too many visiting experts leave too few people with too few resources and too little time to actually do anything? The immediate need is for a forum in which ministerial-level coordination of environmental-management activities can be regularly discussed and implemented, much as is already done for international economic policy. As in the case of economic policy, the existence of such a formal, high-level governmental summit on global issues of environment and development could provide an occasion for parallel discussions involving nongovernment and private sector interests.

in more moderate environments such as temperate or tropical forests.

Three factors—diversity of environmental conditions, harshness of environmental conditions, and the length of time a system has had to evolve—are not the only factors affecting diversity, but they appear to be major controlling influences.

Human interference may also move conditions farther from biological optima. For instance, the addition of sewage to a stream reduces the amount of oxygen available in the water. Only a few organisms are adapted to low oxygen concentrations. As a result, the diversity in the polluted stream is much lower than in a normal, well-oxygenated stream.

It should be emphasized that the actual number of organisms in the polluted and nonpolluted habitat may be similar, but the organisms in the polluted habitat will mostly be members of one or a few species. It is the number of different species that is reduced.

SUCCESSION AND CLIMAX

Succession

Some ecosystems are both characteristic of the area in which they occur and also stable over time. That is, the kinds and proportions of the various plants and animals do not change much. Not all communities have this sort of stability.

Consider the fate of an abandoned farmer's field in a temperate climate such as the northern United States. The first year after the farmer gives up the field, it fills with annual weeds—the kinds of weeds that grow up each year, produce seed, and die. Perennial weeds, which are dormant during the winter months, start to appear the second year. Eventually, small shrubs and trees grow among the weeds and then take over the field. As the shrubs and trees grow larger and begin to shade the ground, the weeds that once grew in the field no longer find conditions suitable for growth. The kinds of animal species found in the field change as the vegetation alters. This rather orderly process is called **succession.** During succession, each community of plants and animals actually changes the environment in which it lives so that conditions favor a new community, one usually involving larger species. The changes may involve such factors as the temperature and acidity of the soil or the amount of water and sunlight available. For example, pines may be the first trees to grow in a field. Pine branches eventually shade the ground, however, and pine seedlings do not do well in shade. Deciduous tree seedlings, such as oaks and hickories, which can grow in shade, may then take over the forest floor and supplant the pines themselves.

Succession occurs not only in abandoned fields but in all kinds of habitats. For instance, after a volcano erupts, tiny plants called algae begin to colonize the cooled lava. Over the years, a series of communities will replace each other until communities similar to those inhabiting the area before the volcano erupted appear. This succession, which starts from bare rock, is called *primary succession.*

Primary succession may also occur in ponds and lakes. With time, lakes and ponds may begin to fill up with sediments and plant debris. The waters become more and more shallow and less and less clear. (This is the process of **eutrophication.**) Eventually, the lake or pond fills so completely that it becomes a bog or marsh.

The term *secondary succession* is used to describe the process by which a community that had been removed from a particular site is reestablished. For instance, when a field is cleared for farming, a natural community is removed. If the field is later abandoned, and the original community begins to reestablish itself, that is called secondary succession.

The Climax Concept

In many areas, a community finally appears that is not supplanted by another one, as long as major climate changes do not occur. This last community does not change conditions to make them unsuitable for itself. Such a community may survive, perhaps for centuries, until other factors (such as climate) change or until disease or human activities are introduced. This relatively stable community is called the **climax community.** Major areas of the world have characteristic, or regional, climax communities and these are what we call **biomes.** They appear to be determined mainly by temperature and rainfall within a given area, although other factors, such as soil type and soil age, can also influence the kind of vegetation that grows.

Succession starting from an aquatic environment, such as a lake or pond, or from a terrestrial environment, such as an abandoned field, tends to lead to the same climax vegetation in a given area, although the path the succession takes may be very different. This supports the idea that the climate of a given area determines what the climax vegetation will be.

Succession and Climax in Natural Ecosystems

This concept of succession leading to a climax vegetation is a clear and straightforward idea. Unfortunately, it does not perfectly fit natural ecosystems. Thus, systems occur in which two or more climaxes appear to alternate. An example is Neusiedler Lake on the border between Austria and Hungary, which seems to appear and disappear in long cycles, perhaps 80 years or more. One theory holds that reeds in the lake grow until they occupy the entire lake (which is shallow). At this point the reeds use up the entire amount of water in the lake. The dry lake bed can no longer support the reed ecosystem, which collapses, only to reappear after the lake fills again.

The main point is that there may be long cycles of change even in climax ecosystems. It is important to take this into account when humans are planning changes in ecosystems, lest the natural and human changes add together and have an unexpectedly greater result. For instance, forest trees such as beech, spruce, and maple do not produce seeds every year but rather at irregular intervals depending on the climate. Passenger pigeons were probably dependent on seeds of this type. Some ecologists believe that large flocks of passenger pigeons were the result of a series of good seed years. The birds may have become extinct because humans killed so many birds that flocks were too small to survive the following series of poor seed years.

We will return to the concepts of diversity, succession, and climax at the end of Chapter 3, after energy flow in ecosystems is discussed.

EVOLUTION AND COMPETITION

Even a short study of the fossil record reveals that the very existence of a species is a dynamic phenomenon. That is, a species is not a static entity, shaped in a particular mold and assured of the same niche for eternity. Rather, fossil history shows a pattern of change in species as they adapt to changing conditions. If species are for some reason unable to adapt, the fossil record shows clearly that they cease to exist; in other words, they become extinct. From fossil evidence it appears that species exist, on average, less than 10 million years. In fact, about 99% of the species that have ever existed are believed to have suffered extinction.

Despite this record, some 1.5 million species have been identified in today's world. Even this number, however, is thought to be only a fraction of the mind-boggling number of total species that exist on earth—5 to 10 million or more. In the following sections we will consider briefly some of the ideas about how evolution has led to such a

great diversity of organisms. We must understand something about this natural process before we examine the effects humans have on the dynamic diversity of natural communities.

Evolution is one of the most exciting areas in biology today. Theories are being devised, torn apart, and revised. There is a great deal of argument, and as yet there are few points on which everyone agrees. Information on this topic comes from a variety of sources. One source is the field of genetics, in which the hereditary material (DNA or genes) of organisms living today is studied. Another source is the field of paleontology, in which fossils illustrating past evolutionary change are unearthed and examined. A third source is the field of ecology, in which the relationships between species alive today are investigated and relationships between species from the past are deduced.

Forces Driving Evolutionary Change

The most commonly held beliefs about the evolution of a diversity of life forms involve two major factors. The first is the adaptation of species to use new habitats. As climates have changed through the eons, as continents have drifted apart and come together, as mountains have risen or worn away, new habitats must have become available for organisms to colonize, and old ones must have become much less hospitable than they once were. These pressures, acting through natural selection of the fittest organisms, could have caused species to change in character over long periods of time. In addition, when geologic changes cause separation of populations of the same species, new species can develop. On the other hand, the same factors of climatic or geologic change must cause some species, unable to live under the new conditions, to become extinct.

But, there is a second factor implicit in ideas about evolution: competition. If environmental change is the force that sets the stage for species to form, competition is the theme of the play itself. It is competition within a species that determines that the fittest individuals will survive to reproduce and that thus determines the direction of a species's evolution. It is competition between species that determines which species will survive to reproduce and which will become extinct. Furthermore, competition between species can be viewed as the force driving them to use new niches in order to avoid extinction. Thus, competition is seen as a major determinant of community structure today as well as an evolutionary force.

Climatic Change. Although the idea of environmental change as a driving force in the evolution of species has great logical appeal, real fossil evidence for it is only now being collected. This is partly because in the fossil record extinction of species and the appearance of new species are hard to distinguish from the migration of various species into or out of an area. One location where fossil evidence for climate-caused evolution is fairly strong is in sediments from the Siwalik Hills in Pakistan, laid down from 1 to 18 million years ago. Here, scientists can see the sudden disappearance about 7 million years ago of a whole related group of apes. This disappearance coincides with the beginning of a drier, cooler climate.

Competition. Many ecologists believe that predation and competition for resources such as space or food are the two main forces that determine what species are found in particular communities. How well a species meets the challenge of being preyed upon is a factor that influences how abundant that species is in a community. Similarly, how well a species competes with the other species present in a community determines whether it will gather enough of the resources it needs to survive and reproduce.

Predation is sometimes said to be less important than competition because predation pressure tends to lessen as a species becomes less abundant. (The predator itself becomes scarce as a result of starvation, or it turns to other prey.) Unlike predation, however, competition between two species can be unremitting and can lead to the loss or exclusion of the weaker species from a community. This is called the **principle of competitive exclusion.** According to this theory, two organisms cannot live in the same habitat and use the same re-

sources—that is, occupy the same niche—indefinitely. Eventually one, the better competitor, will eliminate the other. This principle can actually be demonstrated in the laboratory with single-celled organisms, such as paramecia in a jug of growth medium. However, because of the complexity of natural ecosystems, in the real world it is not so easy to show that a species has disappeared as a result of competition as opposed to some other cause.

The driving force or evolutionary "push" that competition exerts might work either directly or indirectly. A species could evolve directly toward an improved competitive position by becoming the stronger competitor for a given resource. For instance, a plant might evolve in the direction of improved absorption of essential nutrients such as dissolved phosphate in the soil. This sort of strategy has obvious physiological limits, however. The plant will eventually approach a maximum rate of movement of chemicals.

A more indirect method of improving competitive position would be to begin using a different resource or part of a resource that is not presently being used. In this strategy, competing species in a given habitat evolve so that they use different spaces, different resources, or the same resources but at different times. For instance, several bird species may continually occupy and find food in the same trees, but one species will occupy the topmost branches, another the middle ranges, and another the bottommost branches. Bats and swallows would ordinarily compete directly for insects, but swallows feed on the insects until dusk while bats feed only at night.

Relief from competition is also obtained when organisms evolve ways to "mark" a particular resource space as their own. Certain tree species excrete chemicals that prevent the growth of other species or individuals nearby. *Symbiosis,* in which two species live in close touch, and at least one partner provides the other with a material or a service, can be viewed as a way of improving the competitive advantage of one or both partners. The tree that provides a home in its roots for nitrogen-fixing bacteria receives in return a necessary nutrient

CHAPTER 1 Species, Communities, Ecosystems, Evolution, and Competition **35**

that improves its competitive position in a nitrogen-poor environment.

In all these ways, then, competition is believed to exert an evolutionary pressure on organisms to change, to diversify, in fact to become new species in different habitats or to develop a different set of ecological requirements in the same habitat (a new niche).

Competitionists point to the finches of the Galapagos Islands as proof of their theory. There are 14 species found in that habitat and all 14 are believed to have evolved from one ancestral species. The birds differ in food habits—all the way from seed eating to blood drinking—and in body characteristics such as beak size and shape. Certain pairs of closely related finches are never, or almost never, found on the same island. This is considered to be evidence for the principle of competitive exclusion. In one case where closely related finches do coexist, they occupy different parts of the island. Furthermore, one of the species has shifted from eating mainly seeds, which it does on islands where it exists by itself, to eating mainly insects. Competitionists believe this to be an example of a shift in the use of resources caused by competition between species.

Competition versus Other Evolutionary Pressures

Competition theory—the body of evidence and conjecture that attributes the structure of communities and pressure for evolutionary change to competition between individuals and between species—has been a major part of ecological thought for many years. Recently, however, some scientists have questioned whether competition between species is really that common or that important in natural communities. That is, most ecologists believe that competition exists, but not all believe it is the major force in either the present structure of communities or in evolutionary change. In fact, many believe that predation is more important than competition.

Several field studies seem to show that for some species, predators do keep populations well below the level at which they would need to compete for resources. A classic study involved predatory starfish (Schoener, 1982). When scientists removed starfish from intertidal regions, there was a decrease in the number of species the starfish had been preying on. This seemed to be due to competitive exclusion of some of the prey species by others. Such competition had been kept down by the starfish, which had prevented the prey species from using all their available resources. Thus, in this community, competition had an effect only when predation was absent.

The Variable Environment Alternative

Ecologists who do not subscribe to the ideas of competition theory believe that environmental change, which occurs often and without regard to any biological interaction (examples would include floods, hurricanes, cold spells, drought), acts to keep populations well below the level at which competition will occur. These scientists note that it is true that periods of scarcity of resources (such as food) may occur, thus causing competition among species. However, they argue that the more common periods of relative plenty that follow scarcity obscure any evolutionary effects. That is, any characteristics that might have given a competitive advantage to certain individuals during the period of scarcity would no longer represent an advantage during the normal times in which resources are abundant compared to population size. These characteristics would just become part of the normal variation in characteristics within a species.

Examination of natural communities to determine whether competition is occurring (or whether it occurred in the past, leading to the exclusion of some species) is a field of study currently fraught with controversy. It appears that the amount of competition between two species can vary from year to year in some areas, while competition can be a relatively constant fact of life in others. Even in the same environment, abiotic factors such as climate and fire can keep some species well below the level at which competition would occur, while at the same time competition is taking place between other species. In other words, the complexity of the situation regarding competition is pretty much what one might expect from the complexity of the natural world!

Punctuated versus Gradual Evolution

Basic to the theory of competition as an evolutionary driving force is the idea that natural communities are in **equilibrium.** That is, amounts of resources compared to the numbers of organisms remain in balance from season to season or year to year. Whether great or small, all of the available resources are used by a dynamic balance of the species present. These species are in constant and unremitting competition with each other for resources. Further, competition theory predicts a gradual evolutionary change, a fine honing of competitive edges, resulting from this constant pressure.

In some environments, however, the fossil record does not support such gradual changes. Instead, scientists studying the fossils theorize that species remain the same for millions of generations even in the face of environmental change such as cooling of the climate or decreases in rainfall. These scientists believe that evolution does not take place by gradually accumulated changes in a species that, bit by bit, help it adapt to a changing environment. Rather, they feel evolutionary change is abrupt. New species form suddenly and remain the same for a long time. This is called **punctuated evolution.** Such a view of communities and evolution has interesting implications for ecology and environmental science. The idea of communities as perfectly balanced groups of species perfectly adapted to their environment may not always be the case. Natural communities may not be a "perfect and fragile blend of irreplaceable species" (Bakker, 1985).

On the other hand, the concept of equilibrium implies a natural balance of forces that act to correct a push in the population from one direction or another. Equilibrium systems are in balance and tend to remain in balance. If natural systems are often not in equilibrium, natural communities may have less resilience to environmental change than some people have thought. Until we understand more about evolution and what drives species toward extinction or toward better adaptation to their environment, we must be very careful about the environmental pressures we exert on natural systems.

SUMMARY

A group of organisms that can successfully breed with each other, that share ties of parentage, and that therefore have a common pool of hereditary material is called a species. A population is a group of organisms of the same species living together in a particular area. The habitat of a species consists of the biological and physical surroundings in which a species or population is found. Similar but somewhat more comprehensive is the term *niche,* which also includes what a species does in its habitat: what it eats or what feeds on it, whether it is active day or night, and so on.

Within a given habitat, the species are organized into a community. There are interactions between the species in a community. Sometimes these interactions may actually help to preserve the habitat in a particular form. For instance, grazing communities prevent grasslands from being invaded by woodland species. The abiotic factors in an environment along with the community of organisms found there form an ecosystem. Light, oxygen supply, moisture, soil type, salinity, temperature, and fire are all examples of abiotic factors.

Soils consist of several vertical layers. The uppermost, or A horizon, is topsoil, a layer rich in biomass. The B horizon, or subsoil layer, receives inorganic substances from decomposition in the topsoil. The lowermost layer, or C horizon, is parent rock from which the soil was originally formed.

Because soil is composed not only of rock but also of the organic substances contributed by the plant and animal community in and on the soil, the type of soil that develops in a region is related to the region's climate, because climate influences the plant and animal communities that develop. World maps of soil type and climate illustrate this relationship.

In a given area, an orderly series of communities tend to follow one another until a more stable or climax community is reached. This process is called primary succession if it starts on bare rock or in water, and secondary succession if it begins on abandoned agricultural land. Major climatic regions of the world have characteristic climax communities determined mainly by temperature and rainfall and, to a lesser extent, by soil type.

Species are not fixed entities. They can be shown to have changed, become extinct, or arisen over time due to environmental change and the interaction between organisms and species. Competition between individuals and between species appears to be and to have been an important factor, but not the only factor, in shaping community structure and evolutionary adaptation to environmental change.

Questions

1. How would you define a species? a population? What could be the purpose of an executive order prohibiting the introduction of exotic species into the United States?

2. When rats and goats were introduced into the Hawaiian Islands, many native species became extinct. Explain this using the concept of niche.

3. How do the unique properties of water (its high heat capacity and the fact that its greatest density is at 3.94°C) affect living organisms?

4. What forces are believed to shape community structure and evolutionary change?

5. Explain how the concept of punctuated evolution differs from more generally accepted theories of gradual evolutionary change.

Further Reading

If you are interested in ecology, you may want to read some of the following materials.

Cade, T. J. *The Falcons of the World.* Ithaca, N.Y.: Cornell University Press, 1982.

Cargo, D. N., and B. H. Mallory. *Man and His Geologic Environment.* Reading, Mass.: Addison-Wesley, 1977.

Levin, D. A. "The Nature of Plant Species," *Science,* 204 (April 27, 1979), 381.

In this article, Levin states: "For humans the environment has meaning only when its components can be interrelated in a predictive structure. We try to make sense out of nonsense and put the world into some perspective which has order and harmony." The species concept has caused a great deal of argument and confusion. This article is a thoughtful consideration of the problem, as well as a thought-provoking discussion of the human need to impose order where it is not always clear that order exists.

May, R. M., and J. Seger. "Ideas in Ecology," *American Scientist,* 74, May-June 1986.

A good summary of how ecology developed and where it is going.

Our Planet. United Nations Environment Program, Washington, D.C. Tel: 202-289-8456.

This magazine, started in 1989, contains a wealth of articles on international issues in ecology and environmental science.

The following readings all deal with competition theory and evolution.

Kiely, Tom. "Rethinking Darwin," *Technology Review,* May/June, 1990.

Lewin, R. "Finches Show Competition in Ecology," *Science, 219* (March 25, 1983), 1411.

Lewin, R. "Santa Rosalia Was a Goat," *Science, 221* (August 12, 1983), 636.

Lewin, R. "Punctuated Equilibrium Is Now Old Hat," *Science, 231* (February 14, 1986), 672.

May, R. M., and J. Seger. "Ideas in Ecology," *American Scientist,* 74 (May-June 1986), 256.

References

Bakker, R. T. "Evolution by Revolution," *Science, 85* (November 1985), 80.

Ehrlich, P. R., and J. Roughgarden. *The Science of Ecology.* New York: Macmillan, 1987.

Gates, D. M. *Biophysical Ecology.* New York: Springer-Verlag, 1980.

Odum, E. P. *Ecology.* Sunderland, Mass.: Sinauer Assoc. Inc., 1989.

Remmert, H. *Ecology.* New York: Springer-Verlag, 1980.

Richardson, J. L. *Dimensions of Ecology.* New York: Oxford University Press, 1979.

Schoener, T. "The Controversy over Interspecific Competition," *American Scientist, 70* (November-December 1982), 586.

Chapter 2

Global Habitats

A TALL-GRASS PRAIRIE PARK

When the first American pioneers moved westward, they found vast expanses of grassland: the American prairies. Their covered wagons, moving through seemingly endless seas of waving grasses, were called prairie schooners. These prairies once covered more than a million square miles (2.6 million km^2), from southern Canada all the way to the Gulf of Mexico, and from the eastern forests to the Rockies.

Prairie grasses range in size from short grasses a few inches (10 cm) high to tall grasses such as big bluestem, which grows taller than a human. At one time, tall-grass prairie covered 400,000 square miles (1 million km^2), but now barely 1% of that remains. The rest, along with 50% of the short-grass prairies, has been farmed or paved over to make roads, housing developments, and shopping centers.

Tall-grass prairie forms a stable ecosystem composed of characteristic grasses—big bluestem, Indian, little bluestem, and switch grass—which grow to heights of 3–8 feet (1–2.4 m). Many wildflowers are mixed in with the grass, and 80 species

of mammals, including deer, bobcats, coyotes, and badgers, find a home there. In addition, 300 bird species and well over 1,000 kinds of insects inhabit the prairie. However, once the grass is plowed up, it may be difficult or impossible to reestablish the system in any reasonable length of time.

The Nature Conservancy recently bought a 30,000-acre ranch in the Osage Hills of northeastern Oklahoma in order to attempt to regrow part of the tall-grass prairie. The ranch land has been grazed for the past 50 years, which has led to the loss of several species of prairie plants and animals, but the land was never plowed for farming. Conservancy ecologists hope to bring back the tall-grass prairie ecosystem by reinstituting the natural cycles of fire and grazing by bison herds (see Figure 2-1).

Grasslands occur in many other parts of the world, for example the Russian steppes, the South African veld, and the Argentinian pampas (see Figure 2-2). These are all examples of the grassland biome. A **biome** is a major community of plants (with its interacting animals) characteristic of a particular climatic region. There is no exact size requirement for a biome, and different ecologists recognize different numbers of biomes. Here we will

(a)   (b)

FIGURE 2-1 Restoring the Prairie. (*a*) Volunteer collects seeds of prairie grasses and wildflowers to plant on part of the Fermi laboratory's 6,800-acre site in Illinois. Some of this restored prairie covers the Fermi labs' subterranean proton accelerator ring. Laboratory officials from Fermi had approached the Morton Arboretum in Lisle, Illinois for help in landscaping their new site. However, Robert Betz, a Northern Illinois University professor and prairie restoration enthusiast, suggested that the lab restore the original prairie ecosystem instead. So far, over 600 acres have been restored. The Fermi lab prairie is now the largest restored prairie in the United States. (*b*) Annual burn. In order to mimic a natural prairie condition that encourages the growth of prairie grasses, the experimental prairie is periodically burned. (*Photos:* Courtesy of Fermilab Visual Media Services, Batavia, Ill.)

describe six major types of terrestrial (land) biomes, and the climatic factors that influence them. In the last part of this chapter we go on to look at different kinds of water habitats.

In Chapter 10 we will discuss the vast diversity of organisms found in natural biomes and the value of maintaining that diversity.

THE RELATIONSHIP OF CLIMATE, SOIL, AND BIOMES

The world's climate can be described in various ways, but the most useful appears to be a system using temperature and precipitation. These two factors have perhaps the greatest effect on the distri-

FIGURE 2-2 Zebras Grazing in Rwanda. Both fire and animals act with climate to maintain grassland biomes. Different species of animals graze the grasses to different heights and prevent large numbers of tree seedlings from becoming established. (*Photo:* Ruth Massey/UNDP)

bution of soil types, vegetation, animal life, and human activities. In Chapter 1 we noted that the severity and constancy of temperature and rainfall determine the kinds of communities that grow up in a region. We also mentioned that climate (principally temperature and precipitation) determines the soil type that develops in a region. Because of these interactions, it is not surprising that a map of world climate corresponds in many major details to a map of world biomes or to a map of soil types around the world (Figures 2-3a, 2-3b, and 2-4).

Several factors control the climate for a given region. Most important is the amount of sunlight or solar radiation. Figure 2-5 summarizes some of the effects of solar radiation on climate. If this were the only controlling factor, however, the earth's climate would be a series of bands running horizontally around the globe, corresponding to the amount of solar radiation at different latitudes.

A glance at Figure 2-3a shows this is not the case. A major factor modifying the influence of sunlight is the distribution of land and water. Land heats and cools more quickly than water; thus, continental climates tend to be more extreme than marine climates. Similarly, the presence of mountains affects the amount of precipitation in a region, while cold or warm ocean currents cool or heat nearby coastal areas.

To complete the circle of influences, the climate of a region is also affected by the community of

plants and animals that grows up. Plants and animals contribute to the gases, liquids and particles found in the atmosphere. The plant cover in a given area determines how much sunlight will be absorbed or reflected back from a land mass and thus affects temperature and rainfall. For example, when semi-arid areas are overgrazed so that all the plant cover is lost, the temperature in those areas will tend to rise and the area may become desert.

On the other hand, if it is not disturbed excessively, the biota in a region can act as a buffer for temperature changes or other physical changes in the environment. In a healthy ecosystem, the system itself thus displays some elasticity, or resistance to change. This is the basis of James Lovelock's **Gaia theory,** the idea that the earth, through its functioning ecosystems, possesses self-righting mechanisms. Lovelock is not, however, saying that ecosystems are able to resist all change. Such human-induced changes as the global warming caused by the burning of fossil fuels are clearly a threat to ecosystem self-righting mechanisms (as discussed further in Chapter 17).

WORLD BIOMES

Tropical Forest

In a broken band running around the world, roughly at the level of the equator, we find the

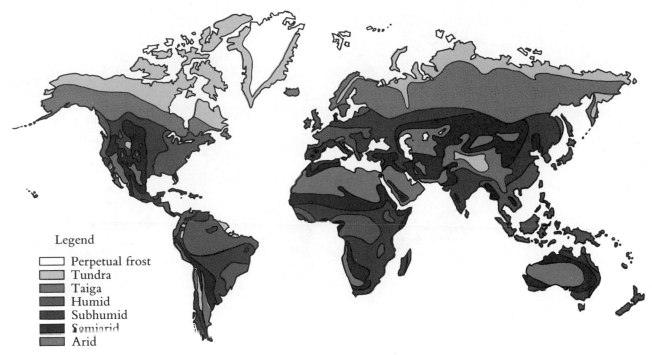

Legend

▢ Perpetual frost
▨ Tundra
▨ Taiga
▨ Humid
▨ Subhumid
▨ Semiarid
▨ Arid

FIGURE 2-3a Map of Major World Climates. (*Source: U.S. Department of Agriculture Yearbook, 1941*)

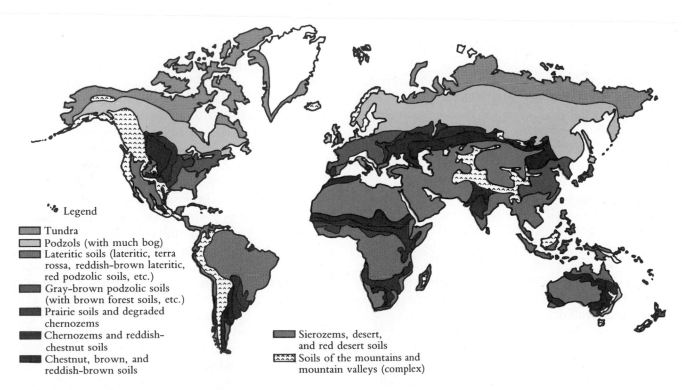

Legend

▨ Tundra
▨ Podzols (with much bog)
▨ Lateritic soils (lateritic, terra rossa, reddish-brown lateritic, red podzolic soils, etc.)
▨ Gray-brown podzolic soils (with brown forest soils, etc.)
▨ Prairie soils and degraded chernozems
▨ Chernozems and reddish-chestnut soils
▨ Chestnut, brown, and reddish-brown soils

▨ Sierozems, desert, and red desert soils
▨ Soils of the mountains and mountain valleys (complex)

FIGURE 2-3b Map of Major World Soil Types. (*Source: U.S. Department of Agriculture Yearbook, 1941*)

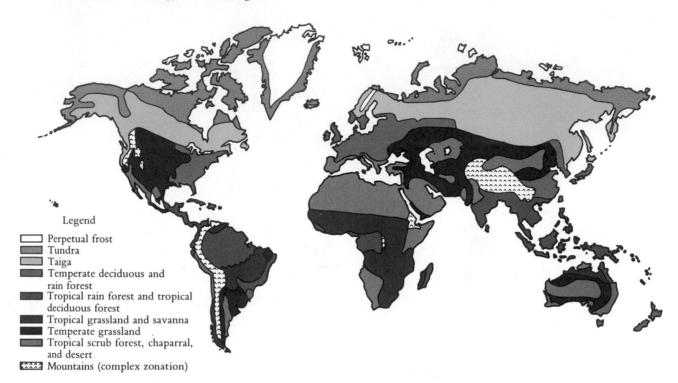

Legend

☐ Perpetual frost
▨ Tundra
▨ Taiga
▨ Temperate deciduous and rain forest
■ Tropical rain forest and tropical deciduous forest
■ Tropical grassland and savanna
■ Temperate grassland
■ Tropical scrub forest, chaparral, and desert
▨ Mountains (complex zonation)

FIGURE 2-4 Map of Major World Biomes. (*Source:* E. P. Odum, *Fundamentals of Ecology*, 3rd ed. © 1971 by Holt, Rinehart & Winston, Inc., reprinted by permission of the publisher.)

world's tropical forests. On Figure 2-4 you can follow the band, starting on the left with Central America and Brazil, following across to Africa and then to Southeast Asia (India, Bangladesh, Burma) and various islands of the Indian and Pacific oceans. In these warm regions, where rainfall is more than 240 cm (96 in) per year and temperatures are relatively constant year round, a typical community, known as the tropical rain forest, grows up (Figure 2-6).

Where rainfall is not as constant, slightly farther away from the equator, there are pronounced wet and dry seasons and tropical deciduous forest occurs. The trees shed their leaves to conserve moisture during the dry season.

Savannah and Grasslands

North and south of the tropical forests, rainfall decreases to 25 to 75 cm (10 to 30 in) of rain per year,

mostly falling during one season. Similar rainfall patterns occur in central North America and Russia, although here the temperatures are much cooler. Such climates do not support large trees. Instead, grasses, which can grow vigorously during the rainy season and die back to drought-resistant roots during the dry season or the frozen winter season, take over. In warmer areas, savannah, which is grassland studded with occasional drought-resistant trees, grades to grassland without trees as rainfall decreases. In temperate regions of North America and Asia, the height of the grasslands varies in a gradient from tall to short to match the amount of rainfall.

Grazing animals and cyclic fires contribute to the stability of grassland biomes. Both grazing and fires prevent most tree seedlings from taking hold. Without fire and grazing in North American, Russian, and some African grasslands, trees would probably grow up. Because forests make climates

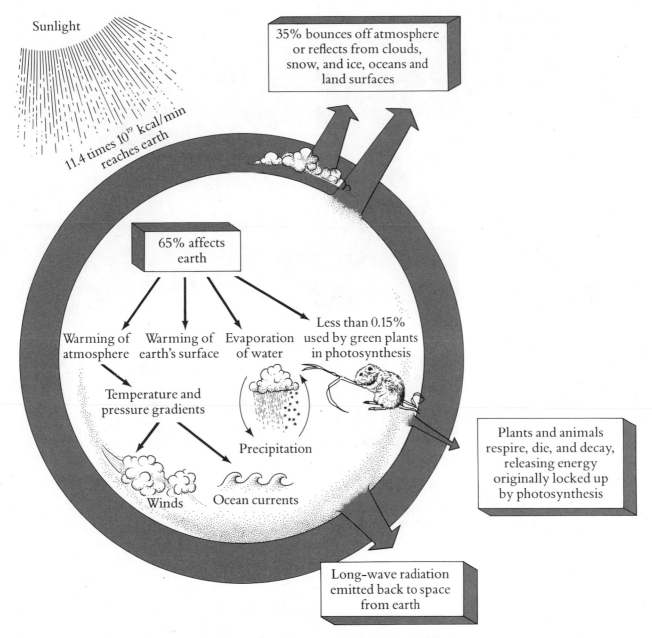

Sunlight

11.4 times 10⁹ kcal/min reaches earth

35% bounces off atmosphere or reflects from clouds, snow, and ice, oceans and land surfaces

65% affects earth

Warming of atmosphere   Warming of earth's surface   Evaporation of water   Less than 0.15% used by green plants in photosynthesis

Temperature and pressure gradients

Precipitation

Winds   Ocean currents

Plants and animals respire, die, and decay, releasing energy originally locked up by photosynthesis

Long-wave radiation emitted back to space from earth

FIGURE 2-5 Solar Radiation and the Earth's Climate. Of the solar radiation reaching the earth and its atmosphere, about one-third is reflected away immediately by clouds, snow and ice, and water or land surfaces. The remaining two-thirds is absorbed by the earth and its atmosphere. Of this amount, less than 0.15% is used by green plants in photosynthesis. The rest causes water to evaporate and also warms the earth's surface and atmosphere. This warming is uneven over the globe, leading to temperature and pressure gradients. Along with the rotation of the earth, these gradients cause winds and ocean currents. All of the radiation absorbed by the earth and its atmosphere (except for a minute amount stored as fossil fuels) is eventually reradiated into space, mainly as long-wave radiation in the infrared range.

FIGURE 2-6 Tropical Rain Forest Biome. Typically, three layers of vegetation occur. A sprinkling of tall trees, which lose their leaves during dry seasons, pokes up through a canopy of broadleaved evergreens and plants. Below this is a third layer of plants that flourish wherever there is a hole in the canopy. Lower levels of the forest are humid and have a constant temperature. Climbing vines and plants growing on other plants are common. So many species are found in tropical rain forests that it may be hard to find two trees of the same species over an area of several acres. Animals and insects are likewise numerous and diverse. (*Photo:* United Nations)

more moist, this would lead to an expansion of the forest biome at the expense of grassland.

Deserts

Deserts occur at latitudes of about 30° north and south of the equator, because of currents of hot, dry air that have lost most of their moisture over the tropics. The Sahara in North Africa, the Kalahari in South Africa, and the Sonoran desert in Mexico and the United States are all located in this band of deserts. However, deserts occur wherever rainfall is less than 25 cm (10 in) per year, and these conditions occur not only at the latitudes mentioned but also in the "rain shadows" of mountains. In these areas, air is dry because it has lost its moisture while rising up and flowing over the mountains.

Desert regions on the eastern side of the Sierra Nevada occur for this reason.

Only organisms adapted to long periods of drought and widely varying day–night temperatures can survive desert conditions. Because there is little or no vegetation to moderate the sun's energy, days on the desert tend to be very hot, but as soon as the sun goes down, night temperatures plummet (see Figure 2-7).

Temperate Forests

In cooler climates, rainfall of 75 to 150 cm (30 to 60 in) and definite summer and winter seasons give rise to the temperate forest biome. Here trees lose their leaves to conserve moisture, just as in tropical deciduous forests, but the loss is in response to the

(a)

FIGURE 2-7 Desert Biome. Desert plants have adapted to survive long periods without water. Some have few, small, leathery leaves, which can be dropped during the dry season to reduce water loss—examples are sagebrush and mesquite. Other plants can store quantities of water in their tissues—these are the cacti and the euphorbias. A third group includes the annuals, which spring up, flower, and set seed in the short period after a rain. Desert animals have similarly adapted to the conditions of their environment. Many are active only in the night periods, burrowing into the ground during the day to remain cool. (*Photos:* [*a*] Richard Frear, National Park Service, Sonoran desert; [*b*] T. Farkas, UNEP, Tunisian desert)

(b)

dry winter, when freezing temperatures lock water up as ice. Deciduous forest occurs in most of the eastern United States, central Europe, and parts of Asia (Figure 2-8).

Tundra and Taiga

Further north is an area called the **taiga,** or **northern coniferous forest biome.** Although this biome is cold in winter, when summer comes the soil thaws completely (Figure 2-9). In the far north, only the top few inches of soil thaw in the summer. Below this thin layer, the soil remains permanently frozen year round. The frozen layer is called **permafrost,** and the whole area is known as the **tundra biome.** Roots cannot penetrate the icy layer, and so vegetation is limited to mosses, lichens (such as reindeer moss), grasses, and small woody plants.

Overall, growth on the tundra is very slow. For this reason, when the tundra is disturbed, as by tire tracks, the scars do not heal. In the summer the tracks fill with water and mud and in the winter they freeze to ice. This particular problem was of much concern during the planning of the Alaskan pipeline, which crosses so many miles of tundra.

(How much land should be set aside as wilderness or examples of natural biomes? See Controversy 2-1 and Controversy 2-2 for opinions on U.S. wilderness.)

FIGURE 2-8 Deciduous Forest Biome. In different areas, the mixture of deciduous trees (trees that shed their leaves each year) making up the forest will vary. For instance, in the north central United States, the forests are predominantly beech and maple, while in the West and South, the forests are composed mainly of oak and hickory. Deer, bear, squirrels, and foxes roam the woodlands, while many bird species—such as woodpeckers, thrushes, and titmice—find a home here. In the fall the leaves turn color and then fall to the ground. (*Photo:* National Park Service)

WATER HABITATS

Availability of Water

We pointed out in Chapter 1 that water is a necessity for all forms of life on earth. As noted earlier in this chapter, in land habitats the abundance of water (a function of rainfall, humidity, and the evaporation rate) determines the kinds of communities that develop. In water environments, the availability of water changes with changes in water levels—for instance, with tides. It also changes according to differences in the salt content of water, which affect the rate at which water enters or leaves

organisms. In water environments, as well as land environments, the type of community that develops depends on this availability of water.

The Watershed

Surface waters such as lakes, rivers, and oceans are highly visible features of the environment. We can easily see that they provide different habitats for living organisms than do land areas. Not as easily seen is that the two kinds of habitats, land and water, are tied together by the cycling of energy,

(a)   (b)

FIGURE 2-9 Northern Coniferous Forest Biome. This biome is made up of conifers such as spruce, fir, and tamarack, along with some deciduous trees such as birch. Bears, wolves, moose, squirrels, lynx, and many other mammals are common, as are many species of birds in the summer. (*a*) A spruce-pine forest in a mountainous region. (*b*) Alaskan taiga. (*Photos:* U.S. Department of the Interior, Bureau of Land Management)

water, and nutrients through the environment. For instance, a river is not a self-contained system. Energy comes from the sun. Organic and inorganic nutrients wash into the river, by erosion and stream flow, from the river's banks and from land bordering all those streams flowing into the river. Even the river water itself cycles through the **hydrologic cycle**—some water leaves as evaporation and some water enters the river as rainfall and stream flows. Pollutants, too, reach the river, not only directly but also from the land areas surrounding it.

We can see, then, that the functioning unit is not simply the river itself but also the whole land area that drains into the river. This area is the **watershed.** In terms of understanding and maintaining

the quality of natural waters, the whole watershed is the ecosystem that must be studied or managed.

KINDS OF WATER HABITATS

Water habitats are usually differentiated on the basis of salt content (saltwater versus freshwater habitats) and whether a current is present or absent (streams with swift-flowing waters versus still lakes or river pools—see Figure 2-10).

Freshwater Habitats

The most important physical characteristics of freshwater habitats are turbidity, temperature, cur-

Controversy 2-1

Wilderness

All this land is being set aside for non-use at a time when public interest in the maintenance of single-use wilderness . . . is evaporating.

R. L. Brown

The U.S. Forest Service should think in terms of generations if not of centuries.

Editorial, *Business Week*, January 29, 1979

Additions to the National Wilderness Preservation System are surrounded by controversy. A study by the U.S. Forest Service, made public in 1979, considered the potential uses of 62 million acres of roadless land in the National Forests. Known as RARE II, for the second Roadless Area Review and Evaluation, the study concluded that the areas in question should be largely given over to other uses than wilderness. Of the 62 million acres, only 15 million acres were proposed for wilderness, while 36 million acres were to be "open" for multiple-use activities. These activities include "mineral entry" (prospecting and mining), grazing of stock, and timber cutting. Eleven of the 62 million acres were not designated either open or for wilderness but were recommended for further study. The next step after the Forest Service proposal was for Congress to consider the study and then allocate areas to wilderness as it saw fit.

Some people thought the area of land that the Forest Service had recommended for wilderness to be quite ample and perhaps even too generous. In a letter to *The New York Times* (May 9, 1979), R. L. Brown asserted:

All this land is being set aside for non-use at a time when public interest in the maintenance of a single-use wilderness, which appears to have been a fad of some three or four years' duration, is evaporating. Entry into wilderness areas last year totaled only seven million mandays, a fraction of the entry by Americans into national parks, and onto other types of Federal land. Sporting-equipment manufacturers report that sales of tents, sleeping bags and other equipment used by hikers for treks into the wilderness are decreasing. . . .

It is not true that all use of land results in permanent loss of wilderness characteristics. Most exploration for mineral deposits, for an example, fails. All signs of preliminary exploration are usually obliterated by new growth in a very short time. Even clear-cut log areas reforestate, and wilderness groups now suggest that many reforested areas are in fact wilderness and should be so designated.

(To put some of Brown's figures in perspective, the National Parks include about 27 million acres in the lower 48 states. Visitor days to the parks in 1990 reached a total of about 258 million.)

Other people felt the Forest Service had recommended too little wilderness:

The U.S. Forest Service should think in terms of generations if not of centuries. But continuing pressure from lumbermen, mining companies, and enterprising recreational developers makes it hard for Forest Service officials to think beyond the day's schedule of appointments. The result is a built-in bias in favor of early utilization, which shows in the recommendations the Forest Service has just drawn up for classifying some 62 million acres of undeveloped land in the national forests. (Editorial, *Business Week*, January 29, 1979, p. 28)

Is Brown right that wilderness use is a passing fad? Brown implies that wilderness is only set aside for human uses such as hiking and camping. Is that a correct interpretation? What criteria should be used in deciding how much public land should be set aside as wilderness compared to the amount of land on which multiple uses are allowed? Are visitor-use days a good measure of the value of parks or of wilderness?

Controversy 2-2

Should Wilderness Be Accessible?

To be precious, the heritage of wilderness must be open to those who can earn it again for themselves. The rest, since they cannot gain the genuine treasure by their own efforts, must relinquish the shadow of it. We must earn again for ourselves what we have inherited.

Garrett Hardin (1971)

My mother is only 63, but totally immobile because of bone cancer. By renting a motorhome she was able to tour several southwestern national parks and never leave her bedroom. . . . Before the young, healthy, and physically active propose limited access to public areas, I hope they consider that someday their own bodies may not permit them to access these public areas . . .

Loretta Campbell (1991)

The views of Garrett Hardin and Loretta Campbell are in conflict over the issue of whether wilderness ought or ought not be easily accessible to people. The sentiments expressed by Hardin suggest that the definition of wilderness as offered by Congress in the Wilderness Act is somehow inadequate.

Hardin is suggesting that wilderness should not be easily accessible. There are, of course, practical reasons to limit accessibility. You should be able to provide such practical reasons. Hardin's point of view, however, is one of principle. The practical implications are not of concern to him, at least not in this passage.

Campbell's comments, on the other hand, suggest that wilderness should be used by people and that accessibility provides the wilderness values to many, rather than to the few.

You may have thought about these points of view before when you were on the trail and looking to escape crowds of people. You may consciously have chosen less-traveled paths. Your opinion on the accessibility of wilderness, however, may have something to do with your age and condition. No doubt her mother's age and condition influenced Campbell's opinion. You should examine your views on this issue because the shape of future wilderness will be influenced by them. Is there a middle ground or compromise between inaccessibility and accessibility?

Sources: G. Hardin, quoted from the foreword by David Brower in *Earth and the Great Weather: The Brooks Range* (San Francisco: Friends of the Earth, 1971); and Loretta Campbell, Letters to the Editor, *National Parks,* September/ October, 1991.

---

rent (or lack of current), and the amount of dissolved materials, including solids (such as nitrate and phosphate salts) and gases (such as oxygen and carbon dioxide). The turbidity of water, which is a measure of its clarity, is important because turbidity affects how far sunlight can penetrate in water. Green plants can only live in the water zone into which sunlight reaches because they need sunlight for photosynthesis.

Lakes and Reservoirs. Most organisms living in lakes, reservoirs, and ponds or in the quiet pools of streams are adapted to life in still waters. In the shallow water zone along the shore, light reaches all the way to the bottom. Here live rooted water plants and floating algae, as well as a variety of animal life (see Figure 2-11).

Farther from shore is the area of open water. The upper layer, which light penetrates, is home to minute plants and animals called **plankton,** as well as to fish. Plankton are microscopic, drifting organisms found in lake waters as far down as light penetrates. Plankton species are, in general, unable to move against currents; they drift along with

(a)

(b)

FIGURE 2-10 Water Habitats. (*a*) In freshwater habitats, the water is either still, as in lakes and ponds, or moving, as in streams and rivers. (*Photo:* Yellowstone Lake, National Park Service) (*b*) In marine habitats, such as oceans and seas, the water moves continuously as a result of various currents. The salt concentration is, of course, much higher than in fresh water. (*Photo:* Jeff Devine)

water movements. Plant species, called **phytoplankton,** include many species of algae; animal species are known as **zooplankton.**

Living in the deeper water layer and on the bottom, where not enough light penetrates for photosynthesis to occur, are organisms that live on dead organic matter. Bacteria, fungi, small clams, and bloodworms all "reprocess" organic matter, which is then carried by currents or swimming creatures back to the other lake zones.

Stratification. Lakes and reservoirs often stratify, or have layers of different temperatures. Such stratification can lead to poor water quality—that is, water with little dissolved oxygen in it. This, in turn, will affect the kinds of organisms able to live in the deeper waters of a lake.

To explain how decreased quality of lake and reservoir waters comes about, we need to discuss the effects of temperature on the water in a lake reservoir. An annual cycle occurs in the temperature profile of such a body of water.

For convenience, we describe the cycle as beginning in late fall, when the weather has begun to cool. The autumn and winter winds transfer their energy to the lake or reservoir in the form of waves, which mix into the body of water. The waters are well mixed during this period. Thus, a fairly uniform quality and temperature of the water exist at all depths. Such a picture continues through the winter months.

In the spring, however, sunlight warms the waters nearest the surface, and warmer stream inflows enter the cold body of water. Above 4°C, warm water is less dense than cooler water and thus floats above it. Hence, the new warmer inflows tend to form layers near the surface of the reservoir. Similarly, surface waters that have been warmed

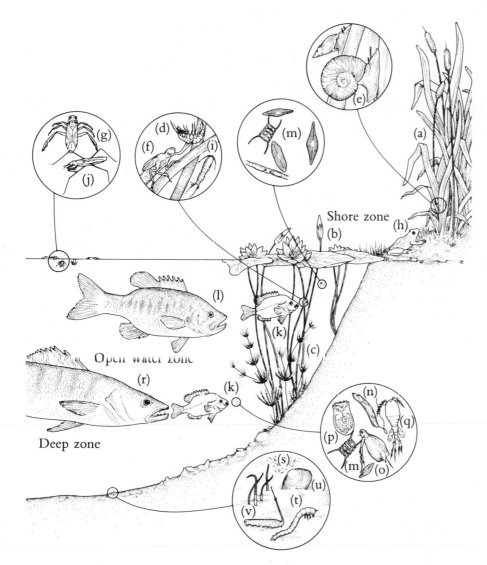

FIGURE 2-11 Simplified Lake Community. In the shallow waters along lake shores grow rooted water plants such as cattails (a), water lilies (b), and muskgrass (c). Also found there are frogs (h), pond snails (e), dragonfly nymphs (f), amphipods (d), and copepods (i). On the surface balance waterstriders (j) and backswimmers (g). In the open-water zone, algae and dinoflagellates (m, n) are found as deep as sunlight penetrates. They are eaten by zooplankton such as copepods (q), cladocera (o), and rotifers (p), which are eaten by small fish such as sunfish (k) who are, in turn, eaten by larger fish, such as walleye (r) and small-mouth bass (l). The deep zones and bottom muds are inhabited by creatures that live on detritus: bacteria and fungi (s), chironomid larvae (t), clams (u), and tubifex (v).

by sunlight tend to remain near the top. The wind's force at mixing is now less effective because the warmer, more buoyant water, though pushed into the interior, rises again toward the surface.

Essentially, three layers of water form at successively warmer temperatures. The warmest layer, called the *epilimnion,* forms at the top; it stays at the top because it has the lowest density. The coldest layer, called the *hypolimnion,* lies at the bottom; it has the highest density. Between these layers, a sharp temperature transition occurs; this middle layer is called the *thermocline*. This formation of layers of differing density and temperature is known as **stratification.**

Stratification of water into temperature layers is one of two phenomena that combine to cause a decrease in the quality of lake and reservoir water. The other phenomenon is the growth of algae in relatively clear waters. While some algae are growing, others are dying. The dead algae sink to the bottom layers; there, microorganisms in the water consume the dead algae as food. The microbes also

Global Economic Justice

by Gro Harlem Brundtland

Gro Harlem Brundtland has been Prime Minister of Norway since 1981. Earlier she served as Norway's Minister of Environment. Mrs. Brundtland chaired the U.N. World Commission on Environment and Development, which authored the report "Our Common Future." She has received many prizes for her work, including the Third World Prize for 1988 and the Indira Gandhi Prize for Peace, Disarmament and Development.

Poverty is a major cause and also a major effect of global environmental problems. It is futile to seek solutions to environmental disturbances without considering them from a broad perspective that encompasses the factors underlying world poverty and the inequalities within and among nations. For developing countries, poverty lies at the heart of all issues.

Yet it is both futile and an insult to the poor to tell them that they must remain in poverty to "protect the environment." What is required is a new era of economic growth—growth that enhances the resource base rather than degrades it. Environment and development have come to the top of the international agenda. Policies to promote sustainable development must be devised by nations both in the Northern and in the Southern Hemisphere, and they must also take into account the imbalances in international economic relations that prevail today.

Those of us who live in the industrialized world have an obligation to ensure that international economic relations help rather than hinder the prospects for sustainable development. It is our duty, as well as in our own self-interest, to do so. Commodity prices must be adjusted to provide a fair international distribution of income. Official development assistance programs and private loans to developing countries, as well as private investment, must be improved, both in quality and quantity. Policies—both national and international—will have to be changed so that capital transfers are sensitive to environmental impacts and can contribute to long-term sustainability.

Energy is another area of vital importance. As nations continue to develop they will require more, not less, total energy; their industrialization and rapidly growing populations will depend on it. Yet global energy consumption, even at its present levels, has already created serious environmental woes. How can an increase in energy use be tolerated without further deterioration of the global ecosystem? The solution, we believe, is to place energy-efficiency policies at the cutting edge of national energy strategies, regardless of the relatively low price of such traditional fuels as coal and petroleum.

The large ecological issues—the greenhouse effect, the disappearing ozone layer, and sustainable utilization of tropical forests—are tasks facing humankind as a whole. Our goal should now be to make the 1990s a decade of rapid social, economic, and environmental cooperation rather than confrontation. A global economic consensus for growth should be developed. To be consistent with sustainable development, such a consensus must observe ecological limitations. It should include socioeconomic policies within developing countries and be particularly sensitive to the poorer nations in Asia, Africa, and Latin America. The time is now ripe to explore these problems both institutionally and financially.

remove oxygen as they grow and maintain themselves. Since the water in the lake has stratified and little mixing occurs between the upper and lower layers, oxygen removed in the bottom layer is not restored quickly. Thus, the bottom waters of a stratified lake or reservoir may become very low in oxygen. Because oxygen is sometimes in short supply in deep lake waters, many organisms living there have adapted to low oxygen concentrations or even no oxygen at all.

As colder weather arrives, the upper layers become cooler and cooler, until they approach temperatures just less than the temperature in the bottom layers. At that point the layering becomes unstable, and the layers "flip." This event is called the *fall overturn,* and the lake or reservoir now becomes relatively well mixed; that is, the water at all depths is of about the same temperature. The well-mixed character is sustained through the winter months.

Rivers and Streams. Three features of the environment in rapidly flowing waters are important to understanding the types of organisms that live there: the presence of a current, the high oxygen concentration, and the source of nutrients. A current is one of the main factors making life in a stream or river different from life in lakes and ponds. However, the difference is not found in all parts of these environments. Streams have pools or areas of quiet flow where organisms find similar habitats to those in lakes. In addition, a lake shore, where waves keep water moving, provides organisms with a habitat similar to a rapidly flowing stream or river. There are thus two types of stream or river communities: those in flowing water and those in quiet water.

A major, and very understandable, feature of organisms living in moving water is that they usually have some way of hanging onto surfaces such as rocks or stream bottoms. Some are cemented firmly to stones or other objects in the flowing waters. Others have hooks, suckers, or sticky undersides. Stream creatures also have streamlined bodies to reduce resistance to flowing water and are often flat so they can crawl under rocks to escape the pull of the current.

Because of the current, rapidly flowing streams or rivers usually have a high oxygen content. The waters, moving and tumbling over rocks, become well mixed with air and so absorb a great deal of oxygen. Organisms living in rapidly flowing water are used to these high oxygen concentrations. When pollutants that use up oxygen in water are added to streams, the clean-stream organisms cannot survive the low oxygen levels.

A large part of the nutrients in streams and rivers either wash or fall into the water from the banks and surrounding watershed. Plant nutrients, such as nitrate and phosphate, and organic material, such as leaves on which detritus feeders live, enter the stream from its watershed. Stream organisms have adapted to this constant flow of fresh nutrients and also to the removal of their waste products by the current. Waters with currents thus provide an environment fundamentally different from the still waters of ponds and lakes.

Organic materials and plant nutrients are not the only materials washed into rivers and streams from watersheds. Pesticides or industrial wastes in groundwaters may also wash in. For this reason, when river and stream pollution problems arise, we must, in examining possible solutions, take into account not only the stream itself but also the land surrounding the stream.

Estuaries and Wetlands

As rivers wind their way to the oceans, they reach at last an area where fresh waters mix with the salt waters brought by ocean tides. River mouths, salt marshes, bodies of water behind barrier islands, and coastal bays are all parts of estuaries (see Figure 2-12). **Estuaries** are coastal bodies of water partly surrounded by land but still having an open connection with the ocean. In these areas, fresh water drains from the land and mixes with tidal currents of salt water. Estuaries, especially marshes, are often looked upon as wasteland, best dredged or filled. But this is a serious misunderstanding of the role estuaries play.

Estuaries are highly productive systems and are generally more fertile than either the neighboring ocean or the fresh waters that flow into them. The

FIGURE 2-12 Estuaries. Chincoteague Bay is an estuary formed by the mainland on one side and the barrier islands Chincoteague and Assateague on the other. Chesapeake Bay is a huge estuary where fresh waters from many large rivers—such as the James, the Susquehanna, and the Potomac—mix with salt waters from the Atlantic Ocean. (*Photo:* NASA)

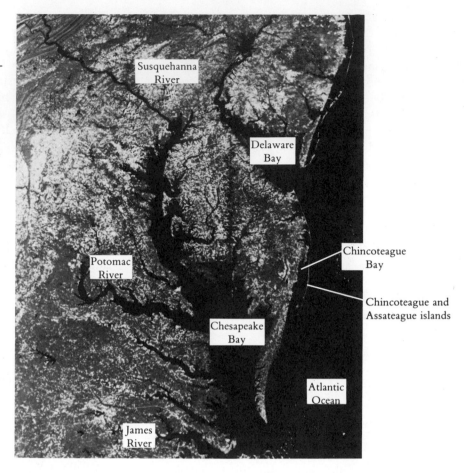

reason is that nutrients are easily trapped in estuaries. The nutrients are trapped in a physical sense, first as sediments settle out from river inflows and then by the action of the tides and fresh water flow (see Figure 2-13). Tides, which cause the water in estuaries to flow back and forth, make it possible for organisms like the oyster, which feeds by filtering sea water, to sit and have their food brought to them. In the same way, their wastes are removed.

Nutrients are also trapped in a biological sense because they are recycled rapidly by a network of producers, consumers, and detritus feeders. Unfortunately, pollutants are also recycled and sometimes biologically magnified in estuaries, so the effect of toxic materials such as DDT can be more serious here than in a river or the ocean.

Estuaries provide good habitats for a variety of organisms, from the large rooted grasses such as eel grass, turtle grass, and salt marsh grass to the tiny floating plants or bottom-dwelling algae. In fact, often more organic material is produced than can be recycled in the estuary itself. The excess nutrients flow out into the ocean and fertilize these waters. Good fishing is the result.

Estuaries serve yet another important purpose: providing a nursery for many ocean species, such as shrimp. The larvae, or immature stages, of these species find protection and food in the estuary. Some fish, such as salmon or Hudson River shad, that live in salt water but return to fresh water to breed require estuaries as places to rest during their journey. Thus, when estuaries are unthinkingly filled in, the effects fall not only upon the creatures that spend their whole lives there but also upon many ocean species that use estuaries or the food produced there.

Coastal salt and brackish marshes, freshwater swamps, prairie potholes, sloughs, bottom lands,

FIGURE 2-13 Mixing Currents in Estuaries. Fresh water, which is lighter, tends to float on the heavier sea water. As one rolls over the other, mixing currents are set up that tend to recirculate nutrients. (*Source:* Adapted from E. P. Odum, *Fundamentals of Ecology,* 3rd ed. © 1971 by Holt, Rinehart & Winston, Inc., reprinted by permission of the publisher, p. 354.)

and bogs all fall into the category of **wetlands.** In the past, attention has been paid almost exclusively to coastal wetlands, but most wetlands are freshwater drainages in inland areas. These wetlands function as natural floodwater storage basins, holding the water during flood time and then releasing it slowly to streams and rivers. In some areas where wetlands have been destroyed, severe flooding has resulted.

Wetlands absorb excess nitrogen and phosphorus from water, thus acting as a natural water treatment system and reducing overgrowths of algae. As in coastal estuaries, freshwater wetlands act as nurseries and food sources for many wild species, including some 80% of the ducks in North America. Almost 35% of the endangered species in the United States and many more around the world depend on wetlands for food or cover (see Figure 2-14).

Some states are attempting to stem the loss of wetland by embracing a policy of "no net loss." Under this policy, wetland development is discouraged and wetlands that are destroyed must be replaced by artificially created ones. Whether the creation of wetlands can be successfully accomplished is still in dispute, however.

Marine Habitats

Currents. Unlike lakes, where layers of water may remain still for long periods, the water in the

(a)

(b)

FIGURE 2-14 Wetland Areas. (a) Vietnamese girl tends an irrigation gate on a canal. During the war the French, and later the Americans, destroyed wetlands by digging canals to drain the wetlands and spraying Agent Orange to help drive out the Viet Cong. Since the war, dikes have been constructed in a few areas and many of the wetland species have returned. (b) Rare eastern saurus cranes, symbol of happiness and longevity, land in restored wetlands. The wetlands and thus the crane face a further threat from population growth, however, as increasing numbers of people look to settle and farm in wetland areas. (*Photos:* Paul P. Rome)

FIGURE 2-15 The Sea in Cross-Section. The shallow water of the continental shelf is called the *neritic zone,* including the area where the tides cover and un-cover the shore twice a day. The rest of the open sea is called the *oceanic zone.* The bottom of the sea along the continental slope and rise is called the *bathyal zone,* while along the deeper plain it is called the *abyssal zone.* As in fresh water, light penetrates only the top layer of water. All below this layer is in darkness.

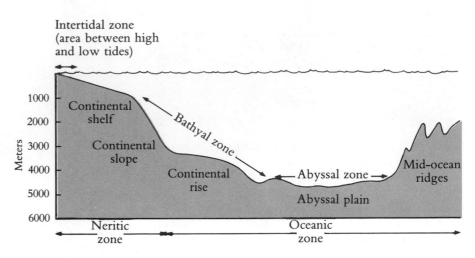

sea moves continually. Currents are caused by a variety of forces, such as temperature differences, differences in salt content, the rotation of the earth, and winds. Because of these mixing currents, even the deep parts of the oceans have a constant supply of oxygen in the water. In some areas, along steep coastal slopes, winds continually blow the surface water away from shore, allowing cold bottom waters, rich in nutrients, to rise to the surface. This is called **upwelling.** The areas where this occurs—for instance, along the coast of Peru—are the most fertile in the seas. In general, although life is found in all areas of the sea, the major commercial fisheries are all located on or near the continental shelf. The reason is that many ocean food chains are based on the microscopic green plants, which grow best in areas of coastal upwelling.

Marine Communities. Organisms that live in the **intertidal zone** (the area between high and low tides—Figure 2-15) are specifically adapted to the periodic absence of water.

Between the intertidal zone and the deeper ocean regions is the area of the continental shelf. In this fertile zone, phytoplankton species, including diatoms, dinoflagellates, and microflagellates form the base of the food chain. Tiny zooplankton such as copepods, pteropods, and jellyfish (medusae), as well as shrimp-like krill, feed on them and are fed on by fish, squid, and sea mammals such as whales.

Sea birds, large fish such as tuna and swordfish, and humans are the final beneficiaries of this rich chain of linkages. Also found in this region are the larvae or immature stages of many marine species. Buried in the bottom muds or clinging to rocks are the worms, clams, snails, crabs, and bacteria that form the **benthos,** or bottom dwellers, which feed on detritus.

In the open ocean, species have adapted to life far from shore. In the top layer of water, where light penetrates, drifting microscopic plants and animals live. Microplankton species such as *Chloramoeba* are the main producers in the open oceans. Krill, as well as small zooplankton species, feed on microplankton. Larger fish and sea mammals such as the baleen whale range over both the open ocean and the shore areas in search of krill and zooplankton, on which they feed. Oceanic birds such as petrels, albatrosses, and frigate birds feed on the open oceans except during breeding time, when they fly to land.

The sunlit zone in the open oceans does not support as much life per square meter as the light zone in coastal areas does. However, the oceans cover 70% of the earth's surface, and much of this is open ocean. For this reason, the photosynthetic organisms in the open ocean are very important in world oxygen and carbon dioxide balances.

We know relatively little about communities in the deep zones of the ocean. Only recently have a

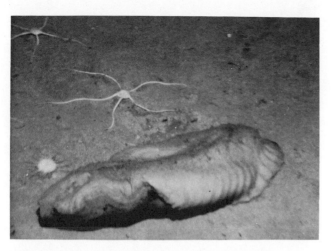

FIGURE 2-16 Life on the Deep Ocean Bottom. Although a few large species are visible on the surface, most of the organisms in the deep sea are found in the mud. Here, a holothurian, or sea cucumber (*Holothuroidea*), an urchin (probably *Lytechinus*), and brittle stars (*Ophiuroidea*) share the sediment surface. (*Photo:* Dr. Fred Grassle, Woods Hole Oceanographic Institute)

number of facts come to light—quite literally, since one of the main physical characteristics of the deep sea regions is relative darkness. Since there is not enough light for photosynthesis, organisms depend on the top layer of water for organic nutrients. The major portion of the organic matter reaching the deep ocean zones is probably composed of fecal pellets from zooplankton on the surface (Figure 2-16).

SUMMARY

Biomes are major communities of plants characteristic of particular climatic regions. Climate affects the type of soil that is formed in a given area both through physical processes and by determining the type of plant community that can grow there. In turn, the plant and animal community has an effect on the climate in a given region. Maps of soil type, climate, and world biomes show striking similarities because of these interactions. Six major world

biomes are: the tropical forest biome, found where rainfall is more than 240 cm per year and temperatures are relatively constant year round; the temperate forest biome, found where rainfall is 75 to 150 cm per year and there are distinct winter and summer seasons; grassland, where rainfall is 25 to 75 cm per year (fires and grazing animals may help maintain this biome); the desert biome, which occurs where rainfall is less than 25 cm per year; tundra, characterized by a permanently frozen subsoil; and taiga, where a long, harsh winter season restricts plant growth.

To fully understand a water habitat, we must consider the land area that drains into the water— the watershed—as well as the stream, lake, or river itself. Water communities consist of producers (microscopic algae and more visible underwater and shore-based green plants) and the consumers that feed on them. Important factors differentiating freshwater habitats include current, turbidity, oxygen content, temperature, and dissolved solids. Marine environments differ in sunlight, currents, temperature, and salt concentration.

Questions

1. Why is the watershed of a lake or river considered the important ecosystem, rather than just the river or lake itself?

2. What major factors define water habitats? Describe some of the major ways in which organisms have adapted to these habitats.

3. In the past, wetlands such as marshes and swamps were considered wasteland, suitable only for draining and filling. Why is this an incorrect notion?

4. Explain the interaction of climate, soil type, and biome.

5. Why can the effect of pollutants such as pesticides be particularly severe in estuaries?

6. UNESCO has a program to identify and preserve examples of all the world biomes. What is a biome? Of what possible use could it be to preserve an example of each type?

Further Reading

Gifford, Jane. "The Desert Peninsula," *National Geographic World*, May 1989, Number 24.

If you think of the desert as a barren place, you should read this article and the one preceding it in the magazine. Both detail the interesting species and the "flower shows" the desert can put on when its scanty moisture arrives.

Lovelock, James. *The Ages of Gaia, A Biography of Our Living Earth*. New York: Norton, 1988.

In this persuasive book, Lovelock argues that the earth is, or at least acts like, a living organism. He then looks at environmental issues from the point of view of which are serious threats to this organism that he has named Gaia. You may not agree with his basic premise, but it's worth thinking about.

Madson, James. "On the Osage," *Nature Conservancy Magazine*, May/June 1990.

This article details the Nature Conservancy program to reestablish the tall-grass prairie ecosystem, which it characterizes as an "extinct" ecosystem.

"Protecting America's Wetlands: An Action Agenda," Report of the National Wetlands Policy Forum. Washington, D.C.: The Conservation Foundation, 1988.

An easy-to-follow treatment of the problem of disappearing wetlands, with some solid suggestions for solving the problem.

Chapter 3

Ecosystem Dynamics: The Flow of Materials and Energy

In the first chapter we discussed the parts of ecosystems—the living organisms as well as important nonliving or abiotic factors. Figure 3-1 is a simplified picture of a forest ecosystem, and Figure 3-2 is a photograph of an actual forest. However, while both the diagram and the photograph are representative of this type of ecosystem, one central fact needs to be emphasized: Ecosystems are not like diagrams or photographs, static in time. Instead, growth and change are characteristics of ecosystems. The living and nonliving components act on each other and cause changes. Further, there is a flow of materials and energy through ecosystems. These ecosystem dynamics are the subject of this chapter.

THE FLOW OF MATERIALS IN ECOSYSTEMS

A unifying feature of the flow of materials in ecosystems is that the flow is cyclic. That is, materials flow through systems in a largely circular manner:

into the living organisms, back to the abiotic environment, and then into the living organisms again.

Hydrologic Cycle

The cycle with which we are most familiar is the **hydrologic cycle.** It consists of three distinct and continuing events: the evaporation of water, condensation and rainfall, and runoff. Water evaporates from the surfaces of lakes, ponds, streams, wetlands, rivers, and oceans. It also evaporates from soil and vegetation and is transpired by plants.★ This water returns to the earth as rainfall. More water evaporates from the surface of the oceans than returns to the oceans as rain, however. On land, the opposite is true—less water evaporates from soils, vegetation, and surface waters than returns by rainfall (except for deserts, where evaporation

---

★ *Transpiration* refers to the release of water vapor from the above-ground parts of plants. Evaporation and transpiration from plants together are sometimes referred to by the term *evapotranspiration.*

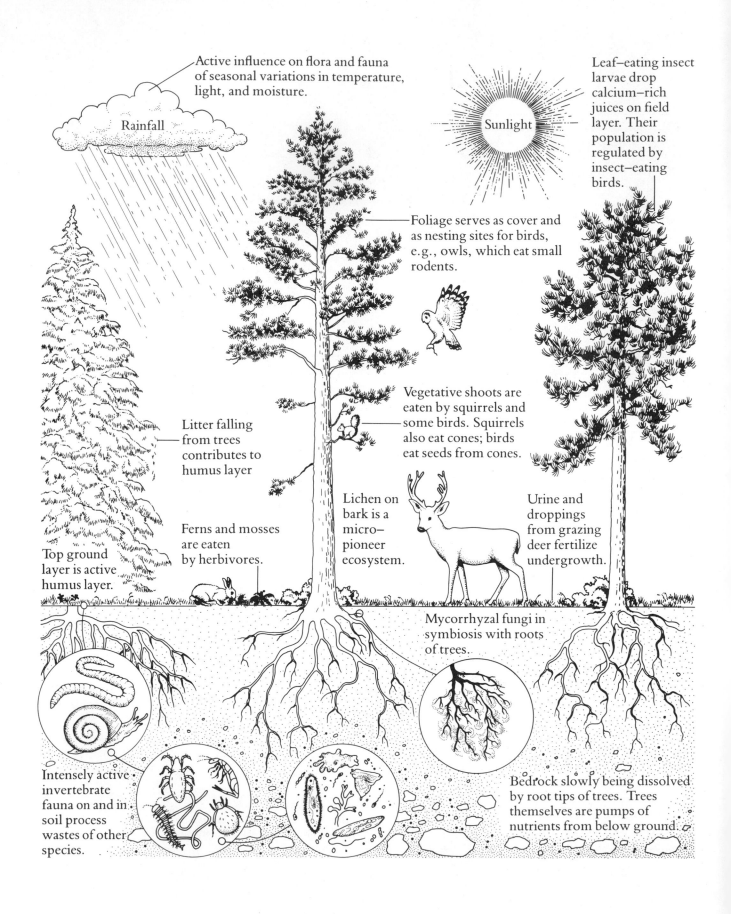

Active influence on flora and fauna of seasonal variations in temperature, light, and moisture.

Rainfall

Sunlight

Leaf–eating insect larvae drop calcium–rich juices on field layer. Their population is regulated by insect–eating birds.

Foliage serves as cover and as nesting sites for birds, e.g., owls, which eat small rodents.

Litter falling from trees contributes to humus layer

Vegetative shoots are eaten by squirrels and some birds. Squirrels also eat cones; birds eat seeds from cones.

Ferns and mosses are eaten by herbivores.

Lichen on bark is a micro–pioneer ecosystem.

Urine and droppings from grazing deer fertilize undergrowth.

Top ground layer is active humus layer.

Mycorrhyzal fungi in symbiosis with roots of trees.

Intensely active invertebrate fauna on and in soil process wastes of other species.

Bedrock slowly being dissolved by root tips of trees. Trees themselves are pumps of nutrients from below ground.

FIGURE 3-2 Old-Growth Forest in the Pacific Northwest. Some of the Douglas firs in these forests are estimated to be 500 years old or more. Only about one-eighth of these forests, never cut by loggers, still remain, a reminder of what the land looked like before the settlers came. The controversy about whether these old-growth forests should be logged is explored in Chapter 10. (*Photo:* Jim Harris/North Cascades National Park)

is greater than rainfall). The balance is maintained by runoff, or water flowing from streams, lakes, rivers, and groundwaters to the oceans (Figure 3-3).

The hydrologic cycle can be compared to the process of distillation, in which water is vaporized by heating it in a flask. The water vapor leaves behind in the flask dissolved materials such as salt. This does not mean that rain is completely free of contaminants—rain and snow may become contaminated with gases and particles in the air. (For example, acid rain may form; see Chapter 16.) However, rain is relatively pure. In some areas of the world, with few rivers and little water in the ground for people to utilize, rain furnishes drinking water. In such places, rainfall is collected in cisterns and stored for later use.

The processes in the hydrologic cycle are being modified by human activities. Some of these changes are intentional; others are accidental. For instance, rainfall has increased in industrial areas because water droplets condense more quickly around minute mineral particles in the air. As another example, runoff increases when vegetation is destroyed. Trees, grasses, and other plant covers capture and hold rainfall, allowing it to percolate down through layers of decaying organic materials and rocks in the soil. Too rapid runoff may lead to flooding. Also, where there is less water slowly percolating through the deep soil layers, the

FIGURE 3-1 Simplified Diagram of an Old-Growth Forest Ecosystem. Trees such as Douglas fir, cedar, hemlock, and sugar pine utilize the energy from sunlight and carbon dioxide from the air to produce the basic materials for growth and reproduction. The trees provide cover, nesting sites, and food for a wide variety of birds and other small animals. Litter from the trees is broken down by soil-dwelling organisms, and some of the nutrients are cycled back into the trees through the roots.

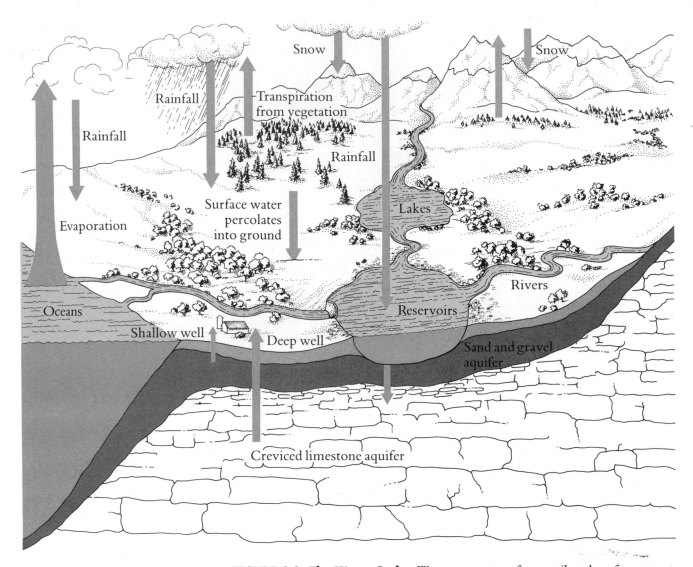

FIGURE 3-3 The Water Cycle. Water evaporates from soil and surface waters and is transpired by vegetation. This water returns to the earth as precipitation: rain, snow, and fog. Water moves from land areas to the oceans as runoff in streams, rivers, and groundwater flows. Humans influence the water cycle in many ways. We dam rivers to form reservoirs, dig wells to tap underground aquifers, decrease the amount of water held in soil by destroying natural vegetation, and increase rainfall via air pollution.

amounts of trace minerals dissolved from buried rocks decreases. These minerals are necessary for plant growth and may have to be added to fertilizer in some areas. On the other hand, the runoff of water via streams, rivers, and lakes to the oceans is interrupted by humans at many points and for many purposes, some of which contaminate the water with chemical and biological wastes. These problems are described in greater detail in Chapters 18 and 19.

Carbon Cycle

All living creatures on earth consist mainly of water. About 80% to 90% of living material is

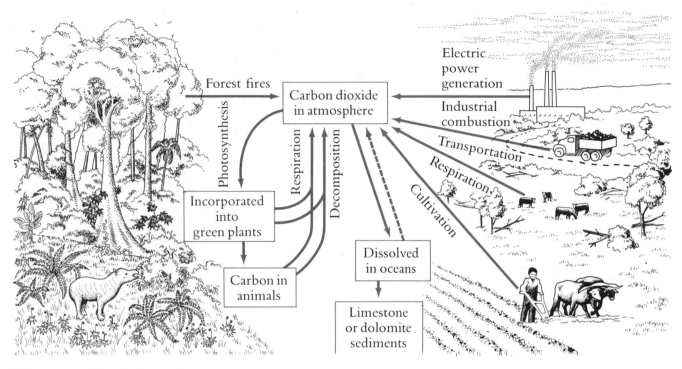

FIGURE 3-4 The Carbon Cycle.

water. However, the most important structural material for life forms is carbon. This carbon, which forms the molecular backbone for all organic compounds in living creatures, comes from carbon dioxide in the atmosphere.

As explained in Chapter 1, plants use carbon dioxide during photosynthesis to manufacture some of the organic compounds necessary to life. Carbon from the atmosphere thus enters living systems through photosynthesis. Carbon moves through an ecosystem until it reenters the atmosphere during respiration or until the organisms in which it is contained die. The process of decomposition forms carbon dioxide again as dead material decays (Figure 3-4).

This is only a part of the **carbon cycle,** however. Most carbon involved in the cycle is in the oceans. This carbon (in the form of carbonates) controls, to a large extent, the amount of carbon dioxide in the air. Excess carbon dioxide in the atmosphere can dissolve in the oceans, forming carbonate and bicarbonate ions. In the opposite direction, the oceans can release carbon dioxide to the atmosphere. The oceans thus act to buffer, or keep

constant, the carbon dioxide concentration of the atmosphere. Scientists believe that this mechanism kept the amount of carbon dioxide in the atmosphere relatively constant until industrialization began.

Human activities appear to be unbalancing the carbon cycle in several ways. An extra 5.8 billion tons of carbon dioxide are added to the atmosphere each year when fuels are burned at their present level of use. Some scientists believe that the rapid cutting of forests to satisfy human needs for farmland and wood products may be decreasing the amount of carbon dioxide used by plants.

Although some of the excess carbon dioxide from burning of fuels dissolves in the ocean, half or more remains in the atmosphere. Measurements show that the level of atmospheric carbon dioxide has increased steadily since the 1950s. The possible effects of an increase in atmospheric carbon dioxide, are explored in Chapter 17.

Nitrogen, Phosphorus, and Sulfur Cycles

Three other important materials cycle through ecosystems along with water and carbon: nitrogen, phosphorus, and sulfur. All three of these chemical elements are essential components of living matter.

Nitrogen Cycle. Nitrogen is present in the atmosphere as nitrogen gas (N_2). The air we breathe is about 80% nitrogen. This nitrogen becomes part of biological matter almost entirely through the bacteria and algae that can "fix" atmospheric nitrogen into organic compounds and nitrates. Legumes, such as clover, alfalfa, soybeans, and locust

NATURAL NITROGEN CYCLE   HUMAN INFLUENCES

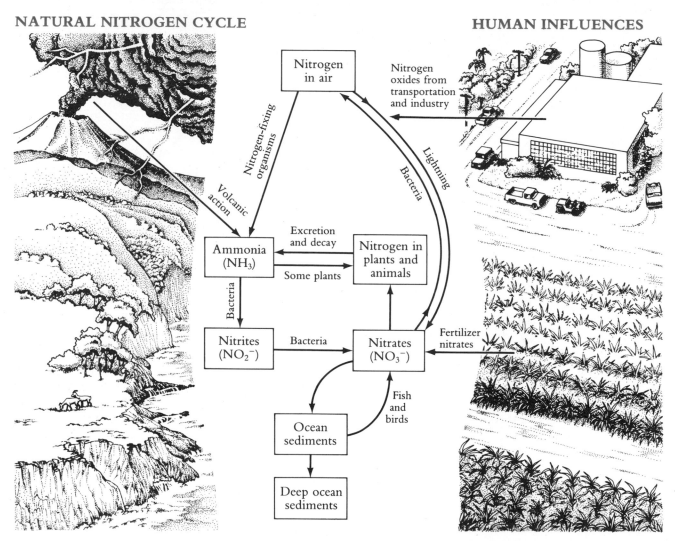

FIGURE 3-5 The Nitrogen Cycle. Plants and animals generally require nitrogen in the form of nitrates. A small amount of nitrate is formed from atmospheric nitrogen by lightning. However, most nitrogen enters living systems through bacteria and algae that can "fix" nitrogen gas from the air into ammonia. Biological matter is broken down into ammonia, which is cycled by bacteria through nitrites and back to nitrates. Some of the nitrates are lost to the cycle when they are buried in deep sea sediments, while nitrogen is added to the cycle by volcanic action. Certain bacteria can "denitrify" nitrates back to nitrogen in the air. Humans influence the nitrogen cycle by adding nitrates in fertilizers and nitrogen oxide gases from transportation and industry.

trees, form little nodules in their roots where such nitrogen-fixing bacteria live. Farmers often fertilize their land naturally by growing these types of crops and then plowing them into the soil.

Nitrogen is lost from the **nitrogen cycle** (Figure 3-5) to deep-sea sediments, but this loss is just about balanced by additions from volcanoes. Humans interfere with the nitrogen cycle by producing large quantities of nitrogen oxide gases, which are normally present in very small amounts. These gases contribute to the formation of smog (see Chapter 15). In addition, excess nitrate from agricultural fertilizers can lead to overgrowths of algae, or eutrophication (Chapter 18).

Phosphorus Cycle.   The sea is a major part of a number of important cycles. One example is the

hydrologic cycle; another is the **phosphorus cycle,** shown in Figure 3-6. Phosphorus enters the environment mainly from rocks or deposits laid down in past ages. Erosion and **leaching** gradually release the phosphorus. Some is used by biological systems, but much of it is washed into the sea, where it settles in the sediments. Phosphorus in shallow sediments is cycled by bottom dwellers through fish and then to birds, which deposit the phosphorus back on land as droppings or guano. But a portion of the phosphorus is not recycled; this is the amount buried in deep sediments.

Large quantities of phosphorus are used as fertilizer, and most is eventually lost as deep-sea sediments. At some time, though not in the near future, shortages could result. Phosphorus is an essential nutrient for plants and, along with nitro-

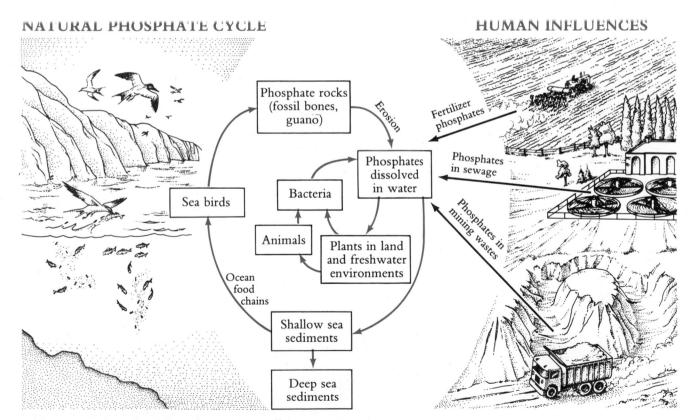

NATURAL PHOSPHATE CYCLE   HUMAN INFLUENCES

FIGURE 3-6 The Phosphorus Cycle. Erosion and mining release phosphates from rocks and other deposits to water environments. Phosphates are eventually deposited in shallow or deep sea sediments. From shallow sediments, some phosphate is recycled back to land environments.

gen, is often in short supply compared to other nutrients in water. Phosphate, which enters natural waters from sewage, fertilizer runoff, and mining wastes, contributes to the problems of eutrophication (Chapter 18).

Sulfur Cycle. In the **sulfur cycle,** sulfur is changed from one form to another by a variety of microorganisms in the soil and sediments (see Figure 3-7). Plants and animals require sulfur as sulfate (SO_4^{2-}) in order to build organic materials such as amino acids and proteins. In the deep sediments and soils, sulfur is changed to iron sulfides at the same time that phosphorus is changed from an insoluble to a soluble form. In this way, the two cycles interact.

Human activities, notably the burning of high-sulfur coal to generate electric power, are affecting

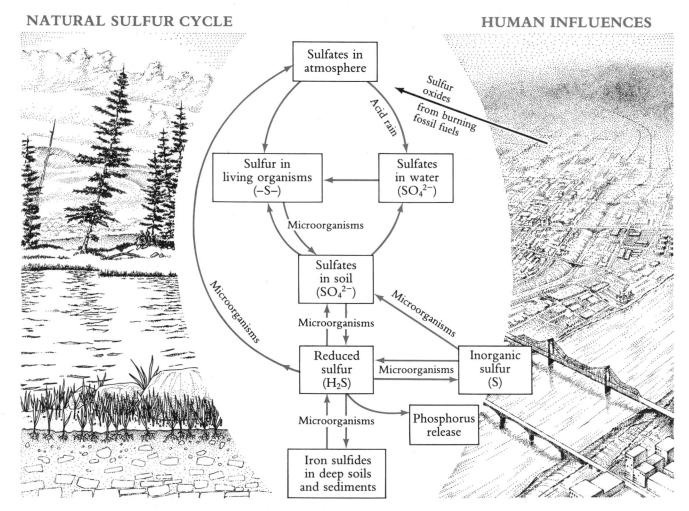

NATURAL SULFUR CYCLE

HUMAN INFLUENCES

FIGURE 3-7 The Sulfur Cycle. There is a large pool of sulfur in soil and sediments and a smaller pool of sulfur in the atmosphere. Plants and animals use sulfur (as sulfates) from soil, water, and air. This sulfur is then incorporated into organic sulfur compounds, such as sulfur-containing proteins. Sulfur is changed from sulfates to reduced sulfur compounds and back again by a variety of microorganisms in the soil and sediments.

the sulfur cycle by overloading the atmospheric pool of sulfur with sulfur dioxide, a compound normally present at very low levels. (The effects are described in Chapter 16.)

Water, carbon, nitrogen, phosphorus, and sulfur are not the only materials that cycle in ecosystems, but from the point of view of their significance to living organisms and their relationship to current environmental problems, they are the most important.

ENERGY FLOW IN ECOSYSTEMS

In contrast to the cyclic flow of materials we have been discussing, energy flow on earth is more like a one-way street. The energy in ecosystems comes from the sun and is finally lost as heat to the cosmic reaches of outer space (see Figure 2-5).

The flow of energy through systems is of major concern to ecologists and should be of interest to everyone else, too. An understanding of energy flow, and the basic laws that govern it, leads to a better understanding of why natural systems work the way they do. Equally important, such an understanding helps us see the limits of our ability to make changes in our environment without damaging it.

Trophic Structure in Ecosystems

Before detailing how energy flows through ecosystems, however, it will be useful to describe the **trophic structure** of ecosystems—the pattern of eating and being eaten that links all the organisms in any particular ecosystem. Such patterns are often described as food chains or food webs.

Food Chains

Food chains can be diagrammed in a relatively simple, straight-line fashion. Creatures in the chain generally feed on only one or a few species and are preyed on by one or a few other species. Food chains are found where conditions are so harsh that few animals or plant species are able to survive—for instance, on the arctic tundra (Figure 3-8) or in the high carbonate concentrations in Lake Nakuru (Figure 1-6).

The food chain illustrated in Figure 3-8 is a grazing food chain. There are several distinct trophic levels in the chain. Organisms at the bottom of grazing food chains are **producers,** plant species that convert sunlight into food energy by photosynthesis (the grasses, sedges, and lichen in Figure 3-8). Creatures that eat producers are **herbivores,** or green-plant eaters (such as the caribou in Figure 3-8), and they are called *primary consumers.* Next in line are the meat eaters, or **carnivores,** which eat the primary consumers. These are the *secondary consumers* (men and wolves in Figure 3-8). Longer food chains include *tertiary consumers* that eat the secondary consumers, and so on.

At another trophic level are the **decomposers,** or **detritus** feeders. This group of organisms is extremely important because it feeds on dead organic matter, breaking it down into inorganic and organic materials. These materials may be used by plants and animals or may inhibit or stimulate other organisms in the ecosystem. Fungi and bacteria are common decomposers, but animal species may also be important. In the freshwater lakes of the Alaskan tundra, especially interesting examples of detritus-based food chains are found. Into these lakes is washed peat formed from plants that lived and died 8,000 to 12,000 years ago. Carbon from the peat is incorporated into insect larvae, which are eaten by consumer species such as arctic graylings and old-squaw ducks (Figure 3-9). In this case there is a delay of thousands of years between primary production and its use by consumers.

Food Webs

In contrast to harsh arctic regions, which have relatively few species, many ecosystems in temperate and tropical climates, where a large number of species interact with one another, have a trophic structure best described as a **food web.** Food webs have more organisms and interconnections than food chains. Figure 3-10 shows an example of only part of a food web from a small stream in South Wales.

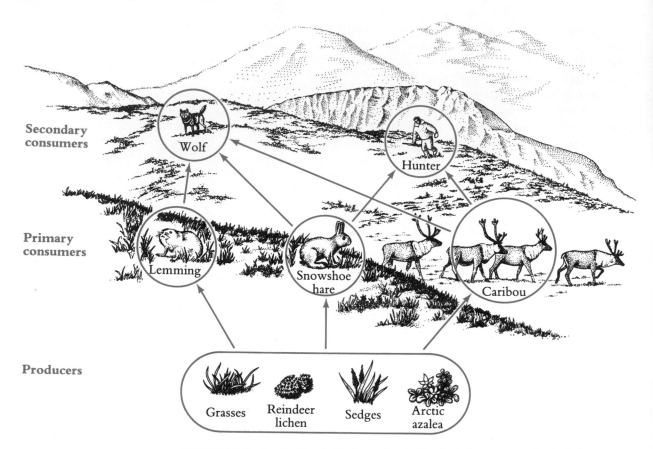

Secondary
consumers

Primary
consumers

Producers

Wolf

Hunter

Lemming

Snowshoe
hare

Caribou

Grasses

Reindeer
lichen

Sedges

Arctic
azalea

FIGURE 3-8 Arctic Food Chains. Arctic food chains are simple and short because few species are able to live in the harsh and unpredictable arctic climate. One arctic food chain is made up of a few arctic tundra plants; the caribou, lemmings, and snowshoe hares that eat the plants; and wolves and humans.

Food webs are more complicated than food chains and are more difficult to sort into the trophic levels of producer, consumer, and so on. One reason is that food webs involve so many species that we cannot always be sure we know all of the creatures in a particular food web. Also, some species occupy more than one position in a web. That is, an organism may eat both green plants and such primary consumers as insects, making it both a primary consumer and a secondary consumer. The net-spinning caddis in Figure 3-10 illustrates just such a complication.

In the small-stream food web, the decomposers feed on materials carried by water from upstream, such as leaves, feces, dead organisms, and so on.

Many food webs, especially in water, are based on detritus. The large arrow on the side of Figure 3-10 indicates that all of the unused organic material produced at various levels of the food chain (feces, secretions, dead plants, or animal bodies) is either broken down by the decomposers to basic plant nutrients or cycled back up the food web as decomposers themselves are eaten.

Figure 3-11 is a simplified diagram summarizing energy and materials flow in a stream ecosystem. The energy from the sun is the driving force. Green plants capture the sun's energy by photosynthesis and use this energy to produce organic materials. The energy stored in these materials serves as the energy source for the primary consumers that eat

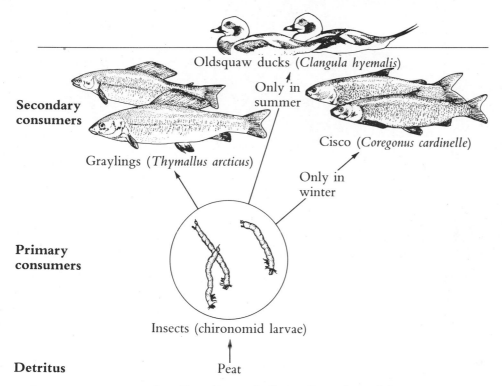

Secondary consumers

Oldsquaw ducks (*Clangula hyemalis*)

Only in summer

Graylings (*Thymallus arcticus*)

Cisco (*Coregonus cardinelle*)

Only in winter

Primary consumers

Insects (chironomid larvae)

Detritus

Peat

FIGURE 3-9 A Detritus-based Arctic Food Chain. Peat, formed from organisms that decayed thousands of years ago, is the carbon source for insect larvae, which in turn are consumed by arctic graylings, ducks, and whitefish. (*Source:* Data from D. M. Schell, *Science, 219* [1983])

the plants and then for the higher consumers that eat primary consumers, and so on. Even in ecosystems called "incomplete" because they lack the producers that capture sunlight, if we follow the energy source back far enough, it will be found in the sun. For instance, in the deep-sea bottom, where no light penetrates, photosynthesis cannot occur. Instead, the energy source is *detritus*. But this detritus originates from organic materials produced in the upper layers of the ocean, where there is light and photosynthesis.

Trophic Structure and Energy Flow

The food an organism eats is its source of energy for growth, reproduction, and all other life processes. When one organism eats another, energy is passed on from one to the other. Let us look again at the trophic structure of ecosystems, this time as a transfer of energy from one set of organisms to another.

Ecological Pyramids. Ecologists draw **ecological pyramids** to show the amount of energy transferred from one trophic level to another in an ecosystem. Figure 3-12 shows an imaginary and highly simplified system in which alfalfa plants in a field use sunlight to produce plant tissue, which is eaten by calves, which in turn are eaten by a boy. The first pyramid shows the *biomass,* or weight of living material, at each level. The second shows the yearly energy transfer in calories through the system.

Productivity

The amount of organic matter produced in an ecosystem or by an individual in a given time is its

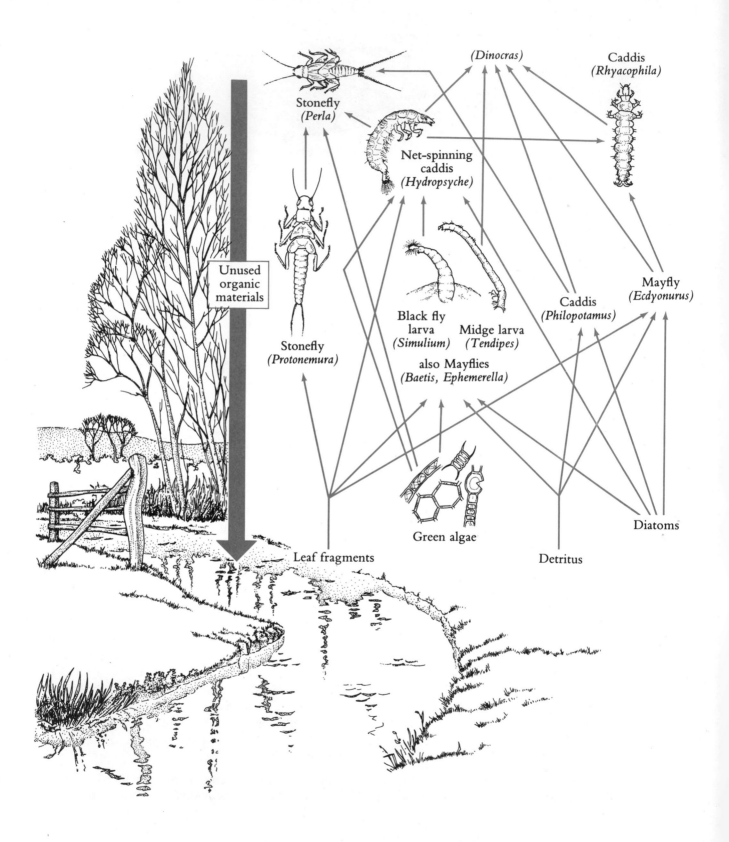

(Dinocras)

Caddis
(Rhyacophila)

Stonefly
(Perla)

Net-spinning
caddis
(Hydropsyche)

Unused
organic
materials

Mayfly
(Ecdyonurus)

Caddis
(Philopotamus)

Stonefly
(Protonemura)

Black fly
larva
(Simulium)   Midge larva
(Tendipes)

also Mayflies
(Baetis, Ephemerella)

Diatoms

Green algae

Detritus

Leaf fragments

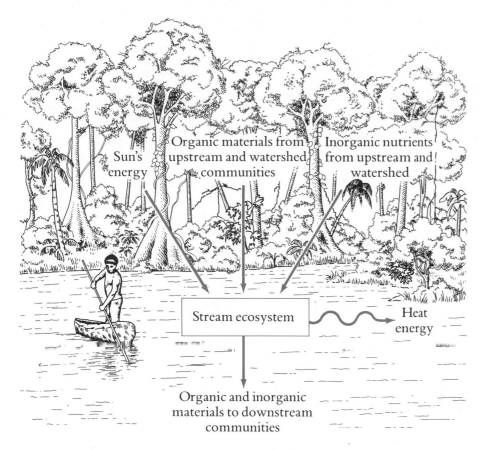

FIGURE 3-11 Energy and Materials Flow for a Stream Ecosystem. Living systems are open systems: Materials and energy flow into the system from its surroundings and out again into the environment.

Sun's energy

Organic materials from upstream and watershed communities

Inorganic nutrients from upstream and watershed

Stream ecosystem

Heat energy

Organic and inorganic materials to downstream communities

productivity. Productivity is measured in a variety of ways. It is often measured as the *increase* in weight of biological matter for a given area over a given time period. (This includes all the new plant tissue, roots, leaves, and so on as well as the increased weight of animals during the time specified.) Productivity may also be stated as a number of calories for a given time period, when measuring the energy captured by green plants and then transferred from one trophic level to another in an ecosystem.

In contrast, the **biomass** of an area or ecosystem is the *total* weight of all living material, plant or animal, in that area at a specified moment. For instance, the productivity of a forest ecosystem might be measured during a year's time. The bio-

FIGURE 3-10 Part of the Food Web in a Small Stream Community in South Wales. Note that the net-spinning caddis is both a primary consumer (eats green plants) and a secondary consumer (eats primary consumers). The complexity of most food webs is emphasized by the fact that this illustration shows only some of the insects involved. Many other creatures—for example, small fish, frogs, and turtles, are a part of this web. (*Source:* Adapted from J. R. Jones, *Journal of Animal Ecology, 18* [1949], 142. Used by permission of Blackwell Scientific Publ. Ltd.)

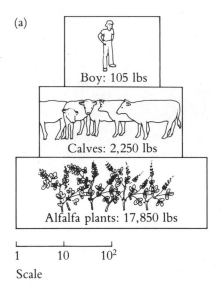

(a)

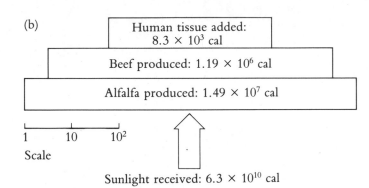

(b)

FIGURE 3-12 Ecological Pyramids for an Alfalfa–Calf–Boy System, Calculated for 10 Acres and 1 Year. (*a*) The biomass of the living material at each trophic level; (*b*) the productivity in calories at each level. (Note that both pyramids are drawn using a logarithmic scale in order to accommodate the large values at the producer level.) (*Source:* Adapted from E. P. Odum, *Fundamentals of Ecology*, 3rd ed. © 1971 by Holt, Rinehart & Winston, Inc., reprinted by permission of the publisher.)

mass at the end of the year would include not only that year's productivity but also plant and animal tissue (such as tree trunks) produced in previous years.

The productivity of an ecosystem can be further divided into primary and secondary production. **Primary productivity** is the amount of organic material produced by green plants (and some bacteria) using the sun's energy. **Secondary productivity** is the organic material produced by organisms that are not photosynthetic—that is, fungi, most bacteria, and animals. These organisms consume organic matter from primary producers to gain energy and materials for their own bodies.

The pyramids in Figure 3-12 clearly illustrate how much primary productivity is necessary to provide the yearly protein consumption of just one boy if his requirement is met by meat alone. The implications of this in terms of the world food supply are discussed in Chapter 9.

Availability of Produced Material. Several factors are not at all clear from illustrations such as Figure 3-12. In the first place, we should distinguish between gross and net productivity. **Gross productivity** is the total amount of organic material produced by plant photosynthesis in a given time period. Part of this, however, is used up by the plants themselves in respiration. The amount left is **net productivity.** This is actually what we measure, and it is the more important figure because only net productivity is available to the next trophic level.

Second, the available organic material is not usually completely consumed by the next trophic level. As a rule, primary consumers utilize only 5–15% of the primary production. There are several reasons for this. One is that some of this primary production is simply not available. In a tropical rain forest, for instance, most of the primary production is in the leaves of the tree canopy high above the forest floor, largely unavailable to browsing animals. Another reason is that dry or cold seasons create a variation in primary productivity: When it is cold or dry, primary productivity drops. The number of animals that can live on primary production is governed by the availability of food at the worst times. There simply are not enough animals in an ecosystem to consume all primary production during periods of high productivity; however, this effect is partly offset by migrations of consumers into areas where productivity is high. Even that portion of the available food actually eaten by animals is not all turned into flesh to be eaten by the next trophic level. Some part of the food is not digestible, and part of the energy in the food that is digested must go to maintain normal vital processes. Finally, energy transfer is not 100% efficient because energy is lost as heat (this will be explained later). In general, only 1–10% of the food eaten by animals is used to form new body materials.

All of these losses are summarized in Figure 3-13, which is a more detailed energy flow diagram than Figure 3-12. Such a diagram is sometimes called an **energy budget,** since it attempts to account for all of the energy entering and leaving a system. Even this complicated-looking diagram is not as complex as a real ecosystem. Several things are not shown in the diagram. For instance, small herbivores (plant eaters) probably migrate into or out of such ecosystems from other areas. Further, some of these small herbivores are eaten by secondary consumers, who are eaten by tertiary consumers, and so on. Note that all of the unused organic material eventually enters the food chains responsible for the decomposition of dead material. On land, these are mainly in the soil; in bodies of water, they are usually found toward the bottom.

Thermodynamic Laws and Ecosystems

Energy budgets follow the **first law of thermodynamics,** which states that energy can be changed from one form to another, but it cannot be created or destroyed. Thus, all the energy entering an ecosystem must balance with the amount remaining there plus the amount leaving the system, as illustrated in Figure 3-13. (Note that the amount of energy consumed by "other herbivores" does not quite balance the amount lost as heat and to decay processes. The remainder represents the "other herbivores" eaten by secondary consumers, which are not shown in the diagram.)

The first law of thermodynamics explains certain facts about the environment. For instance, it can help us understand limits on food production. Food contains stored chemical energy used by living organisms. When we eat food, it is broken down in our bodies as the stored energy is released. Some of the energy is captured and stored in body structure, some is lost as heat, and some powers the reactions essential to life.

In order to increase food production, especially in the developed world, farmers use great quantities of synthetic fertilizer. However, this fertilizer is produced by using fossil fuels, both as raw materials and to run the manufacturing process itself. That is, we are increasing the production of one kind of energy—the food energy in plant crops and the animals that eat them—by using up stores of high-energy fossil fuels. Similarly, synthetic foods cannot be manufactured without using some other energy resource to run the process—energy cannot be created.

This does not mean that no improvements can be made in the efficiency of food production. A major effort involves breeding plants in which more growth takes place in parts useful to humans as food, such as the kernels of a wheat plant rather than the stalk. In plant breeding, as in other sciences, however, ecological energy considerations must be taken into account. Remmert (1980) gives the example of attempts to breed plants that can fix nitrogen from the air rather than requiring soil nitrates (which in many farming areas are supplied in the form of expensive fertilizer). In terms of energy costs to the organism, fixing nitrogen costs more than the uptake of nitrate from the soil. This energy must come from some other biological process. Remmert speculates that if the experiment is successful, the plants will be found to be much less productive than the original variety, which could have the effect of canceling out the cost savings in reduced fertilizer use.

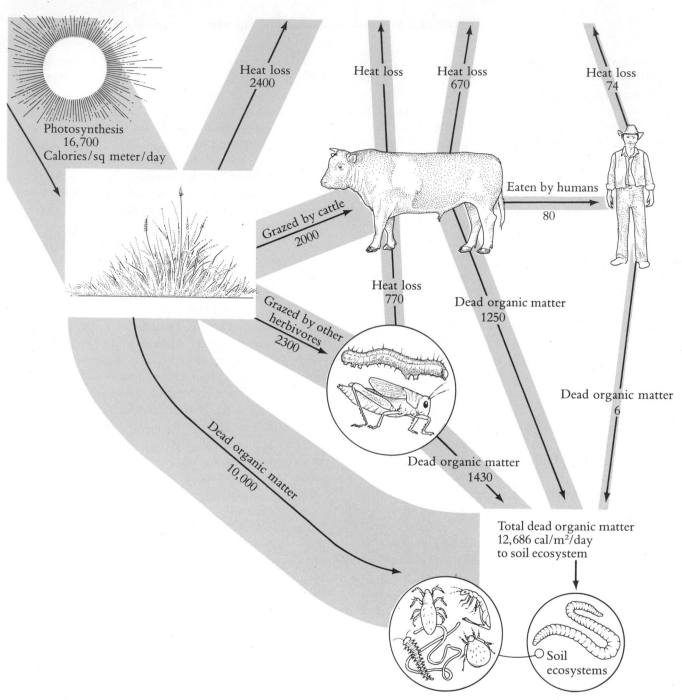

Photosynthesis
16,700
Calories/sq meter/day

Heat loss
2400

Heat loss

Heat loss
670

Heat loss
74

Grazed by cattle
2000

Eaten by humans
80

Grazed by other
herbivores
2300

Heat loss
770

Dead organic matter
1250

Dead organic matter
6

Dead organic matter
10,000

Dead organic matter
1430

Total dead organic matter
12,686 cal/m²/day
to soil ecosystem

Soil
ecosystems

FIGURE 3-13 Energy Budget for a Cow Pasture. The photosynthetic activity of the grasses captures 16,700 cal/m²/day. The energy flow through the system is shown. Note the large proportion of energy that enters detritus food chains in the soil. Note also the proportion of energy lost as heat at each stage of transfer. Eventually the 12,686 calories that enter soil food chains will also be lost as heat when the organic material containing this energy is completely broken down. Note that not all energy flow is accounted for in this simplified diagram—see text. (*Source:* Adapted from H. Remmert, *Ecology* [New York: Springer-Verlag, 1980], p. 211)

While explaining ecological pyramids, we mentioned that energy transfer reactions are not 100% efficient—some energy is lost as heat. In this way, living systems obey the **second law of thermodynamics.** This law was first discovered by physicists attempting to turn heat energy into useful work using machines such as steam engines. They discovered that heat could never be converted 100% into useful work. Similarly, in living systems, energy gained from breaking down energy-rich food substances is not all available for use in other reactions—some energy is always lost as heat.

This is one reason why few individuals (such as large carnivores) stand at the top of food chains compared to the vast numbers of individuals at the bottom. The loss of energy at each step in the food chain makes it impossible for more than a few individuals to be supported. This also explains why it is not energy-efficient to eat from the top of food chains, as humans often do. When we eat meat or fish, we eat food that contains only a small part of the energy with which the food chain began.

The large amount of energy lost as heat during energy transfers in the food web must be made up from outside sources (sunlight, detritus), or the whole ecosystem will run out of energy and collapse. Materials such as minerals or water cycle in the environment, but energy does not. Energy flows into ecosystems and is lost as heat.

A much broader and sometimes more useful statement of the second law of thermodynamics is that all systems tend to become random, or disordered, on their own. For instance, if you dump a bag of marbles onto the floor, they will spread out spontaneously in a disorderly fashion. The release of air pollutants, such as those formed when coal is burned, demonstrates the second law in action. Pollutants released from a power-plant smokestack disperse spontaneously in the atmosphere. We actually depend on this phenomenon: As the pollutants disperse, they become more dilute and less dangerous. Of course, this sort of system only works up to a point. As populations grow, power demands and pollutant levels increase, and dispersal or dilution of pollutants becomes a less and less effective solution.

On their own, the marbles we spill will not regroup and hop back into the bag to restore order in the room. We need to expend energy hunting for them and putting them back in the bag. The formation of order is a nonspontaneous process requiring energy, whether someone is cleaning up marbles from a floor or an organism is growing by the orderly arrangement of molecules.

When we first look at living organisms, it may seem that here is a system become more orderly spontaneously. A growing, living organism, considered alone, might seem to fit this description. However, at the same time that the organism is growing in an orderly fashion, biochemical reactions occurring inside it are producing heat. This heat, which is given off into the environment, increases the random motion of molecules in the organism's surroundings. Thus, the organisms plus its environment is still tending spontaneously toward disorder.

Using the second law, we can project some of the effects of population growth. Increasing numbers of people, who themselves live and grow by the production of order, will cause increasing levels of disorder in their environment. Air pollution caused by increased power demands of growing populations is one example. Another is the erosion of soil from land that was once part of tightly knit forest ecosystems, after the forest has been cleared to plant crops or after the land has been turned over in the search for minerals.

Although the laws of thermodynamics are important in understanding relationships between organisms and the effects of organisms (including humans) on their environment, most people fail to take them into account. A study of how these natural laws operate with respect to power generation, for example, can help us find ways to minimize our impact on the environment.

Productivity of Marine versus Land Ecosystems

Productivity in water habitats is greatest in estuaries, where nutrients are trapped and protective habitats are available for the young of many species. Coastal areas and areas of upwelling are also productive and provide the basis for fisheries.

Towards a Sustainable Society

Implications of the Gaia Metaphor for Lengthening Homo sapiens' Sojourn on Earth

by Lynn Margulis

Lynn Margulis is a Distinguished University Professor in the Department of Biology of the University of Massachusetts, Amherst. In addition to her interest in cells, she collaborates with James Lovelock on investigations concerning his Gaia hypothesis, which states that the surface of the Earth and the atmosphere are actively modulated with respect to tem-

perature, acidity, and chemical composition, and that modulation is due to the growth, metabolism, death and other activities of live organisms, especially microbes. Microcosmos: Four Billion Years of Evolution from our Bacterial Ancestors *(Touchstone Books, 1991) co-authored with Dorion Sagan, explores these issues in greater detail.*

Seeking remote detection of life on other planets, James Lovelock developed the Gaia hypothesis. Lovelock realized that one does not have to visit Mars to realize that it is lifeless. Chemistry and physics alone adequately model the Martian environment. The same standard physics and chemistry that explain the atmospheres of Mars and Venus fail to describe Earth's at-

mosphere. Although invisible to us, our atmosphere is so out of chemical equilibrium that it would be easy for a hypothetical Martian to intuit life on Earth from Mars. Gases that should quickly, indeed explosively, react with each other—for example, oxygen and nitrogen, or oxygen and methane—maintain dynamically stable concentrations here. Lovelock argues that if life evolves on the surface of a planet, it must become planetary in scale because it grows exponentially and therefore must continuously exchange gases, liquids, and solids with its environment. Atmospheres and oceans—that is, the fluid phases of the environment—must be conduits for the connected organismic system embedded in them. The environment and its organisms form not

Compared to most land ecosystems, the productivity of the open oceans is relatively low. Some researchers believe this is primarily due to a lack of nutrients in the open oceans. However, especially in warm oceans, it is probably also due to the fact that the primary producers are nannoplankton and picoplankton. These extremely small plankton species are used as a food source only by very spec-

ialized small planktonic animals. Because only about 10% of the available energy is passed from one trophic level to another the addition of another level at the bottom of the trophic pyramid greatly decreases the production measured at higher levels.

At the moment, humans eat near the top of ocean food chains, thus decreasing even further the amount of productivity available to them. At one

just a house but a body—the proper study of which is geophysiology.

A body differs from an inert place in that it is sentient, it is reactive, and it always metabolizes. Indeed, whereas the difference between referring to Earth as a "living planet" as does David Attenborough, and a planet that is itself "alive" may seem minor, debating it has caused contention and distress among biologists and geologists.

The "textbook" view of life is that it comprises millions of independent beings that inhabit inanimate surroundings. Such a traditional view of the biosphere was espoused even by forward-thinking individuals such as Buckminster Fuller. His metaphor of "Spaceship Earth" perpetuates the conceit of human control and mastery of an essentially inanimate environment.

In Gaia theory, by contrast, the air and the ground are not independent inorganic chemicals; rather, the sediments and atmosphere have been worked into an entire organic, living system. From the Gaian perspective, human air pollution on a global scale perturbs not just the atmosphere but affects all the biota. Feedback between the biological and geological realms is so intense that considering one in isolation from the other is an exercise in frustration.

The Gaian concept leads to a redefinition of life. Metaphysically, Gaia has narrowed the space, or expanded the continuum between life and nonlife, the organic and the inorganic, the animate and the inanimate. In Gaia theory, for example, the atmosphere as part of the biosphere is a global circulatory system. The muddy, bacteria-laden limestones and microbe-rich topsoils are no longer inert substrata but rather living tissues at the planetary surface. In the boldest extensions of the Gaia hypothesis, the living system at the Earth's surface provisionally encompasses not only the atmosphere and its clouds, but lateral plate tectonics, the regulation of ocean salinity, and mammal-like planetary thermostasis. These regulatory properties have persisted over a period of some three billion years—nearly the entire time in the absence of people!

This new-found attention to our surroundings as a body implies a transvaluation of values, giving our technical civilization a chance to recognize that our impacts upon the environment directly alter ourselves and our future.

Several billion trading, settling, warring, citifying, reproducing, largely technological human beings inhabit the surface of planet Earth. From an evolutionary viewpoint, it appears that we must, to survive in present numbers, adopt some version of the Gaia hypothesis: Only science has the status of a belief system necessary to induce human behavioral changes on a global scale. Gaia science, global science, operates out of the metaphor, or noble lie, that the planet is not just a home but a *body*—continuously replacing its components including us by metabolic activity, growth, death, and extinction. Our connection to our planetmates is one we can ignore but never escape.

Source: This essay is based on a chapter by Dorion Sagan, "Views of Gaia: Metascientific, Scientific, Phenomenological, Mythological and Deconstructive," in *Ecological Prospects: Theory and Practice,* C. Chapple, ed., SUNY Press, Albany, New York (in press).

time, scientists thought that plankton might be harvested from the ocean and used as a human food source; however, productivity in the open oceans is too low to make harvesting plankton a reasonable alternative at this time. That is, too much energy would need to be invested in running the fishing boats and processing the plankton compared to the amount of food energy obtained. In addition, of course, we would have to find ways to make plankton appealing to humans as a food. It is largely because of low productivity that once widely held hopes of feeding the world from the oceans seem doomed to disappointment.

In addition, the primary producers in the ocean are important to the world's oxygen and carbon dioxide balance. Schemes to harvest the primary producers in the ocean could seriously interfere with this balance.

ECOSYSTEM STABILITY

Diversity and Stability

Because of their complicated interrelationships, food webs were once thought to be more stable than food chains. That is, food webs should remain in balance despite the loss of a species. According to this theory, in a temperate-region field community, for example, the loss of an animal such as a fox, which preys on another species such as rabbits, should not cause a rapid increase in the rabbit population because there are other predators who also eat rabbits. In a food chain the loss of a predator might lead to an explosive increase in its prey population. However, other factors appear to be more important. For example, most of the food energy in a web may flow along only a few pathways, resembling food chains (Figure 3-14). In addition, the stability observed in communities that have many species could be due to other factors. For instance, mixed fields of crops do not suffer the massive outbreaks of insect pests often seen in fields with only one sort of crop. In some cases this happens because insect pests locate the plants on which they feed by means of chemicals given off by the plants, and the insects have trouble locating these plants in a mixed field. The stability of the mixed-field ecosystem thus results from a sensory phenomenon rather than from additional predator-prey relationships. As another example, tropical rain forests are among the most diverse ecosystems known, yet investigators believe them to be among those systems most easily disrupted by human actions.

We might say that very diverse ecosystems appear to have evolved under fairly constant conditions. Their higher diversity affords many checks and balances that act to keep the system constant as long as there is little outside interference. Changed environmental conditions and new species can have drastic effects on these delicately balanced systems. On the other hand, elastic systems—that is, those that can spring back after an outside influence—may well have evolved under more variable environmental conditions. For instance, the reed communities along lake shores, which are naturally subject to variable conditions such as water-level fluctuations, mowing, and ice movements, appear able to recover relatively quickly from pollution incidents. Like organisms in tropical rain forests, organisms in deep-sea communities live in an area that maintains a stable temperature and energy supply. Although the organisms living here are small, an enormous variety of them exists. In fact, the diversity is comparable to that found in tropical rain forests and in coral reefs, two other areas noted for their great variety of species. These habitats are similar in that they are physically stable (that is, little or no changes in physical conditions take place over long time periods) and have a long evolutionary history.

Diversity, Succession, and Climax

In Chapter 1 we discussed the process of succession, in which a community of plants and animals changes the environment in such a way that a different community eventually grows up. This succession of communities generally ends with the **climax community,** a relatively stable community characteristic of that particular climatic region.

Generally, during succession the number of species increases in each successive community. The first communities that colonize a lava flow, sand dune, or field are simple: They contain few species. As more plants appear, niches arise for more species of insects and other animals. These creatures, in turn, feed on plants and create pressures for species of resistant plants to flourish, and so on, through the various stages of succession. In this way, diversity increases as succession goes forward. However, diversity of species is not greatest in the climax community. Rather, diversity seems to peak sometime before the climax community appears.

Energy Use and Succession

Another community measure that increases during succession is energy use. As different groups of plants succeed each other, taller species grow up. The amount of biomass, or the weight of living material, both plant and animal, increases. Thus,

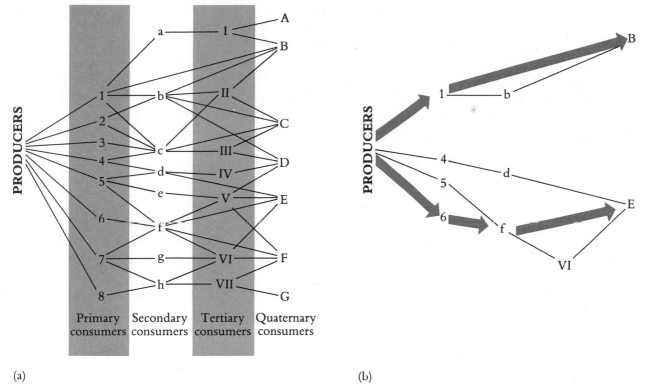

(a)

(b)

FIGURE 3-14 Food Web Diagram. (a) A hypothetical food web, showing the flow of food or energy through an ecosystem from producers to quaternary consumers. (b) Another view of the same system, in which all pathways accounting for less than 0.001 of the total are left out. Now the significant structure more greatly resembles a set of connecting food chains. (*Source:* Adapted from H. Remmert, *Ecology* [New York: Springer-Verlag, 1980])

more and more biomass is produced for the same energy input (sunlight) as succession progresses. However, energy use, too, peaks before the climax community occurs.

In climax communities other factors seem to be more important than those leading to species diversity and increasing biomass. An example is the increasing size of individuals, which gives species the ability to store nutrients or water against seasonal shortages. This and other factors lead to increased competition between species and a loss of species in the climax community.

Because climax communities do not produce the greatest biomass per unit of energy input, productivity is not as great in climax ecosystems as in some earlier stages of succession. In order to in-

crease production of food or wood, humans will try to keep an area at a younger successional stage. Younger stages, however, are less balanced and less able to maintain themselves than are older climax stages. Large inputs of energy and ingenuity are needed to maintain them. For instance, in some areas, paper companies plant vast tracts of forest land with softwood tree species that are fast growing and suitable for pulp. Such stands are much more subject to severe insect damage than the normal, mixed climax community. For this reason, quantities of pesticides must be used to protect the trees. Manufacturing and applying pesticides, of course, requires energy. Pesticides can also have many adverse effects on the environment, as mentioned earlier and detailed in Chapter 8.

SUMMARY

Ecosystems are not fixed but rather dynamic or changing. Materials such as water, carbon, nitrogen, phosphorus, and sulfur tend to cycle in ecosystems, while energy flow is in one direction.

The trophic structure of a community describes how the organisms are bound together in a pattern of eating and being eaten. Producers, which form organic materials by the process of photosynthesis, and detritus, the dead organic residue matter from living organisms, are the basis of either simple food chains or complex food webs. Consumers utilize producers and detritus as sources for their organic materials.

Productivity is a measure of the organic material produced by a system or an individual in a given time period, while the biomass of an ecosystem is the total weight of all living material.

Ecological pyramids, which show the productivity of various levels in the trophic structure, illustrate that energy transfer from one level to another is quite small. This is partly explained by the second law of thermodynamics, which states that energy transfers are never 100% efficient. The first law of thermodynamics, which holds that energy can neither be created nor destroyed, reminds us that all the energy in a particular system can be accounted for and also that schemes for increasing the production of food energy will always require an input of energy from some other source, such as fossil fuels.

Diversity is a measure of the species richness of an ecosystem and also a measure of the dominance of one species over others. Major influences on the diversity of organisms found in an ecosystem include the diversity of environmental conditions, the length of time the ecosystem has been in existence, and the harshness of environmental conditions. Diversity is not a guarantee of stability in ecosystems. In fact, ecosystems evolving under harsh conditions may have low diversity and be quite stable, while highly diverse systems may be very fragile in terms of environmental change.

During succession, diversity and biomass tend to increase. Both peak before the climax is reached, however, when competitive interaction becomes more important. Human beings influence succession by maintaining ecosystems in young, highly productive stages.

Questions

1. Illustrate the cyclic nature of the movement of materials in the ecosystem, using water, carbon, nitrogen, phosphorus, or sulfur. How does the flow of energy differ from such cyclic processes?

2. How does the first law of thermodynamics govern the food energy produced by farmers?

3. Diagram a simple food web that might exist in the area where you live. What are the producers? the consumers? the decomposers?

4. What does an ecologist mean by diversity? Of what importance are measurements of diversity?

5. What is the main characteristic of a climax community? (See also Chapter 1.) What are some of its other characteristics compared to earlier stages of succession?

References

Erlich, P. R., and J. Roughgarden. *The Science of Ecology*. New York: Macmillan, 1987.

Odum, E. P. *Fundamentals of Ecology*. Philadelphia: Saunders, 1971.

Remmert, H. *Ecology*. New York: Springer-Verlag, 1980.

Schell, D. M. "C^{13} and C^{14} Abundances in Alaskan Aquatic Organisms," *Science*, *219* (March 4, 1983), 1068.

Further Reading

Lewin, Roger. "In Ecology, Change Brings Stability," *Science*, *28* (November 1986), 1071.

The dynamic nature of ecosystems, and how this affects the management of parks and reserves, is explored in this article.

Stiak, Jim. "Old Growth, Battle Cry of the Northwest," *Amicus Journal*, Winter 1990.

The special characteristics of old-growth forest in the Pacific Northwest are described in this article.

Wilson, E. O. "Threats to Biodiversity," *Scientific American*, September 1989, 108.

Along with many other points, Wilson explains current thinking on ecosystem stability in this interesting and easy-to-read article.

Interior of home and children in Tunis. Where there are few opportunities for work or education, children may be the only form of wealth a family can accumulate, and having a large family may be the only way a woman can gain prestige. *(Alex McPhail)*

Family planning lesson, Indonesia. Making birth control information and services available and affordable to all couples is the vital first step in limiting population growth. *(UN Photo: R. Witlin)*

Girls being taught—Pakistan. After provision of birth control services, government actions that increase educational and work opportunities for women can have the greatest effect on reducing population growth. *(UN Photo: J. Isaac)*

Women's Agricultural Cooperative, Togo. *(UNDP: Ruth Massey)*

Female assembly line worker, Sweden. *(UN Photo)*

Women's milk cooperative, Bolivia. *(UNDP: R. Witlin)*

Sustainable Cities / Housing

It has been said that the battle for sustainable societies will be won or lost in the cities. Certainly, with an anticipated 60% of the world's population living in cities by the year 2000, the environmental problems posed by cities loom very large. Housing rapidly growing populations is one such problem.

Urban land sharing in Bangkok, Thailand. An innovative program in Thailand allows urban slum landlords to develop one-half of their land commercially, in return for deeding the other half to slum residents. Landlords avoid costly and chancy court battles to oust slum-dwellers. The residents receive a diminished plot of land, but one which is theirs on which to build a permanent home. *(UNDP: Studio Azzurro)*

Elderly derelicts in New York City. In both developed and developing cities, populations are increasing faster than adequate housing can be provided. *(UN Photo)*

Homeless children sleeping outside sports stadium in Addis Ababa, Ethiopia. *(UN Photo)*

Squatter settlement outside of Caracas, Venezuela. Settlements such as this usually have no water supply or sewage disposal. *(UN Photo)*

Chapter 4

Population Ecology

When the rains finally fall in the normally dry regions of Africa, delight is sometimes followed by despair, because the rain necessary for the growth of crops and grazing plants may also be the signal for explosive growth in populations of desert locusts. A swarm of locusts increases 30 times every time it breeds, and it can breed three or four times a year if conditions are right. The young locusts, not yet able to fly, march along the ground eating almost every living plant in their path. Hunger follows in their wake. The adults rise and swarm, traveling with the winds to devastate new areas (Figure 4-1). In 1988–1989 such a plague of locusts spread across Africa and the Middle East, bringing

FIGURE 4-1 Flying Locusts Rise from the Grass Around a Defoliated Tree. (*Photo:* United Nations)

FIGURE 4-2 Locusts in Africa and the Middle East, 1988–89. Desert locusts cut a wide swath in crops and pasturelands. In order to prevent famine, local governments fought the locusts with pesticides sprayed from airplanes. (*Source:* Map from *World Development*, January 1989, p. 5)

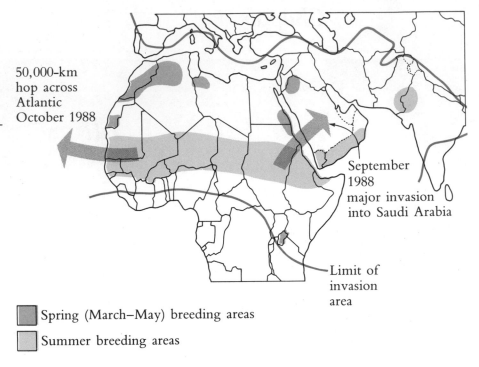

50,000-km hop across Atlantic October 1988

September 1988 major invasion into Saudi Arabia

Limit of invasion area

Spring (March–May) breeding areas

Summer breeding areas

destruction and famine (Figure 4-2). Eventually, when all the vegetation is devoured, the locusts themselves die of hunger, victims of their own population explosion.

But the plague of locusts does not come every year. In dry years only a relatively small number of locusts can be found, feeding on desert scrub. What is the cause of explosive population growth among the locusts? Why do we see such growth in some kinds of organisms and not in others? In this chapter we will look at the factors that govern the growth or decline of populations. We will examine the factors that determine whether a population can survive in a long-term relationship with its environment or whether it will grow explosively until the environment is so damaged that it can no longer support the population, as happens to the desert locust.

Finally, in the next two chapters we examine the growth of another species that appears to be growing explosively—our own species.

GROWING AND DECLINING POPULATIONS

There are two ways that individual members can be added to a population: They can migrate into the population from some other area, that is, they can **immigrate** into the population, or they can be born into the population. The natality or **birth rate** of a population refers to the number of individuals born or hatched or sprouted in a given time period into that specific population. Birth rates are calculated by dividing the number of individuals born into a population during a certain time period by the number of individuals already in the population at the midpoint of the time period.

The birth rate of a population is influenced by natural conditions, but there is also a wide variation among species in **fecundity,** or the ability of females in a population to produce offspring. For instance, the female Pacific herring can produce some 8,000 eggs each year, while the female elephant takes 18 months to produce only one offspring.

Conversely, individuals leave a population by death, or by **emigrating** to another area. Mortality or the **death rate** is a measure of the number of individuals dying in a population in a given time period. The death rate is calculated by dividing the number of individuals who die in a population over a certain time period by the number of individuals in the population at the midpoint of that time period.

Like fecundity, the theoretical maximum age to which an individual in a population could live varies widely from species to species. Some bacteria have a maximum life span of as little as 20 minutes, while humans may live for more than 100 years, and some trees may live for centuries. Mortality is sometimes illustrated by a **survivorship** curve. This kind of graph shows, for a specific population, the percentage of the maximum lifespan achieved by the members of the population (see Figure 4-3).

Age Structure of a Population

In many natural populations, if we compare the numbers of individuals at various ages, we obtain a graph resembling Figure 4-4a. In such a case, younger individuals are present in much greater numbers than older ones. The death rate of the young organisms is very high compared to that in other age groups. Thus, the numbers of individuals that survive to enter the older age categories are relatively small.

The shape of an age distribution graph depends on the specific population under study. For instance, of the 8,000 eggs the female Pacific herring produces each year, 95% hatch. Only 0.1%, however, live to maturity. A bar graph of this population would show a very broad base and a very narrow top (Figure 4-4b, 4-5a). Such an age distribution is also characteristic of populations that are growing very rapidly.

On the other hand, a population distribution for species such as elephants and whales, which produce only one offspring—and that not every year—

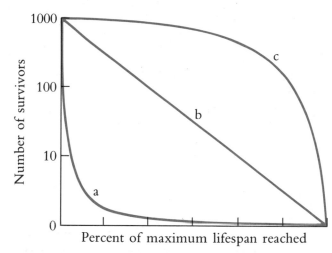

FIGURE 4-3 Survivorship. (*Line a*) In some species, for example oysters or Pacific herring, most of the individuals who are born die at a relatively young age, before they have a chance to reproduce. If individuals do reach adulthood, however, the likelihood of their reaching old age is relatively good. (*Line b*) In other species, death is equally probable at any age. Examples of this group are sea gulls, American robins, and bacteria in laboratory cultures. (*Line c*) A third group of species exhibits low mortality of infants, or prereproductive-age individuals, and high mortality of the elderly, or postreproductive-age individuals. Generally these individuals produce few offspring and invest a large amount of energy in caring for their offspring so that they are likely to reach reproductive age. Death comes as the maximum life span is approached. Humans fall into this category.

would not have as wide a base and would have a larger percent of the population in the adult age categories (Figure 4-5b). This type of age distribution graph is characteristic of populations in which natality and mortality are fairly well balanced; that is, approximately equal numbers of individuals enter and leave the population in any time period.

A third type of age distribution graph occurs when mortality exceeds natality—when more individuals leave a population through death or emigration than enter the population by birth or immigration. This type of bar graph has a narrow

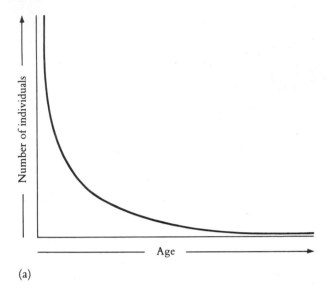

(a)

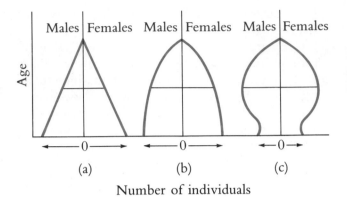

FIGURE 4-5 Bar Graphs of Population Age Distributions. (*a*) Population exhibiting high mortality in the younger age categories. Such a graph resembles a pyramid with a wide base and a narrow top. (*b*) Stable population, in which natality and mortality are approximately equal. Relatively equal numbers of individuals are found in all age categories except the oldest. (*c*) Declining population in which recruitment into the population is less than losses to death or emigration.

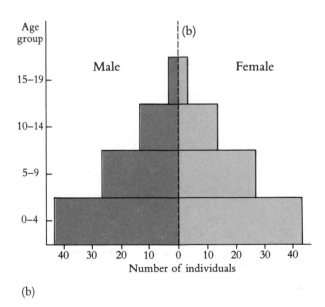

(b)

FIGURE 4-4 Age Distribution Graph. (*a*) Generalized curve showing numbers of individuals in a population versus their age group. (*b*) Bar graph of this population. Note: males and females are recorded separately and each bar represents a group of individuals in a different age category.

base and top and a wider middle (Figure 4-5c). Animals and plants in danger of extinction might exhibit such a population distribution graph.

Population Growth Curves

If a population of organisms grows under conditions in which essentially no death occurs before organisms become sexually mature—that is, if all of the individuals born survive long enough to reproduce—then each member of the population will likely produce, on average, more than one surviving offspring. Such a population grows at an exponential rate. Figure 4-6a shows **exponential growth.** Note that the time period necessary to achieve a specified population increase (e.g. a doubling of the population) continually decreases. This type of growth is also called **geometric.**

Exponential growth occurs in natural systems when organisms colonize a new habitat in which they have no competitors. However, it is obvious that this type of growth does not continue as the

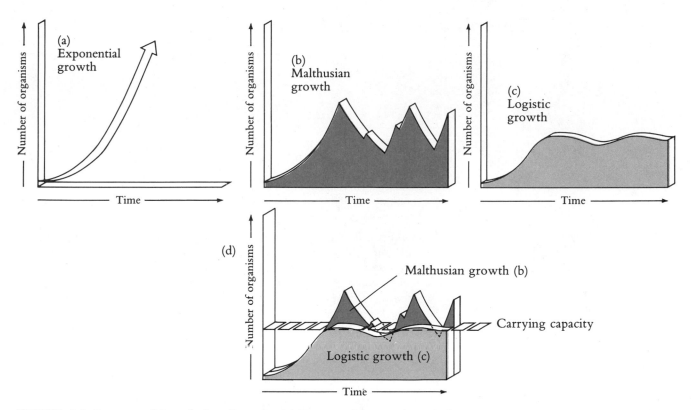

FIGURE 4-6 Patterns of Population Growth. (*a*) Exponential growth typical of organisms colonizing newly formed habitats. (*b*) Malthusian, or irruptive, growth pattern, in which population growth is limited by disastrous population crashes. (*c*) Logistic growth, in which the population gradually levels off. (*d*) Malthusian and logistic growth are superimposed on each other for comparison. Also shown is the carrying capacity of an environment, or the largest population that environment can support without being damaged. Note how the population showing Malthusian growth tends to overshoot the carrying capacity and then fall in a series of sharp population crashes. Populations growing logistically, however, level off around the carrying capacity of their environment.

curve does, because otherwise such an organism would soon cover the earth completely.

Malthus recognized this fact in the late 1800s. He proposed that populations grow until they use up the resources available to them, and then growth is limited by catastrophes such as famine, disease, and violence. The growth curve thus levels off into a series of fluctuations, as shown in Figure 4-6b.

Some animal populations do seem to follow this pattern of explosive growth and then collapse. In 1944, for instance, 29 reindeer were brought to St. Matthews Island in the Bering Sea. By 1963, there were 6,000 deer on the island. Immediately thereafter, however, the population suffered a catastrophic decline to less than 50 animals. Such growth is called **irruptive** or **Malthusian growth.** The desert locusts mentioned at the beginning of this chapter exhibit this kind of growth in wet years. The infrequent rains in these dry regions of Africa in effect create a new habitat that triggers

Towards a Sustainable Society

A Declaration of the Rights of Future Generations

by Jacques-Yves Cousteau

Let us assure for the children to come the same rights that have been declared for their parents.

Jacques-Yves Cousteau is a scientist and inventor who has spent a lifetime exploring the oceanic environment and communicating his findings to the world. Captain Cousteau and his research vessel Calypso *are familiar to Americans from many television specials. He is one of the few foreign members of the U.S. National Academy of Sciences and is the recipient of many awards for his work, including the United Nations Global 500 Award for Environmental Achievement.*

I land by Zodiac on a minuscule, overpopulated island—500 people crammed onto a grand total of 1,000 square meters—in the bay of Port-au-Prince, Haiti, one of the poorest countries in the world. The crowd, drawn from common huts, greets me laughing. The mayor, surrounded by his offspring, bids me welcome and answers my questions: He has three wives and eight children, five by the first and three by the second. I ask: "And the third?" "Oh the third," he says with joy, "that one's for the future!"

Throughout the so-called "developing countries—which are given no chance of economic development—the only thing that develops, and without moderation, is the population. The number of humans on Earth has tripled during

exponential population growth in the locusts. But the locusts then exceed the carrying capacity of their environment by eating all the available food, and their population crashes (see Figure 4-7).

Other populations do not seem to follow such a growth pattern but instead show a similar initial exponential increase followed by a leveling off over a period of time and then an oscillation around a value often referred to as the carrying capacity of their environment. (Carrying capacity is discussed more fully shortly.) Organisms with simple life histories demonstrate this type of growth, called **logistic growth,** very well—see Figure 4-6c. As life

histories become more complex, however, no curve may fit a population's growth patterns very well, or a particular curve may fit only at certain periods of time.

r and K Selection

Habitats such as undisturbed forests are relatively stable over long periods of time. That is, unless humans intervene, conditions do not change rapidly (with the notable exception of natural disasters). Most of the organisms in these ecosystems have adapted in ways that allow them to make the maximum use of their environment without harming

my lifetime and is increasing by a full billion every ten years. By 2030, it will certainly have doubled and probably will have tripled by 2100! This human tidal wave, multiplied by economic growth, is already causing a veritable pillaging of the irreplaceable resources of our planet.

In Africa, my heart broke to see little girls running ten kilometers to fetch a small pail of potable water instead of going to school. In Amazonia, intrigued by the children swarming around a cottage on stilts, I asked the master of the house how many children he had: "I don't know any more," he said. "My wife knows, surely!" And to one pregnant Haitian mother of eleven I asked: "How many children do you want?" "It's not me who decides," she replied, "It's God . . . and my husband!"

One look from these youngsters is enough to stir rebellion: Let us stop this delayed-action genocide!

Let us cease thinking only of ourselves and reasoning only in the short term. Let us assure for the children to come the same rights that have been declared for their parents.

But our cherished children, who will have to pay the debts our generation accumulated, who will seek to live on a desertified and poisoned planet, who will have to assume the risks that we have decided to force on them, and from whom we will have confiscated most options—who will they be?

Their parents, preoccupied by the car bumpers they gloomily follow for several hours a day, obsessed by their professional concerns, contemplating their navels and their appearance, are scarcely looking after their children except to get rid of them by handing them over to television or by offering them one of those expensive solitary games, a Nintendo or a computer. To ease their conscience,

they give their offspring a kiss or a "cootchy-coo," condemning them sweetly to an infernal concentration camp.

An interminable succession of absurdities imposed by the myopic logic of short-term thinking will engender tragic prospects for future generations. Such an inexorable mechanism can only be averted by recourse to Utopia. But we must have a fulcrum if we are to use the leverage at our disposal.

We demand that the rights of future generations be solemnly declared so that all human beings may inherit an undamaged and uncontaminated planet. The petition we propose for signature by millions of fathers and mothers worldwide is, in fact, the most reasonable of Utopias.

Source: A longer version of this essay appeared in *Calypso Log*, August 1991. Copyright 1990 The Cousteau Society Inc.

it. In other words, these organisms are adapted to the capacity of the environment. A growth curve for such a population of organisms might resemble Figure 4-6c, the logistic growth curve. There are other habitats, however, that develop rapidly and disappear again—for instance, seasonal ponds that fill with water only during rainy seasons. The growth curve for organisms colonizing such habitats commonly resembles Figure 4-6a.

Organisms characteristic of stable habitats are often termed **K-selected,** where *K* is a symbol for the capacity of the environment. *K*-selected organisms are generally long-lived, have few offspring, and are successful in situations where they must compete for scarce resources. In general, trees and animals with long life spans are *K* strategists. A second type of organism, characteristic of fleeting environments, is called **r-selected,** where *r* refers to their high rate of reproduction. In addition to showing a high reproductive rate, these organisms generally develop rapidly. They are not good competitors, however, and can establish themselves only where there is little or no competition. Small animals and the plants that first colonize habitats after a disaster (pioneer plants) are *r* strategists.

Of course, there is no neat division of all organisms into one or the other type. Many organisms are better classified somewhere between the two categories. Furthermore, even stable habitats have subdivisions that favor *r* strategists. The bodies of organisms that die in forests, for example, provide a habitat for *r* strategists (such as fly maggots) in an area where *K*-selected species are usually favored.

Factors Determining Carrying Capacity

Populations have certain space requirements that ensure such things as adequate food supply, space to seed or to raise young, the availability of reproductive partners, and a necessary minimum of stress-producing encounters. The **carrying capacity** of an ecosystem is the maximum-sized population for which the ecosystem can provide these requirements for an indefinite period of time. Carrying capacity is shown in graphic form in Figure 4-6d. We might now ask, what are the factors that determine the carrying capacity of an environment for a particular species, and how do organisms in nature adjust to this capacity?

Density-Dependent and Density-Independent Factors. Most, if not all, factors that adjust population size and carrying capacity are density-dependent; that is, they may kill off 80% of a dense population but only 10% of a sparse one. An example would be a disease that spreads quickly in dense populations with many contacts between individuals but that does not make much headway in a sparse population whose individual members rarely come in contact.

Fire and extreme climatic conditions usually act as density-independent factors in population regulation. For instance, a severe winter frost in the intertidal zone can cause rock surface to crumble away, removing snails that cling there without regard to the number of snails present. In many other cases, however, climatic factors act in a density-dependent manner. For example, during a flood, a larger percentage of individuals in a sparse population may find refuge (such as higher ground) than in a denser population.

FIGURE 4-7 Spraying for Locusts in Morocco. Humans do not wait for natural population crashes to bring down the numbers of pests. Here a worker sprays pesticides that kill desert locusts before they reach the stage where they are able to fly. But this may, in the long run, cause more problems, because the most effective pesticide appears to be dieldrin, a pesticide so toxic it is no longer allowed to be used in the United States. Unfortunately, less toxic insecticides used in spraying programs also appear to be much less effective. (*Photo:* G. Tortoli, FAO)

Predation, parasitism, competition, and stress all appear to act as density-dependent factors controlling populations either by decreasing the birth rate in a population or by increasing the death rate.

Predator-Prey Relationships. Predator-prey relationships appear to play a part in controlling population size. The example given of a disease controlling a population size once it reaches a certain level can be considered a special case of predator-prey relations. The disease is the predator and the host the prey. However, each system must be studied to determine whether the predator is controlling the prey or vice versa. One famous example is the nine-year population cycle of hares and the lynxes that prey on them. The hare population peaks in approximately nine-year intervals, and each peak is

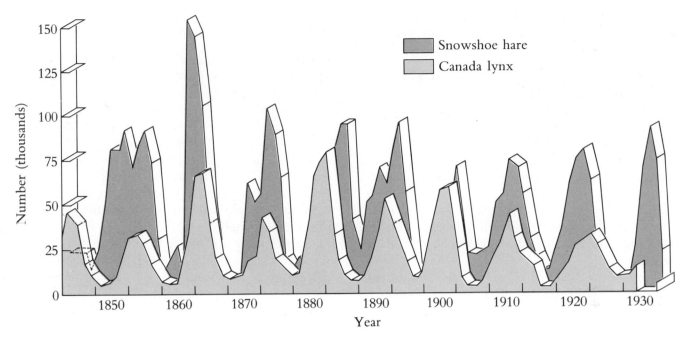

FIGURE 4-8 Variation in the Populations of Hares and Lynx. The snowshoe hare and the lynx in Canada show a periodicity in which the population of the hare rises and then is followed by a rise in the population of the lynx. It is not known what causes the hare population to cycle. It seems clear, however, that the lynx, in years when the hare is abundant, is better fed and therefore has more offspring and is more successful at raising them to adulthood. (*Source:* Data from D. A. Maclulich, "Fluctuations in the Number of the Varying Hare [*Lepus americus*]" [Toronto: University of Toronto Press, 1937, reprinted in 1974])

followed by a peak in the lynx population. But as the lynx population peaks, the hare population crashes. This was originally interpreted as an example of a species (the lynx) exceeding the carrying capacity of its environment by consuming too much of its food supply, following which the lynx population collapses and the whole cycle starts again. However, in regions where the lynx has become extinct, the hare population still cycles. Whatever the reason for this cycling, it is clear that the hare population was controlling the lynx and not vice versa (Figure 4-8).

On the other hand, predators much smaller than their prey (some scientists would then call them parasites) may be able to control the prey population. For instance, a European leaf beetle imported

into this country successfully controls the introduced weed St. John's wort (*Hypericum perforatum*).

In areas of great species diversity, several predators may keep the population of a prey species much smaller than it would be under the same environmental conditions with fewer predators. Several species with similar ecological needs can then occupy the same area. This may be a partial explanation for the richness of species on coral reefs and in rain forests.

Food Supply and Food Competition. On the face of it, food supply and the competition for food appear to be likely limiting factors for populations. However, field researchers have not been able to show that population density varies in any consistent way with food supply. Probably food supply acts with other factors to limit populations.

Autoregulation. In some cases, population size appears to be regulated by factors other than those already mentioned. Scientists have described this situation as **autoregulation.** The stress caused by overcrowding may be a factor in autoregulation. Stress is normally increased by crowding because there are more aggressive meetings with other organisms. Autoregulation can take several forms; for example, parental care of offspring can improve or deteriorate depending on density, or mass migrations out of a habitat may occur at peak population densities.

Sometimes an actual physical basis for autoregulation behavior is known. That is, some biochemical reaction to crowding affects births or deaths or triggers behavioral patterns. As an example, crowding in tree shrews (*Tupaia glis*) causes an increase in blood urea concentrations. Offspring mature more slowly or not at all. Mothers no longer protect their young by marking them with a glandular secretion, and the young are then eaten by other tree shrews. Population size is kept constant in these ways, even if food is present in excess. If crowding is increased artificially—for instance, by decreasing the size of the cage in which the population is kept—blood urea concentrations rise even higher and some of the animals die. In the field, lemmings have been shown to have similar blood urea concentrations during peak population densities.

The factors we have mentioned cannot give us a complete explanation of either the carrying capacity of an environment or how populations adapt to that capacity. In fact, the science of ecology has not advanced to a point at which it could give a complete explanation. However, there are fascinating questions raised by the insights ecology does give us. Considering mechanisms by which animal populations appear able to adjust to the carrying capacity of their environment leads us to wonder what mechanisms might or might not adjust human populations to the carrying capacity of our environment. How do we determine this capacity? Will we recognize it before we have exceeded it?

SUMMARY

Individuals can be added to a population by being born into the population or by migrating into it. The birth rate is the number of individuals born into a population in a given time period, divided by the number of individuals in the population at the midpoint of that time period.

Individuals leave a population by death or by emigration. The death rate is the number of individuals in a population who die, divided by the number of people in the population at the midpoint of the time period.

Species vary widely in their theoretical maximum life span. A survivorship curve shows the percentage of the maximum life span achieved by the members of a population.

Populations can be characterized by their growth curves and age distribution curves. The age structure of a population can be shown as a bar graph of the number of individuals in each age category at a specific time. Populations that are growing exhibit a pyramidal-shaped bar graph with a wide base and a narrow top. Bar graphs for populations that are declining have a narrow bottom, a pointed top, and a wider middle. Populations that are neither growing nor declining have an obelisk-shaped bar graph, with relatively equal numbers of individuals in all age categories except the elderly.

A population that grows until it exceeds the carrying capacity of its habitat and then crashes is said to exhibit Malthusian growth. A population that grows until it levels off at the carrying capacity of its environment is said to exhibit logistic growth. Stable environments characteristically support K-selected organisms, which are good competitors adapted to the carrying capacity of their environments. Fleeting environments encourage r-selected organisms, which have higher reproductive rates but are poor competitors.

The carrying capacity of an environment, or the size of populations that can be supported indefinitely, is determined by density-independent factors, such as some climatic disasters and by density-dependent factors, such as disease, that act more strongly as a population increases in density.

Questions

1. What type of growth curve does the desert locust described in this chapter exhibit? Explain your answer.

2. How does fire act as a density-independent factor regulating population growth?

3. The human population of Brazil is growing very rapidly, while that of Sweden is fairly stable, neither increasing nor decreasing. On the other hand, the population of Hungary appears actually to be decreasing. What shape age distribution graph would you expect each of these countries to have?

References

Ehrlich, R. R., and J. Roughgarden. *The Science of Ecology*. New York: Macmillan, 1987.

Hanley, M. L. "Ancient Enemy, New Threat," *World Development,* 2 (1), January 1989.

May, R. M., and J. Seger. "Ideas in Ecology," *American Scientist,* 74 (May-June 1986).

Odum, E. P. *Ecology*. Sunderland, Mass.: Sinauer Assoc. Inc., 1989.

Pianka, E. *Evolutionary Ecology,* 3d ed. New York: Harper & Row.

Part Two

Human Population Issues

Tokyo City Pool in June. (*Source:* Picture Group Inc./C. Cole)

It is undeniable that there is too much of many things in the world today—too much mercury in the water, too much sulfur in the air, too many wrecked automobiles. But surely the most curious excess is people. How has it happened that human populations have grown so rapidly that food and job shortages have gripped some countries, that both wildlife and wilderness are threatened, and that cities have grown to unmanageable sizes?

There are many reasons. Throughout the history of humankind, children have been valued. They have provided hands to work on the farm, to help in the blacksmith and carpentry shops and in the kitchen. Children represent security for parents in old age because they provide for parents too aged and infirm to work. And, for different reasons to different people, children are desirable in and of themselves. Children are a form of immortality, both of genes and of values. Through their children, a people's physical characteristics and also their beliefs can survive into the future. In traditional African religion, people are immortal as long as their descendants remember them. All societies, from the most primitive to the most cultured, consider the rearing and teaching of children one of their most important tasks.

Children are not only a precious resource; they have also been a most fragile one. In the United States and other countries, before the development of modern medicine and sanitation, five or six children, on the average, were born to each family. Of these, perhaps only two or three lived to adulthood. Because the survival of a child was so uncertain, people customarily wanted large families. Among other considerations, this helped ensure that at least two children would live to care for the parents when they grew old.

In many societies, especially where most of the population is engaged in farming, the tradition of large families has remained. At the same time, however, modern medicine has made child survival much more certain. Within the past 50 years, the death rate (or the number of people who die, each year, per 1,000 people in the population) has been reduced in most societies by one-half or more. This reduction in the death rate is due only partly to the medical advances that help adults to live longer; it is due in greater part to the survival of infants and young children who now live to become adults. This means that, in many countries, the number of people who die each year is much smaller than the number of people who are born. And so the population of these countries grow rapidly.

As the population of a country grows, many facets of life undergo stress. Food supplies must grow or shortages, malnutrition, and finally starvation will result. Job opportunities must increase or unemployment spreads. New housing must be constructed, new parks opened, more roads, hospitals, and schools built or unbearable crowding will occur. Even if construction needs are met, the stresses of city living are forced on many people.

How, and how well, a country meets the stresses of rapid population growth depends to a large extent on how technically advanced that country is. For instance, technically underdeveloped countries may find it difficult or impossible to feed, house, and educate a rapidly growing population. Technically developed countries, on the other hand, can often expand production of food, goods, and services, but cannot cope with increased pollution, vanishing wilderness, or the mushrooming of social problems in growing cities.

Population growth is thus an underlying cause of, or contributor to, many of the environmental problems we know by other names: food crisis; disappearance of wilderness; energy crisis; air and water pollution; urban sprawl.

The following two chapters explore the problem of rapid growth in human populations. How has the population problem come about? What are the effects of rapid population growth in developed and undeveloped nations? What means do we have of controlling population growth? And, finally, what is the outlook for the future?

Chapter 5

Human Population Problems

By at least one measure, humans are a very successful species. That measure is the size and distribution of the human population. Except among the insects, it would be difficult to find another species that has adapted so well and reproduced so successfully in such a variety of habitats. Yet it is that very success that is now the underlying cause of many environmental problems.

HUMAN POPULATION GROWTH

As Figure 5-1 shows, the human population grew very slowly throughout most of the history of the world. Early humans were hunters and gatherers, dependent upon a variable food supply, and victims of periodic natural disasters. There were probably no more than 10 million humans in the world until about 8000 BC, when people first learned to domesticate animals and to grow and store their own food. With a more certain food supply, the human population grew more quickly. Experts estimate there were perhaps 300 million people in the world by the year 1. This population doubled to about 600 million over the next 1,500 years—a steady but slow increase interrupted by war, famine, and plague. Then, just before the start of the Industrial Revolution, a tremendous growth spurt began.

In the eighteenth and nineteenth centuries the world population grew at an estimated rate of 0.5% a year. In only 150 years, from 1750 to 1900, the world population doubled to 1.7 billion. But faster rates were yet to come. In only 30 years, from 1950 to 1984, the world population, achieving growth rates of 2% per year, doubled once again from 2.5 billion to almost 4.8 billion.

By 1990, the world population was 5.3 billion. Although growth rates have slowed somewhat over that last 10 years, according to many experts the world population is expected to double again by 2050.

Looking at Figure 5-1, it is clear that the major portion of world population growth has occurred in the last 50 years. Although this may seem to be an astonishing figure, this type of population growth curve is not unique to humans. The curve is called **exponential** (see page 84). Such growth occurs when individuals in a population more than reproduce themselves—that is, when they have more than two surviving offspring per couple. The

FIGURE 5-1 World Population Growth Through History. There has been a steady increase in the human population since 8000 B.C., when agriculture became a significant way of obtaining food. However, the current enormous population growth spurt began much more recently, just before the start of the Industrial Revolution. (*Source:* Elaine M. Murphy, *World Population: Toward the Next Century* [Washington, D.C.: Population Reference Bureau, 1981])

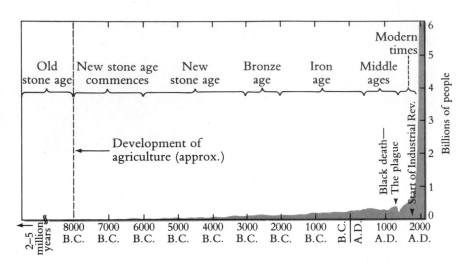

peculiar velocity of exponential growth is illustrated by the old story about the water lilies that grow on the surface of a pond. If the lilies double the area they cover each day, and if they have covered half the pond by day 28, the story asks, how soon will they cover the whole pond? The answer is: by day 29. A characteristic feature of exponential growth is that it speeds up, moving faster and faster as time goes on.

But there are limits in nature to this type of population growth. When all the food or water or living space has been used up, when populations become so dense that epidemic diseases spread easily, the population will crash. It will fall to a level far below the dizzying heights reached earlier.

Common sense tells us that unchecked exponential growth is not possible for the human species any more than for any other species on earth. It is only a successful strategy for survival if there are new wildernesses to conquer, and we have run out of wilderness. We no longer have suitable lands into which populations can expand when they outgrow their own living space, and we no longer have wilderness that will absorb the waste products of our living.

A living and nonliving complex of organisms and materials has in the past renewed the air we breathe out, purified the wastes we added to water, and recycled our organic wastes into the elemental materials usable by the plants and animals that provide our food. But it is a system that has limits.

The human species has evolved with a formidable set of abilities to ensure its survival: an ability to profit by past mistakes, an ability to plan for the future, an ability to find new ways to solve new problems. In order to use this complex of talents, in order to turn them to solving the problem of human population growth, we must first understand the factors that drive this growth.

Developed versus Developing Nations

The areas of the world in which population growth is taking place have shifted with time. From the middle 1700s well into the 1900s, populations grew in the countries we now call the **developed nations,** such as the United States and Great Britain. Since 1950, however, the major portion of world population growth has been taking place in the **developing nations.**

In general, the terms *developed* and *developing* refer to whether a country is industrialized (developed) or not industrialized (developing). Because industrialization leads to a higher standard of living, "developed versus developing" usually (although not always) means wealthy versus poor as well.

If a country's total economic production—called its gross national product (GNP) or gross domestic

TABLE 5-1 Per Capita GNP in 1988 for Selected Countries (in U.S. dollars)

	Per Capita GNP
Developing countries: Low-income economies	
Zaire	$ 170
Mali	230
Uganda	280
India	330
China	330
Senegal	630
Developing countries: Middle-income economies	
Mexico	1,820
Brazil	2,280
South Korea	3,530
Developed countries	
United Kingdom	12,800
Canada	16,760
Sweden	19,150
United States	19,780
Switzerland	27,260
High-income oil-exporting economies	
Saudi Arabia	6,170
Qatar	11,610
United Arab Emirates	15,720

Source: Population Reference Bureau, *1990 World Population Data Sheet.*

product (GDP)—is divided by the population of the country, a number is obtained, the per capita GNP, that is a rough indicator of the economic status of people in that country. For countries classified as low income, the per capita GNP is less than $410 per year. India, for instance, had a per capita GNP of $330 in 1988. In comparison, the U.S. per capita GNP was $19,780 in 1988 (see Table 5-1).

In Table 5-1 countries are divided into developing or developed on the basis of how industrialized they are. However, a third grouping is necessary to accommodate oil-exporting countries in which a relatively nonindustrialized population still enjoys many of the same benefits found in developed nations. This is due, of course, to the large income derived from oil.

Several qualifications must be given about such per capita figures. In the first place, the income in any country is not evenly distributed. Some people benefit by a much greater share of the GNP than others. Thus, there can be, and are, very poor people living in countries with a high per capita GNP. Nevertheless, when differences in GNP are as great as those shown in Table 5-1, it is clear that vast differences in living standards must exist as well.

A second qualification is that the absolute difference in living standards between developing and developed countries is not quite as great as the difference in GNP. Not only incomes but also prices are lower in developing nations.

Even when adjustments are made for purchasing power, however, large gaps exist between the real incomes of people in developed and developing nations. In 1987, Japanese citizens enjoyed an average real income of $13,135 in U.S. dollars, while citizens of the African country of Niger had an average of only $425 each.

Birth Rates, Death Rates, and Growth Rates

In the developed nations, **death rates**—the number of persons out of every 1,000 who die each year—began to fall in the middle of the eighteenth century. This decline was attributable to a variety of medical and sanitary improvements that we will discuss in the next section. The drop in death rates continued to the middle of the 1900s. Because fewer people out of every thousand were dying each year, populations in these countries began to grow. Such growth did not continue indefinitely, however, because **birth rates**—the number of births each year per 1,000 people—also began to decline.

Those countries in which both the birth and death rates have fallen are said to have undergone the **demographic transition.** Most industrial nations have already undergone this transition. Further changes in birth and death rates in these countries in the near future are likely to be small.

It would be easy to conclude that birth rates in developed nations fell *because* people became aware of the decline in death rates. In other words, people could see that more children would survive to adulthood and so chose to have fewer children. However, there is evidence that birth rates actually began to fall *before* the medical and sanitary advances that lowered death rates. Further, this seeming paradox is an important clue to why rapid population growth continues in developing countries today.

The Decline in Death Rates. In countries all over the world, death rates are being lowered by public health measures, by improved medical care, and by improvements in nutrition.

Diseases such as malaria and yellow fever, which are spread by mosquitoes, are prevented by the use of insecticide sprays and by draining and filling the swamps where these insects breed. Cholera, typhoid, and other intestinal diseases are prevented by chlorinating and filtering public water supplies. The pasteurization of milk can prevent the spread of bacterial diseases through this most common of childhood foods. General food sanitation, made possible by refrigeration and a pure water supply, also contributes to reducing disease.

Antibiotics save many children who might once have been victims of diseases such as pneumonia and scarlet fever. A vaccine that prevents tuberculosis and a drug that cures it are available. Vaccinations can also prevent most children from ever having smallpox, diphtheria, tetanus, whooping cough, polio, and measles. Finally, better nutrition and care for pregnant women have improved both the health of mothers and the chances that their babies will survive.

All these medical and public health advances have combined to cause a dramatic drop in the death rate among infants and small children, not only in developed countries but in developing countries as well. But even though the odds on child survival have increased in developing countries, and even though more of a couple's children survive to adulthood, there has not always been a corresponding drop in the birth rate. That is to say, many parents still have as many children as they did when it was necessary to have five or six children to be sure of raising two to adulthood.

Growth Rates. In developing countries the birth rate is, on average, 30 to 35 births per 1,000 people in the population each year, while the death rate is 10 to 11 per 1,000 per year. In contrast, among the developed countries birth rates have fallen to an average of 15 per 1,000 people per year while death rates are close to those in developing countries, 9 per year per 1,000 people (see Figure 5-2).

If we subtract the death rate from the birth rate, we obtain the **rate of natural increase,** a number that indicates how fast a population is growing. In countries classified as developing, this rate ranges from 14 to as many as 40 people per year for every 1,000 already in the population. For developed countries, on the other hand, the rate is much lower—in some cases, zero.

The actual **growth rate** of a country includes not only the rate of natural increase but also the amount of migration into or out of the country. This is called the **net immigration rate,** or immigration minus emigration. The growth rate is thus the rate of natural increase combined with the net immigration rate.

In some developed countries with low birth rates, immigration may be a major part of the growth rate. In the United States, for instance, net immigration accounted for almost one-third of population growth in 1988.

Immigration can have a significant impact in some undeveloped countries as well. In Nigeria, for instance, the government issued a decree in 1982 that all aliens were to leave the country. Hundreds of thousands of workers had entered Nigeria from countries such as Ghana to work in jobs generated by Nigeria's oil boom. When falling world oil prices dried up the job market, the Nigerian government determined that Nigerians should fill all remaining jobs. (Immigration problems are discussed further later in this chapter.)

A Comparison of Growth Rates. Growth rates vary among the developing nations and among the developed nations as well. Of the developed na-

Developed countries

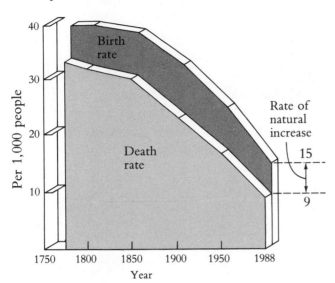

Developing countries

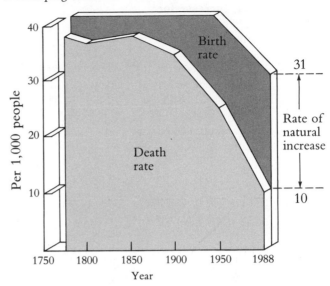

FIGURE 5-2 World Birth and Death Rates. The rates of birth and death are shown for both developed and developing countries. By subtracting the death rate from the birth rate, we obtain the rate of natural increase. (*Sources:* Elaine M. Murphy, *World Population: Toward the Next Century* [Washington, D.C.: Population Reference Bureau, 1981] and *World Population Data Sheet, 1990*)

tions, Denmark, Germany, and Hungary are hovering around zero growth, while in Canada and the United States, birth rates still exceed death rates. As a group, however, growth rates in developed countries are much lower than in developing countries. The major portion of the world's population growth is occurring in the developing nations (see Figure 5-3).

Causes of Rapid Population Growth— The Value of Children

Understanding the cause of high population growth rates in developing nations requires understanding the value of children in these countries compared to the value of children in developed nations. In developed societies today, most of the benefits of raising children could be called psychological. The pleasures of parenting, the gratification of passing on values to another generation, the fulfilling of other people's (such as grandparents') expectations—none of these bring any economic reward

to the parents. Most of these psychological rewards are gained by having one or two children (although a third child may be wanted if the first two are the same sex). These factors, combined with the high cost of raising children in Western society today and with the availability of effective contraceptive methods, have made the two-child family more and more the accepted norm.

The situation is different in most developing nations, where children may increase a family's wealth or provide parents with more leisure, with old-age security, or with status.

Children as a Labor Resource. In parts of rural Africa, labor is a scarce resource and land is not. The family that has many working members can farm more land and become wealthier. As Jones (1970) noted of Mali:

Except for recently introduced plows and carts, the physical factors a man needs to produce food are readily available. Land is abundant, "capital goods"—

FIGURE 5-3 World Population, Average Annual Increase for Each Decade. This graph divides the average annual increase in the world's population every 10 years into the portion that occurred in developed countries and the portion that occurred in developing countries. (*Source:* T. W. Merrick, "World Population in Transition," *Population Bulletin, 41* [6] [1986])

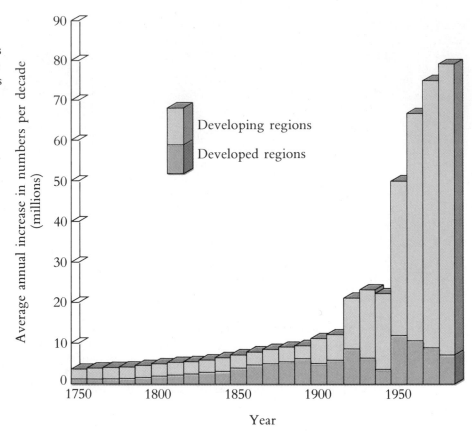

hoes and oxen—are cheap, and the wood and iron for making them are abundant. The crucial factors of production are the family's labor, of course, and "technology."

While in Uganda:

Extensive labor is needed for herding. . . . A moderately prosperous herd owner with say 100 to 150 cattle, 100 sheep and goats and a few donkeys needs about six herd boys ranging from 6 to 25 years of age to maintain a herd by himself. A man with many cattle but few sons must herd together, and share the yield of his stock, with a man who has few cattle and many sons. (Dyson-Hudson and Dyson-Hudson, 1970)

Further, in some parts of Africa—for example, Burkina Faso and the Sudan—private ownership of land does not exist. A person owns the crops grown on land, but no one can own the land itself. Land-use priorities are often given out according to the number of people in a family who can work on the land.

Besides providing labor to free the parent from household or field chores so the parent can do other work, working children allow the parent to have some leisure time. Younger children even allow older children more freedom. In developing nations, children can be useful at as young an age as 5 (Figure 5-4). If they cannot do an adult's labor in the fields, they can help take care of younger brothers and sisters and do some of the household chores. In developing countries such as Bangladesh, marketing and preparing meals may be a full day's work for one person in the family. Children can be trained to help with meal preparation chores. Cain (1977) estimated that a man living alone in Bangladesh would spend 90% of his working time

FIGURE 5-4 Child Worker. This Venezuelan boy is one of what the International Labour Organization estimates as at least 52 million child laborers in the world today. (*Photo:* UNICEF)

on household chores—tasks that women and children would otherwise do.

African and Asian families are often not as child-centered as families in the West. Parents may be expected to eat more than a proportionate share of food and to use more of the family resources for clothing and so on than are the children.

Children as Security. Children can provide security against old age or ill health, especially where there are no government old-age programs. In at least one sense, children are better than pensions or government social security, since the benefits they promise will not be eaten away by inflation. Even when parents must invest resources in children during the years of child rearing, they can expect to reap some return when the children are grown. This enables parents to even out their own lifetime consumption: They spend more when they are young, vigorous, and able to work, and they draw on this

investment when they are old or infirm. In Africa, parents who can expect their children to support them when they are old tend to respond to arguments that fewer children are needed as medical care improves. Thus, they have fewer children. However, African parents living in cities, who seem to feel less certain that the old values will hold, tend to have even more children because it is then more likely that at least a few will provide for the parents' old age.

Children and Inheritance. Another factor that affects population growth rates is the way in which property is passed from generation to generation. In many developing countries the definition of family differs from that in the West. In parts of Africa a father, his sons, and their wives and children may live together, or at least work together, under the father's direction. The economic unit of one man, his wife, and their children is not necessarily the usual one. In fact, in parts of Africa a man may have more than one wife. In such situations, property rarely belongs to a husband and wife together and may not be passed down from father to son. In parts of Africa where land is not held privately or where a father's property is not divided among his sons, parents do not feel the need to limit family size to avoid splitting inherited land among too many heirs.

In some Indian states the problems of inheritance are seen as the problems of the next generation. The father has the right and the duty to work for the maximum benefits for himself and the family he heads. This may very well mean more children now to provide more labor and produce more goods in the present, with no thought as to how the children will fend for themselves in the future.

The Value of Children and the Status of Women. In parts of Africa or the Middle East, women have little official status. They may not hold or inherit property. As mothers, however, they may gain power and influence through their children. In situations like this, where women have little opportunity for improving their lot except by bearing children, it is understandable that fertility rates remain high.

Educating Children. In some countries, parents can make choices about how they will educate their children. They may educate all of them, splitting the family's resources; they may educate only the brightest, sending that one child as far up the educational ladder as possible; or they may educate none of them. In countries that have enough economic development and in which social classes are not rigid, parents may see a benefit in producing only a few, well-educated children. These children can be expected to make something of themselves and add to the family's prestige and wealth. Further, in most of these countries, parents cannot benefit from their children's labor because of laws against child labor and because children are often required to be in school. In such a climate, parents limit family size in order to gain extra income by working themselves.

In poorer countries, such as Bangladesh, parents may not have this choice; their resources are often so limited that not even one child can be educated, or schools may not be available. In such a situation, the only wealth available to a family is a large number of children.

To summarize, in many developing nations, children provide parents with wealth (labor), with leisure, with status, and with security in old age. These factors, which promote large families, are largely absent in industrialized societies. In addition, social factors that act to limit family size in developed countries, such as education opportunities for children and the inheritance of property from a father to his children, are often missing in developing countries.

Population Profiles

Before we go on to look at the consequences of rapid population growth and what can be done to change its course, it is useful to look at a particular way of representing the population of a country: the **population profile.** The males and females in a population can be represented as groups called *age cohorts*. These cohorts consist of all the males and females born in the same 5-year period.* For instance, all the girl or all the boy babies born in the United States from 1955 through 1959 would constitute one age group. In Figure 5-5 the U.S. population is shown as a series of profiles over time. The 1955–1959 cohort of men and women first appears as the bottom bars on the population profile for 1960. In the 1970 profile, these people, then 10 to 14 years old, are represented by the third bar up from the bottom of the pyramid, and so on for the later decades.

Pinched Profiles of Developing Nations. Certain features of populations show up well in population profiles. For example, many developing countries show a characteristic "pinched profile." In this case, a decreased death rate in younger portions of the population, brought about by better health care, has swollen the younger age groups compared to the older ones. The profile thus has a wide base and a narrow top (Figure 5-6, left). The increased size of childhood age groups is the result of better infant and child survival as health care and sanitation have improved.

Profiles of Developed Nations. Figure 5-6 also shows the population profile for a typical developed country (right). In this case the profile is approaching an obelisk shape, which is characteristic of countries that have achieved replacement-level fertility. That is to say, each couple has only two children, on average, and so only replaces themselves. In such a situation the distribution among the age groups becomes more uniform.

Population Momentum

One more feature of population growth that can be seen well in these bar graphs is **population momentum,** the growth that can take place in a country's population even if each couple has, on an average, no more than two children. Momentum can be understood by considering people in terms of age ranges: those 0–15 years who are not yet old enough to have children, those 15–45 who are now in their childbearing years, and all those older than 45, who are no longer likely to have children. In terms of a country's future population growth, the two important groups are those 0–15, who will

* Sometimes the population may be divided into 1-year age groups, but 5-year groups are more commonly used.

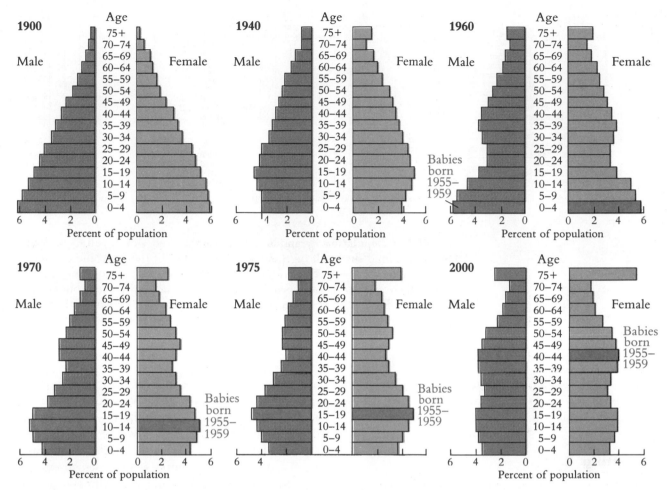

FIGURE 5-5 Population Profiles for the Population of the United States at Various Times. From these graphs you can see how a large group of babies born during one period (1955–1959) swells the size of age groups in later years. (*Source:* Population Reference Bureau, 1975)

have children in the future, and those 16–45, who are having their families now. People in all the older age groups can cause no further increase in the population. In most developing countries the large numbers of children now 0–15 years old are likely to marry and have at least two children per couple. As these large numbers of parents and their children grow older, they will swell the older age groups, which are now relatively small.

Because changes in the near future are the result of the age structure existing today, population reduction programs started right now would have a 40- to 60-year lag time before they could result in

stable populations. This would be the case even if programs were immediately and successfully implemented. (Actual experience shows that population reduction programs are rarely successful immediately but take a number of years to become accepted.)

In Figure 5-5, which shows the age structure of the U.S. population from 1900 to 2000 as a series of population profiles, the large group of babies born in 1950–1964 forms a bulge, the "baby boom." The females in this age group will be in their childbearing years through the 1990s. Even if their fertility rate remains at less than replacement

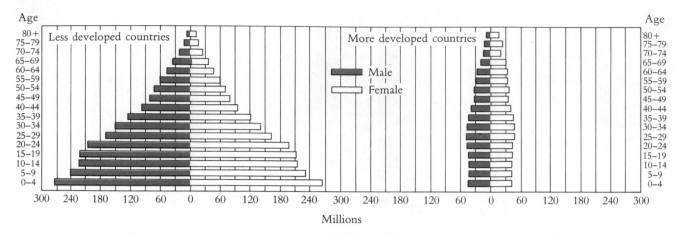

FIGURE 5-6 Population Pyramids for Developing and Developed Countries. The left pyramid shows the age and sex distribution of the population in the less developed countries. The profile has a wide base and a narrow top, showing that there are many more people in the age 19 and under age groups than in other age groups. In contrast, the pyramid for developed countries has a more uniform distribution of people in the various age groups. (*Source: World Population Profile 1989,* U.S. Census Bureau, WP-89, 1989)

level (1.8, for instance), the large actual number of children born to these women will cause a growth in the U.S. population.

Total Fertility Rate

The birth rate and death rate defined and used at the beginning of this chapter are often referred to as the *crude birth rate* and *crude death rate*. The adjective *crude* points out that there could be something misleading in these numbers. One problem is that the crude death rate does not take into account the age structure of a population. For instance, the crude death rate for Sweden in 1985 was 11 deaths per 1,000 in the population, while for Mexico it was 6. This might seem to indicate that Mexicans are receiving better health care. In fact, the difference arises from the fact that Mexico's population has proportionately more people in the younger age groups. Only 4% of Mexicans are in the over-65 age group and thus subject to the likelihood of dying from old age, while 17% of Swedes are in this group. Actually, the life expectancy in Sweden is 75 years, while in Mexico it is about 66.

The crude birth rate is less subject to this particular kind of misinterpretation because the pro-

portion of women in childbearing age groups is similar in most countries. Both Mexico and Sweden had 23% of their population in the 15–49 age group in 1980. Problems do arise, however, in the cases in which the proportion of women of childbearing age differs between countries, or cases in which more women in the age group 15–49 in a particular country are in the subgroup 20–29, the most fertile period of a woman's life.

A more sensitive measure of a country's fertility than crude birth rate is the **total fertility rate (TFR):** the total number of live births a hypothetical average woman would be expected to have during her reproductive lifetime. This figure is based on the fertility rates current when the calculation is made. Because this hypothetical woman will be part of several different age groups over her lifetime, the TFR is derived by combining all the fertility rates for the different age groups in the population. Whether the number of women in the childbearing age group is large or small does not affect the TFR, which measures only how many children each woman can be expected to have. For this reason, TFR gives much earlier warning of changes in reproductive behavior than the crude birth rate does. The crude birth rate for a country may remain high or continue to increase as long as there are much larger numbers of women in the childbearing age groups than in the older age groups. TFR, however, tells whether the couples reproducing now are choosing to lower their family size toward replacement levels or are continuing to have more than the average two children per couple.

EFFECTS OF RAPID POPULATION GROWTH ON HEALTH AND WELFARE IN DEVELOPING NATIONS

The types of problems caused by rapid population growth are different for developing countries than for developed ones.

Food Production

In developing countries the most pressing need is often simply to produce enough food to feed the rapidly growing numbers of people. Government programs must be heavily weighted in this direction to prevent starvation.

The graph in Figure 5-7 shows India's rate of population growth from 1950 to 1984 and the increased production of food grains in India during that period. While India managed a significant increase in food production, the population increase used up all but a small part of the gain, and during bad years there was no improvement.

Investments in food production are also important for the stability of a developing country's government. A hungry population is a discontented one, and discontent can flare into revolution and overthrow of those in power. This possibility sometimes leads governments to act in ways that are not economically wise but that will help them stay in power. For instance, food prices are often kept at a low level in large cities. However, this policy results in low prices for the farmer, which in turn discourages increases in food production. Farmers will not want to raise more food if they

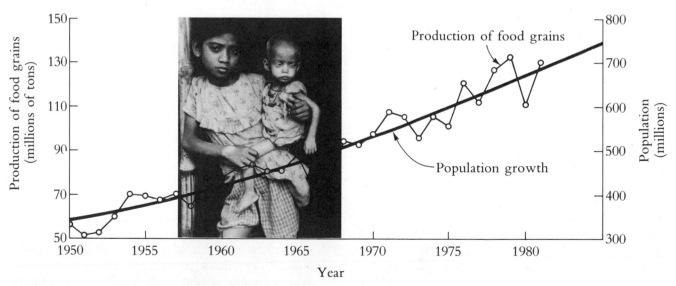

FIGURE 5-7 Population Growth and Production of Food Grains in India, 1950–1984. Although grain production increased almost 250% over the period, population growth resulted in barely a 20% increase in food-grain production on a per person basis. Severe malnutrition affects about 10 million children under age 5 in developing countries. (*Source:* Data from The World Bank, *World Development Report 1984* [New York: Oxford Press, 1984], p. 93) (*Photo:* Abigail Heyman/UNICEF)

FIGURE 5-8 Impoverished Shacks Contrast with Public Housing. Disease flourishes in shantytowns such as this one, in the Dominican Republic. Because of population growth, government spending on housing, health, and, sanitary measures cannot keep pace with the public's need for such services. (*Photo:* United Nations)

do not receive a reasonable price for their efforts. Low farm prices also mean that farmers cannot invest in modern farming methods that would increase their crop yields. Thus, the countries that most need more food may, in some ways, be hindering greater food production. In this manner, population pressures can force a government to slant its policies in ways that are not in the country's long-term best interest. The world food situation is covered in more detail in Chapter 9.

Health Consequences

Because so much money must be spent on food production in developing nations, little is left for health programs. Among women who have many children, the rates of maternal illness and death are higher than in developed countries, and the babies born to these women tend to suffer from malnutrition. The lack of sufficient food in childhood leads to poor health and decreased mental ability.

A developing nation's annual investment in health activities must cover medicines, rents, equipment, salaries of physicians and nurses, and so on. Yet in most developing countries the total annual investment in health activities, when divided by the population, comes to only $1–$2 per person per year. Obviously, not much health care can be obtained for this sum.

Ill health has its effect on productivity. Burdened by ailments of many sorts, individuals are not likely to be able to pull themselves and their families out of poverty by their own labor. Thus, the expanding populations of developing nations diminish the

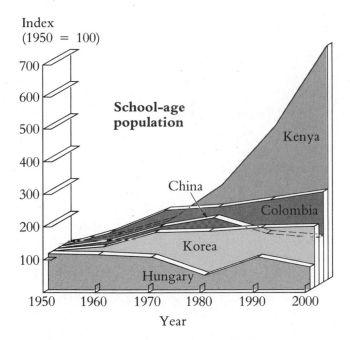

Index
(1950 = 100)

700
600
500
400
300
200
100

School-age population

Kenya

China

Colombia

Korea

Hungary

1950   1960   1970   1980   1990   2000

Year

FIGURE 5-9 Projected Growth in School-age Popula tions for Several Countries. (*Source:* Data from The World Bank, *World Development Report 1984* [New York: Oxford Press, 1984])

health resources available to each person and so reduce each person's potential to succeed (see Figure 5-8).

Educational Consequences

Education is also likely to be slighted in developing nations, as governments are often unable to increase educational services at the same rate at which the population is growing (Figure 5-9).

Developing countries have made tremendous gains in primary education for their young people over the past 20 years. Improvements in enrollment figures have been recorded in almost all countries. However, government spending on education in developing countries, as a whole, has become a significant burden—about 4% of the gross national product. Predicted increases in school-age children will make programs difficult to maintain. In fact, recessions in the world economy have already put severe strains on the ability of developing nations to sustain educational spending. In some cases the amount spent per student has dropped in real terms,

even though there is not much margin for decrease. In Malawi and Kenya, class sizes are often greater than 60 students. Whereas Scandinavian countries spend over $300 per year per student for classroom supplies, countries such as Bolivia, El Salvador, and Malawi spend less than $2 per student. It is difficult to see how improvements in class size or improvements in the materials for each student can be achieved if populations continue to grow.

As increasing numbers of young people go out to look for jobs each year, their low educational levels and the scarcity of jobs force them into un- skilled positions at best. People who accept these low-paying jobs have limited upward social mo- bility and little opportunity to improve their eco- nomic lot even by hard work.

Environmental Consequences

To feed increasing numbers of people, developing countries usually attempt to increase farm outputs. However, increased agricultural production carries environmental costs. The clearing of large forest tracts and the soil erosion that accompanies inten- sive agriculture have led to landslides, floods, and the silting of reservoirs needed for hydroelectric power. Animal habitats are being endangered as more and more land is turned over to agriculture or the gathering of fuel wood. Agricultural pesti- cides and fertilizers have polluted waters and pose new health problems for agricultural workers.

In some environmentally fragile areas the com- bination of population growth and drought has turned large areas into virtual desert (see Chapter 7). Erosion, pollution, loss of species, and loss of land have all resulted from unchecked population growth.

We catalog these events because they matter to us. Our perspective is influenced, however, by the mountain of plenty on which we stand. Well-fed, well-clothed, well-educated, we can afford the lux- ury of seeking quality in our environment.

It is not hard to understand why wise land-use policies, pollution control, and protection of en- dangered wildlife are sometimes low priorities in developing nations. Where children and parents are perpetually hungry, often sick, and without ade- quate clothing, where there is little hope for people

Towards a Sustainable Society

Environmental Problems and the "Demographic Connection"

by Susan Kalish

Susan Kalish is editor of Population Today *newsletter, published by the Population Reference Bureau.*

If population growth does not necessarily cause environmental problems, it surely *aggravates* them.

This is one reason why many population experts and policy makers around the world are looking to family planning programs to slow population growth. In an increasing number of developing countries, family planning is seen as a key strategy to improve health status, educate a greater portion of the population, enhance the quality of life, moderate the crisis of uncontrolled growth around many Third World cities, and further global environmental aims.

The population of the world has doubled over the past 50 years to 5.4 billion. At current rates of growth, it will double again in about 40 years. Almost all of the growth will occur in developing countries, where women average

over four children in their lifetimes. By contrast, in more developed countries, such as the United States, European nations, Australia, and Japan, fertility levels are at or below "replacement level," with two or fewer children per woman.

In addition to the much publicized case of China, countries as diverse as Colombia, Mexico, Indonesia, Thailand, the Republic of Korea, Singapore, and Sri Lanka have strong family planning programs. Other areas lag behind. Iran and Pakistan have recently adopted new family planning initiatives. In Africa, fertility has not yet changed much, and women average about six children.

Population experts John Bon-

to better themselves, the immediate future of the environment does not seem to matter very much. Until people's primary needs are met, they will have little enthusiasm about seeking a quality environment.

Nonetheless, certain elements of the environment are of long-term importance to people everywhere. Without good agricultural methods, such as proper irrigation techniques, careful use of pesticides, and control of erosion, the productivity of the soil will eventually be lost and food production

will fall. Without adequate treatment of water supplies and wastewaters, diseases will continue to ravage and weaken the population and periodic epidemics of chemical poisoning will occur. (See, for instance, Agarwal et al. [1982] on environmental problems in India.)

These are but a few of the potential long-term problems. The point is, even in developing nations where the most pressing needs are the most basic human ones—food, shelter, and good health—consideration must be given to the environment.

gaarts, Parker Mauldin, and James Phillips* have measured the effects of family planning on world population size to date and projected potential effects into the future. They estimate that past programs have already produced a population reduction of 412 million births through 1990. Population momentum, the effect of high birth rates in former years on current growth of population, obscures this. However, the impact could grow to 700 million by the year 2000 and 3.1 billion in 2050, as the force of momentum wanes. By the beginning of the twenty-second century, family planning has the potential to have prevented a whopping 4.6 billion births.

As Mauldin points out, sometime in the next one to two decades, there will be a year when the

* John Bongaarts, W. Parker Mauldin, and James F. Phillips, "The Demographic Impact of Family Planning Programs," *Studies in Family Planning*, 21(6) (1990).

number of babies born is less than in the year that preceded it. The timing of this event will give a good indication of what is likely to be the final population level of the world. If it occurs relatively soon, the population will top out at about double what it is today. If it occurs later, ultimate world population size will be closer to three times the population of today.

People concerned about threats to the environment have good reason to take an interest in world population trends. It is important to note, however, that determining the exact connections between population numbers and environmental problems is a very tricky matter. Causes of pollution include such wide-ranging factors as how much fossil fuel consumption it takes to satisfy the demands of a modern lifestyle, the kinds of products people purchase and use, the types of industries in a country, the waste disposal systems in place, the amount of "clean" and "dirty" technology that is used, and so on.

The demographic connection is further complicated by the fact that as developing countries modernize and population levels off, the standard of living generally goes up and, with it, per capita consumption of energy and manufactured goods. Headlines sometimes overlook these complexities, suggesting, for example, that "population pressures" are destroying tropical rain forests. However, one can also discern other factors at work, such as *economic* pressures, driving timber cutters into the forests and supplying them with the chain-saw technology that speeds up the devastation.

Many developing countries are finding a wide variety of reasons for making efforts to slow population growth. These measures seem likely to at least buy time for individual countries to cope with their resource crises. Taken as a whole, these steps will influence the ultimate numbers of people who will share the resources of the planet.

For unless the environment remains healthy, it cannot long support a human population.

POPULATION GROWTH AND ECONOMIC DEVELOPMENT IN DEVELOPING NATIONS

Economic development is one of the major aims of governments in developing nations. It is through economic development that governments hope to raise the living standards of their people.

Population Growth as a Block to Economic Development

In the Western nations, economic development took place at the same time as the discovery of the health and sanitation measures that led to rapid population growth. In these countries, industrialization provided jobs to absorb the increasing labor force that resulted from population growth, and incomes rose steadily. Within the same time frame, birth rates in these countries began to fall. Eventually, a point was reached in most of the developed nations where birth rates and death rates balanced each other. Today these nations are approaching a state in which their populations are not growing at all (zero population growth).

To many people there seems a clear relationship: Increasing economic development leads to a lowering of the population growth rate. Therefore, to achieve decreases in population growth in developing countries, the first step must be economic development. However, looked at from another point of view, there is a great deal of evidence that population growth itself, at the level taking place in developing countries today, is blocking their economic development.

According to the analysis of experts at the World Bank, economic development alone would not bring down birth rates quickly enough to prevent serious consequences in developing nations. Moreover, rapid population growth may in some ways make economic development impossible. There are several reasons for this opinion.

In the first place, population growth in developing countries is both quantitatively and qualitatively different than it was in the now-developed countries 200 years ago. In the second place, rapid population growth causes governments to spend their limited capital in ways that do not speed economic progress. In the third place, rapidly growing populations place stresses on resources and social institutions, thereby hindering economic progress.

How the Situation Differs in Developing Nations Today. Even during the time of their most rapid growth, Western nations never experienced the growth rates now prevalent in the developing nations. In Europe, population growth peaked at about 1.5% in the early 1800s and declined from there. In North America, relatively high fertility combined with heavy immigration raised population growth rates to more than 2% in the 1800s, but the rates had declined well below 2% by the early 1900s. In contrast, growth rates are near to or exceed 3% in many developing countries today. An additional difference is that a large part of that increase is taking place in rural areas. In Africa and Asia rural populations are growing at well over 2% per year, whereas in developed countries, rural populations grew at a rate of less than 1% during the 1800s.

This rural growth is a problem because population growth is less easily absorbed in rural areas, where most jobs are in agriculture. Land suitable for farming is a scarce commodity in many countries. Further, modernization of agriculture tends to decrease the number of jobs available rather than increase it (see Chapter 9 for more on this subject).

Population Growth and the Capital Needed for Development. Rapid population growth forces governments to choose between making investments that would improve the long-term economic welfare of their people and spending money on the short-term health and food requirements of the people. For instance, education through at least the primary level has become a prerequisite for economic improvement in the modern world. But, as populations grow, the number of children who must be educated increases. If a government attempts to continue spending the same per capita amount on schooling, larger and larger sums of money must be allocated to education each year. This is a form of **capital widening.** In contrast, slower population growth would free some of this capital for improvements in education or job training. This would be **capital deepening,** an increase in available capital per person. Countries that are faced with food shortages and that must take emergency actions to prevent starvation or the spread of epidemic diseases may be forced to spend their limited resources on food and medical care and decrease the amount spent on education.

A second example of capital widening involves growth of the labor force in developing countries. To increase productivity per worker and thus increase incomes, capital must be invested in roads, energy sources, farm machinery, parts, and factories. If it is not, each additional worker will produce less with the reduced land and capital available to him or her. Wages will fall in relation to profits, while rents and income inequalities will increase. Table 5-2 shows how much investment could have been available for each new worker in selected countries in 1980 (if all available investment were allocated to new workers). Rapid population growth in developing countries leading to increases in the size of their labor force will widen these differences even more in the future.

In short, the human capital (an educated, skilled labor force) and the physical capital to invest in the physical requirements of manufacturing are difficult or even impossible to accumulate when a country's population is growing rapidly.

Population Growth and the Resources Needed for Development. Because there is little advanced technology in developing countries, there is little demand for the kind of resources that fuel an industrialized society. The one serious exception is materials used to produce fertilizers. Developing nations need large amounts of fertilizer to produce food, but production of fertilizers requires nitrates (which are produced from natural gas), phosphates, and energy. For this reason, high world oil prices affect not only the developed parts of the world but also developing countries such as India.

Increasing populations put pressure on scarce resources such as land and water and may make wise use of these resources impossible. In many developing countries today, large areas of tropical forest land and steep mountainous slopes are being cleared to grow food for increasing populations. Erosion of fertile topsoil often follows, leaving land unfit for cultivation in the future. Similarly, over-grazing of semiarid lands can turn them into deserts. In such cases the welfare of future generations is being mortgaged to serve the needs of the present.

In developing countries that possess an abundance of natural resources (such as Brazil, Ivory Coast, and Zaire), more people could theoretically be supported in the long term. However, rapid population growth will hinder the investment in roads, public services, and training programs that would allow use of these resources.

Developing countries whose natural resources are already scarce (such as Bangladesh, Burundi, China, Egypt, India, Java, Kenya, Malawi, Nepal, and Rwanda) must look to investment in manufacturing and agricultural modernization to improve their economic picture. Again, this will be difficult if increasing numbers of people must be fed and cared for.

TABLE 5.2 Investment per Potential New Worker in Selected Countries, 1980

Country	Gross Domestic Investment per Potential New Worker*
Bangladesh	$ 1,090
Ethiopia	1,530
Nepal	1,260
Rwanda	1,660
Kenya	4,700
Egypt	8,960
Thailand	10,660
Colombia	10,100
Korea	29,850
Brazil	40,360
Japan	535,040
Australia	219,350
France	461,340
Germany	481,330
United States	188,990

* In 1980 dollars, if all available investments were allocated to new workers.

Source: The World Bank, *World Development Report 1984* (New York: Oxford Press, 1984).

Social Inequalities and the Reforms Needed for Development

As the population grows in a developing country, the per capita income (the Gross National Product divided by the number of people) generally decreases. There are two ways of interpreting this particular fact. Some experts emphasize the points we have been making: Lower per capita income decreases savings, cuts down on the amount of capital available for investment, and prevents people from buying manufactured goods, thus retarding industrialization. Others point out that in many developing countries the capital and most of the income is in the hands of a privileged few anyway. This has led to the development of two groups:

one rich and well fed, one poor and ill nourished. Furthermore, the rich are likely to remain rich and privileged, while the poor and the children of the poor have little hope of escaping their fate. These experts argue that unless population programs are combined with some form of redistribution of wealth, population reduction among the poorer people in a developing nation will not help improve their economic status. In the next chapter we discuss this issue further with reference to several South American countries.

When governments do attempt to make changes, rapid population growth can cause difficulties in instituting the social and economic reforms that can lead to increased economic development. For instance, social and political pressures to employ large numbers of young people have contributed to the growth of a large government workforce in many developing nations. Yet such a use of scarce resources is not always in the long-term best interests of a developing country. Egypt's guarantee of a job to all college graduates tends to siphon funds away from the uneducated who might otherwise benefit from government spending and toward those who are already relatively well off.

POPULATION GROWTH IN DEVELOPED NATIONS

Resources and Technology

In developed countries, technology and the scarcity of resources are primary issues raised by population growth. The energy crisis has made many people aware of the depletion of such resources as natural gas and oil. Shortages are also predicted by the turn of the century in many minerals, among them copper, tin, magnesium, and zinc.

Looking back in history, it is hard to find instances in which we have actually run out of some critical resource. What commonly happens is that scarcity causes a price rise that eventually forces a switch to some other resource. Thus, a scarcity of wood in England in past centuries led to the burning of coal. Whether this mechanism, which economists call *substitution,* can be counted on to continue to

work in the face of increasing population growth is not clear. For instance, will technology provide us with solar or fusion power before we run out of uranium, oil, and gas? We are at least gambling with the possibility of future resource shortages.

The example of the switch from wood to coal fires in England brings up another problem. By the 1900s, coal fires were responsible for a level of air pollution that made London almost uninhabitable at certain times of the year. Air pollution incidents, such as the London fog of 1952 that caused 4,000 deaths, were primarily due to pollutants derived from the burning of coal.

Pollution is one of the most serious problems faced in developed countries. We need more fertilizer and pesticides to grow ever increasing quantities of food. We need more petroleum to produce the gasoline required to get increasing numbers of people to ever more distant places of work. The result is increasing levels of smog. More people need more housing and more farm products. Housing and farming use up forested lands, leading to increased soil erosion. More people generate more sewage and solid wastes, which either foul natural waters or demand technological solutions for their disposal. And more people consume more products whose manufacture generates chemical wastes. Although technology may be able to solve some of these problems, more and more of our money and effort go to maintaining the quality of life. Like the Red Queen in *Through the Looking Glass,* we run in order to stay in the same place.

Effects of Crowding

Population growth limits not only our choices about spending society's money but also our personal choices. For example, whole areas of the United States (such as the Eastern seaboard) are becoming urban (Figure 5-10). Recreational areas are threatened by throngs whose presence may even destroy the appeal of the area (Figure 5-11). Furthermore, as population increases, available open space decreases or becomes more costly. Wilderness turns into overcrowded parks, and parks degenerate into outdoor slums.

Scientists who have studied animals under

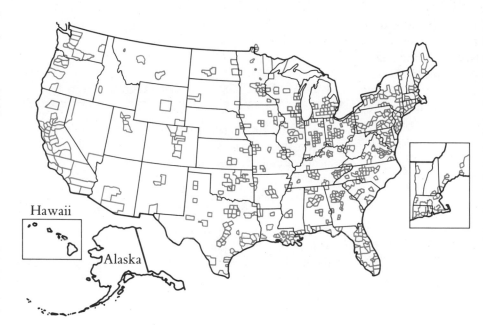

FIGURE 5-10 Urbanization of the United States. The map shows the 281 metropolitan areas scattered across the United States. For purposes of gathering statistics, there are 20 Consolidated Metropolitan Areas and 261 smaller Metropolitan Areas. Most of the metropolitan areas are concentrated in the eastern part of the United States; the eastern seaboard is in danger of becoming one continuous Consolidated Metropolitan Area. (*Source:* Population Reference Bureau, *Population Today, 18* [3] [March 1990])

crowded conditions have reported some results worth noting. For instance, rats in crowded cages begin to lose their normal patterns of social behavior. They neglect their young and sometimes resort to cannibalism. Some rats become overly aggressive, while others withdraw from the community.

Sexual behavior becomes abnormal. Monkeys also show some of this same behavior when crowded together.

In the wild, animal populations occasionally experience rapid growth, and the needs of the expanded population may exceed the food supply or

FIGURE 5-11 Crowded Campground in South Tyrol. In developed countries, rapid population growth leads to overcrowding of recreational and wilderness areas. In a real sense, some of our freedom of choice is lost. (*Photo:* Werner H. Muller/Peter Arnold, Inc.)

living space available. In such cases, starvation, disease, and reduced fertility lead to a decline in the animal population. Some scientists think the mass migration of lemmings is a response to rapid population growth.

Can the results of animal studies be applied to human populations? Probably not directly. Nevertheless, the implications of the changes that occur in animal communities under stress from rapid growth and crowding warrant consideration.

Perhaps humans can survive under relatively crowded conditions. On the other hand, we may prefer not to see the changes such crowding will cause. If we wish to influence the future, we must make decisions about population growth. Otherwise, the choice will have been made for us.

ZPG

In a number of developed countries the fertility rate has reached replacement level or even dropped slightly below. Populations in these countries are thus no longer growing. Zero population growth or ZPG can bring its own set of problems. The main concern is the "aging" of the population that accompanies increasing life expectancy and decreasing birth rates.

Low fertility rates eventually produce populations with higher proportions of the elderly than in the past. For most countries, people in the working age groups will then be supporting more retired people than in past times. This is partially offset by the fact that there will be fewer children to be supported per family, but because older people consume about twice as much as children, problems will arise.

In Sweden, for instance, where population growth is at zero and there is a comprehensive welfare system, costs for support of the elderly have been rising much faster than other welfare costs. Proposals designed to help solve these problems include increasing the retirement age and changing tax policies to encourage older people to remain productive longer. Families might also be helped to care for their elderly members so that costly institutionalization is not necessary. Flexible work arrangements in which some "retirement" could be

taken at younger ages, for education or retraining, might also help.

RURAL TO URBAN MIGRATION

Although the rapid growth of the world's population in general is a major cause for concern, another equally far-reaching phenomenon is occurring in this century that affects both the environment and how people interact with one another: the way in which society is organizing itself. We are in the midst of transition from a mainly rural society to a mainly urban society. Although at one time most people lived on farms, soon most will live in cities. In the early 1900s, only one-quarter of the world's

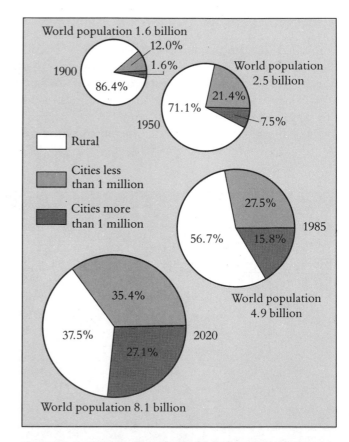

FIGURE 5-12 Patterns of World Urbanization.
(*Source: Population Reference Bureau, World Population: Towards the Next Century, 1985*)

TABLE 5-3 Largest Cities in the World, 1950 and 1989

1950	Population (in millions)	1989	Population (in millions)
1. New York–N.E. New Jersey	12.3	1. Tokyo–Yokohama	26.9
2. London	10.4	2. Mexico City	20.2
3. Rhine–Ruhr	6.9	3. Sao Paulo	18.5
4. Tokyo–Yokohama	6.7	4. Seoul	16.3
5. Shanghai	5.8	5. New York–N.E. New Jersey	14.6
6. Paris	5.5	6. Osaka–Kobe–Kyoto	13.8
7. Greater Buenos Aires	5.3	7. Greater Bombay	11.8
8. Chicago–N.W. Indiana	4.9	8. Calcutta	11.7
9. Moscow	4.8	9. Greater Buenos Aires	11.5
10. Calcutta	4.6	10. Rio de Janeiro	11.4
		11. Moscow	10.4
		12. Los Angeles	10.0

Source: Population Reference Bureau and World Population Profile, 1989, U.S. Census Bureau, Publ. #003-024-07074-0.

population lived in cities. By the year 2000, it is believed that 60% will live in cities (Figure 5-12). Furthermore, the cities themselves are getting larger. There were only 2 cities with more than 10 million people in 1950, but 12 had reached that level by 1989 (Table 5-3).

Advantages of Cities

Cities have certain advantages. They allow for greater division of labor, providing more jobs. Cities offer more specialized occupations for people to find work—for example, taxicab or rickshaw driver, police officer, firefighter—jobs that may not even exist in the hinterlands. Even crime and begging provide ways to sustain life in the cities. On average, 75% of migrants to cities are economically better off than they were in rural areas.

While cities provide more job opportunities for growing populations, the number of jobs in rural areas is decreasing. In both developed and developing nations, fertilizers, pesticides, and modern farming equipment (when available) make it possible for fewer people to till the same area of land.

Employment opportunities are then fewer and people must move to the cities to support themselves.

Another advantage of cities is that the more concentrated population can be more easily provided with health and welfare services. In sub-Saharan Africa, for instance, only 10% of the rural population has a safe water supply, whereas 66% of the urban population does. Studies in India show that substantial economies of scale are found in supplying water and electricity to cities of at least 150,000 people. However, whether a point is reached at which cities are too large to provide such services economically is not yet clear.

Disadvantages of Cities

In developing nations, poor people who move to cities to find work often find conditions of extreme squalor. The services needed in cities—housing, traffic control, sewerage, water supplies—are difficult to provide when cities double in size in only 10 years. Administrators may have neither the money nor the skills to cope with such growth. In the major cities of India, many people must live on

FIGURE 5-13 Sidewalk Dwellers. These typical sidewalk-squatter dwellings in Bombay contrast starkly with the modern high-rise apartment buildings that house a fortunate few. (*Photo:* UNICEF)

sidewalks, making their home on nothing more than the pavement (Figure 5-13). The water and sanitary conditions of these wretchedly poor people may be worse than in the rural areas from which they came. Cardboard and tar-paper shacks seem a step up to people who have so little. Sanitation conditions are a modest improvement in communities of shacks, but they remain extremely primitive, with no running water and only ground disposal of waste. Intestinal diseases and tuberculosis are rampant in these unsanitary and crowded conditions.

In the wealthier, developed countries, poor people who move from rural areas to the cities may find noise, dirty air, violence-ridden schools, crime, readily available drugs, and, too often, ugly surroundings.

These problems of cities in the developing and developed world are due in large part to the speed of the transition from rural to urban society. Laws, managerial skills, and customs have not evolved quickly enough to cover situations in which enormous numbers of people are crowded together into cities. Perhaps new laws and methods will help solve some of these problems. As an example, wise land-use programs may preserve open space, limit "urban sprawl," prevent strip development, or confine industrial operations.

Reversing the Trend

A number of countries have attempted to slow the growth of cities. China has successfully kept the proportion of its urban population constant over the past 30 years using a system of restrictions in movement and a resettlement program.

In Korea, schemes to attract population and industry to small towns through economic incentives have been successful. Elsewhere, however, such schemes have had no visible impact on the growth of major cities. In fact, the World Bank has concluded that in economic terms, the money used in urban–rural resettlement plans would be better spent to intensify production in already settled areas. This view is admittedly a purely economic one, however. Indonesia's resettlement program, which relocates families from populous Java to the country's sparsely populated other islands, has dealt mainly with families from the poorest strata of society. These families have enjoyed a better standard of living once resettled. In purely economic terms the money spent on relocation might have brought greater returns in other programs, but in terms of economic justice the government considers the program a success.

MIGRATION BETWEEN COUNTRIES

In the eighteenth and nineteenth centuries, emigration provided something akin to a safety valve for population growth in Europe, absorbing some

10%–20% of the increase in population. Today, migration between countries is reaching historic proportions if we include legal immigration, refugee movements, and illegal (and often temporary) movements into and out of countries by workers in search of jobs. Yet, for developing countries today, emigration cannot provide relief from problems of overpopulation, for two major reasons. First, the size of growing populations in developing countries makes it unlikely that any significant fraction can be absorbed by the more developed countries. Only 0.2% of the population growth in India was siphoned off by emigration between 1970 and 1980, and that figure is less than 1% for Africa or Asia as a whole. The World Bank points out that even if 700,000 immigrants from developing nations were allowed into the developed countries each year between 1985 and 2000, this flow would account for only 2% of the projected population growth in these countries, while it would account for 20%–40% of the population increase in the host countries. A larger migration from developing to developed countries in the near future is not only of little use; it appears unlikely. Second, the receiving countries place severe restrictions on the number of immigrants they will accept. Host countries are concerned about foreign workers taking jobs from natives. They also fear social changes or political tensions caused by large immigrant groups. Thus, host countries not only restrict numbers of immigrants but also try to ensure control over the type of immigrants allowed so that particular needs in their country will be met (skilled versus unskilled laborers, professionals versus nonprofessionals).

Although immigration is not a solution for rapid population growth, it can offer benefits to both sending and receiving countries. For receiving countries, immigration provides a flexible labor supply—one that can be tuned to the particular needs of the country. For sending countries, emigration of particular groups can ease job pressures at home, raising wages for those who remain. This has been true for construction workers in Pakistan and agricultural workers in Yemen Arab Republic. Emigrants themselves often send home money, which helps not only their own families but also their government's trade deficit. Such monies provided almost the same amount of foreign exchange as exports for Bangladesh and Burkina Faso in 1980. Many governments recognize this benefit and have designed taxation and incentive policies that encourage emigrants to send money home.

Immigration to the United States

The United States accepts almost twice as many immigrants as all other countries combined, close to a half million people a year in recent years. To this figure should be added the number of refugees, who are not counted as part of normal immigrant quotas. The number of refugees accepted each year is determined by the President in consultation with Congress. On average, the United States has accepted about 200,000 refugees per year over the past decade. There is a further category to consider, however, and that is illegal immigration. It is not clear how many illegal immigrants enter the United States each year, but the number appears to be between 100,000 and 200,000. The total number of legal and illegal immigrants plus refugees accounts for somewhere between one-fourth and one-third of U.S. population growth.

Opinions about the economic effects of immigration, especially illegal immigration, vary. Many people feel that unskilled immigrants take jobs away from U.S. citizens and use social services for which they are not paying a fair share. A blue-ribbon government panel, the Interagency Task Force on Immigration Policy, reported in 1979 that the situation is complex. In times of high unemployment, immigrants may take jobs from U.S. citizens, but at other times they fill jobs in which pay is too low and working conditions are too poor to attract U.S. citizens. On the other hand, the availability of cheap labor acts to prevent wages in these jobs from rising to a level where they would attract U.S. workers. However, if raises did occur, some manufacturers would go out of business and some goods and services might become unavailable or unaffordable to the majority of people.

Legal immigrants appear to consist only one-third of males, according to a Labor Department study. Apparently, two-thirds of legal immigrants are women and children and thus represent less of

Controversy 5-1

U.S. Population Growth: Who Is Responsible?

The growth of any country's population is governed by the country's birth rate, death rate, and rates of immigration and emigration. The United States occupies a somewhat unique position among the developed nations because these rates sum to a population growth rate of 0.8% per year, the highest for any developed nation except Iceland. Current projections are that the U.S. population will continue to grow until 2040, when there would be 309 million people, and then possibly decline to a fairly stable 292 million people by 2080. That would be 16% higher than the current population of about 250 million people.

One cause of the current high growth rate is undoubtedly immigration. The United States accepts more immigrants than any other country in the world. Although immigration is not *the* major cause of U.S. population growth (it accounts for between 25 and 30%), it is significant. Experts at the Population Reference Bureau estimate that if net immigration were reduced to zero, the population in 2080 could stabilize at 220.3 million, or about one-quarter lower than if immigration rates re-

mained at today's level. Of course, most Americans recognize the value of immigration; most of us are the descendants of immigrants. And, as Lawrence Fuchs, former executive director of the Select Commission on Immigration and Refugee Policy, points out, "All research shows that immigrants are extremely productive. They contribute to economic growth. They enrich our cultural and social life. Accepting immigrants into the United States also shows the world how confident we are about our ideals and institutions."

In any case, current population growth in the United States is not primarily due to immigration but rather to an excess of births over deaths. But whose babies are swelling the U.S. population? Are they mostly babies born to the white majority, or are they babies born to minority-group mothers? Some confusion appears to exist over this point, possibly due to misunderstanding about the difference between fertility rates and the number of babies actually born each year.

There were 3,809,394 babies born in the United States in 1987, the latest year for which final fig-

ures have been released. Of these babies, 816,906 were born to minority-group mothers while 2,992,488, over three times as many, were born to white mothers. Why then is there a perception that population growth in the United States is due primarily to minority groups?

One reason may be that population reporting has emphasized the fact that for white Americans the total fertility rate (TFR), or the number of children a woman can be expected to have over her whole lifetime, had dropped to 1.77 in 1987. This is less than replacement level. (In order to replace themselves, each couple must have an average of 2.3 children.) How can a group that is reproducing at less than replacement level be responsible for population growth? The answer lies in population momentum. The superimposed U.S. population pyramids for 1960 and 2050 in Figure A illustrate how a large group of under 15-year-olds will swell a country's population when they come to reproductive age, even if they only have an average of 1.77 children per couple.

What about the minority groups? For black Americans the

TFR in 1987 was 2.29, and for Hispanics 2.6. Their percentage of the population can be expected to increase somewhat over time, if their TFR remains above that of the majority group (see Figure B). But because they make up a smaller percentage of the population, their marginally higher fertility does not now result in their producing as great a percentage of the babies each year as does the white majority.

Do you favor stricter controls on immigration, or do you think we should take in more immi-

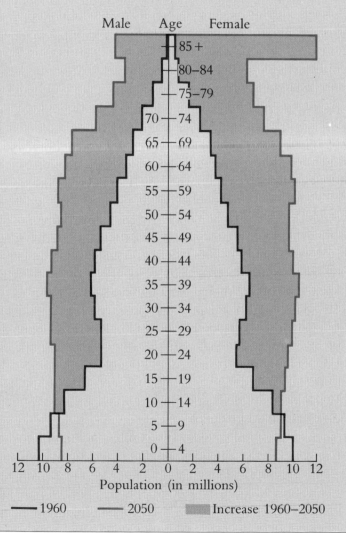

FIGURE A U.S. Population Changes 1960–2050. The two overlapping "population pyramids" give a vivid picture of the changes in U.S. population size and composition projected to the year 2050. Because both pyramids are drawn to the same scale, they give a comparable picture of overall size in both years. In 1960, as the "baby boom" began to wane, U.S. population was 179 million and the pyramid had a wide base as a result of prior years' high fertility. By 2050, continued low fertility should cause the pyramid to take on a relatively uniform appearance. (*Source:* From Population Reference Bureau, *Population Today,* February 1984, p. 5)

(Continues)

Controversy 5.1 (Continued)

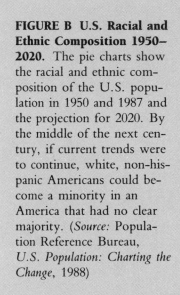

FIGURE B   U.S. Racial and Ethnic Composition 1950–2020. The pie charts show the racial and ethnic composition of the U.S. population in 1950 and 1987 and the projection for 2020. By the middle of the next century, if current trends were to continue, white, non-hispanic Americans could become a minority in an America that had no clear majority. (*Source:* Population Reference Bureau, *U.S. Population: Charting the Change,* 1988)

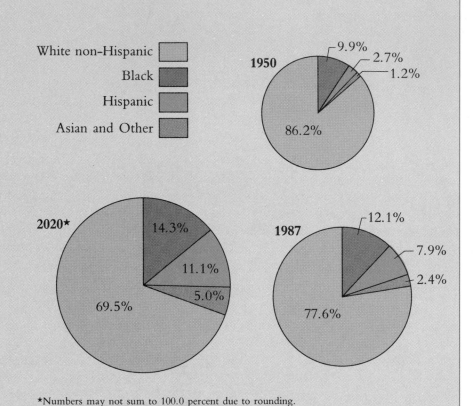

*Numbers may not sum to 100.0 percent due to rounding.

grants? Does the United States have an historic mission to accept refugees? Will we benefit or lose if we continue to accept large numbers of refugees? Does it make a difference that the cultural mix of immigrants has changed over the past 100 years (Figure 5-14)?

How do you feel about the changing ethnic and racial composition of the U.S. population? Does it appear from Figure B to promise significant changes in American life?

Source: L. Fuchs quoted in P. Murphy and P. Cancellier, *Immigration: Questions and Answers,* Population Reference Bureau, 1982.)

a threat to the unskilled labor market than do illegal immigrants.

Data are scant on the use of government services (welfare, schooling, health care) by illegal immigrant families. Those few studies that have been done indicate that most illegal immigrants do in fact pay income and social security taxes and hospitalization premiums, through employer withholding channels. Further, few appear to use government services. In one study, 27% were found to have used hospitals or clinics, less than 4% had children in school or collected unemployment benefits, and only 0.5% were on welfare (Population Reference Bureau, 1982).

Of equal concern with the economic effects of immigration are the social and political effects on

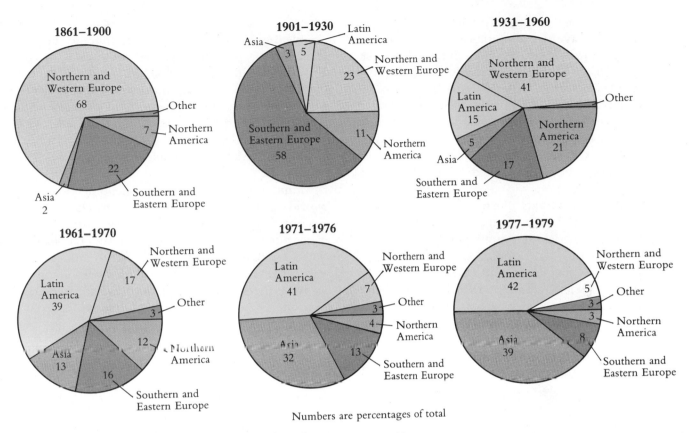

FIGURE 5-14 U.S. Immigrants by Region of Birth, 1861–1979. (*Source:* from L. F. Bouvier, *Immigration and Its Impact on U.S. Society,* Population Trends and Public Policy Series #2, Population Reference Bureau, 1981.)

U.S. society. Figure 5-14 illustrates how the origins of immigrants have changed. The proportion of the immigrant population that is of Hispanic origin (Mexican-American, Puerto Rican, Cuban, and so on) has risen through the years. Although the earlier European immigrants usually adopted American customs and language quickly, parts of the recent Hispanic immigrant population have desired to retain their own language and customs. This has raised fears of separatist difficulties, such as those between French-speaking Quebec and the rest of Canada. However, since the Hispanic immigrants themselves come from a variety of cultural backgrounds and, in fact, share only a common language, these fears may be unjustified.

It is clear, however, that the composition of the U.S. population is slowly changing in response to the preponderance of Hispanic immigrants, both legal and illegal. Hispanics are the fastest growing U.S. minority both because of their immigration levels and their relatively high fertility level (2.6 children per woman compared to 2.0 for the United States as a whole).

SUMMARY

When a country's death rates and birth rates have both declined to similar low levels, it has undergone the demographic transition from the older type of high-birth-rate–high-death-rate society to the more modern low-birth-rate–low-death-rate society. However, if death rates decline due to modern sanitary and health advances without a corresponding decrease in the birth rate, the result is rapid population growth. Birth rates may not decline if, besides the more personal satisfaction they bring parents, children have an economic value to the parents as well. In some countries, children can add to the family's income by working, can justify additional land allotments, may free parents from simple household and child-care tasks, and represent a source of security for the parents' old age. A lack of educational opportunities also contributes to high birth rates, as may certain social patterns such as the way property is distributed or inherited, and low status for women.

Population pyramids illustrate the comparative sizes of the various age groups in a population. In developing countries the population of children is much greater than the population of older people. This is due to decreasing death rates, especially among infants and children, that have not been matched by decreased birth rates. Population pyramids for these countries have a wide base and a narrow top. In contrast, population pyramids in developed countries are approaching an obelisk shape because converging birth and death rates tend to result in the same numbers of people in all the various age groups. Population momentum refers to the fact that even where successful population control programs are in effect, the populations of most developing countries will increase greatly over the next 20 to 40 years. This is because the large numbers of children now age 0–15 are likely to marry and have at least two children per couple. This will swell all of the older age groups (which are now relatively small).

Total fertility rate is a measure of the number of children a hypothetical woman will have over her lifetime. It is a more sensitive measure of reproductive behavior than crude birth rate.

Rapid population growth makes it difficult for a country to feed, educate, and provide health care for increasing numbers of people. Environmental degradation is often found as larger numbers of people try to live off land that cannot support them. There is much evidence that population growth itself is a block to economic development. Available funds must often be spent on short-term needs— medical care, food disaster relief—rather than on long-term investments such as roads, industrial development, and job training that would provide a better standard of living for people in the future.

In developed countries, population growth problems include absorption of immigrants into the mainstream, possible scarcities of resources, and crowding (which limits choices).

The world is tending to become an urban rather than a rural society. Advantages associated with living in cities include easier delivery of health care and social services and greater economic opportunities. Disadvantages include crowding, violence, and crime.

Immigration is a growing phenomenon in the world today as people move in search of better economic opportunities and escape from political persecution. Between one-fourth and one-half of U.S. population growth is now due to immigration rather than natural increase. Still, emigration cannot provide the safety valve it once did for overpopulation. There are not enough unpopulated countries to absorb the excess of people.

Questions

1. Why do demographers use fertility rates to measure the success of population limitation programs rather than birth rates and death rates?

2. Contrast the value of children to families in developing countries, such as those in Africa, and to families in developed countries, such as those in Western Europe.

3. Explain what factors drive population growth in the United States.

4. It has been said that the problem of rapid population growth contributes to all other environmental problems. What does this mean?

5. In many countries, population growth is forcing people to leave rural areas and move to the cities. What advantages and disadvantages are there in this increasing urbanization of the world?

Further Reading

Espenshade, T. J. "A Short History of U.S. Policy Towards Immigration," *Population Today, 18*(2) (February 1990).
  A useful, brief summary of U.S. immigration history, policy, and laws. Good selection of further references at the end.

Faucett, J. T., et al. "The Value of Children in Asia and the United States: Comparative Perspectives," *Papers of the East-West Population Institute,* No. 38, July 1974.

Human Development Report (1990), United Nations Development Program.

In a new way of looking at world development, this publication attempts to "quantify the human condition and rank countries by their success in meeting human needs."

Population Reference Bureau, 2213 M Street N.W., Washington, D.C. 20037.

Publishes a monthly newsletter as well as many position papers, teaching aids, wall posters, and population data sheets. Memberships, which entitle the owner to almost all of the publications (a real wealth of information), are available to teachers and students at reduced rates. The writing is clear and at a level intended for the general public.

Ware, Helen. "The Economic Value of Children in Asia and Africa: Comparative Perspective," *Papers of the East-West Population Institute,* No. 50, April 1978

This and the Faucett paper are available in single copies from the East-West Population Institute, East-West Road, Honolulu, Hawaii 96822.

World Development Report 1984. New York: Oxford University Press, 1984.

This is a comprehensive report on population issues, although the slant is heavily, and understandably, economic.

References

Agarwal, A., et al. *The State of India's Environment.* Washington, D.C.: International Institute for Environment and Development, 1982.

Cain, M. "The Economic Activities of Children in a Village in Bangladesh." Paper presented at the IUSSP International Population Conference, Mexico City, 1977.

Dyson-Hudson, R., and N. Dyson-Hudson. "The Food Production System of a Semi-Nomadic Society: The Karimojong, Uganda." In P. F. McLouglin (Ed.), *African Food Production Systems.* Baltimore, Md.: Johns Hopkins University Press, 1970.

Fuchs, L. Quoted in L. F. Bouvier and R. W. Gardner, "Immigration to the U.S.: The Unfinished Story," *Population Bulletin, 41*(4) (November 1986).

Population Reference Bureau. *U.S. Population: Where We Are, Where We're Going.* Washington, D.C.: Population Reference Bureau, June 1982.

Jones, W. "The Food Economy of the Ba Bugu Ijoliba, Mali." In P. F. McLouglin (Ed.), *African Food Production Systems.* Baltimore: Johns Hopkins University Press, 1970.

Population Reference Bureau. *World Population Data Sheet 1991.* Washington, D.C.: Population Reference Bureau.

World Population Profile 1989. Washington, D.C.: U.S. Census Bureau, Publication #003-024-07074-0 (1989).

Chapter 6

Limiting Population Growth

COMPONENTS OF THE PROBLEM

Two important lessons have been learned in the past 20 years of population research. The first is that reductions in population growth are possible for countries at all levels of economic development. It is not necessary to progress through the traditional stages of industrialization before population growth can be controlled. The second is that the mix of methods that will be successful in a particular country will vary, just as beliefs and social customs vary from country to country.

The Value of Factors Other than Economic Development

At the 1974 World Population Conference, a popular saying among delegates from developing nations was "Development is the best contraceptive." The examples of Korea, Singapore, and Hong Kong, all developing nations that were rapidly industrializing and at the same time experiencing fertility declines in the 1960s, seemed to prove the truth of this slogan. Now, however, we have other examples that do not fit this picture. Birth rates have fallen faster in Thailand than in Brazil and Venezuela, despite the fact that these last two countries have been industrializing more rapidly, have

had better economic growth, and have achieved higher average incomes. What is the reason for this? A closer look at the three countries shows that incomes and social services are distributed more evenly in Thailand than in Brazil or Venezuela. Further, family planning services are more available in Thailand. Thus, other factors besides economic development are able to affect fertility.

Untangling the various factors that affect fertility is both a difficult and an important task. To design successful population programs, we must understand how individuals make decisions about family size and how various programs affect these decisions.

The Proximate Determinants of Fertility

Fertility, or the number of children a family will actually have, is determined by the parents' age at marriage, their use of contraception, and their decisions about breastfeeding and abortion. These are called the **proximate determinants** of fertility. These behaviors are the result of decisions the family makes on how many children they want, whether they will educate the children, whether the mother will work outside the home, and other savings and consumption decisions.

To go one step further back, the decisions a family reaches in these matters depend on the so-

124

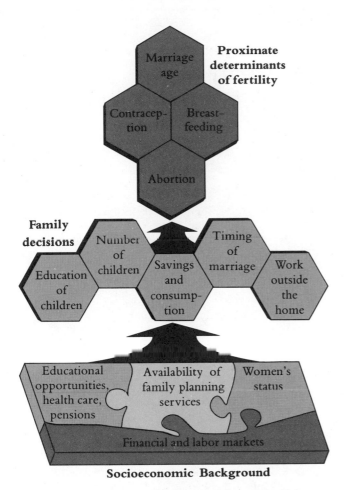

FIGURE 6-1 Factors Affecting Fertility. The behaviors that determine fertility, called the *proximate determinants of fertility,* are the result of family decisions. These decisions crystalize from the socioeconomic climate in which the family lives. Governments can have their strongest and most lasting effect on fertility with policies that change this socioeconomic climate: restrictions on marriage age and child labor, provisions for health care and universal education, improvements in the status of women, old age pensions and incentives for small families, promotion of breastfeeding, and provision of contraceptive services.

cioeconomic climate in which the family lives (see Figure 6-1). When a government wishes to affect fertility, it can attempt to influence the proximate determinants. However, it can also alter the socioeconomic climate. Although such government ac-

tions will be indirect, they can have the strongest and most lasting possible effects on fertility.

The Ethics of Population Control

When a government attempts direct control over the proximate determinants of fertility, ethical issues often arise. Forced contraception, forced abortion, and insistence on breastfeeding are generally felt to be unacceptable interference with personal liberties. For instance, suppose a government decided to try to take active control of individual reproduction. In such a situation, a license might be issued to allow a couple to have a child, or forced sterilization programs might be carried out, as they were in parts of India in the 1970s.

There are a number of valid objections to these policies. Who would decide, and on what basis, which couples deserve to have children? Minorities and the poorer segments of society are rightly concerned about such decisions.

On the practical side, the technical capability does not yet exist to institute a program of forced contraception. There is no magic chemical that can be put into the water to prevent fertility without other serious effects. In most countries there are not enough doctors and nurses for forced, large-scale contraceptive or sterilization procedures.

Another possible means of population control that is usually ruled out immediately is allowing mortality to rise or remain high when measures exist to prevent this. Most people agree that a government's role should include improving the lives of its people. It is for this reason that population control programs are begun: to prevent the miseries that can accompany rapid population growth. Failure to reduce mortality when it is possible works counter to this goal. (Not everyone subscribes to this belief. See Controversy 6-1.)

Only one of the determinants of fertility—marriage age—is commonly legislated. This is usually for social and health reasons, to prevent childbearing by young girls whose health would suffer. On the other hand, in at least one country, China, the allowed marriage age has been raised to decrease fertility (because the span of married women's childbearing years will then be decreased).

The Ethics of Limiting Family Size

Any choice and decision with regard to the size of the family must irrevocably rest with the family itself....

United Nations Universal Declaration of Human Rights (1967)

Freedom to breed will bring ruin to all.

Garrett Hardin

Many difficult decisions are involved in the control of population growth. One of the most difficult is whether couples should have the complete freedom to decide how many children they will have. That is, should governments set and enforce upper limits of family size?

In 1967, the United Nations passed the Universal Declaration of Human Rights, which stated in part:

> The Universal Declaration of Human Rights describes the family as the natural and fundamental unit of society. It follows that any choice and decision with regard to the size of the family must irrevocably rest with the family itself, and cannot be made by anyone else.

In the past few years, however, a few nations have decided that this concept is unworkable. Thus, in Bangladesh, Singapore, China, and India, governments have begun to use both economic threats and bonuses designed to limit population size.

Demographer Garrett Hardin believes that the decision to limit family size cannot be left to the individual. He says that such a decision is similar to one that faced cattle owners in eighteenth-century England. At that time, pastureland was held in common, so there was a great advantage to a herdsman to add more cattle to his herd, if he could. If everyone did that, however, the pasture would be overgrazed and thus ruined. Hardin argues that, in a sense, our welfare-oriented society is like a commons. Individuals can choose to use up more than a fair share of resources, both social and environmental, by having more than their fair share of children.

Hardin (1968) wrote:

> Perhaps the simplest summary of this analysis of man's population problems is this: the commons, if justifiable at all, is justifiable only under conditions of low-population density. As the human population has increased, the commons has had to be abandoned in one aspect after another.

> First we abandoned the commons in food gathering, enclosing farm land and restricting pastures and hunting and fishing areas. These restrictions are still not complete throughout the world.

> Somewhat later we saw that the commons as a place for waste disposal would also have to be abandoned. Restrictions on the disposal of domestic sewage are widely accepted in the Western world; we are still struggling to close the commons to pollution by automobiles, factories, insecticide sprayers, fertilizing operations, and atomic energy installations.

> . . . I believe it was Hegel who said, "Freedom is the recognition of necessity."

> The most important aspect of necessity that we must now recognize, is the necessity of abandoning the commons in breeding. No technical solution can rescue us from the misery of overpopulation. Freedom to breed will bring ruin to all. At the moment, to avoid hard decisions many of us are tempted to propagandize for conscience and responsible parenthood. The temptation must be resisted, because an appeal to independently acting consciences selects for the disappearance of all conscience in the long run, and an increase in anxiety in the short.

> The only way we can preserve and nurture other and more precious freedoms is by relinquishing the freedom to breed, and that very soon.

Do you agree with Hardin? Should the decision on family size be made by each couple, or should governments have a voice in it? If you feel that population growth should be slowed, should appeals to conscience be tried first? What did Hardin mean when he said "an appeal to independently acting consciences selects for the disappearance of all conscience in the long run"? Suppose such appeals don't work—can you think of economic measures, such as the use of taxes, that could influence family size? Suppose neither appeals nor economic measures are effective—are penalties justifiable?

Source: Garrett Hardin, "The Tragedy of the Commons," *Science, 162* (December 13, 1968), 1243.

As the rest of this chapter illustrates, the possible range of population control measures can differ somewhat depending on whether a country is governed by a freely elected government or by a dictatorship. A freely elected government that must answer to its electorate is not in a position to impose measures such as forced sterilization or fines for having too many children on a large segment of its population. If it tried to do so, such a government would be voted out of office at the very next opportunity. But even a dictatorship must tread lightly when dealing with such strongly emotional issues as the right to have children.

Governments currently rely on a complex of population growth control measures: (1) provision of birth control information and services, (2) incentives and fines to induce people to use birth control, and (3) manipulation of the social factors that make people want many children. The discussion about how much authority a government should have over the reproductive behavior of its citizens is not over, however. It will become more and more of an issue, as population growth, with all its attendant problems, continues. (See Controversy 6-1.)

METHODS OF LIMITING POPULATION GROWTH

Providing Birth Control Information

When a government wishes to limit the growth of its population, the first policy it usually adopts is to provide people with birth control information and materials. In many cases, abortions are made legal and thus easier for the poor to obtain. Although several religious organizations object to both abortion and the distribution of birth control information, there is usually also a great deal of popular support for this type of policy. In most situations, people will at least tacitly agree that couples should be able to limit their family size if they wish to do so. For instance, in mostly Roman Catholic Colombia, despite initial opposition by the Church, wide government distribution of contraceptives has helped reduce the fertility rate from 4.8 to 3.4.

A policy of providing access to information and materials on birth control can be justified on grounds of humanitarianism. Fewer children will, in general, be better fed and cared for, since a family's resources will not be spread too thin. These children may even be healthier, since repeated, closely spaced pregnancies have been shown to be harmful both to mothers and to babies. (See Figure 6-2.) Furthermore, if only wanted pregnancies occur, mothers have no need to resort to abortion, which, like any operation, carries some risk. For this reason, many antiabortion groups support contraceptive programs. The cost to society of unwanted children who may become wards of the state in one way or another is also reduced.

Birth Control in Developing Nations. There is still an unmet need for contraceptive services in many developing countries today, although the size of this need is not easy to determine. Up-to-date information on contraceptive use is not available for all countries. Furthermore, the concept of unmet need implies a judgment about the motivation of couples with respect to their nonuse of contraceptives. How many of the nonusers would, in fact, use contraception if it were both available and affordable?

Nonetheless, some estimates can be made by looking at available statistics for contraceptive use, by interviewing women about their desire for more children and by checking the costs of contraception in various countries.

The World Resources Institute has used a variety of studies to estimate the unmet need for contraception. Their estimates for a few countries are shown in Table 6-1. These figures include only those women who want no more children. Those who would like to space births are not included.

A study of 25 developing countries (Thapa et al., 1991), indicated that, among women of childbearing age, contraception is currently being used by 15% in sub-Saharan Africa, 41% in North Africa, 48% in Latin America, and 59% in Asia. Some of the women not using contraception are protected from pregnancy because they are nursing a baby or because of traditional customs of abstinence after the birth of a child. Thapa and colleagues estimate

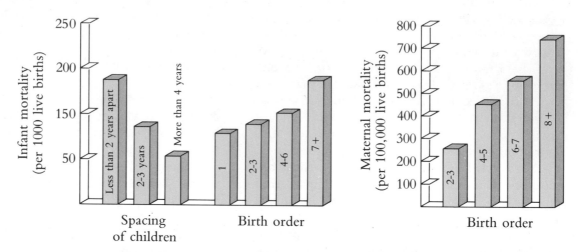

FIGURE 6-2 Mortality of Infants and Mothers Compared to Birth Order and Spacing. Infants and mothers both suffer higher death rates as more and more children are born into a family. (*Source:* Data from The World Bank, *World Development Report 1984* [New York: Oxford University Press, 1984], pp. 128–129)

that about 20% of the women in the study, all of whom had recently given birth to a child, were actually exposed to pregnancy and not using contraceptives. Figure 6-3 looks specifically at this group of women and charts those who do not want any more children or who want to space the next child.

Couples wishing to use birth control must solve several problems. Financial costs may be a significant problem for couples in many developing countries. The availability of affordable contraception in developing countries is thus another way of measuring unmet need for contraception. This point is discussed and illustrated later in the chapter.

In addition to being able to afford contraception, couples must have access to medical care for many of the modern methods of contraception. Furthermore, social pressures may work against contraceptive use. Government programs can attack all of these problems, helping to increase contraceptive use.

Table 6-2 notes the major forms of contraception available for family planning programs today. Material on the human reproductive system and a more detailed description of contraceptive methods can be found in Belcastro (1986).

Birth Control in the United States. Only contraceptive implants and improved barrier methods such as contraceptive sponges and cervical caps have been recently added to the available selection of contraceptives in the United States. In addition, contraceptive research and development by U.S. firms has come to a virtual halt. This is partly due to corporate fears of lawsuits by users and partly due to the relatively slow rate of FDA approval for new contraceptive methods. A recent National Research Council Report recommends that U.S. product liability laws be changed and that FDA approval procedures be streamlined to stimulate research and development on promising new methods of contraception such as transdermal patches, vaginal suppositories and rings, and under-the-tongue tablets.

Instituting Measures That Improve People's Social and Economic Well-Being

Access to birth control services alone is not enough to ensure a reduction in population. As previously mentioned, there are a number of reasons why couples may choose to have more children than is considered ideal for society as a whole. A massive program of public education and contraceptive

TABLE 6-1 Unmet Need for Contraception, Selected Countries

	Unmet Need (percent)
Africa	
Benin	3
Ghana	5–8
Kenya	6–10
Mauritania	6
Sudan	6–9
Tunisia	10–19
Latin America	
Costa Rica	6–11
Guatemala	21
Honduras	9–21
Panama	13
Asia	
Nepal	22–27
Pakistan	17–27

Source: World Resources 1988/1989, 3rd ed., World Resources Institute, 1989, p. 258.

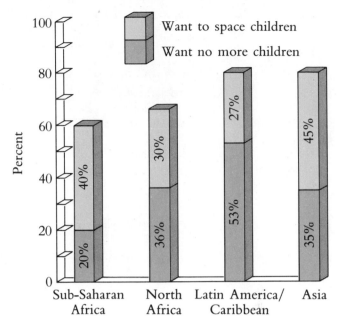

FIGURE 6-2 Childbearing Preferences among Women Who Have Recently Given Birth and Who Are Not Using Contraceptives. The graph shows the percentages of women surveyed who want no more children, or who would like to space their children further apart, but who are not using contraception. (*Source:* Adapted from S. Thapa et al., *Contraceptive Use and Needs among Postpartum Women in 25 Developing Countries* [Washington, D.C.: Population Association of America, 1991])

distribution in Pakistan from 1965 to 1980 failed almost completely, because of social factors. The failure was partly administrative: Information about the program failed to reach a large part of the population. But, in addition, a demand for contraceptives was not generated in this society.

Two other types of policies are available to governments: those that improve the social and economic well-being of people in general, which as a by-product spur a reduction in population growth, and those that offer specific rewards and incentives for individual families who reduce fertility and economic punishments for those who do not.

Old-Age Security Programs. Recall from earlier discussion that children represent security for parents in old age. If old-age pensions, such as the social security program of the United States, are created in developing nations, parents may be able to give up the idea that they need many children. Bangladesh, for instance, has begun a program of social security benefits. To emphasize the desirability of small families, these benefits are awarded only to parents of two or fewer children.

Reductions in Infant and Child Mortality. Another reason many parents have more than two children is to ensure that they will be able to raise at least two children to adulthood. Africa, the region with the world's highest birth rate, also has the world's highest death rate.* Continuing reduc-

---

* In 1990 the birth rate was 44 and the death rate near 15 per 1,000 per year.

TABLE 6-2 Birth Planning Technology

Method	Effectiveness[a]	Disadvantages
Rhythm (timing of intercourse)	67–80%	Poor effectiveness
Barrier methods:		
Condoms	88–97%	Inconvenient, hard to store or dispose of in developing countries
Diaphragms, sponges, cervical caps	88–97%	
Spermicides	79–97%	
IUD	97–98%	Can alter bleeding patterns,[b] medical backup required for side effects
Birth control pills	97–100%	Medical backup required for side effects
Injectable contraceptives	100%	Can alter bleeding patterns,[b] medical backup required
Contraceptive implants	100%	Can alter bleeding patterns[b]
Menstrual regulation (vacuum aspiration of uterus within 14 days of missed period)	95–98%[c]	May be religiously or culturally unacceptable
Antiprogesterones (the "abortion pill," RU 486)	96%[c]	May be religiously or culturally unacceptable
Male or female sterilization	100%	Generally irreversible, requires trained medical staff, expensive
Still under development: Transdermal patches, under-the-tongue tablets, vaginal suppositories, male contraceptive pills, antipregnancy vaccines		Not likely to be approved before the end of this century

Source: Information from The World Bank, *World Development Report 1984* (New York: Oxford University Press, 1984); *Developing New Contraceptives: Obstacles and Opportunities,* Committee on Population, The National Research Council, National Academy of Sciences, ISBN 0-309-04147-3 (Washington, D.C.: National Academy Press, 1990); Hatcher, R. A., et al. *Contraceptive Technology: International Edition* (Atlanta, Ga.: Printed Matter Inc., 1989).

[a] Effectiveness is a measure of the number of women who become pregnant while using the method. Thus, an effectiveness of 98% means 2 out of every 100 women using the method become pregnant within one year.

Although methods such as the pill can be 100% effective in controlled studies, and even condoms can be 97% effective, in actual use the effectiveness of most methods is lower due to mistakes and failure of motivation. Couples who wish no more children are more successful in using contraception than those who wish to space births.

[b] May cause spotting between periods, increased flow, or no flow.

[c] Reflects the percent of women who remain pregnant after use of the method.

FIGURE 6-4 Child Labor. Young, nimble-fingered children toiled long hours at low pay in the nineteenth-century factories and mines of today's more developed countries. (*Photo:* Lewis Hines, courtesy of U.S. Library of Congress)

tions in infant and child diseases in developing nations will pave the way for a reduction in births.

Child Labor and Child Education Laws. In many developing countries, children may be sent to work and so represent to the parents the possibility of additional family income. The passage and enforcement of laws prohibiting child labor can make additional children less desirable by removing their income potential. Parents must then feed and clothe each child for a longer time during which the child cannot work. Such laws benefit children by allowing them time for schooling and, depending on what work they would have done, possibly improving their health (Figure 6-4). The state of Kerala in India has a per capita income below the average for all of India, yet it devotes 39% of its

budget to education and 16% to health and family planning services. Almost all children in Kerala attend at least the primary school grades. The result? Birth rates in Kerala declined from 37 per 1,000 in 1966 to 25 per 1,000 by 1978.

Education, besides helping the children themselves and society as a whole, has several benefits related to population control. Educated people tend to marry later and to have fewer children. This is related to the fact that education allows people to move upward in economic and social status. Upward mobility is hindered by large numbers of children to feed, clothe, and care for. Educated women tend to limit their families to allow themselves the satisfaction of a career and additional family income.

Improvements in Status of Women. Improvements in the status of women may act as a brake on population growth. Given the opportunity to take advantage of new or better job openings, women often limit their family size to reduce their child-care responsibilities. In the United States the educational achievements of women, as well as men, have been steadily growing. In addition, the percentage of women who work has been increasing. These factors have probably contributed to the downward trend in the U.S. birth rate.

In some developing countries, women have very little status. They do not have equal access to education and may not be able to hold property or work outside the home. In such circumstances a woman can exert influence only through her children. It is not surprising that birth rates remain stubbornly high in such countries. But it is also true that birth rates can be induced to fall in these countries by improving the status of women.

Indirect Influences on Marriage Age. Additional ways to influence population growth are to control housing availability and to require a period of military or other national service for all young people. These actions tend to increase the age at which marriage occurs, reducing the span of years in which a couple can conceive.

Promotion of Breastfeeding. Breastfeeding has a definite contraceptive effect. In fact, as recently as 10 years ago it was responsible for more contraception in developing countries than were family planning programs. The contraceptive effect of breastfeeding is not lasting, however; it decreases with time after childbirth. Furthermore, although failure to menstruate as a result of breastfeeding is a reasonable guarantee of contraception, about 7% of women become pregnant without resuming menstruation. Despite the fact that breastfeeding is well recognized as contraceptive, the trend appears to be toward less and shorter periods of breastfeeding in developing countries. This is partly due to women working outside the home, especially if the workplace is far from the home. But it is also due to feelings that bottle-feeding is more modern or that breastfeeding is difficult or does not provide enough food for the child.

A decrease in breastfeeding not only increases the risk of pregnancy (if no other contraceptives are used) but also may endanger the health of the baby. In countries without a safe water supply and where mothers cannot read or understand formula-making directions, bottle-fed babies suffer much more diarrhea and malnutrition.

Government programs pointing out the health benefits of breastfeeding and discouraging the use of formula in hospitals and clinics can increase the percentage of mothers breastfeeding their babies. In Papua New Guinea a campaign to discourage advertising of infant formula, combined with restrictions on formula use and distribution in hospitals, increased the proportion of breastfed children under age 2 from 65% to 88% in only two years. The additional benefit of breastfeeding, over and above child health improvements, is, of course, a "free" contraceptive effect.

Raising of Incomes. There is no question that raising incomes decreases fertility in the long run. In the short run, however, raising incomes for poor families can increase fertility. This occurs in areas where marriages are often delayed by the costs of setting up a household or by the need for a dowry. Higher income allows earlier marriage in such cases as these.

Over the long term, however, fertility decreases with increasing income, because children's incomes become less important, and the education of children becomes a good investment. Furthermore, money is available to save and invest for old age.

The various population control methods that affect the socioeconomic climate in which people live allow individuals some freedom of choice in the number of children they plan to have. These methods open other areas of satisfaction, and they also make people aware of the additional costs that children bring. (In 1990 it was estimated that each child costs a middle-income American family $100,000 in direct costs.★ This does not include lost opportunity costs, income the mother went without while taking care of the child.)

Through such mechanisms, population growth can be reduced without coercion. Evidence shows that, under the right circumstances, people become aware that having more than two children is not in their own best interest. Countries offering the greatest possibility of upward movement in economic and social status have shown the most dramatic decreases in birth rate. Thus, the ideal of bringing population under control may be achieved by means that, at the same time, help people reach a satisfying standard of living.

However, as detailed in the previous chapter, the size of the human population and its rate of growth may no longer allow us the luxury of waiting for these humane and desirable policies to work. While there is no justification for abandoning attempts to improve the human condition, if we rely on such measures alone to reduce population growth, we risk starvation and disease for a large portion of the world's population, as well as the possibility of irreversible damage to our ecosystem.

Let us examine a second set of policies designed to reduce population growth: incentives and disincentives.

Providing Incentives and Disincentives

The second group of policies for controlling population growth consists of rewards for families with

---

★ B. Cutler, "Rock-a-Buy Baby," *American Demographics,* January 1990, 36.

few children and penalties for those with more than a designated number. Although such schemes are in effect in over 30 countries, it is difficult to determine how much of an effect they have had, because they are usually accompanied by social change and an increase in family planning services.

Incentives and disincentives have included such things as educational or other bonuses for having few children and fines for having more than a specified number of children. The main objection to such policies is that children in the larger families, who had no control over whether they were born, suffer along with the parents who are subject to penalties or forgo rewards. Another objection is that verification that couples are in fact complying with the limits on children can be difficult. Further, the cost of the rewards may be high, and money might be better spent on other investments.

Incentives are transfer payments. That is, people are paid not to have children who, if they were born, would require government money in other ways (education, health care, and so on). In this sense, incentives do not use up government resources but rather use them in a different way. But, unless parents save for such things as old-age care, which the child would have been expected to provide, the transfer will not succeed.

Despite these drawbacks, such policies are, in fact, being followed in many countries and are planned in others. Government employees in certain Indian states are not eligible for housing loans and land grants if they have more than three children. Singapore levies increasing fines for the birth of a third, fourth, fifth, or sixth child. Maternity leave is not allowed for the birth of a third or subsequent child, and hospital fees rise with the number of children in a family. On the other hand, sterilization after two children is rewarded with education and employment for the children and extra vacation time for the parent. Foreigners who wish to marry Singapore nationals must agree to be sterilized after the birth of their second child.

China has instituted the most extensive set of incentives and disincentives of any country in its attempt to achieve a fertility level of only one child per family. The specific example of China is discussed later in this chapter.

TIME SCALE AND CONTROL OF RAPID POPULATION GROWTH

Population Momentum

As mentioned in Chapter 5, programs designed to reduce population growth have one very serious built-in problem: It takes some 10 to 20 years before the results of any such program are seen. The reason is that fertility reduction programs have an effect only on the number of babies currently being born; they can obviously have no effect on the group of children, ages 0–15 years, already born. These children will grow to adulthood and marry and have children themselves during the next 10 to 20 years.

In most countries the size of the 0–15 age group is larger than that of any other group in the population. If the people in the 0–15 age category turn out to have only enough children to reproduce themselves, they will still swell the size of their country's population. Thus, most countries would continue to grow in population for a time even if birth control programs immediately reduced the birth rate to about 2.1 to 2.3 children per couple, the birth rate that provides for each couple to reproduce themselves.

The fact that population programs take such a long time to make their effects felt is a great handicap to effective action. It takes 5 to 6 years before decreased school enrollments are seen, 15 years before a reduction in the labor force occurs, and 15 to 19 years before stabilization begins in the amount of food needed. A government may thus seem to be spending a great deal of money for many years with very little obvious effect. Because of this time gap, it is important to try to separate birth control programs from politics and politicians, as political movements and ideologies have a way of changing or going in and out of favor in less than 10 or 20 years.

The Speed at Which Different Policies Take Effect

Besides the inherent problem of population momentum, various fertility control methods differ in the time it takes for their effects to be seen. The long-term effect of raising incomes is clearly to lower fertility, although the short-term effect may be just the opposite. Other methods that tend to require a long time to be effective include educational programs, reduction in infant and child mortality, and improvements in the status of women. In contrast, promoting later marriage, encouraging breastfeeding, and making contraception easier to obtain all have more immediate effects.

EXPERIENCE OF POPULATION PROGRAMS IN FOUR REGIONS

The main problem in devising ways for reducing population growth is, of course, the fact that the issue is not some abstract scientific problem solvable by dollars and technology. Instead, it is a problem that touches people directly. We can program computers to give us projections of population, but only people's behavior, plans, and aspirations can determine what the future will be. People's needs and feelings affect how they react to incentives and plans. People also exert a degree of control over policies that affect them. In the United States, for instance, population control policies must be seen as desirable to the majority of people before they have any chance of being put into action.

The experience of population control programs in four countries or regions is instructive because it illustrates not only successes versus failures but also how population control programs must be tailored to the specific values and sociopolitical system of each country.

China: The One-Child Family

The most ambitious experiment in controlling rapid population growth is taking place in China today.

Almost a quarter of the world's population, 1.1 billion people, live in China. (India is second to China in population, with 853 million people, the Soviet Union is third, and the United States fourth.) Population growth in China was not considered a problem until relatively recently. China had a **pronatalist** policy (in favor of population growth) until 1957. By 1971, however, Chinese leaders clearly felt that population growth was making it difficult

to achieve their goal of a better living standard for all Chinese people. Late marriage was legislated, and a spacing of three to seven years between births was encouraged, as was a maximum of two children per family. Local governments were charged with the responsibility of seeing that fertility goals were met through incentives, disincentives, and social pressure on individual families.

In 1978, however, Chinese leaders learned that the situation was worse than they had realized. Better counting procedures revealed that there were almost 10% more people in China than had been thought. In addition, a huge group of young people was about to enter their reproductive years. The population was close to 1 billion and growing, while new studies of land and water resources showed that no more than 1.2 billion could be supported at a reasonable standard of living. Thus began a campaign to convince each family to have no more than one child. The goal of this campaign was to stop the growth of the Chinese population at 1.2 billion people by the end of the century and thereafter to allow it to shrink toward 800 million.

Couples were encouraged to sign a pledge to have only one child. In return, they received a certificate entitling them to a variety of benefits, depending on where they lived. Examples of benefits include: free medical care and schooling for the only child, cash bonuses or work points usable for extra food, old-age pension benefits, preferential housing treatment, and job preference for the child when grown up. If the couple, after signing the pledge, had another child, they were not only to surrender all privileges, but also to pay fines as well.

Although the "one-child" policy was never entirely implemented, it did have a significant effect on China's birth rate. By 1982 some 37% of eligible couples had signed the pledge, helping to bring the fertility rate down from 6.0 in the late 1960s to 2.1 by 1984. Compliance with the policy was spotty, however; rates of acceptance were higher in the cities than in rural areas and some 5% to 34% of couples went on to have another child anyway. Couples whose first child was a girl were more likely to renege on their pledge than those whose first child was a boy.

Meanwhile discussion of the policy continued. A number of experts voiced concern about what

Total population 1.05 billion

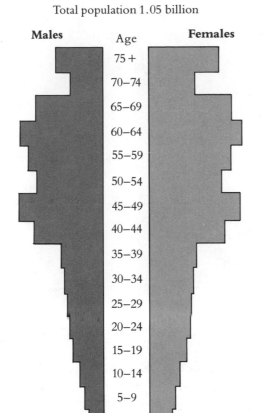

FIGURE 6-5 Projected Chinese Population in 2032 If Fertility Rate Reached 1.0 by 1992. (*Source:* H. Yuan Tien, *Population Today*, April 1984, p. 7)

would happen if the campaign was successful. It might result in a China that had a huge number of old people, dependent on a relatively small group of working adults for support. (Figure 6-5 shows what China's population pyramid would have looked like if a fertility rate of 1.0 were reached by 1991.) Other experts wondered about the effect on society of raising children without siblings or of consigning parents to a lifetime of worrying about whether their one child would survive. Few Chinese are covered by an old-age pension system. What would happen to parents if their one child was unable or unwilling to take care of them when they became too old to work? The relative lack of

compliance, in some areas as low as 10%, indicated that the people, too, were not happy with the policy. There were rumors of forced abortions and sterilizations and of possible female infanticide. Although fines were legislated for renouncing a pledge, the amounts were, at the same time, small enough not to be a deterrent to wealthier families and high enough that there was no likelihood of collecting them from the poorer families.

Eventually it became clear that Chinese officials were backing off from strict enforcement of a one-child-per-couple policy. In many cases where couples had a second or even third child, officials turned a blind eye, especially in the rural areas where children are needed to help work farms. Among minority groups, which constitute 8% of the Chinese population, enforcement was also lax.

It is possible that it was never the intention of the government to enforce a strict one-child per couple policy against the will of a major portion of the people. A stated goal of the Chinese government is that policies must achieve not only social betterment but also maintain a unity of feeling among the people. The clear lack of acceptance of one child as the norm for family size obviously does not meet this criterion. This idea is supported by the fact that the policy was never codified into a national law; instead, it was carried out by administrative directives and ad hoc local regulations.

Equally clearly, however, the government does not intend to leave control of family size to the individual couple. Instead, emphasis has shifted from enforcement of the one-child norm to education of people on the need for population control measures. This is combined with pilot programs to test the acceptability of allowing two children per family, at least in rural areas, but with a mandatory spacing of 10 years between the children. Such a policy would, for the first 10 years, have the same effect as a successful one-child policy. After that time, it is expected that some portion of the couples who had originally planned to have two children would have become so used to having only one that they would no longer want a second.

Furthermore, China is becoming more urban. Between 1982 and 1990 the percentage of China's population that lived in cities rose from 20% to 26%. The urban population in China has in the past been much more receptive to the concept of smaller families. Officials feel that a spacing policy combined with a 30% acceptance of the one-child concept would level off the Chinese population at between 1.2 and 1.3 billion by the year 2000. Although this is higher than the original goal of 1.2 billion, it could presumably be reached with less social upheaval and the desired popular consensus.

Meanwhile there is a large group of young people in China now entering their 20s. This group, born after the famine of 1959–1961 (see Figure 6-6), has already begun to swell the birth rate, and the fertility rate has slowly crept back up to 2.5. Whether China can successfully damp this baby boom is of vital importance to attempts to bring the growth of the world's population under control.

Latin America: An Unequal Distribution of Wealth

In many Latin American countries, income and population are unequally distributed. The poorest 20% of households in Brazil have one-third of the children and only 2% of the income. The richest 20% of households have 8% of the children and 64% of the income. These differences are much greater than those found elsewhere in the world, even in such countries as India.

Until 1974, Brazil's government was pronatalist, on the theory that Brazil's vast land resources could support a much larger population. In addition, the Catholic church's official position against any but natural contraceptive methods (such as rhythm) inhibited the spread of modern birth control methods.

In this climate (lack of government support of birth control policies and widely unequal distribution of wealth), even a doubling of per capita real incomes between 1972 and 1982 failed to make a large impact on fertility.

Some population experts insisted that economic development would eventually bring down birth rates in Latin American countries such as Brazil; other experts predicted that high birth rates would prevent economic progress by requiring the government to spend money for social services rather than for economic development. Furthermore, this

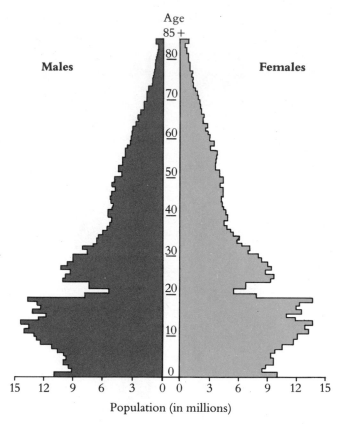

FIGURE 6-6 Population Pyramid for China in One-Year Age Groups.★ From the top to about age 20, China's pyramid resembles a country with rapidly slowing growth and might suggest a country on a rapid demographic transition. Below age 20, the pyramid gives China a most unusual demographic appearance. Despite the recent declines in Chinese fertility, those below 20 account for nearly half of the population. (*Source:* Population Reference Bureau, *Population Today*, March 1985, p. 5; data from the 10 percent Sample Survey of the 1982 Third National Census of China, as reported in *Beijing Review*, January 16, 1984)

latter group argued, there would be no significant decrease in fertility levels until there was a redistribution of income—that unless the poorer mem-

---

★ Because of the Chinese belief in astrology, everyone knows the year and date of his or her birth. In many developing countries, one-year age groupings are inaccurate because people do not pay much attention to their age and tend to report it as the nearest 5- or 10-year interval. In Bangladesh's 1974 census, for example, 2.8 million people reported they were 30 years old and only 124,209 said they were 31.

bers of society were able to share in the economic growth of the country, they would have no incentive to reduce the number of children they wanted.

However, the reality of the situation seems to fall somewhere between the two extreme points of view. In Brazil, even without central government support, birth control filtered into most regions, usually through commercial sales or private agencies such as International Planned Parenthood Federation (IPPF). By 1986, when the central government agreed to support family planning through its social services agencies, Brazil's fertility rate had already begun to fall. From 4.3 in 1980 the fertility rate fell to 3.5 in 1984 and 3.3 by 1990.

In Mexico, on the other hand, both the economy and the population have continued to grow at a high rate. This confounds both those who expected rapid economic growth to slow population growth and also those who expected rapid population growth to slow economic progress. It does not rule out the idea that redistribution of income may be necessary if economic growth is to affect population growth. The poorest 20% of Mexican households receive 3% of the income, while the richest 10 get 41%.

Experience in Latin America supports the view that economic development and strong birth control programs act together to bring down birth rates, and that the two factors enhance each other's performance. Where policies lead to more equal distribution of income, the rate of progress in lowering fertility rates may well be faster.

India: The Limits to Coercive Measures

Among the nations of the developing world, India has had one of the fastest-growing populations. At 300 million just after World War II, India doubled its population by the mid-1970s. Efforts to limit population have been underway there since the early 1950s. In fact, India was the first nation to create a national program to limit population through family planning. Even into the 1970s, however, the results were barely noticeable. In 1976, it was estimated that only 17.5 million couples out of 103 million in the reproductive age groups were using contraceptives.

India's program up to that time was traditional: Sterilization or birth control methods and devices were made available to those who asked for them. Although no one was forced to seek sterilization, incentives were offered. For a time, a man could obtain cash or a transistor radio (a coveted article) in return for having a vasectomy.

In April 1976, a new policy was adopted emphasizing sterilization by vasectomy and, in many ways, compelling men to submit to the operation. Indira Gandhi, prime minister of India, was quoted as saying, "We must act decisively and bring down the birth rate. . . . We should not hesitate to take steps which might be described as drastic. Some personal rights have to be kept in abeyance for the human rights of the nation: the right to live, the right to progress." The government's goal: a reduction in the birth rate from 35 per 1,000 to 25 per 1,000 by 1984. The Indian government had declared a state of emergency in June 1975 and a number of civil rights, including free speech, had been either suspended or decreased since that time; the intensive program of sterilization was begun in this political climate. Although the government did not mount a national campaign of compulsory sterilization, individual states were encouraged to do so.

The state of Maharashtra passed laws calling for compulsory sterilization for the father of three living children and compulsory abortion of a pregnancy leading to a fourth child. Incentive payments to those who submitted to vasectomies were a part of the law, as were payments to informers. In India's capital, Delhi, and in the states of Punjab and Haryana, laws were passed withdrawing vital government benefits and services from married men with two children who did not submit to vasectomy. Loss of subsidized housing, loss of free medical care and loans, and even loss of employment were possible if a man did not comply with the sterilization laws.

Widespread abuses, in which people—especially poor people—were compelled to submit, were reported as the state governments attempted to fill sterilization quotas. Riots broke out in northern India over the issue. In the final months of Mrs. Gandhi's rule, sterilizations numbered a million per month. Then, in early 1977, Mrs. Gandhi's government fell, as the voters sent her and her Congress

Party from office. It is not clear whether her government fell because of her near dictatorial rule and her suspension of civil liberties or because of the highly visible, highly controversial program of sterilization she promoted. Many regarded the sterilization program as the largest factor in her defeat. The government that succeeded hers, led by Prime Minister Desai, abandoned the use of force and punishment for failure to be sterilized, presumably because the issue remained highly charged politically. In 1977–1978, sterilizations fell to 11% of the previous year's total. Although she was reelected in January 1980, Mrs. Gandhi afterward kept a low profile on population control efforts.

This episode raises some basic questions about government birth control policies. Kaval Gulhati asked, in an article in *Science* (1977): "Should they stand by and wait for economic development and family planning programs to motivate contraception? Or should they take the destiny of the people in their hands, and force a fertility decline?"

Gulhati asked this question before Mrs. Gandhi's government was rejected. In light of her government's defeat, the question might be expanded to ask: Can a government successfully undertake a compulsory program of population control and itself survive?

India still has not met its 1984 goal of 25 births per 1,000. By 1990 its birth rate had dropped only to 32 per 1,000 in the population. However, it is perhaps misleading to consider India as a single country in terms of population growth experience. Differences in background and customs have led to differing successes in population growth control in the various regions of India. In Uttar Pradesh, infant mortality was 171 per 1,000 in 1978, only about 1 in 10 rural women were literate, and fertility was 5.6 children per woman. In Kerala, on the other hand, infant mortality was 47 per 1,000, 75% of rural women were literate, and fertility was the lowest in India: 2.7 children per woman. The apparent explanation for such differences is found less in economic differences between the two areas, which are small, than in differences in social development, such as availability of health services, women's education, and family planning services.

Similarly, in another South Asian state, Sri Lanka, where per capita income was only $420 in 1990, fertility had fallen to 2.3 children per woman from 5.5 in 1960. The fall is the result of decreased infant mortality, virtually 100% school enrollment of primary-age girls, and increased contraceptive availability.

Africa below the Sahara: A Preference for Large Families

The Sahara Desert runs in a large band across the top of the African continent. The 42 countries that form the sub-Sahara are home to an extraordinarily diverse group of peoples—800 ethnic groups speaking 1,000 different languages or dialects. What these countries have in common, however, is the highest rates of population growth in the world. With a few exceptions these countries are increasing at close to 3% per year. At this rate of growth a country's population will double in 23 years. In comparison, growth rates in Asia are about 1.9% per year and in Latin America about 2.1% per year. African growth rates are the result of the world's highest birth rates, an average of 44 births per 1,000 in the population (the world average is 27). Yet, at the same time, the region suffers the world's highest death rates, 15 per 1,000 compared to a world average of 10.

These high death rates are mainly due to high infant and child mortality. One out of 10 babies dies before its first birthday, compared to less than 1 out of 100 in the United States and Western Europe. In some of these countries the deaths of children under 5 make up half of the total number of deaths every year. Such high death rates are largely the result of a lack of adequate health care.

In addition to a lack of health care, modern birth control and family planning services are largely unavailable. Rates of contraceptive use commonly hover around 5% or 6%.

Most of the region is rural. Families live mainly by subsistence farming. Although Africa is relatively rich in land, food production continues to lag behind population growth, condemning a large portion of the population to live continually on the brink of starvation.

In many African countries the status of women is low. They often cannot own land or find work outside the home, and they do not have equal access to education.

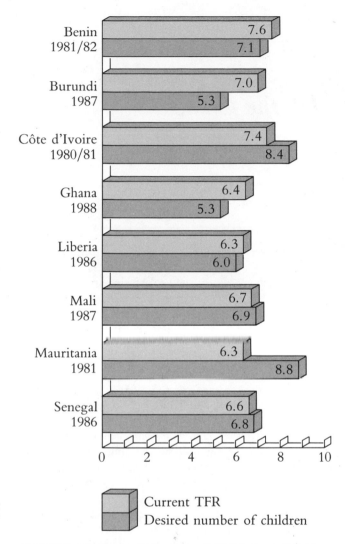

Benin
1981/82   7.6
            7.1

Burundi
1987   7.0
           5.3

Côte d'Ivoire
1980/81   7.4
           8.4

Ghana
1988   6.4
           5.3

Liberia
1986   6.3
           6.0

Mali
1987   6.7
           6.9

Mauritania
1981   6.3
           8.8

Senegal
1986   6.6
           6.8

0   2   4   6   8   10

Current TFR
Desired number of children

FIGURE 6-7 Desired Number of Children and Esti-mated Total Fertility Rate (TFR): Selected Sub-Saharan Countries. (*Source:* T. J. Goliber, "Africa's Expanding Population," *Population Bulletin, 44*[3] [No-vember 1989], 39; data from: World Fertility Survey and DHS Reports)

All of these factors—high infant and child mor-tality, a mostly rural, subsistence economy, and the low status of women—combine to reinforce a tra-ditional preference for large families (see Figure 6-7). Yet, while decisions to have many children may be understandable on an individual family basis, the effect on a country as a whole is devastating. At least 45% of the population in most African coun-tries is under 15 years of age and in several cases

the majority of the people are under 15. Govern-ments find it impossible to keep up with the de-mand for health care and education. In some African countries, 20% to 25% of the budget goes for ed-ucation. Efforts to provide adequate housing, or food supplies, or to develop jobs and industries are continually being swamped by expansion of the population.

African governments have been generally slow to acknowledge the threat that population growth represents to improvement in the life of their peo-ples. In the past this was partly due to a lack of real statistics on the growth rates in many countries and partly due to suspicion about the motives of Western countries that offered or demanded birth control as a part of aid packages. Government at-titudes have changed gradually, however, so that by the end of the 1980s, more than half of the sub-Saharan countries were willing to admit that their birth rates were too high.

Nigeria, with 21% of the population of sub-Saharan Africa, is already the largest country in the region. At current growth rates, Nigeria bids fair to become the third largest country in the world, after China and India. Yet, because Nigeria is rich in petroleum, little attention was paid to population growth. The country's leaders felt the petroleum-based economy would provide for population in-creases. It was not until the price of oil dropped in the 1980s that the government was forced to ac-knowledge that population growth would hinder further development. Current goals are to reduce the fertility rate from 6.5 to 4.0 children per year by 2000.

Similarly, Zambia hopes to reduce fertility rates from 7.2 to 6.0 by the year 2000 and to 4.0 by 2015. Liberia plans to reduce total fertility from 6.7 to 4.0 by 2000.

There are indications that population programs are already beginning to lower growth in Africa. But the question remains: Will these goals be met? And, if they are, will they slow population growth quickly enough to prevent environmental damage, such as degradation of land by overfarming, or large-scale epidemics and famines that will reduce population without human help?

Another question that population experts pon-der is the effect of the AIDS epidemic on population

---
Towards a Sustainable Society

Sustainable Growth for the Chinese Economy, Population, and Environment

by Geping Qu

Geping Qu is Administrator of China's Environmental Protection Agency and Vice Chairman of the Environmental Commission of the State Council of China. He is considered the architect of Chinese environmental protection efforts and is the recipient of a gold medal from the United Nations Environment Programme.

Sustainable development can be achieved when population and economic growth are in balance with the long-term supporting capacity of the natural environment. Like other developing counties, China faces a great challenge in this respect.

Historically a country of large population, China had a population of 1.16 billion in 1990, which amounts to approximately 22% of the world population. This large population imposes severe and long-lasting impacts on the Chinese environment.

In the early 1950s the agricultural land available per person was 0.19 hectare, compared to 0.1 hectare today; per capita water resources have been decreased by half within a period of 40 years, and forest resources are also declining rapidly, as a result of the huge pressure the growing population puts on agricultural land, timber, and fuel wood. At present, the level of population growth in China is 16 million each year. The large population has posed increasing pressure on urban and rural environ-ments and has, as well, caused the failure to settle environmental problems more efficiently. In one word, *population* is the ultimate reason for environmental problems in China.

Family planning has been faithfully practiced by the Chinese since the 1970s and has prevented the birth of 0.2 billion people, which means that it has delayed the "World 5 Billion Population Day" by two years.

This state policy of family planning will be continued in China and efforts will be made to control average population growth within 12.5%; meanwhile, China will develop and make full use of its rich population resource in agricultural land development, control of water and soil erosion, large-scale forestation, and other ecological development for sustainable growth.

growth in Africa. Recently the World Health Organization estimated that 3.5 million people in sub-Saharan Africa are infected with the AIDS virus—this is 1 out of every 50 adults. In Africa the virus infects an equal number of men and women. The best guess at the moment is that at current rates of prevalence and without a cure, AIDS might reduce population growth in African countries by 25%, or from 3% per year to 2% per year.

Clearly, provision of birth control and family planning services is a vital need in most sub-Saharan countries today. This is a need that wealthier countries can help to fill, as is improvement in infant and child survival. If population growth is to be damped to reasonable levels in the little time available, however, the governments of the countries themselves must work to improve educational and economic opportunities for women, legislate later age at marriage, promote longer spacing between children, and encourage breastfeeding—measures that contribute to lower birth rates as well as better maternal and child health.

OUTLOOK FOR POPULATION GROWTH IN THE FUTURE

In the late 1970s demographers were encouraged by a small but real decrease in world population growth rates. From a high of 1.98% per year in 1965–1970 the world's growth rate fell to 1.88% in 1977–1978 and then to 1.7% in 1982. But by 1989 and 1990 it was back up to 1.8%.

Fertility Rate Trends

The above figures obscure some good news about population growth. And that is that fertility rates are dropping. Remember that crude birth and death rates depend on the age structure of a population. If a large percentage of a population consists of women of childbearing age, the crude birth rate tends to be high. This is the situation in developing countries today. The real hope that population growth is slowing comes from looking at the total fertility rate for each country. Because this rate measures the number of children each woman of childbearing age is expected to have, it can reveal changes in reproductive behavior that are not confused by the size of various groups in the population. On a worldwide basis, the average total fertility rate fell from 4.6 in 1968 to 3.5 in 1990. Fully 80% of the world's population is in countries with declining fertility rates.

Even in sub-Saharan Africa, where population growth patterns have been most resistant to change, there are declines in fertility rates. Kenya, once labeled the country with the world's highest fertility, has declined from 8.0 children per woman in 1986 to 6.7 in 1990.

What influence will this drop in fertility rates have on the total size of the world's population? The growth of the world's population will slow in the 1990s as a result of fertility rate declines, but, due to population momentum, it is likely that we have not yet seen the end of extraordinary growth. Because of the age structure in most developing countries (a large group of children yet to enter their childbearing years), birth rates and growth rates are expected to remain high for at least the next decade.

In fact, it now looks as though the 1990s will be the historic peak decade of population growth in terms of absolute numbers (see Figure 6-8). There is still a great deal of uncertainty about the final size the world's population might reach. The United Nations has proposed three growth scenarios depending on how fast fertility rates drop (Figure 6-9).

The growth rates caused by lowering mortality will not play as large a role in the future as they have in the past. This is partly because much of the fall in mortality has already been accomplished. But it is also because mortality declines are not as significant at low birth rates as they are at high birth rates. When fertility is high, saving a new baby's life means that child will add many more people to the population when he or she comes to reproductive age. When fertility is low, children can be expected only to replace themselves. Similarly, increasing the life expectancy to 80 of someone who now expects to live to age 60 adds only one person to the population, since the years being added are not reproductive years.

In 1991 the United Nations Fund for Population Activities predicted that the world population would level off at 11.5 billion sometime in the twenty-second century, somewhat higher than the medium series prediction shown in Figure 6-9. "The choices of the next 10 years," writes Dr. Nafis Sadik, executive director of the U.N. Fund for Population Activities, "will decide whether the world population trebles or merely doubles before it finally stops growing. . . ."

It would be well to remember, however, that

FIGURE 6-8 World Population:
Average Annual Increase for
Each Decade, 1750–2100
(projected). Each decade's total
increase is shown as the average
annual increase over that decade.
The 1990s are predicted to be the
historic peak of population
growth in terms of absolute
numbers. (*Source:* T. W. Merrick,
Population Reference Bureau,
"World Population in Transition," *Population Bulletin, 41*[2],
[1986])

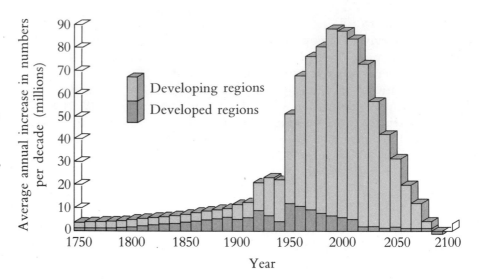

these numbers are merely projections of trends.
They do not take into account the possibility that
at certain population levels natural restraints on
population size may come into play. It is possible
that limits to food production or the spread of diseases may lower population growth rates long before the world population doubles or trebles. It is
possible that increased pollution and efforts to feed
a world population double or treble the current size
will so damage the environment that the number
of people the earth can support will actually decrease. Furthermore, the effects of environmental
damage will not be limited to the developing countries in which the major portion of population
growth takes place. Most of this book details problems that could be eased or eliminated simply by
reducing the size of the world's population, rather
than allowing it to grow. Global warming, loss of
the ozone layer, erosion of soil, and the loss of
tropical forests and the creatures that live there are
all examples of problems that affect us in whatever
country we live. And they are problems whose size
is tied to the size of the world population.

Actions to Address the Problems

What sorts of actions can we take, now, to slow
population growth more quickly? There are at least

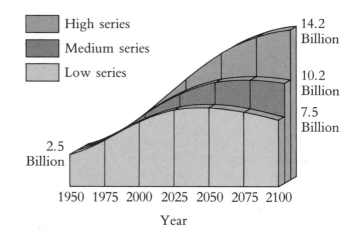

**FIGURE 6-9 World Population Growth, 1950–2100,
Three Scenarios.** The projections differ due to the assumptions made about world fertility rates. The middle series assumes that world fertility will decline to
about two children per woman by 2035. In this case
the world population would level off at 10.2 billion by
the end of the twenty-first century. The low prediction assumes greater success in lowering fertility rates,
so that the two-child family was reached by 2010,
while the high series assumes that this norm would
not be reached until 2065. In the case of the low series, the world population would level off at 7.5 billion, but if the high-series assumptions are accurate,
world population would almost treble to 14.2 billion.
(*Source:* Population Reference Bureau, *World Population
Data Sheet Workbook,* 1988)

four areas in which we can take action. The first is in provision of birth control and family planning services. As long as there is an unmet need for contraception anywhere in the world, it means that people still have more children than they want.

Figure 6-3 portrayed unmet need for contraception as the percentage of fertile women who wanted no more children but who were not using contraception. The reasons why these women are not using contraception can be several. Effective, modern contraception may simply be unavailable. Or if it is available, it may cost too much for a family in a developing country to use regularly.

The Population Crisis Committee suggests that in order for contraception to be widely adopted, it must cost less than 1 percent of monthly income. In many developing countries, if provided by the private sector, the cost for the insertion of an IUD is 5% to 70% of yearly income and the cost of sterilization is 10% to 250% of yearly income. In Ethiopia a year's supply of condoms costs 30% of yearly income unless obtained from subsidized sources, but these reach only 30% of the adult male population. In the Western industrialized countries the cost of sterilization is generally under 5% of yearly income, while pills, condoms, and IUD insertion are all less than 1 percent of yearly income.

Table 6-3 shows the percentage of people in various countries that have access to affordable contraception. These percentages include both private sector and governmental sources of contracaption. In order to achieve the ideal of an average family size of two children, about 75% of reproductive-age couples must use some sort of contraception, although if only the most effective methods are used, an average of two children per family could be achieved with somewhat lower contraceptive use.

The Population Crisis Committee estimates that the cost of providing family planning services to 75% of all reproductive-age couples in developing countries would be about $10.5 billion per year. Currently about $3.2 billion per year is spent on contraception, most by the developing countries themselves. Only about 20% currently comes from foreign donors. The needed increase in spending could come from loans by multilateral development banks and from industrialized countries themselves,

as outright grants, or from allocating more development aid to population planning efforts.

The second area in which we can help is in supporting efforts to lower infant and child mortality in developing countries. When the death rate in a country is due one-half to the deaths of children under the age of 5, as it is in many sub-Saharan countries, it is naive to believe that parents will accept the concept of a two-child family. None of us would settle for only two children if the survival of those children were so uncertain.

The third area in which we can work is that of improving conditions and opportunities for women. Studies show again and again that the most effective socioeconomic changes in terms of reducing desired family size are those that provide women with education, status, and employment opportunities.

These are solutions that mainly require money and good will. The fourth group of solutions is more difficult, because they involve a change of lifestyle. As you read further in this book, you will find many examples of environmental problems whose root cause is the way energy is used in the industrialized countries, or the way resources are used rather than reused, or the diet eaten by citizens of developed countries. This is the lifestyle that citizens of undeveloped countries hope to emulate—wasteful, unmindful of the damage it does to the environment. There are fewer of us in the developed world than in the developing world, 1.2 billion compared to 4.1 billion, and this inequality will probably become larger. Yet, though there are fewer of us, we use a disproportionate share of many of the world's resources—some 75% of the nonfuel mineral resources produced each year, for instance. The United States, alone, uses 30% of the petroleum extracted in the world every year.

Because of our wealth, those of us living in developed countries have the opportunity to support efforts to develop a more sustainable lifestyle, one that takes into account the long-term cost to the environment of the way we live today. If we do not do this, the problems caused by increases in the world's population will become unbearable and they will affect all of us, rich or poor, citizens of developed countries or of undeveloped countries.

TABLE 6-3 Percentage of People with Access to Affordable Contraception, 17 Countries

Country	Type of Contraception			
	Condoms	Pills	Male or Female Sterilization	Abortion
Argentina	50	45	2	5
Canada	100	100	100	83
China	84	84	92	92
Cuba	100	100	98	100
Egypt	84	97	53	58
Ethiopia	30	30	3	NA
Guatemala	65	60	50	NA
Guinea	2	2	NA	NA
Jordan	20	30	25	NA
Kenya	58	54	21	NA
Lebanon	28	29	25	29
Nepal	9	14	29	NA
Nigeria	29	24	6	15[b]
Pakistan	39	30	3	NA
Uganda	6	22	6	NA
United States	100	90	80	78
Former USSR	20	10	NA	90

Data Source: from Population Crisis Committee, "Access to Affordable Contraception," 1991 Report on World Progress Towards Population Stabilization (Washington, D.C.: 1991: Population Crisis Committee, 1991).

[a] Method not used, or no data available.
[b] Figure is for menstrual regulation, rather than abortion.

SUMMARY

Industrialization and economic development may eventually lower population growth rates. However, lower growth rates have also been achieved by means of social welfare policies: universal education, easily accessible birth control services, improvements in the status of women, better health care, and old-age security plans. When the socioeconomic climate is altered so that families can increase their economic welfare by having fewer children, evidence is accumulating that they will do so.

Future programs need to be tailored to the specific needs of each country. Some populations still lack adequate birth control services; others need health care programs to reduce infant and maternal mortality and infertility. In other countries, improvements in the status of women will help to lower population growth rates.

Further progress may depend on government incentives and disincentives. These should increase the cost of children to a family or generate opportunities that cannot be enjoyed if parents choose to have large numbers of children.

Current world population projections predict a more than doubling of the world population, to 11.5 billion by the end of the twenty-second century. It is by no means clear that the earth can support this many people without serious damage to the environment.

Those of us in the developed world can help to supply birth control and family planning services where there are unmet needs for contraception, and health care services where infant and child mortality is high. We can also consider lifestyle changes that would bring the actions of our own population more into line with the ability of the planet to support human life.

QUESTIONS

1. What are the proximate determinants of fertility? What result would you expect if a government tried to control population growth by making laws pertaining to these proximate determinants of fertility?

2. Population reduction policies that penalize families with more than a certain number of children can be viewed as unfair to innocent children. Are policies that reward small families similarly unfair? Explain, using examples such as housing loans, employment and education bonuses, old-age social security, and so on.

3. How do economic development and population growth affect each other?

4. Why is the status of women (education, employment opportunities) an important factor in fertility levels?

5. Ninety percent of future population growth is expected to take place in the developing nations. What can citizens of the developed nations do to help dampen this population growth?

Further Reading

Fawcett, J. T. *Perceptions of the Value of Children,* Reprint #183. Honolulu, Hawaii: East-West Population Institute, 1983.

Understanding rapid population growth requires understanding of the value of children in different cultures. This publication is an in-depth look at children and how various societies value them.

Keyfitz, Nathan. "The Growing Human Population," *Scientific American,* September 1989.

Excellent graphics and good examples of countries that have and have not managed to reduce population growth make this an article worth reading.

Merrick, T. W. "Population Pressures in Latin America," *Population Bulletin 41* (3) (1986), Population Reference Bureau.

Weeks, J. R. "The Demography of Islamic Nations," *Population Bulletin 43* (4) (1988), Population Reference Bureau.

Goliber, T. J. "Africa's Expanding Population: Old Problems, New Policies," *Population Bulletin, 44* (3) (1989), Population Reference Bureau.

These three issues give an in-depth view of population problems, causes, and solutions in three critical regions of the world.

ReVelle, R., A. Khosla, and M. Vinovskis. *The Survival Equation.* Boston: Houghton Mifflin, 1971.

A thoughtful, humanitarian approach to rapid population growth and possible solutions to the problems it causes. Still worth reading for the arguments against coercion in birth control programs and the arguments that, under the right circumstances, all peoples can see that control of rapid population growth is in their best interest.

References

Belcastro, P. A. *The Birth Control Book.* Boston: Jones and Bartlett, 1986.

Coale, A. J. *Recent Trends in Fertility and Nuptiality in China. Science,* 251 (January 25, 1991).

Gulhati, K. "Compulsory Sterilization: The Change in India's Population Policy," *Science, 195* (March 25, 1977).

Mastroianni, L., Jr. "Developing New Contraceptives: Obstacles and Opportunities," Committee on Contraceptive Development, National Academy of Sciences. Washington, D.C.: National Academy Press, 1990.

Merrick, T. W. "World Population in Transition," *Population Bulletin, 41* (2) (1986).

Population Crisis Committee. *Access to Affordable Contraception, 1991: Report on World Progress Towards Population Stabilization.* Washington, D.C.: Population Crisis Committee, 1991.

The State of World Population Report 1990, United Nations Population Fund, 220 East 42nd St., New York, N.Y. 10017.

The Statistical Abstract of the United States 1989. U.S. Department of Commerce.

Thapa, S., S. Kumar, J. Cushing, and K. Kennedy. Contraceptive Use and Needs among Postpartum Women in 25 Developing Countries. Presented at the Annual Meeting of the Population Association of America, Washington, D.C., March 19–23, 1991.

World Resources 1988/1989. Washington, D.C.: World Resources Institute, 1989.

Part Three

Land and Wildlife Resources

Chestnut-sided Warbler. Populations of this migrating bird are down nearly 30 percent from 1978. (*Photo:* Bates Littlehales)

In the introduction to this book, we traced the development of the concept of setting aside land resources for wildlife habitat, for timber resources, and for preservation of wilderness itself. In Chapters 7, 8, and 9, we look at land resources from another point of view — from the point of view of land as an agricultural resource, capable of feeding the world's growing population.

There is no shortage of land physically able to grow crops. In fact, the earth may have as much as twice again the amount of arable land as is now farmed. Some important qualifications must be made, however. In the first place, most of the land that is easily cropped is already being farmed. Using the remaining land would require a great deal of energy and labor for such tasks as clearing forests, building irrigation systems, or transporting crops to distant markets. Furthermore, the land that is considered most fertile is generally already in cultivation. Some of the land not now being farmed is only marginally fertile. Thus, if new land is farmed, expected yields may not be as great as on present farmland.

Thirdly, severe environmental problems might result from farming some of this unused land. Steep hillsides, for instance, erode easily when their tree cover is removed for farming. Arid lands are especially susceptible to the salinization of soil that results from irrigation. And, finally, plans for clearing new lands for farming put food production experts on a direct collision course with those concerned about preserving endangered plant and animal species. In South America, as well as in Africa, a large part of the land that could be farmed is now under forest cover and provides habitats for large numbers of animals and even larger numbers of plant species. The concept of preserving a wide diversity of species in the world comes into conflict with the vision of providing enough food for everyone. As human populations increase, so that more land is necessary for food production, other desirable uses, such as species protection, are edged out of the picture.

The soil that forms the basis of the world's agricultural resource is threatened in several ways. The main threat is soil **erosion,** the loss of soil to winds or water flow. Erosion occurs when soil is left with little or no vegetation as a result of farming, overgrazing, mining, or construction. In certain areas, **salinization,** the accumulation of salts in soil, is a problem. Salinization often occurs when irrigation water evaporates, leaving behind the salts it contains. For this reason, it is a problem in dry climates such as the American Southwest, where a great deal of irrigation water is used. In other areas, the structure of the soils has been hurt by traditional farming methods that compact soil with heavy equipment, or by recreational vehicles run over delicate desert soils.

Acid rain leaches needed minerals from both agricultural and forest soils, especially in the northeastern United States. Also, in the United States, we are paving over some 3 million acres (1.2 million hectares) a year of our soil, almost one-third of it prime farmland, as cities and suburbs grow to accommodate a growing U.S. population.

The most tragic loss of soil and land resources is the process known as **desertification.** All over the world are areas where groundwater tables are declining as people pump water out faster than it can be naturally replaced, or where erosion or salinization is destroying soil resources. In some of these places, especially the semi-arid regions of the African Sahel and the American Southwest, vegetation has vanished.

Although it may appear that desert is creeping along and engulfing more and more land, this is not what actually happens. *Desertification* is a term applied to the severe degradation of land, to the point where it resembles a desert. It results from overuse by humans, sometimes in combination with variations in climate such as droughts. Desertification is the ultimate human insult to land and soil resources.

Like desertification, other soil resource problems are not unique to the United States. Erosion, for instance, is a serious problem in many countries today, especially in areas where tropical

forests have been cleared for crops. Similarly, acid rain affects forests and croplands in a number of European countries. Erosion and desertification are the subjects of the first chapter in this part.

An equally important environmental problem associated with food production is pesticide use, covered in Chapter 8.

In Chapter 9 the world food situation and prospects for the future are reviewed. We first look at the scope of the food problem. What is the extent of the food supply crisis? How can farmers, especially those in developing countries, where population growth is most rapid, grow more food? But these questions deal with only part of the story. Social and political realities control, to a large extent, how much food is actually produced and where it goes. Chapter 9 also deals with the issue of world grain reserves, because here may lie the solution to both unnecessarily high food prices and catastrophic famine.

Water resources, which along with soil resources determine an area's food-producing ability, are covered in Chapter 18. Acid rain, which leaches needed minerals from both agricultural and forest soils, is discussed in Chapter 16.

The last chapter in this part, Chapter 10, examines what many scientists feel is one of the most serious environmental problems we face today, shrinkage of the resource of **biodiversity.** This is another way of describing the loss of a major portion of the world's wildlife. Such a loss is taking place primarily because of destruction of **habitat,** the places where these organisms live.

Loss of biodiversity is often discussed in the context of tropical forest loss, and it is true that the greatest number of species facing extinction live in countries with large amounts of tropical forest. Such losses have the potential to affect U.S. residents in many ways, as detailed in Chapter 10. There is at least one way in which we are already being affected, however.

Scientists have been tracking the size of U.S. bird populations for many years by sophisticated radar techniques and by annual surveys of the number of birds breeding in various locations. Radar images of bird flocks migrating across the Gulf of Mexico show shocking changes: Within the past 20 years, the density of the flocks appears to have decreased by half. The North American Breeding Bird Survey indicates declines of 6% to 78% in some of our migrating land birds — bay-breasted warblers, Tennessee warblers, black-billed cuckoos, rose-breasted grosbeaks, wood thrushes, indigo buntings, northern orioles, and scarlet tanagers. All these birds are long-distance migrators. They may spend their summers in our northern forests, but they winter in the rapidly dwindling tropical forests of Central and South America. Thus, in what may be a sort of global repercussion, tropical deforestation may be having a real and direct effect on one of the most well-loved parts of the North American environment.

Not only the tropical forests are disappearing, however. Northern forests, in which the songbirds breed, are being cut for lumber. Some of the critical areas where the birds rest and refuel during migration are being lost to development.

These and other wildlife issues are discussed in Chapter 10.

Chapter 7

Erosion and Desertification

Producing enough food to feed the world's growing population is one of the major challenges faced by scientists and governments today. But the problems involved are not simply those of quantity, growing *enough* food. Also at issue are the social and political realities that control the distribution of food and the harmful effects that agricultural practices can have on the earth and its inhabitants.

In this chapter we explain the problems caused when fertile topsoil is eroded by wind and water. Then we discuss **desertification,** a phenomenon described as the ultimate insult to the land. It is a process in which once fertile land becomes a dry, forbidding desert.

SOIL EROSION

What exactly is **erosion?** A short scenario can explain this phenomenon.

Storm clouds gather and a brisk wind stirs the poplars in the hedgerow. A tiny drop of rain falls on the freshly plowed earth. Then another drop, and another, and the storm begins in earnest. Each drop hits the earth like a miniature meteor—soil particles spray in a circle around the drop and a small crater is formed. As more droplets reach the earth, their arrival rate begins to exceed the rate at which the water can be absorbed into the soil. Puddles form, then rivulets. The looser and finer soil, the best soil, is picked up by the rivulets and carried downslope. The velocity of the rivulets increases; more and more soil is carried in suspension. Rivulets join to form temporary streams, which flow in gullies, and the rapidly flowing water, en route to a true stream, cuts sharply into the earth.

This event is not isolated or uncommon—it is any rainstorm on a plowed field. Multiplied by thousands of farms or millions of acres, it results in as much as 4 billion tons of soil being carried off each year by water erosion in the United States, about three-quarters of it from farmland. Wind may scour away another billion tons of soil (Figure 7-1).

The four major food-producing countries (the United States, the Soviet Union, China, and India) may lose as much as 13.2 billion tons of soil from their croplands every year. In some countries the situation is even more severe (Figure 7-2).

All erosion carries away soil nutrients and plant residues, essential components of a productive earth. Pesticides and even disease-causing organ-

FIGURE 7-1 Gully Erosion in Montana. This gully cuts deeply through a hay meadow. The farmer will have to do significantly more plowing to prepare his land—now in two fields instead of one. (*Photo:* D. J. Anderson, USDA, Soil Conservation Service)

FIGURE 7-2 Erosion in Ethiopia. Overgrazing by cattle of hilly pastures, the clearing of 200,000 hectares of forest each year for fuelwood, and farming on steep hillsides has led to severe erosion problems in Ethiopia. (*Photo:* FAO/F. Botts)

isms can be absorbed onto the soil particles and can later contaminate waters into which the soil is carried.

Environmental Effects

It is important to remember that erosion is a natural process. It has been observed for centuries; it even has beneficial effects. The rich delta lands built up at the mouths of the Mississippi, the Rhine, and the Nile all exist because soil was carried off the land in enormous quantities. The richness of the river deltas is a two-edged sword, however. If the delta soils are rich, the soil that remains on the land upstream must have been robbed of some of its value. This, in fact, is one of the principal concerns we have about soil erosion: the decreasing productive capacity of the soil.

Although erosion is a natural process, the massive extent to which it is presently occurring is the result of human activities. The farming of more land (only in this century made productive by irrigation), the grazing of cattle, the construction of buildings and highways, the activities associated with mining—all disturb the soil and accelerate erosion. In addition, the pavement that now overlays so much of the world contributes to faster erosion. Because water cannot be absorbed by paving materials, it collects and may run swiftly off the pavements. Its increased volume and velocity will erode and suspend soil, carrying it into streambeds.

Rate of Soil Formation versus Soil Loss. Soil is formed in a slow and continuous process. The rate of new soil formation is about 1 inch (2.5 cm) of topsoil every 100–1,000 years. However, the rate varies widely, depending on climate, vegetation, soil type, and land use.

Soil erosion is measured in tons of soil lost per acre (metric tons/hectare, or t/ha). To understand what rates of soil loss means, we need to know a few facts. About 6 inches (15 cm) of topsoil is usually cultivated in modern agriculture. This 6 inches weighs approximately 1,000 tons/acre (2245 t/ha). If soil erodes at about 15 tons/acre/year (33 t/ha/year), about 0.10 inch (0.25 cm) of soil is lost each year and the whole plow layer in 60–70 years.

Experts estimate that, depending on soil types, only 1–5 tons of soil can be lost per acre each year (2.2–11 t/ha) without decreasing productivity over the long term.

Loss of Topsoil in the United States and Worldwide. The 2.7 billion tons of soil eroded from U.S. farmland each year come from individual farms, where erosion could be more or less than some average figure. From sloped land that is unprotected and has been freshly plowed, under an intense rain, annual erosion losses could reach 60–100 tons per acre (132–220 t/ha). On a national basis, cropland erosion losses average about 4–5 tons per acre (9–11 t/ha) per year, but averages are deceiving. Only 6% of U.S. cropland accounts for some 43% of the soil erosion. The Soviet Union may be losing even more soil than the United States, as Soviet leaders try to reduce grain imports by bringing marginal, more easily eroded land into cultivation.

Such losses create numerous problems. The productive capacity of the soil may decrease, depending on the depth to which the topsoil extends and the character of the subsoil. The loss of 6 inches (15 cm) of topsoil will make most cropland much less productive, if not unsuitable for farming. For example, losses of this magnitude in Tennessee have reduced corn yields by 42%. These decreases in productivity may occur even if the farmer tries to make up for lost nutrients by adding more fertilizer. Loss in productivity is due not only to loss of the more fertile topsoil but also to changes in the soil structure. When topsoil has been carried off, the remaining soil may not absorb water as well. Hence, more runoff is likely to occur, making less water available to the crop. Since the subsoil is generally less permeable, less water can be stored between rains, making the likelihood of damage from droughts greater.

The less desirable subsoil remaining is also more difficult to till; rills make plowing more difficult yet; and gullies may block plowing entirely, resulting in the complete loss of portions of the land.

Effects on Streams, Reservoirs, and Aquatic Life. Soil particles carried in suspension and bumping along the bottom of streambeds will eventually settle when the velocity of the stream decreases sufficiently. These sediments accumulating on the bottom of the stream channel use up part of the room in the channel. Thus, more water will be coursing down a stream channel than it is able to handle. Compounding the problem is the fact that the volume of runoff is further increased by the volume of the soil particles carried in suspension. Thus, flooding by streams flowing through badly eroding areas is more likely.

One extreme case of erosion has been documented on the Yellow River (Hwang Ho) in China. At flood stage, the flow in that river has been as much as 50% sediment by weight. The yellow color of the river is due to the color of the soil particles eroded from the uplands.

Not only are stream channels filled up by sediments, but reservoirs fill up as well. These structures, which are used to store water for irrigation, for hydropower, and for water supply, bring the flowing waters to a standstill. When this occurs, most of the sediments, which were in suspension, drop down. The buildup of sediments in reservoirs decreases the quantity of water available on a reliable basis. Large reservoirs are actually designed with extra capacity to hold the sediments. Of course, this added capacity drives up the cost of the reservoir.

Besides using up the capacity of rivers and reservoirs, sediments carried in suspension affect aquatic life. Sediments may bury the habitat of bottom feeders. The turbid water allows less sunlight to enter, thus hindering the growth of aquatic plant species.

Finally, we must list among the effects of water erosion the poor water quality caused by the substances carried into our streams in runoff. Fertilizers and animal wastes use up vital oxygen in the water and destroy the habitat of aquatic life. Erosion is the most common route of pesticide entry into water. In fact, although loss of productivity due to a shrinking layer of topsoil is a serious problem for some 10% of U.S. farms, overall, the off-farm effects, such as water pollution by fertilizers and pesticides, are probably the most serious effect of water erosion in the United States.

Effects of Wind Erosion

Annual soil losses due to wind erosion have been measured at levels up to seven tons per acre. People and livestock have difficulty breathing in dust storms and develop respiratory and eye ailments. Crops, especially seedlings, cannot survive such conditions.

Although dust storms are distinct and noteworthy events, blowing soil is common. Its effects are the same as those of dust storms, though slower and less dramatic. Scour of plant leaves by soil particles may reduce crops. If plant roots are uncovered, the crop will not survive. Soil is stripped of its richer portions. (See Figure 7-3.)

Methods of Controlling Erosion

The most important single activity that brings about soil erosion is farming. When soil is turned over, exposing a surface with no cover—indeed, with no protection whatsoever—the possibilities for erosion are greatly increased. One set of alternatives to control erosion, then, concentrates on how soil is tilled.

Reduced Tillage Farming. The fastest-spreading soil conservation technique today is undoubtedly **reduced tillage** farming. This is actually a group of methods in which some sort of crop cover is left on the soil at all times. The soil is never plowed and left bare to erosive wind and rain. Herbicides are applied to kill weeds or the previous crop. New crop seeds are often planted directly into the old stubble using special equipment. For instance, rye may be planted in a field in the fall and then killed by an herbicide in the spring before corn is planted into the residue of the rye crop. This residue reduces soil erosion by decreasing the impact of raindrops and slowing the flow of water across the field. Reduced tillage farming can decrease soil erosion to almost zero.

Developing countries might profit from this technique, especially in tropical climates, where the topsoil layer is very thin and quickly eroded. Although reduced tillage is now primarily used by large farmers in developing nations, small farmers could benefit from the reduced plowing labor in-

FIGURE 7-3 Effects of Wind Erosion. A United Nations Development Program employee stands next to a tree whose roots have been laid bare by wind erosion. While water erosion with its off-the-farm effects is the most important erosion problem in the United States, in dry areas of the world, such as the African Sahel, wind erosion is the more serious problem. Dry, sandy soil, unprotected by vegetation, is easily picked up by the winds and blown great distances. Roads, farmland, even whole villages are buried by the moving sands. People suffer more respiratory disease from breathing dust constantly. Farm productivity suffers as valuable topsoil blows away. (*Photo:* Mary Lynn Hanley/UNDP)

volved. The energy involved in plowing fields with hand tools often limits the amount of land a farmer can plant.

Is reduced tillage farming the environmentally sound way to farm? Maybe, but it's not entirely clear yet. Large quantities of herbicides must be used in these methods. The long-term effect of such

use on the environment is still to be determined. "Before we shift 90% of the nation's cropland into a farming technique that relies on increasing use of pesticides, we should take a hard look at where those pesticides are likely to end up and what their effects will be" (Speer and Paulson, 1984).

Crop Rotation. On plowed land the method of plowing and the type of crops planted can be planned to reduce erosion. When crops are **rotated,** by planting cash crops such as wheat alternately with grasses or legumes, the soil gains protection from erosion and may be nourished as well.

Contour Plowing, Terracing, and Shelterbelts. An important factor in the severity of erosion is the slope of the soil: The greater the slope, the more severe erosion is likely to be (other factors such as rainfall and soil types remaining the same). This has led to the development of soil management practices such as contour plowing or terracing. Such methods are designed to interrupt, divert, and absorb the flow of water in its path down a field (Figure 7-4).

Methods involving the use of vegetation can protect the soil not only from water erosion but from wind erosion as well. Protection against wind erosion, however, may also involve planting trees such as willow or poplar, two fast-growing species. Arranged in long lines, called shelterbelts, the trees decrease the wind speed downwind from the belt. Earth banks, wooden fences, and rock walls may also be useful in checking wind erosion.

A model soil conservation program in Kenya, which includes strip cropping, tree planting, and drains, has improved farm incomes and shown that soil conservation is possible for small-scale farming in developing nations.

Encouraging Soil Conservation

One would think that soil conservation is in the farmer's best interests. It may be, but only in the long run. In the short run, the farmer must survive to plant another year. Soil conservation measures that involve restructuring the land cost money. And land taken out of production is land that will not produce a crop and an income. Furthermore, the

FIGURE 7-4 Soil Conservation or Modern Art? The aerial view of a field of peach trees (*left*) in New Bridgeton, New Jersey resembles nothing so much as a tufted bedspread. Yet the pattern actually reflects good soil conservation practice. Between the rows of peach trees are strips of clover sod, which simultaneously enrich the soil and help to anchor it in place. (*Photo:* Clarence Deland, USDA, SCS) (*Right*) One of the first Soil and Water Conservation Districts in the United States was founded in Lancaster County, Pennsylvania in 1937. From a wasteful pattern of straight-line furrows that climbed up hillsides, the pattern of cultivation evolved to its present state. This aerial view shows furrows following the contours of the hills and strip cropping (growing alternate strips of the main crop and a ground cover, such as hay or grass), two soil conservation practices that check erosion and hence preserve the soil. (*Photo:* Don Schuhart, USDA, SCS)

loss in fertility of the soil due to erosion can temporarily be overcome by liberal doses of fertilizer.

The U.S. Department of Agriculture (USDA) has sponsored soil conservation programs since the middle 1930s, when the Dust Bowl era dramatized how very fragile our soil resource is. Yet a 1977 study by the U.S. General Accounting Office, investigating conditions and practices on 283 U.S. farms, showed that 84% were losing soil by erosion at an annual rate of 5 tons per acre (11 t/ha) or more. Of the 119 farms with conservation plans, fewer than half were actually using them.

The 1985 farm bill was designed to help solve some of these problems. The bill was designed to reduce the number of acres U.S. farmers cultivate by paying them *not* to grow crops on up to 40 million acres of erosion-prone grasslands and fragile wetlands. Furthermore, farmers who destroy such lands will be ineligible for government farm programs the following year. Farmers already cultivating fragile and erodable lands were given five years to develop a soil and water conservation plan and have another five years to put the plan into effect.

The United Nations Environment program encourages farmers in developing nations to put into place these same erosion control methods, as part of its plan of action to control desertification.

DESERTIFICATION

Drought and the needs of a growing human population sometimes combine with erosion to cause one of the harshest of environmental consequences—**desertification.** This term describes a deterioration of land so severe that the land becomes, in fact, a desert.

After Man, The Desert*

I stood on the Great Wall of China high on a hill near the border of Mongolia. . . . The slope below the Great Wall was cut with gullies, some of which were 50 feet deep. As far as the eye could see were gullies—a gashed and gutted countryside.

. . . The whole valley, once good farmland, had become a desert of sand and gravel, alternately wet and dry, always fruitless. . . . Its sole harvest now is dust, picked up by the bitter winds of winter that rip across its dry surface in this land of rainy summers and dry winters. . . .

The farmers of a past generation had cleared the forest. They had plowed the sloping land and dotted it with hamlets. . . . Each village was marked by columns of smoke rising from fires that cooked the sim-

* Old World saying, reported by J. R. Smith.

Towards a Sustainable Society

Tree Crops: A Permanent Agriculture

by J. Russell Smith

J. Russell Smith was a professor of economic geography at Columbia University. In 1929 he published a book entitled Tree Crops—A Permanent Agriculture, *from which*

this essay is excerpted (reprinted courtesy of Island Press). This visionary volume is still available from bookstores today.

As plants, the cereals are weaklings. They must be coddled and weeded. For their reception the ground must be plowed and harrowed, and sometimes it must be cultivated after the crop is planted. This must be done for every harvest. When we produce these crops upon hilly land, the necessary breaking up of the soil prepares the land for ruin—first the plow, then rain, then erosion. Finally the desert. . . .

Testing applied to the plant kingdom would show that the natural engines of food production for hill lands are not corn and other grasses, but trees. A single oak tree yields acorns (good carbohydrate food) often by the hundredweight, sometimes by the ton. Some hickory and pecan trees give us nuts by the barrel; the walnut tree yields by the ten bushels. There are bean trees producing good food for cattle, which food would apparently make more meat or milk per acre than our forage crops now make. . . .

For experiments in breeding, the tree has one *great advantage* over most of the annuals. We propagate

ple fare of those sons of Genghis Kahn. Year by year the rain has washed away the soil. Now the plow comes not—only the shepherd is here with his sheep and goats, nibblers of last vestiges. These 4-footed vultures pick the bones of dead cultures in all continents. Will they do it to ours? The hamlets in my valley below the Great Wall are shriveled or gone. Only gullies remain—a wide and sickening expanse of gullies, more sickening to look upon than the ruins of fire. You can rebuild after a fire. (Smith, 1980, p. 3)

J. R. Smith's graphic description of a human-made desert could be matched in many parts of the world, including the United States. The Sonoran Desert in Arizona was lush grassland before overgrazing turned it into a scrub desert. In Syria, once fertile Roman farms are now bare rock. Today in

the sub-Saharan region of Africa known as the Sahel, the worst drought in modern history has speeded up this process of desertification. But, contrary to popular belief, desertification is not a problem limited to lands directly adjoining deserts or to Africa. Lands in the American Southwest are undergoing desertification, as are parts of Bolivia, Australia, and Brazil.

Causes of Desertification

Drought. Drought is by and large a natural crisis, one that occurs periodically in many parts of the world. It is a frequent visitor to the lands on the southern borders of the Sahara (Figure 7-5). This huge desert, the largest in the world, runs from

trees by twig or bud, by grafting or budding. Therefore, any wild, unstable (though useful) freak, any helpless malformation like the navel orange which cannot reproduce itself, can be made into a million trees by the nurseryman. The parent tree of the Red Delicious variety of apple grew, by chance, in an Iowa fence row. . . .

Not only is the tree the great engine of production, but its present triumphant agricultural rivals, the grains, are really weaklings. . . .

Moreover the grains are *annual* plants. They must build themselves anew for each harvest. They may, therefore, become victims of the climatic peculiarities of a certain short season. It is rain in July that is so vital to the American corn crop. The rains of June cannot bring a good crop through. . . . Trees are much better able than the

cereals to use rain when it comes. They can store moisture much better than the annuals can store it, because they thrust their roots deep into the earth, seeking moisture far below the surface. They are able to survive drought better than the annual crops that grow beside them. . . . Trees living from year to year are a permanent institution, a going concern, ready to produce when their producing time comes.

Therefore, the crop-yielding tree offers the best medium for extending agriculture to hills, to steep places, to rocky places, and to the lands where rainfall is deficient. . . . When we develop an agriculture that fits this land, it will become an almost endless vista of green, crop-yielding trees. We will have plowed fields on the level hilltops and strip crops on the gentle slopes. The level valleys also will be plowed, but the steeper slopes

will be productive through crop trees and will be protected by them—a permanent form of agriculture. When we have done all this, posterity will have a chance.

Smith goes on to propose an Institute of Mountain Agriculture to create a whole new set of crop trees and to devise an agriculture based upon them. His institute would locate parent trees and hybridize them. Then the institute would test the new trees, setting up experimental farms. Smith envisioned orchards of shagbark hickory, shellbark hickory, pecan hickory, butternut, and black walnut trees, among others, for human use. He saw acorn-yielding oaks, honey locust trees, chestnut, persimmon, and mulberry trees providing food for animals.

Smith's book and proposal illustrate that the search for pathways to sustainable societies is not a new idea, but an idea whose time has finally arrived.

east to west across northern Africa. Geologic records indicate that similar droughts have occurred in this area at least six times since 1400 and may occur as often as three times in a century.

Like the total rainfall, and to some extent in synchrony with it, the toll of human life and suffering has waxed and waned in the region's past. As the populations continue to grow, however, humans begin to have an environmental effect that adds to and intensifies the effects of natural drought.

The result of 15 years of the latest drought in countries bordering the Sahara, where there is little or no extra food to tide people over and no money to buy food from somewhere else, has been famine (Figure 7-6). And, although seasonal rains fell on schedule for several years in the late 1980s, growing

populations continue to ask more of these fragile lands than they are capable of giving. More people require more intensive farming, more wood for cooking fires, and more land to graze their cattle.

Overgrazing and Burning of Rangeland. One of the major causes of desertification is stocking of rangeland with more cattle than the range can support. The animals strip the land of vegetation, leaving it bare to wind and water erosion.

In Africa, raising cattle (as opposed to native species) entails another problem: Cattle are not as resistant to drought. They require four times as much water as camels. Unlike desert animals, which respond to higher temperatures by decreased

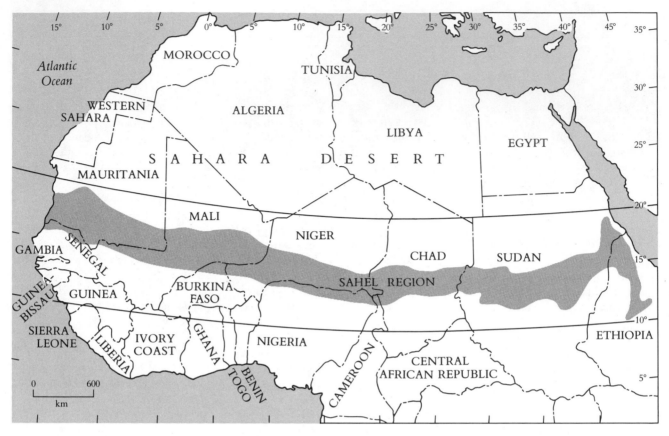

FIGURE 7-5 The Sahel. The lands on the borders of the Sahara desert are known as the *Sahel*, which translates loosely as *shore*.

urination of a higher concentration, cattle respond by increasing volume and decreasing concentration. Apparently they cool their bodies through increased water consumption. During drought they are thus more vulnerable than native species would be.

In the Sahel region, herders burn bushland in the belief that the new growth after a fire will provide tender green forage for wildlife and cattle, thus improving both hunting and grazing lands. If done regularly, however, this burning results in normal vegetation being replaced by grasslands, with few shrubs and trees, mostly pyrophytes—plants that have most of their mass underground rather than above ground. The general effects are a simplification of ecosystems, loss of nitrogen released by the burning itself, and loss of nutrient cycling previously accomplished by deep-rooted trees. Cattle graze on the grasses, reducing nutrients in the soil

until the range will support only goats and sheep and, finally, when desert results, only camels.

Agriculture. A second cause of desertification is intensive farming of marginally fertile arid lands. When farmers attempt to increase crop yields by eliminating traditional fallow periods, soil fertility can be exhausted. Again, the resulting bare land is subject to erosion by wind and water. Topsoil washes or blows away, leaving infertile subsoils or rock.

Firewood Gathering. A third contribution to desertification occurs when increasing human populations strip areas clean of firewood. In many developing nations wood is the major fuel for cooking. In the Ethiopian highlands, increasing populations have led to the elimination of fallow

FIGURE 7-6 Death from Starvation. Famine victim is borne by stretcher away from the camp at Bati, northeast of Addis-Ababa, in 1984. (*Photo:* John Isaac/UN)

periods on croplands, cultivation of steep slopes, and loss of forests to farmers and wood gatherers. The result is rocky deserts in the highlands, the extent of which have been greatly increased by the additional stress of the drought.

Political and Social Factors. In addition to population growth, political and social factors have in-

fluenced the spread of desertification in Africa. The lands of the western Sahel were inadvertently protected from human exploitation by raiding tribes from the thirteenth century to the early twentieth century. When colonial occupation made the area safe for herders and their cattle, agricultural populations moved northward into the Sahel, bringing their livestock. At the time the area was experiencing a relatively wet period. Thus, before the beginning of the current drought in 1968, the land appeared to support a greater number of cattle than it actually can.

The introduction of firearms in the sixteenth and seventeenth centuries led to a steady loss of wildlife in the area. Environmental consequences have been severe. Birds and herbivores involved in seed dispersal were killed at the same time as habitat losses due to agriculture and human settlements decreased the number of seeds to be dispersed. In forested areas, hunting eliminated wild carnivores and made wooded areas safe for grazing cattle, sheep, and goats. These animals, grazing and browsing in the forests, destroyed the habitats of native animals. They also decreased the ground cover, which captures rainfall and thus recharges groundwater, and eliminated wild plants formerly used by rural populations in times of drought.

Cities that have expanded or new ones that have been founded have put severe stress on the surrounding area to provide food and wood for fuel and construction.

Salinization. In more developed countries, such as the United States, desertification has resulted from overgrazing of rangeland and agricultural erosion, just as it has in the less developed countries. Another serious problem in the United States, which has occurred to a lesser extent in Africa, is **soil salinization.** Arid lands can be irrigated to allow growth of crops requiring more water than a region provides naturally. However, evaporation of pure water from irrigation water leaves behind water concentrated in salts. If this water does not drain away, it can build up to such an extent that plant growth is stunted. Further, an impermeable crust of salt may form over the soil surface. The Senegal Delta, the Niger Delta and Lake Chad Valley, and the Tigris-Euphrates Valley join the Imperial and San Joaquin valleys in the United States as subject to this type of salinization. Thousands of acres of once fertile cropland in the United States have been sterilized in this manner (Figure 7-7).

Groundwater Overuse. In the United States, desertification is also accelerated when groundwater is withdrawn faster than it can be recharged. As groundwater levels drop, native vegetation cannot

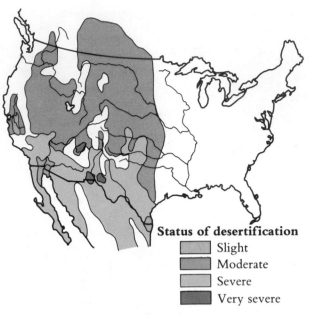

Status of desertification
- Slight
- Moderate
- Severe
- Very severe

FIGURE 7-7 Status of Desertification in Hot Arid Regions of the United States.

survive. To save water for the needs of people in western cities such as Tucson, Arizona, many acres of once irrigated farmland have been abandoned. Without natural cover, these lands are subject to wind erosion. In the lower Santa Cruz basin of Arizona, blowing dust from abandoned or idle fields has been so severe that at times it has caused highways to be closed.

It is clear that desertification is not a simple extension of the margins of desert due to drought. Rather, overuse of a relatively fragile environment appears to push the system past the point from which it can recover naturally, especially when further stressed by drought.

Consequences of Desertification

The consequences of desertification are severe: loss of soil fertility resulting in a reduced ability to grow food, clouds of atmospheric dust that interfere with radio transmission and cause respiratory diseases, and even the possibility that desertification itself prolongs drought.

This last consequence may result from two weather phenomena. Land stripped of vegetation

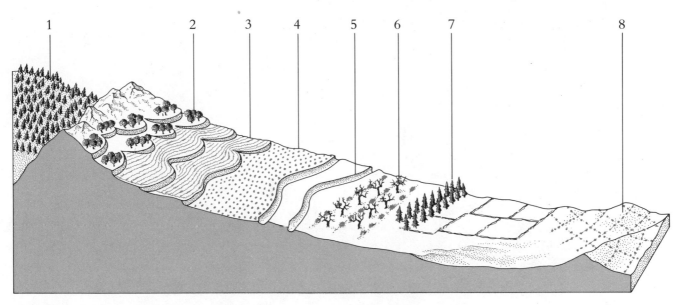

FIGURE 7-8 Eight Ways to Prevent Desertification. 1. Reforestation of slopes 2. growing tree crops on eyebrow terraces 3. growing crops on terraces 4. cultivating along the contour 5. building bunds to control runoff or planting moisture-conserving grasses (e.g., vetiver grass) 6. agroforestry 7. planting shelterbelts or windbreaks 8. stabilizing sand dunes

reflects more sunlight back into the atmosphere than land with a plant cover. This can cause more dry air to sink toward the earth. Secondly, the dust clouds that result when winds blow the desert soils into the air may stabilize wind currents and reduce rainfall.

According to U.N. estimates, 850 million people are threatened by the consequences of desertification today. One-fifth of the world's land area is now covered by desert, and that area continues to grow yearly.

Halting Desertification

Is there any hope for halting desertification and recovering land already degraded? A number of suggestions have been made, and some appear to hold promise (Figure 7-8).

Agricultural and Grazing Restrictions. On relatively level land, shelterbelts can break the force of winds that scour away soil. If the trees and shrubs planted in the shelterbelt are carefully chosen, they can provide food for humans and animals, and a wildlife habitat as well (Figure 7-9).

Grazing restrictions of some sort may be a necessity for arid lands and yet may be the most difficult kind of solution to impose. Often in the developing countries and on America's own Indian reservations, grasslands are exploited because people are too poor to have another choice. As populations increase, herds must increase to feed additional mouths. Rangeland is encroached upon by farming, causing remaining grasslands to be further overgrazed. The suggestion has been made that regional cooperatives based on existing local nongovernmental units (such as religious groups) might be given governance of specific land areas. This has been done successfully in Saudi Arabia and Syria where the ancient *hema* system of range reserves has been revived.

Agroforestry. Agroforestry is a mixture of herding or farming and the growing of woody plants on the same land. Such systems appear to hold great promise for arid and semi-arid lands. They allow more crops to be grown on the same amount of land, provide insurance against crop failures because more than one species is harvested,

FIGURE 7-9 **Sand Dune Fixation in Tunisia.** Sand dunes can be prevented from engulfing villages and roads by stabilizing them with plantings of drought-resistant trees or by establishing windbreaks made of dead branches and leaves. (*Photo:* T. Farkas/UNEP)

improve nutrient cycling, and improve the local microclimate.

Furthermore, the system is usually acceptable to local farmers. This last point is one of the most important in any consideration of methods for halting desertification or reclaiming wornout lands. Unless systems are economically appealing to local populations, they will have little chance of success. (See Chapter 9 for more on farming systems for arid lands.)

Comprehensive Plans. Desertification is the culmination of a series of environmental problems: overpopulation, erosion, salinization, drought, overgrazing, inappropriate farming methods. It does not occur instantaneously, and we should not expect it to be halted instantaneously. Rather, ef-

forts to address the various parts of the problem need long-term solutions. In 1977 the United Nations devised its Comprehensive Plan of Action to Combat Desertification. All of the ideas noted here were included in the plan. Yet, some 15 years later, U.N. observers report that the problem is worsening rather than improving. Why is that? Part of the answer is that developed countries have not funded the Plan to Combat Desertification at the level requested. Another part of the problem is that most of the developing countries involved have not taken the problem seriously enough to prepare national plans of action. Both of these problems can be remedied by public education as to the serious consequences of desertification.

Nonetheless, the underlying problem is still population growth. Increasing numbers of humans put intolerable pressures on fragile, semi-arid lands. This is the problem that must be addressed at the same time that we institute the more direct methods of combating desertification.

SUMMARY

Erosion is the loss of topsoil due to water or wind. New topsoil is formed slowly—at most, 1 inch every 100 to 1,000 years. Only 1 to 5 tons of soil per acre can be lost each year before a loss in productivity will result. In addition to lost productivity, erosion increases the chance of flooding from local streams, intensifies the effects of drought, makes plowing more difficult, decreases the capacity of reservoirs, and increases the organic matter and pesticide burdens of natural waters. Wind erosion also leads to decreased productivity and may result in dust storms. Erosion can be controlled by reduced or minimum tillage farming, crop rotation, contour plowing, terracing, and shelterbelts.

Desertification is a degradation of land so severe that it resembles desert. It results from drought combined with overuse of land by overgrazing, farming practices that lead to erosion, salinization, overuse of groundwater, and excessive firewood gathering. The consequences are severe: loss of soil fertility, dust storms, the prolongation of drought. In order to prevent desertification, it may be necessary to restrict agriculture and grazing in semi-arid areas, institute methods to prevent erosion, promote agroforestry schemes, and control population pressures on fragile lands.

Questions

1. If erosion lessens soil productivity, why are farmers so slow to adopt erosion control methods? What solutions do you see for this problem?
2. What is meant by *desertification*? Is it caused by drought?
3. What effect do you think global warming (Chapter 17) will have on desertification? Why?

Further Reading

Eisenberg, Evan. "Back to Eden," *The Atlantic Monthly*, November 1989, p. 57.

At least one scientist wants to revise the whole concept of agriculture. Read about Wes Jackson and his attempt to devise a system of agriculture based on the prairie ecosystem.

Hanley, M. L. "Anchoring the Dunes of Mauritania," *World Development*, March 1989, p. 10.

A few countries have begun attempts to combat desertification. Mauritania is one. This article details some of its successes.

Middleton, N. "Wind Erosion in the Sahel," *Geography Review*, 1(2) (November 1987), 26.

A well-written summary of the causes and consequences of desertification in Africa.

"Sands of Change," UNEP Environment Brief #2. United Nations Environment Programme, 1987.

This eight-page pamphlet is full of facts and figures about desertification.

References

Benbrook, C. M. "New Tools and Policies in the 1985 Farm Bill," *Water Science and Technology Board Newsletter*, 3(2) (March 1986).

Council on Environmental Quality. *Desertification of the United States*. Washington, D.C.: U.S. Government Printing Office, 1981.

Larson, W. E., et al. "The Threat of Soil Erosion to Long-Term Crop Production," *Science*, 219 (February 4, 1983), 458.

National Research Council. *Environmental Change in the West African Sahara*. Washington, D.C.: National Academy Press, 1983.

National Research Council. *Soil Conservation: Assessing the National Resources Inventory*. Committee on Conservation Needs and Opportunities, Board on Agriculture, National Research Council. Washington, D.C.: National Academy Press, 1986.

Nelson, R. "Dryland Management: The Desertification Problem," World Bank Technical Paper #116. Washington, D.C.: The World Bank, 1990.

Osuji, O., and O. Babalola. "Tillage Practices on a Tropical Soil," *Journal of Environmental Management*, 14 (1982), 343.

Smith, J. R. *Tree Crops: A Permanent Agriculture*. New York: Harper & Row, 1980.

Walden, J. H. *Soil Culture*. New York: Saxton, Barker, and Co., 1860.

Chapter 8

Pesticides

PESTICIDES AND FOOD PRODUCTION

Any material used to kill pests is called a **pesticide,** and usually any organism that competes with humans for food, fiber, or living space is called a pest. The use of chemicals to kill pests is not a new idea. For centuries, farmers have used minerals such as arsenic, lead, and mercury or natural plant substances such as pyrethrum (obtained from a daisy-like plant) to kill insects and other pests.

In 1945, however, a new era in pest control began, when DDT came into widespread use to control the lice and fleas that plagued the armies of World War II. DDT was the first widely used *synthetic* (laboratory-produced) pesticide. In the years that followed, many other synthetic pesticides were introduced. In a number of cases, spectacular increases in crop yields resulted where the new pesticides were used. By 1967, half of all the pesticides used were, like DDT, in the chemical family of chlorinated hydrocarbons. Slowly, however, evidence began to accumulate that the synthetic pesticides were a mixed blessing.

Biological Magnification

Problems with pesticides arose in three main areas. In the first place, certain pesticides* tend to accumulate in living organisms. In some cases, pesticides not only accumulate to levels greater than are found in the environment, but concentrations keep increasing as they move up food chains. This is the effect known as **biological magnification.**

DDT is an example of a pesticide that is magnified biologically. DDT is soluble in fat. When an organism ingests DDT—whether from water, from the detritus of plants that have been sprayed, or from insects that have eaten the plants—the DDT becomes concentrated in the organism's fatty parts. DDT is lost very slowly from these fatty tissues. If another creature in the food web eats the first organism, the consumer will be consuming a concentrated dose of DDT (Figure 8-1). Organisms at the top of their food chain (such as humans and predatory birds such as eagles and falcons) are eating foods with a much higher level of DDT than is

* Mainly, chlorinated hydrocarbons such as DDT and mercury-containing compounds.

generally present in the environment. One effect of such DDT levels on birds is that they lay eggs with shells that are much thinner than normal. These thin shells break easily and so are no protection for the developing chick inside the egg. In this way the Eastern peregrine falcon failed to reproduce and so became extinct in the 1960s (see Chapter 1).

Persistence

A second area of concern is the length of time pesticides remain in the soil or on crops after they are applied. The chlorinated hydrocarbons, such as DDT, and pesticides that contain arsenic, lead, or mercury are known as **persistent** pesticides. This means that they are not broken down within one growing season by sunlight or bacteria. The *half-life* of DDT, for instance, may be as long as 20 years. (That is, after 20 years, only one-half of an amount of DDT used has been broken down to simpler compounds.) Mercury and arsenic are never really broken down—they are moved around or buried in muds.

Persistent pesticides can build up in the soil if a farmer applies them year after year. In some orchards where lead arsenate has been used to control insects, arsenic in the soil has built up to a level that kills the fruit trees. The long life of persistent pesticides is a major factor in the process of **secondary contamination,** whereby foods that were never treated with pesticides still become contaminated. For example, DDT sticks to soil particles after it is applied. In many areas, dust storms have picked up this contaminated dust and blown it, literally, around the world. Rain washes this dust out of the air in places where pesticides and even farming are practically unknown. Thus seals, penguins, and fish in the Antarctic all show traces of DDT in their fat. In the 1960s, when DDT use was at its height, 40 tons of DDT were dumped on England every year in rainfall. In this way, pastures and crops of all kinds received an unintended and unwanted treatment with DDT.

Resistance

Biological magnification and persistence are not the only problems associated with the use of pesticides.

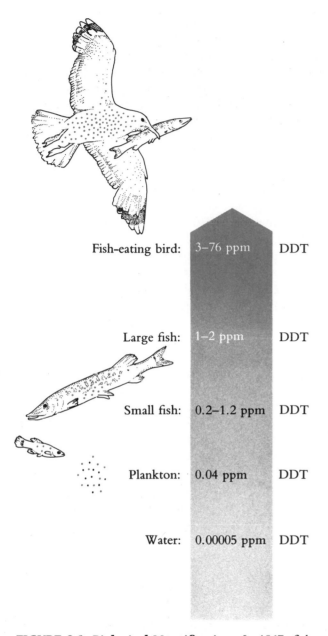

Fish-eating bird:	3–76 ppm	DDT
Large fish:	1–2 ppm	DDT
Small fish:	0.2–1.2 ppm	DDT
Plankton:	0.04 ppm	DDT
Water:	0.00005 ppm	DDT

FIGURE 8-1 Biological Magnification. In 1967, fish-eating birds from a Long Island salt marsh estuary contained almost a million times more DDT than could be found in the water. At each step of the food chain, DDT was concentrated, as organisms consumed and absorbed more DDT than they were able to excrete. If you are not familiar with the term *parts per million,* see inside back cover. (*Source:* Adapted from W. Keeton, *Biological Science*, 3rd ed. [New York: Norton, 1980])

A third serious problem is that pests can become **resistant** to pesticides—the pesticide will no longer kill them. This can come about because of mutations occurring in some of the enormous numbers of insects hatching each season. **Mutations** are changes in an organism's inherited genetic material, the material that determines the organism's characteristics.

A pesticide may kill off most of the insects in a certain area. However, a few that have mutated so that they have slightly different characteristics than the others may survive. These few can repopulate the sprayed area, passing on their pesticide resistance to their offspring. In some cases, pesticides themselves may cause the development of resistance by stimulating the production in pests of enzymes that act to break down pesticides. Those insects that have been stimulated to produce the largest amounts of the enzymes will be most likely to survive and reproduce. In several generations, insects with sufficient enzyme to break down any reasonable amount of pesticide will appear. This sort of effect has led to the development of houseflies resistant to all of the major types of pesticides used.

The commonly used "broad-spectrum" pesticides, which kill a wide variety of insects, make the development of resistance simpler. They not only ensure that the newly resistant insects will have little competition for food but also kill off many parasites and predators of insect pests. In fact, predators may receive a higher dose of pesticide than their prey because of biological magnification. Resistant insects are thus given a good chance to establish themselves, free from normal controls. In a number of cases, pesticides have created new pests in this manner. For instance, the ladybug normally controls a type of citrus scale insect. If an orchard is sprayed with DDT, however, the ladybugs are killed while the scale insect is not. The scale insect can then multiply unchecked and cause severe damage to the citrus crop.

In some cases, extensive use of pesticides has left farmers worse off than before. For instance, cotton has long been grown in Peru in the Cañete Valley. Before World War II, insects were controlled with arsenic and nicotine sulfate. Yields of cotton were about 470 bushels per acre (42.5 kl/ha). In 1949, crops were severely damaged by cotton bollworms and aphids, causing growers to try the new chlorinated hydrocarbon insecticides such as DDT and toxaphene. At first, it seemed to be a successful move. Yields nearly doubled. However, by 1955 the picture had changed. Not only had insect pests become resistant to synthetic insecticides, but new pests were appearing because the insecticides had killed off the beneficial insects that preyed on pests. Chemicals were unable to control insect populations, and by 1956 the cotton-growing industry had collapsed.

A similar sequence of events occurred in the Rio Grande Valley in Texas. By 1968, cotton pests were resistant to all available insecticides. Despite as many as 15–20 treatments with all possible combinations of pesticides, many fields were totally lost due to insect damage (but see Figure 8-2).

Even the successful public health uses of pesticides are threatened by insect resistance. In many countries, walls inside houses are sprayed with DDT and dieldrin (see Figure 8-3). For months after the spraying, mosquitoes that land on the walls are killed. In this way, diseases like malaria and yellow fever, which are spread by mosquitoes, can be controlled. Worldwide, malaria is the largest single cause of death and debilitation. In the 1950s, campaigns to eradicate malaria were begun. Based mainly on spraying with chemical pesticides such as DDT, the campaigns were at first successful. However, the mosquitoes became resistant to DDT and then to propoxur, the spray that replaced DDT. Now cases of malaria are once more on the rise. In 1955, when eradication programs began, 250 million cases were reported and 2.5 million people died. By 1965, only 107 million cases were reported, but in 1976, the number rose to 150 million, and by 1989 270 million people were infected. Furthermore, the malarial parasite is becoming resistant to drugs used to treat the disease itself.

Between 1970 and 1980 the number of insects resistant to pesticides doubled from 224 to 428.

In line with the development of insect resistance to insecticides, weeds are becoming resistant to her-

FIGURE 8-2 The Boll Weevil. Cotton growing has resumed in the Rio Grande Valley in Texas as a result of integrated pest management methods. Short-season cotton, which matures before boll weevil populations become large, cultural techniques such as destroying crop residues, and the use of small amounts of insecticides control pests without destroying beneficial insects or causing pest resistance to develop. In 1985, using a similar set of methods, USDA reported that it had reduced the boll weevil population in North and South Carolina to the point where economic damage to cotton was negligible. (*Photo:* Lewis Riley, USDA)

FIGURE 8-3 Spraying House Walls with DDT. In countries where malaria is common, house walls are sprayed with DDT to kill the mosquitos that carry the malarial parasite. (*Photo:* United Nations)

bicides. In 1968, the first herbicide-resistant weed was discovered. Resistant weeds are rare in fields never treated with herbicides. However, as the use of herbicides has increased, a result of more farmers practicing reduced tillage farming, herbicide-resistant weeds are becoming more common.

Soil Microbes and Pesticides

A fourth problem has only recently been recognized. In the late 1970s, scientists trying to find out why certain pesticides worked well at first but slowly became ineffective discovered they were not dealing with resistant weeds or insects but rather with soil microbes that break down pesticides. These microbes adapt to pesticide chemicals so they can break down, or use them, making the pesticides useless in controlling weeds or insects.

To summarize, synthetic chemical pesticides have not proven to be as easy to use nor as beneficial as was originally hoped. Insects and other pests such as rats have shown the ability to develop resistance to chemical pesticides. While pesticides that are persistent can accumulate from year to year in the soil and in the muds at the bottom of lakes and rivers, other pesticides are broken down by soil microorganisms before they can kill pests.

Further, fat-soluble pesticides absorbed from water, grass, or crops become concentrated in the milk and body fat of many animals, including humans, at the level of parts per million or parts per billion.

PESTICIDES AND HUMAN HEALTH

Besides concern about the effectiveness of pesticides against pests and worries about the effect of pesticides on nontarget wildlife species, there is concern about the effect of pesticides on human health. Many pesticides are extremely toxic to humans. These materials pose a hazard to workers applying them, especially if they do not wear protective clothing (Figure 8-4). Furthermore, pesticides may become a contaminant in water or food consumed by humans.

Pesticides in Food

How do pesticides, toxic chemicals intended to kill pests, get into food? In many cases, small amounts of pesticides used to treat crops or animals remain on produce or in meat when they are marketed. These small amounts are called **residues.** Certain government regulations state exactly how high residues can legally be and list procedures that must be followed to keep residues below the legal limit.

In other cases, however, foods become contaminated with pesticides that were not even used on food crops. This is a process of secondary contamination in which pesticides in dust or rain land on food crops. For instance, most food products from animals (milk, meat, cheese) contain measurable amounts of the pesticide DDT. This comes about because of widespread contamination of the environment with DDT, which is picked up and blown around the world on dust particles. Rain washes DDT out of the air and onto pastureland. Grazing cattle eat DDT-contaminated grass and incorporate the DDT into their meat and milk.

Pesticide Use in the United States

Regulation. The Environmental Protection Agency (EPA) is responsible for protecting people in the United States from the risks involved in using

FIGURE 8-4 Spraying Without Protective Clothing. Many workers in developing countries do not wear enough protective clothing when spraying pesticides. This is sometimes because they do not understand the need for such clothing, but it is also because the design of protective clothing rarely takes into account the hot and humid conditions common in many such countries. (*Photo:* F. Botts/UN/FAO)

pesticides. The most recent major pesticides law, passed in 1972 and amended in 1988, is the Federal Insecticides, Fungicides and Rodenticides Act, or FIFRA. Under this law, manufacturers must supply the EPA with data showing that a pesticide they wish to sell is effective against pests and will not harm humans or the environment. If the EPA is satisfied with the data, it will register the pesticide. In some cases a **tolerance** is allowed. That is, a certain amount of pesticide residue may safely remain on food or feed when it is marketed. If the EPA later finds that a pesticide is hazardous to human health or the environment, it can suspend or cancel the registration for the pesticide.

Regulation of pesticides has proven to be a major problem for the EPA. By 1976, $2.4 billion in pesticides were sold every year. By 1984 this had grown to $3.3 billion. Industries on this scale have political muscle. Industry and other special-interest groups are almost certain to challenge regulations through lawsuits and by stimulating Congressional pressure to reverse decisions. For instance, when aldrin/dieldrin was suspended, both Shell Oil (the manufacturer) and the Environmental Defense Fund (EDF) filed suit, because neither group was happy with the decision (although for exactly opposite reasons).

This sort of pressure has, to some extent, caused a situation in which the EPA seems to make regulations only when it is forced into complying with toxic substances laws by lawsuits brought by public interest groups.

The House Commerce Committee has been critical of the EPA's tolerance-setting program. In many cases, pesticide tolerances have been set without all the needed information. On pesticides registered more than 10 years ago, there is a lack of information on carcinogenicity and data on birth defects and mutations. Furthermore, the EPA relies on safety data supplied by the pesticide manufacturer. The committee, noting that the manufacturer is hardly a disinterested party, suggests that a better program to check the accuracy of such data is needed. A major provision in the 1988 amendments is that EPA reregister the active ingredients in all pesticides approved before 1972.

The Delaney Amendment. The Federal Food Drug and Cosmetic Act contains a section that directs that no chemicals that cause cancer may be added to foods. This clause, known as the Delaney amendment, has far-reaching effects. It was responsible for the ban on the artificial sweetener saccharin, a ban that was overturned by Congress after vast public outcry. The clause is also the basis for a large part of the regulation of pesticide residues in foods. If any portion of a crop to which a carcinogenic pesticide has been applied is processed in a way that will concentrate residues of the pesticide, the EPA's current policy is not only to deny a tolerance for the pesticide on the raw commodity but to deny registration for the pesticide. Some people feel that this strict interpretation of the De-

laney amendment, which allows no room for the consideration of possible benefits from the pesticide compared to the risk it presents the consumer, is unfair. (See Controversy 8-1.)

Testing for Pesticides in Food. The U.S. Department of Agriculture is responsible for checking that meat and poultry do not contain more than the legally allowed residue of hazardous chemicals such as pesticides, drugs (such as antibiotics or hormones), and other substances (such as lead or mercury). The Food and Drug Administration (FDA) checks all foods except meat and poultry. The FDA is also the agency that is supposed to actually take contaminated foods off the market if the USDA or FDA monitoring programs find excessive residues. In addition, the FDA can prosecute growers for sending contaminated food to market.

However, neither the FDA nor USDA monitors all shipments of food or all toxic substances known to occur as residues in food. This is partly a matter of economics. Both agencies rely mainly on tests that detect whole groups of chemicals at one time. The tests for some chemicals are difficult and take a great deal of time to carry out. Furthermore, in some cases there are no good tests for a particular chemical.

Pesticides in Imported Foods. Although the FDA has a monitoring program to detect harmful substances in imported food, the program is too small to sample more than a tiny percentage of food imports. In 1982, the FDA took one sample out of every 200 million pounds of imported oranges, every 8 million pounds of imported grapes, every 4 million pounds of imported tomatoes, and every 5 million pounds of imported coffee. A 1986 study showed FDA sampled less than 1% of imported produce shipments.

Even then, FDA tests do not check for the presence of some commonly used pesticides that are banned in the United States but used overseas, such as the suspected carcinogens EDB and DBCP. In general, tests detect only half of the kinds of pesticides that may be used on imported foods.

Controversy 8-1

Alar and the Delaney Amendment

One has to conclude that the publicity Alar got really had nothing to do with the science.

Gary Flamm, private
toxicology consultant

You have to view these risk assessments as understatements.

Lawrie Mott, NRDC
staff scientist

The Delaney amendment, which directs that no chemicals proven to cause cancer may be added to foods, played a part in the controversy over the chemical Alar. Alar can be sprayed on apples to slow ripening, and it was widely used in the United States in the 1980s. An environmental organization, Natural Resources Defense Council (NRDC), targeted Alar as a dangerous chemical in the 1970s when studies first indicated that it might be carcinogenic—that is, it might cause cancer. Because the studies were inconclusive, the Environmental Protection Agency did not act to prohibit the use of Alar on apples, but instead commissioned more studies.

Before these studies were finished, NRDC made public a report about hazardous chemicals in food that specifically branded Alar a health risk for children, who commonly consume more apple products than adults. The resulting publicity caused a temporary drop in the market for apples and apple products and led the manufacturer of Alar, Uniroyal, to withdraw the chemical from use in the United States.

Further studies have neither clearly confirmed nor denied Alar's health risk. EPA regulators feel new studies still label Alar a carcinogen. Thus, according to the Delaney amendment, it cannot be used on apples because it would later be found in foods processed from the apples, such as juice. A United Nations panel, however, did not feel the studies indicated that Alar presented much of a health risk and recommended a relatively high tolerance for Alar in foods.

This scientific uncertainty about the actual hazard presented by Alar has led a group of U.S. apple growers to sue NRDC for the lost sales that resulted from what they call NRDC's unwarranted attack on Alar.

NRDC notes that apple crops are at record high levels and apple growers seem to be doing very well without Alar. For this reason, and because people are exposed to many chemicals in their environment that may interact in unknown ways, the organization still feels that the possible risks Alar presents are not worth the minor benefits of its use.

Several issues are highlighted by this controversy. When should the public be alerted to the possible hazards of a chemical? Should we wait until final results are obtained before making this decision? Are chemicals "innocent until proven guilty?" Does the Delaney amendment serve a useful purpose in protecting people from carcinogens and their possible interaction? Or does the amendment unnecessarily hamper regulators by viewing chemical carcinogens as uniformly harmful rather than as substances with risks and benefits that must be weighed and balanced?

Sources: All quotes are from "News and Comment," *Science, 254,* (October 4, 1991), 20.

Ironically, the source of much of the pesticides used in developing countries is the United States itself, because it is not illegal for U.S. manufacturers to ship banned pesticides overseas. Tougher laws on pesticide use in the United States have led to new higher-priced, low-toxicity pesticides being sold in the United States while the older, lower-priced, more toxic and persistent pesticides are exported. The United States supplies 30% of the pesticides used worldwide, approximately one-third of

FIGURE 8-5 Nicaraguan Children Bathing in a Pesticides Barrel. (*Photo:* Don Cole and Doug Murray/Red, Green, Black and Blue Photos)

which consist of products that are not approved for use in the United States.

Pesticide Use in Developing Countries

Not only are pesticides that are considered too dangerous for use in the United States being used in developing countries, but the pesticides are often misused or misapplied by workers who are unaware of the risks involved. In Nigeria, large drums of pesticides are delivered to fields where they are often left in the open, under intense sun and torrential rains. "Some or all of the labels, including instructions for use, are washed off. Some containers get rusty and leak pesticides that may leach down to the groundwater . . ." (Atuma and Okor, 1985). In Ecuador, pesticides are usually sold without instructions for use or with instructions that farm workers are not likely to understand. "Many farm workers are poorly educated, and often illiterate. They commonly think of pesticides as a medicine which is used to cure plants of the diseases caused by insects or other pests. As a result there is a total lack of awareness that pesticides are poisons which can, if improperly used, harm their

health and their environment" (Sevilla, 1984) (Figure 8-5).

Protective devices such as waterproof clothing and respirators are often not available in developing countries or are not affordable. In tropical climates, workers find it difficult to work while wearing heavy clothing or goggles and so forgo such protection. And when pesticide workers do wear heavy clothing, it may be all they own and, as is the case with the heavy wool clothing worn by workers in the mountains of Ecuador, it may not be washed after being worn to spray pesticides. Finally, in the small one- or two-room houses where workers live, they often have no place to store pesticides out of the reach of children or animals.

In Nigeria, empty pesticide containers are dumped into rivers and streams or, worse, are used to store drinking water. In some cases, pesticides are even used as medicines. In rural areas, γ-HCH, a member of the DDT family, is used to cure people of intestinal worms.

In April 1985 the World Bank and the U.S. Agency for International Development, two agencies that fund a major portion of agricultural development projects in developing nations, adopted

---

Towards a Sustainable Society

Durable and Environmentally Friendly Pest Management
by Thomas R. Odhiambo

Dr. Thomas R. Odhiambo is founder and director of the International Centre of Insect Physiology and Ecology in Nairobi, Kenya. He is also a founder of the International Commission on Food and Peace and was awarded the Albert Einstein Medal by UNESCO.

Fifty years after the discovery of the potent chemical powers of DDT to control insects by killing them and the subsequent dawn of the Age of Pesticides for what promised to be the final solution to insect pests by the use of synthetic chemical poisons, we are almost where we were at the beginning of World War II. While the size of the pesticide industry is substantial worldwide, standing at nearly $20 billion U.S. in 1988, resistance to pesticides has dramatically increased since the early 1950s when the phenomenon became generally known. The worldwide preharvest losses due to insects, weeds, and plant diseases have not substantially changed since that time, standing at about 36% of potential yield, and post-harvest losses are stable at an additional 14%.

Several carefully designed experiments carried out between 1965 and 1989 in the United States have suggested that one can reduce pesticide use by as much as 35 to 50% without concomitantly reducing crop yields. Since 1945 the use of synthetic pesticides in the United States has grown 33-fold, now totaling some 350,000 tons annually. It is estimated that the social and environmental damage from the overuse of pesticides in the United States is costing the public at least $1 billion U.S. a year—to replace poisoned pollinators, to offset the loss of natural enemies, and to fund the increased application of pesticides in the light of increased pest resistance to chemical pesticides. Such acute environmental impacts in other parts of the world have led several nations to enact laws for a progressive reduction of pesticide use within 5 to 10 years. Sweden, for instance, passed a law in 1988 to reduce pesticide use by 50% within 5 years, and the Netherlands is developing a scheme to reduce pesticide use by 50% in 10 years.

strict new guidelines for pesticide use, handling, and storage.

In the long run, the real solution to pesticide problems in developing countries and in the United States lies in decreased use of pesticides and increased use of other methods of pest control such as the techniques of *integrated pest management (IPM)*. For example, in Ibadan, Nigeria, tiny South American wasps in capsules are dropped to prey on mealybugs that threaten the cassava, an especially important crop that withstands the drought now affecting Africa.

This type of solution offers hope for both the victims of pesticide use in developing nations and the unsuspecting consumers in the United States. But in light of low literacy levels and the relative

One can envisage the marginalization of poisonous chemicals as a pest management strategy by the end of the current decade. Then one can echo Rachel Carson's words in *Silent Spring*, when she cried out bitterly 29 years ago, "How could intelligent beings seek to control a few unwanted species by a method that contaminated the entire environment and brought the threat of disease and death to their own kind?" The World beyond Silent Spring will be a very different pest management world.

It will be a world in which what is critical in a pest is not its population size but the actual economic losses it brings about. Pest management will not be synonymous with keeling over and being dead; it will be a silent but continuing battle of hide-and-seek so as to retain for the human population the section of the crop yield that it regards as its own. Translated into an actual scenario, this rational pest management strategy will be more demanding, more knowledge-intensive, more answerable to sustainability and to environmental sensitivity.

An instance in which this future-oriented strategy can be tested under a large-scale circumstance is the possible sustainable control of the age-old scourge, the desert locust. Its ravages pepper Biblical accounts and continue to destabilize locust-affected countries from time to time, as it did in Africa's Sahelian zone during 1986–1989. The classical approach for attempting control since the 1940s is to locate, from aerial surveys and surveillance, the sites of aggregating breeding locusts and to spray them with highly poisonous chemicals while they are still on the ground. If the locusts do escape and form into migrating swarms, they are tracked all day and bombarded with insecticides while roosting at night in their staging locations. Although such tactics are dramatic in their immediate effect, in fact many swarms escape detection, and numerous locust populations remain in their rather inaccessible and scattered breeding grounds. Furthermore, we know little of the factors that lead to the ebbing of the swarming behavior at the very end of the locust outbreak, nor of the factors that originally lead to the multiplication, crowding, and eventual swarming and migration. Most years the locusts remain in their breeding areas in solitary, dispersed state—behaving, if you like, like nonswarming grasshoppers.

A year ago a long-term research project was initiated under the auspices of the International Centre of Insect Physiology and Ecology (ICIPE), based in Nairobi, Kenya, to undertake an in-depth study of the natural biochemicals responsible for the switch from solitary behavior to gregariousness and swarming; those regulating sexual maturation and its synchronization during the gregarization process; those that regulate synchronized and communal egg-laying; the process of marching of the non-adult nymphs and its semiochemical regulation; and the biochemical control of solitarization after a spate of swarming. It is believed that these behavior-modifying semiochemicals are at the heart of the emerging rational control of the desert locust. The strategy is to control the desert locust by permanently modifying its behavior so that it remains a grass-eating insect, domiciled in its home range, rarely if ever swarming away to new pastures.

poverty in developing countries, it may take decades or longer for such integrated pest management techniques to be adopted. (See Controversy 8-2.)

The Organic Farming Solution

If pesticides are now seen as a somewhat tarnished miracle, what might be a better strategy in growing food and fiber? One possibility is to apply no synthetic pesticides at all and to use only manure or special crops for fertilizer. This is, of course, **organic farming.** Once the only possible type of agriculture, organic farming became associated with health-food faddists and back-to-nature cultists after the development of synthetic pesticides and fertilizers. Today organic farming is often viewed as a fine ideal for the home gardener but not a reasonable

Controversy 8-2

Should the United States Sell Dangerous Pesticides Overseas?

In a world of growing food interdependence, we cannot export our hazards and then forget them. There is no refuge.

D. Weir and M. Shapiro

It is simply ridiculous to suggest that my country can be or should be able to undertake the extensive testing analysis and reviews which are carried out in the U.S. in order to decide whether or not to allow the use of a pesticide. . . . To a Latin American our concern about the export of banned pesticides is not much different than the United States' concern about exports from Latin America of cocaine and marijuana.

Roque Sevilla, president of an environmental protection organization in Ecuador

For Nigeria and all developing countries, pesticide use is indispensable to the struggle against hunger and disease. Emphasis should be placed on judicious and safe use rather than the barring and/or restriction of pesticides.

Samuel Atuma, chemistry professor, University of Benin, Nigeria

Risks and benefits must be balanced differently in a nation on the edge of famine.

John E. Davies, Department of Epidemiology and Public Health, University of Miami

The United States currently sells overseas some pesticides that are banned in the United States (except for public health emergencies), including DDT, aldrin, dieldrin, heptachlor, and chlordane. In 1976, several environmental groups successfully sued to prevent any sale of these unregistered pesticides that involved the use of money from the U.S. Agency for International Development. Chemical companies can still ship unregistered pesticides and other countries can still buy them, however, as long as they don't use U.S.A.I.D. money. Ten percent of U.S. pesticide production consists of unregistered or banned products destined for overseas markets.

What do you think? Should we allow sales to other countries of pesticides we restrict severely in our own country? Do we have the right to make this decision for other people? Do we have the responsibility? What about the argument that if we do not sell pesticides to other countries, someone else will?

Sources: D. Weir and M. Shapiro, "The Circle of Poison," *The Nation* (November 15, 1980); R. Sevilla, "Pesticides South of the Border," *The Amicus Journal,* Winter 1984, p. 12; S. Atuma, "Pesticide Usage in Nigeria," *Ambio* 14(6) (December 1985), 340; J. Davies, *Technology Review,* November/December 1984, p. 72.

goal for large-scale farmers. In 1971, Earl Butz, then Secretary of Agriculture, said in an interview, "Before we go back to an organic agriculture in this country, somebody must decide which 50 million Americans we are going to let starve or go hungry." Nonetheless, evidence is accumulating that in some situations, and when properly carried out, organic farming may be a match for what is now called conventional farming—that is, using synthetic pesticides and fertilizers (see Controversy 8-3).

The USDA estimates that if no pesticides at all were used in the United States, farmers would lose some 70% of their crops to pests, but other experts do not agree with this figure. Professor David Pimentel (1978) of Cornell University counters that one study of organic farming in the corn belt seemed to show that yields of corn and soybeans were almost as good as on conventional farms (corn yields were about 10% lower and soybean yields about 5% lower). However, wheat yields were as

Controversy 8-3

Organic Gardening Economics

You would never have believed it—we outyielded our neighbors by 100% or better on everything.

K. C. Livermore, Nebraska
organic farmer

. . . The result of abandoning the use of pesticides? . . . Silent Autumn.

ChemEcology, January 1978

Although most agriculturists remain unbelievers, a small but growing number of people believe that even large farms can be run, profitably, without synthetic pesticides and fertilizers. The high prices of fertilizer and pesticides, due partly to the energy crunch, have led many farmers to experiment with using fewer synthetic chemicals.

K. C. Livermore, a Nebraska farmer, grows alfalfa, oats, soybeans, and corn on 260 acres (104 hectares). He says:

We've done much better without chemicals. We hurt some at first when we switched over because we had to get the soil back in balance, get the poisons worked out of it. But in our

fourth year there was a big turn-around and now we're outyielding our "chemical neighbors" by far.

Mr. Livermore says about insect and weed problems:

We don't have an insect problem like our chemical neighbors do. We don't have an altered plant. Our plants are natural and healthy. They pick up antibiotics from the soil, which turns insects away as nature intended. And we have insects, like ladybugs, which fight off the enemy insects. Ladybugs thrive on our farm.

Also, as soon as you get natural, healthy soil, there isn't any weed problem. Nature puts in weeds to protect the soil. Weeds grow down in the soil and pick up trace minerals, and as they die they deposit these minerals on the soil's surface.

And when you have your soil in balance, weeds just don't grow as fast and you don't grow as many of them. Another thing is that when we used chemicals we had a clotty soil. Now it will run through your hands just like flour at times. Earthworms and other life in the soil are alive

and can loosen it. It's easy to push the weeds right over when we cultivate.

Dow Chemical, on the other hand, has published a book, *Silent Autumn*, that describes the plagues of Biblical times as well as a variety of famines caused by uncontrolled pests in recent years. The book emphasizes the idea that careful use of pesticides is necessary to feed people in an ever more crowded world.

For the experimenting organic farmers, though, K. C. Livermore sums it up:

We'd like to see this thing get turned around. . . . We'd like to see the wildlife and the birds back here like it was in the 1940s and 50s. Is that a profitable way to farm? You bet it is. We use one-fourth less input and get as much or more back than anybody else. That should be real easy to calculate in your mind. . . .

Sources: All quotes from *EPA Journal*, March 1978, pp. 24–25.

much as 25% lower on organic farms. When energy cost savings on organic farms were taken into account, profits were almost the same for both kinds of farming.

Pimentel (1991) further argues that the use of crop varieties resistant to pests, and other non-

chemical techniques—such as changing the kinds of crops grown in different areas—could allow U.S. farmers to cut pesticide use in half with only a 0.6% increase in food costs, and no decrease in yields. According to a 1989 report by the National Research Council, some 5% of U.S. crops are al-

Towards a Sustainable Society

Reducing Pesticide Use in the Home Environment

by Russell J. Balge

Russell Balge has degrees in both agriculture and horticulture. He has been the Baltimore County Commercial and Home Horticulture Agent since 1973. He has won numerous awards for his public education programs in plant science and culture.

Each year, homeowners use billions of pounds of fungicides, insecticides, and miticides. I would like to propose some practical cultural means of (1) altering the plants' susceptibility to insects and diseases, (2) modifying the environment so that it does not as readily predispose plants to insects and diseases, and (3) reducing the availability of insects and diseases, as alternatives to this heavy use of pesticides.

Select a sunny, somewhat breezy, well-drained planting site. Such a site guarantees a rapid drying of the foliage, deterring moisture-loving foliar pathogens and reducing crown and root rots. Prepare the soil properly for planting. Incorporate large amounts of organic matter, test the soil, modify the soil pH, and add the necessary nutrients. Organic matter helps hold moisture, adds nutrients as it biodegrades, and helps retain existing and added positively charged nutrient ions by virtue of its own weak negative charge. Organic matter also improves soil structure, increasing oxygen penetration and water percolation and encouraging greater root depth. The humic acids absorbed by plants from organic matter breakdown aid plants in the synthesis of enzymes necessary for protein formation and improved plant vigor. A proper pH guarantees that soil nutrients will be available to the plants.

Grow those species and cultivars of plants with natural resistance. Over eons, plants have evolved many chemical and physical barriers that make them naturally dis-

ready grown without the use of synthetic chemicals or with reduced use of such chemicals.

Integrated Pest Management and Biological Controls

A second possibility is to use small amounts of synthetic pesticides in combination with a variety of other techniques to control pests. This solution is called IPM (for integrated pest management). The farmer practicing IPM chooses from a variety of pest-control methods, including:

- Cultural practices, such as plowing, disposing of crop wastes at the end of the season, crop rotation
- Planting resistant crops
- Scouting for the actual presence of pests
- Selective use of pesticides

Cultural Techniques and Resistant Crops. Before synthetic pesticides were invented, farmers used many cultural practices to reduce insect damage. Some of these old techniques and some newly

tasteful, unattractive, or indigestible to insects and resistant to pathogens. Consider using native plants or their derivatives in the landscape. Native plants may not be as "exotic," but they have withstood the test of time.

Make every effort to maintain your plants in good vigor. Research has shown that when plants that produce allelopathic or protective chemicals are grown under the most ideal conditions, they produce higher amounts of these chemicals. Water infrequently but deeply, feed the plants when they need to be fed, and space the plants far enough apart to allow the foliage to dry by evening. Do not replant the same kind of plant into the same site where a similar plant died without replacing and/or treating the soil. Mulch to conserve soil moisture, moderate soil temperature, inhibit weeds, and, in the vegetable garden, reduce contact between the fruit and the soil.

Eliminate weeds so that they do not act as hosts for insects and diseases. At the same time, remember that some weeds shelter the predators and parasites of many garden pests. As a compromise, grow a hedgerow of native grasses and wildflowers.

Avoid planting large blocks of the same species or cultivars together to avoid a disease running rampant or an insect easily finding all of the identical plants. In the vegetable garden avoid planting members of the same plant family together, such as eggplant, pepper, potato, and tomato, all members of the *Solanaceae*.

Practice crop rotation in the vegetable garden and grow different flowers in the same flower bed from year to year to prevent the buildup of soil-dwelling insects and diseases that attack certain plants.

I remain skeptical of companion planting as no legitimate research has yet to show more nutritious or insect-free produce in the vegetable garden as a result of it. Trap plants, with the possible exception of marigolds for nematodes, may actually serve as a springboard for an insect attack on other plants.

Rototill the soil in the fall to expose insects and their eggs to birds and to improve the soil structure, courtesy of the alternate wetting and drying and freezing and thawing of the soil during the winter months. At the same time, practice good sanitation. Relentlessly rogue out and destroy diseased, damaged, or dead plants. Do not prune when foliage or stems are wet. Bury, burn, compost, or dispose of all plant refuse.

At the same time that you are following the above cultural practices, monitor the home grounds for pest problems and then respond to them in an environmentally conscious manner should they reach an unacceptable level. Once a pest problem is discovered, spot-treat it with short-lived, biorational, natural pesticides such as horticultural oils, soaps, bacteria, or nematodes that do not impact beneficial populations of natural predators and parasites. Use synthetic, long-lasting, nonselective pesticides only as a last resort, and then only on a spot-treatment basis.

developed ones are very useful. A book published in 1860 lists this control for apple worms:

The insect that produces this worm lays its egg in the blossom-end of the young apple. That egg makes a worm that passes down about the core and ruins the fruit. Apples so affected will fall prematurely and should be picked up and fed to swine. This done every day during their falling, which does not last a great while, will remedy the evil in two seasons. The worm that crawls from the fallen apple gets into crevices in rough bark, and spins his cocoon, in which he remains till the following spring. (Walden, 1860, p. 22)

Plowing alone can destroy up to 98% of the corn earworm pupae that winter in the soil. Rotating the kinds of crops grown in a field each season, or mixing crops in a field rather than growing large fields of the same kind of crop year after year, can prevent the buildup of pests. Destroying crop residues after harvest destroys the winter home of pests such as the boll weevil. By growing certain

(a)

(b)

FIGURE 8-6 Insect Traps. (*a*) A scout collects insects from a trap in a field. The trap serves as an early warning of insect pests for farmers in the area. (*Photo:* USDA) (*b*) Technician in Burkina Faso checks a tsetse fly trap. (*Photo:* FAO/J. Van Acker)

kinds of hedgerows around fields, a farmer can increase the number of predatory insects in a field, leading to better control of the plant-eating insects that damage crops.

Some plant varieties have been bred so that they are resistant to major insect pests. In some cases, this has been accomplished by breeding plants that look or taste unattractive to pests. Wheat resistant to Hessian fly has been available for 30 years. As with pesticides, however, new insect mutants may develop and begin to attack the resistant species, making it necessary to again breed new crop varieties.

Monitoring and Treatment. In integrated pest management, farmers must carefully monitor their crops to watch for the beginnings of insect attacks. Traps baited with a variety of substances lure insects and give the farmers early warning of a pest invasion (Figure 8-6). Only when something must be done to prevent serious crop damage do the farmers choose a pest-control treatment. This need not be a chemical spray in all cases, since a number of methods of biological pest control are known.

Biological Controls and Use of Natural Biochemicals. Investigations of how insects reproduce and how they interact with each other have identified several points at which humans can interfere in order to reduce insect damage to crops (Table 8-1). For example, insects produce chemical substances called *pheromones*. Some pheromones are

TABLE 8-1 Biological Control Techniques

Control by other organisms
Parasites

Predators

Pathogens

Reproductive control
Release of sterile insects

Use of chemical sterilants

Release of incompatible pest strains

Hormones
Pheromones or other behavioral chemicals

sex attractants, which help insects find mates; other pheromones mark paths to food sources. If large amounts of a pheromone can be obtained, it can be used to bait traps. This has been done with the gypsy moth, whose sex-attractant pheromone has been artificially synthesized. Traps baited with pheromone can be used either to catch insects and kill them with a poison or to give early warning of a pest's appearance in the field.

Insects and weeds are sometimes imported from other countries without their natural parasites, predators, or diseases. Such pests may then spread unchecked and cause great damage. Successful attempts have been made to control many of these undesirable immigrants, as well as some native pests, by introducing parasites, predators, and diseases. For instance, a tiny wasp, *Trichogramma,* controls cotton bollworms by parasitizing bollworm eggs. Two kinds of leaf-eating beetles have been able to keep Klamath weed, once a serious problem in California, under control. In such cases, of course, it is necessary to determine in advance that the new species will not begin to eat crops or kill desirable insects if it runs out of pests.

Bacteria that attack only pest species also can be used as a control measure. Bacteria causing milky-spore disease will kill Japanese beetles and can be applied much like a synthetic insecticide.

Certain kinds of insects can be grown in large numbers and then sterilized by radiation or chem-

icals. Sterile males of these species, when released, mate in the wild with normal females, but the females then lay eggs that do not hatch. Screw worms have been eliminated from several Caribbean islands and the United States by the release of sterile males. Mediterranean fruit flies are partially controlled in California and Florida by the release of sterile flies. However, not all insects can be grown artificially in large enough numbers, or sterilized easily enough, to use this method (Figure 8-7).

Economics of IPM. For a number of crops, integrated pest management is cheaper than conventional techniques, which involve spraying with chemicals at regular intervals. Even though farmers must pay to have their crops monitored, cotton, apples, and citrus fruits all can be grown more economically using IPM methods. The savings are mainly due to the use of less chemical spray, although yields are sometimes increased as well. In one example, 600 acres (243 hectares) of California tomatoes were being sprayed with chemicals four or five times a season, at a cost of $20–$30 per acre ($50–$75 per hectare). In spite of this, fruit worms continued to damage the crop. A company specializing in IPM was able to control the fruit worms as well as reduce costs to $8–$10 an acre ($20–$25 per hectare), and during the second year of the program, no chemical sprays were necessary at all. As the costs of fertilizer and pesticides go up due to fossil fuel shortages, the savings in such IPM programs will become more and more attractive.

In a similar way, the use of a biological form of pest control may prove much less expensive than repeated spraying with costly chemicals. Even in developing countries, biological control methods, such as the release of parasites, are being tried. Experts hope such methods will prove cheaper than chemicals and also less harmful to people and the environment in developing countries.

Low-Impact Sustainable Agriculture

Similar to IPM, but more comprehensive, is a new set of techniques that have come to be known as **low-impact sustainable agriculture,** or **LISA.** The philosophy behind LISA is that the long-term

FIGURE 8-7 Screw Worms. Screw worms, the most feared insect pest of livestock in the Western Hemisphere, showed up for the first time in Libya in 1988. The worms lay eggs anyplace they can find a break in the skin of an animal. The eggs hatch into larvae that feed on the animal. Without treatment, infected animals usually die within two weeks. Millions of Arab and African families who depend on their livestock for subsistance were at risk.

Screw worms have been eradicated in the United States and most of Mexico by the use of the sterile insect technique. Despite strained diplomatic ties with Libya, the United States allowed travel to Libya by personnel trained in the technique and also allowed sale of sterile screw worms for the campaign from U.S. facilities. In late 1991, the United Nations Food and Agricultural Organization announced that the campaign had been successful. No new cases of screwworm infestation had been reported since the previous April. (*Above*) Libyan farmers apply insecticide to the umbilical cord of a newborn calf to prevent screwworm infection. (*Photo:* Mary Lynn Hanley/UNDP)

fertility of soil and the protection of the environment are more important than short-term profit, and must be considered. LISA deals not only with pesticides use, but also with fertilizer use, irrigation problems such as salinization of soil, and erosion control. An expert in LISA would advise a farmer not only on pest control, but also on wetland and groundwater safeguards, mixes of crop and animal culture suitable for the area, and how to preserve soil fertility. (See Box 9-2, page 198, for more on LISA.)

LISA will probably require extensive government funding for research and development and then for training of experts able to communicate its benefits to farmers. IPM is already a viable option for farmers, but, again, government training of advisors in the technique will be useful.

Understandably, farmers are slow to change their farm practices. Their income depends on the crops they raise, and so they want to be sure of the effectiveness of a new method before they risk using it. Nonchemical pest-control methods tend to be more complicated to use than chemical sprays, and they usually do not have the immediate and obvious "knockdown" effect that sprays have.

Farmers and experts who are used to reducing pest populations as close as possible to zero may be uncomfortable with one of the basic ideas of IPM: that pest populations should be kept just below the level at which they cause economic injury, in order to maintain predators and parasites in the ecosystem. Furthermore, farmers get a good deal of advice from pesticide manufacturing companies, which are hardly disinterested parties.

A report by the Environmental Protection Agency's Science Advisory Board recommended that EPA actively attempt to reduce pesticide use in the USA by offering education and incentives to farmers using IPM or LISA. The report also suggested that pesticide companies be required to show efficacy data for pesticides—that is, data that show they actually work in reducing pests—and that registrations be canceled for ineffective pesticides. Commercial operators might be held responsible, the board noted, for monitoring to prevent pesticide damage to environmentally sensitive areas.

Finally, the advisory recommended that the public be better informed about what pesticides are being used commercially in their area and be encouraged to use less of the pesticides available to homeowners on store shelves.

SUMMARY

Pesticides are chemicals used to kill pests. The use of pesticides has led to a variety of problems. The chemicals may accumulate in living organisms by a process called biological magnification. If they do not break down within one growing season, they can persist and even accumulate in the environment. Pests often become resistant to pesticides that formerly controlled them. Furthermore, soil microorganisms can adapt to pesticides, breaking them down in the soil to useless by-products.

There is also concern about pesticides and human health. Small amounts of pesticides are left on foods after the spraying of crops. The EPA registers pesticides for use against pests and sets tolerances for the amount of pesticides that can remain on crops after harvest. The FDA and the USDA are responsible for checking that foods meet the criteria set by the EPA. The use of pesticides in developing nations poses a problem because of the lack of education of farmers with respect to the hazards presented by pesticides. In addition, foods imported to the United States may have excessive residues of pesticides, sometimes even residues of pesticides banned in the United States.

Alternatives to pesticide use include organic farming, integrated pest management (IPM), and low-impact sustainable agriculture (LISA). In IPM, a variety of techniques are used, including cultural techniques, resistant crops, and monitoring for pest outbreaks, combined with limited pesticide use. Both IPM and the use of biological controls may prove more economical for a farmer than the use of chemical sprays. However, farmers must be informed about these alternatives and LISA and how they can benefit from them. This is the role of specially trained pest-control experts.

Questions

1. What are the major environmental problems associated with the use of pesticides? What are the major public health problems?
2. Explain the basis of integrated pest management.
3. What factors might prevent a farmer from adopting IPM rather than depending exclusively on chemical pest control? How can these barriers be overcome?
4. If you were a farmer, would you be an organic farmer, would you use integrated pest management or LISA, or would you use chemical pesticides whenever you felt you had a pest problem? Why?

Further Reading

Graham, F., Jr. *Since Silent Spring.* New York: Fawcett, 1970.
The classic book *Silent Spring* by Rachel Carson began a public controversy over the effects of pesticides that continues today. Carson was eventually proven correct in many of her claims, although, as detailed in Graham's

book, they were attacked violently when her book was first published.

"Integrated Pest Management: A Second Look," *Journal of Pesticide Reform*, 8(4), (Winter 1989).

This entire issue is devoted to the pros and cons of IPM.

Josephson, J. "Pesticides of the Future," *Environmental Science and Technology*, 17 (1983), 464A.

New directions in pest control are predicted in this interesting article.

National Research Council. *Regulating Pesticides in Food: the Delaney Paradox*. Committee on Scientific and Regulatory Issues, Board on Agriculture, National Research Council. Washington, D.C.: National Academy Press, 1987.

This report illuminates the controversy about the Delaney amendment and carcinogenic food additives.

Phillips, R. E., et al. "No-Tillage Agriculture," *Science*, 208 (June 6, 1980), 1108.

No-tillage agriculture is a fast-spreading solution to soil erosion problems on cropland. The pros and cons are carefully detailed in this paper.

References

Atuma, S., and D. Okor. "Pesticide Usage in Nigeria," *Ambio*, 16(6) (December 1985), 340.

Batra, S. "Biological Control in Agroecosystems," *Science*, 215 (January 8, 1982), 134.

Fox, J. L. "Soil Microbes Pose Problems for Pesticides," *Science*, 221 (September 9, 1983), 1029.

Lockeretz, W., et al. "Organic Farming in the Corn Belt," *Science*, 211 (February 6, 1981), 540.

"Pesticides," in *Reducing Risk, The Report of the Strategic Options Subcommittee* (Appendix C, section A.13, page 101), U.S. Environmental Protection Agency, Science Advisory Board, EPA SAB-EC-90-021C, 1990.

Pimentel, D. (Ed.). *World Food Pest Losses and the Environment*. AAAS Selected Symposium 13, 1978. Washington, D.C.: American Association for the Advancement of Science, 1978.

Pimentel, D. "Environmental and Economic Impacts of Reducing U.S. Agricultural Pesticide Use," *Handbook on Pest Management in Agriculture*. Boca Raton, Fla.: CRC Press, 1991.

Sevilla, R. "Pesticides South of the Border," *Amicus Journal*, Winter 1984.

Speer, L., and G. Paulson. Letter to the Editor. *New York Times*, October 24, 1984.

World Health Organization. *The Work of WHO 1988–1989*, WHO Biennial Report. Geneva: World Health Organization, 1990.

Chapter 9

Feeding the World's People

HOW MUCH FOOD?

Famine and Malnutrition

The worst famine in African history struck the continent in 1983–1985. The world was shocked by photographs and figures detailing the tragedy (Figure 9-1). A major drought, the most severe in modern history, had caused massive crop failures. This led inevitably to famine for populations that had little or no food in reserve for bad years, had no money to buy food from the rest of the world, and often lacked even a road or transportation system that could distribute the food aid finally sent by other nations.

As dreadful a crisis as the African famine was, it was but the acute form of a chronic problem. In all parts of the world, areas of chronic starvation exist where day after day, people eat fewer calories or less protein than they need. Despite this lack of food, people do not commonly die of starvation. In most cases a person who has too little food is more likely to develop diseases than someone who eats well. Furthermore, the undernourished victim is more likely to die of diseases from which a well-nourished person could recover. Typhus, cholera, smallpox, plague, influenza, tuberculosis, and re-lapsing fever all commonly strike people weakened from lack of food. This means that the actual cause of death is listed as something other than starvation, even though starvation is clearly an underlying or major cause of death.

The United Nations Food and Agriculture Organization (FAO) distinguishes two categories of people who do not have enough food. In the first category are those who are *severely undernourished.* These people eat less than 1.2 times the number of calories their bodies would need if they were completely inactive and fasting, a quantity known as the **basal metabolic rate,** or **BMR.** Some 350 million people have only this much food each day. Another group is called *moderately undernourished.* These people have a little more food—1.4 times their BMR. Together, the two groups total about 512 million people. For normal activity, such as working or going to school, nutritionists estimate that people need 1.5 to 1.7 times their BMR.

Children and Poor Nutrition

Children suffer from two diseases specially related to malnutrition. **Kwashiorkor** occurs when a child's diet may have enough calories but too little protein. A major symptom of the disease is edema,

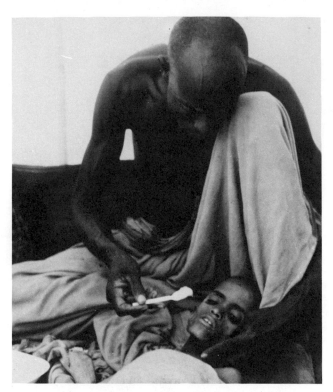

FIGURE 9-1 Ethiopian Famine Victims. A father who had lost both his wife and daughter during their 100-km journey to this camp in Bati, Ethiopia feeds his dying son. (*Photo:* O. Monsen/UN)

FIGURE 9-2 A Hungry Child. The effects of lack of food or protein are felt especially severely by children. Twenty percent, or 100 million, of the poorly nourished people in the world are children under the age of 5, and 10 million of them will die from the direct consequences of this lack of food or protein. (*Photo:* Lynn Millar/UNICEF)

or swelling, of the abdomen (Figure 9-2). Kwashiorkor usually occurs after children are weaned. **Marasmus,** which involves a shortage of both protein and calories, occurs when infants less than 1 year old are fed overdiluted formula from unsterile nursing bottles. Severe diarrhea almost always occurs in both diseases. Children with kwashiorkor and marasmus have higher death rates and may also suffer permanent brain damage.

If mothers nurse their babies, infantile marasmus can be prevented because human milk provides needed protein for the child. In addition, because human milk is a completely sanitary food source, chances are less that the child will be infected with diarrhea-causing organisms. Even kwashiorkor is

uncommon if a child is nursed through the second year or longer. Furthermore, nursing has an incomplete but significant contraceptive effect. Women who nurse are less likely to conceive again while nursing. This can have a positive effect in terms of population control where other birth control methods are not available or are unacceptable.

Unfortunately, in some developing countries, companies that produce infant formulas have engaged in campaigns to sell parents on formula feeding of infants. In many of these countries the cost of infant formulas is high compared to workers' incomes. In some cases, commercial formula, if fed at the proper strength, would cost one-fourth to one-third of a worker's income. Thus, the formula is often overdiluted. The high cost and the lack of necessary sanitary conditions for preparing formula mean that in many parts of developing countries a switch from breastfeeding to bottlefeeding or earlier weaning will cause infant and child health to suffer.

According to the United Nations (1990) the nutritional status of children, which began to improve during the 1970s, failed to show further improvement in the 1980s.

A Food Crisis?

Over the past 25 years, technical advances in farming have enabled the world's food supply to keep slightly ahead of population growth. That is, conditions have improved somewhat, for some people. In Asia, North Africa, and Central America, people are better fed now than they were 10 years ago. But there has been no net gain in South America as a whole, and conditions are much worse in sub-Saharan Africa. Figure 5-7, on page 105, shows how population growth has used up all of the gains in food production in India, leaving no increase in food supplies to improve people's nutrition.

Even when there is a reasonable surplus of food, the world remains troubled by uneven distribution. The developed countries, especially the United States and Canada, produce about one-half of the world's food. Yet they are home to only 20% of the world's population. One part of ending malnutrition, then, involves transportation: getting food surpluses to where the needy people are. Another aspect involves decreasing the portion of crops lost to insects and disease in the field, in storage, and in transportation. As noted in Figure 9-3, some 25% more grain could be available if such losses were prevented. The highest losses occur in developing countries, which can least afford them.

A third concern is damping the price fluctuations of grain on the world market. These fluctuations are caused mainly by bad weather, which decreases harvests in an unpredictable fashion. Because an increasing part of the world's grain harvests is spoken for in long-term contracts between the wealthier nations, any decreases in harvest seriously affect small, poor nations. These nations do not have the

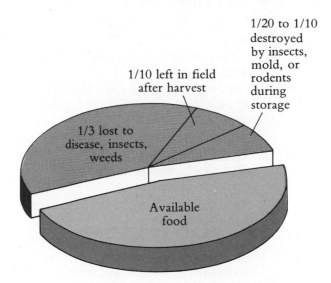

FIGURE 9-3 Crop Loss in the Field and in Storage. In the United States, more than one-third of the crops grown are lost to insects, disease, and rodents in the field and during storage. One-third are lost in the field, another 10% are left in the field after harvest, and 5%–10% are lost during storage. In other parts of the world, these figures are even higher. More than one-half of the world's food crop is lost to disease, insects, and rodents during growing, shipping, and storage.

money or political clout to compete for grain when world supplies are small and prices high.

Fourth is the problem of changing income distributions so that the countries and the people currently too poor to purchase enough food can afford a healthful diet. The social, political, and economic problems involved are enormous and will be discussed later. Before we look at these problems, however, let us look at the prospects for increasing the world's food supply in absolute terms.

INCREASING THE WORLD'S FOOD SUPPLY

Fishery Resources

At one time, humans looked to the oceans as a vast reservoir of food, waiting only for the technology to harvest and turn it into tasty dishes. However, reality, in the form of declining fish catches and even the complete collapse of some fisheries, has caught up with this notion. The California sardine fishing industry collapsed in the 1950s, the North Sea herring industry in 1969, the West Africa/Namibia pilchard industry in 1970, and the Peruvian anchovy industry in 1972.

The seas hold a finite food resource. If we over-exploit this resource, it appears that commercial enterprises will no longer be worthwhile and some species may be driven to extinction.

In fact, the total world marine catch has remained relatively constant over the past 10 years, despite improved technology and increased fishing activity. This suggests that many currently harvested species are fully exploited and in some cases are decreasing in abundance. Rather than increasing the harvest, technology will be hard put to keep it from decreasing in the near future.

Aquaculture

One possible bright spot in this fairly dismal scenario is the growing science of **aquaculture.** Certain aquatic species, such as oysters, clams, mussels, and a variety of fish can be raised successfully in pens or enclosures in natural bodies of water, or in tanks on land. Some clever farmers have even made use of warm water effluents from power plants to grow species such as oysters in otherwise cold northern waters. Three possible problems may limit the use of aquaculture, however. First, there is the problem of waste disposal. Just like farms on land, aquaculture farms produce animal waste. This waste can contaminate water or fertilize it, thus causing excessive growths of algae.

The second problem is that many aquatic species, for example clams and oysters, are filter feeders. They filter large quantities of water to obtain their nutrients. They may also filter out toxic materials and concentrate them to harmful levels. For this reason, warm water effluents used in aquaculture must be free of even trace concentrations of toxic metals, radioactive substances, or carcinogenic organic compounds.

Like farms on land, aquaculture farms may use up habitat formerly occupied by native, wild species. Aquaculture schemes should be measured against the yardstick of what wild species may be lost as well as what food resources will be gained.

The Supply of Arable Land

As noted in the introduction to this part, there is only a finite amount of land that can be easily farmed without severely damaging the environment. Most of this fertile, readily cropped land is already under cultivation. Marginal lands—those that are on hillsides, or beneath tropical forests, or in semi-arid to arid climates, or those that are wetlands—present serious environmental problems when they are farmed. Soil erosion and flooding result from farming sloped lands. Soil salinization is a common hazard of irrigated farming in dry climates. Loss of wetlands, forests, and other essential wildlife habitats often follows attempts to increase the amount of land under cultivation.

The problem of increasing food supplies, then, comes down to the question: How can we grow more food on the land already under cultivation?

Today's Agricultural Technology

Traditional Farming versus the Modern American Farm. In the central highlands of the Philippine island of Luzon are the villages of a fierce mountain people, the Igorots. These people were once noted as head hunters, but their fame now rests on their outstanding ability to farm the steep mountain slopes of the island's central region. In the incredibly short period of a few hundred years, these people have built a series of terraces on the mountainside, by hand labor with only a few primitive tools (Figure 9-4). On these terraces, using no artificial fertilizers, they grow rice in amazingly high yields. A single hectare of land (2.47 acres) yields a whole year's supply of rice, their main food, for a family of five.

The high yields are due partly to the enormous amount of labor the Igorots put in. On the terraces, rice is grown by water culture. The terraces must be weeded continually to keep the water-retaining walls from crumbling. Another important factor appears to be nitrogen-fixing algae that grow in the water along with the rice. These algae provide nitrogen, which fertilizes the rice crop, while the rice provides carbon dioxide and some necessary shade for the algae. The Igorots have developed an environmentally sound and self-renewing agricultural system that supports them well. Along with the agricultural system, a social system has developed. Villages are organized into work groups that construct irrigation canals, terrace new slopes, plow the fields, and harvest crops, far more efficiently than solitary workers could. From these work groups the whole social structure of the villages has grown:

They sponsor rituals, and they help to resolve disputes; they form political parties and in times of trouble they become military units. They enter into virtually every phase of the communities' activities. Perhaps most importantly, they provide the Igorots with a stability of association, continuity in their personal relationships that in our own affluent, mobile society is becoming ever more rare and valued. The interdependence of the working groups has made the Igorots so culturally conservative that almost a century of contact with Western Society has resulted only in superficial changes in their way of life. (Drucker, 1978, p. 22)

The wet culture of rice is a special type of farming. All over the world, farmers grow crops in a manner such as this, requiring much manpower but little or nothing of modern agricultural technology. Such crops are usually well adapted to the climate, the soil type, and the availability of water. But, in many cases, these farming operations are at or near the subsistence level. The farmer grows enough food for his own family and some to trade for the other goods needed to live. Increasing numbers of people cannot be fed by traditional subsistence-level farming.

In contrast, let us now look at the modern American farm. In the United States, profitable farms are big. This may mean 600–800 acres (240–320 hectares) in the corn belt, where one family can work this much land alone with the proper machinery and a small amount of help at harvest time. A dairy farm must have 40 cows per worker

FIGURE 9-4 Rice Terraces. Igorot rice terraces are marvels of engineering and skill, practiced by a people with no modern tools or equipment. (*Photo:* Charles Drucker)

to see a profit because, again, a great deal of machinery is involved.

Fertilizer, Energy, and the Modern Farm. With few exceptions, the American farmer uses large amounts of artificial fertilizer. In fact, 30%–40% of increased U.S. productivity has been attributed to increased use of fertilizer. Nitrogen fertilizers, which account for half of all fertilizer in the world, are produced mainly from fossil fuels such as natural gas and coal. Energy is also needed for the manufacturing process itself. Shortages of fossil fuels have raised the cost of fertilizers over threefold in recent years, which, in turn, has contributed to the higher cost of food.

An especially unfortunate result of higher fertilizer prices is that poorer countries can now afford less fertilizer—yet these areas are precisely where it would do the most good. The reason is that as more and more fertilizer is added to a field, the

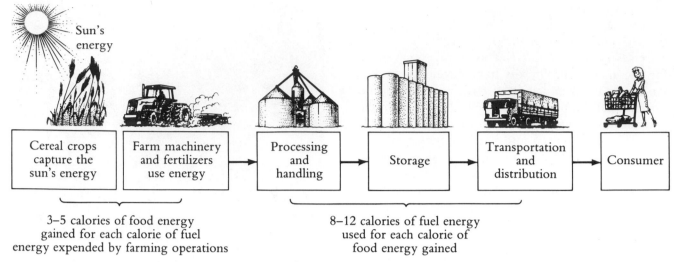

3–5 calories of food energy
gained for each calorie of fuel
energy expended by farming operations

8–12 calories of fuel energy
used for each calorie of
food energy gained

FIGURE 9-5 Energy Costs for Producing Food in a Developed Country Such as the United States. Farming itself shows a net gain of energy because more of the sun's energy is captured by plants than is used by farming procedures. After this, however, processing, handling, storage, and distribution of food use up this energy gain and more, so that by the time food reaches the consumer, 5–7 calories of fuel energy have been used to produce each calorie of food energy.

increased crop yield per pound of fertilizer begins to decrease. The field is, so to speak, saturated with fertilizer. Most large farms in developed countries, such as the United States, fall into this category. In contrast, farms in developing countries, where little or no fertilizer has been used in the past, show a much larger increase in yield for a smaller amount of fertilizer. In terms of the total world food supply, then, the distribution of fertilizer is uneven.

Energy is used in modern agriculture not only to produce fertilizer but also to run the machines that plant and harvest crops and in the after-harvest processes: handling, storage, processing, and distribution. (See Figure 9-5.)

One further point should be made in relation to energy and agriculture. Most people prefer to eat meat if they can afford it. Yet, as the second law of thermodynamics predicts, meat is an inefficient way of obtaining food energy because of the energy transfers involved. As a general rule, an animal eats 3–10 pounds of grain to produce 1 pound of meat. A much more efficient use of food resources is for people to consume grain directly, as is now done in most developing nations. Figure 9-6 illustrates the way in which meat consumption tends to increase as incomes rise. Such an increase in meat consumption, of course, puts even more of a strain on world food resources.

Animals and animal products still have an important place in improving agricultural systems of developing nations, however. For instance, farmers can use animals to pull machinery such as plows or harvesting equipment. In many parts of the world, this means that a small family can tend the same amount of land as used to be tended by a larger family without animal help. This could lead to improved diet or excess crops for sale. The animal must be fed, of course, but it can graze on land that is not as suitable for human food crops (too steep, too cold, too rocky) or can be fed a second crop harvested at a different time from the main human food crop. In any case, animals and animal feed are generally easier to come by in developing nations than tractors and gasoline.

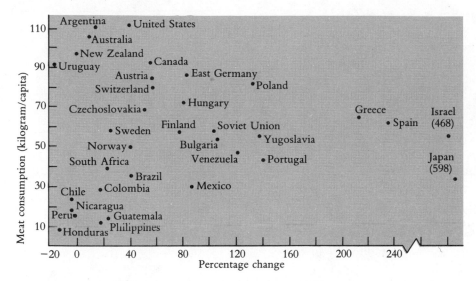

FIGURE 9-6 Change in Meat Consumption Between 1961 and 1980. As people earn higher incomes, they spend more money on meat. The actual meat consumption per person is shown on the vertical axis, while the percent change from 1961 to 1980 is shown on the horizontal axis. Argentina and the U.S. lead in the amount of meat eaten per person, but the greatest changes have taken place in countries such as Israel and Japan. (From T. Barr, *Science*, **214** [December 4, 1981], 1087)

Animal products such as milk and meat can also provide the farmer with year-round income, as well as some small insurance against starvation in bad crop years.

Irrigation and Salinization. In many areas, notably the American Southwest, fertile lands that receive little rainfall are successfully farmed after the development of irrigation systems. Some 15% of the world's farmland is irrigated, and 30% of the world's food is produced on these acres. Again, energy is a necessary component of the system. In most cases, fossil fuel is needed directly for pumping or draining systems.

In many areas, however, irrigation brings hazards along with benefits. In tropical countries, irrigation canals serve as a breeding place for the snails that carry the disease schistosomiasis. Although this disease is not fatal, it takes a great toll of strength from people living in areas where the disease did not exist before irrigation.

Furthermore, irrigation water evaporates to some degree, leaving behind salts that were in the water. In some areas, including parts of the American West, this has left soils so salty that crops will no longer grow there. Soils can also become waterlogged if drainage systems are not included in irrigation plans. Irrigation schemes may even have

adverse social effects, such as causing overpopulation in newly irrigated areas.

Some scientists have expressed concern that within the next hundred years, irrigation may become so widespread that the flow of major rivers into the sea may completely stop. The Nile and other rivers entering the Mediterranean are most likely to suffer that fate. The environmental effects of such an occurrence are unknown, but might include such things as decreased fishing, as the flow of nutrients from land into sea is stopped. Water as a scarce resource is discussed in Chapter 18.

The Green Revolutions

Green Revolution I. Perhaps the biggest success technology has achieved is the development of high-yield grains. New varieties of wheat and rice have been developed that far outproduce traditional varieties. Many new wheat and rice varieties are shorter in stature than older varieties and so channel more energy into seed production than into stem growth. Further, they often mature more quickly than older varieties, allowing a farmer to plant and harvest up to three crops a year. Using the new varieties, a farmer can grow more grain even without increasing the amount of land under cultivation.

Towards a Sustainable Society

Ensuring Safe Use of Pesticides in Developing Countries

by Donald Cole

Donald Cole is trained both in medicine and public health. Dr. Cole has worked in Latin America on pesticide health and safety programs. He currently works in a community-based health program in Ontario, Canada and does research on the effects of pesticides on the health of farm families in developing nations.

Pesticides have caused numerous poisonings among farmers and their families in developing countries. In addition to the personal tragedy this represents, such poisoning reduces the energy and the work output of farm labor. Human labor is an essential resource for development. The health impacts of pesticides technology may thus lessen the sustainability of agricultural production.

Overuse and excessive exposure both contribute to these unnecessary poisonings. The reasons for overuse are many. Large areas of monoculture promote the growth of pest populations. Biological control methods require long periods to develop and may require considerable training and labor to implement. Pesticide company vendors are often more numerous and receive better pay than agricultural extension agents who could promote more integrated approaches to pest management.

The major source of excessive exposure is skin contamination during the mixing and applying of pesticides. Pesticide suppliers do not commonly supply protective equipment, such as gloves, at reasonable prices. Furthermore, the protective clothing and equipment developed in industrial countries are often poorly adapted to the crops and climates of developing countries. Although clothing such as long-sleeved shirts and pants, gloves, and boots can reduce exposure significantly, in many parts of the world, even such simple protective measures as wearing this type of clothing during pesticide application are not taken. Education in the safe handling of pesticides is not routine, and low literacy levels in some developing countries prevent people from reading or understanding hazard warnings and other teaching materials on the safe use of pesticides.

Poor farmers and farm workers with little job security are severely limited in their capacity to generate demand for safety products and services. In addition, the regulatory structure of many developing country governments has traditionally been weak.

A number of ideas have been developed to deal with these inadequacies. The Ottawa-based International Development Research Centre has financed the design and production of cheaper and safer backpack sprayers in Africa. Popular education techniques and materials such as radio spots, dramatic skits, calendars, and comic book–type literature have been used successfully in Latin America to help people decode hazard information and improve safety practices with pesticides.

In some developing countries, government programs have been started to train personnel in integrated pest management techniques. In Nicaragua the Ministry of Agriculture promoted crop diversification and even set and monitored regional planting dates for cotton in order to reduce the buildup of cotton pests. Seasonal frequency of pesticide application almost halved during these efforts.

FIGURE 9-7 Triticale—A New Grain. On the right is triticale, a cross between wheat (left) and rye (middle). Triticale gives better yields than wheat, corn, or soybeans on marginal land, especially with acid soil. (*Photo:* USDA)

This development has become known as the **Green Revolution.**

In practice, however, difficulties remain. The new grains are very responsive to fertilizers—in fact, the best yields depend on the use of large amounts of fertilizer. In addition, the new varieties need more water than older varieties to reach their full potential, and in some cases they are more susceptible to disease and insects. All this means that a farmer must have the technical knowledge of how to use the new varieties and, often, the money to spend on necessary supplements such as fertilizers, pesticides, and irrigation mechanisms. Without these supplements the new grain varieties may be no better and are sometimes worse than the older ones. Further, the intensive farming encouraged by the Green Revolution can cause serious erosion, salinization, and pesticide pollution unless farmers are educated to deal with such problems.

This is not to say the Green Revolution is without value. Even without optimum amounts of fertilizer, the new varieties often yield substantially more than older varieties. In a period of six years, from 1965 to 1971, farmers in the northwest area of India achieved spectacular increases in food grain production, in some cases averaging almost 10%

more grain per year. A combination of high-yield grain, more fertilizer, and good rainfall led India to announce in 1971 that she soon expected to be self-sufficient in food. Although the lack of the monsoon rains in 1973 and 1974 caused a setback, India is now largely self-sufficient in cereal grains.

In short, however, the new varieties are best suited for certain environments where water, energy, education, and capital are not severely limited. On some 80% of the world's acreage, traditional varieties are still grown with little or no chemicals or machinery.

Green Revolution II. New advances in agricultural production involve breeding crop varieties adapted to special local conditions—varieties that produce high yields on marginal lands. Agricultural researchers have developed new varieties that are tolerant of salt or aluminum, that can survive swamping during monsoons, or that have natural defenses against plant pests (Figure 9-7).

Scientists hope that many more of these advances will come from techniques such as genetic engineering or the use of chemicals to regulate plant growth. These relatively new kinds of biotechnology are sometimes labeled Green Revolution II.

Leaf tissues are placed in enzyme solution to separate cells. Cell walls are removed, leaving "naked" protoplasts.

Protoplasts are exposed to selection pressure (e.g. high salt concentration or toxin).

Surviving protoplasts are treated to encourage cell division.

Protoplasts develop into calluses of undifferentiated cells. Calluses are cultured with hormones to promote cell differentiation.

New plant manifests desired trait.

FIGURE 9-8 Growing Whole Plants from Single Cells. Single cells are isolated from a plant and then treated so each one regenerates a whole new plant. In most cases, each cell will produce a plant exactly like the parent plant. (This is the process of cloning.) Orchids, Boston ferns, African violets, and oil palms are all propagated this way. When scientists use the method to develop new plant varieties, however, they look for those few cells that have some different characteristics than the parent plant. The number of these "different" cells can be increased by treating the cells with certain chemicals or ultraviolet light. Scientists can screen a group of cells to see whether any would develop into plants with useful characteristics, such as tolerance to high salt or high aluminum concentrations. Those single cells that survive and reproduce in such conditions in the laboratory are likely candidates for growing into whole plants that are tolerant to these conditions. (*Source:* Adapted from R. Cooke, "Engineering a New Agriculture," *Technology Review,* May/June 1982, p. 24, drawing by Dan Collins)

Genetic engineering involves such things as the transfer of genes governing desirable traits between different species. Not long ago such feats were held to be still 10 years in the future. However, scientists have already been able to transfer genes responsible for traits such as resistance to certain herbicides to crop plants such as tomatoes, potatoes, and tobacco. Such resistance enables farmers to use herbicides to kill weeds in a field without damaging the crop plants.

Also being used are techniques in which whole plants are regenerated from single cells in tissue cultures. Rapid screening of large numbers of plants for desirable traits is possible with tissue culture techniques (Figure 9-8).

Newly discovered plant-growth regulators may eventually be able to increase crop yields or, conversely, prevent weed growth. Other newly found chemicals seem to stimulate natural plant defenses against insect damage and so may eventually be used in reducing pesticide needs.

One unfortunate result of Green Revolution I was the virtual disappearance of local varieties of crop plants in some areas, when all the farmers switched to new hybrid varieties. As Green Revolution II gets underway, we can see even more clearly the need to preserve as many different species of plants as possible. For example, some of the traits that will be used to produce improved crop varieties by genetic engineering will probably be found in wild plants and locally adapted varieties of crop plants (see Figure 10-4, page 155).

A number of countries have now established plant germ banks. These facilities store seeds or plant parts from local varieties of the important food crops or other possibly useful food plants. In this way, useful varieties won't be allowed to disappear as a result of most farmers' switching to one or a few "super" varieties of corn, rice, and wheat.

Social, Economic, and Political Aspects of Increasing the Food Supply

Technology offers farmers in developing countries hope for increasing food production. Whether the farmers can take advantage of this help depends in large part on political and economic conditions. For instance, before small farmers in a developing country can take advantage of many kinds of improved technology, credit must be available so they can purchase seeds, pesticides, and other equipment. Large banks are usually wary of lending money to small farmers, however. Some of these farmers may turn to local moneylenders, friends, or relatives. The energy crunch is apparently making the credit problem worse, since prices for fertilizers, fuel, and related goods are rising. In the long run, price increases will be a curb on the success of the Green Revolution.

In the long run, too, land reform may be necessary in countries where a few wealthy landowners hold most of the political power. Such landowners are able to obtain new technological information for themselves fairly easily and see no need to make such information available to the small farmer. Yet the small farmer must have help, especially education in the technology of using high-yield grains, if the developing countries are to significantly increase agricultural production.

Another political restraint on agricultural production in the past has been that politicians have often tried to hold down food prices. This is often done to keep living costs down so that the large numbers of city dwellers will continue to vote for the politicians in power. The effect of this policy is to remove any incentive for farmers to grow more food than their families need. Market prices simply remain too low to justify the work and investment involved in more crops. As an extreme example, a careful study in Mali showed that it cost a farmer 83 Malian francs to produce a kilo of rice,

but the government paid the farmers only 60 francs per kilo. As a result, farmers smuggled rice across the borders into countries where they could get 108–128 francs per kilo for it.

In the Sahelian states (Mali, Niger, Upper Volta) it has been a practice to assure a job to any high school graduate. Such a policy has led to vast increases in the number of civil servants, whose salaries can be kept low by keeping food prices at low levels. This has acted to slow food production because the farmers see no reason to grow more crops at current prices.

Experience shows that government policy can have a significant effect on a country's ability to feed itself. Several developing countries have successfully improved food production over the past 10 years as a direct result of government actions.

In some cases, leaders have improved production by decreasing government regulation of agriculture. China is a good example of increasing agricultural production by allowing farmers to profit from their own schemes.

In the oil-rich countries, food production has increased as a result of heavy government inputs and subsidies. In some countries, notably India, government promotion of agricultural technology such as irrigation and the use of high-yielding grains has produced impressive gains. Other countries, such as Malaysia, have improved their position in terms of agricultural production by focusing on export crops.

International Food Policies and Grain Reserves. Although there are a number of ways in which a government can affect its country's agricultural output, some issues can only be dealt with on an international basis. Tariffs and subsidies fall into this category. (See Box 9-1 for an explanation of terms dealing with governmental agricultural policy.) Protective tariffs in developed countries have prevented some developing countries from profiting from their main exportable crops, for example, sugar and meat. Along the same lines, heavy subsidies given by temperate-zone developed countries to their own export crops, such as grains, have inhibited developing countries from exploiting

Box 9-1

Farm Programs

The federal government attempts to stabilize farm prices and provide a floor under farmers' earnings on wheat, corn, rice, and cotton with a number of programs.

Price support loans: Loans made at Treasury interest rates with a farmer's crop put up as collateral. The per bushel loan rate is set by the Agriculture Secretary. These loans, plus interest, may be repaid after nine months. Or they may be forfeited, without interest, by transferring the collateral crops to the Agriculture Department, which may not sell them until the market rises to 105% of the per bushel loan rate.

Subsidies: Called "deficiency payments." The per bushel rate at which these are paid is the difference between the "target price" set by Congress and the average free market price in the first five months after harvest. An eligible farmer receives these automatically, whether he or she sells the crop, takes a loan on it, or stores it.

Reserve: Eligible farmers may designate part of their crops for the reserve, holding them on their own farms or country elevators. They receive a loan, at the loan rate, when they do. When the market reaches a "trigger price" set by Congress, these reserves may be sold and the loan, plus interest, paid off. When the market reaches a "release price" the farmers must pay off their loans and are no longer given storage payments if they hold reserves.

Paid diversion: When the Secretary offers a "diversion," a farmer who idles a percentage of the land normally planted in these crops is paid in cash, based on the average per acre yield on the land diverted. He or she may not plant another controlled crop on that land.

Payment-in-kind: Farmers who leave idle additional land are given crops from government stores in proportion to the average yield from the land idled.

Source: S. King, *The New York Times,* August 8, 1983.

these markets. International cooperation on issues of tariffs and subsidies could be of great help in increasing food production in developing countries.

Whether or not people can obtain food depends not only on its availability but also on its price. For this reason, maintaining a relatively stable, low price for grain on the world market would mean that poorer people would have better access to the world's food. One way to achieve this would be through an international grain reserve.

Resistance to an international grain reserve is great, but the benefits are large. Consider how an international agency operating a grain reserve might function. Two prices might be used to trigger the operation of the reserve. A price for grain falling below a preset low price would signal the agency to buy grain. The low-price signal to buy serves two functions. First, low prices are the time to set grain aside; holding or investment costs for the agency are kept low in this way. Low prices also mean an abundant harvest relative to demand, indicating that now is the time to buy and store grain without driving the price up significantly. Second, purchase of the excess harvest acts as a price support for grain. Farmers would find that a good portion of their excess harvest is thus absorbed without the price falling still lower. Thus, the presence of a grain reserve helps to ensure the income and prosperity of farmers in times when too much good weather works against them.

In similar fashion, when the price for grain rises above some predetermined high limit, the agency would offer its grain on the international market. The grain would be available for purchase by those poor nations for whom higher prices are a burden. The price at which the grain is sold essentially puts a lid on the international price of grain: Who would pay more than the high-signal price if grain can be purchased at that price from the international agency? True, farm profits are dampened when the international agency decides to sell its grain, but the diminished profits are not the normal profits that keep a farm in business but the profits built of hardship and malnutrition for the poorest. The farmer selling grain at the grain reserve price still makes a sturdy profit.

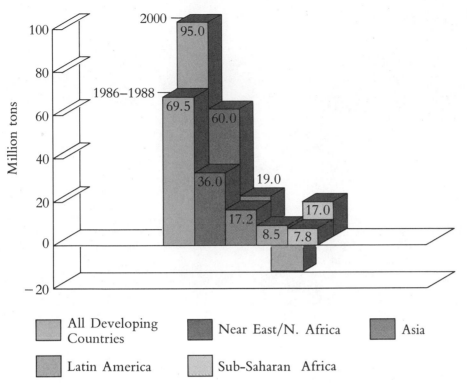

FIGURE 9-9 Projection of Net Cereal Import Requirements of Developing Countries.

All Developing Countries   Near East/N. Africa   Asia

Latin America   Sub-Saharan Africa

AGRICULTURE AND THE FUTURE

In 1990, the United Nations predicted that the world food situation in the year 2000 will not have changed much. Based on Food and Agriculture Organization figures, the United Nations estimates that the number of hungry people in the world will still hover around 500 million, with gains in South America being offset by losses in Africa (Figure 9-9). U.N. predictions are based on the assumption that food production in developing countries will, in general, keep pace with population growth. A lack of improvements in income and income distribution will remain the major problem for most developing countries, according to the United Nations. Food aid will be required by some countries into the next century. (See Controversy 9-1 for some other thoughts on food aid.) Let us look now at what agricultural changes might be made to improve on this glum scenario.

New Agricultural Methods and Ideas

Need for Alternative Agricultural Schemes. Policy cannot solve all countries' food problems. For some developing countries, especially in semi-arid parts of Africa, natural conditions such as drought have frustrated government attempts to increase food production. In other countries, where much of the available land is covered by rain forest, farming is successful for only a few years, until the soil nutrients are used up. It appears that these fragile lands may not be suitable for Western-style, Green Revolution farming. Environmental consequences including erosion, salinization, pesticides poisoning, and desertification have too often been the result of intensive farming in these areas.

Moreover, agricultural technologists do not all agree that the flow of Green Revolution–style agricultural advances will continue. Many of these scientists are pessimistic about increasing crop yields to keep pace with population growth by

Controversy 9-1

The Lifeboat Ethic

For posterity's sake we should never send food to any population that is beyond the carrying capacity of its land.

Garrett Hardin

This obscene doctrine . . .

Roger Revelle

It is just as obscene to let people die in the future as it is to let them die now.

J. D. Martin, Sociologist,
Lakehead University,
Ontario, Canada

Garrett Hardin has proposed an analogy, related to population growth and the supply of food in the world, that is known as the "lifeboat ethic." In this analogy, so many people crowd onto a lifeboat that it sinks and all are lost. If fewer people had been in the boat, the argument goes, those few might have reached shore safely.

Roger Revelle stated in an editorial in *Science* (1974):

The specter, unseen by some and ignored by others, looming over the World Food Conference this week in Rome is the continuing rapid population growth of the world's poor countries. Some scientists and publicists have seriously advocated a "lifeboat ethic," saying that nations which do not *compel* human fertility control (by what means is never stated) are endangering the survival of our species—hence they should be starved out of the human race by denying them food aid. This obscene doctrine assumes that men and women will not voluntarily limit their own fertility when they have good reasons and the knowledge and means to do so.

The sharp decline in birth rates during the past decade in a dozen developing countries belies the assumption. But one

thing is clear from this experience: environmental changes can bring down birth rates only if they affect the people who have the children—the great mass of the poor who now have little hope for a better life.

Many people sent letters to the editor in reply to this editorial. J. D. Martin, a member of the sociology department at a Canadian university, wrote:

The idea of letting people die, Revelle says, is "obscene." Well, if so, it is just as obscene to let people die in the future as it is to let them do so now.

. . . non-Western populations will keep growing until we can't feed them, even at great cost to the quality of our soils.

We Westerners brought it on ourselves, by saving lives through medical skill and humanitarian generosity. . . . The millions of lives saved by our medical help became the

---

breeding new, ever-higher-yielding varieties of the traditional crops such as wheat and rice. What hope can technology offer farmers, especially in the countries that are most in need of food?

LISA. In farming the new operative word is "sustainability." There is compelling logic to the idea that farming methods should be such that a farmer can expect to grow crops or raise animals on his or her land far into the foreseeable future.

A farming system that is truly sustainable must meet a number of criteria (see Box 9-2). This set of principles is sometimes called low-impact sustainable agriculture, or LISA.

Appropriate Technology. Although the criteria in Box 9-2 can be applied to farming systems in all countries, a further point needs to be made about technology intended for developing countries. In these countries the goals of agriculture may be dif-

hundreds of millions of lives that are due to be lost in famines.

. . . Shall we impoverish the West in order to make the problem even worse, and in the process weaken both our land and theirs?

I think not; this is the essence of the "lifeboat ethic" which Revelle criticizes. Let too many people into a lifeboat and all will sink. The same may be true of our spaceship called Earth.

F. A. Cotton, a member of the chemistry department at Texas A & M University, echoed Martin's position:

Nobody can look without horror on the prospect, let alone the actual spectacle, of fellow human beings starving to death. It is a monstrous thing, but we live in an age of monstrosities—some still latent but imminent, unless actively forestalled—and it is literally necessary to consider not only relative degrees of monstrousness, but the fact that some monstrosities are qualitatively more ghastly than others.

Overpopulation and starvation are interdependent monstrosities, but of a qualitatively different nature. I believe that the former is far more dire than the latter.

If a quarter of the people in the world starved to death next year, the human condition, in the larger sense, would not be basically or permanently changed. After a few generations, this calamity would leave no basic imprint on our collective consciousness, any more than did the deaths of one-fourth of the people in Europe in the great plague of the 14th century.

However, if the population of the world goes on increasing at the present rate for much longer, the human condition will be basically and catastrophically altered, in an irreversible way.

What do you think of Martin's argument that "we Westerners brought it [a food crisis] on ourselves" by providing medical aid and knowledge to developing countries? Should we have denied them this aid in the first place? Do you agree with Cotton that worldwide starvation can be equated with the deaths from plague in the fourteenth century? Do you agree with Revelle that the lifeboat ethic is an obscene one, or do you feel that the horrors of overpopulation call for such a drastic response?

Another way of looking at this issue is to ask: Is the nutrition problem really a population problem, as Revelle's critics contend, or is the population problem, at least in part, a nutrition problem? Could better nutrition help people in undeveloped countries solve population problems themselves? Beverly Winikoff in a 1978 *Science* article (see References), examined some of the ways these questions can be answered.

Sources: Garrett Hardin, *Atlantic Monthly,* 247 (May 1981), 60; Roger Revelle, Editorial, *Science, 186* (November 15, 1974), 589; J. D. Martin, Letter to Editor, *Science, 187* (March 21, 1975), 1029; F. A. Cotton, Letter to Editor, *Science, 187* (March 21, 1975), 1030.

ferent than in developed countries. In the first place, saving labor may not be a goal. On the contrary, it may be important to increase agricultural production while employing as many people as possible in rural areas. In the second place, attaining high yields may not be as important as ensuring a relatively constant food supply. That is, in areas where the market infrastructure is weak or nonexistent—where farmers cannot get loans to buy new seed if their harvest fails, or where food cannot easily be bought if a crop doesn't do well—farmers will place more importance on methods that ensure a reasonable harvest every year rather than those that promise high yields.

Rather than simply promoting a wholesale transfer of modern agricultural technology, many experts now recommend a careful study of what people in developing nations need and can use in the way of technology. This idea has come to be known as "appropriate technology." For instance, farm machines do not have to be labor-saving to be useful. In many developing countries, farmers

---

Box 9-2

Low-Impact Sustainable Agriculture (LISA)

Local and Technical Criteria

1. Soil nutrients removed by crops are replaced.
2. Soil structure is maintained or improved (this refers mainly to the amount of humus in the soil).
3. Weeds, pests, and diseases do not build up.
4. Soil acidity and toxic elements do not build up.
5. Soil erosion is controlled.

Regional and Global Criteria

6. Dependence on nonrenewable energy and mineral resources is minimized.
7. Off-farm pollution by nutrients or chemicals is reduced to levels where self-cleansing can take place.
8. Wildlife habitat is maintained.
9. Genetic resources of agricultural plants and animals are maintained.

Source: Adapted from M. Dover and L. Talbot, *To Feed the Earth* (Washington, D.C.: World Resources Institute, 1987).

---

must wait for the rainy season before plowing. Machines to help farmers plow the hard caked earth allow them to have their crops planted in time to take advantage of the monsoon rains (Figure 9-10).

Polyculture. One especially important factor involves how many different crops a farmer grows. **Monoculture**—growing large stands of only one crop—has often increased yields in highly mechanized, energy-intensive, Western-style agriculture. With a monoculture, large areas can be planted, cultivated, and harvested with a minimum of labor.

Pests can be detected and killed with chemical controls. Marketing is easy, as long as the market infrastructure and transportation networks are in place. However, this type of agriculture leaves farmers vulnerable to vagaries of weather and price fluctuations for crops and energy. Monoculture fields are subject to pest outbreaks, erosion, and weather-caused crop failures.

Where rainfall is uncertain, farmers need to diversify crops and planting times, in order to be sure to have at least some successful harvests. Where farm families are completely dependent on the food they raise, a mix of crops and animals must be grown to ensure good nutrition.

Increasingly, agricultural experts are concluding that **polyculture,** growing several crops together or one after the other, serves these purposes better than the currently more fashionable methods of monoculture.

In many parts of the world, traditional agricultural systems already involve a mixture of crops, sometimes grown in a riotous mixture that would bewilder a practitioner of Western-style farming (Figure 9-11). In one study of Javanese home gardens, for instance, researchers counted 607 plant species, a diversity of species comparable to that found in a subtropical forest. In Nigeria, farms often combine eight or more crops, including bananas, beans, cassava, melons, and yams.

Polycropping has a number of advantages. Certain crops can replace soil nutrients, such as nitrates, that other crops remove from soil. Other crops leave a residue that improves soil structure. Mixtures of crops may thus reduce the need for fertilizer and soil conditioning.

Combinations of crops that have different heights can take better advantage of sunlight than monocultures. When crop species use all the available sunlight, weeds are crowded out, reducing the need for herbicides. Some combinations of species can take fuller advantage of moisture or nutrients in the soil because of different nutritional requirements or root depths. In many polycultures, insect damage is lower than in monocultures, apparently because insects have more trouble finding their preferred food and thus are not as successful at reproducing.

FIGURE 9-10 Appropriate Technology. Modern labor-saving devices on farms tend to displace agricultural workers, shifting them to cities where they must live in overcrowded, unsanitary conditions. Developing countries must find ways to increase yields while at the same time not reducing the number of laborers needed in agriculture. (*Left*) This pedestrian tractor is used in Philippine rice paddies, along with an easily built and repaired rice thresher (*right*) designed to thresh Philippine rice. (*Photos:* Courtesy of J. K. Campbell, Cornell University, Department of Agricultural Engineering)

(a)   (b)

FIGURE 9-11 Slash-and-Burn Agriculture in Fiji. Native forest people often practice what is known as slash-and-burn agriculture. (*a*) After trees are cut down and brush is burned, a mixture of crops, such as yams, taro, bananas, yaquona, and paw-paws, are planted. (*b*) In the second photo we see the same plot 18 months later. Yams and taro have been harvested, leaving yaquona, bananas, paw-paws, and taro suckers. (*Photos:* S. Siwatibau)

Towards a Sustainable Society

Sustainable Agriculture

by Norman Uphoff

Norman Uphoff is Director of the Cornell International Institute for Food, Agriculture and Development (CIIFAD). His research has taken him to Ghana, Nepal, and Sri Lanka. Dr. Uphoff is a consultant to many international food and development agencies.

By the year 2010, we will need to be producing 40 to 50% more food to meet likely demands. This figure is suggested by estimates of continuing population growth in the world, and allows for the increased demand for food that accompanies rising per capita incomes. Yet most of the "easy" gains in agricultural output appear to have been made, leaving us with more difficult and complex changes to be introduced into highly varied farming systems worldwide.

Researchers in biotechnology anticipate some remarkable advances in the future using recombinant DNA and other techniques. But moving innovations from the laboratory to the field is a long, costly, and uncertain process. Few of the heralded new technologies are likely to have an impact on production within the next decade or two. Our best hope is that they will give agriculture a desperately needed boost sometime in the future when we have exhausted our present resource-based and technology-based production possibilities.

The main point for the present is that we start using our resources and technologies now with more attention to not compromising future production capabilities. We need to be achieving production gains year by year while maintaining the fertility of our natural resource base for generations to come. In a number of areas, existing or evolving technologies and institutional changes can be utilized more beneficially to increase food

Some successful mixtures of crops give higher yields than monocultures. In other cases the yields may be lower, but, because less money needs to be spent on fertilizer, pesticides, or irrigation water, the net return to the farmer is higher than with a monoculture.

Agroforestry. One type of species combination is known as **agroforestry,** because it combines trees with field crops and animals. Trees may be used as shelterbelts to control erosion from both wind and water. Trees with long tap roots draw nutrients up from lower soil layers and can utilize deep underground water sources. Furthermore, trees provide many useful products, from fruit and cattle fodder to fuel wood and poles. For example, a tropical tree, *Acacia albida,* that adds nitrogen to the soil and drops its leaves during the wet season can be grown with crops such as millet or sorghum. The tree loses its leaves during the time that the grains are grown and so does not shade the soil. During the dry season the tree produces leaves and

production if fitted into the institutional and social settings of Third World agriculture.

- *Irrigation management:* applying scarce water more efficiently through improvements in physical and social infrastructure (the latter includes farmer organizations that have authority to manage collectively the water they receive). With improper water application, soil can become chemically degraded and infertile.
- *Integrated pest management:* reducing use of chemicals by utilizing biological controls, natural predators, weather information, changes in cultivation practices and cropping systems, etc.
- *Soil and nutrient management:* enhancing soil structure and fertility by practices that incorporate the benefits of plentiful microorganisms and the cycling of organic material in the soil.
- *Agroforestry:* combining field and tree crops that give multi-crop production that protects and even enriches the soil.
- *Aquaculture:* producing more marine and freshwater plants and animals through ecologically efficient technologies that harvest solar energy and utilize organic by-products.
- *Post-harvest technologies:* saving more of what is produced through a variety of techniques that guard against pests, spoilage, etc. This will reduce pressures on our land, water, and labor resources (post-harvest losses reduce food supply by 20–30%).
- *Renewable energy:* shifting to use of solar, hydro, wind, and other sources as much and as soon as practical.
- *Land tenure:* providing farmers long-term access to land, which gives them greater incentives to invest in conserving soil and biotic resources, particularly trees.
- *Training and maintenance of an agricultural labor force:* we must find a way to stem the migration from rural to urban areas of the younger generation in Third World countries. Increasingly we find urban unemployment occurring simultaneously with rural labor shortages.

These comments have not addressed the issue of the size of our world's population in the future. There are limits to what agricultural development can or should try to achieve for an expanding world population. We have also to appreciate that an expanded food supply does not necessarily reach those with the greatest nutritional needs, since the latter usually lack purchasing power. Sustainable agricultural solutions thus require attention to socio-economic dimensions and dynamics such as population growth and income and asset distribution. An overcrowded, inequitable world will not be sustainable no matter what our agricultural technology can potentially achieve.

pods that can be eaten by cattle, whose dung is returned to the soil. In another example, rubber trees are intercropped with tea bushes.

Adapting Agricultural Systems to Local Needs. No one system of agriculture will be able to embody the principles of LISA and appropriate technology for all regions of the world. Rather, agricultural systems will need to be tailored for specific conditions and social structures. Factors that can be varied include the kinds of plants grown, the timing of planting and harvesting, the spacing of individual plants, and the inputs of fertilizer, water, and pest-control agents.

Wherever possible, native species, crop mixtures, and management practices should be incorporated. The main innovations will be in the areas of "farm architecture"—that is, adding forest shelterbelts, ponds for aquaculture, and raised beds for crops. A second group of innovations will try to ensure that farming systems integrate sources of fertilizer and soil-conditioning materials into the

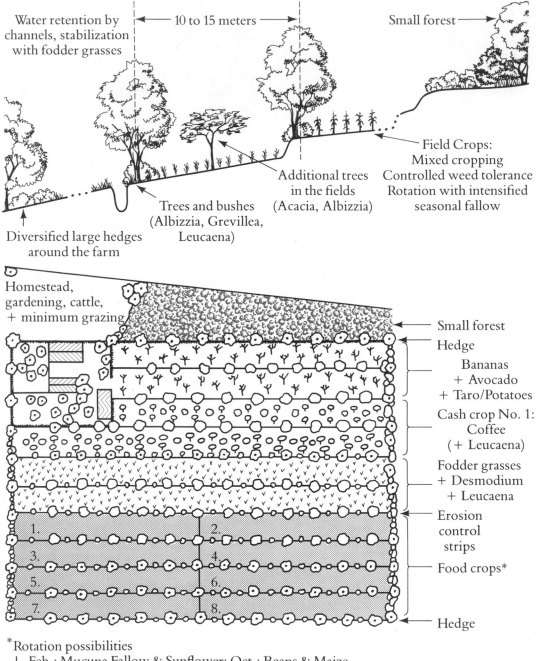

Water retention by channels, stabilization with fodder grasses

←— 10 to 15 meters —→

Small forest

Additional trees in the fields (Acacia, Albizzia)

Field Crops:
Mixed cropping
Controlled weed tolerance
Rotation with intensified seasonal fallow

Trees and bushes (Albizzia, Grevillea, Leucaena)

Diversified large hedges around the farm

Homestead, gardening, cattle, + minimum grazing

Small forest

Hedge

Bananas + Avocado + Taro/Potatoes

Cash crop No. 1: Coffee (+ Leucaena)

Fodder grasses + Desmodium + Leucaena

Erosion control strips

Food crops*

Hedge

*Rotation possibilities
1. Feb.: Mucuna Fallow & Sunflower; Oct.: Beans & Maize
2. Feb.: Soja & Sorghum; Oct.: Soja & Maize
3. Feb.: Cassava & Mucuna 4 Seasons; Oct.: Cassava & Mucuna 2 Seasons
4. Feb.: Cassava & Mucuna 4 Seasons; Oct.: Cassava & Mucuna 4 Seasons
5. Feb.: Soja & Sorghum; Oct.: Soja & Maize
6. Feb.: Mucuna Fallow & Sunflower; Oct.: Beans & Maize
7. Feb.: Sweet Potatoes & Soja; Oct.: Soja & Maize
8. Feb.: Soja & Maize; Oct.: Beans & Maize

farm system. For example, animal dung, pond sediments, and crop residues should be added back to the soil. (See Figure 9-12.)

Rethinking Agricultural Goals

A question that will be asked about non–Western-style agricultural systems, of course, is whether they have the potential to feed a continually increasing world population. But perhaps that is not the first question that should be asked. Rather, we should ask whether the energy-intensive, Western-style system we are now using is capable of feeding the world on a long-term basis.

China provides a case in point. China embarked on a program of high-input agricultural modernization in the 1970s. The program required large amounts of chemical fertilizers and pesticides. At the same time, the government began increasing the country's ability to manufacture these materials. The use of chemical fertilizers increased threefold in the first few years of the program, with half of all crops being treated. Over the past 10 years, however, larger and larger amounts of fertilizers and pesticides have been needed in order to keep production high. In some cases, production is declining despite these greater inputs. Furthermore, environmental damage due to agricultural pollution and erosion has become a problem. Human health is also suffering. According to a recent official news release, 27,000 people are poisoned by pesticides in one Chinese province every year, 10% of them fatally.

In contrast, sustainable agriculture meets criteria that ensure that the land will be fertile indefinitely. Soil nutrients removed by crops are replaced. Soil structure is maintained or improved. Weeds, pests, diseases, toxic elements, and soil acidity do not build up. Erosion is controlled. In addition, wildlife habitat is maintained, off-farm pollution is controlled, genetic resources are maintained, and use of nonrenewable energy and mineral resources is minimized. But it is not clear that farms run according to these principles can match the yields of traditional Western-style agriculture.

It may be that agriculture in the future will become a hybrid of the two systems—high-input Western agriculture and low-input sustainable agriculture. What is clear is that productivity and sustainability must both be considered if we are to feed the world's people far into the future.

It is also clear that attention needs to be paid to methods of promoting acceptance of new techniques. When agricultural systems fail entirely—for instance, when the last available free tree is cut for firewood—then there is evidence that new technologies are adopted readily. For example, at that point, tree-planting schemes become very popular. What is needed is technologies that will be adopted before the point of failure is reached, and this means technologies that are economically attractive to farmers.

It must be obvious to farmers that the cost of inputs such as fertilizer or improved seeds can be recouped by increased harvests or more reliable harvests. If this is true, then farmers are likely to adopt the new technologies readily.

Farm credit schemes can also make a difference in whether technologies are accepted. It is difficult to convince farmers in areas where the climate is variable to buy fertilizer, even when it can be shown that fertilizers improve yields dramatically, if there

FIGURE 9-12 Polycropping on Model Farm in Nyabisindu, Rwanda. (*a*) Side view. Note the use of trees for soil and moisture retention, as well as for the fruit, fodder, and soil-conditioning residues they produce. (*b*) Typical horizontal layout of model farm, ±1 hectare. (*Source:* Friedrich Behmel and Irmfried Neumann, "An Example for Agro-Forestry in Tropical Mountain Areas," Presented to the workshop on *Agro-Forestry in the African Humid Tropics*, Ibadan, Nigeria, 1981, as reported in M. Dover and L. Talbot, *To Feed the Earth*, World Resources Institute, 1987)

is a possibility that there will be no yields at all in certain years due to a failure of the rains. Some form of crop insurance could allow farmers to take advantage of new technologies while averaging out their losses over good years. Such schemes may be difficult for primarily rural, agricultural countries to develop on their own.

Education of farmers about the long-term benefits of sustainable-agriculture techniques is necessary and may be very effective if carried out on a local level.

Finally, of course, we come back to the problem of population growth. It seems logical to conclude that, at some point, the size of the human population could outstrip the ability of the earth's system to provide enough food to sustain everyone at a reasonable level, on an indefinite basis. We do not really know where that point is. We don't know whether there is still sustainable food capacity for more people or whether, perhaps, we require food supplies in excess of that capacity already. Intertwined with discussions of how to produce more and more food for more and more people, then, should be discussions about how to determine the number of people the earth can support on a sustainable basis, and how we can keep the human population within those limits.

SUMMARY

Periodic famines, such as the mid–1980s famine in Africa, occur against a background of chronic malnutrition for over 4 million people in the world. Children suffer from kwashiorkor and marasmus, diseases caused by too little protein or too few calories. Both are preventable by breastfeeding.

The specter of a food crisis has periodically been raised throughout history, but ensuring an adequate food supply involves more than simply growing enough food. Transportation of food to areas of need, reduction of losses due to pests, a damping of food price fluctuations caused by bad weather, and changing income distribution are all problems to be solved in order to achieve a fair distribution of food.

Issues involved in growing more food include energy requirements for fertilizers, pesticides, and machinery (a problem in poor developing nations short on energy resources); irrigation problems such as salinization, water-borne diseases, and water management; and cultivation of suboptimal land.

The Green Revolution promises great increases in food production due to high-yielding varieties of rice and wheat. But in order for the Green Revolution to work, there must be energy, water, and management inputs that may be unavailable in developing nations. Also of concern is loss of diversity in crop plants due to widespread adoption of new hybrid varieties.

The Green Revolution II promises even greater benefits from genetic engineering of plants to withstand a great variety of suboptimal farming conditions such as drought or high salt. Seed banks are important for preserving the genetic diversity on which the Green Revolution II depends. Economic and social changes are needed in many developing countries if the full benefits of agricultural technology are to be realized. Appropriate technology, or fitting technology into people's traditional way of life, is also necessary for full acceptance of the new crops and management practices. Grain reserves are a possible solution to fluctuating grain supplies and the accompanying price rises.

Sustainable agriculture meets criteria that ensure that the land will be fertile indefinitely. Polycropping, especially agroforestry, helps agricultural systems meet these goals. Productivity and sustainability should be equally important goals for agricultural systems.

Questions

1. If people die from too little food every day in the poorer countries, how can we say people rarely die of starvation?

2. What are the Green Revolution I and Green Revolution II? What problems are tied to the Green Revolution?

3. Explain how economic and political problems can be as important as introducing new technologies in terms of food production in developing countries.

4. What is meant by the statement "Agriculture without sustainability is mining"?

5. Debate the statement that sustainable agriculture is the right system to follow even if it cannot, in the short term, produce as much food as can Western-style agriculture.

Further Reading

"Can Africa Feed Itself," *World Development*, November 1990.

Dover, M., and L. Talbot. *To Feed the Earth: Agroecology for Sustainable Development*. Washington, D.C.: World Resources Institute, June 1987.

This well-written article explains the alternative agricultural systems proposed for developing nations—their advantages and disadvantages.

Franke, R. W., et al. *Seeds of Famine*. Montclair, N.J.: Allanheld, Osmun, 1980.

Food and population problems in Africa are perhaps the most severe in the world. Twenty-two of the poorest countries in the world are African. Population growth continues at high rates while food production languishes. These articles detail why the Green Revolution seems to have bypassed Africa and what social and economic barriers appear to prevent progress in food production.

Gasser, C., and R. Fraley. "Genetically Engineering Plants for Crop Improvement," *Science*, 244 (June 16, 1989).

This article explains the techniques of genetic engineering and the promise it holds for improvements in agriculture.

Intercom: The International Population News Magazine. Population Reference Bureau, Inc., 1337 Connecticut Ave. N.W., Washington, D.C. 20036.

This publication carries a capsule on the world food situation each month, prepared by FAO. Good for up-to-the-minute information.

Popkin, B., et al. "Breast-Feeding Patterns in Low-Income Countries," *Science*, 218 (December 10, 1982), 1088.

The authors discuss the interrelationship between the food and population problems, as well as advantages and social aspects of breastfeeding in developed and developing countries.

Scrimshaw, N. "The Politics of Starvation," *Technology Review*, August/September 1984, p. 18.

The effects of government economic and social policy on food supply in developing nations are well described in this paper.

References

Campbell, J. K. *Dibble Sticks, Donkeys, and Diesels: Machines in Crop Production*. International Rice Research Institute, P.O. Box 933, 1099 Manila, Philippines, 1989.

Drucker, C. "The Price of Progress in the Philippines," *Sierra*, October–November 1978, p. 22.

Global Outlook 2000. New York: United Nations Publications, 1990.

Holden, C. "Pioneering Rural Technology in India," *Science*, 207 (January 11, 1980), 159.

Nelson, Ridley. *Dryland Management, the Desertification Problem*. World Bank Technical Paper #116. Washington, D.C.: The World Bank, 1990.

Ward, G. M., et al. "Animals as an Energy Source in Third World Agriculture," *Science*, 208 (May 9, 1980), 570.

Winikoff, B., "Nutrition, Population and Health: Some Implications for Policy," *Science*, 200 (May 26, 1978), 895.

Worthington, E. B. "The Greening of the Desert: What Cost to Farmers," *Civil Engineering—ASCE*, August 1978, p. 60.

Chapter 10

Wildlife: Endangering Biodiversity

Some 213,000 fires burn each year in Brazil's tropical rain forest. Satellite photos show the black smoke from the smoldering fires rising into the air over the forest.

Below the smoke in rain forests like these, which clothe the earth in a belt running around the equator, live at least 2 million species, more than half of all the species that live on earth. But 2 million species is only a conservative estimate. There could be 5 million different species living in rain forests. We simply don't know. So far, only about 1.4 million rain forest species have been described and cataloged. Yet this ecosystem is disappearing at an alarming rate. Forty-five percent of the original forest cover has been logged and burned already. Another 1%, an area equal to the state of Massachusetts, is lost each year.

In most cases the forests are first logged for valuable tropical hardwoods. Then, once the logging roads are in, settlers follow and clear the remaining trees in order to farm or ranch. But little tropical forest is suitable for agriculture. In as little as 2 years or as much as 7 years, soil fertility is exhausted. Farms and ranches are abandoned to erosion and flooding. If current rates of destruction were to continue, in 20 years there would be no tropical forests at all, outside of the negligible portion in parks or reserves.

After viewing areas where loggers had **clear-cut** tropical forests, Nicholas Guppy (1984) wrote:

Visiting such areas, it is hard to view without emotion the miles of devastated trees, of felled broken and burned trunks, of branches, mud and bark crisscrossed with tractor trails. Such sights are reminiscent of photographs of Hiroshima, and Brazil and Indonesia might be regarded as waging the equivalent of thermonuclear war upon their own territories.

(See Figure 10-1.)

Guppy's reaction is the point of view of a biologist from a developed country, however. From the point of view of the developing country itself, these same tropical forests are a resource wealth, sometimes the only wealth that it has. "People are starving on one side of the Andes," says Mariano Prado (1983), who is developing a resort on the other, tropical forest side of the mountains, "and here there are so many riches." The Peruvian government is trying to shift some of the desperately poor population along the coast into the relatively unpopulated interior forests.

Estimates of deforestation rates (thousands of hectares per year)

FIGURE 10-1 Tropical Forest Destruction. The graph shows how the rate of tropical deforestation has increased over the past 10 years. The dark gray bars show the rate of deforestation in the early 1980s; the green bars show the rate of deforestation as shown recently by satellite imaging. (*Source:* "Deforestation in the Tropics," by Robert Repetto, *Scientific America,* April 1990, p. 40. *Photo:* George Seddon)

In order to weigh these two conflicting views of the rain forest, we must first understand what is lost when any ecosystem is destroyed and the species living there face extinction.

VALUE OF BIODIVERSITY

A Hard-Won Resource

As Harvard biologist E. O. Wilson points out, all countries have three kinds of wealth: material, cultural, and biological. The last, a country's biological wealth or biodiversity, has been the least valued. Yet a diverse biota is an important form of wealth. It is also a hard-won form of wealth. Figure 10-2 shows, in terms of marine organisms, the slow in-

crease of biological diversity since life began on earth. Of special interest are the five points shown on the diagram at which some great natural cataclysm appears to have caused a massive extinction of species. During the last such event, at the end of the Cretaceous period, the dinosaurs became extinct. After each mass extinction, new species evolved to fill in the gaps—but look at the time scale for recovery! After the great Permian extinction, during which some 77% to 96% of marine species became extinct, 5 million years went by before the number of families of species began to recover. Almost 1 million years passed before the number of families increased to their former number after the Cretaceous extinction. For comparison, consider that our own species, *Homo sapiens,* is believed to have evolved only 200,000 years ago.

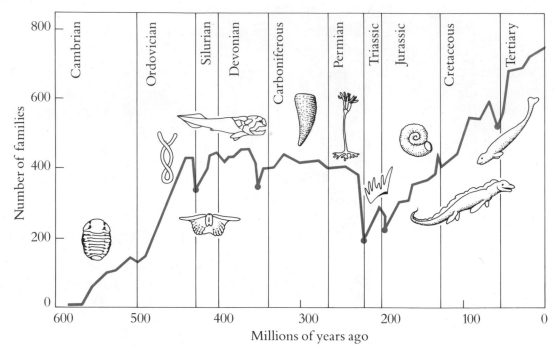

FIGURE 10-2 The Level of Biological Diversity. Biological diversity, as shown by the number of families of marine animals, has increased slowly over time. Marine animals are used to track biological diversity because their fossil record is the most complete, but data from other sets of organisms support the theory that there have been five mass extinctions over the course of evolutionary history. These extinctions are marked in the diagram by dots. (*Source:* E. O. Wilson, "Threats to Biodiversity," *Scientific American*, September 1989, p. 111)

Today, as a result of the clearing of tropical forests, Wilson estimates that we may be losing 4,000 to 6,000 species per year, 10,000 times the natural rate of extinction and far faster than new species can evolve.

Wildlife as a Harvestable Resource

Even in highly developed countries such as the United States, wildlife species provide humans with food and fuel in the form of fish, nuts, berries, and wood for heating. The value of fresh foods from wild organisms in the United States is estimated at $2.8 billion per year. In Vermont, over half the homes now use wood as their primary heat source.

In developing countries, wild sources of food and fuel are even more important. Fish protein pro-

vides 10% of the animal protein in human diets worldwide. In many developing countries, wood is the only source of heat for cooking or heating.

Practical Value in Medicine, Agriculture, and Industry

Lost species can be viewed as lost opportunities. In addition to providing food and fuel, plants and animals are sources of drugs, pest control substances, and raw materials for industry. Twenty-five percent of prescription drugs dispensed in the United States contain plant extracts that cannot be synthesized. These drugs include the tranquilizer reserpine as well as a variety of antibiotics, pain killers, and drugs used to treat heart disease and high blood pressure. Vincristine, a drug extracted from a trop-

Towards a Sustainable Society / Maintaining Soil Fertility and Wise Use of Biological Resources

Humans depend on the fertility of the natural world for food and medicines and for fuel resources such as wood. The maintenance of soil fertility and wise harvesting of natural biological resources is essential for a sustainable society.

Fuelwood plantation in Ethiopia. The UN is increasing efforts to plant trees that can be harvested for fuelwood in deforested, dry lands. In addition to helping supply fuel, such tree plantations will help prevent erosion, and may even moderate climate. *(UNDP: Louise Gubb)*

Aquaculture in Mexico. Growing fish or other seafood in pens in coastal waters or in ponds is an industry that may help increase the world's food supply. *(UNDP: Emma Robson)*

Making compost in Benin. Composting organic wastes can provide a needed soil conditioner at the same time that it helps dispose of solid wastes. *(UNDP: Ruth Massey)*

U.S. old growth forest. In the United States, as in many other countries, timber is being harvested on National Forest land faster than it will regrow. Taxol, a compound that appears to be a potent anti-cancer drug, was recently isolated from certain trees in old-growth forests like this one. *(DITTLI/NPS: North Cascades National Park)*

Indigo Bunting. This migratory U.S. songbird is endangered by the loss of both tropical rainforest and nesting areas in the U.S. *(Bates Littlehales)*

Rainforest plant. A wealth of medicinal and food species is found in the rainforest. *(UN Photo Library)*

Howell's gumweed. Medicinal plants are not only found in the rainforest. This rare plant is a close relative of one used by Native Americans as a sedative, expectorant, and cure for poison ivy. *(Bob Keisling)*

Egret. Protected on an Indian wildlife reserve. *(UN Photo Library)*

Tiger cubs. Protected on Indian wildlife reserve. *(UN Photo Library)*

FIGURE 10-3 Medicinal Plants Used by Amazonian Indians. The natives of Amazonia use about 300 different plants as medicines. Above are shown: (a) *Phytolacca rivinoides,* used to treat head lice; (b) *Renealmia,* which is brewed into a tea for coughs and colds; (c) *Marcgravia coriacea,* useful for centipede stings; and (d) *Cordia nodosa,* from which a fever-reducing tea is made. A number of plant-based medicines in common use today were first discovered by native forest dwellers. An example is the muscle relaxant curare, frequently used during surgical operations. (*Photos:* Mark J. Plotkin)

(a)

(b)

(c)

(d)

ical periwinkle, is used in the successful treatment of Hodgkins disease, a cancer that strikes 5,000–6,000 Americans each year. However, only 5,000 plant species have been investigated for useful drugs. Scientists feel that another 5,000 usable drugs could be found among the 500,000 species of plants believed to grow in the world (Figure 10-3).

Agricultural researchers have found uses for a number of organisms. For instance, an important technique in farming is the use of biological controls, which involves using one species to prevent another from harming crops. As an example, certain wasps can successfully prevent the sugar-cane borer from destroying whole fields of cane. Another technique of modern agriculture involves the cross-breeding of various plant species to develop crops with higher yields or resistance to disease, drought, or heat. (In some parts of the world the spread of modern hybrid grain varieties threatens the survival of traditional varieties, many of which have useful characteristics. This problem is discussed in Chapter 9.)

Many plants produce chemicals that are natural *insecticides* (insect killers) or *herbicides* (weed killers). Still other plants provide waxes, lubricating oils, resins, oils for perfumes and flavorings, and dyes. The list could go on. And these are only the useful plant and animal products discovered so far. Many other agricultural, drug, and manufacturing substances await discovery.

Value as Part of the Gene Pool

The science of genetic engineering is in its infancy, yet it is already clear that in the future scientists will be able to transfer, from one plant to another, desirable genes for certain characteristics. Examples might include disease or drought resistance, insect resistance, drug-producing ability, and higher protein content (Figure 10-4). Reducing the number of species in the world reduces the size of the gene pool. Every time we allow a plant or animal to become extinct, we run the risk of losing a possibly helpful organism or gene.

Value as Part of Food Webs

The loss of a particular species or group of species may have far-reaching effects on the community in which the species live. Complex food webs are common in temperate and tropical climates; however, since only a relatively few webs have been thoroughly studied, we usually lack the knowledge to predict the effects of the extinction of any particular plant or animal species. Many rare insects, snails, and birds depend on a particular kind of plant for food or as a place to live. If the plant becomes extinct, the animal is also likely to become extinct. In another case, a predator that normally keeps some pest under control might be lost. As an example, sea otters were almost wiped out by fur trappers in the eighteenth and nineteenth centuries.

Ecological studies show that the sea otter is a vital member of the shore community. By feeding on species such as sea urchins, otters protect seaweeds such as kelp from being overgrazed. In turn, kelp beds are at the bottom of the food webs that sustain species such as harbor seals and bald eagles. Now, due in part to laws such as the Marine Mammal Protection Act, sea otter populations are recovering.

Concern about endangered plant species has come much more slowly than concern about endangered animal species; yet the two are so intimately related that they cannot be conserved separately. Many examples are known of animals driven to the brink of extinction because a particular plant on which they feed or under which they shelter became scarce. Peter Raven, of the Missouri Botanical Garden, has estimated that for every plant species that becomes extinct, 10 to 30 species of insects, higher animals, and other plants may also face extinction.

The red-cockaded woodpecker is threatened with extinction because it nests only in mature longleaf and loblolly pines. In many areas these mature trees are being replaced by young trees grown for pulp. Maturation of the longleaf pine itself appears to depend on a ground cover of wiregrass (*Aristida stricta*), which encourages fires that help the pine seedlings germinate and grow. Wiregrass grows, slowly, from stolons rather than from seed. Often, an area of wiregrass and longleaf pine will not grow back when logged, apparently because the slower-growing wiregrass cannot compete well with the faster-growing species.

Ecosystem Services

In addition to the easily quantified value of wild species as food, fuel, and raw materials, wildlife species provide the planet with a set of what might be termed **ecosystem services.** Plants produce oxygen that humans and other animals need for respiration. In addition, plants and microorganisms remove air and water pollutants, recycle nutrients, and moderate climate. While some of these services might be carried out by technological processes (the

FIGURE 10-4 Wild Corn. A kind of wild corn (*Zea diploperennis*) was recently discovered on a hillside in Mexico. This wild corn is a perennial—that is, it doesn't need to be planted each year, as cultivated corn must. In addition, the corn is resistant to various viruses and grows well in wet soil. These are all desirable characteristics to transfer to cultivated corn by traditional plant-breeding techniques or by genetic engineering. The new species has so far been found only in this one location. The discovery was made just before the hillside was to be plowed up. (*Photo:* Larry Daughters/The World Bank)

removal of phosphates in runoff water by a coastal wetland area could be accomplished at much greater cost by a sewage treatment plant), others are clearly irreplaceable.

Intrinsic Value of Species

Besides all the practical reasons we might give, there are philosophical arguments in favor of preserving as many species as possible. Any species lost is gone forever. If we fail to do what is in our power to prevent these losses, we make a choice not only for ourselves but also for future generations. We are saying that they will never see the same living creatures we can see; they will never enjoy the diversity we enjoy. It may not even be a question of enjoyment—having evolved in the midst of such diversity, humans may require it to maintain their own mental health.

All these reasons, of course, consider other species only from the viewpoint of their usefulness to humans. Henry Beston (1928) wrote:

Remote from universal nature, and living by complicated artifice, man in civilization surveys the creature through the glass of his knowledge and sees thereby a feather magnified and the whole image in distortion. We patronize them for their incompleteness, for their tragic fate of having taken form so far below ourselves. And therein we err and greatly err. For the animal shall not be measured by man. In a world older and more complete than ours they move finished and complete, gifted with extensions of the senses we have lost or never attained, living by voices we shall never hear. They are not brethren, they are not underlings; they are other nations, caught with ourselves in the net of life and time, fellow prisoners of the splendour and travail of the earth.

WHY SPECIES LOSS IS ACCELERATING

Hunting

Tropical forests are the most species–rich ecosystem on earth. For this reason the clearing of tropical

Towards a Sustainable Society

Wise Use of Resources
by Faith Thompson Campbell

Faith T. Campbell is a Senior Research Associate in charge of plant conservation projects for the Natural Resources Defense Council. Dr. Campbell has been a nongovernmental observer at meetings of the Con-

vention on International Trade in Endangered Species (CITES) and has won awards for her work in plant conservation.

We humans are actively destroying the life-sustaining systems of our only home, earth. By the middle of the next century, scientists predict, we will have caused the extinction of up to one half of all species now living. Over the same period, global climate change, stratospheric ozone depletion, loss of soil fertility, and waste and pollution of water supplies will further degrade earth's habitability.

To attain a sustainable society, we must

- Reduce human population numbers as rapidly as possible (while maintaining standards of equity)
- Improve the efficiency of our resource use

Americans harm the biosphere primarily through our disproportionate use of global resources and equally disproportionate contribution to pollution. Americans contribute 22% of CO_2 caused by burning of fossil fuels. We log virgin forests here and abroad, threatening species residing there and adding to CO_2 buildup in the atmosphere.

Even biological resources are *not* renewable when used at current, excessive rates. Humans, livestock,

forest land is responsible for the greatest part of species loss today. At other times and in other places, however, hunting has contributed to the loss of a number of animals, especially *vertebrates* (animals that have a backbone). In certain well-managed wildlife populations, hunting need not harm the population—in fact, it can contribute to its welfare, most notably in cases where a population threatens to grow too large for its habitat. Unregulated hunting, however, has contributed to the loss of species. The buffalo of the American plains was hunted almost to extinction in the 1800s. Trainloads of hunters came for the sport, often carrying

home no more than a buffalo head to mount as a trophy. In Africa, game officials have stopped or limited the hunting of many game species lest these animals cease to exist except in zoos. (See Controversy 10-1.)

Collection of Plants

Certain plants, especially cacti, orchids, certain spring-flowering bulbs, and carnivorous plants, are so desirable that they have been collected almost to extinction. Dealers in Texas and Mexico dig up huge piles of cactus and truck them to market,

and wildlife depend on plants' "excess" energy—the energy (stored in leaves, fruit, etc.) produced by plants above the minimum needed for their own survival. According to Dr. Paul Ehrlich, people already use or destroy through carelessness 25% of all the world's terrestrial plants' "excess" energy. If human population grows as projected and living standards in Third World countries improve somewhat, in 50 years humans may use *all* the available energy produced by plants—leaving *none* for wildlife.

Given our role in causing environmental destruction and our relative wealth and technological skills, we Americans have a moral and practical duty to work for sustainability. First, we must limit both our numbers and our own consumption of all natural resources. Furthermore, we should press suppliers of "renewable" natural resources such as wild, garden, and houseplants to ensure that they are obtained by environmentally sustainable practices.

At home and abroad, we must actively conserve biological diversity—especially the plants and invertebrates that perform the bulk of the "work" in sustaining a functioning ecosystem. (Protecting birds and mammals—at the top of the food chain—cannot by itself repair environmental degradation.)

We must modify capitalism to raise standards of living in the Third World and reduce the debt they are currently paying to ourselves, Europe, and Japan. Otherwise, the over one billion people now living in "absolute poverty" must continue ruthlessly exploiting whatever resources they have, regardless of the damage to the global environment.

We must also *multiply* the funding for conservation and environmental protection activities by governmental agencies and nongovernmental organizations. The $63 million that U.S. organizations spent on conserving biological diversity in developing countries in 1989 pales beside the $5 billion Americans spend per year on video games. It is a matter of priorities.

Private industry can also contribute by *paying* for use of valuable chemicals and genes extracted from tropical plants and animals.

Citizens should demand the following governmental actions:

- Increasing support to population control programs and eliminating restrictions tied to concerns about abortion
- Adopting legislation that mandates a high priority for protecting biological diversity at home and funds programs abroad
- Adopting stringent energy efficiency standards for transportation, buildings, and industry
- Increasing funding for environmental protection programs

selling them to collectors and for use in Southwestern landscaping schemes. Half the cacti go as far afield as Europe and the Far East.

Competition with Introduced Species: The Special Case of Islands

A number of species have become endangered or are already extinct because they were unable to compete with new species introduced into their habitat. Island ecosystems are especially fragile in terms of species loss due to competition with introduced species.

Of the 161 birds that have become extinct in their native habitat since the year 1600, 149 lived on islands. On some islands—for instance, the Hawaiian Islands—many species have evolved fairly recently. These islands exhibit a variety of different habitats due to differences in soil, rainfall, and elevation. During the evolution of native plants, competition from other species was different from what happened on the continents, allowing many new species to survive. In Hawaii, 97% of the native species are *endemic* (found nowhere else). Unfortunately, many of these species have been unable to compete with plant species or survive predation by animal spe-

Endangered Sea Mammals versus
Endangered Eskimo Culture

We are eskimo, we can't write a check to purchase something—Sea mammals. It's our living. . . .

John Henry, Native American

Whaling is an affront to human dignity.

Sir Peter Scott

In 1972, the U.S. Congress passed the Ocean Mammal Protection Bill. This law protects arctic fur seals, walruses, and whales, among other ocean mammals, from commercial hunting, which has reduced some species almost to extinction. However, during the hearings before the bill was passed, it became clear that a total prohibition of the hunting of sea mammals or the sale of products made from sea mammals would threaten something else that was endangered: native Eskimo culture.

The following testimony is excerpted from hearings from the Subcommittee on Oceans and Atmosphere of the Committee on Commerce of the United States Senate in the spring of 1972 (before the Ocean Mammals Protection Bill was passed):

Statement of Myrtle Johnson: I am a resident of Nome, and was born and raised in the village of Golovin. . . . I will draw from people I know personally to paint an imaginary picture based upon the truth.

John and Mary are in their mid-50s. John works part-time seasonally in casual labor, and they care for four foster children plus one grandchild. John is a successful seal hunter. He also catches Beluga. If he had a chance, he would join a crew and hunt black whale as well. This would bring him a share of meat and muktuk—something his family otherwise must buy at $3 per pound or receive as a gift that will oblige him to return in some other form.

John's family depends heavily upon sea mammal meat and oil all year long. The spring greens are stored in fresh seal oil, some of this being sent to family and friends living in the cities. The meat is dried, frozen, or in other ways preserved for the time when it is not so plentiful. . . .

The skins will end up as mukluks, parkas, parka-pants, and vests for the family, as well as surplus skins or garments to be sold or traded to others. Both raw and stretched, skins are a source of income and add to the internal welfare system of their village. . . .

Caucasians speak of bread as the staff of life. For coastal Eskimos the seal represents the single basic food staple with all the meanings others may associate with bread. . . .

To take away our Eskimo bread is to deny the men and women of the villages the right to work to meet their needs as they see them and can mean the final end of our way of life before we are fully adapted to the modern world.

As a result of the hearings, the final act allowed exemptions for subsistence hunting (hunting for food or clothing) and the sale of native handicrafts.★

On the issue of whales, however, even the Eskimo right to subsistence hunting has been questioned. For centuries, humans have hunted whales for oil and meat. In the 1700s and 1800s, right and bowhead whales were the main targets. Now these whales, along with the blue whale, the humpback, and the gray whale, are near extinction.

Although they swim in the oceans, as fish do, whales and their smaller relatives, the dolphins, are mammals. Whales are warm-blooded and suckle their young. They are also social animals, living in herds and possibly even in families. Within the past few years, scientists have realized that whales can "talk" to each other. Some beautiful records have been made of the singing sounds they make under water.

Whaling was once a dangerous occupation. The small crew of men, with their harpoons and in their fragile boat, and the huge whale were relatively well matched. Mostly the men won, but sometimes the whale did, too.

★ When the bill was renewed in 1981, the subsistence exemption was changed to one for rural users, rather than specifically mentioning Eskimos.

Modern methods, however, have tipped the balance far in favor of men.

Modern non-Eskimo whaling fleets consist of fast killer boats, which kill the whales with harpoon guns, and large factory ships, which process the whales at sea. Whales are located by sonar or small planes, then driven by high-frequency sound waves until they are exhausted. A harpoon carrying a grenade, which explodes within the whale, is used to kill them. With these methods, modern whaling fleets have killed more whales in this century than whalers did in the sixteenth, seventeenth, eighteenth, and nineteenth centuries combined. Within the past 50 years, the numbers of blue, humpback, and gray whales have been reduced from hundreds of thousands to a few thousand.

About 30 nations belong to the International Whaling Commission, which sets yearly whaling quotas (the numbers of each type of whale that may be caught in the various oceans). Nations that have whaling fleets, such as Japan, and those that no longer have fleets, such as the United States, Canada, and South Africa, send delegates to the Commission meetings. In past years, quotas were slowly reduced as new scientific data came to light on the population sizes and reproductive ability of whales. However, quotas also declined because, in a number of cases, whalers were simply unable to find enough whales to fill them.

A moratorium on commercial whaling is now in effect, although some of the smaller whales such as the minke and fin whales are still hunted by a few countries who claim they are conducting "research."

In 1946, the IWC treaty noted that the bowhead whale was the most endangered whale species. The Commission at that time forbade all but subsistence hunting. U.S. Eskimos had been catching about 10 to 15 bowheads per year since 1946. However, in the 1970s, the catch increased. Further, the number of whales struck but lost steadily increased.

The increased whale catch was related to the increase in whaling crews. This was a result of the greater availability of jobs and money for Eskimos. Traditionally, to be a whaling captain was not only a matter of great prestige, but also of great difficulty. One had to either inherit the equipment, marry to obtain it, or gain sufficient wealth to purchase it. The latter option was seldom possible. Recently, however, such construction projects as the Alaskan pipeline, and oil drilling operations, as well as the Alaskan Native Claims Settlement, have changed this. An ambitious Eskimo can save $9,000 for an "outfit" plus another $2,000 for provisions for a whaling crew.

The IWC was concerned about the effect this increased hunting would have on an already severely endangered species. In 1976 the commission called for a total ban on subsistence hunting of the bowhead.

The Eskimos were outraged by the ban, as were many other people who sympathize with the native Alaskans' difficult fight to survive and preserve their culture in a relatively hostile natural environment. W. H. DuBay (1977) wrote, in defense of the Eskimo hunters:

People outside Alaska don't seem to realize that the Eskimos are the residents of the Arctic and that, were it not for their aggressiveness in protecting their Arctic homeland from those who would destroy it, there would be no effective environmental safeguards at all operating in the U.S. or Canadian Arctic.

In the end, the commission allowed the Eskimos a small quota of bowheads.

Should the United States continue to ask for an exemption for Alaskan Eskimos to hunt bowhead whales, even though this makes it more difficult for the United States to support a total moratorium on whaling at IWC meetings?

Most of us would agree that it would be wrong to hunt whales to extinction. But to go a step further, should we "harvest" them at all? When the moratorium on commercial whaling ends, should limited commercial whaling be allowed, as long as no whale species are driven to extinction?

Sources: John Henry, quoted in the Hearings on the Ocean Mammal Protection Bill, U.S. Senate Committee on Commerce, Subcommittee on Oceans and Atmosphere; Peter Scott, quoted in The New York Times, June 8, 1982, p. A25; W. H. Dubay, Letter to the Editor, The New York Times, November 15, 1977.

cies introduced in modern times. For example, imported mouflon sheep threaten both the mamane tree and the honeycreeper, a bird dependent on the tree as a food source. Of the native plant and animal species of the Hawaiian Islands, 36% are in danger and more than 10% may already be extinct.

Pesticides and Air Pollution

Many habitats that are otherwise undisturbed are poisoned by air pollution, acid rain, or pesticides. Pines in the mountains near Los Angeles are injured by smog from the city. The large-scale use of pesticides in agriculture places further stress upon many endangered species. For instance, birds in the raptor group, which includes hawks and falcons, are affected by the use of DDT.

As part of a pest-control program in the American West, attempts were made to kill coyotes, foxes, and wolves by using poisoned baits. This method had a severe effect on populations of endangered species, among them the bald eagle, that also took the bait.

Habitat Destruction

As human populations grow, they require more houses, roads, and shopping centers. Forests are cut down; marshes, estuaries, and bays are filled in; and land is overturned in the search for coal. All of these processes reduce the land or food supply available to various animals and plants. In a sense, humans are increasing their own habitat at the expense of the habitats for other creatures.

Habitat destruction is the main reason why species are threatened with extinction today. Although the greatest problem exists in the tropical rain forests, it would be wrong to suppose that this is the only place where habitat alteration is a problem.

Nor is tropical forest the only type of forest whose loss concerns us today. In the United States the fight over a small owl highlights the loss of old-growth forests. The spotted owl lives in old-growth forests of the Pacific Northwest. **Old-growth forest** means stands of trees 200 years old or more. Some of the Douglas firs in these forests

began their growth more than 500 years ago (Figure 10-5).

Forested land anywhere is a valuable resource. Forests absorb pollutants from the air and water. Tree roots hold onto soil, thus preventing erosion, while the humus-rich soils formed by rotting leaves slow the flow of rainwater, preventing floods. Carbon dioxide is absorbed and oxygen is given off by forests. All of these "ecosystem services" can be provided by any forest. If the land is carefully replanted, we can expect to regain many of these forest benefits even in the young forests that grow up after an area is logged. But old-growth forests provide something more—biodiversity. Over the centuries required for their growth, a vast web of interconnected species has grown up in these forests. Just as in the tropical forests, the sheer variety of organisms promises new finds in medicine, agriculture, and environmental improvement. Moreover, as almost any visitor to these forests will attest, the cathedral-like beauty of an old-growth forest grove, cool and shady, with a floor of springy mosses and ferns and tree trunks upholstered in velvety epiphytes, provides a peaceful and contemplative setting that reforested land will not achieve for centuries.

In the Pacific Northwest a whole industry has grown up around logging the old-growth forests. There are saw mills that can handle only the giant trunks of the ancient trees. Communities of loggers, their families, and the services they use dot the area. But the old-growth forest is a limited resource. Only about one-eighth of the original forest, about 2.4 million acres, remains. Some 800,000 acres are protected in parks and wilderness areas, mostly at high elevations. Almost all the rest is on lands under jurisdiction of the Forest Service or the Bureau of Land Management (see Figure 10-5).

The U.S. Forest Service, as directed by Congress, is meant to manage federal lands under its jurisdiction for a variety of purposes, one of which is the provision of lumber. Old-growth forests that once stood on private lands have long since fallen to the loggers' saws and, at current rates of logging, the old-growth trees on federal lands will be gone in another 10 years. Environmentalists working to

FIGURE 10-5 Spotted Owl and Its Habitat. The map shows the extent of old-growth forest in the Pacific Northwest. The amount is about 12% of the original forest cover. Only a small portion is protected in wilderness areas or parks. Almost all of the remaining forest is on federal land, overseen by the U.S. Forest Service or the Bureau of Land Management. (*Photo:* U.S. Fish and Wildlife Service)

save more than the tiny fraction of old-growth forest locked up in parks find themselves pitted against the interests of lumber companies and the people they employ. There are few other forms of employment in the forested areas, and people are loath to leave the area where their families have lived and worked, sometimes for generations. Yet the jobs

will be gone anyway in a few decades, if the forests are cut at the present rate.

Enter the spotted owl. The owl nests in the broken-topped dead trees or "snags" found in old-growth forests. It eats from the top of a food web whose base is set firmly on the plant species found in the old forest. It is clear that without the forest in its present form the spotted owl could not survive. Realizing that the owl was their best hope for saving the forest, environmentally concerned citizens and officials pushed to have the owl listed as an endangered species. Under the Endangered Species Act, this would prohibit the government from taking actions on federal lands that would threaten the survival of the owl, such as allowing logging of the owl's habitat in old-growth forest.

In June of 1990 the U.S. Fish and Wildlife Service formally declared the spotted owl a threatened species. While not quite as much in danger as an endangered species, threatened species are also protected by the Endangered Species Act. Predictably, timber companies and loggers were dismayed that the interests of a small owl could seem to be put before human interests. Yet the owl, like the snail darter, an endangered three-inch fish that held up completion of the $116 million dollar Tellico dam in the 1970s, must be viewed as an indicator species. Like the canary in the coal mine, which warns of danger, these endangered creatures are indicators of the values lost when ecosystems are changed or destroyed. In the case of the snail darter, the fish represented the value of a free-flowing river compared to a dammed reservoir. The spotted owl stands for all the material and spiritual treasures found in an old-growth forest.

PROTECTING WILDLIFE RESOURCES

The protection of wildlife resources can be approached in a variety of ways. Laws can be written to protect species or to enhance their survival on an individual basis. This is the way the U.S. Endangered Species Act works. Samples of species can also be collected in zoos, botanical gardens, or seed banks to ensure that we have representative examples of all living organisms. International seed banks preserve seeds and tubers of several species of food plants. For many species, however, this second approach does not appear feasible. Special requirements for habitat or the population size for breeding may be too difficult to meet in captivity.

A third approach is to set aside biological reserves containing entire ecosystems. In this way, not only obviously threatened species but also the organisms tied to them in complex food webs can be saved.

Laws Protecting Wildlife

In the United States, the major law protecting individual species is the Endangered Species Act (ESA). Last reauthorized in 1988, the act directs that plants and animals in danger of extinction be identified (listed) and that a recovery plan for each of these species be designed by the U.S. Fish and Wildlife Service or the National Marine Fisheries Agency. The law distinguishes between **endangered species,** those species that are in imminent danger of extinction, and **threatened species,** those that will become endangered if no action is taken, although species in both categories are protected. The ESA prohibits the government from undertaking projects that would further harm endangered or threatened species or their habitats, but it does not apply to projects on private land. The act does, however, prohibit anyone from harming or taking endangered or threatened animals, even if they are on private land (see Figure 10-6).

In the spotted owl controversy, the U.S. government, in order to comply with the Endangered Species Act, finally agreed to set aside areas of old-growth forest as "habitat conservation areas" for the owl. (But this issue almost provoked a challenge to the ESA. See Controversy 10-2.)

Internationally, the major law protecting endangered species is the Convention on International Trade in Endangered Species of Wild Fauna and Flora (CITES). The countries that have signed CITES have agreed to abide by a system of permits for both exporting and importing threatened and endangered species, or products made from them. Trade in nearly extinct species is practically prohibited, while strict controls are set for other endangered or threatened species (Figure 10-7).

Several laws have been passed to decrease the effects of U.S. actions on endangered species worldwide. Under the National Environmental Policy Act (NEPA), U.S. government agencies are re-

FIGURE 10-6 Endangered Boott's Rattlesnake Root. Unlike endangered animals, which are protected by the Endangered Species Act from being "taken" at any place in their natural habitat, endangered plants are protected only where they occur on federal lands. Furthermore, it is only illegal to "take" plants. Vandalism, uprooting, or trampling endangered plants is not, strictly speaking, illegal. (*Photo:* Larry Master, Heritage Task Force)

quired to examine their actions abroad for possible ecological harm.

The United States has signed the Convention on Nature Protection and Wildlife Preservation in the Western Hemisphere. Because of this convention, special plans were developed during Pan American Canal negotiations by the United States and Panama to protect endangered vegetation on Barro Colorado Island.

Wildlife Management Techniques

A variety of special techniques have been developed to preserve species in danger of extinction or to increase the range of animals considered highly desirable (i.e., those that people like to hunt). In some cases, animals may be transferred from their natural habitat to a similar area where they were not previously found. This has been done mainly with nonendangered game species such as Canada geese. The wild turkey, which has been introduced in a number of areas, now occupies more territory than it did during Colonial times.

When the judgment has been made that a species will not survive on its own, even if given a fair chance, eggs may be collected and hatched in captivity, or breeding programs can be instituted at zoos. The animals can in some, but not all, cases be successfully reintroduced into the wild.

In some cases, management procedures on preserves are so successful that limited hunting can again be allowed. One hundred years ago, the American bison lived in herds so huge it sometimes required several hours to pass by a herd. Fifty years ago there were only a few hundred bison left. Within the past few years, bison numbers have increased enough to again allow some hunting.

Refuges and Reserves

In the United States during the early 1900s, Congress began to set aside areas of wildlife habitat, or **refuges,** to help protect endangered wildlife. In a similar way, the United Nations Educational, Scientific and Cultural Organization (UNESCO) has begun to identify "biosphere reserves" or "ecological reserves," a network of protected samples of the world's major ecosystem types. The reserves must be large enough to support all the species living there, buffer them from the outside world, and protect their genetic diversity. In this way the reserve allows both growth and evolution and acts as a standard against which human effects on the environment can be measured.

How Big Do Reserves Need to Be? Many wildlife experts point out that refuges must be large areas, measured in thousands of square kilometers. Smaller areas may not be able to support certain species, often those most endangered. For example, large predators such as wolves or the big cats must roam vast areas to find food. In addition, larger reserves are able to buffer species from border pressures, such as pollution or human disturbance.

Controversy 10-2

Do We Need Flexibility in Laws Protecting Endangered Species?

No compromise is possible when the problem is stated in terms of the question "Do organisms have the right to exist?"

Wayne Grimm, National
Museum of Canada

We survived without the dinosaur. What's the big deal about the owl?

Bruce Goetsch, salesman

When the Endangered Species Act halted construction of the Tellico Dam because it appeared that a completed dam would wipe out the endangered snail darter, many legislators began to feel that the act was "inflexible." That is, the act had no provision for considering a project's value compared to the value of an endangered species. People began thinking of cases in

which, they felt, a project or action could have more value to humans than the continued existence of a species. Senator William Scott of Virginia (1978) argued:

Suppose a bird of some endangered species was in front of an intercontinental ballistic missile. . . . They could not release that missile. To me that would be a ridiculous offense. . . . Any commander worth his salt . . . would go ahead and release the missile, but he would be disobeying the law and would be subject to a fine of $20,000 and imprisonment for up to a year.

In a similar way, when protection of the spotted owl seemed to take precedence over jobs for citizens of logging communities, the administration announced that it would ask for changes in

the Endangered Species Act, so that it would be easier to allow a species to dwindle to extinction if severe economic hardship would result from protecting it.

Do you feel there are instances in which a project could have more significance to humankind than the survival of an endangered species? Can you think of an example? Or do you think that no species should become extinct because of a construction project or an industry, however beneficial to humans? Can you justify this view?

Sources: Wayne Grimm, quoted in *Science, 196* (June 24, 1977), 1427–28; and Bruce Goetsch quoted in *Time Magazine,* June 25, 1990, p. 61.

Certain research done on islands has a bearing on how big parks or reserves must be. The size of an island seems to influence how many different species can exist there. Ecologists E. O. Wilson (1984) and Robert MacArthur found in a study of animals on Pacific islands that a doubling of the area of an island is not accompanied by a doubling of the number of species found. Rather, an island ten times as big is needed to support twice the number of species. The reason this research applies to parks or reserves is that such areas are more and more becoming like natural islands in the midst of a sea of human-influenced habitat destruction.

Following the rule of island biogeography, if 90% of a natural habitat is destroyed and 10% is set aside in a reserve or park, we might expect to save no more than half the original number of species found in the area. By this reasoning, if we save only as much of the Amazonian tropical forests as is now found in parks or preserves, we may well be unable to save two-thirds of the half-million species found there.

It is not yet certain that the island theory applies to parks. However, studies now being done in some tropical forests by ecologists seem to show that it does. Thomas Lovejoy, of the Smithsonian Insti-

FIGURE 10-7 Declining Elephant Populations. African elephant herds have decreased dramatically in the past 20 years, due mainly to poachers seeking the ivory tusks. In 1970, approximately 5 million elephants lived in Africa; by 1989 there were about 600,000. In 1990 an international ban on the trading of ivory was accepted by members of the Convention on International Trade in Endangered Species (CITES). Without an international market, it is hoped that ivory poachers will find it unprofitable to continue to kill elephants. (*Photo:* Judy Rensberger/*New York Times* Pictures)

tution, gives the example of a 25-acre preserve that lost its far-ranging piglike animals called peccaries. In an unanticipated chain reaction, ten species of frogs also disappeared because they needed the moist wallows created by the peccaries.

Preserving Genetic Diversity. In addition, wildlife experts are concerned about the size of reserve needed to preserve genetic diversity within a particular species. As the population of a particular species becomes smaller and smaller, animals have fewer choices in breeding. As a result, the offspring become more and more alike in their genetic composition.

In evolutionary terms this is not a good thing. A population in which all the individuals contain almost the same genes is vulnerable to any changes in the environment. Without a range of different characteristics among members of the population, there is no longer the possibility that some members will be able to stand disease or a change in the environment better than the average individual.

There is always the danger that climatic change, disease, or competition from a new species could wipe out the whole population.

Furthermore, studies on endangered animals such as the cheetah, which has little natural genetic variability, show that there is a higher mortality of young born in the wild or in zoo breeding programs. This is apparently due to the large number of birth defects that can show up whenever close relatives breed. Small reserves that can support only small populations of a species (especially the larger mammals) force this kind of genetic uniformity (see Figure 1-2).

The Economics of Preserving Endangered Species Worldwide

Most people would agree that other creatures have a right to survive on the earth. People rarely intentionally set out to wipe out other species. Yet, as a number of experts have shown, our economic system is set up in such a way that we tend to do just that.

Towards a Sustainable Society

Debt-for-Nature Swaps

by Thomas E. Lovejoy

Thomas Lovejoy is Assistant Secretary for External Affairs of the Smithsonian Institution. He has done much ecological research in tropical forests and was the first environmentalist to receive Brazil's Order of Rio Branco. He founded and for many years advised the public television series "Nature." Lovejoy is generally credited with having brought the problem of disappearing tropical forests to the fore as a public issue and was the originator of the concept of debt-for-nature swaps.

The germ of the concept of debt-for-nature swaps came in a Congressional hearing in 1984. The subject was the environmental effects of the loans of multilateral development agencies (e.g., the World Bank or the Inter-American Development Bank). At one point the testimony of José Lutzenberger (who became Brazil's Secretary for the Environment in 1990) veered off to problems of social inequity.

As I listened, I realized there was a third concern—namely that the debt itself was generating environmental problems. For example, the drive to generate foreign exchange could produce land use changes that in turn could produce colonization pressure in ecologically sensitive areas. Surely, I mused, there should be some way to use the debt *for* the environment?

Three years later the first debt-for-nature project took place in Costa Rica. Taking a leaf from the book of the world of commerce, Conservation International, based in Washington, had purchased debt owed by Bolivia to some U.S. commercial banks at a discount on the secondary market. With Bolivian conservationists, this debt was redeemed at full face value by the

Species, like air and water, are, in a sense, a common resource. That is, we all stand to benefit from having a wide variety of plants and animals on the planet. None of us, however, "owns" any particular wild species and so no one is directly responsible for the survival of any particular species. Individuals can easily see the benefits gained from hunting tigers, capturing apes, or building a housing development on some other creature's habitat. Much harder to keep in mind are the benefits, to all of us, of having a great variety of species, since these benefits (medical uses, agriculture) are long term or less visible (aesthetic or moral). In other words, the short-term, visible benefits go directly to the individuals involved, while the losses are mainly long term and are spread over society as a whole. As a result, we are as wasteful of the resource of species as we have been of air and water, other resources that no one owns.★

★ These principles were first clearly applied to environmental problems by Garrett Hardin in his "Tragedy of the Commons," *Science, 162* (December 13, 1968), 1243.

Central Bank of that country. In the process, land was set aside to create the Beni Biosphere Reserve, an area of rain forest and savannah. The banks had retired a modest amount of debt, at a loss to be sure, but one that was essentially inevitable in any case. Bolivia had been relieved of a modest amount of foreign currency obligation and was able to underwrite an environmental activity of interest to that country. While the sum was not large, in terms of funds available for vital conservation activities, this represented a significant addition of financial resources.

A great deal has been learned about this financial mechanism in the ensuing four years, and debt-for-nature swaps have been carried out in many other countries: Ecuador, Costa Rica, Guatemala, Mexico, Philippines, Madagascar, Dominican Republic, Argentina, Peru, Zambia, Sudan, Bolivia, and Poland. The notion of using debt as a financial resource on behalf of the environment did not come easily. Somehow, substituting the use of a financial instrument generated by the ordinary world of finance for environmental purposes smacked of arm twisting. Yet in the end, no project would work unless there was indigenous support for it. More than anything, the reluctance was based on lack of understanding by the world of finance and government of the importance of environment to finance and to society. Often debt-for-nature was misunderstood as a proposition to solve all debt problems and environmental problems simultaneously and in their entirety. While debt-for-nature could make truly significant contributions on both counts, a lot of other help is needed. The indigenous peoples saw debt-for-nature as yet another ploy to take their lands, but later began to recognize it could be used to secure their own lands.

The most recent entry into the field has been by Brazil, the country most noticeably resistant principally on sovereignty grounds, but also because previous administrations had placed less value on environment. In July 1991, Brazil announced a debt-for-nature package of $100,000,000/year. The debt (selling at 34 cents on the dollar) will be redeemed at full face value with bonds. Indexed to avoid inflation, they will pay 6% in perpetuity. As a consequence, it will be possible to endow activities, whether park protection, environmental research, training, recovery of degraded lands, et cetera. This will provide a vital long-term stability that has been lacking all too often.

In a world of ever less available financial resources, debt-for-nature will play a significant role. It should be just the beginning of a whole series of innovative financing mechanisms.

A hunter who poaches an elephant for its ivory exemplifies this type of problem. The hunter reaps the benefit of the poaching, often a large sum of money. The loss represented by extinction of elephants would be spread among all of us, however. An economic answer to the particular problem of poaching elephants has been for all countries who were importing ivory, for such uses as jewelry, piano keys, and billiard balls, to ban such imports. Without a market for the ivory, would-be poachers have no reason to kill elephants.

In other cases, however, species are lost incidentally to other human actions, such as cutting tropical forests for farming or cattle grazing.

Because these sorts of effects are not an intended result of people's actions, economists call them *externalities,* or spillover effects. People who undertake more economic activities are likely to cause greater spillover effects. People in developed countries use the most raw materials, which are often obtained by disturbing the habitat of creatures in less developed countries. Those of us in developed countries have been, in this sense, most responsible for loss of many species.

A third economic reality is that the wildlife resources that conservationists wish to protect are largely found in those developing countries or undeveloped areas of the world where the native peoples themselves are engaged in a struggle for survival.

This is no accident, of course. Civilization has brought both riches and ease to most of the population of the developed countries. At the same time, civilization has destroyed much of the habitat for wildlife in those same countries. Precisely because they are undeveloped, the poorer countries in Africa and southwest Central America still have much natural wildlife habitat.

Add to this the fact that the tropical rain forest habitat found in many of these countries is home to a staggering richness of species, and the stage is set for a conflict between the rights of poor but growing human populations and the rights of wild plant and animal species. Again and again, around the world these poignant conflicts are played out. Whose rights are paramount: our fellow human beings struggling to feed their families and live with dignity in the old ways, or the wild species, struggling perhaps for their very existence on the earth?

Economic Solutions and International Cooperation in Africa. "It's crazy to try to educate an African to your point of view [on wildlife conservation] unless he's living in the same circumstances you are" (Parker, 1982). This lesson has been a bitter one for many conservation organizations attempting to influence African policies on wildlife conservation. In a country where large portions of the people don't have enough to eat and very few people have a living standard close to the average for the developed world, wildlife conservation simply isn't a priority issue.

There is a growing feeling that wildlife conservation in Africa will be possible only if it can be made to pay. The development of tourism based on visits to parks and reserves is one possibility. If people are willing to pay enough to see wild animals in their natural habitats, it makes sense to set those habitats aside. The area that is now set aside in this way is too small to preserve any significant portion of Africa's wild species, however. In most cases the preserves are only gathering places for large numbers of animals at certain times of the year. At other times the animals disperse over a much wider area outside the preserves. Increasing the size of the preserves is not usually possible. Even if the large sums of money needed to purchase the areas were available, many of these areas are already settled by human populations.

Another possibility is to "crop" the wild animals—that is, to allow them to live and grow on ranches and in reserves without artificial feeding or watering and then to harvest surplus animals and sell the meat. It is not clear yet whether this is economically feasible or ecologically desirable. What *is* clear, however, is that the best solutions so far have been devised by people born and raised in the country concerned. Perhaps this is because they have the sensitivity to local customs and concerns, without which it is difficult to work out a plan acceptable to all factions.

A recent success is worth noting. The Amboseli region in Kenya has been used by humans as well as animals since the late Pleistocene. For the past 400 years the Masai, nomadic cattle herders, have dominated the region. As in the rest of Africa, in recent years the Masai population has been growing rapidly. As a result, the tribes have been looking for additional pasture lands for increasing numbers of cattle. But, at the same time, increasing tourism has encouraged the Kenyan government to plan to set aside the entire Amboseli area as a park. To protest the park plan, the Masai began to kill large numbers of rhinoceroses.

David Westein, an African-born ecologist, has devised a plan whereby 150 square miles, constituting the most important area for wildlife conservation and tourism in the Amboseli region, will be protected from human intrusion. In the surrounding area, wildlife will coexist with cattle. There will, however, be some cost to the Masai ranchers in animals lost to predators and in land unusable for grazing. The government will pay in money and in services (health care, water development schemes) for these losses. So far the compromise appears to be working.

Tanzania, which has the largest wildlife population in Africa, has asked that other countries contribute to the cost of guarding wildlife from poaching. Needed equipment, such as surveillance helicopters for game wardens, is beyond the reach of many developing countries. That such measures can help is shown by the success of Project Tiger to preserve the Bengal tiger in India. This program, supported by international conservation groups, has increased the tiger population by 65%. Key features of the project include preserves, surrounded by buffer areas, in which humans are not allowed, and payments to farmers who lose stock to the tigers.

Proposals to Stem Tropical Forest Loss

Organizations such as the World Bank and the U.N. Food and Agricultural Organization have given a great deal of thought and money to attempts to stem the tide of loss of the world's tropical forests.

In October 1985 an international task force organized by the World Resources Institute published a 56-country plan to halt tropical forest destruction. The report, funded by the World Bank and the United Nations Environment Plan, recognized that forest preservation must take its place beside agricultural and industrial development as an important goal in developing nations. The report also recommended more local participation and more participation by women (who traditionally gather and use many forest resources in developing nations) in plans to preserve forests. (See Figure 10-8.)

The economic reality of life in the developing nations is that unless the countries can profit in some way from conserving their forests, they cannot afford to save them. Conservation plans that take this into account have the best chance of being adopted.

Thomas Lovejoy has spearheaded that kind of conservation effort—the debt-for-nature swap. In this plan, developing countries that possess both tropical forests and large international debts are allowed to swap some of that debt in return for promises to set aside land in parks or reserves. Of course, the banks to whom the countries owe money must be enticed into accepting the plan as well. Several

FIGURE 10-8 Tree Nursery in India. Several demonstration tree nurseries have been set up in India to encourage reforestation and to provide practical business experience for women. (*Photo:* U.N. Environment Program)

successful swaps have been arranged in countries such as Costa Rica, Bolivia, Ecuador, Madagascar, Zambia, and the Philippines. In some cases, banks are encouraged to restructure loans that they are unlikely to collect in any case; in other instances, governments in the developed countries can offer tax considerations that make it less of a loss for a bank to grant discounts or credits against loans. Sometimes conservation groups buy a developing country's debt at a reduced price from a bank. The debt is then redeemed by the country, which sets aside an amount of land, equivalent to the full debt, in a preserve.

Thomas Eisner of Cornell University has engineered a project with Costa Rica's Instituto Nacional de Biodiversidad and Merck & Co., a U.S. drug firm, to carry out "chemical prospecting" in Costa Rica's nature preserves. Merck has been promised first rights to market drugs developed from rain forest insects and plants. In return, Merck is donating money for the training of Costa Rican biologists, as well as a portion of future profits from the sale of drugs developed from the project. This money will be used in forest preservation efforts. The importance of a project such as this is not only that useful plants or insects may be located before they become extinct. It is also important because it enhances the value of rain forest to the country in which it is located. The citizens of Costa Rica receive an "up front" payment for training of their own biologists and also a portion of future profits from their tropical forest resources. When people are able to benefit directly from having a resource, they will naturally be more interested in preserving it.

An interesting proposal by Guppy (1984) would involve an organization of timber-producing countries modeled in some ways on the successful OPEC oil cartel. According to Guppy, tropical forest woods are now grossly undervalued in the world market. As an example, when a forest is cut it is worthwhile to carry out only about 10% of the trees found there. Another 55% are irreparably damaged, and the remaining 35% are left standing. Yet many of the trees not sold are excellent woods with the potential for use and export. Market prices simply don't justify the cost of transporting them

out. Because tropical forest woods bring so little on the world market, projects to maintain these lands as forest do not compete well with agricultural projects, hydroelectric dams, or other development schemes. A cartel, by artificially raising the price of tropical forest woods on the world market, could make the forest themselves more valuable as forest. In addition, part of the increased price could be set aside for reforestation projects.

If developing nations themselves are not able to set up such a plan, importing countries could levy a tax on tropical hardwoods and use the revenues collected to help conserve tropical forests. All of these plans meet an important criterion: They do not cause the entire burden of saving endangered species to fall on those members of the human race least in a position to bear it—the citizens of the developing countries.

Different Viewpoints

Some conservationists feel that human impact criteria are laudable, but secondary to the most important issue. That, they say, is saving species from extinction. Other experts point out that any solution that sacrifices human needs to animal or plant welfare simply will not work. This remains a central point of debate about conserving wildlife resources.

Those of us in the developed countries, for the most part well fed and well clothed, with our own welfare secure, are in a position to consider the welfare of the entire planet. We have today a unique chance to influence the evolution and future of those "other nations," as Henry Beston termed other species, that share time and space with us.

SUMMARY

Over half the world's species live in tropical rain forests, an ecosystem that is disappearing at an alarming rate. The loss of biodiversity this represents is of major concern to environmentalists.

Wild plants and animals represent harvestable resources of food, fuel, and building materials. Natural communities also provide ecological services such as oxygen production and reduction of air and water pollution. Individual species manufacture chemicals useful as drugs, pesticides, flavorings, and a variety of other industrial raw materials. Additional agricultural uses for some species are found in programs for biological control or species improvement through cross-breeding. All species are important complements of the food webs of which they are part. Finally, species have an importance and a right to exist in and of themselves.

In a variety of ways, this right to exist is being threatened. Hunting and collecting, habitat destruction, competition from introduced species, and pollution all threaten wildlife resources. Species can be protected individually by laws, such as the U.S. Endangered Species Act, which directs federal agencies to discover the needs and protect the habitats of specific endangered or threatened species. Worldwide, species are protected by the Convention on International Trade in Endangered Fauna and Flora (CITES), which prohibits trade of endangered species or products made from them between countries that have signed the treaty. Examples or seeds of endangered species can be collected in zoos, seed banks, and botanical gardens. The most comprehensive and most-likely-to-succeed solution would be to save whole ecosystems in parks or reserves. It is important, however, that such reserves be large enough to fully protect an ecosystem and allow it to function normally.

Most of the species in danger of extinction are found in the poorer nations. Plans designed to save endangered species or endangered ecosystems such as tropical forests must recognize that these countries have little money to spend on conservation efforts. Successful plans such as the debt-for-nature swap make it economically attractive for countries to conserve species or ecosystems.

Questions

1. How would you explain the value of preserving a wide variety of species, both plant and animal?

2. Briefly list the main reasons that plant and animal species become extinct or endangered. Which is the most important reason?

3. Explain why efforts to conserve endangered species so often seem to be complicated by the plight of native peoples.

4. Do you think solutions based on the economic value of wild species are a good idea? What if it turns out that other uses of the land are more valuable?

5. How does the fact that wildlife species are usually viewed as a common resource, in the same way that water or air are considered common resources, contribute to the rapid loss of species today?

6. Recount some of the ways in which attempts are currently being made to preserve species from extinction. What further measures could be taken?

7. Are genuine human needs always paramount in a conflict between native peoples and wildlife species?

Further Reading

Animal Welfare Institute Quarterly, Summer 1990, P.O. Box 3650, Washington, D.C., 20007.

Although 10 species of large whales are now protected by a whaling moratorium, 65 other species of small whales, dolphins, and porpoises are still in danger from hunting, drift nets, and purse seining. The EIA has published a book detailing the problem and possible solutions, "Global War Against Small Cetaceans." The Animal Welfare Institute keeps track of the situation in its quarterly newsletter.

"Biological Diversity." Washington, D.C.: The Global Tomorrow Coalition, Natural Resources Defense Council, 1985.

A good review of the causes of and possible solutions to species extinction.

Canadian Nature Federation, 75 Albert Street, Ottawa, Ontario, K1P 6G1.

Information on endangered species in Canada and Canadian wildlife laws can be obtained from this organization.

DiSilvestro, Roger L. (Ed.). *Audubon Wildlife Report 1987*. Orlando, Fla.: Academic Press, 1987.

This volume features a comprehensive compilation of federal wildlife conservation activities.

Egan, T. "Energy Project Imperils a Rain Forest," *New York Times*, January 26, 1990, p. B8.

The United States actually owns some rain forest—in Puerto Rico, the U.S. Virgin Islands, and on the Hawaiian Islands. In Hawaii the islands' major industry, tourism, threatens the last large rain forest in the United States.

Gup, T. "Owl versus Man," *Time Magazine*, June 25, 1990, p. 56.

Although it is not commonly thought of as a conservation magazine, *Time* does a good job of covering the spotted owl controversy. Both the owl and the loggers are treated sympathetically and with understanding.

Jackson, D. D. "Searching for Medicinal Wealth in Amazonia," *Smithsonian*, February 1989, p. 95.

The variety of possible drugs to be found in rain forests is illustrated in this article. Featured is Mark Plottkin, director of plant conservation for the World Wildlife Fund, who explores the jungle with Amazonian Indian medicine men.

Jones, R. F. "Farewell to Africa," *Audubon,* September 1990.

This article is by a long-time big game hunter and Africa watcher. Although it sometimes lapses into sentimental reminiscence about the way things used to be, it also does a thorough job of assessing current efforts in Africa to save what is left of the larger animals. Schemes to crop the animals for meat or preserve them for tourists to look at are detailed, as are the various problems involved, such as poaching, politics, racial conflict, and human population growth. Well worth reading for its realistic view of Africa today.

Lewis, D. M., and G. Kaweche. "The Luangwa Valley of Zambia: Preserving Its Future by Integrated Management," *Ambio*, December 1985, p. 362.

All of the problems of wildlife management and protection are evidenced in this Zambian valley: poaching, agricultural encroachment, watershed deterioration, and conflicts between human and wildlife needs.

Morse, L. E., and M. Henifin (Eds.). "Rare Plant Conservation: Geographical Data Organization." New York: New York Botanical Garden, 1981.

Citizens interested in helping with studies necessary before plants can gain official endangered species status can get an idea of the type and quantity of needed data from this publication.

Plumwood, V., and R. Routley. "World Rainforest Destruction—The Social Factors," *The Ecologist*, *12*(1) (1982), 4.

The social, political, and economic factors involved in rain forest destruction are thoroughly explored in this article. Its conclusions are not the same as those in the *National Geographic* article on India and wildlife (below).

Putnam, John J. "India Struggles to Save Her Wildlife," *National Geographic*, September 1976, p. 299.

India provides one of the best examples of how an expanding human population exerts intolerable pressures on wildlife populations in developing countries. The almost unresolvable conflicts between human and animal needs are highlighted in this perceptive article.

Repetto, Robert. "Deforestation in the Tropics," *Scientific American*, April 1990, p. 36.

Repetto explains the economic factors that contribute to tropical deforestation and recommends solutions that would make it possible for developing nations to conserve their forests.

Stiak, J. "Old Growth," *The Amicus Journal*, Winter 1990, p. 35.

Efforts to save the old-growth forests of the Pacific Northwest are detailed in this issue of the journal.

Wilson, E. O. *Biophilia*. Cambridge, Mass.: Harvard University Press, 1984.

A famous ecologist explains his fascination with the natural world and why it is important to all of us to preserve the variety of species we now enjoy.

Wilson, E. O. "Threats to Biodiversity," *Scientific American*, September 1989, p. 108.

Wilson, one of the first scientists to alert the environmental community about the threat to biodiversity, details the rise of biodiversity through history and notes what we lose when biodiversity decreases.

References

Beston, H. *The Outermost House*. New York: Henry Holt and Company, Inc., 1928.

Bolandrin, M. F., et al. "Natural Plant Chemicals: Sources of Industrial and Medicinal Materials," *Science*, *228* (June 7, 1985), 1154.

Guppy, N. "Tropical Deforestation: A Global View," *Foreign Affairs Quarterly*, Spring 1984, p. 928.

Grier, J. W. "Ban of DDT and Subsequent Recovery of Reproduction in Bald Eagles," *Science*, *218* (December 17, 1982), 1232.

"International Ban on Ivory Trade Approved," *New York Times*, October 18, 1989, p. 5A.

Kiss, A. (Ed.). *Living with Wildlife: Wildlife Resource Management with Local Participation in Africa*, World Bank

Technical Paper #130, Africa Technical Department Series, 1990.

MacBryde, B. "Why Are So Few Endangered Plants Protected?" *American Horticulturist*, October/November 1980, p. 29.

O'Brien, S. J., et al. "Genetic Basis for Species Vulnerability in the Cheetah," *Science*, *227* (March 22, 1985), 1428.

Official World Wildlife Fund Guide to Endangered Species of North America. Washington, D.C.: Beacham, 1990.

Parker, I. "African Born White," *New York Times Magazine*, September 12, 1982.

Prado, M. Quoted in *The New York Times*, August 11, 1983.

Shiva, V., et al. "Reforestation in India: Problems and Strategies," *Ambio*, December 1985, p. 329.

Sun, M. "The Lovejoy Effect," *Science*, *247* (March 9, 1990), 1174.

Tropical Forests: A Call for Action. World Resources Institute, 1985.

Wise, Jeff. "The Role of Debt-for-Nature Swaps in Preserving Tropical Habitats," *Endangered Species Update*, 7(12) (October 1990).

Part Four

Energy Resources and Recycling

LUZ solar-thermal concentrator power plant. (*Photo:* Courtesy of Electric Power Research Institute)

*T*he environment as a concept is composed of a number of interlocking parts: ecology, population, land and species preservation, air and water pollution, human health, energy, and other facets. The energy component of the environment, the topic we focus on in this section of the book, is not, as one might suppose at first glance, simply an issue of declining resources or of resources unevenly distributed across the globe. Energy interacts with many of the other parts of the environment. Energy resource extraction and transportation threaten sea, land, and species; energy use leads to urban air pollution and acid rain; fossil fuel combustion puts carbon dioxide in the atmosphere and places the climate of the globe in jeopardy. We do not study energy here simply because it is a resource that we need, but because it is a resource that we abuse and that we need to learn to control before our misuse does irreparable harm.

In this section of the book, we examine our current patterns of energy use and the fuels upon which we and the world draw (Chapter 11). We consider how we divide our use among the various fuels at our disposal, and how we distribute that use across activities such as heating, transportation, and electric power generation. With these uses in mind, we then investigate how we obtain and utilize the conventional fuel resources on which we currently depend. Coal, the fossil fuel resource in which we are richest, the fuel we depend on for electric power, turns out to destroy the landscape, cause air and water pollution, and damage miners' health. Oil, the fuel we depend on to furnish gasoline, we find is distributed in a distinctly uneven fashion—with two-thirds of the world's oil in the highly unstable Middle East, where it is under the control of an oil cartel with tremendous power to manipulate prices. Natural gas appears to be our most benign fossil fuel and to be in reasonable supply in North America. Nuclear power, on the other hand, is a resource at once safe and dangerous—safe in day-to-day emissions from the operation of nuclear plants, dangerous if an accident ever occurs, as happened at Chernobyl, dangerous in the wastes that it generates, and dangerous in the risks associated with the production of plutonium, the substance of atomic bombs.

It is remarkable to think that only two centuries ago, society had, besides human and animal energy, only three forms of energy at its disposal. All three of these forms could be traced to the sun. Hydropower was used to operate mills, which ground grain or wove cloth. Hydropower required water running downward to the sea from the uplands, where water fell as rain. Of course, the sun caused the water to evaporate in the first place. Wood was another source of energy; it was used for cooking, heating, and smelting iron. Again, the sun's energy used in the process of photosynthesis is responsible for the existence of wood. Also, wind was used to pump water for irrigation and to fill the sails of the great wooden ships. Wind, the movement of air, is the result of temperature differences in the atmosphere caused by uneven heating by the sun. The giant windmills of Holland are vivid reminders of an early era when only such ingenuity and muscle were available to do our work. Today, these same sun-origin sources are still available to us. In addition, we have learned how to harness the sun itself.

In the past hundred years, however, our industrial society became dependent on the heat from fossil fuels and the heat from nuclear fission to power the enormous development that has taken place in our civilization. Hydropower remained an important source of energy, but wind has been utilized to only a minor extent. Nor has heat been withdrawn from the earth, or the sun's energy tapped directly to any significant degree. These natural sources of energy, which stem from the earth's natural processes, are all around us. Furthermore, much of the technology to use these sources is available now, and new technologies are developing rapidly.

In the last decade, we have increasingly been turning to these natural sources of energy because, in many respects, they provide energy without limit. Furthermore, the pollution that comes from them is often minor compared with that from fossil fuels and fission. We have been turning to these sources for another fundamental reason, though. As fuel supplies become less secure and more expensive, these sources become more attractive and more economical. The rising prices of oil and gas have in a large measure been responsible for our renewed interest in water, wind, and sun. It seems strange to be saying "Thank you" to the oil cartel, but it has made the point of dwindling energy resources more vividly than the arguments of any resource economist.

In Chapter 12, we look at renewable sources of power: hydropower, tidal power, wind energy, and geothermal energy. In Chapter 13, we investigate how the sun's energy can be harnessed and how we can save energy. The sun is an energy source that is virtually unlimited, and energy saved is energy you never run out of. These sources of energy and energy conservation promise softer impacts on the environment than combustion of the fossil fuels or the fissioning of uranium. In addition, most of these energy sources are self-renewing, in the sense that nature makes them available on an almost continuous basis. In Chapter 14, we examine recycling, an activity that saves both energy and resources.

Chapter 11

Conventional Energy Resources

HOW WE POWER MODERN SOCIETY

Energy Conversions

We commonly utilize energy resources in just three ways. First, we may release heat energy by burning fossil fuels and use this energy directly as heat for homes, schools, factories, and shops. Second, we may convert this heat energy into work, using refined oil to drive machinery and to power automobiles, trucks, trains, planes, and ships. Last, we may convert the heat energy from burning fossil fuels or from the fissioning of uranium into electricity and then use this transformed energy either for heat or to do work. Falling water is also commonly used to generate electricity. In effect, electricity acts as a middleman between energy resources and final use (Figure 11-1). Just as the presence of a middleman in a market creates higher prices, the use of energy in the form of electricity creates a markup as well—in this case, an energy loss, or penalty.

The use of coal and other fossil fuels to generate electric power for machines is appealing. Since electric power can be transmitted from place to place, machinery can be located far from the site of elec-

tricity generation. But there is a penalty for using energy in the form of electricity, a penalty far beyond the extensive pollution at the point of electricity generation. This penalty is a loss of efficiency—an enormous waste of the heat energy in fossil fuels. This penalty is codified in the second law of thermodynamics. According to this law, there is an inherent limit to the amount of heat energy that can be converted into work and hence into electricity. The reverse is not true; that is, other forms of energy can be converted completely into heat. This limit to the efficiency of converting heat into work was not an obvious concept to the early designers of engines that used heat for power, but was discovered experimentally.

An example of the impact of the second law is the generation of electric power. The heat from the combustion of fuel is used to boil water to high-pressure steam. The steam is then used to turn a turbine that rotates an armature in a magnetic field, producing electric current. According to the second law, there is a limit to the amount of the heat energy that can be converted into work—in this case, into the turning of the turbine. As a consequence, there is a limit to the amount of electric energy that can be generated from the combustion of a fossil fuel.

In fact, most of the possible design improve-

FIGURE 11-1 How Fossil and Nuclear Energy Resources Are Utilized. Increasingly, electric energy is acting as a "middle-man" between energy resources and energy use.

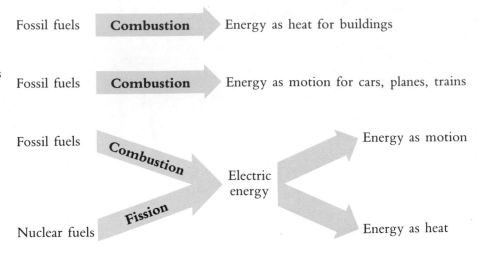

ments to increase the efficiency of generating electric power from steam have now been made. The modern coal-fired power plant, which produces steam to turn a turbine for generating electricity, has reached 40% efficiency; that is, 40% of the heat energy in the coal that is burned is converted into electric energy. The remaining 60% of heat energy is wasted to the environment as hot stack gases and heated water. The efficiency of oil-fired power plants is close to this range as well. Conventional approaches to electric power generation cannot be expected to increase this efficiency by very much. The reason is the inherent limit to the portion of heat energy that can be converted to work and hence to electricity—this is the result of the second law of thermodynamics. Nuclear power plants also produce steam to turn a turbine, and these plants have attained efficiencies only of 30%–32%; that is, only 30%–32% of the heat of fission is converted into electrical energy. The rest of the energy, an enormous amount, is wasted to the environment. Attempts to increase this conversion percentage have yet to succeed.

Electric Power

Electric power provides us with light, sound, visual communication, heat, hot water, refrigeration, and air conditioning. At the same time, it causes burying of river valleys in sediment, nitrogen oxides and sulfur dioxide air pollution, acid rain, acid mine drainage, oil pollution, particulate air pollution, smog, strip mining, thermal pollution, radioactive wastes, and plutonium for bombs.

Electric energy is one of the most easily used forms of energy. One electric line enters a house, and the energy to light the home, cook and bake, heat water, and run machines and appliances is all at our fingertips. The use of electricity for household tasks such as cooking, water heating, air conditioning, and dish washing is steadily increasing. According to the Energy Information Administration, the quantity of energy used to produce electric energy in the United States will increase by about 45% from 1985 to 1995, even though the total of all our energy use will increase by only about 19% in that same period (Figure 11-2).

It should be noted again that the quantity of energy *consumed* in the process of electric generation at power plants is not, in fact, the same as the quantity of *electrical* energy generated at power plants. Nor is it the quantity consumed in end uses such as heating water. It is, instead, the far larger quantity of energy that was released in the burning of coal or fissioning of uranium at the power plant. The quantity of electrical energy that can actually be put to use is, on average, only about 30% of the raw energy consumed for electricity generation. This is a result of the inherent inefficiency of electricity generation, a consequence of the second law

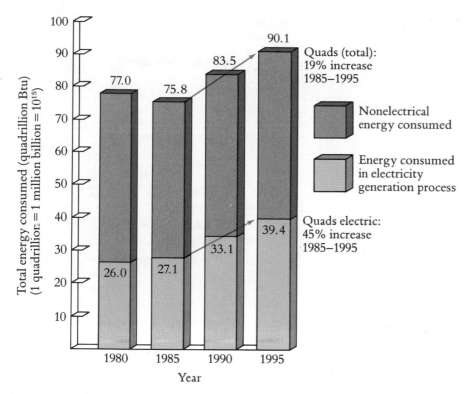

FIGURE 11-2 Growth in Total Energy Consumption and Growth in Energy Consumed in Electricity Generation in the United States. The energy consumption numbers are given in quadrillions of *Btu* (British thermal units). A Btu is the amount of heat needed to raise the temperature of 1 pound of water by 1°F. A quadrillion Btu, or *quad* as it has come to be known, is equal to the heat energy in about 180 million barrels of oil, or about 40 million tons of coal.

To understand the term *energy consumed in electricity generation,* examine the data for 1980, when 26 quads of energy were consumed in the generation process. This is the amount of energy required to produce the electric energy used in end uses. It is about 3.3 times larger than the amount of electrical energy actually utilized. It is the energy in the coal, oil, and gas that was burned at the power plant plus the total energy produced by the fission process at nuclear power plants. Of the 26 quads consumed in the generation process, only 30%, or 7.8 quads, was actually utilized. In contrast, photovoltaic electric energy wastes almost no energy to the environment but is consumed almost entirely. (*Source:* Data from Energy Information Administration)

of thermodynamics, as well as due to additional losses in transmission.

To understand how fuels are used to generate electricity, we need to examine the operation of a typical thermal electric plant (Figure 11-3). By *thermal electric plant,* we mean a power plant that utilizes heat to produce steam, which turns a turbine. A

coal-fired plant is a thermal electric plant; so also is a plant that burns oil or gas and a plant that utilizes the heat from nuclear fission. The principle of operation is the same in all three.

Heat is produced by combustion or fission. That heat is used to boil water for steam. The steam, at a high temperature and under high pressure, is used to turn a turbine. The turbine rotates an armature in a magnetic field, inducing the flow of electric current and thus generating electricity. As the steam leaves the turbine, its pressure and temperature are much reduced. This "spent" steam is converted back to water by a condenser, through which cooling water flows. The water produced from condensing the steam reenters the boiler to be reconverted to steam and recirculated to the turbine.

The combination of power plant types from which we draw electricity has been in flux for a variety of reasons. During the late 1960s, coal-fired power plants were being converted to residual oil in an effort to reduce sulfur dioxide levels in urban areas. With the onset of the 1973 oil embargo and the massive increase in oil prices, coal plants with better pollution control, or those burning lower-sulfur coal, began to replace the oil-fired plants because of more certain coal availability and lower cost. From the late 1960s to the 1970s, new nuclear plants were being added quickly to the stock of generating stations. By 1979, however, orders for new nuclear plants in the United States had come to a complete and seemingly permanent halt. Concerns about safety and waste disposal blocked the nuclear juggernaut. Thus, the combination of fuels used for electric energy, as shown for 1985 and projected for 1995 (Figure 11-4), reflects the evolution of a changing system.

Electric generation from coal is neither efficient nor clean. In terms of air pollution, the production of electric power accounts for about 15% of airborne particles, 80%–85% of the sulfur dioxide, and 30% of the nitrogen oxides produced annually in the United States. Nearly all of the airborne particles and sulfur oxides produced in electric generation are the result of coal-fired electric generation.

Energy Today

In the material that follows, we describe how we produce and apply our principal energy resources: coal, oil, natural gas, and nuclear energy. This information will help us determine how we can conserve energy without diminishing our standard of living.

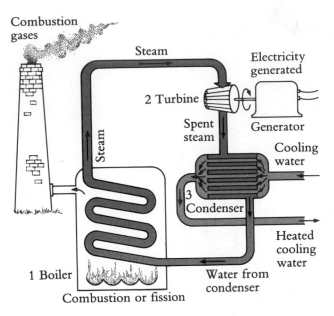

FIGURE 11-3 Elements of a Typical Thermal Electric Power Plant.

Figure 11-5 shows how the United States consumes energy in the various sectors of its economy: transportation, industry, and residential/commercial activities. In general, the pattern of consumption has not changed drastically over the past 40 years. However, actual energy consumption increased by more than 100% between 1950 and 1990 due to an increase in population of over 50% and a parallel increase in energy use per person.

Transportation accounts for about 25% of the energy we consume each year. Nearly all of this transport energy in the United States is consumed as some form of petroleum. In 1985, about 41% of this transport energy was burned in automobiles, 25% in transportation of goods by truck, and 13% in airplane operations. Railroads, buses, pipelines, ships and barges, and other minor consumers used the remainder of U.S. transport energy.

The residential/commercial sector of our economy consumes about 35% of our annual energy budget. Based on 1985 data, about 57% of this energy expenditure was used to keep people warm and 4% to keep them cool. Water heating consumed 16% of the energy in this category, and refriger-

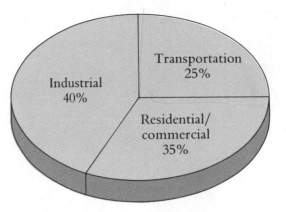

FIGURE 11-5 U.S. Energy Consumption by Economic Sector.

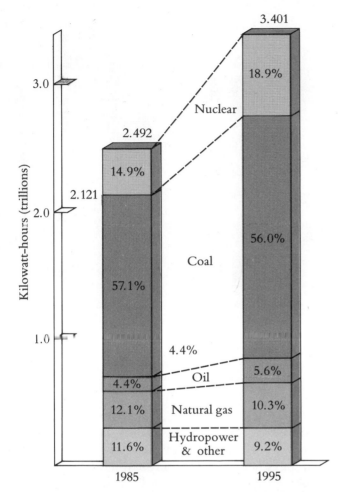

FIGURE 11-4 Fuels for Electric Generation in the United States. (Numbers may not total due to independent rounding.) (*Source:* Data from Energy Information Administration)

ation, freezing, and cooking 23%. Natural gas was the primary fuel for heating, providing 56% of the energy in this category; oil furnished 18%, and wood 17%. Coal, electricity, and bottled gas provided the remainder of heating energy.

Our energy use in all sectors of the economy is expanding, so our use of fuels must expand as well. Figure 11-6 displays U.S. energy growth by fuel type from 1965 to 1995. From this chart, we can see that petroleum and natural gas together will have fallen from 74% of total energy use in 1965 down to 61% of energy use by 1995 even though

the total energy drawn from these fuels grew by about 40% in the period. Coal, nuclear power, and hydropower in aggregate will have grown from 26% of energy use in 1965 to 39% in 1995. Coal use alone will have more than doubled in this interval. These three energy resources, coal, nuclear, and hydro, are used in electric power generation, so this increase reflects a steady increase in our reliance on electrical energy.

Since the oil embargo of 1973–74, which caused sharp increases in oil prices, the nation has begun to reevaluate the importance of its coal resource. It is the fossil fuel in which we are richest; perhaps 20% of the world's supply of coal lies within our borders. All strategic plans to fill the growing U.S. demand for energy focus upon coal as a central element. Our coal, however, is a mixed blessing. It has serious effects upon the land and upon our health. And because of its high carbon content compared to other fossil fuels, its contribution to carbon dioxide in the atmosphere and to potential global warming is very great. Because coal is now seen as so important to the nation's economic health, and because it also has a large negative impact, we need to consider fully our plans for its use.

Energy in the Future

Fusion. Fusion is not only a specific atomic event that scientists hope to harness to produce electric

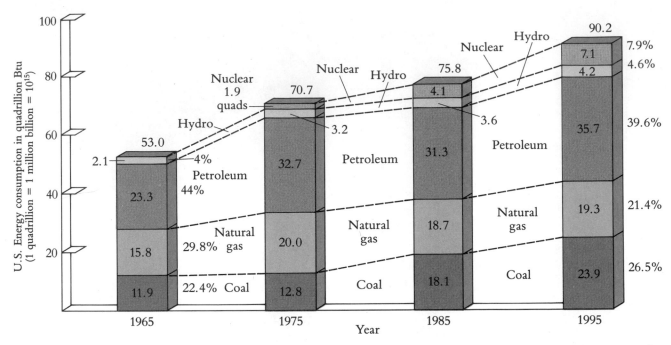

FIGURE 11-6 Pattern of Growth in United States Energy Consumption by Fuel Type.

power. To many, it has become the name for the "dream of limitless energy." While **nuclear fission** refers to the *splitting apart* of the nuclei of large "heavy" atoms with a release of energy, **nuclear fusion** refers to the *combining* of the nuclei of certain "light" atoms, such as two atoms of deuterium, an isotope of hydrogen. This combination takes place constantly in the sun and other stars, releasing vast quantities of energy. The hope is that the fusion reactor of the future will capture this energy from fusion and convert it to electric power.

In fact, deuterium is so abundant in the surface waters of the earth that if the energy from deuterium fusion reactions were fully extracted, only 8 pounds of water (about a gallon) could supply the energy equivalent of 300 gallons of gasoline. Unfortunately, it is not clear that the fusion reaction can ever be exploited because we seem unable to "house" the fusion reaction. Containment is needed for a fusion reaction because fusion takes place only at the temperature of a star: 100,000,000°C. Since

no substance is known to remain solid at this temperature, scientists have devised the famous *tokamak* concept in which the fusion reaction is held in place by powerful magnetic fields. Many nations are now conducting fusion experiments.

When active research on fusion began in the late 1950s, the first fusion power was estimated to be 20 years away. Today, more than a third of a century later, scientists are saying, "20 years away and, maybe more." In contrast, active and passive solar heating systems are ready now. And photovoltaic (solar electric) energy is on the verge of widespread commercial application.

Fuel Cells. The **fuel cell** is the name given to the concept of producing electricity from the chemical reaction of hydrogen and oxygen. At the site of electric generation, fuel cells produce very little in the way of air pollution. Hence, as urban neighbors these modular units are expected to be more welcome than the smoky, sooty, coal-fired plant or the nuclear power plant with its built-in hazard potential.

Whereas the oxygen needed for a fuel cell can be supplied from the air, hydrogen gas must be obtained by chemical processing. Hydrogen can be obtained by processing a liquid hydrocarbon fuel such as naptha or by processing natural gas or petroleum gas. Two first-generation fuel-cell plants, each with about 5% of the power capacity of large modern coal or nuclear plants, have been installed, one in New York City and the other in Tokyo, to demonstrate the feasibility of fuel cells. The Tokyo plant began successfully producing electric power in 1983, but the plant in New York City never generated power due to equipment failures. United Technologies, Westinghouse, Fuji, and Mitsubishi are all building fuel cells for commercial applications.

Hydrogen is not a new energy resource, however. Instead, it is a new way to convey energy. Hydrogen might be produced from the electrolysis of sea water using electricity from conventional power plants; in that case, the fuel that fired the plants would be the base energy resource. In addition to being used in fuel cells, hydrogen is being considered as a fuel for the internal combustion engines of automobiles, but such uses are not imminent. In contrast, solar energy for heat and hot water is available now.

Developments in Conventional Electricity Generation. Although improvements in the efficiency of conventional electricity generation have come almost to a halt, novel and unconventional routes of improvement remain open. The thrust of most of this research is to put processes together to capture the waste heat from electric generation. There are three promising ideas. The first, called **district heating,** uses spent steam from thermal power plants for heating. It requires costly piping systems and nearby power plants, so its application in cities is probably limited. The second concept, known as **combined cycle power generation,** puts together the turbine engine and the conventional boiler/turbine system. Combined cycle

power plants use the hot gases from fossil fuel combustion to first turn a turbine much like that of a jet engine and thus produce electric energy. The hot gases are then used to generate steam to turn a second turbine. The last idea, **magnetohydrodynamics,** is designed to extract energy from the hot exhaust gas of a coal-fired electric plant. Potassium is injected in the exhaust gas and ionizes. The ions flowing through a magnetic field generate electric energy. Corrosion of required materials, however, is slowing the development of this process.

COAL—RICH RESOURCES, SERIOUS IMPACTS

Coal and Its Uses

Coal took us out of the era in which only human muscle, wind, and water power were available to manufacture goods. Coal was also the fossil fuel that first changed our methods of transportation—coal powered the steam locomotive.

Although the major use of coal in the United States today is as a fuel for steam electric power plants, it was once an important fuel for home heating and for transportation. After World War II, homeowners began to switch from coal to oil and to the newly available natural gas. Railroads also converted from coal-fired locomotives to the dependable and cleaner diesel engine.

There are a number of kinds of coal, but subbituminous and bituminous coal are by far the most important. Our discussion focuses on these fuels. Coal contains, in addition to carbon and hydrogen, inorganic minerals that remain after coal has been burned; we know the residue material simply as *ash.* Sulfur also occurs in coal, sometimes as iron sulfide and sometimes combined with organic compounds. This sulfur, when burned, is responsible for much of the acid rain that falls on the northeastern United States. Arsenic is also present in coal, as are radioactive elements. In fact, coal is the dirtiest of the fossil fuels. Dirty though it is, it is a magnificent source of heat energy. Furthermore, coal is the most plentiful fossil fuel we possess in the United States.

How Much Coal Is There?   Of the 430 billion metric tons★ of discovered coal reserves in the United States, 55% occurs in the western states. Of these western coal reserves, 44% can be obtained by surface-mining methods, while the remaining 56% requires underground mining. Eastern coal, in contrast, is concentrated as underground reserves, which constitute about 80% of total eastern coal. The total coal reserves in the United States amount to about 20% of the world's coal reserves.

The coal that can be obtained from underground mining is only about 50% of the actual coal in the deposits, since supporting structures, or pillars, must be left in the mine. In comparison, surface mining recovers 80%–95% of a coal deposit, leaving only minor amounts remaining in the ground. Even with these recovery factors, coal reserves in the United States are sufficient for several centuries at the present rate of use.

Certain states have much more coal than others. In the East, coal resources are concentrated in Ohio, Illinois, Pennsylvania, West Virginia, and Kentucky. In the West, North Dakota, Montana, Wyoming, and Colorado have the richest coal resources. About 45% of the land area of North Dakota and 41% of Wyoming contain substrata of coal-bearing rock. About 35% of Montana and 28% of Colorado sit atop coal resources. Taken together, Montana and Wyoming account for 40% of the tonnage of U.S. coal reserves.

Nearly 85% of the coal that is less than 1% sulfur by weight is found west of the Mississippi. Thus, to obtain low-sulfur coal in the eastern United States, where a larger percentage of the coal is used, the eastern power plants must bring coal from the western United States. These imports may come in by train or barge, or if the newest technology takes hold, by coal-slurry pipeline.

How Is Coal Being Used?   The use of coal is growing, after a period in which it had fallen stead-

★ One metric ton = 1,000 kilograms = 2,200 pounds = 1.10 English ton.

ily (see Figure 11-7). The long decline in coal consumption came about as the railroads switched from coal to diesel fuel and as homeowners switched from coal to gas and oil. The present upward trend is the result of the growing demand for electricity, a demand that is increasingly being filled by coal-fired electric plants.

In 1985, about 817 million metric tons of coal were mined in the United States. Of that tonnage, about 55% was obtained by surface-mining methods. The dramatic growth in surface mining is shown in Figure 11-7. In 1985, more coal was surface mined in the United States than was produced by all methods in 1960. By 1990, annual coal production had reached 940 million metric tons with about 60% of coal from surface mining (estimated).

Coal is used most in the electric utility industry. In 1985, coal consumed in the generation of electricity amounted to about 84% of the annual coal consumption in the United States. Other uses of coal include coking in the iron and steel industry (5.5%) and general industrial use (9%).

Environmental Impact of Coal Mining

With so much coal available to the United States, coal will undoubtedly become a "bridge fuel." We will likely use this secure fuel extensively during our transition to new low-carbon or noncarbon fuels in the future. Unfortunately, coal mining, especially surface mining, is an activity that violently disrupts the natural environment. Moreover, at its point of use, the burning of coal pollutes the air, injures vegetation, and affects human health.

Surface (Strip) Mining.   Some deposits of coal lie so near the surface that it is economical simply to remove all the layers of soil and rock above the coal seam, lay this overburden aside, and remove the coal. Surface mines tend to be huge in extent, with giant and costly equipment removing the overburden and coal (Figure 11-8).

Contour mining, one of the two basic types of surface mining, is used on hilly terrain. A power shovel cuts a notch into the hillside, exposing the coal seam for removal. Prior to the passage of fed-

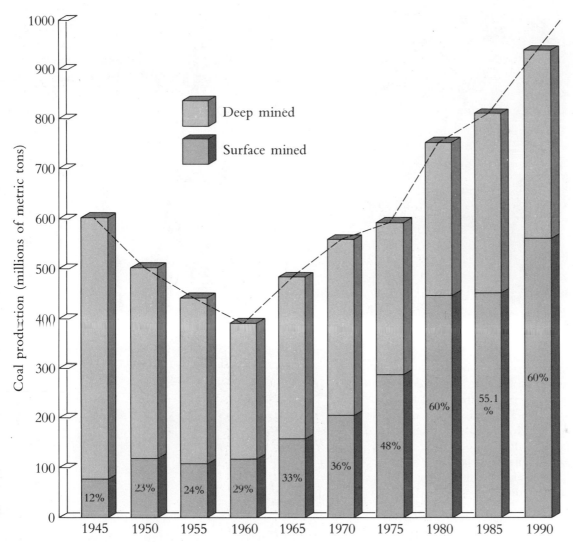

FIGURE 11-7 Coal Production in Millions of Metric Tons in the United States, 1945–1990. (*Source:* Data from U.S. Department of Energy)

eral laws requiring reclamation and restoration of surface-mined sites, coal companies would simply leave the hillside with the groove exposed and move on to other areas. Soil erosion and landslides were likely occurrences from these abused sites. Now the law requires the coal company to fill the groove with earth and to replant the fresh soil with grasses. Still, thousands of miles of *highwalls,* the name given to the back of the notch, ring the hills of Appalachia where no reclamation was practiced.

Area mining, in contrast to contour mining, operates on flat terrain (Figure 11-9). Area mining lays up the soil in rows, exposing the coal in a long path. When the coal is removed from that open path, the overburden on the coal next to the path is excavated and dumped into the mined area, exposing another long path of coal. The process is repeated for row after row, leaving hills of rubble resembling miniature mountain ranges.

Even into the middle 1970s, strip miners were

FIGURE 11-8 Strip Mining. The equipment used in strip mining is massive. (*a*) This is the bucket of a dragline machine at the Medicine Bow Coal Mine in Hanna, Wyoming. The bucket holds 78 cubic yards, a volume equal to that of a 16-foot-square room with an 8-foot ceiling. (*b*) This dragline operating at a surface mine at Marrisa, Illinois, is so large (20 stories tall) that it had to be assembled at the mining site. (*Photos:* U.S. Department of Energy)

allowed to remove coal and simply depart. The result was a surrealist picture of huge mounds of rubble, sometimes arranged in rows, sometimes strewn haphazardly over the landscape. The land from which the coal was torn was often left useless and without vegetation. Black-striped highwalls ringed the tops of hills, cutting off any plant and animal life from the nearby surroundings.

When land is left unreclaimed, soil particles can be washed off the barren slopes of the hills and can fill streambeds. Because the stream channels are decreased in volume, the flows from large rainstorms cannot be carried in the channel and the stream will flood over its banks more frequently. Furthermore,

the barren hillsides with loose earth are unstable. A soaking rain can increase the weight of a soil mass and decrease its hold to the stable earth; the result is landslides.

Eventually, vegetation will return to many of these areas, but the process is slow because the rubble left on the land is acidic due to impurities in coal. This acid condition hinders the regrowth of grasses and trees. In addition, acid rivulets run off these lands and enter nearby streams. Acid waters do not typically support aquatic life, and humans cannot drink such stream water.

Reclamation can prevent such scenes of devastation. The concept of **reclamation** is to restore

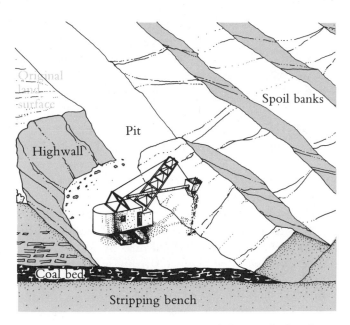

FIGURE 11-9 Area Mining, One of the Methods of Surface Mining for Coal. Area mining is used when the land above the coal seam is flat or gently rolling.

the original contour of the land—if possible, with topsoil on top—and reestablish vegetation to "anchor" the soil and prevent erosion. The concept is simple, but reclamation costs a small amount of money. As a consequence the coal companies fought legislation requiring reclamation for many years.

With rainfall of 10 inches (25 cm) or more, reclamation works, in the sense that vegetation returns and erosion can be checked. In regions where rain is sparse, the best of reclamation methods may be inadequate to restore vegetation to the land. The concern here is mainly with the vast coal fields of the West, where huge strip-mining operations are underway and increasing in scope; the consequences of such operations in low-rainfall areas are difficult to predict. The best revegetation, however, cannot soon bring back forested areas. Forest wildlife cannot survive in grassland; their food supply and nesting places do not exist. Thus, the ecological balance is unavoidably altered by strip mining, even with the best reclamation.

In 1977, after years of bitter debate and disagreement, Congress passed a law establishing partial control over strip mining. The Surface Mining Control and Reclamation Act demands that strip-mined lands be returned to approximately original contours. Prime farmlands, according to the legislation, are not to be mined unless they can be returned to their original productivity. Furthermore, a tax is collected on coal currently being produced. This tax is to be used to pay for restoration of land that was marred in the era before reclamation. While enforcement of these standards is left to the states, the Department of the Interior may step in when states fail to act.

There are several flaws in the legislation. When a state fails to enforce the law, allowing illegal and destructive strip mining, much damage can be done before the federal government discovers the operation and is able to take action. The act dictates that prime farmlands cannot be strip mined unless their productivity can be restored, but who is to judge what has not yet been determined even by scientists? In addition, there is no prohibition on surface mining the desert, where we know that recovery of the land is extremely unlikely. Finally, it appears that an administration unsympathetic to the law has the power to limit enforcement of the law. It does so by simply cutting the budget and the staff of the enforcement agency until it is powerless. This is what occurred in the 1980s under the Reagan administration, according to the House Government Operation Committee.

Surface mining is now increasing dramatically in the West. To illustrate, 101 million metric tons of coal (17% of total production) were produced west of the Mississippi in 1975. By 1985, production had increased to 288 million metric tons, and by 1995 it is expected to reach 445 million metric tons, or 40% of total production. Why is surface mining capturing such a large share of the coal-mining market? It is a matter mainly of economics: The price of surface-mined coal at the mine is roughly about half the cost of coal from underground mines. The low price of surface-mined coal is due to the technology of surface mining, which has eliminated a great deal of human labor.

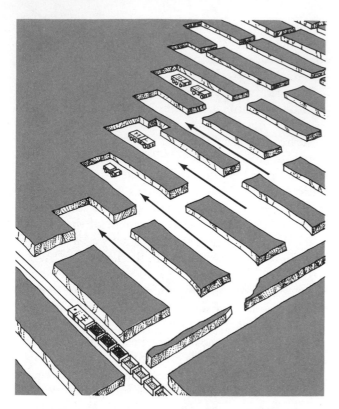

FIGURE 11-10 Looking Down on a Room-and-Pillar Mining Operation. Arrows indicate the direction of further mining. The tunnels may be up to 20 feet (6 m) wide.

Thus, the issue of coal surface mining is not yet laid to rest. As the 1990s proceed, you may wish to observe the effect of vastly increased surface mining on the states of the western plains and ask your legislators and president why the surface mining law is not being enforced.

Underground Mining. In an underground coal mine, men and machines cut the mineral from the coal face and load it into cars or onto conveyors for removal to the surface. The *room-and-pillar method* of mining is the traditional means of extracting the coal (Figure 11-10). In room-and-pillar mining, about 45%–50% of the coal in the seam is actually brought out.

Once coal has been extracted from a mine, it may be sent directly to customers, such as the elec-

tric utilities. Two-thirds or more of current bituminous coal production moves directly to users in this way. The remainder is sent to a preparation plant, where it is crushed, washed, and graded by size.

Coal Refuse Banks. The wastes from the preparation plant consist of low-grade coal, shale, slate, and coal dust. These wastes are stored in huge hills known as *refuse banks* or "gob" piles. Water contaminated with coal dust may be produced from the washing process. This water may be settled in ponds to remove the coal particles, but in some cases the water is discharged directly into streams. One practice is to dam a stream with the refuse bank, thus creating a settling pond behind the dam. In West Virginia in 1972, such a coal waste pile gave way on Buffalo Creek, resulting in a devastating flood. One infamous coal pile in Aberfam, Wales, collapsed in the 1960s, burying a school and all inside. These mounds of coal debris may often catch fire, producing air pollution; the fires can smolder for years.

Subsidence. The removal of coal from underground mines leaves another legacy: **subsidence,** the sinking, or settling, of the ground surface. As the roof supports in a mine give way, the mine fills with overburden; sink holes and cracks may appear at the surface, and tremors may shake the area.

Though only a nuisance when it occurs in farmland or forest, subsidence is a serious problem when human dwellings are nearby. Roads and foundations may crack, buckle, and crumble as the earth settles into a firmer position below. Gas mains may break and threaten explosion, and sewer lines may crack. In some areas of Pennsylvania, homes have had to be abandoned for safety.

Acid Mine Damage. Another effect of underground coal mining, and of surface mining as well, is **acid mine drainage.** The process that creates acid mine drainage is much the same for underground or surface mines. Water may enter an underground mine directly through the mine shaft, or groundwater may seep into the mine through the layers of soil or through sink holes. Iron pyrites from the coal remaining in the mine dissolve in these waters. And the water drains from the mine into nearby streams and rivers.

Iron pyrite, known chemically as ferrous sulfide, is also called "fool's gold." When ferrous sulfide dissolves in water, a series of chemical reactions takes place that leave the water stripped of dissolved oxygen, which is necessary for normal aquatic life, and highly acidic as well. In addition, a yellow-brown precipitate of ferric hydroxide, called *yellow boy*, may settle out and coat the stream bottom, preventing such species as crayfish from feeding.

Acid mine drainage has historically been a regional problem. Pennsylvania, West Virginia, and neighboring coal states have had the greatest share of the problem. Because so much of the nation's coal now originates in the West, the regional aspect of the problem of acid mine drainage is disappearing. Its control is now a problem of national scope.

One option to control acid drainage from abandoned mines is to prevent surface water from entering the mines by filling sink holes and by rerouting gullies that may sometimes flow above an abandoned mine. Another method of controlling acid mine drainage is to treat acid waters chemically with crushed limestone to neutralize the acidity.

Safety and Health of the Coal Miner

Mine Safety. Coal mining, more than any other process of fuel resource extraction, has an impact on human life itself. Several hundred coal-mining deaths occur each year in the United States in individual accidents, cave-ins, or explosions. Coal mining is one of the most hazardous jobs in modern times. Some dangers are immediate—such as explosions or roof falls. Other dangers are delayed. The sooty air of the mine, laced with coal particles, may implant in a miner's lungs and eventually destroy the ability to breathe.

Explosions in coal mines result from the ignition of methane gas (though coal dust itself can explode). Pockets of methane commonly occur in underground coal deposits. If these pockets go undetected and gas builds up in the mine, a simple spark can detonate an explosion. The high accident rate in the coal industry leads to a great number of disability cases. Not only do accidents contribute to disability, but working conditions do as well. Performing heavy labor in a stooped position and crawling on hands and knees both lead to inflammations of the joints—conditions known as *beat hand* and *beat knee*.

Black Lung Disease. A miner who escapes accidents and crippling deformities may finally succumb to **black lung**—a wheezing and shortness of breath, an inability to climb stairs or perform any labor, a disease so disabling that some victims are only able to sit in chairs, their lungs destroyed by the particles they inhaled. The public and the coal miners call this condition *black lung disease* because the lungs of miners who die from it are black (Figure 11-11). Physicians know the disease as *coal workers' pneumoconiosis* (pronounced new-mō-cō-ni-ō'-sis), abbreviated as CWP.

The disease is caused by the inhalation of coal dust. Fibers grow within the lungs around the sites where particles have been deposited and gradually destroy the elasticity of the lungs. There appears to be no treatment, no cure, for black lung, only for the bacterial infections that are side effects of the disease. The risk of black lung disease appears to be influenced by the specific mining task (cutting at the coal face is worse than hauling) and by the years spent underground.

How many individuals are afflicted with black lung disease? Over 250,000 claims of black lung disease have been approved by the Social Security Administration. These claims were submitted either by current or former miners or their widows, and more claims are continually being approved.

Impact of Coal-Fired Electric Power

Coal, as we pointed out earlier, is used mainly in the generation of electricity. The burning of coal (which is about 80% carbon) produces carbon dioxide, a gas that is of concern because of its potential effect on the earth's climate. (See Chapter 17 for further discussion of carbon dioxide and climate.) The three most important other air pollutants in the stack gases of coal-fired power plants are sulfur dioxide, particulate matter, and nitrogen oxides.

Sulfur dioxide injures plants, materials, and peo-

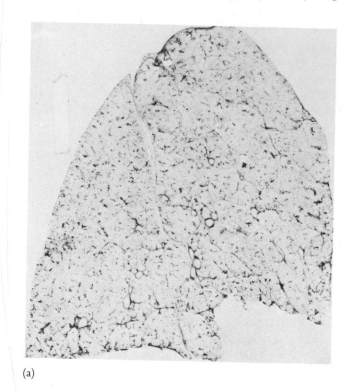

(a)

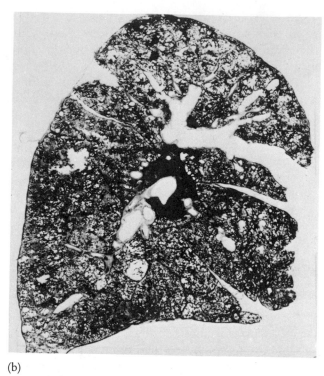

(b)

FIGURE 11-11 A Comparison of the Lungs of a Nonminer and a Coal Miner. (*a*) A section from the lung of a man who died at age 86 and was never a coal miner. (*b*) A section from the lung of a man who died at age 78 and was an underground coal miner for 36 years. Although the man did not smoke, he suffered from severe emphysema, a lung disease in which breathing is badly impaired. (*Photos:* Courtesy of Dr. Frank Green, Chief, Pathology Section, Appalachian Laboratory for Occupational Safety and Health)

ple's lungs (see Chapter 16). Sulfur dioxide was present in the air in the air pollution disasters at Donora, Pennsylvania and in the infamous "London Fog." A single 1,000-megawatt coal-fired electric plant burning 2.5% sulfur coal (not an unusual level) will discharge 200,000–250,000 *tons* of sulfur dioxide per year if the plant has no emissions controls. Controls typically consist of ridding the coal of some of its sulfur by water washing, and "scrubbing" the stack gases to remove sulfur dioxide. Such controls are necessary to decrease air pollution levels and to diminish acid rain (see Chapter 16).

Particles or particulate matter are "the partners in crime" of sulfur oxides. Particles are known to aggravate human respiratory problems. Particles discharged into the atmosphere when coal is burned at power plants are known as *fly ash*. Assuming that the emissions of fly ash are controlled by the electrostatic precipitator or by baghouse technology, the annual production of particles from a 1,000-megawatt coal-fired electric plant could still be as high as 20,000–25,000 tons. (See Chapter 15 for further descriptions of these technologies.)

Nitrogen oxides are also produced when coal is burned at electric power plants. Although nitrogen oxides have direct effects on our health, they are noted primarily for their interaction with hydrocarbons to produce ozone, a gas that aggravates diseases of the respiratory tract. Nitrogen oxides are also implicated in acid rain.

Coal also contains arsenic, a carcinogen, emitted in the fly ash. A last category of emissions from coal-fired power plants is unexpected: radioactive elements, which are found naturally in fly ash. The quantity of radiation from a coal-fired electric plant is very low, less than 1% of natural background radiation.

OIL AND NATURAL GAS —GLOBALLY MALDISTRIBUTED

Scientists believe that oil and natural gas are derived from algal plankton in the ocean. In much the same fashion that coal was derived from woody land plants, buried plankton were broken down by bacteria in the absence of oxygen. Chemical and physical processes, operating over many thousands of years, converted the organic material into petroleum compounds.

Oil consists mainly of liquid hydrocarbons, compounds of carbon and hydrogen. About 80% or more of oil by weight is carbon. The remainder is principally hydrogen, but sulfur and oxygen may each account for up to 5% of the oil's weight. Raw oil is distilled, or *refined,* in a distillation column where trays are used to separate the components. From the various levels of the distillation column come such products as gasoline, aviation fuel, heating oil, diesel oil, and asphalt.

Natural gas, in contrast to oil, may be as little as 65% carbon by weight, but hydrogen furnishes much of the energy when natural gas is burned. Because of its lower carbon content, natural gas produces less carbon dioxide; hence, its use contributes less to the potential greenhouse effect. Although the sulfur content of natural gas is usually low, nitrogen levels may be high, up to 15%.

It is not unusual to find oil and gas together. Often the gas is found dissolved in the liquid hydrocarbons, but natural gas is also often trapped above the liquid petroleum. Most often, however, gas is found alone. Nonetheless, about 25% of natural gas is found in the search for oil.

Oil and Gas Resources

Until the 1950s the United States produced nearly all the oil it consumed. In that decade the United States found itself producing less and importing cheap foreign oil in larger and larger quantities.

Even with the dramatic price rise after the oil embargo of 1973–74, we had difficulty curbing our oil appetite. By the late 1970s the proportion of U.S. demands met by imports had grown to about 45%, a level that we have been unable to decrease up to the present time. In 1990 our appetite for petroleum caused us to import about 44% of our annual oil needs of 6.3 billion barrels. The portion of our total oil use that was met by imports from the politically unstable Middle East stood at 12% that year.

With demands still growing, and domestic production falling, the proportion of our consumption met by imports is projected to continue to grow—to 53% by the year 2000 and to 61% by the year 2010, unless we can learn to conserve. Since we utilize about 65% of our total oil consumption in all forms of transportation, this is a sector to target for conservation.

The proved oil reserves in the United States were estimated at 26.2 billion barrels as of January 1, 1991. The term *proved oil reserves* means that this oil is known to remain in portions of the oil fields where production drilling has already begun. Furthermore, we are assured that this oil is profitable to recover. These proved reserve quantities, however, have been falling in the United States since the early 1960s because new discoveries have failed to keep pace with our rate of production.

The low figure for proved oil reserves does not mean that our oil supply is in imminent danger of exhaustion, even though we produce 3.5 billion barrels of oil per year. We have, in fact, perhaps 39 billion barrels of oil in our indicated and inferred reserves. *Indicated reserves* include oil that we know exists and that we think can be produced by new methods of recovery.* The term *inferred reserves* refers to oil for which we already have limited evi-

---

* The quantity of oil that flows out of the well by natural pressure alone is referred to as *primary recovery* and averages about 20% of the oil in place. Since about 1960, petroleum engineers have developed methods to force up more of the petroleum. These *secondary recovery* techniques involve either injection of water beneath the oil or injection of gas above the reservoir to place increased pressure on the oil in place. Secondary methods can increase the yield of oil reservoirs to 50% or 60% of the oil in place. Newer *tertiary* methods, such as injections of carbon dioxide, nitrogen, or steam, may push recovery to the 90% level.

dence of existence, perhaps in fields nearby those currently in production.

In addition to indicated and inferred reserves, new oil is still being found from our *undiscovered resources,* which the U.S. Geological Survey estimated at only 35 billion barrels in 1989. The projection combines geologic evidence, statistical methods, and extrapolation of past trends in various measures. This low level of undiscovered resources means that our petroleum production will probably continue to fall, and that unless we find means to dampen demand, the proportion of our needs met by imported oil will continue to rise.

At the current rate of oil use in the United States and our total resource base of about 100 billion barrels (proved, indicated and inferred, and undiscovered), we will run out of oil in about 33 years— but only if we continue to import 50% of our needs. Without any importation our resource base would last us just 16 years.

In 1988, world oil production was 64.2 million barrels per day. This is the combined figure for the market economies of the world and the centrally planned economies of the former U.S.S.R., China, and Eastern Europe. Of this total, the United States used 17.3 million barrels per day, or 27% (Figure 11-12a). Projections for the year 2010 are a worldwide production of 70 million barrels per day with U.S. consumption of 20.3 million barrels per day, or 29%. The United States previously consumed over a third of world oil production, but other nations have increased their consumption dramatically, thus decreasing the U.S. share.

Our oil consumption has been on a roller coaster ride. In 1979, it was 18.5 million barrels per day; in 1981, 16 million barrels/day due to recession; in 1984, conservation measures had taken hold and oil use had declined to 15.7 million barrels/day. By 1988, an increased number of vehicle miles and an increased demand for jet fuel had driven our consumption back to 17.3 million barrels per day, the figure that describes 1990 U.S. oil use as well. Yet, efforts by Congress in 1990 and 1991 to require increased vehicle efficiencies failed, despite the invasion of Kuwait by Iraq and war in the Middle East, a war that probably had something to do with oil.

In 1988, gasolines accounted for 43% of consumption of refined petroleum products; middle distillates, which are used for home heating oil, diesel fuel, and kerosene (jet fuel), made up 26% of consumption; and residual fuel oil, which is used for heating commercial and industrial buildings and as a fuel in a decreasing number of steam electric plants, accounted for 8% of oil consumption (Figure 11-12b). The total of all other uses of oil as the base for asphalt, plastics, rubber, chemical manufacture, and so forth, accounts for the remaining 23%. Clearly, oil's other uses, in addition to energy, are very important. Again, the amount of oil (as gasoline, jet fuel, diesel fuel) used in all forms of transportation is about 65%.

Proved reserves of oil are not distributed equally throughout the world. Figure 11-13 shows the inequity. As we can see, the Middle East has by far the greatest proved reserves in the world. Nonetheless, discoveries and production in other parts of the world have been growing since the price increases of the 1970s. The dominance of the Middle East in the world oil market has thus been reduced, to a degree. Nonetheless, the production of these other nations will be decreasing by the late 1990s as their resources are drawn down, returning the Middle East to its dominant position in the oil market.

How OPEC Works. Established in the early 1970s, the **Organization of Petroleum Exporting Countries (OPEC)** has had enormous influence on the price of oil. OPEC controls about 60% of the world's oil and the price of all of it. Even though OPEC consists of a number of countries, these countries have still been able to dominate the marketplace as though they were a single firm. That is, they set the price at which they sell their oil. Such an organization, which attempts to dominate the international market, is referred to as a *cartel.* In order to ensure that each member of the cartel is able to obtain the price set by OPEC, each country participating in OPEC agrees to produce so many million barrels of oil per day and no more. Since OPEC both sets a price and allocates production to the member nations, each member is,

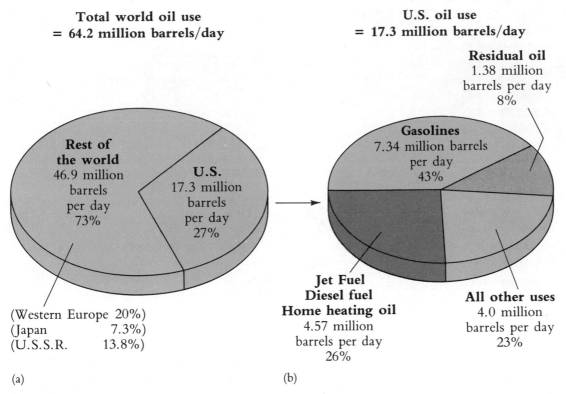

Total world oil use
= 64.2 million barrels/day

U.S. oil use
= 17.3 million barrels/day

Rest of
the world
46.9 million
barrels
per day
73%

U.S.
17.3 million
barrels
per day
27%

(Western Europe 20%)
(Japan   7.3%)
(U.S.S.R.   13.8%)

Residual oil
1.38 million
barrels per day
8%

Gasolines
7.34 million barrels
per day
43%

Jet Fuel
Diesel fuel
Home heating oil
4.57 million
barrels per day
26%

All other uses
4.0 million
barrels per day
23%

(a)

(b)

FIGURE 11-12 U.S. Oil Consumption, 1988. (*a*) In relation to world use. (*b*) By category.

in effect, agreeing to a particular revenue from oil sales. The cartel may not be stable if one of its members needs increased revenues or if new suppliers appear on the scene.

Natural Gas Resources and Use. We can describe natural gas resources in the United States in the same way we described oil resources. Proved reserves are in place and profitable to produce. The proved reserves of natural gas in the United States were estimated at 166 trillion cubic feet as of January 1, 1991. We have a comparable quantity of indicated and inferred reserves for which we have some degree of evidence, and our undiscovered resources, resources yet to be found, are estimated at about 263 trillion cubic feet (U.S. Geological Survey, 1988).

The U.S. position in natural gas as compared to other countries of the world is quite good. Sev-

eral Persian Gulf countries—Saudi Arabia, Qatar, and Abu Dhabi—have comparable reserves. Iran has proved reserves of 600 trillion cubic feet, and the former U.S.S.R. has proved reserves of 1,600 trillion cubic feet, nearly 40% of the total of the world's proved reserves.

Annual consumption of natural gas was 18 trillion cubic feet in 1988. This consumption is expected to rise to 22 trillion cubic feet by 2010. Of the current annual consumption, about 1 trillion cubic feet is imported annually from Canada by pipeline.

There is another potential source of natural gas. It is **geopressured methane.** If there ever was a phantom resource, it is the natural gas known to be dissolved in salt water in deeply buried caverns of the earth. Trapped subterranean waters are at high temperatures and under enormous pressure. In this environment, natural gas may be formed

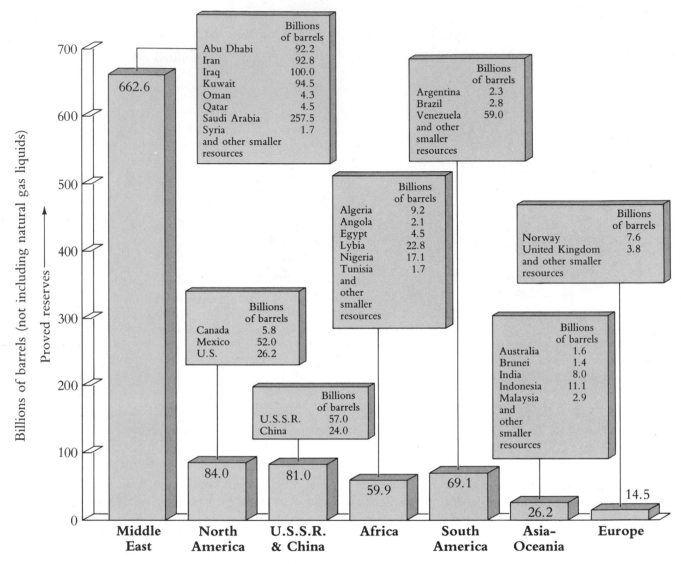

FIGURE 11-13 Distribution of World Crude Oil, 1991. (*Source:* Reserves data are from *Oil and Gas Journal* and are as of January 1, 1991)

from the breakdown of oil deposits and should be found dissolved in the salt water. If the salt water caverns themselves can be tapped, a very large resource of natural gas may await us. The U.S. Geological Survey estimates that there may be 24,000 trillion cubic feet (680 trillion cubic meters) of gas in the geopressured zone of the continental United States. This is a 1,200-year supply at the current rate of use. Controversy abounds over whether this gas can, in practice, be recovered, but experts agree

it is there. We may also be able to produce natural gas from tight sand formations and from coal deposits.

Synthetic Fuels from Coal, Tar Sands, and Shale

The term **synthetic fuels** refers to liquid and gaseous fuels derived from coal or shale oil or tar sands, rather than from naturally occurring petroleum and natural gas. Synthetic fuels have been around for a long time. In the first half of the nineteenth century, before we learned to exploit petroleum, the lamps of North America were lit by whale oil, coal oil, and shale oil. In addition, gas was manufactured from coal in the early 1800s on a wide scale, first in Britain and then in the United States. The product of the local "gasworks" was known as *town gas* or *illuminating gas*. This low–heating-value gas was used for community lighting, for heating homes, and for cooking. By the end of World War II, natural gas had displaced town gas in the United States.

Synthetic Fuels from Coal: Gasification and Liquefaction.

Coal gasification processes are of two types, based on the quality of the product. One process produces a gas of relatively low heating value, consisting primarily of carbon monoxide and hydrogen; the process is referred to as *low-Btu gasification*. The second process produces a gas with a heating value nearly that of natural gas, and the process is known as *high-Btu gasification*. The gas from this second process is referred to as *synthetic natural gas (SNG)*, and it consists primarily of methane. It is a reasonable substitute for the natural gas transported by pipeline to many sections of the country. In both these processes the undesirable constituents of coal are replaced with hydrogen, eventually producing methane.

In the 1980s the Great Plains coal gasification plant was built in Beulah, North Dakota, as one part of an effort to develop synthetic fuels. The plant produced 137.5 million cubic feet of high-Btu gas per day in 1984 and 1985, consuming about 4.7 million tons of coal per year. In total, a dozen commercial-scale demonstrations of synthetic fuel production were planned around the country as a response to the oil embargo of 1973–1974. With an aggregate value of $23 billion, shared between industry and government, these projects would have provided the technology for coal gasification, coal liquefaction, and oil extraction from shale, but Congress and President Reagan withdrew government support and left the synthetic fuel industry in a shambles. One by one, the projects folded.

In 1985, one of the few commercial-scale projects remaining, the successful Great Plains coal gasification plant, was put on notice that its government support would end in 1986. The federal government tossed away its $1.5 billion investment, and the industry partners lost $543 million. It will be understandable if future corporate interest in long-term energy projects with government co-sponsorship is low. These projects, had they been continued, would have provided a considerable security to U.S. oil and gas supplies.

Tar Sands of Athabasca.

In the United States, synthetic fuel developments are now largely confined to the laboratory scale, but in Canada a different resource is being determinedly developed. In the Athabasca region of the province of Alberta are deposits of a sand that is coated black with tar; these deposits are being exploited to produce oil. The tarry material can account for up to 16% of the weight of the sandstone. Geologists estimate there may be 300 billion barrels of oil in the tar sand deposits in Athabasca, more than ten times the proved oil reserves in the United States.

Efforts in Alberta to extract the oil initially had a difficult history. The oil was costly to produce, and mechanical breakdowns plagued the operations, but oil companies such as Sun Oil, PetroCanada, Imperial (Exxon of Canada), and Amoco Canada have now had some commercial success in producing a high-quality product from the tar sands.

Tar sands are found in the United States in Utah: 20–30 billion barrels of liquid hydrocarbons might be produced from these deposits. Venezuela also has large deposits of tar sands, which it has been working to exploit.

Shale Oil from the Rocky Mountains.

Another source of liquid hydrocarbons is shale rock that contains the organic material known as **kerogen.** A liquid that is much like oil can be extracted from the kerogen by distillation. The organic matter locked in the shale is the result of geologic processes acting on the ancient sediments accumulated in inland lakes. The world's largest deposits of this oil-

Towards a Sustainable Society

What Business Must Do
by Stephan Schmidheiny

Stephan Schmidheiny is a Swiss businessman who chairs the Business Council for Sustainable Development located in Geneva, Switzerland. He has been the main link between the United Nations Conference on Environment and Development and the international business community.

Free markets, in which individual business people decide what goods and services they want to offer at a price they hope to get, are the most efficient way to set prices. But the market has never been designed to express the needs of future generations. Today's market conditions and price signals encourage more misuse of resources than nature can bear. So we have to build into this free market system a new rationality that will make the market reflect costs to the environment and benefits to the environment. Then business, following its own best interests, will intrinsically be following the way to more sustainable development.

Sensible solutions will only come about as a result of a spirit of cooperation between governments and the private sector. You need governments. There are clear limits for the private sector, which cannot go beyond the rationale of the market. And there are clear limits where governments understand the function of markets.

Governments are already very heavily interfering in markets, looking out for what they can tax. Traditionally they have been taxing the process of creating wealth, of adding wealth. I believe that this, in the long run, is not the right thing to do. Governments should be taxing the impact on the resource base—on nature—and, at the same time, taxing the process of creating added value less heavily so that the overall tax burden shouldn't be increasing.

Governments should impose bans, regulations, and legislation where there is imminent danger to human beings, species, or watersheds from, for example, ozone-depleting substances. But where you want incremental progress, governments must build incentives into the business process, and that is only possible through signals from the market, costs and benefits, to which business will respond very fast.

In the past, business always went against environmental legislation. It was always seen as representing additional cost, government interference, and tax restrictions, and business instinct was to push away as much as possible. But, frankly, I think what we are in the process of learning is that it makes more sense to accept that change is going to come about anyway. Governments are going to legislate, so it's better for us—and in our own interest—to get involved at an early stage in these legislative processes, to show alternatives, and to assist in costing them and so forth, so our interests are represented to legislators.

I'm not suggesting this as a humanitarian mission—I don't want to appear a better citizen than other business people. I do this in my and in my successor's best interests. I am a businessman and I am profoundly convinced that environment and development is the number one issue that is going to shape tomorrow's—my children's—business environment. I cannot see any more important, more far-reaching trend.

bearing rock are apparently in the Rocky Mountains of Wyoming and Colorado, where the equivalent of 600 billion barrels of oil may be present. Compared to ordinary U.S. proved reserves (about 26 billion barrels of oil), this resource is enormous.

Why have we been so slow to develop this resource? Clearly, it could solve any current oil shortage. There are several reasons for the long delay. First, removing the oil requires the mining of rock. Between half and two barrels of oil can be extracted from each ton of rock, leaving 1,700 pounds of waste rock to dispose of. If we were to produce 1 billion barrels of oil from this shale, or about one-sixth of our annual oil consumption, we would produce about 900 million tons of waste rock. This waste rock would have a huge impact on the land and the mining operation would be massive, requiring extensive reclamation. Brine from the mining operation would need to be disposed of as well. Clearly, the environmental impact would be very large.

The second reason we are not producing oil from shale is cost. The Office of Technology Assessment (OTA), an arm of Congress, estimated that shale oil would have to sell for $48 per barrel to give the manufacturer a 12% return on investment and, hence, a reasonable profit. In 1991, after the rescue of Kuwait, oil was selling at $15 per barrel. With such high prices needed for shale oil, energy companies have been reluctant to invest in its production.

NUCLEAR POWER—HIGH-TECH SERVANT WITH COMPLEX PROBLEMS

It began under a cloud—a mushroom cloud rising over a Japanese city. The reputation acquired by the first public display of atomic power in 1945 has been transferred by association to the nuclear electric power industry and has proven very difficult to change.

The scientists who created the atom bomb also envisioned that the atom could be used peacefully as a means of generating electric power. In the 1950s under the "Atoms for Peace" program of President Eisenhower, private corporations were given the privilege of owning nuclear reactors. Industries then began to join in projects with the Atomic Energy Commission to develop electric plants powered by nuclear energy. The first experimental production of electricity from a nuclear reactor occurred in 1956, when a boiling-water reactor began operating at Argonne National Laboratory in Illinois. In the following year a pressurized-water reactor at Shippingport, Pennsylvania began delivering 60 megawatts of electrical power. The size of new plants increased quickly as operating experience grew.

A tide of commitments to nuclear plants began in 1965. Seven orders for plants were placed that year, 20 the following year, and 30 in 1967. The rate continued strong into the 1970s. By mid-1974, almost 240 nuclear plants had been ordered, and most new plants on order were to provide 1,000 megawatts or more of electrical power. The new technology had taken hold with remarkable speed. However, between 1974 and 1978 just 13 new orders were placed for nuclear reactors to be sited in the United States, and only 2 were ordered in 1978. The fate of nuclear power in the United States was sealed in 1979 by a nuclear accident at the Three Mile Island power plant near Harrisburg, Pennsylvania. Not a single order for a nuclear reactor to generate power in the United States has been placed since 1978. Cancellations of earlier orders followed quickly. In all, 66 reactor orders were canceled between 1978 and 1984. The tide had begun to recede.

The course of nuclear power development was slowed at first by debate in the scientific community and in Congress about the possible levels of radiation released routinely from the plants. Scientists have also argued over the safety of the containment structure in terms of its ability to prevent the accidental release of radioactive material. Debate continues on whether plutonium ought to be used as a replacement nuclear fuel for uranium as a means to extend fuel supplies, because plutonium might be stolen and used for making atomic bombs. Finally, no assuredly safe method of disposal of nuclear waste has yet been devised.

Is it the cloud at the beginning that has alone limited the acceptance of nuclear electric power? Or is there more substance to the debate than simply poor public relations? Understanding the controversy that swirls around nuclear power requires a discussion of the complete nuclear power system as it has evolved to the present time. In no other way can the reader formulate sound opinions.

Nuclear Power Plants: How They Operate

To understand the operation of nuclear power plants, it is helpful first to examine the nuclear reaction known as **fission.** Fission occurs when a neutron strikes the nucleus of uranium-235 or certain other heavy atoms. The reaction consists of the breaking apart (fissioning) of the large uranium atom into two medium-size atoms, accompanied by the release of a large amount of heat energy and gamma rays. The two medium-size atoms are often radioactive and decay in gradual steps to stable atoms, releasing radiation and heat at each step.

Not only are fission products, energy, and gamma rays released, but neutrons are also ejected in the fission reaction. When one of these neutrons strikes another uranium-235 atom, it can cause that uranium-235 atom to fission in turn. Still more fragments, heat energy, and neutrons are released, and the fission reaction is thereby continued or sustained. The sustained fission reaction is the basis for the design of both the atomic bomb and the nuclear power plant.

Two fundamental reactor types are commonly used to capture the heat energy from the fission process: the *boiling-water reactor (BWR)* and the *pressurized-water reactor (PWR).* In both reactor types, uranium-235 undergoes controlled fission in a core, generating heat energy. In the interior of the core, long cylindrical metal rods containing the nuclear fuel are arranged vertically (Figure 11-14). Fission takes place within the fuel rods and provides the energy to heat water that is flowing through the core, around the rods. The core of the nuclear reactor is thus the "boiler" of the nuclear power plant. The core is heavily shielded by concrete and steel to prevent the exposure of workers to the dangerous neutrons and gamma rays.

About 3% of the uranium in the fresh fuel is in the form of uranium-235; this is the isotope that undergoes fission. The remainder of the uranium in the fuel rod is uranium-238, an isotope that cannot undergo fission. As the reactor operates over a period of time, the amount of uranium-235 within the rod decreases and fission fragments build up. The fission process gradually slows down because the fission products capture some of the neutrons that sustain the chain reaction. After about three years the rod is no longer an efficient source of heat because of a low rate of fission; it is then replaced by a fresh fuel rod. The spent fuel rod is now relatively low in uranium-235 and rich in the dangerous fission products.

This, in general, is how the core operates, both for the BWR and the PWR, with the heat energy of fission being transferred to the water that passes through the core. The boiling-water reactor functions in precisely the same way as the boiler in a fossil fuel power plant—that is, the water flowing through the core is converted directly to steam, and the steam is used to turn a turbine (Figure 11-15).

The pressurized-water reactor, in contrast, does not convert the water flowing in the core to steam. Instead, the reactor maintains enormous pressure on the water to prevent it from boiling. All the heat energy from fission goes into raising the temperature of the water, which is cycled from the core to a steam generator, where its heat is transferred to water flowing in a secondary loop. The water from the core returns from the steam generator back to the core to be heated again. This water, circulating between the core and the steam generator, flows in what is called the primary loop. The water in the secondary loop boils to steam as it leaves the steam generator under pressure. This steam in the secondary loop is used to turn a turbine and generate electricity. Thus, in the BWR, steam is generated in the core itself and is used directly to turn a turbine. In contrast, in the PWR, steam to turn the turbine is produced in a steam generator and flows only in the secondary loop. The spent steam from the boiler in either the BWR and PWR is condensed and recirculated to be boiled once again.

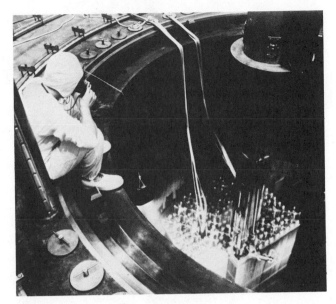

FIGURE 11-14 Fuel-loading Operation. A technician monitors the fuel-loading operation at Unit No. 1 of the Calvert Cliffs Nuclear Power Plant, owned by the Baltimore Gas & Electric Company. Each fuel bundle—of a total 217 bundles—is being positioned by an atomic fuel-handling machine, shown extending down to the upper core level. (*Photo:* Combustion Engineering, Inc.)

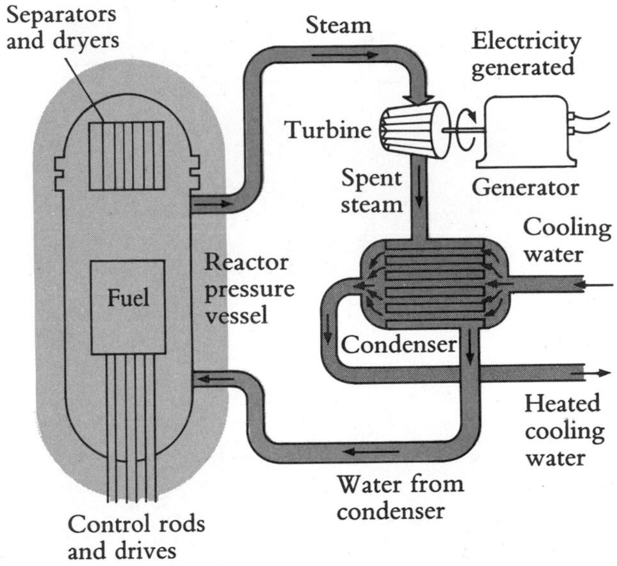

FIGURE 11-15 Boiling-Water Reactor (BWR) Power Plant. Water is boiled to steam in the reactor pressure vessel, just as in the boiler of a coal-fired electric plant. The steam turns a turbine to generate electric power and then is condensed to a liquid prior to return to the "boiler."

Safety of Nuclear Power Plants

Just as fossil fuel power plants emit pollutants, so also do nuclear power plants, but routine releases of radioactivity are negligible. That is, on a day-to-day basis, a resident near a nuclear power plant is exposed to very little radiation. Most plants are meeting the rules set by the federal government on releases. The rules call for routine releases of less than 5% of the natural background radiation. It should be added that these guidelines were not always so strict and that criticism by scientists helped to bring about new and stricter guidelines. Day-to-day emissions are no longer the target of critics, however. It is the potential release of radiation from a serious accident or from sabotage that concerns people. One particular form of accident is of more concern than all others.

Recall that water circulates through the reactor core to withdraw the heat produced by the fission process. If the circulating water were suddenly lost, the heat in the core would accumulate rapidly, and the contents of the core could melt. In the jargon of the nuclear industry, this is called a *loss-of-coolant accident.* This kind of accident might occur if a steam or water line carrying water into or out of the core should break. The high pressures in the line would probably cause most of the water or steam to be rapidly ejected from the core through the break. The temperature in the core would rise rapidly, melting the fuel rods. This extreme event is known as a *meltdown.* Radioactive xenon and krypton gases would be released from the melted rods and would enter the building through the break in the pipe.

Controversy 11-1

Is Nuclear Energy an Inevitable Result of Technical Progress?

The anti-nuclear movement . . . seeks to undermine the scientific and technological revolution which has created the modern world.

Alex A. Vardamis

If man is to survive on this earth, . . . it will be through his wisdom in choosing between those innovations that he can control and those that he cannot.

George Dryfoos

The excerpted letters that follow appeared in the *New York Times* on successive July days in 1978, shortly after demonstrations at the nuclear plant site at Seabrook, New Hampshire. They raise issues and questions that are worth exploring.

To the Editor:

The recent anti-nuclear-energy demonstration in Seabrook, N.H., should be placed in perspective. The animating rationale of the protest movement is based upon a rejection of progress and technology. . . .

The anti-nuclear movement is doomed to failure, for it seeks to undermine the scientific and technological revolution which has created the modern world. . . . The Seabrook demonstrators . . . are temporary and inconsequential impedimenta to the tide of history and are destined to become a forgotten footnote to the constructive advancements of science in this century. . . .

Alex A. Vardamis, July 6, 1978

To the Editor:

Questioned as to the possibility of another blackout in New York this summer, Con Ed Chairman Charles Luce sensibly pointed out that in a complex system of machines, operated by fallible human beings, there can be no 100 percent guarantee.

His words should be carved in stone for the benefit of those who see nuclear power as the answer to our future energy needs. . . .

The catalogue of hazards ranges from an admitted inability to guarantee that storage of nuclear wastes will not fatally pollute our land, water and atmosphere, to the very real possibility that proliferation of weapons-grade fuel will make possible the production of explosive devices. . . .

If man is to survive on this earth, it will not be through his genius for technical innovation. It will be through his wisdom in choosing between those innovations that he can control and those that he cannot.

George Dryfoos, July 7, 1978

Who was Ned Ludd? And who were the Luddites? Is Vardamis suggesting that antinuclear demonstrators are modern-day Luddites? Is the comparison a valid or invalid one? Defend your position. Has the United States ever rejected an otherwise useful technology, simply for environmental reasons, that others have gone on to develop?

Sources: The Vardamis letter appeared on July 6, 1978; the Dryfoos letter appeared on July 7, 1978, both in the *New York Times*.

The molten mass of fuel and fuel rod shells would fall to the floor of the reactor vessel, perhaps melting through the floor and falling into the containment room that surrounds the reactor core.

To meet the emergency of a loss–of–coolant ac-cident the reactor core is equipped with a spray system. The *emergency core cooling system* is designed to inject water automatically into the core in the event of a break in the coolant line; its purpose is to cool the reactor core and prevent melting. The ability of the emergency core cooling system to flood the core with water was finally tested in 1979 at a test reactor, more than 20 years after the first commercial nuclear power plants went on line.

Worst-Case Possibilities. The severity of a loss-of-coolant accident, in terms of its impact on the population, would depend on how effectively the emergency core cooling system functioned as well as on the wind speed and direction if radiation escaped from the plant. According to one safety study led by Professor Norman Rasmussen of MIT, the odds against such a worst-case accident occurring were estimated at 10 million to 1, given that 100 reactors are in operation (Report of the Nuclear Regulatory Commission—WASH-1,400). The probability of a meltdown, however, is not so small. With 100 light-water reactors in operation, the probability of a meltdown is 1 in 100 per year. Thus, although the worst-case accident is estimated as only a remote possibility, the meltdown alone is not such an unlikely event. Safety devices engineered into the plant, though, are likely to prevent the serious consequences of the worst-case accident. The Rasmussen study was criticized severely for underestimating the uncertainties of reactor safety.

Until 1979 the issue of nuclear safety lay buried in the jumble of questions that had piled up about nuclear power. In 1979, however, at a pressurized-water nuclear reactor near Harrisburg, Pennsylvania, an accident occurred of a character not thought possible. The reactor incident at the Three Mile Island (TMI) Nuclear Power Station in Middletown, Pennsylvania began at 4 a.m. on March 28, 1979, with the failure of two pumps in Reactor 2. This was the first in a series of events that eventually resulted in a partial meltdown of the reactor core, the most serious accident at any commercial nuclear reactor in the United States. In the incident the metal rods and some of the fuel began to melt. Releases of significant and potentially lethal amounts of radioactive material were fortunately avoided. Although no one died as a result of the TMI accident, it could have easily escalated into an event far worse—as happened in Chernobyl in 1986. Cleanup operations at the damaged plant were completed in the late 1980s at a final cost of about $1 billion.

Chernobyl: The Worst-Case Disaster Occurs. Early in the morning on April 26, 1986, a violent explosion followed a series of experiments at Reactor IV of the multiunit Chernobyl Power Station near Kiev on the Black Sea. The explosion blew the roof off the unit and ejected vast quantities of radioactive materials high into the atmosphere. The materials were detected across much of northern Europe. A seemingly unquenchable fire followed the explosion.

Among the radioactive elements released were cesium-137 and iodine-131. Iodine-131 is a substance that can enter the human diet (by falling on grasses that milk-producing cows may eat) and that concentrates in the human thyroid gland. Up to 50% of the radioactivity in the emissions may have been from iodine-131. Estimates of total radiation from fallout have varied, but one source suggested that the radiation released to the atmosphere rivaled that from about 300 atomic bombs. Some Western experts suggested that as much as 10% of the 180 tons of fuel in the reactor core had entered the atmosphere. Evacuation of almost 50,000 people was completed in the two weeks following the explosion.

Helicopters dropped sand, boron, dolomite, and clay onto the open reactor to fight the fierce fire in order to decrease the production of heat and radioactivity. While the fire was being fought, sandhogs began tunneling beneath the reactor, hollowing out a space in which to pour a several-foot layer of concrete to isolate the reactor from the groundwater and nearby river. Much of the agricultural land around the reactor remains contaminated and will remain closed for years until radioactivity levels subside. The officially reported human toll was 31 deaths; a European commission studying the tragedy estimated that 1,000 people were killed. The commission estimated that perhaps 1,000 more people would ultimately die due to exposure to radiation from Chernobyl, although for most of these people whether Chernobyl was the cause will not be known.

Reports out of the Soviet Union in 1991 suggested that the health status of the population of Byelorussia has deteriorated. The province of Byelorussia is just 10 miles north of Chernobyl, and its area and population were widely contaminated when winds spread Chernobyl's atmospheric debris northward. The reports of health status deterioration were difficult to verify.

What went wrong at Chernobyl? Could a similar accident occur in the United States? Reactor IV at Chernobyl appears to have had much of the modern safety equipment that U.S. reactors have. The reactor itself, however, was of a special design favored by the Soviets, known as the RBMK-1000. The RBMK is known to be susceptible to surges of heat, and a surge apparently occurred that could not be cooled quickly enough, causing a water line to rupture with the water flashing to steam. The RBMK reactor uses graphite in the core to capture neutrons and slow the fission process. It was a reaction of steam with the graphite that produced hydrogen and the terrible explosion that blew the roof off the building.

The common view of many U.S. nuclear experts is that American reactors are not susceptible to the heat surges that the RBMK design is. However, experts disagree on the ability of the American-style containment structure to withstand the type of steam explosion that occurred at Chernobyl.

Problems in the Nuclear Fuel Cycle

From the Mine to the Power Plant. The system for nuclear electric generation involves a cycle that begins with the mining of uranium and proceeds through the use of uranium at the power plant to the recycling and/or disposal of the contents of spent fuel rods.

The first operation in the cycle is the actual mining and milling of uranium ore. Both uranium-235 and uranium-238 are found in the extracted uranium oxide. However, only about 0.7% of the uranium is present as uranium-235, which is the isotope necessary for fission. In the *gaseous diffusion enrichment process* the level of uranium-235 is increased to 3% of the total uranium present, although it can be

increased further if, perhaps, a bomb were being made. Two gaseous diffusion plants currently operate in the United States, one in Paducah, Kentucky, the other in Portsmouth, Ohio.

The fuel now enriched in uranium-235 is next placed in fuel rods at a *fuel fabrication plant*. The fuel rods are shipped, in turn, to the power plant, where, as we discussed earlier, they produce heat in the core of the reactor. When fission products have built up in the rods to a level that slows the chain reaction, the spent rods are removed from the core. Such spent rods were originally intended to go to a fuel reprocessing plant, where remaining fuel resources could be recovered. At the moment, however, in the United States the rods are simply piling up. The reason for this buildup will be discussed shortly.

Fuel Reprocessing and Spent Fuel Rod Storage. The most serious environmental problems in the fuel cycle begin after the spent fuel rods have been removed from the core of the power plant. Because quantities of reusable fuel are still in the rods, the advocates of nuclear power have viewed the step of *fuel reprocessing* as a crucial one. However, hazardous radioactive elements—the fission products—are also in the rods.

Of the reusable fuels in the rods, there is first the uranium-235 that has not been fissioned and can still be used if it can be recovered. Another substance present in the spent rod that can also be used as a nuclear fuel is plutonium. Plutonium-239 is not present in the rod initially but is formed, or "bred," from uranium-238 during the process of fission. Recall that uranium-238 does not participate in the fission process, even though it is the most abundant uranium isotope in the rod. However, during the fission process a small but significant portion of the uranium-238 is converted by nuclear bombardment to plutonium. The fuel reprocessing plant is designed to separate the useful uranium-235 and the plutonium from the hazardous and unwanted fission products (Figure 11-16).

Through most of the 1970s and 1980s, no reprocessing plant was operating in the United States.

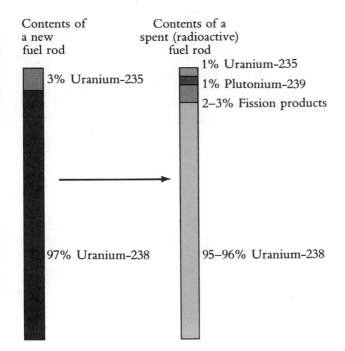

Contents of
a new
fuel rod

Contents of a
spent (radioactive)
fuel rod

3% Uranium-235

1% Uranium-235

1% Plutonium-239

2–3% Fission products

97% Uranium-238

95–96% Uranium-238

FIGURE 11-16 New and Spent Fuel Rods. Plutonium-239 is created when neutrons are captured in the nucleus of uranium-238. This capture process creates uranium-239, which decays in two steps to plutonium-239.

The only fuel reprocessing plant ever to operate in the United States was at West Valley, New York. It had been in operation only since 1966 when it closed for extensive repairs in 1972; it never reopened. The plant left a legacy of improperly stored liquid nuclear wastes as well as workers and environment recklessly exposed to nuclear radiation.

Storage at the Power Plant. Although a fuel rod is not particularly hazardous when it enters the core, a spent fuel rod contains the intensely radioactive and lethally dangerous fission products from the fissioning of uranium-235. Each year about one-third of the rods in the core are removed and replaced; this amounts to the removal of 36 tons of spent fuel annually for the typical 1,000-megawatt light-water reactor. The spent rods are removed via an underwater canal to storage in a water-filled basin where much of the fast initial radioactive decay takes place. Most of the dangerous iodine-131 disappears via the decay process in the first few months of storage.

Because no fuel reprocessing plants have been operating in the United States for almost two decades, spent fuel rods have simply been accumulating at the power plants. The Carter administration planned for the creation of away-from-reactor storage sites, but the Reagan administration ignored the problem, saying it was a matter for private industry to solve.

By the late 1970s a number of nuclear plants had already begun reracking the spent fuel rods in their storage basins to make more room, in order to proceed with refueling on schedule. There is, however, a limit to the number of spent fuel rods that can be stored at power plants. A number of plants will probably run out of storage space in the 1990s. Utilities are now building their current plants with very large water-filled basins; these basins can store as much as 15 years' accumulation of spent fuel rods. In fact, we may soon find shipments of spent fuel rods moving on major highways as utilities transport the rods from plants that are short of storage capacity to newer plants with remaining capacity for fuel rod storage (Figure 11-17). Fundamentally, the reactors themselves have become the storage site for spent fuel rods, a situation not envisioned by the architects of the nuclear fuel cycle. A repository is being built at Yucca Mountain, Nevada. Nonetheless, scientific uncertainties about eventual water movement in the shale rock make it an open question as to whether significant quantities of radioactive wastes will ever be stored there.

Arguments for and Against Reprocessing. Three reasons have been put forward for the reprocessing of spent fuel. First, some experts have asserted that there "may be" a reduction of costs for nuclear fuel if the uranium and plutonium remaining in the spent fuel are purified and recycled. But there is controversy over whether these savings are significant. The second reason cited for fuel reprocessing in the United States is to decrease de-

FIGURE 11-17 Crash Test of a Spent Fuel Cask. A rocket-propelled rail car carrying a 74-ton spent fuel cask smashes into a concrete wall at a speed of 81.4 mph. The impact demolished the front of the rail car, turning it into a mass of twisted metal, but the cask was essentially undamaged. Such crashes are meant to duplicate the worst possible accident conditions in order to predict how well containers will survive. (*Photo:* Sandia Laboratories)

pendence on foreign sources of uranium. France and Germany, two industrial nations, have decided to reprocess nuclear fuel because they have little uranium resources of their own. They also have relatively low amounts of other energy resources. Reprocessing makes these nations less dependent on uranium fuel imports. The United Kingdom is also reprocessing spent nuclear fuel, as are Japan and India. The third reason given for reprocessing is to reduce the difficulty of disposing of radioactive wastes. This reason, however, has been vigorously debated, since if no reprocessing takes place, the high-level wastes remain neatly packaged inside the fuel rods.

Probably one of the reasons for the halt to reprocessing in the United States was that reprocessing produces plutonium, the raw material for atomic bombs. The plutonium would need to be shipped by road or rail from the reprocessing plant to the plant that manufactured the fuel rods. If plutonium were hijacked, the risks would be great. The plutonium could be used by terrorists for either

atomic bombs or dispersal weapons. If spent fuel were not reprocessed, there would be no plutonium recovery or plutonium shipment.

The PUREX (Plutonium and URanium EXtraction) reprocessing technology produces three products (1) uranium, a portion of which is uranium-235; (2) plutonium; and (3) wastes (the fission products). The amount of plutonium that could be recovered annually from the spent fuel of a single 1,000-megawatt reactor is about 550 pounds (about 250 kg), or enough to produce about 15 atom bombs per year.

International Safeguards. A foreign nation building a nuclear power plant with the help of another nation may be subject to international treaties that force it to accept inspection and monitoring by the International Atomic Energy Agency (IAEA). This inspection process is designed to prevent the misuse of nuclear materials for weapons purposes. However, the IAEA does not itself protect fissionable material or attempt to prevent theft or sabotage, even if it is aware of them. All "police-type" responsibilities are reserved to the nation that supplies the nuclear material or technology. If a prohibited act is detected, all that the IAEA can do is notify the supplier nation.

The nuclear Non-Proliferation Treaty (NPT), which gave the IAEA its power to monitor and inspect, is designed to prevent new nations from obtaining nuclear weapons or from obtaining nuclear explosives for "peaceful uses." However, a party to the treaty can legally make all the preparations needed to manufacture a nuclear weapon as long as it does not actually assemble the warhead. A summary of the treaty, which was established in 1970, is given in Table 11-1.

Since 1970, more than 100 nations have signed the treaty, and most have approved it internally as well. Nevertheless, many nations have not signed, among them Argentina, Brazil, Chile, France, India, Israel, Pakistan, South Africa, and Spain. China agreed to IAEA guidelines in 1983. Of the nations that have not signed the NPT, India was able to explode an atomic bomb in 1974, violating a treaty with Canada, which was supplying it with nuclear technology for a power plant—illustrating the haz-

TABLE 11-1 The Non-Proliferation Treaty

Article I prohibits the transfer of nuclear weapons or other nuclear explosive devices (including devices for peaceful nuclear explosions) to any state. . . . Nuclear-weapon states are also forbidden to assist non–nuclear-weapon states to acquire nuclear weapons or explosive devices.

Article II prohibits non–nuclear-weapon signatories from manufacturing or otherwise acquiring nuclear weapons or devices, including peaceful nuclear explosives.

Article III obligates the non–nuclear weapon parties to accept international safeguards . . . to ensure that there is no diversion of nuclear material to the manufacture of nuclear explosives.

Source: Stockholm International Peace Research Institute, "Preventing Nuclear Weapons Proliferation" (Stockholm, Sweden, January 1975).

ard of giving nuclear technology to a nation that has not signed and ratified the NPT. Sales of full nuclear technology, including reprocessing, have also been made to Brazil (by West Germany) and to Pakistan (by France). These nations deny intentions to obtain nuclear weapons, but neither has signed the Non-Proliferation Treaty and hence cannot be inspected by IAEA. In 1985 a citizen of Pakistan was arrested in the United States for attempting to ship an A-bomb trigger to Pakistan.

Interestingly, Iraq was an early signatory of the NPT. Yet, as inspections after the war in the Persian Gulf have shown, Iraq was well on its way to assembling an atomic bomb at the time of the war. Apparently a signature on the NPT is not a guarantee of safety. Unless strict inspections are carried out, the nuclear genie seems to have a way of escaping.

The Future of Nuclear Power

The fraction of our electrical power supplied by nuclear energy has been steadily increasing as new nuclear plants have come on line. On the other hand, there have been no orders for nuclear reactors to be constructed in the United States since 1978.

Only orders for reactors in overseas countries have kept the U.S. nuclear industry afloat. What are the barriers that have stalled and halted, at least for the moment, the spread of nuclear technology in the United States?

The factors that have slowed construction and halted new orders for nuclear reactors are several. Difficulties in obtaining full licensing for the operation of new plants have so delayed these plants that their costs have soared. From about $1 billion for a 1,000-megawatt nuclear plant in the mid-1970s, the cost rose to on the order of $1.5 billion by 1985. The delays in licensing are part of an effort to ensure the safety of each nuclear plant. Safety has become an even greater concern since the reactor incident at Three Mile Island. In addition, the search for disposal sites for radioactive wastes has been slowed by hostile receptions in many states. The concern is that storage will not be as safe as promised. Although the nuclear industry's orders for new plants have ground to a halt, about 140 nuclear plants have already been built in the United States.

We are witnessing a very unusual event in the history of any nation: We are gradually rejecting nuclear electrical power. The current nuclear plants will be with us for a long time, but the trend is clear. For the moment, coal appears to be the route chosen for the next generation of power plants; other choices are not on the horizon.

Overseas, the trends are not so clear. Smaller nations want nuclear power; they want to be part of the nuclear club. France, Germany, and Britain, though public opposition exists, are building the entire fuel cycle, including reprocessing. Nuclear electrical energy will fill a large portion of their energy needs. The United States is either being left behind or is choosing another route to the future.

SUMMARY

How We Power Modern Society. Electricity acts as a middleman between energy resources, such as coal or falling water, and the final use of that energy. This middleman allows energy to be transported easily or to be used in a more convenient form. The cost of using electricity as a middleman is a loss of efficiency as the energy resource is transformed first into work and then into electricity. The second law of thermodynamics states that there is a limit to the amount of heat energy that can be transformed into work. Modern coal-fired plants are 40% efficient; nuclear plants are 30%–32% efficient.

In a thermal power plant, heat from combustion or fission boils water to steam. The steam then turns a turbine and generates electricity. The spent steam is condensed back to water in a condenser and then circulated to the boiler again. Coal will increasingly be used to generate electricity in the future because of public resistance to new nuclear power plants. Electric generation from fossil fuels, especially coal, releases many pollutants, including particles, sulfur oxides, and nitrogen oxides.

Although U.S. energy consumption increased by more than 100% between 1950 and the present, the relative use in different sectors remains approximately 40% industrial, 35% residential/commercial, and 25% transport. Transportation energy is mostly used in the form of petroleum. Petroleum provides about 40% of total U.S. energy use; natural gas and coal account for about 25% each; and hydropower and nuclear power account for about 5% each.

One possible future source of energy is fusion, the combining of the nuclei of certain light atoms. However, serious difficulties in the design of a "vessel" to contain the fusion reaction make it hard to predict if, or when, fusion power will become a reality. Similarly, the fuel cell, in which hydrogen and oxygen react, is a power source that seems to be some years away, at least on a commercial scale. The fuel cell does not provide a new source of energy in any event—only a new way to produce energy in a local area.

Coal. The most important type of coal is bituminous coal. Two major impurities in coal are sulfur and ash. Of the total tonnage of U.S. coal, 55% of the reserves are in the West; these reserves are often low in sulfur. About half of Western coal must be mined underground, and the other half is surface-mineable. Most U.S. coal (84%) is used for electricity generation. Coal resources in the United States appear sufficient for the next several centuries.

Surface mining of coal is cheaper than deep mining. The two basic types of strip mining are known as contour mining and area mining. Both types, unless the land is properly reclaimed, can lead to useless wasteland that is unable to support vegetation. Soil sterility, erosion, and acid drainage are all problems that occur when strip-mined land is left unreclaimed. The most important factor in reclamation is replacement of topsoil over the exposed strip-mined earth.

Underground, or deep, mining proceeds mainly by room-and-pillar mining. Underground miners are exposed to explosions and cave-ins. They may be crippled as a result of working conditions, and they breathe coal dust that eventually causes black lung disease.

Acid mine drainage occurs from both surface and deep mines as water dissolves iron pyrite (ferrous sulfide). This low-oxygen, high-acid water destroys aquatic life, but acid water can be treated with crushed limestone to neutralize the acidity. When coal is burned, it produces many air pollutants, including carbon dioxide, sulfur oxides, particulates, nitrogen oxides, arsenic, selenium, and radioactive materials.

Oil and Natural Gas. *Petroleum* is a term for liquid hydrocarbons, which are formed by physical and chemical processes acting on algal plankton that were buried in ocean sediments. Crude oil is refined into less complex mixtures for specific uses; examples are gasoline, heating oil, and residual fuel oil. Crude oil may contain up to 5% sulfur. Natural gas generally contains less carbon than oil does, but it has more hydrogen and nitrogen; it contains little or no sulfur.

Worldwide, the largest amount of crude oil is located in the Middle East (663 billion barrels of proved reserves). The United States has 26.2 billion barrels of proved reserves—reserves we are confident exist and can be profitably extracted. We also have about 39 billion barrels of indicated and inferred oil reserves and about 35 billion barrels of undiscovered oil resources in the United States.

Shale oil constitutes another oil resource but is currently too expensive to produce. Nearly 600 billion barrels of shale oil could be produced from American oil-shale rock, most of which is in Colorado.

The United States used an average of about 17.3 million barrels of oil per day in 1990. Imports accounted for 44% of this consumption. The United States now uses about 27% of all oil consumed worldwide, but its share has been declining as other nations have increased their use of oil. In 1990, about 12% of U.S. oil consumption was imported from the Middle East. OPEC is a cartel of oil-producing countries formed to control the pricing and production of oil for the world market. The largest portion of oil consumed in the United States is used for gasoline (43%), with lesser amounts used for home heating, diesel and jet fuel, and residual fuel oil.

In 1988, U.S. consumption of natural gas was 18 trillion cubic feet. The United States has some 166 trillion cubic feet of proved reserves of natural gas. Another possible source for natural gas is geopressured methane, but it is not clear that this resource can actually be recovered.

Liquid and gaseous hydrocarbons can be produced from coal (by liquefaction or gasification); oil can be produced from tar sands and from shale rock. Except for efforts on the tar sands in Canada, most projects to recover synthetic fuel from these sources have come to a halt due to lack of government funding. Oil shale represents a possibly huge resource of fuel, but the environmental problems, especially waste rock, that accompany its production are very serious.

Nuclear Power. Nuclear electric power dates only from 1956, when the first experimental reactor produced power at Argonne National Laboratory. The industry experienced rapid growth until 1974, when a decline in orders set in. Since 1978, no new reactors have been ordered for power production in the United States and many reactor orders have been canceled.

The principle of nuclear electric power is the sustained fission (breaking apart) of uranium-235 in fuel rods located in the reactor core. This fission produces heat, radioactive wastes, gamma rays, and neutrons. Water is boiled to steam by the heat from the fission process. The steam turns a turbine, generating electricity. The two reactor types in wide use in the United States are the boiling-water reactor (BWR) and pressurized-water reactor (PWR).

The waste products from the fissioning of uranium-235 include the radioactive forms of krypton, cesium, strontium, and iodine. Remarkably little radioactive material escapes to the environment during normal operations of a nuclear plant. The safety concerns for nuclear plants center on the possibility of a loss-of-coolant accident, in which water is lost from the core (such as through a pipe break), causing the fuel rods to heat up uncontrollably, and on the misuse of plutonium, which forms in the rods during fission.

The architects of nuclear power originally intended that the fuel in spent rods would be reprocessed to recover the fissionable plutonium and uranium-235. Unfortunately, production and shipment of plutonium from reprocessing creates the risk of hijacking or diversion of the plutonium for use in nuclear weapons. Although Britain and France are reprocessing spent fuel, the United States no longer does so, and spent fuel rods are piling up in huge water-filled basins at the electric plants.

The International Atomic Energy Agency has the power to monitor and inspect the nuclear activities of nations that have signed the nuclear Non-Proliferation Treaty (NPT) as a means of preventing the production of nuclear weapons, but the IAEA has no power to halt such activities.

The United States appears to be abandoning nuclear power as a permanent means of power generation. Yet, other nations are increasing their reliance on nuclear energy steadily and plan to continue to do so. The citizens of the United States appear to have decided that nuclear energy is not worth the multiple risks associated with it.

Questions

1. From what you have read about electric power, do you think that the use of electric automobiles will help solve the pollution problems of the United States? Explain your position as fully as possible. Might it help one geographic area and hurt another?

2. What were two very significant uses for coal before World War II that are not significant uses today? Explain what happened.

3. List at least four pollutants from coal-fired electric power plants (in addition to carbon dioxide).

4. What is the name of the accident that is the worst that could occur in a nuclear power plant? How could it cause a "meltdown"? What safety system is in place in nuclear plants to prevent a meltdown? How does it work?

5. What element that undergoes fission is produced in the core of a nuclear reactor? Why is it important in the debate about the safety of the nuclear power system? How is it recovered?

6. Compare oil, natural gas, coal, and uranium-235 as fuels for the generation of electric power in terms of the pollutants they generate and the economic, political, or environmental upheaval that obtaining them causes.

7. Compare the use of oil, coal, natural gas, and electricity for home heating. Which is the most efficient? Which causes the least pollution? (Be sure to include the possible production of pollutants at the electric generating plant in your answer.)

Further Reading—General References

Energy for Planet Earth, special issue, *Scientific American*, September 1990.

This issue brings together world-class energy experts with competence in areas from resources to electric power to conservation.

Energy: The Next Twenty Years. Report of a study group sponsored by the Ford Foundation and administered by Resources for the Future. Cambridge, Mass.: Ballinger, 1979.

Oil, coal, nuclear power, solar power, projections, economics—all are here, thoroughly documented and comprehensive; one of the most complete studies of that era.

Kash, Don, et al. *Our Energy Future*. Norman, Okla.: University of Oklahoma Press, 1976.

As thorough a description of energy technology and resources as can be found. Language is largely nontechnical and new words applying to the technologies are defined as they are used.

Further Reading—Coal

The American Coal Miner. The President's Commission on Coal. Washington, D.C.: 1980.

A report on community conditions and living conditions in the coal fields. Many photographs. Covers housing, health, safety, black lung disease, company towns. The meaning of coal as a resource is expanded by this document.

Balzhiser, E., and K. Yeager. "Coal-Fired Power Plants for the Future," *Scientific American*, *257*(3) (September 1987), 100–107.

Fulkerson, W., R. Judkins, and M. Sanghvi. "Energy from Fossil Fuels," *Scientific American*, *263*(3) (September 1990), 128–135.

An examination of all the major fossil fuels and how they may be used in the future in a way to decrease their impact on the environment.

Perry, H. "Coal in the United States: A Status Report," *Science*, October 28, 1983, p. 377.

Harry Perry is a renowned expert on coal, and this article is complete and authoritative.

Further Reading—Oil and Natural Gas

Burnett, W. M., and S. D. Ban. "Changing Prospects for Natural Gas in the United States," *Science*, *244* (April 21, 1989), 305–310.

Carrigy, Maurice A. "New Production Techniques for Alberta Oil Sands," *Science*, *234* (December 19, 1986), 1515–1518.

Fulkerson, W., R. Judkins, and M. Sanghvi. "Energy from Fossil Fuels," *Scientific American*, *263* (September 1990), 128–135.

A discussion of new technologies to minimize environmental effects of the fossil fuels.

National Research Council. "U.S. Strategic Oil Reserve May Need Some Pumping Up," *The Logistics of the U.S. Strategic Petroleum Reserve in the World Petroleum Market: 1990–2000*. Energy Engineering Board, Commission on Engineering and Technical Systems. Washington, D.C.: National Research Council, 1986. 144 pp.

"World-wide Report," *Oil and Gas Journal*, December 31, 1990, pp. 41–45.

Further Reading—Nuclear Power

Bupp, I., and J. Derian. *Light Water: How the Nuclear Dream Dissolved*. New York: Basic Books, 1978.

Haefle, W. "Energy from Nuclear Power," *Scientific American*, *263*(3) (September 1990), 136–145.

Haefle suggests a new generation of nuclear reactors whose safety will be ensured by improved technology and a new system of nuclear security.

Hansen, K., et al. "Making Nuclear Power Work: Lessons from around the World," *Technology Review*, February/March 1989, pp. 30–40.

Spector, L. "Nonproliferation—After the Bomb Has Spread," *Arms Control Today*, December 1988, pp. 8–12.

Sweet, W. "Chernobyl—What Really Happened," *Technology Review*, July 1989, pp. 43–52.

Taylor, J. J. "Improved and Safer Nuclear Power," *Science*, *244* (April 21, 1989), 318–325.

Wicks, G., and D. Bickford. "Doing Something about High-Level Nuclear Waste," *Technology Review*, November/December 1989, pp. 50–58.

Chapter 12

Renewable Energy Sources: Hydro, Tidal, Wind, and Geothermal

HYDROELECTRIC POWER

Water, an ancient source of power, today remains a good but not perfect option for supplying electrical energy to our industrial civilization. In the past the energy from a turning water wheel was used directly to grind grain, or cut lumber, or weave fabrics. But the gristmills and sawmills on our rivers began to fade when, in the 1880s, the generation of electric power began at waterfalls. In 1882 the first hydroelectric power plant in the United States was built on the Fox River in Appleton, Wisconsin. In 1895 the power of the mighty Niagara River was harnessed and used to produce electricity. This was the first large-scale production of hydropower in the United States. No one will say that hydroelectric power is without problems, but when we consider the pollution and the potential hazards of other forms of power generation, hydropower begins to look much less menacing.

Hydropower provides about 12% of the nation's electrical energy needs. A generating capacity of 81,000 megawatts was available in 1985 at some 1,200 hydropower plants across the country. By the mid-1990s, hydropower capacity was expected to reach about 90,000 megawatts. In the 1930s, hydropower furnished 30% of the nation's generating capacity, but decreasing costs at fossil fuel power stations gradually made hydropower generation at smaller sites (up to 25 megawatts) uneconomical. Many of the smaller hydropower plants in the eastern United States closed, and newer, larger hydropower plants were constructed at western sites at Hoover Dam, at Grand Coulee Dam, and elsewhere.

Conventional Hydroelectric Power Generation

The principle of hydropower generation is simple. The energy of falling water is used to turn a turbine, which is linked to an electrical generator. Most modern hydropower installations use dams to increase the volume of water that can be steadily discharged through the turbine. Dams do more than provide a reservoir of water from which to draw; they increase the height of the water surface. The increased pressure provided by this higher water surface gives the falling water a higher velocity and hence more energy to turn the turbine.

In practice, water is drawn from the reservoir downward through a long smooth channel, called

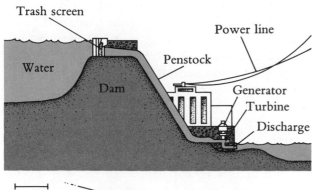

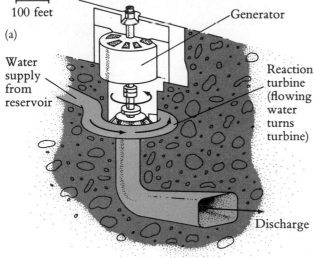

FIGURE 12-1 Hydropower. (*a*) Components of a hydropower system. (*b*) Turbine-generator unit. (*Source:* Adapted from D. Kash et al., Energy Alternatives, *Report to the President's Council on Environmental Quality*, 1975)

a penstock, and is directed across turbine blades that rotate horizontally (Figure 12-1). The turbine shaft is directed upward into the generator unit. Many turbine/generator units are needed at a typical installation. About 60%–70% of the energy in the falling water is converted to electricity.

Hydropower units are costly to install and require maintenance, but they use a fuel, water flowing to the sea, that is free and not subject to inflation. Unfortunately, hydropower is not free of environmental impacts. Reservoirs not only flood the land behind the dam, but also modify the quality of the water that is stored in and released from the reservoir. The loss of land habitat is an obvious effect. The decrease in the quality of water is surprising, though. Water released from a reservoir, depending on the season, can be very low in dissolved oxygen and hence an unfavorable environment for fish and other normal aquatic species. In addition, the water released from a reservoir erodes and scours the stream channel to a greater extent than the undammed stream would have. Finally, dams block the way for fish that swim upstream to spawn. To enable fish such as salmon and shad to reach their spawning grounds, concrete fish ladders are built alongside many dams. Certain fish are capable of jumping up these ladders between water pools in order to enter the waters of the reservoir above and continue their upstream journey.

The hydropower resources of North America make up 11% of the world's hydropower potential. Although most sites in the United States with large hydropower potential have already been put to use, much of the capacity at low-head sites remains to be exploited. (*Head* refers to water height above the turbine; low-head sites have a small height above the turbine.)

In Canada, on the other hand, huge hydropower resources are just now being tapped. Hydro-Quebec is building hydropower projects on a massive scale, including an installation on James Bay that will be the largest hydropower plant in North America. Power from these projects has already been sold to New York State and is likely to be available in other parts of the eastern United States as well. High-voltage transmission lines will carry the power down from Quebec to New York and elsewhere. The projects will provide a source of money for Quebec. In agreeing to use electricity from Hydro-Quebec, we are potentially damaging the environment of the Canadian North.

Small-Scale and Low-Head Hydropower

It is a surprising fact that hundreds of hydropower sites, with dams already in existence, are no longer in use for electric power generation. Many of these sites are small in capacity, 5 megawatts or less, but their potential is real. Abandoned in favor of central electric power stations during an era of cheap fuel, the sites could nearly double our capacity for hydroelectric power generation, if they were all put into service once again.

The U.S. Corps of Engineers estimates that by restoring the abandoned dams and adding generating equipment to those dam sites never equipped for hydropower, 55,000 megawatts of capacity could be added. Since a new thermal power plant is usually rated at about 1,000 megawatts, adding 55,000 megawatts is equivalent to building 55 major plants. Moreover, there would be little more disruption than has already occurred because the sites have been previously developed. All over New York and New England, small-capacity sites are being restored to production or are producing hydropower for the first time.

In the early 1950s a French firm, Neyrpic, invented a new kind of turbine—the **bulb turbine**—that is so versatile it can generate power just from rapidly flowing water. Not even a dam is required. This development has dramatically changed the potential contribution of hydropower to electric power needs. The bulb turbine has made tidal power, with its low heads of 30–50 feet (9–15 m), technically feasible as well. The tidal power plant on the Rance River Estuary in France uses the Neyrpic bulb turbine. The bulb turbine can be installed at sites previously too small to use, and it can also be used to convert existing dams to hydropower installations. On existing dams, it could be installed just downstream of the outlet works in such a way that reservoir releases could be channeled through the turbine.

Even irrigation canals are now being tapped for electric power. In California, hydropower has been generated since 1982 from water flowing in the Richvale Irrigation Canal. Using a Schneider generator, the power plant generates a steady 75 kilowatts from water falling only 9.5 feet (2.8 m). A similar power plant is opening on the Turlock Irrigation Canal in California, as well. Also in California, the Metropolitan Water District, which supplies water to Los Angeles and San Diego, has been installing generating turbines in their water supply system. Their water supply from Northern

California and from the Colorado River in Arizona has to be pumped over mountains to reach the city. It arrives with heads of up to 1,500 feet (450 m), ripe for conversion to electricity.

The redevelopment of hydropower is not without problems, however. Breaking through tangles of red tape at both the state and the federal levels is one such problem. Cost is another, but free fuel for the life of the structure often tips the balance in favor of redevelopment. Finding a market for this power is a potential problem as well. Fortunately, federal law now requires utilities to purchase such power at fair prices.

POWER FROM THE TIDES

Franklin Roosevelt, president of the United States from 1932 to 1945, made his summer home on Campobello Island, which lies along the western edge of the Bay of Fundy. From his home, he could see the rise and fall of some of the highest tides in the world. He recognized and spoke of the potential of this region for power generation. Though Roosevelt's vision has not been fulfilled, the promise in the tremendous Fundy tides remains.

Tides are the result of the gravitational pull of the moon and, to a lesser extent, of the sun on the great oceans. As the earth rotates, a portion of the ocean waters is lifted and held in position for a time by this gravitational pull. When the swell of water in the grip of the moon reaches land, as it must because of the rotation of the earth, it appears as a high tide. Further rotation of the earth releases the grip of the moon on that portion of the ocean and the tide falls away. Tides rise and fall twice each day, although the times shift with the season and the moon's position.

The average height of the tidal swell is only a few feet (half a meter), *except* when the ocean tides move within relatively narrow bodies of water. In this case an oscillation wave is set up that may be 10 to 20 times the normal height of the tidal swell. Bay of Fundy tides, the largest in the world, run up to 53 feet (16 m). Between England and the European coast (France, Belgium, and Holland), such large tides are also created.

FIGURE 12-2 La Rance Power Station. The facility lies across the estuary of the Rance River, which empties into the Atlantic Ocean between St. Malo and Dinard on the coast of Brittany. (*Photo:* Courtesy of Electricité de France)

The possibility of using the energy in the tides has been made a reality in France. In 1968, Electricité de France finished a tidal power station on the Rance River, which flows into the Atlantic Ocean. To understand how tidal power works, we can discuss the operation of the station on the Rance (Figure 12-2).

The Rance River experiences tides nearly as high as those in the Bay of Fundy, up to 44 feet (13.5 m). A half-mile-long dam has been built across the Rance and is used to store the waters of the arriving high tide. When tidal waters are receding, the stored

water is released through sluice gates and then through bulb turbines below the dam to the ocean. Electricity is generated by the turning bulb turbines. To many people, this is the way tidal power is expected to operate, but at La Rance Power Station, energy can be generated on the rising tide as well as the falling tide.

At low tide, most of the water behind the dam has been released. As the tide builds again on the seaward side, it does so against the closed gates of the dam, so the water levels on the seaward side exceed those on the land side of the dam. When a sufficient head is built up, the water is allowed to flow upstream through the turbines, again generating electricity. Thus, electricity is generated both on the receding tide and on the arriving tide. The generation of electrical energy from these low heads of water is made possible by the use of the bulb turbine. La Rance Power Station has 24 separate bulb turbine units, capable of generating a total of 320 megawatts of electricity (see Figure 12-3).

Because of the enormous cost of these structures, governments have been reluctant to invest in tidal power. Yet once the initial investment is made, the production of power requires no fuel. Only maintenance of the structure is required. The Rance station is proof that the concept of tidal power can work on a large scale. Other drawbacks to tidal power do exist besides cost. If the tidal project is a great distance from the nearest large load center, long and costly transmission lines will need to be built to provide the tide-generated electricity an entry into the transmission network.

Tidal Power Resources

A number of sites located around the world have tides that could be used to generate electricity. The potential exists for the generation of about 27,000 megawatts of electricity at inlets of the Bay of Fundy. The coast of France has sites that could produce 11,000 megawatts, and the U.S.S.R. has along the White Sea, an arm off of the Arctic Ocean, the potential for more than 14,000 megawatts of power generation.

Although the United States has studied several tidal power proposals for the U.S. side of the Bay

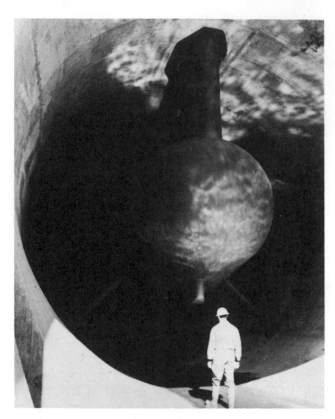

FIGURE 12-3 The Bulb Turbine at La Rance Power Station, as Viewed from the Basin Side. Note the size of the workman for scale. (*Photo:* Courtesy of Electricité de France)

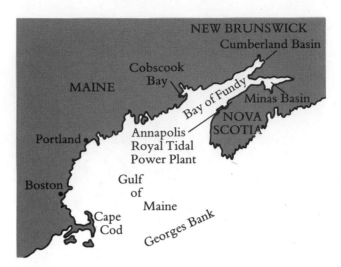

FIGURE 12-4 Tidal Power Projects and Proposals on the Bay of Fundy.

of Fundy, Canada has forged ahead with a 20-megawatt tidal power plant. Located on the Annapolis River near the town of Annapolis Royal on the Nova Scotia side of the Bay of Fundy, the plant was completed in 1984 at a cost of $55 million. The Annapolis plant is the first operating tidal power plant in the Western Hemisphere and was built as a forerunner of a proposed massive Canadian development 200 miles to the north and also on the Bay of Fundy (Figure 12-4).

The project to the north is most likely to be sited in the Minas Basin, where the world's highest tides sweep in and out. The Minas Basin power complex is forecast to cost $23 billion. Depending on the number of turbines, between 3,800 and 5,300 megawatts would be generated by the Minas Basin power plant. The construction cost per kilowatt of generating capacity is not far different from the cost of conventional coal-fired capacity or nuclear capacity—and the fuel is free, unlike coal and enriched uranium.

Cheap power? Yes. Environmentally sound? Not necessarily. There are unknown and troublesome features to tidal power, some peculiar to the Bay of Fundy. The concerns center on the impact on the intricate biological community that lives in and uses the bay.

Environmental Impacts of Tidal Power at Fundy

A large-scale tidal power plant on the Bay of Fundy is likely to have both local and distant biological effects. In the basin behind the tidal dam, the operation of the power plant is likely to have an effect on an important biological area. The area that extends along the shore of the ocean is known as the **intertidal zone,** and it stretches from the point of the highest tide (or spray from the tides) to the lowest point exposed when the tide recedes. (Both of these points vary with the seasons, within limits.)

Sometimes the intertidal zone consists of mud or sandy beaches, sometimes of rocky shores. On beaches live burrowing creatures such as crabs, shrimp, worms, and clams. Rocky shores support organisms attached to the rocks, such as mussels, oysters, barnacles, and the larger algae. The waters of the intertidal zone contain another set of organisms: the phytoplankton. These microscopic floating green plants include the diatoms, the dinoflagellates, and the microflagellates, organisms that are swept in and out with the tides. One of the species of dinoflagellates is responsible for the infamous *red tides,* which kill fish and sometimes make the flesh of shellfish poisonous to humans.

The phytoplankton, along with the attached larger red, brown, and green algae, or "seaweeds," are the "producers" of the intertidal region. A variety of "consumers" also live in the intertidal zone. Some consumers come in with the tide, among them zooplankton and the larval stages of crabs, jellyfish, sea urchins, snails, starfish, and other creatures. The intertidal zone is thus an extremely important part of the sea's "nursery grounds." Still other consumers are present even at low tide, including the mature stages of crabs, clams, barnacles, snails, and starfish.

Tidal power has the potential to change the relative balance among species that make up the communities of the intertidal zone. We are not at all certain how or if the larval stages of marine species will survive passage through the turbine. Moreover, it is conceivable that nuisance species, such as those responsible for red tide, could be favored while the spawning of desirable species such as crabs or oysters could be harmed. In addition, we are not sure whether erosion could be accelerated or the deposit of sediments hastened by such projects.

While local species may be altered by the presence of a tidal power plant on the Minas Basin, migrating species also may be severely damaged. Shad, an important commercial species, migrate each summer to the top of the Bay of Fundy, feeding in the many small embayments there. Passage through the turbines of a tidal power plant is unlikely to do them any good. At the Annapolis Royal tidal power plant, 15% of the shad are killed with each passage through the turbines. Screens may be used to block the entrance, but the usefulness of fish ladders to provide them a way around is still an open question. Migrating birds that feed on the tidal flats, such as sandpipers and plovers, are likely

to find a reduced food supply in the tidal basin behind the power plant due to the mortality caused by the turbine. The birds stop for sustenance at Fundy each fall on the way from the Arctic to their temporary homes in South America. All of these effects take place locally, though their effects may be felt more widely. Thus, tidal power may have unwanted, even severe, environmental impacts. Caution in the development of this resource is in order.

POWER FROM THE WIND

A Brief History of Wind Power

Wind has been in the service of humankind since primitive people first raised a sail above a fragile log canoe. The prevailing "westerlies" were the winds that powered the voyages of discovery to the New World, and wind carried the Spanish Armada to victory after victory. The trade winds caught the sails of the great clipper ships and opened India and China to commerce with the West.

Long before the wind was harnessed by the ingenious windmills of the durable Dutch people, the ancient Persians had captured the wind to grind their grain. The Persian windmill turned on a vertical shaft, a design reinvented in the modern age. The windmills in Holland were used not only to grind grain but also to pump water out of the low-lying lands (*polders*) so that the fertile delta of the Rhine River could be farmed.

The Dutch windmills, in contrast to the Persian windmills, had the familiar horizontal axis (Figure 12-5). The blades of these wooden windmills reached 80 feet (24 m) in diameter, and the windmill could operate in winds of 25 miles per hour (42 km/hr). Many of the Dutch windmills, now more than 500 years old, are still in operation.

In the 1850s a new type of windmill was invented in the United States. This American innovation, the multivane windmill, became common in rural America in the following years and was first used to raise water from wells. The multivane windmill pumped water for the steam locomotives that began crossing the American continent in the

FIGURE 12-5 A Basic Dutch Windmill Design. This windmill has a *cap*, which rotates so that the blades can be oriented to the wind.

FIGURE 12-6 Multivane Windmill. The multivane windmill, invented in the United States in the 1850s, is still used on farms today to lift water from wells for livestock. The windmill is the product of Dempster Industries, Inc. (*Photo:* Courtesy of Dempster Industries, Inc.)

1870s. The multivaned windmill is still in production today, but steel blades are now used in place of the handmade wooden blades of early models. With blades up to 30 feet (9 m) in diameter, multivaned fans could produce up to 4 horsepower (3 kilowatts) in a wind of 15 miles per hour (25 km/hr) (Figure 12-6). In the 1930s about 6 million multivaned windmills were in use, pumping water, across the United States.

A new invention from Denmark gave windmills another chore on the American farm. In 1890 the Danes became the first people to generate electricity from a windmill. This windmill used a propeller with two or three thin blades instead of the multivaned design, and it could capture the wind's energy more efficiently and at higher wind speeds. Windmills brought electricity to the farms of America long before power lines were extended from central power stations. By the 1930s these 1-kilowatt windmill generators were helping rural America "tune in" to an exciting medium, the radio.

The windmill generators were used to charge automobile-type batteries, which could then be used for lights or radio even when the wind was calm. As central station electric power reached more and more of rural America through public power programs like the Tennessee Valley Authority, the use of such wind generators decreased.

For a while, though, about 50 years ago, it looked as if electricity from the wind could compete with electricity from fossil fuel generating stations. It was 1941, and a Smith-Putnam Generator rated at 1,250 kilowatts in a wind of 35 miles per hour (60 km/hr) was installed at Grandpa's Knob, near Rutland, Vermont. Hooked into a power grid, the 110-foot-tall windmill delivered commercial power for over three years. But in 1945 a sudden strong wind broke one of the 175-foot blades. A wartime shortage of materials prevented the windmill from ever being rebuilt, but the windmill at Grandpa's

Knob proved that wind could be used to deliver commercial power.

In the present era of high fuel prices, it appears that such windmills can become cost-competitive and contribute to the electricity needs of the nation. Sail power, as well, abandoned on commercial ocean vessels around 1910, is becoming once again a viable option. Combining motor and sail on a single vessel and using durable new fabrics for sail-cloth may return us to the era of the square-rigger, but with none of the delays and uncertainties of arrival.

Windmill Design

Windmills produce power when the wind pushes on the blades. The greater the *reach* of the blade, the more wind energy it can capture. Also, the greater the velocity of the wind, the greater the force on the blades and the greater amount of energy captured. This is why engineers lean toward big windmills and why they try to capture the higher winds.

Most large windmills now being built or already in use are designed to operate at wind speeds of 10–35 miles per hour (17–58 km/hr). Winds less than 10 miles per hour produce little useful energy; winds higher than 35 miles per hour could wreck the windmill. In a sense, the accident at Grandpa's Knob was an early indication of design problems in windmill technology. The serious accident indicated that the huge propeller blades could fatigue, that is, lose their structural strength as they are subjected to strong forces.

Windmills should not be designed to capture gale winds. Even though such winds deliver far more power than low-speed winds, they exert such a strong force on the blades that the machine itself may be destroyed. To combat the problem of gale winds, windmill blades are curved in such a way that they turn slightly to one side, out of the direct force of the wind, so that the full impact of large gusts does not damage the propeller. This old practice is known as *feathering*.

Another problem in using the power from windmills is the nature of wind itself. From little freshets to great gusts, the speed of the wind varies over a wide range. As a consequence, the cycles per second of the electrical output from a windmill vary. To correct this, the alternating current generated by the turning shaft is *rectified;* that is, it is converted into a steady, one-directional flow. For large windmills, this steady flow of current is fed to an *electronic inverter,* which produces a stable alternating current that can be fed into a power grid. Small windmills could also feed the rectified output to a large storage battery, instead of to an inverter, to store electrical energy for periods when the wind is calm.

Wind Resources of the United States

Wind varies with the features of the landscape; it varies with the nearness to bodies of water, with the weather and the season, and with the height above ground. Winds over the land tend to be slower, on average, than those on the coast or over the ocean. Ocean winds are not only stronger; they are steadier as well.

Across the United States the average annual wind speed is about 10 miles per hour (17 km/hr). It varies from a lowest average of 6.5 miles per hour up to 37 miles per hour, the average wind speed at the top of Mount Washington, New Hampshire. In fact, the winds on Mount Washington have been known to reach an incredible 150 miles per hour (250 km/hr). Interestingly, there is a steady wind across the Great Plains, though the Plains are relatively free of obstructions.

The President's Council on Environmental Quality has estimated that wind resources, if rapidly developed, could be used to displace 4–8 quads of thermal energy by the year 2000. This is energy that would be consumed to generate electricity. Depending on how well we conserve energy, this could equal 5%–7% of annual U.S. energy needs. One study estimates the wind potential of the United States at 1–2 trillion kilowatt-hours per year. U.S. consumption of electricity in 1985 was on the order of 2.5 trillion kilowatt-hours, indicating remarkable potential for wind power.

Environmental Impacts of Wind Power

Wind power causes no air pollution; it requires no water for cooling and causes no thermal pollution. It consumes no fuels. It does cause noise, it does

Towards a Sustainable Society

A Call to Action

by Russell W. Peterson

Russell Peterson has had a distinguished career in public service. He was Governor of Delaware from 1969 to 1973. He served as Chairman of the Council on Environmental Quality from 1973 to 1976 and Director of the Office of Technology Assessment of the U.S. Congress from 1978 to 1979. In 1979, Dr. Peterson was elected President of the

National Audubon Society, a position he held until 1985. He is currently on the board of directors of or is advisor to a number of environmental organizations and international committees.

*T*oday the world is at a crossroads. The systems that support life on earth are deteriorating at an increasing rate. At the same time the knowledge of how to cope with this global predicament is mounting.

Both the problem and the knowledge for its correction are the creations of humans. At this juncture the problem is winning, but only because we *Homo sapiens* have not summoned the will and allocated the resources to apply the available knowledge.

Here is how Dr. Mostafa Tolba, Executive Director of the United Nations' Environment Program, recently described the problem:

The more months that pass, the more prominently the environment features on the world's political agenda. With good reason. Water supplies become increasingly scarce and contaminated. Millions of hectares of agricultural land are rendered unproductive each year through erosion and salinization. Desertification threatens the health and survival of one quarter of the global population. Tropical deforestation continues to degrade land and erase species. Urban pollution continues to worsen. The depleting ozone layer lets increasing quantities of harmful ultraviolet radiation through to the surface. And global warm-

use land, and it does take materials to construct. It also has a visual impact, but the towers of long-distance electric power lines have a height near that of the tallest windmill being considered, and cooling towers are even taller. Also, for a distance of up to 1 mile, large windmills may interfere with television reception. Small windmills are unlikely to cause such a problem. Birds may be hurt by windmill blades, but it is difficult to predict to what extent this would occur. Basically, when we count all the environmental costs, wind power comes out very low in environmental impact.

During the late 1970s and early 1980s the Department of Energy funded the building of a succession of windmills around the country. Their capacities ranged from 100 kilowatts up to 2,500 kilowatts. Few survive in the larger ranges of capacity. Instead, small- to moderate-scale wind power proved to be more cost-efficient and reliable. Thousands of small windmills have been built to generate electric power; small companies have taken the lead.

Private interest in wind power has been spurred by federal and state tax credits for renewable energy

ing looms larger and more threatening by the day.

It is essential that our leaders develop a sense of urgency commensurate with this threat, and then a commitment to provide the resources to cope with it. Environmental policy needs to emphasize development that is sustainable and thus respects the quality of life of future generations—that ensures intergenerational equity.

There are three basic causes of our environmental problem. They are human population growth, escalating resource consumption, and environmentally deleterious fallout from research and development.

World population growth now increasing by over 90 million per year must be stopped. The Population Crisis Committee believes that the most optimistic goal at which such growth can be stopped is about 10 billion. This will require worldwide access to family planning information and services by the year 2000, increasing con-

traceptive use to 75% of all fertile couples. To produce such services in poor countries will cost $10.5 billion per year, up from the current level of $3.2 billion. No other investment would do more to further global security.

Consumption of the world's resources is projected to increase five-fold by the middle of the next century. Such exponential growth cannot go on forever. Each human, in increasing his standard of living, has increased his ability to impact on the environment. The cumulative impact of all of us is pushing the natural world to the limits of its ability to sustain us.

Research and development has been the principal source of humankind's fantastic advances and can be the solution to many of today's ills, but nearly all of our current environmental problems are by-products of research and development. We must do more to steer the world's escalating research and development to minimize the negative fallout, while maximizing the positive.

We must work to lower all three of the basic causes of environmental degradation—first, stabilize population; second, reduce average consumption per person by recycling, reusing, recovering, and preventing waste; and third, develop and select more environmentally benign technology, such as renewable sources and more efficient use of energy.

What is required is the leadership to bring our knowledge and resources to bear on the problems. The world is ripe for such environmental leadership. A spirit of international cooperation not dreamed of a few years ago is now alive. And millions of citizen activists around the world are now demonstrating their determination to rescue our battered planet.

Now is the time to marshal our forces. It is not the time for a doomsday attitude. It is time for a call to action—for a message of hope.

investments. California tax law has made such investments particularly attractive in that state. In addition to tax incentives, a 1978 federal law has given small-scale wind power (and also water power) a real boost. Known as PURPA, the Public Utility Regulatory Policies Act requires public utility electric companies to purchase power from small producers at their *avoided cost rate*—that is, at the cost that would be incurred by the utility to produce the power itself. Until the act, utilities were free either to refuse to purchase small-scale power or to offer discouragingly low rates for it. PURPA and

tax credits have led to substantial wind power development.

In 1981, Windfarms Limited, a San Francisco-based firm, began a project to produce and sell electricity, up to 80 megawatts, from a cluster of 30 windmills on the island of Oahu, Hawaii. In the Altamont Pass, 50 miles east of San Francisco, the same firm has built some 600 relatively small windmills, with a total power capacity of 30 megawatts. Another firm, U.S. Wind Power, Inc. (USW), has also installed windmills in the Altamont Pass. By the end of 1984, USW had a total of 1,400 wind turbines operating in the pass, enough capacity to supply 15,000 residential customers. USW designs and manufactures its own wind machines (see Figure 12-7).

All together, nearly 10,000 wind turbines were expected to be built by 1990 in the Altamont Pass. The pass was chosen because of its strong summer winds; summer is the time the power is needed most in California because of air conditioning loads. Two other wind farm development areas have sprung up in Southern California, in the Tehachapi Mountains north of Los Angeles and in San Gorgonio Pass near Palm Springs. By 1990, more than 1,400 megawatts were being delivered from the total of these California wind farms, enough to supply a city of 350,000 homes. Nationwide, the wind can now deliver about 1,500 megawatts of electric power. The costs of wind power electricity are projected to drop substantially over the next 20 years— to levels below that for electricity from coal-fired power plants. They are already competitive with fossil fuel generation at some sites.

Germany and the United Kingdom both launched wind initiatives in 1989. Germany will be producing wind power electricity at the rate of 100 megawatts by 1994. Britain is studying three sites for wind power development, acting on studies that show that 20% of the nation's electric needs could be supplied by wind.

In 1991, the Dutch government announced plans for a wind power development program that would lead to 2,000–3,000 new windmills capable of generating 1,000 megawatts of electricity by the year 2000. About 300 new windmills had already been erected at the time of the announcement. The wind is coming home to Holland.

Not to be forgotten, however, are the small windmills that have served the countryside since the early 1900s. These modernized private wind systems include 8- to 40-kilowatt machines that could be used on farms, at rural suburban residences, and even at city residences. According to one study, if these wind systems can be made reliable, can be given a 20- to 25-year life, and can be made cost-competitive because of quantity manufacture, a U.S. market for over 17 million machines awaits the industry.

FIGURE 12-7 The Wind Farm of U.S. Windpower, Altamont Pass, California. Power is sold by the firm to Pacific Gas & Electric. Winds in the pass average 18–27 miles per hour from May to August. By 1990 more than 17,000 windmills (with capacities of 50–200 kilowatts) had been erected in the United States and were delivering 1500 megawatts of electric power. (*Photo:* Ed Linton, courtesy of U.S. Windpower)

GEOTHERMAL ENERGY

In the late nineteenth century, residents of the bustling city of San Francisco would travel some 75 miles to the north to Lake County on the California coast to be "restored" at the hot geyser baths that dotted the area. The odor of hydrogen sulfide gas was so noticeable in the area of the hot springs that the local stream became known as Big Sulphur Creek. Restorative though the baths must have been, no one saw any other commercial potential in the hot springs until the 1920s. Then, perhaps inspired by success in Italy in the early 1900s, drilling for steam began in the area. The drillers, how-

FIGURE 12-8 A Geothermal Power Plant at the Geysers in northern California. This is one of nearly 30 plants in the steam fields of northern California. Nearly 2,000 megawatts of electrical capacity were in place by 1990. A bank of mechanical-draft cooling towers in the foreground of the plant are a reminder that thermal discharges are a part of geothermal electric power. (*Photo: Courtesy of The Marley Cooling Tower Company*)

ever, could not interest the electric companies in their steam.

Although Italy began to produce electricity using steam from the earth as early as 1904, it was not until the 1950s that Pacific Gas & Electric became interested in using the steam that came bursting forth in clouds in Northern California. By 1960, Pacific Gas & Electric was generating electric power using that geothermal steam at the rate of 11 megawatts. The capacity of the sprawling plant had reached 1,400 megawatts in 1983. Nearly 2,000 megawatts of electricity were being produced at the Geysers by 1990 (Figure 12-8). The capacity of a modern coal-fired or nuclear power plant is about 1,000 megawatts, so this production is indeed substantial. Wells are going ever deeper at the Geysers. Although the first steam was found at about 1,000 feet, recent wells have been drilled to more than 9,000 feet. In the past year, however, a decline in steam production has set in, perhaps because water was not being recharged to the basin. Table 12-1 identifies areas producing large quantities of geothermal electric power around the globe.

What is geothermal heat? How can it be used,

and where can we find it? Is it a clean and renewable source of power?

Origin of Geothermal Heat

Simply put, geothermal heat is the energy from the earth's interior. Of course, the eruption of a volcano, such as Mount St. Helens, is visible evidence of the enormous heat inside the earth. Scientists estimate the temperature in the core of the earth at thousands of degrees Celsius. In the intensely hot interior of the earth, molten metal and molten rock are thought to be the only forms possible.

Only a few miles beneath the surface, one can occasionally find molten rock at 1,000°C or more. The more likely find, however, is hot solid rock at temperatures of perhaps 300°C. At a number of points on the earth's surface, usually in the areas of volcanic and earthquake activity, this immense heat comes bubbling to the surface in the form of water and steam at temperatures as high as 300°C.

This water and steam come from groundwater that has wound its way down from the surface, down through porous rock and through rock fis-

TABLE 12-1 Worldwide Geothermal Power Production, 1984

Country	Generating Capacity (in megawatts)
United States	1664
Philippines	891
Mexico	700
Italy	467
Japan	228
New Zealand	203
El Salvador	95
Iceland	41

Source: R. DePippe, "Worldwide Geothermal Power Development," Geothermal Resources Council Bulletin, May 1983.

sures, into a region of very hot rock. Heated by the rock, even boiled, this water comes bursting to the surface under pressure as steam and hot water. We call this erupting column of water and steam a **geyser.** Old Faithful in Yellowstone National Park is our best-known geyser because of its towering spray and its insistent punctuality.

Two Important Uses for Geothermal Heat

Geothermal heat has the potential to be used in two basic ways: in the production of electricity and in the heating of homes, offices, and factories. Whether the heat is used for electricity or for heating homes and factories depends on the form in which the resource makes its appearance. Sometimes the water comes billowing up from the earth as pure "dry" steam—that is, entirely as vapor with no water droplets mixed in. This dry steam can be used directly to turn a turbine and generate electricity. Water condensed from the steam may be reinjected into the earth or, if the quality is good enough, disposed of in a nearby body of water.

The Geysers field in California where Pacific Gas & Electric has its plants and the Larderello field in Italy are both examples of fields that produce dry steam. But dry steam discharges are hard to find.

In some fields the geysers spew forth a mixture of steam and water droplets. This mixture of steam and droplets cannot be used directly for the generation of electricity; the impact of the droplets would damage a turbine. In addition, geothermal water contains corrosive salts that make the use of wet steam even less advisable. The mixture must be separated into dry steam and water by a centrifugal separator, a device that whirls the heavier water droplets to the outer edge of the separator for collection. The steam is then directed to the turbine for the generation of electricity, while the hot water is disposed of in various ways, typically into deep wells. The steam that turns the turbine is condensed and also reinjected into the earth. The water is often high in dissolved salts and could damage any body of water receiving it.

The largest electric power plant in the world that uses wet steam is in Wairakei, New Zealand, where a plant with a power rating of 192 megawatts is in operation. The plant began operation in 1958. Whereas the Geysers plant and the plant at Larderello, Italy, are the models for power production with dry steam, the New Zealand plant is the model for power production with wet steam. Two small plants that use wet steam to produce electricity are operating in the United States. The 10-megawatt plant in Brawley, California, and the 50-megawatt plant at Valles Caldera, New Mexico, were both built in the 1980s.

A third type of geothermal field, in addition to the dry-steam and wet-steam fields, is a field that produces hot water only. Such fields are even more common than wet- and dry-steam fields. Reykjavik, the capital of Iceland, with a population of 85,000, is heated almost entirely by hot water drawn from deep geothermal wells under the city (Figure 12-9). The use of geothermal water in Iceland began only in 1943. After the water has been used to heat the city, it is pumped to 40 acres of greenhouses that produce fresh fruit and vegetables for Icelanders. Their crop includes bananas! In the United States, geothermal heat has been used for several decades to heat homes in Boise, Idaho, and Klamath Falls, Oregon.

Hot water may be used for more than heating homes and offices. Geothermal water can be used

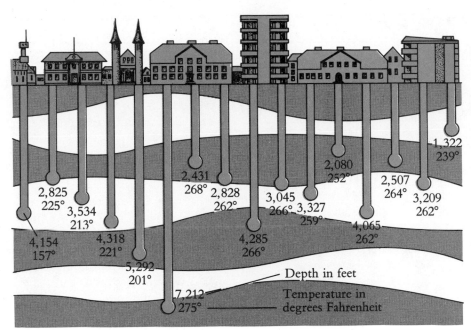

FIGURE 12-9 Geothermal Heating. The city of Reykjavik, Iceland, has been using geothermal water to heat its homes, offices, shops, and factories since 1943. To provide the city with pollution-free heat, 32 holes have been drilled through the underlying lava beds to tap reservoirs of extremely hot water. A number of the holes have been productive, as shown in this diagram. Nine holes are currently in use. (*Source:* © 1974 by The New York Times Company. Reprinted by permission.)

to produce a steam, or vapor, out of a *working fluid* that boils at a lower temperature than does water. Isobutane, one such fluid, might be boiled to an isobutane "steam" in a heat exchanger by using hot geothermal water as the heat source; this "steam" is then used to turn a turbine. The spent isobutane vapor is condensed and returned to the heat exchanger to be boiled again. A 45-megawatt power plant using this principle began operation in 1985 at Heber in the Imperial Valley of California. Successful operation of this plant opens the way to use hot-water geothermal resources for electric power production.

There is at least one additional way to extract energy from the earth. Geologists have noted that buried dry rock at temperatures as high as 300°C is about 10 times more abundant than water-bearing hot rock. Experiments indicate that this dry rock can be fractured by pumping down water under very high pressure. This technique, known as **hydrofracturing,** originated in the petroleum industry to get at gas deposits that were cut off from one another. Once the rock is fractured, water can be forced through the cracks and returned to the surface in a heated state—even as hot as ordinary

geothermal hot water. There may be, however, significant energy costs for pumping, depending on the depth at which the hot rock is found.

In 1986, scientists at Los Alamos National Laboratory succeeded in a commercial-scale trial of this concept. Millions of gallons of water were pumped into a fractured region two and a half miles beneath the earth's surface. The water was returned to the surface at nearly 180°C, hot enough to heat homes or factories or even to generate electricity. Since such a process does not depend on the initial presence of hot water or steam resources, it could be used almost anywhere. Japan, Britain, and France are all conducting their own experiments on this process.

Resources of Geothermal Heat and Projections of Use

The U.S. Geological Survey estimates that our known reserves of high-temperature water and steam (those useful for the generation of electricity) are at a level capable of producing 11,700 megawatts each year for the next 30 years. (These resources and reserves exclude those in national parks.) A

Controversy 12-1

Geothermal Energy Development— Should It Take Precedence over the Risk to a National Park?

The grizzly bear can't survive if Yellowstone Park is its only refuge. It also needs portions of the five adjacent national forests.

John Townsley, Superintendent of Yellowstone National Park

Any activity that would tend to damage them (the geothermal features of Yellowstone Park) . . . would be an insult of the worst kind—insensitivity typical of nineteenth-century America.

Ralph Maughan

One must simply accept the conclusion that our geothermal resources

should be developed promptly, regardless of their location.

Alan Buck, Stewart Capital Corporation

Union Oil has pioneered the development of geothermal resources in the United States. The Union Oil Company operates the Geysers geothermal plant for Pacific Gas & Electric and is a partner in the geothermal development at Brawley, California, and at Valles Caldera, New Mexico. The company is now seeking to develop the Island

Park Geothermal Area (IPGA) in Wyoming. The potential of this area is thought to rival that of the Geysers in California.

Unfortunately, the IPGA lies directly alongside Yellowstone National Park, the first (1872) National Park to be established in the United States. Yellowstone, as you know, is the home of Old Faithful, the world's most famous and most unique geyser. Yellowstone is also home to the grizzly bear, a threatened species in the lower 48 states, as well as home to bison, elk, and such western waterfowl as the

plant of 1,000 megawatts, the size of a modern nuclear or coal-fired power plant, is needed to supply an average city of 1 million people. These reserves, then, are capable of supplying the electricity needs of about 12 million people, or about 5%–6% of current demands.

The resource base we have described so far is only that portion useful for the generation of electricity. In addition, lower-temperature water at 90–150°C is abundant. Such water is useful for heating, and the U.S. Geological Survey estimates the heating value of identified resources as equivalent to that of 14.3 million barrels of oil. Given that the United States uses about 6–7 billion barrels of oil

each year *for all purposes* and has only about 26 billion barrels of proved reserves, this amount of heat is staggering. We must be cautious, however, in interpreting these numbers, since population centers are not often on top of geothermal resources as is Reykjavik, Iceland.

In addition to the resources of underground water and steam, there is also abundant hot rock beneath the surface, which may be useful for heating water pumped into it. Finally, geothermal energy in many cases may be renewable. Where the rock contains the heat and not merely the water, the heat in the rock can continue to be extracted by circulating water through the formation. In sum-

trumpeter swan and Canada goose. The IPGA is outside the park, but many are concerned that the proposed development will affect not only the geothermal features of the park but its wildlife as well.

The grizzly bear is the species thought to be most at risk from development of the IPGA. About 20% of the IPGA, which is in the Targhee National Forest, has been classified as land so critical to the grizzly that decisions about its use must first take into account the need to protect the bear. In fact, much more of the IPGA is crucial habitat for the bear, whose range includes both Yellowstone and parts of six adjoining National Forests. The presence of the additional people who would come to the area with geothermal development is thought to be the largest threat to the bear from geothermal-related activities.

The unique features of the 2.5-million-acre park may also be at risk from development at the IPGA. Even though Old Faithful is inside Yellowstone and is some 13.5 miles from the IPGA, the possibility certainly exists of a deep underground connection between the thermal area and the geyser. Geologists have been unable to rule out the existence of such a connection, though they think it is unlikely. Could Old Faithful fall silent if development proceeds?

The opening of the Wairakei geothermal plant in New Zealand silenced the Great Geyser of Geyser Thermal Valley. Once the fifth most active geyser area in the world, this valley last had a geyser eruption in 1965. Similar declines in activity have occurred with development and drilling in Italy and Iceland, as well as at Beowaive and Steamboat, Nevada. Geysers in the

Boundary Creek area of Yellowstone are within a few miles of the proposed development; thus, an effect on this geothermal area would seem likely.

Can the United States take a chance on geothermal development at the IPGA? What will be saved or replaced by this development? Given that power from the development will still be almost as costly as conventional power, what would be the benefits of development? To whom would the benefits go? What would be the risks? Who would bear the risks? Should we preserve areas that would have economic value to the nation if they were developed?

Sources: All quotes are from "The Incredible Shrinking Wilderness," *National Parks*, January/February 1982, p. 21.

mary, the geothermal potential of the continental United States appears to be large and worth developing.

Cautions and Environmental Impacts

When geothermal energy is used, hot water must be disposed of. This is true even if dry steam is used to generate electricity. When hot water is "wasted" from wet-steam plants, it often has considerable amounts of salts dissolved in it.

Brines from the Imperial Valley may be as much as 20% salt, or about six times the salt concentration in seawater. This brine and the brine from other types of systems may be reinjected into the earth. Certainly, disposal in a body of surface water is not an option.

Reinjection may prove to be more than a way to dispose of brine. It may also prevent the surface above geothermal wells from subsiding as water is drained from the deposit. Not only may it prevent subsidence; it may also provide a **recharge** to the geothermal deposit. Such recharging may be needed in the geothermal basin that feeds the Geysers in California. That is, if the rate of withdrawal exceeds the rate at which surface water descends through the earth to the deposit, reinjection may prevent the well from going dry. Geothermal power may also threaten the natural activity of nearby geysers (see Controversy 12-1).

Geothermal electric plants require a source of cool or cold water, in addition to requiring steam. The cool water is needed to condense the steam prior to its disposal. In this regard, then, a geothermal electric power plant is no different from a coal-fired or nuclear power plant. The water used to condense the steam may come from a nearby freshwater source, such as a lake or river, or it may come from the ocean. If it comes from a freshwater source, cooling towers will be needed so that the heated fresh water from the condenser can be cooled and used again for condensing the steam.

The volume of cooling water needed by a geothermal power plant is larger than that for a nuclear or coal-fired power plant of the same electric capacity. This is because geothermal steam is under lower pressure and at a lower temperature than steam used in conventional electric plants. Because of this, the transfer of electricity to the turbine blades is less efficient, requiring more steam and hence more cooling water. Geothermal water is also likely to contain hydrogen sulfide. Hydrogen sulfide not only smells bad (like rotten eggs); it may affect human health at high-enough levels. Emissions from the Wairakei plant in New Zealand have caused silverware to blacken in a nearby village.

To summarize briefly: Geothermal energy may have a real, even dramatic contribution to make to our energy resource base. It is worth exploring further, even with its drawbacks.

SUMMARY

Hydro and Tidal Power. In the generation of hydroelectric power the kinetic energy of falling water is used to turn a turbine that is linked to an electric generator. Hydropower installations are expensive to build, but they are relatively cheap to operate because the fuel is free. Environmental impacts of hydropower include loss of land and habitat, low oxygen in the water released from the dam, and increased downstream erosion.

The U.S. hydroelectric capacity could easily be expanded by restarting abandoned small hydro-

power stations and by utilizing existing dams not currently used for hydropower, such as those used for municipal water supply reservoirs. Newly developed turbines allow power generation with much smaller water height differences, or heads.

Tidal power is generated from the flow of water caused by the rotation of the earth and the gravitational pull of both the moon and the sun. La Rance Power Station in France uses bulb turbines and has demonstrated that tidal power can be produced on a commercial scale. Construction costs for tidal power are high, but the fuel is free. Aquatic food chains and intertidal communities may be affected by changing water levels and stronger currents caused by the tidal power installation. Passage through the turbines may harm aquatic organisms and alter their abundance in a linked ecological community.

Wind Power. On the American farm the multivane windmill pumped water for livestock and brought electricity to the rural homestead. The emphasis today is on wind-generated electric energy. Windmills are built to capture only moderate winds (10–35 miles per hour); gale winds could destroy them. The wind potential of the United States is 1–2 trillion kilowatt-hours per year, a figure that can be compared to 1985 U.S. electricity consumption of 2.5 trillion kilowatt hours. The technology for smaller windmills (50–200 kilowatts) is already well advanced; federal and state energy tax credits caused the wind power industry to grow quickly, especially in California.

Geothermal Energy. Geothermal power is generated by using steam and hot water from the interior of the earth. The first geothermal development in the United States began at the Geysers in Northern California, where Pacific Gas & Electric has about 2,000 megawatts of generating capacity using dry steam (without water droplets). At other sites where a water-steam mixture (wet steam) is all that is available, the steam is separated out and then used to turn a turbine; the water droplets would harm the turbine. Hot water can also be used directly to heat homes, commercial buildings, and factories. Such use is called *district heating*.

Geothermal development can have adverse results. In geothermal power production the steam that turns the turbine must be condensed, requiring a source of cooling water just as a coal-fired or nuclear power plant does. In addition, where a water-steam mixture is drawn from the earth for a wet-steam power plant, the water must be disposed of. The water can be incredibly salty, up to 20% salt, and may need to be pumped to the ocean or reinjected into the earth.

Questions

1. What are the environmental advantages and disadvantages of hydropower? Briefly compare these to the environmental disadvantages of power from the burning of coal.

2. Explain how tides could be used to generate electric power. Where does the energy come from? Do you think Canada and the United States should develop the Bay of Fundy for tidal power generation?

3. How can the wind be used to generate power? Where does the energy that is captured originate? What environmental problems does wind power have?

4. Briefly describe two ways that geothermal heat can be used as a substitute for other energy sources. What environmental impacts are associated with the use of geothermal heat?

Further Reading—General

Twidell, J., and T. Weir. *Renewable Energy Resources.* London: Spon, 1986.

This book covers the gamut of renewable energy resources from an engineering viewpoint. It includes all the renewables we have discussed in this chapter plus wave energy. There is extensive descriptive material here as well as technical treatment.

Further Reading—Hydroelectric Power, Tidal Power

Britton, P. "Tapping the Tides for Power," *Popular Science,* January 1985, p. 56.

A thorough physical description of the tidal power plant at Annapolis Royal, Nova Scotia.

"Hydropower," *Civil Engineering/ASCE,* July 1984, p. 58.

The up side of hydropower development in which clever engineering provides hydropower without a dam.

Larsen, P. "Potential Environmental Consequences of Tidal Power Development Seaward of Tidal Barrages," *Oceans,* September 1981.

An overview of biological and physical impacts of the Bay of Fundy tidal power plan.

Palmer, T. "What Price Free Energy," *Sierra,* July-August 1983, p. 40.

The down side of hydropower development is described, in which valuable areas and free-flowing streams are lost.

Further Reading—Wind Power

Kahn, R. "Harvesting the Wind," *Technology Review,* November-December 1984, p. 56.

Excellent writing distinguishes this up-to-date treatment of wind power prospects.

Putnam, Palmer C. *Power from the Wind.* New York: Van Nostrand, 1948; reprinted, Van Nostrand Reinhold, 1974.

This book is listed for historical as well as for practical interest. Note the author's name and recall the generator at Grandpa's Knob.

Weinberg, C., and R. Williams. "Energy from the Sun," *Scientific American,* 263(3) (September 1990), 147.

This article devotes a good portion of its length to wind power development.

Further Reading—Geothermal Energy

Bowen, R. *Geothermal Resources,* 2nd ed. London and New York: Elsevier Applied Science, 1989.

Geological orientation but useful general information on geothermal energy.

Johnson, T. "Hot Water Power from the Earth," *Popular Science,* January 1983, p. 70.

Color illustrations and no mathematics make this article relatively easy to read. Probably the best "concept" pictures of geothermal power you will find.

Chapter 13

Solar Energy and Energy Conservation

SOLAR ENERGY

Legend tells us that Archimedes saved his home city of Syracuse in Greece with solar energy. Ordering a thousand soldiers to turn their shields to the sun and lining them up in the shape of a parabola, Archimedes focused the sun's rays on the sails of the ships of an invading navy and burned them. No further practical applications of solar energy are recorded until the nineteenth century, when inventors began to experiment with the sun's ability to heat and even to boil water.

In the early decades of the twentieth century, it was still an open question as to what fuels would power society. Early and exciting efforts to harness solar energy took place in the late nineteenth and early twentieth centuries. In France Mouchot invented a solar steam engine; his collector and engine were first displayed at the 1878 World's Fair (see Figure 13-1). By the early 1900s, farmers in California and Arizona had constructed solar irrigation pumps. By focusing the sun's rays on a boiler, they were able to produce steam, which was used to turn a pump. Such a steam engine was even introduced in Meadi, Egypt, in 1912. Built by Shuman and Boys of Philadelphia, this engine was powered by a long parabolic collector that could be turned to track the sun. The collector provided enough heat to boil steam for a 100-horsepower piston engine.

Solar Water Heaters—A Brief History

Solar pumps and engines were not the only solar devices being built in this era. In 1891, Clarence Kemp of Baltimore invented and patented a solar water heater. His new water heater consisted of a tank painted black that was packed in an insulated and glass-covered box. The box, which could be mounted on a roof or attached to a wall, faced south to the sun. The sun's rays warmed the blackened tank and the water inside it.

Kemp's water heater was not entirely new. Such water tanks, painted black, were already in use by the residents of Southern California, where the price of coal to heat water was very high. But they had not thought of packing the tank in an insulated and glass-covered box. As a consequence, the water in their simple tanks would not be warm enough for use until the afternoon and then would cool quickly. The insulation in Kemp's box prevented heat losses so that the water warmed more quickly and retained its heat longer. The idea caught on, and Kemp's water heater became popular. It was selling for $25 in Pasadena, California, in 1900.

Kemp's design and improvements to his design did not meet the need for water early in the morning

FIGURE 13-1 Solar Collector Exhibited at the 1889 Paris Exposition. The collector is driving a steam engine, which is furnishing the power to drive a printing press. The first solar steam engine was displayed at the 1878 World's Fair. (Source: Courtesy of the Bettmann Archive)

FIGURE 13-2 Day-and-Night Brochure of 1923. In the first two decades of the century, solar water heaters were popular items in southern California. In fact, the basic design still in use today was invented in California in that era. The arrival of inexpensive natural gas brought an end to the industry, however.

when people awoke. That need still had to be met by water heated by coal or gas. Somehow solar energy needed to be stored from one day to the next in order to avoid the use of coal or gas.

In 1909, William Bailey created the basic elements of the modern solar hot-water system. Bailey's design, called the Day-and-Night Solar Water Heater, separated the component used for water heating from that used for heat storage. A collector with copper tubes, much like a modern collector, was mounted on the roof, and an insulated tank within the attic of the building stored the heated water. Water rose from the collector to the tank because warmer water is lighter than cool water. Bailey's system could hold heated water through the night and into the next day. Although the Day-and-Night sold for $100, it could cut gas heating bills by 75%, or about $25 per year. In four years the water heater paid for itself (Figure 13-2).

In 1913, however, a record freeze hit some parts of Southern California. The water in the system froze and cracked the metal tubes; water leaked into houses. Bailey set about to invent a new system

that would not freeze. The revised design simply mixed alcohol with water, creating an antifreeze that was used as the collecting liquid. The heat-collecting loop was separated from the hot-water loop. The collector liquid, now resistant to freezing, passed through a coil in the storage tank to heat the water (Figure 13-3). By the end of World War I, more than 4,000 units of the Day-and-Night had been sold.

When natural gas discoveries in California made

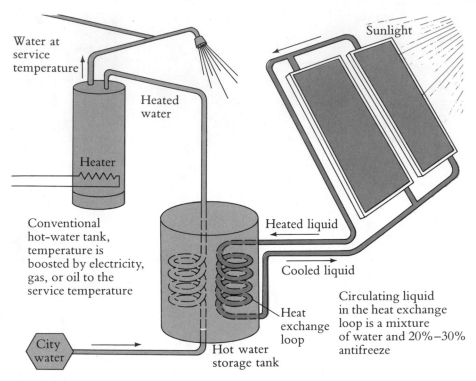

FIGURE 13-3 A Typical Arrangement of Collector and Storage Tank for Solar Hot Water. The water and antifreeze mixture in the collector loop circulates through the collector where the sun's energy is captured. The fluid then passes through a heat exchanger within a water-filled tank, transferring its heat to the water in the tank. The heat in the tank water is extracted by cold water, which flows through a second heat exchanger in the tank. The heated water in this service loop is now available for use in the house, either directly if it is hot enough, or with a boost from a conventional hot-water heater. The large water-filled tank is used to store heat from sunny days for use on cloudy days. The design is basically that of the improved Day-and-Night waterheater invented by William Bailey.

solar hot water less attractive in the 1920s, Day-and-Night built and sold gas water heaters. In 1923, Bailey sold the rights to manufacture the solar water heater to a company that saw gold in solar water heat in Florida. New design features were added to the basic Day-and-Night model.

Because the basic patents on the Day-and-Night had expired by the 1930s, other companies entered the business as well. In 1941, when America entered World War II, annual sales of solar water heaters in Miami were twice that of electric and gas water heaters. The war brought the business to a quick halt, though; civilian uses of copper were forbidden.

The industry did not recover after the war because electric rates were falling while costs in both labor and materials were shooting up. Yet, some 250,000 solar hot-water units are still in service in Florida. Today, as electric rates rise, solar hot water is once again looking attractive in Miami. From coast to coast in south Florida, new homes are once again being offered with solar hot water. In a very real sense, it is something of a "homecoming."

Solar Heat and Hot Water: Active Systems

When people talk about the promise of solar energy, they may be talking about any of a number of solar

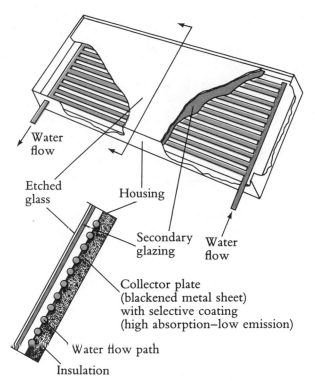

Water flow

Etched glass

Housing

Secondary glazing

Water flow

Collector plate (blackened metal sheet) with selective coating (high absorption–low emission)

Water flow path

Insulation

FIGURE 13-4 Flat-Plate Solar Collector. Cold water is pumped in at the bottom of a row of parallel metal pipes. Warm water exits from the top pipe. The pipes are bonded to a blackened metal sheet. Below the sheet and around the outside of the box in which the pipes are housed may be glass-wool insulation. Two glass plates cover the top of the box. (*Source:* Adapted from *Solar Energy Handbook*, Honeywell, Form 74-5436, p. 9)

Bailey invented. The designs are meant to decrease the loss of heat energy. Typically, the collector is flat and stationary. This *flat-plate collector* is set on a roof at an angle roughly equal to the local latitude. At this angle the rays of the sun fall nearly perpendicular to the surface of the collector. In one typical design, parallel metal tubes are welded to a metal plate, and either liquid or air flows through the tubes. Figure 13-4 illustrates the design of the collector with a liquid flow.

When the rays of the sun fall on the metal plate, the plate is warmed. The metal pipes that are welded to the plate are warmed in turn. The liquid pumped through the pipes receives this heat and carries it off. The pipes and backing plate are of metals such as aluminum, copper, and iron, chosen because they are good conductors of heat. Both pipes and plate may be painted black in order to increase the absorption of heat.

Glass or clear plastic is used to cover the pipes and plate to prevent loss of heat from the metal plate to the sky. The cover also provides a barrier between the warm interior and colder air outside the collector, preventing loss of heat by conduction and convection. The box in which the metal collector is housed is made of a low-conducting material, such as wood or plastic. Insulation is placed in the bottom of the box, and the box itself is usually mounted on the roof in a stationary position.

The Storage System. The collector itself is the exterior symbol of a home or building that uses solar energy. Inside the building is a system of heat exchangers and a storage tank, which together store and transfer the sun's heat.

The conventional design uses an antifreeze-water mixture as the collector fluid, which circulates through the tubes of a flat-plate collector. The heated antifreeze mixture is pumped to and through a heat exchanger (usually a coil of pipe) inside a large water-filled storage tank. The heat in the flowing liquid is transferred through the coil to the water in the tank, which stores the heat for later use and for rainy days. (See Figure 13-3.) The antifreeze-water mixture then cycles back to the collector. Just as in Bailey's original design, an antifreeze-water mixture is used as the collector fluid instead of water

options. If they are pressed for the solar option that can deliver energy today, however, they will tell you that one option is available that does not require further research and development. It is ready now. It is the flat-plate collector that has been used for so many years to provide home heating and hot water. The systems we will discuss in this section, including the flat-plate collector, are termed *active* because they require assistance from conventional energy sources, such as the use of an electrically driven pump to move liquids.

The Collector. To collect the sun's rays efficiently for the production of heat, special solar collectors have been designed, much like the one that

to prevent the fluid from freezing in very cold weather.

The water in the storage tank serves as a heat reservoir. Hot water can be extracted from the tank through a heat exchanger for bathing, washing dishes, washing clothes, and the like. The water flowing through the heat exchanger is heated by the hot water in the tank. The heated water then passes to the conventional electric or gas water heater, where it can be given a temperature boost if it is needed.

If solar heating of homes and other buildings is desired in addition to solar hot water, modifications of this basic design are needed. The use of solar energy for space heating requires a far larger investment in collectors than solar hot water does.

Passive Solar Energy

Unlike active solar-heating systems, some solar equipment uses little or no outside energy to assist in providing heat for the home. These systems are termed *passive*.

South-Facing Windows. One design for passive solar heating captures the sun's energy in the winter, when heat is needed, and avoids collecting heat from the sun in the summer. Large-paned windows are installed on the south wall of a building. These windows face the sun, and a roof overhang extends out over the windows (Figure 13-5). In the summer, when the sun is high, the overhang shades the windows from unwanted heat. But the winter sun hangs low in the southern sky throughout the day, and the sun's rays can enter and provide welcome heat for the dwelling. Interestingly, a deciduous tree can serve much the same purpose as an overhang. The leaves of a deciduous tree growing in front of a south-facing window will block out much of the searing summer sun. In winter the sun's rays can penetrate through the bare branches to enter the window.

The overhang concept can be extended to multiple-floor office buildings. Here an overhang extends over the outer rim of every floor, blocking the sun in summer but letting it enter in winter.

Although a large south-facing window admits and captures more sunlight than a smaller one, it

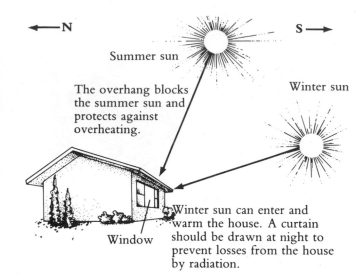

FIGURE 13-5 **Positioning in Relation to Sun.** Proper orientation and design of a house can decrease heating and air-conditioning requirements. The south-facing house has an overhang that blocks the sun's rays in summer but does not block them in winter. (The house illustrated is in the Northern Hemisphere.)

also provides a wide surface that radiates heat into the night sky, an undesirable loss of energy. Opaque insulating curtains offer one solution to the problem of back radiation. Also, several manufacturers are now producing a clear polyester film coated with an extremely thin layer of metal. When the coated film is applied to a glass window, the window remains completely transparent to entering sunlight. However, the metal layer blocks the passage of heat energy from the house to the outside. The special layer can be either added to a film, which is then applied to glass, or coated directly onto the glass in a factory process.

Trombe Walls. A clever design for passive solar heating is the Trombe (rhymes with prom) wall, a solar collector that is a part of the house itself. In a sense, it, too, is a large panel of windows facing south to catch the sun, but it is more. The large windows allow entrance of the sun's rays, and a few inches behind the windows is a concrete wall. Behind the concrete wall is the living space of the home. The side of the wall that faces south is

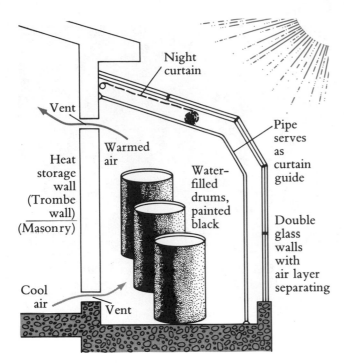

FIGURE 13-6 The Solar Greenhouse, or Solarium, a Passive Solar System. This old idea from the Victorian era uses a greenhouse attached to and open to a residence. The furniture, floor, and perhaps drums of water are heated by the sun's rays. These fixtures radiate heat to the solar room and to the rest of the house when sunshine has ceased.

painted black so that a maximum amount of sunlight is absorbed as heat. The wall heats up, and the air space between the wall and the window heats up as well. Openings near the top of the wall allow the warm, less-dense air in the air space to rise up and out to the living area. That is, natural convection carries warm air into the room and cool air out of the room. The dense concrete structure acts as a heat storage device as well.

The Solar Greenhouse. Another architectural feature used for passive collection of the sun's energy is the solar greenhouse, or solarium. The device is simply a greenhouse attached to a larger structure. Solar energy passes through the glass and into the greenhouse. Drums painted black, which are filled with water, may be stored in the greenhouse. These drums and their contents are heated,

and they store this solar heat for periods of no sunshine. A combination of a solar greenhouse using drum heat storage and a Trombe wall for further heat storage is shown in Figure 13-6. Solar greenhouses are widely available.

Photovoltaics

The process of converting sunlight directly to electricity is known as **photovoltaic conversion.** The basis of the solar cell is the *semiconductor,* the silicon device that has so transformed the computer industry. The solar cell is constructed by layering two wafers of silicon crystal and establishing junctions between them. Light falling on one of the wafers "boils" electrons out of the crystal and across the junction into the other wafer. This current is a direct current (dc), and so typically requires conversion to alternating current (ac) before it is used by a consumer.

The efficiency of converting solar energy to electricity by commercially available solar cells is low but increasing. Only about 12%–14% of the arriving solar energy is converted to electricity by the currently available silicon-based cells. Although silicon is the only material available commercially, cadmium sulfide and gallium arsenide can also be used in solar cells. Gallium arsenide, in particular, holds promise for higher conversion efficiencies. Up to 35% of the arriving solar energy has been converted to electrical energy in gallium arsenide solar cells constructed in the laboratory.

Solar cells were first used in dramatic applications where cost was not a matter of concern. For instance, solar cells furnished the power for the Apollo moon rockets and the Viking space stations. In addition, the cells have been used for mountaintop radios, ocean signal buoys, and highway call boxes. Typically, these uses are far removed from an electric transmission grid. More recently, outdoor lights powered by solar cells have become available to the general public. And to those willing to investigate more deeply, whole-house power systems are actually on the market. In a region where the sunlight is only the average over all the United States, only 430 square feet (40 square meters) of photovoltaic collectors would be sufficient to power the average U.S. home—this at only 12% collector efficiency. A fledgling photovoltaics industry supplies these needs.

Costs of power from photovoltaic arrays have declined dramatically in the last two decades. In 1970 a kilowatt-hour of electricity cost an outrageous $60. By 1990, it was down to 20 to 30 cents. In the offing is a new class of solar cells that uses thin films of semiconductor material. Still only about 16% efficient, the cost of the cells could fall to as little as one-tenth of the 1990 commercial price because of the ease of mass production. The manufacture of solar cells has increased as prices have dropped. From about 4 megawatts of capacity sold in 1981, 40 megawatts were sold around the world in 1990.

The utility industry has already begun to anticipate the dawning of central-station photovoltaic power. Numerous medium-scale applications were underway in the early 1990s. Not only are the medium-scale applications moving forward; solar cells are also now being linked into huge arrays to produce electric power at central stations. Arco Solar (now Siemens) took the lead in this activity. By 1981 the company had built and was operating a 1-megawatt (peak) photovoltaic power plant near Hespera, California; power was being sold to Southern California Edison. And in late 1983, Arco completed a 6.4-megawatt (peak) photovoltaic power plant near California City, California.

In the early 1980s a remarkable concept in photovoltaics was made a reality in Frederick, Maryland. There a photovoltaic plant, powered in part by solar cells, has begun operations. The Solarex Corporation has named it the *solar breeder* (Figure 13-7) because it manufactures solar cells with the energy captured by solar cells.

In a world where technology advances at a rapid pace, there is hope that the cost of semiconductors can be markedly reduced, especially by mass production. If cost barriers can be overcome, and utility experts believe they can be, then photovoltaic electricity becomes very attractive indeed. No steam is generated; nothing is burned, heated, or fissioned; no fuel is mined and transported. No parts move and wear out. No cooling water is needed. The plants function unattended, and the cells are ex-

FIGURE 13-7 The Solar Technology Center. This unique plant in Frederick, Maryland manufactures photovoltaic cells and panels using energy from the sun. The 200-kilowatt array of solar cells that forms the roof of the facility provides electricity for computers and control systems in the plant's production lines. A large battery storage system puts away energy on sunny days for continued production on cloudy days. (*Photo:* Solarex Corporation)

pected to last a long time when enclosed in glass or plastic. Finally, the supply of fuel is inexhaustible. Photovoltaic development should be a national priority—as opposed to oil production from the Arctic National Wildlife Refuge.

Central-Station Electricity from Solar Energy

Power Tower. Picture again the invasion of ancient Syracuse and envision Archimedes directing his solar assault on the approaching warships. This is the principle of the power tower: Banks of mirrors concentrate the sun's rays on a single point. The mirrors, known as *heliostats,* follow the sun across the sky, reflecting the sun's rays on the power tower, where water is boiled to steam. The steam, piped to a turbine on the ground, turns a turbine and generates electricity.

The largest operating power tower was Solar One, a 10-megawatt (at peak) power plant in the Mojave Desert near Barstow, California (Figure

FIGURE 13-8 Solar One. This 10-megawatt solar power tower, located near Barstow, California, was the most successful of the solar thermal central receiver experiments. A field of tracking mirrors followed the sun, focusing its rays onto a central tower-mounted boiler. Water was boiled to steam, which was then piped to a turbine generator unit at the base of the tower for the generation of electricity. (*Photo:* Electric Power Research Institute)

13-8). Begun in 1978, the joint project of the Southern California Edison Company and the U.S. Department of Energy started delivering power to the grid in 1982, but went out of service in the late 1980s.

The 1,818 heliostats of Solar One tracked the sun through the sky, focusing the rays of the sun at the top of the power tower. At the top of the 310-foot (95-m) tower, water was boiled to steam. The steam turned a turbine on the ground, generating enough power for a community of 7,000–10,000 people.

The power tower had provision for heat storage—in hot rocks—to produce steam during hours of darkness. But heat storage for off-sun hours may not be necessary if the power tower is viewed only as a devise to provide power at peak times of demand.

Although Solar One has gone out of service, the power tower concept is being explored else-

where in the United States, Europe, and Japan. There are units at Sandia Labs (Albuquerque, New Mexico), and solar power towers have been built at Almeria, Spain; Adrano, Sicily (Italy); Themis, France; and Nio Town, Japan, though none are as large as Solar One.

The LUZ System. The power tower is not the only concept for central-station power plants that would use the sun's energy to produce steam. A system developed by the LUZ International Corporation differs from Solar One in that it uses no power tower. Instead, an array of mirrors is aimed at its own attached local collector, consisting of oil-filled pipes (see photo on page 230). Inside the pipes of the collector, the oil is heated by the sun's reflected rays. The heated oil is used to boil water to steam, which is used to turn a turbine. Several plants using this modular concept have already been built by the LUZ Corporation in the Mojave Desert of California. Their generating capacity totals 400 megawatts. Another 380 megawatts are either under construction or planned for the area near Harpers Lake in California. The units can be built quickly, in less than a year, in contrast to the 10-year construction time for conventional power plants.

Biomass: Biological Conversion of the Sun's Energy (Alias Photosynthesis)

The fact that oil, gas, and coal all owe their energy to the sun (see Chapter 11) reminds us strongly that nature is constantly converting the sun's rays to energy-laden molecules. We know the process as **photosynthesis,** the conversion of carbon dioxide and water to energy-rich organic molecules through the use of the sun's energy. Why not take greater advantage of the energy being captured by green plants here and now, by using wood, sugar cane, corn, hevea?

Wood. Until the twentieth century, most American families cooked and heated their homes with wood-burning stoves. Some people never stopped heating their homes with wood; they are typically rural people largely concentrated in Maine, Vermont, New Hampshire, and parts of the rural South. Wood was always cheaply available to them, and it made sense to be economical. Now we are emulating them: More than 15 million new wood-burning stoves have been sold since 1974 as people convert to wood as a primary and secondary source of heat. Newer stoves are often equipped to burn wood or coal and may have catalytic combusters to make the wood burn even more efficiently. Wood is also the fuel used by traditional societies throughout the developing world.

Wood is a fairly clean fuel; sulfur levels in wood are very low. The heat content of wood is high: A cord of wood (a stack 4 feet by 4 feet by 8 feet) has about 20,000,000 Btu on average; a ton of coal has 24,000,000 Btu. The price of a ton of coal and that of a cord of wood vary by region and season, but they are not far apart.

If wood biomass were to become a major fuel, thousands upon thousands of new acres of trees would need to be planted; most of our present tree resources are already devoted to timbering and recreation. One proposal for producing wood for fuel in quantity is to grow sycamore trees for only five years to immature size, harvest them mechanically, and replant. Poplar is another fast-growing variety that may produce high yields. Although the burning of wood adds carbon dioxide to the atmosphere, just as the burning of oil, gas, or coal does, the growing trees that accompany the burning would be withdrawing carbon dioxide from the air for photosynthesis. A rough balance of carbon dioxide addition and removal seems possible.

Field Crops. Sugar cane may be the best biological converter of the sun's energy that we have. Its energy can be made available for nonfood use by fermenting it to ethyl alcohol. Sugar cane does not grow as well in this country as other crops, particularly corn. Brazil, on the other hand, is well suited for sugar cane and is seriously pursuing the commercial production of fuel alcohol from sugar cane. Brazil has half a million cars that run on ethyl alcohol and has alcohol-based fueling stations to serve them.

One unusual species of plant, the hevea rubber plant, first found wild in Brazil, produces hydrocarbons that are used to make natural rubber.

Grown now almost exclusively in Indonesia and Malaya, the plant yields almost a ton per acre (0.9 metric tons). Though this is half the yield of sugar cane, the growers think hevea yield can be tripled. Enthusiasts see the hydrocarbons it produces as substitutes for oil. Hevea has competition, however, from another plant that produces hydrocarbons.

The wild desert shrub known as guayule (pronounced gwy-oo'-lee), native to the deserts of Mexico and the American Southwest, was in the early 1900s one of our principal sources of rubber. It was the hevea plant that replaced it in the marketplace. During World War II, when Southeast Asia was dominated by the Japanese, we again established a rubber industry based on guayule. That industry collapsed, however, when the rubber-producing nations of Malaya and Indonesia were liberated. Now a number of scientists want to give guayule another try after first selecting the best strains for cultivation. Still other desert plants have potential for cultivation as oilseed crops, such as jojoba and buffalo gourd.

Corn has also been suggested as a source of biomass fuel. Corn can be fermented to produce the grain alcohol component of the blended fuel known as **gasohol.** Gasohol is a mixture of 90% unleaded gasoline and 10% grain alcohol (ethyl alcohol).

The potential for biomass fuels is very large, but the environmental impact of this development is uncertain. If cropland that is devoted to food plants becomes cropland that is devoted to energy plants, a rise in the price of basic foodstuffs could result. For a nation that serves as a breadbasket to the world, the choice of energy crops over food crops could have wide effect. The use of residues left after harvesting conventional crops, rather than going to an agriculture that grows plants for energy, might be a sounder course of action while we learn about biomass energy.

Of greatest concern, however, is the soundness of biomass proposals from a biological point of view. Planting only a single crop has a tendency to deplete the soil of particular nutrients, attract insect pests, and reduce the survival of a diversity of animals. Caution is needed lest tropical forest be destroyed to produce a single crop as a source of energy. Field crop research on these ideas is needed to evaluate biomass further. And careful economic analysis of the effects on food prices is needed as well.

The Potential of Solar Energy

Solar energy can benefit people in a number of basic ways. First, by replacing fossil fuels, air and water pollution are decreased. Carbon dioxide production can also be reduced. Second, the replacement of fossil fuels means a decrease in fuel imports, especially of oil, and this will help secure the value of the dollar in the international market and at home. Third, by replacing nuclear fuels here and abroad, the threat of the spread of nuclear weapons is decreased. Finally, solar sources can provide us some protection by making our fuel supply less subject to interruption.

However, some form of government intervention will be needed in the market for solar technology. Government intervention in markets is nothing new and nothing radical for Democrats or Republicans. Before the OPEC era, oil from overseas was brought in on a quota system for many years to protect the American oil industry. Strategic metals have been stockpiled for many years, both to have a store of the metals for emergencies and shore up the markets for these materials. In order to keep crop prices up, farmers have been paid to keep acreage out of production. In addition, a system of agricultural extension agents provides free advice to farmers on all aspects of farm operations. Why not have a system of energy extension agents who would provide free advice to homeowners on the most appropriate ways to heat homes and who would lay out choices that include solar options and energy conservation?

The federal government, through the Atomic Energy Commission, has done most of the research and development on nuclear power and still provides the insurance against a nuclear catastrophe. In fact, the entire nuclear industry has been backed by government involvement from the start. If nuclear power research and development merit government support, why not solar energy research? The suggestion that the government stimulate the solar market by incentives and by bearing some development costs is not at all a radical proposal.

Incentives are necessary because active solar heating systems are expensive. For a house with an area of 1,500 square feet (135 m^2) and two or three days of heat storage, the cost of installation, of equipment, and collectors may reach $20,000–$30,000 for the entire solar house-heating system.

Basically, two kinds of costs need to be reduced to help people buy solar technology. The cost of collectors can be brought down by mass production—that is, by expansion of the annual market to many thousands, even millions, of units. The cost of installation of pipes, plumbing, and the instruments for solar heating can be brought down by having a number of experienced companies willing to compete with one another for jobs. Again, a mass market is the key. These two costs, collectors and installation, make up the bulk of the cost of a solar heating system.

One mechanism the government has used to influence people to buy solar equipment is tax credits. Until 1986, 40% of the investment in solar energy, up to a total credit of $4,000, could be subtracted from taxes owed. Thus, a family that invested $5,000 in solar hot water was able to deduct from the taxes they owed 40% of $5,000, or $2,000, effectively reducing the investment in solar equipment from $5,000 to $3,000.

A number of states also had offered tax credits for solar installations. All these incentives had a positive effect on the manufacture and sales of solar equipment for heat and hot water. Tens of thousands of solar installations occurred in the 1980s before the incentives expired. Why were the incentives allowed to expire? The price of oil fell, and government decided that the incentives were not needed, or more accurately, that solar wasn't needed. The 1991 U.S.-Iraq war over Kuwait illustrated how shaky a conclusion this was.

We could use better incentives. To further stimulate solar purchases, a federal Solar Development Bank could be created to loan money at low interest rates for the purchase and installation of solar equipment. Although President Carter wanted to open such a bank with $450 million to loan, President Reagan asked Congress to rescind its appropriations to the bank.

The preceding discussion on solar energy incentives has focused on solar heating of buildings

Towards a Sustainable Society

Sustainable Technology

by James Gustave Speth

James Gustave Speth was chairman of the Council on Environmental Quality for two years from 1979 to 1981. He has served as President of the World Resources Institute since it was founded by him and others in 1982. In 1988 he was elected to the

Global 500 Honor Role of the United Nations Environment Programme.

Countries around the globe have set two potentially conflicting goals for themselves: improving environmental quality, in part by reducing *current* levels of pollution and resource consumption; and achieving large, sustained increases in economic activity. Indeed, by the middle of the next century, the world economy is projected to be five times larger than it is today. Quite possibly, political leaders will face no greater challenge in the decades ahead than reconciling these two goals. Doing so will demand continuing effort at the highest levels of government, including

international cooperation on a scale seldom seen.

What will this reconciliation require in practical terms? If a doubling and redoubling of economic activity is accomplished with the technologies now dominant in energy production, transportation, manufacturing, agriculture, and other sectors, truly catastrophic impacts are likely on global climate, human health, and the productivity of natural systems. Seen this way, reconciling the economic and environmental goals societies have set for themselves will be possible only through a transformation in technology—a shift, perhaps unprecedented in scope and pace, to new technologies designed with environmental sustainability in mind.

and on solar hot water because these uses of solar energy are ready now; their application is not held up by lack of fundamental research. Furthermore, in a number of major cities the annual cost of solar heat or hot water is less than that of electric heat or electric hot water. The only barrier is penetration of the market.

Allowing the demise of tax credits for solar installations seems an unwise choice by Congress. The credits no more favored solar for the home than massive government research efforts favored the nuclear power industry. Solar and conservation remain keystones in the prevention of another en-

ergy crisis in the United States. They likewise serve the cause of decreasing carbon dioxide emissions and hence the potential for global warming.

ENERGY CONSERVATION

Why Save Energy

In Chapter 11, we described the use and environmental impacts of the conventional fuels that power society today. We found risks and dangers in nuclear power that many regard as unacceptable. We

Of course, it is not only technology that must change; values, lifestyles, and policies must change also. But, however much consumer values shift, economic growth on an unprecedented scale will occur. For much of the world this growth is essential to meeting basic human needs and achieving acceptable levels of personal security and comfort. The bottom-line question remains: With what technologies will this growth occur? Only the population explosion rivals this question in fundamental importance to the planetary environment.

The good news is that many emerging technologies offer exciting opportunities to achieve an ecological modernization of industry and agriculture. We can design a new agriculture, one that is sustainable both economically and ecologically and that stresses low inputs of commercial fertilizers, pesticides, and energy. Industry and transportation can be transformed from an era of materials-intensive, high-throughput processes to an era that uses fuel and materials with great efficiency, generates little or no waste, recycles residuals, releases only benign products to the environment, and is, hence, more "closed."

The bad news is that there is no guarantee that these opportunities will be fully explored or exploited. Neither discernible trends in technological change nor current approaches to environmental protection will be sufficient to bring about the needed technological transformation.

Guiding and speeding the application of solution-oriented technologies will require major changes. Today the Environmental Protection Agency stands outside the economy, imposing "end-of-pipe" pollution control standards. In the future, the EPA must come inside, adopting a pollution prevention approach that stresses the need to change products, processes, and pressures that give rise to pollution. A new type of cooperation among the private sector, EPA, traditional Cabinet agencies, and environmental advocates must be forged. Together, they must work "upstream" to integrate environmental factors into the basic design of transportation, energy, and other systems. Technology-forcing regulations and economic incentives must both be harnessed. Most importantly, we must make the market mechanism work for us by ensuring that energy and other prices reflect the full environmental costs.

Environmentalism began on the periphery of the economy, saving a bit of landscape here, bottling up some pollution there. The challenges ahead are such that it must spread as creed and code to permeate to the core of the economies of the world.

found that coal, which is responsible for slightly over half of our electric power, had impacts on the land, on miners' health, on air pollution from sulfur oxides and particles, and on acid rain. We found that oil, the source of our gasoline, diesel, and jet fuels, was predominantly located in a politically unstable region of the globe, and that the fuels that it provides pollute the air of our cities with carbon monoxide, hydrocarbons, and nitrogen oxides, which combine to produce photochemical smog. Even natural gas, the cleanest of our fossil fuels, produces nitric oxide when it is burned. And all the fossil fuels produce carbon dioxide, whose increasing levels in the atmosphere threaten the ecology of the globe itself. Earlier we learned of the steady growth in the population of the world and thus of an increasing appetite for energy.

These facts seem depressing, but in this and the preceding chapter, we discovered new sources of energy: electricity from the tides, the wind, and from geothermal energy; heat and hot water from solar energy; and electricity from photovoltaic devices. There is one more source of energy to replace the energy we use today. There is a way to go on living just as abundantly and comfortably as we do now—with more security, with less air pollution,

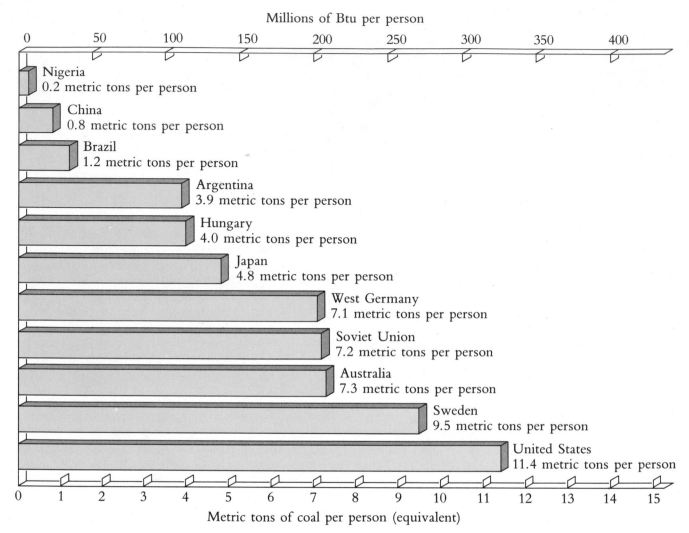

FIGURE 13-9 Annual Energy Consumption per Capita by Countries of the World, 1988. Figures do not include use of wood fuel. People in the United States used an average of the equivalent of 11.4 metric tons of coal per person in 1988. (*Sources:* Data from *World Population Profile, 1988*, U.S. Bureau of the Census, and *International Energy Annual, 1988*, Energy Information Administration)

with less acid rain, and with less carbon dioxide. It is by conserving energy through the introduction of greater efficiency—the same warmth with less heat, the same light with fewer watts, the same power for motors with less electricity, and the same mobility with less gasoline. The savings are likely to be dramatic and can be achieved at low cost. In some cases, we can even make money while we save energy! Energy conservation is not harsh denial; it can easily be achieved by a society that wants to achieve it. Energy efficiency may even be sought for economic reasons. An efficient society can compete better in a global market.

What can we achieve and how can we do it? What are the key uses that we should target? Where are the opportunities? To answer these questions

TABLE 13-1 Proportional Use of Energy by Function

Function	Percentage of Energy Use
Lighting	8%
Heating	20%
Transportation	25%
Electric motors	20%
Other uses (refrigeration, freezing, cooking, air conditioning, etc.)	27%

we first need to compare our energy lifestyles to those elsewhere in the world.

How We Can Save Energy

Figure 13-9 shows the average energy consumption per person for the major regions of the world. As we can see, the energy use of people in the United States is about 50% more than that of people in Western Europe. Yet the Europeans live, from an energy standpoint, as well as we do. What do they do differently—or, to be more precise, what can we do differently, since our society and traditions are different in many ways from theirs?

In brief, we can install more insulation in homes, apartments, public buildings, and factories. We can utilize more efficient appliances and machines. We can replace inefficient refrigerators with better-insulated refrigerators. Gas stoves without pilot lights can be utilized in place of models with pilot lights. Fluorescent lamps can be substituted for incandescent bulbs. Total energy systems in industry may both generate electricity and produce process heat (heat for industrial processes), as well as space heating. Automobiles can be made far more fuel-efficient. In short, energy conservation, if we are willing to achieve it, holds as great an opportunity as discovering new sources of energy. Energy conservation is similar to discovering a source of energy that lasts forever, because you never run out of fuel that you do not use.

We have selected three areas on which we shall focus attention in our discussion of energy conservation. These are (1) the way we heat buildings and make hot water, (2) the way we light our indoor and outdoor spaces, and (3) the way we transport people and freight. The heating of buildings and water heating together account for about 20% of our annual use of energy. Lighting accounts for about 20% of our electric energy consumption each year. Since the energy used in generating electric power is about 40% of our annual energy consumption, it follows that lighting is responsible for 8% of our total annual energy consumption. Transportation consumes about 25% of the energy we use each year. (See Table 13-1.)

Consumers or businesspeople can make choices in these areas now that can influence energy consumption. New technology is not necessary in all of these areas; methods presently available are sufficient to make dramatic differences both in energy consumption and in pollution. Each of these areas we will review is what is called a *point-of-use*. Other improvements at points-of-use are possible.

For instance, a very effective and even charming method for saving energy is to use the old-fashioned ceiling fan for cooling instead of using air conditioning. The breeze from such a fan, whose power usage is about that of a standard light bulb, produces a cooling effect that is about equal to a 6°F drop in temperature.

More efficient appliances can be utilized. Spark-ignition gas stoves can replace pilot-light gas stoves; better-insulated refrigerators using 10%–20% of the energy of current models are now available; better-insulated water heaters are being sold as well; and high-efficiency oil and gas furnaces are now on the market. The labeling of appliances with their energy consumption per unit of time has become a valuable aid to consumers, not only helping them save energy but helping them save money as well.

Nonetheless, we return to the three areas mentioned earlier because of their importance in energy consumption and because of their potential for change.

How We Heat Buildings and Make Hot Water. The choice about how to heat a home or how to heat water is simple to make in most cases, at least from the standpoint of what to reject. In the recent past, there have been only three options, but solar energy has now entered the picture as a real alternative. The three traditional options are natural gas, oil, and electricity. Let us look at these choices carefully.

Suppose you are in the market to purchase a home, and you have seen three houses; all of them are affordable and similar in other respects, except in the fuel used for heating. One heats with natural gas, another with home heating oil, and the third with electricity. In each house, hot water is produced in the same way that the home is heated; that is, the gas-heated home heats its water with natural gas, and so forth. Which home is preferable from the point of view of energy conservation, and which is preferable from the point of view of monthly energy costs?

The price of natural gas naturally keeps rough pace with the price of oil, so that heating a home with natural gas is not too far different in cost from heating with oil. Gas had been much cheaper for some years, but the pattern changed as the government allowed the price of natural gas to rise in order to correct shortages. The energy efficiencies of an oil-fired or gas-fired heating system are about the same. About 80% of the energy derived from burning the fuel goes into raising the temperature of the house.

Electric heating, on the other hand, even when the house receives extra insulation as the electric company suggests, still costs much more than heating by gas or oil. How much more depends on the local electric rates. In nearly all cases the electric home is considerably more expensive to heat than the home heated by gas or oil. The cost of creating hot water using electricity is large as well. About half of the electric bill of a home that uses an electric water heater as opposed to gas or oil is due to water heating alone. Solar energy is an available alternative for heating homes and water in many sections of the country. Its economics relative to electricity are good if the homeowner is willing to wait the payback period of 10 to 15 years.

Not only is the electric home more costly to heat, but it is extremely wasteful of resources. We noted in Chapter 11 that only about 40% of the heat liberated by burning coal, oil, or natural gas can be converted to electric energy. The remainder of the heat from burning the fuel, the portion not converted to electrical energy, is wasted to the air or into the water. By the time electric energy reaches the home, only a third of the original combustion energy of the fuel is left to heat the home.

In contrast, new oil and gas furnaces attain 80% efficiency, although after some use the efficiency falls to 60%–70%. It is reasonably clear in such circumstances that electric resistance heat, which is produced by a generating plant that burns oil or gas, is wasteful of that fuel. The same conclusion follows immediately for hot water.

In the near future, however, the **heat pump** could change both the economics and energy cost of electric heating. This electrical device, a sort of refrigerator or air conditioner in reverse, is capable of heating a home during many, though not all, winter days; it exhausts cold air to the outside and warm air to the inside of a house. Measurements of the performance of these units have indicated that two units of heat energy can be produced for every one unit of energy (as electricity) delivered to the house. This cuts the cost of electric heating in half.

The heat pump can also heat water, and manufacturers are now offering heat pump water heaters. Their electric requirements are expected to be about half that of conventional electric water heaters.

How we heat and cool a building and how we heat water have a large influence on energy consumption and on cost. Nonetheless, there are numerous additional steps that can be taken to reduce the energy requirements of buildings. Of course, many of them come under the heading of insulation, the addition of materials that prevent the exit of heat from the building.

A caution about insulation is in order. Gases and particles from cooking and smoking may accumulate in a house made too tight. Fresh air filters on the furnace, which are used to allow dust-free circulation, become even more important to maintain. In addition, radon gas from the walls of homes built of stone can accumulate. Though formerly uncommon in U.S. homes, air-to-air heat exchangers are being used more frequently to bring in fresh outside air with little heat loss. The heat exchangers become important when houses are made very tight in terms of air and heat loss.

Other possibilities for decreasing the heating and cooling requirements of buildings range from earth-sheltered housing to passive solar heating to the planting of windbreaks. Windbreaks of trees can be especially effective in reducing heat requirements. Other energy-saving devices for the home include flow restrictors on faucets and showers, ceiling fans, automatic setback thermostats, interior airtight shades on windows, awnings on the outside of windows, and jacket insulation on hot-water heaters.

The Way We Light Our Indoor and Outdoor Spaces. We noted earlier that lighting is responsible for about 8% of our annual energy consumption. In most homes and in many factories and businesses, the commonest form of lighting is Edison's incandescent bulb. Of the energy that the incandescent bulb consumes, only about 10% is converted to light. The remainder is wasted as heat to the surroundings. In fact, lights and appliances may warm a home by up to five degrees above its "natural" temperature. This wasted energy and consequent warming cause increased air conditioning loads in the summer.

We have long known that fluorescent fixtures could save energy, but such fixtures are not suitable for spot lighting. Now, however, new fluorescent lighting products are on the market. These "light capsules," as they are called, are not much larger than light bulbs, screw into lamp sockets, give a warm colored light, and use a fifth of the energy to give the same light (Figure 13-10). The capsules are more costly, with prices ranging from $10 to $30 per capsule, but the capsules last about 10,000 hours, or 8 to 13 times the lifetime of a standard incandescent bulb.

To see how these capsules fare economically, we need to know the electric rate. Assume the cost of electricity is at the 1990 national average of eight cents per kilowatt-hour (a 100-watt bulb burning for 10 hours consumes a kilowatt-hour of energy). A 15-watt capsule gives about the same light as a

FIGURE 13-10 Fluorescent Light Capsule. Light capsules like this provide the light of a 75-watt bulb with only about one-fifth the energy. Over the 10,000-hour lifetime of the capsule, consumers can save $25–40 in electricity and replacement costs, depending on the purchase price of the capsule. (*Photo:* OSRAM Corporation)

75-watt incandescent bulb. Assume that the 15-watt capsule costs $15 and lasts 10,000 hours and that a 75-watt bulb costs $0.50 and needs to be replaced every 1,000 hours. The cost of the same light from these two different bulbs consists of both electricity costs and the costs of the bulbs or the capsule. Over the lifetime of the capsule, the cost of light from the incandescent and its nine replacements is $67. The cost of light from the fluorescent capsule (electricity plus the capsule itself) is $27, providing a savings of $40. A well-known energy analyst,

Amory Lovins, put it succinctly: "This is not a free lunch; it is a lunch you are paid to eat."

The fluorescent capsules cannot now be used in sealed fixtures, but they can replace many of the bulbs in the ordinary home. In addition, new energy-saving fluorescent fixtures are available to replace older ones. These new fixtures combine more efficient ballasts and reflectors to give the same light with 60% less energy. Motion sensors are now on the market that automatically turn lights off when no motion is detected in a room after a period of time. Finally, "light piping," a duct system with mirrors that brings daylight into the windowless interior of a building, has great potential for large buildings.

Capsules, new fluorescent fixtures, and motion sensors save energy directly and indirectly. By producing less heat, the capsules and new fluorescent fixtures reduce air conditioning loads in the summer months. Given that lighting accounts for about 20% of annual electric consumption and that 60%–80% of this demand could be eliminated, the nation's *total* electric consumption needs might be reduced by anywhere from 12%–16% by use of these new lighting forms and systems.

Transporting People and Goods

Passenger Transport. No nation has more automobiles per person than the United States (57 per 100 people). Nor do other people drive as far as we do. In 1989, all vehicle classes together traveled almost 2.1 trillion miles (3.5 trillion kilometers), about double the distance that all U.S. vehicles traveled in 1970. Truck miles tripled in this interval. No society consumes as much energy per person in auto travel as ours.

Americans are often accused of wastefulness in this regard compared to Europeans, who consume far less energy in travel. Part of the reason for the higher U.S. consumption has been our tradition of large cars. That tradition results from a low price of gasoline in the United States over many years. The taxes we placed on gasoline were always small in comparison to the taxes Europeans placed on their gasoline. So we hung onto our tradition of large cars, while the Europeans typically manufac-

tured smaller cars that used less gasoline. In that sense, because we were never willing to tax gasoline sufficiently to discourage larger cars, the accusation of wastefulness is true. In another sense, however, the accusation of American wastefulness compared to that of Europeans is false.

If we compare the United States to Europe, we see very different societies. Population centers are much closer together in European countries; families are, in general, less widely separated by distance. People in Europe tend to stay in the nations of their birth, and the nations are small, on the order of the size of our states. The huge distances between cities and towns in the American countryside are not characteristic of Europe.

Nonetheless, in Europe, auto purchases are heavily taxed; special road taxes levied on car owners increase the burden still further. Furthermore, the price of gasoline in European countries is two and a half to three times that in the United States.

Public transportation developed in Europe before the era of the auto. Because of this, the service and networks of the bus, train, and streetcar systems are excellent. Thus, Europeans generally have available to them a public transport system that, by appropriate transfers, can link almost any city address in Western Europe with any other, nearly door-to-door.

Even though such systems are available, the importance of the auto to European travel is growing at a phenomenal rate, as fast as the growth of personal wealth allows it. In Holland, for example, virtually all the growth in passenger kilometers is going into auto travel. Mass transit ridership is only holding even. Similar patterns are seen for other Western European nations. The Europeans enjoy their cars every bit as much as Americans do. If they could afford to waste more energy in auto travel, they probably would. We can "afford" to drive so far because our gasoline prices are so low. At the same time, we can attempt to reduce our gasoline consumption.

Try to imagine a society such as ours with 140 million private automobiles traveling as many miles as we do and using 50% less gasoline. Fuel efficiency is a trick the Europeans learned long ago. The average mileage for all cars in the United States

TABLE 13-2 Average Efficiencies of All Cars in the United States, Old and New

Year	U.S. Passenger Car Registrations (millions)[a]	Average Miles Traveled per Gallon of Fuel Consumed[b]
1973	101.1	13.10
1978	116.5	14.06
1983	126.7	16.70
1988	141.3	19.95

Source: [a]U.S. Department of Energy, Energy Information Administration. [b]*Motor Vehicles Facts & Figures*, 1984, 1985, 1990.

was 20 miles per gallon in 1988. If our fleet of cars had an average efficiency of 40 miles per gallon, not an unreasonable goal, each million miles our fleet logged would require 50% less fuel. Put another way, a car that travels 20 miles on a gallon of gas requires 500 gallons to go 10,000 miles (an average yearly figure). The car that travels 40 miles on a gallon of gas needs only 250 gallons to go the same distance.

How do we arrive at an era of fuel-efficient automobiles? It is reasonably clear that high gasoline prices have encouraged the production of efficient cars in Europe and Japan. These high prices include, in general, taxes that amount to half or more of the total price of a liter of gas. The United States has chosen in the past to place only modest taxes on gasoline, choosing instead to fine manufacturers when the average fuel economy of the vehicles they sold in a year was less than a federal standard. The standard raised the required fuel economy of new cars in stages from 18 miles per gallon in 1978 to 27.5 miles per gallon in 1990.

Even though more efficient new cars will be sold as time goes on, it will take time for energy-efficient cars to replace inefficient ones. The state of the nation's economy in terms of unemployment and inflation will influence how fast new cars are purchased and how fast older cars are retired. Table 13-2 shows the agonizing slowness of improve-

ments in the average fuel efficiency of automobiles in the United States. You would have expected gasoline consumption to have declined significantly with the 50% increase in fuel efficiency (19.95 mpg from 13.10 mpg) that occurred from 1973 to 1988. It fell by only 10% during the interval, though, because of a 40% increase in the number of vehicles on the road. Controversy 13-1 addresses the effects on individuals of various options for encouraging fuel conservation.

What can we do while we wait for higher fuel efficiencies to kick in? Individual action and responsibility will help a great deal. First, and most simply, there is a speed at which automobiles and trucks are most efficient in terms of fuel consumption. For automobiles, that speed is 35–40 miles per hour (56–64 km/hr); for trucks it is a bit higher. During World War II a nationwide speed limit was imposed of 35 miles per hour to conserve fuel.

As a result of the oil embargo of 1973–74, Congress mandated an energy-saving 55-mile-per-hour (89 km/hr) speed limit. In 1987, however, Congress passed a new law that allowed states to raise the speed limit to 65 miles per hour on rural portions of their interstate highways. The 55-mile-per-hour limit turned out to be a life-saving device as well as an energy saver. Motor vehicle fatality and accident rates fell significantly when the speed limit was reduced and have remained lower ever since.

There are other features in the way we drive that influence mileage. Properly inflated tires and radial tires can increase mileage. Racing starts, uneven acceleration, and braking in city traffic can reduce the mileage a car obtains by up to 30%. Driving in lower gears takes more gasoline, as does an untuned engine.

When talk turns to saving gasoline, someone inevitably raises the possibility of the electric car. In the early days of the automotive industry the electric vehicle (EV) was in competition with the auto that was powered by an internal combustion engine. But cheap gasoline for the internal combustion engine car and a limited range for the EV determined that the EV would not survive. In recent years, research on new and longer-lasting batteries has again raised people's hope for an electric vehicle. Such vehicles, however, are not much more

Controversy 13-1

How Do We Get Fuel-Efficient Cars on the Road?

We should adopt a surtax on all cars weighing more than 3,000 pounds escalated upward to as high as $1,000 tax on the big luxury cars weighing over 5,500.

John Quarles

I would like to describe a proposal for a stiff gasoline tax, specifically, an increase in the tax to $2 a gallon (with rebates on a per adult basis). . . . A $2 tax is not much higher than present taxes in countries like France and Italy.

Robert Williams

We must be cautious to see that a national policy of energy conservation does not unfairly burden the poor and those living in rural areas.

C. ReVelle

To stimulate oil conservation, we need a generation of high-mileage cars, but how do we get them? We can tax new car purchases by their weight or by their horsepower; we can tax gasoline; we can give income-tax rebates to individuals who purchase efficient new cars; we can ration gasoline, allowing one or two gallons per car per day. The many possible ways to direct people's attention to fuel-efficient cars are not all equal in their market effect; nor are they equal in their impact on upper-, middle-, and lower-income families.

There are four basic options listed above: (1) tax the purchases of inefficient new cars, (2) tax gasoline, (3) give rewards for purchasing efficient new cars, or (4) ration gasoline. We can assemble many plans from these basic options, but for each plan there is a set of questions to be answered:

1. How will it work? That is, what is the effect on the rate of sales of different kinds of autos? On the sale of gasoline today and in the future?
2. (a) If the government pays, where should the money come from? From general tax revenues? From a special fund?
   (b) If a tax raises money that goes to the government, what should be done with the money? Should it go into general tax revenues with no special earmarks? Or should it be set aside in a special-purpose fund? (To

efficient than autos with internal combustion engines. That is, the energy consumption values per mile are similar. Thus, electric vehicles are not significant energy savers. Instead, they are energy shifters. They shift the energy burden and the pollution burden to other substances and to other sites—to coal and to the sites of the electric power plants. A nation plagued with acid rain should think long and hard about a switch to electric vehicles.

So far, we have argued principally for changes in the automobile itself, not in the way our society transports itself. Public transportation (buses, train systems, and the like), if properly implemented, can have an important role in reducing energy consumption. Figure 13-11 illustrates the relative efficiency of various means of transportation.

A vehicle not listed is the "auto in city traffic with a load equal to 75% of capacity." Such a vehicle is known as a **car pool.** The four-person car pool with an average load equal to 75% of capacity consumes only about 3,000 Btu per passenger mile, an efficiency level about that of a train traveling between cities.

To induce a large proportion of people to ride the bus, train, or subway, routes must cover a large portion of the geographic area, so that access to

give you an idea of what amounts of money are involved, each cent of federal gasoline tax raises $1 billion each year.

3. Who is affected? Are the poor hurt more than the well-to-do? That is, is the policy progressive, taking dollars from those better able to afford the expense? Can you think of ways that the impact on the poor can be softened?

4. What are the political chances?

5. Is there an impact on the national economy? On local economies?

To focus the way you answer these questions, here are some hypothetical individuals, all of whom are very much concerned about such policies. Explain how the various conservation policies could affect the following people.

• Juan Lopez and his family live in Chicago; he maintains a set of apartments in the inner city in return for his own apartment. He just bought a gas-guzzling 1976 Zonker Grand Viscount.

• Arthur Williams and Sally Adam-Williams have moved back to their home town of Wayside, Nebraska, but the nearest job is in Omaha, some 70 miles away. They do not want to leave their rural environment for a city, but they need to make a living. They are about to buy their first car.

• Calvin and Nancy Beale own and run a diner in Ellsworth, Maine. Their diner, the Ellsworth Eatery, is well patronized and locally famous for homemade pies and the "Maineburger." The bulk of their business comes in the summer, when tourists flock to nearby Acadia National Park. Tourists with tents and motor homes come from all up and down the Eastern Seaboard, even from as far south as Virginia. No trains serve Ellsworth.

Can you think of other scenarios showing how people will be hurt by the various gas-conservation policies? Can you think of people who will hardly be affected at all by the listed methods?

Sources: John Quarles, speech before Coal and the Environment Conference, Louisville, Ky., October 1974; Robert Williams, in Daniel Yergin, ed., *The Dependence Dilemma* (Cambridge, Mass.: Harvard University Press, 1980; and C. ReVelle, "Public Transport and the Netherlands: Implications for Transport Policy in the U.S.," Center for Metropolitan Planning and Design (Baltimore, Md.: Johns Hopkins University, 1977).

public transport is not difficult. Stops must be frequent enough and spaced closely enough on the route. Equipment must be clean; conditions must be safe and comfortable; and costs must be reasonable when compared to use of the automobile.

Even when all conditions are favorable, ridership on public transport may still be so low that the costs of providing the service cannot be paid by the revenues generated from fares. Even in Western Europe, where public transport runs quite full, governments make up the difference between revenues earned and the costs of actually operating and maintaining the system. Such support can be justified on the basis of energy savings as well as by the reduction of air pollution. In addition, those who continue to drive have some benefits in terms of less-crowded streets and fewer accidents. Should gasoline be taxed more heavily to pay for this support? The tax revenues could be used not only to help pay for public transport, but would simultaneously make such transport economically attractive to more people.

Freight Transport. About 30% of the energy we spend each year on transportation goes into the movement of goods; the remainder is expended on

FIGURE 13-11 Relative Efficiency of Various Modes of Travel. (*Source:* Data for capacity assumptions and all bars except Automobile are from E. Hirst and J. Moyers, "Efficiency of Energy Use in the United States," Science, *179* [March 30, 1973], 1299, Copyright 1973 by AAS. Automobile bars calculated from 1990 data from Motor Vehicle Manufacturers Association.)

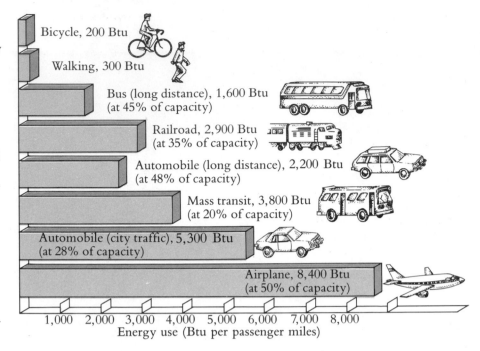

Bicycle, 200 Btu

Walking, 300 Btu

Bus (long distance), 1,600 Btu (at 45% of capacity)

Railroad, 2,900 Btu (at 35% of capacity)

Automobile (long distance), 2,200 Btu (at 48% of capacity)

Mass transit, 3,800 Btu (at 20% of capacity)

Automobile (city traffic), 5,300 Btu (at 28% of capacity)

Airplane, 8,400 Btu (at 50% of capacity)

1,000   2,000   3,000   4,000   5,000   6,000   7,000   8,000

Energy use (Btu per passenger miles)

moving people. Of the various modes of freight transport, railroads, pipelines, and waterway transport all have comparable levels of efficiency. Trucks consume four to five times more energy per ton-mile than those other modes.

The transport of goods, especially between cities, has evolved in much the same way as the transport of people. Whereas waterways and trains initially carried the bulk of goods moving between cities, trucks have been increasing their share of the load quite steadily. Thus, the energy-efficient modes of transport—barge and rail—are losing ground to an inefficient mode, the truck. Certain bulk goods such as coal, however, are unlikely ever to give way to truck transport. Instead, coal-slurry pipelines might capture a portion of the coal transportation market.

The reasons for the growth in trucking are rooted in the door-to-door nature of truck service. Once goods are loaded, they often need not be reloaded before arriving at the final destination. If the particular goods are not moving in sufficient quantity to justify a rail track from door to door, truck transport, though costly, becomes a very attractive alternative. A routing that involves first a truck, then a train, and then a truck may be low in transport cost because of the rail savings, but the two transfers consume time and money and also increase the likelihood of damage to the shipment or of theft.

A promising means of energy-efficient freight transport is the truck container. The container, which attaches to a truck rig, is loaded at the origin, moves by truck to the railroad yard where it is loaded on a flatbed car, moves by train to the destination terminal, and is reattached to a rig. The truck rig delivers the container to its final destination.

SUMMARY

Solar Energy. In active solar systems, pumps powered by electricity move air or water from one part of the system to another. A solar heating or hot-water system is composed of a collector and a storage tank. The collector is warmed by the sun's rays and transfers the heat to a collecting medium: water or a water-antifreeze mixture. The heat is

Towards a Sustainable Society / Renewable Energy Sources Can Provide Sustainable Societies with Virtually Unlimited Energy

House in Katmandu with solar panels for hot water. Solar hot water systems are feasible for use in many areas of the world including the United States. *(UN Photo: J. Isaac)*

Solar panels heat water for showers at beach in Crete. *(UN Photo: M. Tsovaras)*

Modern windmill in U.S. The use of renewable sources of power such as wind and sun not only can provide power, but also can prevent the air pollution that results from the use of fossil fuels to generate power. *(U.S. Department of Energy)*

Silicon BBs — part of new, low-cost solar cells. In 1991 Texas Instruments announced a joint effort with Southern California Edison to develop a new technology for converting sunlight to electricity. The Spheral Solar™ cell, made from tiny beads of low-cost, low-purity silicon, achieves conversion efficiencies of 10–11%. This new material may make central station and rooftop generation of electricity by photovoltaics cost effective for the first time. *(Southern California Edison: G. O'Loughlin)*

Voluntary recycling in Baltimore, Maryland. Every Saturday morning hundreds of citizens bring their recyclable paper, glass, aluminum, and plastics to this center staffed entirely by volunteers. Profits from the sale of recycled materials are awarded as grants to community projects. *(Charles ReVelle)*

Truck collecting newspapers, glass, and plastics in curbside recycling plan in Florida. Although recycling is still voluntary in this community, all residents share part of the money the county saves on trash disposal costs. A discount appears on residents' utility bills. This discount represents the real savings that result from recycling, or from using in energy generation schemes those materials that would otherwise need to be disposed of in landfills. *(Max Rottmann)*

Recycling aluminum cans. A beverage can made from recycled aluminum consumes only one third of the energy per use of a can produced from virgin materials. *(EPA: S. C. Delaney)*

then stored in a heated tank of water. Hot water for direct use is obtained by passing water through a coil inside this heated storage tank. Passive systems use little or no assisting energy to capture heat from the sun. Passive solar devices include large south-facing windows with overhangs, Trombe walls, and greenhouses.

Photovoltaic cells convert sunlight to electricity using semiconductors. The cells are falling in cost and will soon be competitive with coal and nuclear power for central-station electricity generation. Widespread home generation of electricity with solar cells is a distinct and exciting possibility.

Steam electric generation at central stations using solar energy is already possible using the power tower concept; mirrors focus sunlight on a tower in which water is boiled to steam. In a related concept, mirrors reflect sunlight onto smaller focal points, and heat is then collected centrally. The sun's energy can be used indirectly by photosynthesis, in which sunlight converts carbon dioxide and water to biomass. Biomass products such as wood or field crops can be burned for heat or converted to alcohol for use in automobiles. Trees, sugar cane, guayule, and hevea are all possible fuel crops.

Government programs are needed to help offset the high initial costs of installing solar technology and to help commercialize photovoltaic manufacture. Studies have concluded that solar water heating is economical over almost all of the United States, and solar space heating is economical in many areas.

Conservation. Americans use much more energy per person than any other group of people in the world, so our potential for energy savings is great. Energy conservation measures can help postpone scarcity of fuel resources, save money for energy users, slow fuel price increases, and decrease pollution. Conservation measures include more building insulation, more efficient appliances, more efficient automobiles and machines, and replacement of incandescent bulbs with fluorescent lamps. Using electricity to heat buildings and heat water is much less efficient and much more expensive than using oil or natural gas. However, heat pumps that use

electric energy may prove an efficient way both to heat and to cool buildings.

One way to encourage automobile efficiency is to increase gasoline taxes; another is to set fuel efficiency standards for new cars and enforce penalties for manufacturers who fail to meet the standards. Reducing the speed limit to 55 miles per hour saved fuel and also reduced traffic deaths and injuries. Electric cars would not save energy, but would shift the location of the pollution they cause from cities to rural areas where power plants are located. Car pools and public transportation systems (such as buses and trains) also promise energy savings. In addition, such systems reduce air pollution.

Questions

1. Contrast active and passive solar energy systems.
2. What environmental advantages does a photovoltaic (solar cell) system have over generating electricity by burning coal or oil?
3. Why is electric hot water more wasteful of energy resources than gas-fired or oil-fired hot water?
4. Are electric vehicles energy savers? Do they cure air pollution problems? Explain.

Further Reading—Solar Energy

Butti, K., and J. Perlin. *A Golden Threat: 2500 Years of Solar Architecture and Technology*. New York: Cheshire Books/Van Nostrand Reinhold, 1980.

"Energy from Biological Processes." Washington, D.C.: Office of Technology Assessment, July 1980.

Lees, A. "Sunspace," *Popular Science*, September 1988, p. 261.

About 20 pages on these popular heat-capturing home additions.

Moore, T. "Thin Films: Expanding the Solar Marketplace," *EPRI Journal*, March, 1989, p. 4.

These photovoltaic cells could transform the market despite relatively low efficiencies because of their low cost.

Passive Solar Design Handbooks, vol. I, II, and III. Washington, D.C.: U.S. Government Printing Office, 1981.

Weinberg, C., and R. Williams. "Energy from the Sun," *Scientific American*, *263*(3) (September 1990), 147.

A fairly comprehensive treatment of the many faces of solar energy.

Further Reading—Energy Conservation

Bleviss, D. "Saving Fuel: We Have the Way . . . Do We Have the Will?," *Technology Review*, November-December 1988, p. 47.

Argues that the technology is already on the shelf for cars with fuel economy up to 80 miles per gallon (highway).

Energy for Planet Earth, special issue, *Scientific American*, *263*(3) (September 1990).

This issue has four authoritative articles on energy conservation.

Lamarre, L. "New Push for Energy Efficiency," *EPRI Journal*, April-May 1990, p. 4.

From the article: ". . . if today's most efficient electric end use technologies were applied in every case, the U.S. [could save] . . . between 24 and 44% of electricity . . . [needed] . . . in the year 2000."

Lave, L. "Conflicting Objectives in Regulating the Automobile," *Science*, *212* (May 22, 1989), 893–899.

Chapter 14

Solid and Hazardous Wastes and the Recycling Alternative

In the previous three chapters we examined the way modern industrial societies use energy resources. The mineral energy resources such as coal and oil are, of course, not the only mineral resources needed by an industrial society. A number of metals—for instance, aluminum, copper, cobalt, platinum, and molybdenum—arc also necessary. Mining and refining the ores from which these minerals are obtained destroy wildlife habitat and cause air and water pollution in ways similar to the mining for coal or the extraction and refining of oil. Both mining and refining of minerals also require energy.

At the same time as modern societies require energy, minerals, and other resources, they produce wastes that need disposal. Some of the waste—for instance, toxic chemicals or radioactive waste from power plants—must be carefully disposed of because it is intrinsically harmful to humans or the environment. Some of the waste, such as old newspapers or broken washing machines, merely needs to be disposed of in an esthetically pleasing manner. A further portion, such as food wastes, might become harmful if it is not disposed of properly.

These two topics, modern society's requirement for minerals and problems with waste disposal, are both addressed by a process that is as almost as old

as civilization itself but that is only today being recognized as a basic process necessary to sustainable societies. That process is recycling.

In this chapter we first look at how solid and hazardous wastes are now handled. Then we examine the alternative of recycling as one that promises to be a better way of disposing of a major portion of the wastes we generate. But this is not the only benefit to be derived from recycling. Recycling also promises to ease shortages of essential minerals. Furthermore, by providing recycled resources for use instead of virgin materials, it promises to decrease energy use and the environmental impacts of mineral extraction and refining.

DISPOSING OF SOLID WASTES

Just as a weed is a flower in the wrong place, garbage can be viewed as resources in the wrong place. It is possible to present the composition of municipal solid wastes, or garbage, in familiar resource categories—metals, glass, paper, rubber (Figure 14-1). Nevertheless, it is hard for most people to see solid waste as a repository of resources. The prob-

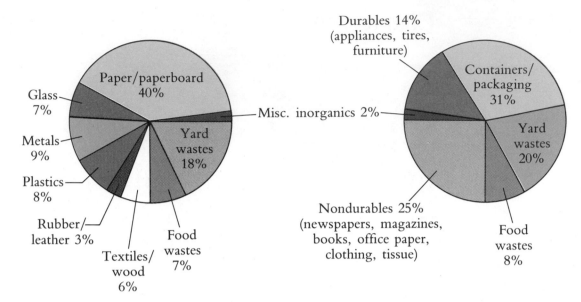

FIGURE 14-1 Typical Composition of U.S. Municipal Solid Waste, 1988.
For the most part, the materials in municipal solid wastes are no different than the objects and substances that, every day, pass through our hands. (*Source:* Franklin Associates, Ltd., *Characterization of Municipal Solid Waste in the United States, 1960 to 2000,* prepared for U.S. EPA)

lem is that it *is* all mixed together, along with food and yard wastes, and it doesn't smell very good.

Americans generate over 180 million tons of municipal solid wastes every year. This waste consists of materials discarded by households, offices, restaurants, hospitals, and schools. The total amount of solid waste generated in the United States is greater than this, however. There is also some 300 million tons of sewage sludge generated in sewage treatment plants (see Chapter 18), as well as the solid waste generated by industry and the construction trades (Table 14-1).

Dumps and Sanitary Landfills

The collection and disposal of solid waste is a problem with which governments have had to wrestle since people started living together in settled communities.

At first the primary method of disposal was the open dump. Open dumps, however, are smelly and may be infested with insects and rodents that carry disease. By the 1940s a better method, called **sanitary landfilling,** had been developed.

In sanitary landfilling an earth cover is added to the solid waste pile on at least a daily basis. The application of an earth cover has been found to enhance a number of aspects of the disposal operation. Besides checking the spread of flies, fire and consequent air pollution are prevented. The earth layer also compacts the refuse into a smaller volume and prevents the wind from spreading it.

The land that has been filled may become suitable for use as a recreational area, although settling and gas production from decomposing wastes may delay such use.

In a modern sanitary landfill the trenches or pits are lined before the solid wastes are dumped in. This is done to prevent pollution of groundwater with materials that can be leached out of buried wastes by rainfall. Typical liners include plastic sheeting and layers of absorbant clay. A porous rock layer may be included, as well, to collect and vent methane gas formed by the waste material. Pipes

TABLE 14-1 Solid Wastes Generated Yearly in the United States

Source	Million Tons
Municipal solid wastes	180
Sewage sludge (wet)	300
Dredged materials	400
Industrial waste (wet and solid)	400

Source: D. Spencer, "The Ocean and Waste Management," *Oceanus, 33*(2) (Summer 1990), 6.

to collect leachate may be buried in the lining materials. Test wells are often drilled around the landfill so that water samples can be taken to ensure that hazardous materials are not leaking from the landfill and polluting groundwater. (Hazardous materials such as toxic or radioactive wastes are subject to even more secure burial. See page 313 for an illustration of a hazardous waste landfill.)

However well this system may work, the simple fact is that in the United States we are running out of room in our landfills. According to the EPA, 80% of landfills now in operation will be full within 20 years. Furthermore, citizen opposition prevents siting new ones, even where there is space for them.

The odyssey of the garbage barge that roamed the world in 1987, looking for a place to offload its cargo, highlighted the immediacy of the problem. The garbage, originally from Long Island, New York, had been destined for burial in North Carolina, but it was turned away because of lack of space. The barge owners next tried to unload at a site in Louisiana, but the garbage was refused there, as well. In a well-publicized series of attempts to dispose of the garbage, the barge tried to dock at numerous other places, going as far south as Belize. By this time, however, media coverage had ensured that no city or country was going to admit to being the one that accepted someone else's garbage.

Two months after embarking on its voyage, the garbage returned to New York City, the barge owners pointing out that it could not sail the seas

forever. Here legal challenges by citizen groups, worried that the garbage must contain unusually toxic materials, blocked unloading for three more months. The case was fought all the way to the New York State Supreme Court, which finally decided that the garbage should be incinerated and the ash transported for burial back to the town of Islip, the origin of most of the garbage.

The unusual part of the story is not that a town tried to ship its garbage far away for burial, however. Some northeastern cities still send their garbage all the way to Michigan or Kansas. Opposition by the receiving towns may make this particular solution to the shortage of landfill space less and less likely.

Incineration

In situations in which the cost of transporting wastes to the nearest landfill site is excessive or where land for filling is in short supply, a community may choose to burn its wastes at a centrally located incinerator. The choice between incineration and landfilling may hinge on social and political considerations as well as economics, because the economically desirable sites for an incinerator may not be politically acceptable to the community. Incineration is a 24–hour operation that produces noise (trucks and operation) and air pollutants.

The operation of a large incinerator begins on the "tipping floor" of the facility, where trucks maneuver to a foot-high bumper rail and discharge their contents into a large, rectangular "storage pit." The pit typically holds one and a half times the daily weight consumed by the incinerator. Cranes mix and distribute the wastes within the pit and haul them into charging hoppers, which discharge them down chutes into the furnace.

The process of **incineration** reduces the wastes to a solid residue and to gases—water vapor, carbon monoxide, carbon dioxide, sulfur oxides, et cetera. The solid residue consists of combustion products along with glass and metal, and these require further disposal, typically by landfilling. Particulate matter may also be removed from the gas stream of the incinerator to prevent its entering the atmosphere as a pollutant; this material joins the solid residue. Glass bottles and metal cans may actually be desirable components of wastes that are to be incinerated; they provide greater porosity to the bed of burning wastes and enhance combustion. As much as 80% of the weight and 90% of the volume of the wastes are eliminated in incineration. With compaction of the residue, the final volume may be reduced to as little as 1.5% of the original volume. Of course, some bulky items may not be incinerated, and these materials are reduced in volume by only about half at the landfill site.

Composting

The compost heap has been utilized for centuries by farmers to reclaim organic matter. From this practice a set of mechanized biological processes known as **composting** has evolved to reduce organic municipal wastes to stable substances. From its introduction in the 1920s and 1930s to the present, it has been the object of derision and hope.

There are two types of composting, outdoor and indoor. In the former, piles of refuse are laid in long lines called windrows; the piles may be 10 feet (3 meters) wide and 5 to 6 feet (1.5–1.8 meters) deep. Occasional turning of the piles promotes microbial activity and gas exchange. Two to three weeks of processing produces a stable humic material. The availability of nearby suitable land for the windrow method is not likely in the United States. In the indoor or factory method, the refuse may be spread in drums, which rotate at slow speeds and agitate the wastes. As microbial action proceeds, the temperature of the refuse quickly rises to 140°–150°F where further biodegradation takes place. In the 7- to 10-day detention required to "cure" the wastes, most disease vectors are eliminated by the elevated temperature. No special inoculum appears to be needed to start the process. It should be noted that not all domestic wastes are capable of being composted. Metal and glass, in particular, may be removed prior to processing.

The product of composting is a brown to black humic material that finds use, especially in Europe, as a soil conditioner. As a soil conditioner, compost fosters the absorptive properties of soil for water.

The substance has less than 1% nitrogen and less than 0.2% phosphate. Thus it is not a particularly good competitor with commercial fertilizer, and it finds little, if any, use in basic agriculture.

Compost has found use in Europe, however, in luxury agriculture. Holland disposes of a sixth of its municipal wastes by composting. Much of the product goes into intensive gardening, such as bulb growing, and into city parks. Germany and Switzerland also engage in composting, although to nowhere near the same extent as Holland. A use in Germany is in preventing erosion of steep hillsides in the German wine country. Still, less than 1% of the municipal wastes of Germany are composted. There is some luxury gardening in the United States—nursery gardening and park gardening are examples—but given the mass of wastes produced annually, it is unlikely that a sufficient market exists for the profitable sale of municipal compost.

This is not to say that municipal composting is not an alternative worthy of consideration. Simply put, it is unwarranted to *assume* a market for compost. Instead, the choice of composting would need to be founded on the economics of the process within the total waste management system. It may be possible for a centrally located mechanized composting process to be competitive with a centrally located incinerator, if air pollution controls make incineration exceedingly costly. Furthermore, a landfill site to which compost has been applied has more potential future uses than does land filled with untreated wastes.

Garbage Grinding

The practice of grinding wastes in the home and discharging them to the sanitary sewer has grown in the last decade. Of course, this activity does not eliminate the need for collection and disposal of other household wastes, but it can change the composition of such wastes. Additionally, the notion of hauling wastes to a central grinding station has been raised. In this operation, as well, the wastes would enter the sanitary sewer. Both methods place a burden of added solids disposal on the sewage treatment plant (see Chapter 18).

HAZARDOUS WASTES

What Hazardous Wastes Are

Harzardous waste is a term applied to any waste materials that could be a serious threat to human health or the environment when stored, transported, treated, or disposed of. Most hazardous waste is produced by the chemical products manufacturing industry, but quantities are also produced by metals industries, paper products manufacturers, the electronics industry, transportation equipment manufacturing, and the petroleum and coal products industries. There are several categories of hazardous waste.

Toxic substances include solids and liquids that damage human health or the health of plants and animals in the environment. They are especially a hazard if they leach into groundwater and enter drinking water supplies. Many such instances have been documented. Toxic chemicals from nearby waste disposal facilities have leaked into individual wells used for drinking water as well as into the drinking water supplies of whole communities. This particular aspect of hazardous waste problems is discussed further in Chapter 19, "Drinking Water Resources."

Ignitable wastes present a potential fire hazard. In Elizabeth, New Jersey, a warehouse filled with stored wastes exploded with a thunderous roar in April 1980. A mushroom-shaped cloud of smoke rose over the city as 55-gallon drums of alcohol, solvents, pesticides, and mercury compounds exploded like bombs and rocketed into the air.

Corrosive wastes, such as acids, present another type of hazard. These wastes can dissolve storage containers and contaminate soils and water supplies.

A fourth category of hazardous wastes includes *reactive wastes,* those materials that can react with each other or with air or water in a dangerous fashion. In 1978 a young truck driver in Tennessee was killed while discharging wastes from his truck into an open pit. Toxic fumes were formed by liquids mixing in the pit.

Officials in Pennsylvania recently began monitoring an abandoned mine, which they learned had been used as a dump for cyanide-containing chemicals. They fear that the chemicals could react with acid mine waters and form deadly cyanide gas that could then escape to the surface.

A fifth category of hazardous wastes includes radioactive materials. These wastes are most commonly generated by nuclear power plants, scientific research laboratories or by medical procedures involving diagnosis or treatment of patients with radioactive materials. The disposal of radioactive wastes from power plants is covered in Chapter 11.

Disposing of Hazardous Wastes

Old Dump Sites: Love Canal. There are actually two major problems with hazardous wastes today. One is what to do with the more than 200 million metric tons of hazardous waste generated yearly. The other is what to do about the hundreds of abandoned dump sites across the country that have been used for hazardous wastes in the past.

The most infamous example of an abandoned dump site is Love Canal near Niagara Falls, New York. At the turn of the century, William T. Love dreamed of building a model community based on the cheap power he would generate by digging a canal between the upper and lower Niagara Falls. But the project failed, leaving only a partly dug ditch. In the 1920s the city and various industries began to use the ditch as a waste disposal dump. In 1953, Hooker Chemical Company, which then owned the dump site, capped it with clay soil and sold it to the school board for $1. In the property deed was a warning that hazardous chemicals were buried in the old canal ditch.

The events that followed are still not entirely clear, but it appears that construction activities (a school and 100 homes were built encircling the canal), together with unusually heavy rains, caused the dump to fill up with rainwater and then overflow. Chemicals from this dump and three others in the area leached into groundwater. Corroding drums of waste collapsed, forming sinkholes from which chemicals evaporated into the air. Backyards, basements, swimming pools, and playing fields built over or adjacent to the old dump site were contaminated by a variety of noxious and hazardous chemicals. Preliminary studies seemed to show a higher than normal incidence of birth defects and chromosome damage in residents living near the canal. Over 850 families were eventually moved from the area, and their houses were purchased using federal disaster emergency funds.

It is still unclear what kind of health effects residents of the area may have suffered and how severe these effects might be. The Love Canal tragedy pointed up how poorly equipped the government was to deal with hazardous waste emergencies at former dump sites. The mechanisms did not really exist to clean up these old sites or to protect the people living near them.

Superfund. In 1981, spurred by the Love Canal disaster, Congress passed a toxic wastes cleanup bill. Known as the "Superfund," this law initially provided $1.6 billion to be used to clean up hazardous waste sites when there was immediate danger to public health or to the environment. In 1986, after the initial appropriation had allowed no more than a good start at cleaning up dump sites, Congress appropriated another $2.5 billion per year while reauthorizing the bill. This money was raised by a $12 tax on every $10,000 of corporate income for corporations earning over $2 million per year. Polluters, when they can be found, are fined. Other monies come from general revenues and taxes on crude oil, motor fuel, and chemical feedstocks. The fund does not, however, provide for the compensation of people injured by hazardous waste dumping. As directed by the bill, the EPA has already identified 400 sites needing top priority cleanup.

Current Methods of Hazardous Waste Disposal. Hazardous wastes can be disposed of in several ways. Chemical treatment can make some wastes nonhazardous. For instance, acids and bases can be neutralized. Organic wastes without heavy metals can be composted or spread out over soil so that soil microbes can use them up. Incineration is the method of choice for particularly hazardous organic wastes such as the herbicide Agent Orange, left over from the Vietnam War. However, incineration is an expensive alternative. A somewhat more common method of disposing of hazardous wastes is to bury them in a secure landfill, or house them in an above-ground storage facility (Figure 14-2). Landfilling of hazardous waste is the least desirable alternative for disposal because of the risk that the waste might eventually leak into groundwater. Recycling is the best alternative for hazardous waste, because it then becomes not waste but a resource. For instance, waste solvents from the electronics industry are still pure enough to be used in other industrial processes. The EPA has been encouraging the establishment of waste-clearing houses to match up wastes with potential uses. Most hazardous waste generated in the United States is disposed of or treated on the grounds of the industry that produces the waste. Figure 14-3 shows the eventual fate of hazardous wastes generated in the United States.

Siting Landfills: A Political Matter. It is important that the monitoring of a landfill go on for a long time, at least 20–30 years and possibly forever, to be sure that the site is secure and that nothing has disturbed the cover. Disturbance of the cover was probably a major cause of leakage from the Love Canal site in upper New York State. Because of the possibility of leaks, and in spite of the technology that exists to build a modern, secure hazardous waste landfill, the public as a whole remains wary. This is understandable in light of past disposal practices and their legacy of chemical contamination of the environment. To quote Jackson B. Browning, Director of Health, Safety and Environment for Union Carbide:

It is not terribly difficult to elicit a political consensus in support of the need for siting sound hazardous waste treatment facilities. The majority of voters will readily agree that such sites are necessary and that you should move with all deliberate speed to locate them—at the other end of the state.

Local community opposition often makes it nearly impossible to site hazardous waste landfills. In such a climate, politics rather than technology decides where a disposal site will go.

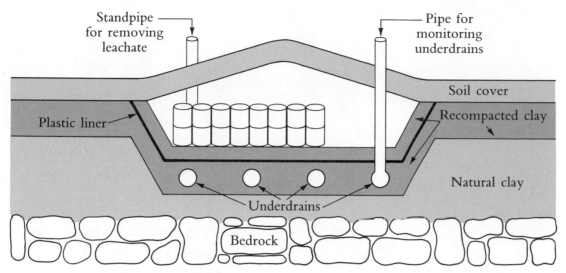

(a) Secure Landfill for Nonradioactive Hazardous Wastes

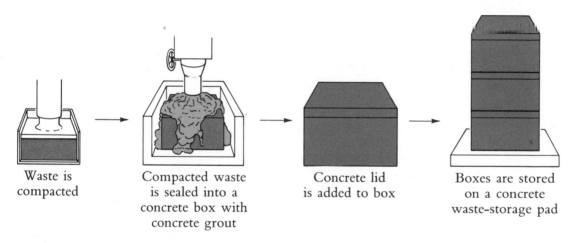

(b) Disposal of Low-Level Radioactive Wastes

FIGURE 14-2 Secure Hazardous Waste Disposal. Part a shows a cross-section of a secure hazardous waste landfill. Hazardous wastes are packed into sealed drums and shipped to this type of landfill for burial. Note the pipes for removing rainwater that leach into the landfill and might become contaminated with wastes. Note also the underdrains, which are monitored for possible leakage of the plastic and clay liners. In part b are shown the additional steps taken for secure disposal of low-level radioactive waste, such as might be generated by a scientific research laboratory. This waste is first compacted and then sealed into a concrete box with concrete grout. The boxes are then stored on a concrete pad in a secure facility.

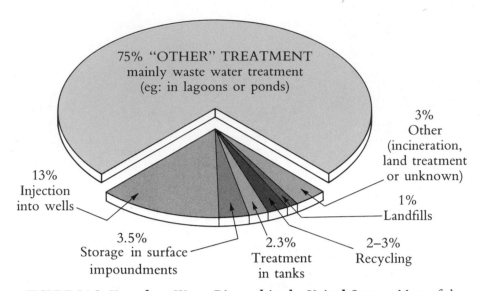

75% "OTHER" TREATMENT
mainly waste water treatment
(eg: in lagoons or ponds)

3%
Other
(incineration,
land treatment
or unknown)

13%
Injection
into wells

1%
Landfills

3.5%
Storage in surface
impoundments

2.3%
Treatment
in tanks

2–3%
Recycling

FIGURE 14-3 Hazardous Waste Disposal in the United States. Most of the approximately 230 million tons of hazardous waste generated in the United States each year is water contaminated with hazardous materials. A large portion of this waste undergoes wastewater treatment (75% of the total amount of hazardous waste handled). Another 13% of the total, mainly corrosive and reactive waste, is injected into deep wells. The Environmental Protection Agency has been discouraging disposal of hazardous waste in landfills because of the possibility that waste may leak out and contaminate groundwater. Only about 1%–2% of the total is now disposed of in this manner. Some 2%–3% of hazardous waste is currently recycled. (*Source:* 1987 National Biennial RCRA Hazardous Waste Report, U.S. Environmental Protection Agency, and Information Management Branch, EPA Office of Solid Waste (1991))

Global Hazardous Waste Issues. It is not known exactly how much hazardous waste is generated each year worldwide. The U.N. Environment Programme estimates that 60 million tons are generated in the United States and about half again that much by the European Economic Community.

A special concern of developing countries is that, as disposal of hazardous wastes becomes more expensive in the industrialized countries and as laws there become more strict, the industrialized countries are attempting to dispose of hazardous waste by shipping it to the developing countries. The 1989 Basel Convention on the Control of Transboundary Movements of Hazardous Wastes and Their Disposal specifies that countries may ban the import of hazardous wastes and that all shipments of hazardous waste that are made must be properly packed and labeled. The treaty also calls for attempts to reduce the amount of hazardous waste generated and shipped. The main problem with the treaty is that there is no effective way to enforce its provisions.

THE RECYCLING ALTERNATIVE FOR SOLID WASTES

Faced with a shortage of landfill space and a lack of any other obvious solutions to their solid waste problem, many waste management authorities in the United States are beginning to consider an alternative that environmental groups have advocated

TABLE 14-2 Years Left until Global Mineral Resources Are Depleted If Developing Countries Increase Their Use of Resources to the Same Rates at Which Developed Countries Now Use Resources*

Resource	Years Left
Coal	477
Aluminum	427
Cobalt	60
Platinum	59
Molybdenum	53
Copper	46
Petroleum	27

Source: R. Frosch, and E. Gallopoulos, "Strategies for Manufacturing," *Scientific American,* September 1989, p. 146.

* These figures assume (1) world population will reach 10 billion by 2023, and (2) all of the resources thought to exist are extracted. Resources would last an even shorter time if only those amounts are counted that are known to be profitably extractable by currently existing technology.

for years—recycling. In addition to solving the solid waste problem, effective recycling also promises to help stave off the steep price rises for mineral resources that will occur as developing nations attempt to increase their consumption to the levels of the developed world (see Table 14-2).

Recycling in the United States

The basic principles of municipal recycling programs are similar to those in voluntary recycling programs. In both cases the idea is to separate out those materials that can be reused economically—the resources—from those that must be discarded. Here the similarity ends, however. Voluntary programs have in the past been mostly small-scale. They have sometimes generated income for charitable groups, and they have helped participants feel they are not using up more than their fair share of the earth's resources. But even curbside voluntary programs, in which a government agency picks up sorted recyclables at the householder's curb, have, in the past, succeeded in recycling only a disappointingly small portion of the total solid waste stream—rarely more than 10% to 15%.

Current municipal programs, in contrast, are large-scale. They are usually associated with some other form of waste reduction, such as incineration, and they are often compulsory. It is interesting to compare several programs in different parts of the country. In New York City, where 20,000 tons of garbage are produced each day, recycling is seen as the only way to cope with dwindling landfill space. Recycling has been required for residences since early 1990. Special sanitation police check garbage for discarded recyclables, give warnings, and, if the warnings are ignored, fine homeowners or landlords. About 5% of New York's trash is being recycled, but that amount is scheduled to rise to 24% by the end of 1994. New York's long-term garbage reduction plans include incineration. However, the city has been unable to site a single incinerator, despite years of trying, due to citizen opposition. This problem, encountered in the siting of sanitary landfills and hazardous waste dumps as well, is known as the NIMBY, or not-in-my-backyard, problem.

In the city of Baltimore, Maryland, incineration and metals recovery are carried out at the BRESCO (Baltimore Resource Energy Systems Company) plant. Mixed waste is collected in the city and incinerated at the plant in three furnaces that handle up to 2,000 tons of waste per day. Heat from the furnaces is used to generate enough electricity for 60,000 homes. The electricity is sold to Baltimore Gas and Electric. Both ferrous (iron) and nonferrous metals are recovered from the ash before it is landfilled. In processes such as this, one ton of garbage generates about 525 kilowatt-hours of electricity and is reduced to about one-eighth of its original volume. On the negative side, air pollution control devices must be added to the incinerator stack to prevent harmful emissions, and this adds to the high capital costs of building incinerators.

In 1988 the Florida legislature passed a bill requiring all counties to begin recycling programs by July 1989. In Pinellas County, Florida, voluntary

Towards a Sustainable Society

Ending the Throwaway Society

by Judie Hansen

In 1984, while a manager in the Oregon Department of Fish and Wildlife Services, Judie Hansen conceived the idea of a beach cleanup—a day set aside for citizen volunteers to collect and bag all the flotsam washed up on Oregon's beaches. Hansen has won many accolades,

most recently the Goldman Environmental Award, for her idea, which has spread to all 22 coastal states in the United States and to several foreign countries.

In 1984, I organized the first statewide coastal cleanup in the State of Oregon. On October 13th, 1,200 citizen volunteers collected 26.3 tons of floatable trash in just three hours along 125 miles of coastline. As they gathered the debris they filled out a short questionnaire listing the trash by categories such as sheeting, bottles, buckets, polystyrene foam, and eating utensils. A large percentage of the debris collected was polystyrene foam in hunks larger than a foot-

ball. Coastal cleanups are now held in all coastal states in the United States and several foreign countries. The volunteers are still completing questionnaires listing items collected and their estimated weight.

Of special concern was the polystyrene foam. Because it is white and lightweight, it floats on the surface of the water and is more visible than most other floatable trash. But in addition to being aesthetically displeasing, the polystyrene foam debris causes harm to marine life. Seabirds, turtles, and marine mammals are known to ingest the foam pieces, resulting in a blockage of their intestines and death by starvation.

In Oregon, several large rivers,

recycling is combined with energy-generating incineration. Residents are given a bright blue recycling can in which they are asked to place newspapers, aluminum beverage cans, steel cans, clear or green glass containers, and plastic milk and water jugs. In the first five months of the program, residents recycled about 10% of the solid wastes generated and saved the county $26,250 in tipping fees. By 1994, however, the county is required by law to raise the percentage of waste recycled to 30%. Whether this can be done with a voluntary program is yet to be seen. The nonrecycled part of the coun-

ty's municipal solid wastes is burned at a resource recovery facility capable of generating electricity from the waste heat.

Although many waste system managers state that energy generation from waste and recycling are compatible activities, there is disagreement on this point. Recycling and energy generation compete for some of the same materials—for example, paper and plastics. The removal of paper and plastics from the waste stream can make energy-generating incinerators unprofitable to operate. Moreover, the energy recovered by burning these

including the Columbia, empty into the Pacific Ocean. In taking a closer look at the polystyrene foam, it has been determined that most of it does not come from items such as food trays, cups, or picnic coolers. The foam beads are larger and the chunks more dense. The source of much of this debris is the flotation blocks used at boat marinas in the rivers and small coastal communities. Because of tidal action, floating docks are preferable to allow for movement.

In talking to marina and boat owners, I learned that much of the material used for floating docks is surplus material available at a very low cost. Unfortunately, most of this surplus material was never designed to be used outdoors or in our nation's waterways, but was intended for use as dunnage to protect cargo shipped by rail or ship. Foam dunnage used for docks has a life of little more than a year before it begins to deteriorate.

When used as a dock material, the polystyrene foam is exposed to petroleum products in the water and to sunlight. In addition, beavers and muskrats are attracted to the foam and are known to chew out the interior of the blocks. So after the foam is weakened by oil, sun, and mammals, all it takes is the bump of a boat or driftwood to knock off a portion and have it enter the natural environment as floatable trash.

A solution to this problem would be to encapsulate these foam blocks in fiberglas or other stabilizing material to protect them from these elements. Even a covering of heavy plastic sheeting can double or triple the life span of the foam blocks. The cost of surplus blocks is about one-third the cost of encapsulated blocks, but this could change if such treatment were a requirement for docking material. When covered in fiberglas, the blocks have a life of at least 10 years.

My recommendation is to reg-

ulate the type of material used for floating docks of all sizes. When a U.S. Army Corps of Engineers permit is issued for a private dock or marina, special provision should be included to regulate the kind of material acceptable for floating docks. Having a floating dock standard would help institutionalize the use of appropriate material.

This is only one suggestion for reducing the amount of floatable trash. A real challenge for future generations is to turn the tide on the use of one-time use or disposable products. Our fresh crop of engineers and scientists might best concentrate their efforts on the development of material and products that are kinder to our natural environment. Finding ways to make more items easy to compost or recycle is preferable to developing more new products to float around on our oceans and rivers for years to come.

---

materials is less than the amount that is saved if they are recycled. Recycling high-density polyethylene containers into new containers can save twice the energy recovered by burning them, for instance, while recycling paper can save up to five times the energy recovered by incinerating it.

Seattle calls itself the recycling capital of the nation, and perhaps that name is appropriate. Through a series of entirely voluntary recycling projects, most run by local charities, Seattle has been recycling almost 25% of its municipal solid waste since the early 1980s. Nonetheless, in 1986

both of the city's landfills were almost full and leaking methane gas into neighboring areas. The city hired two contractors to step up recycling efforts. One contractor distributed three bins per customer for the sorting of scrap paper, newspaper, and glass-tin-aluminum. The other contractor gave out only one bin in which customers were to put all their recyclables. Materials are mechanically sorted after collection. (see Figure 14-4). The program is billed as voluntary, but those who do not recycle are charged higher rates for trash removal. Compliance has been extraordinary. Between 70%

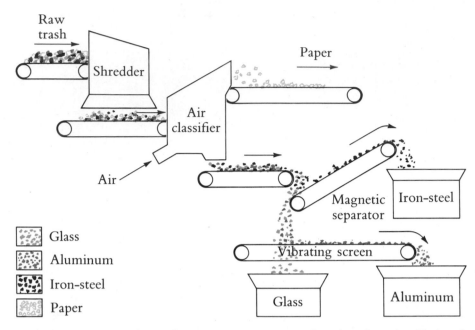

FIGURE 14-4 Mechanical Sorting System. Mixed trash is first shredded and then subjected to an air stream that blows out light materials such as paper. Next, iron and steel are segregated by a magnetic separator. Finally, a vibrating screen differentiates pieces of glass from pieces of aluminum.

and 90% of the population is involved in the recycling effort, and 37% of the city's waste was being recycled by 1989.

This success has brought to light one of the major problems remaining to be solved in recycling schemes: A successful scheme can overpower the market's ability to absorb recyclables. In 1990 the price for newspapers fell from $60 to $20 per ton because more newspapers were being collected than could be recycled into newsprint again by American mills. Not only did this depress the price for recycled newspapers in the United States, but it also disrupted European recycling systems; huge quantities of recycled newspapers were shipped to countries such as the Netherlands, where recycling of newspapers has been a way of life for decades. "It's amazing that it's cheaper to haul surplus paper all the way to Europe rather than storing or burning it in America," said Paul Nouwen at the Netherlands Environmental Ministry. "It's offered here practically for free and ruined the market in all of Western Europe."★

Part of the solution lies in generating new markets for recycled products. A spate of recent laws requiring newspapers to increase the amount of recycled paper they use has already begun to ease the paper glut. One of the strongest laws was passed in Suffolk County in New York State. It requires all newspapers with weekly circulation of 20,000 or more that are printed or sold in the county to be printed on entirely recycled paper by 1996. The law will affect some of the largest newspapers sold in the United States, including the *New York Times,* the *Daily News,* and *USA Today.*

In the developed countries, further progress depends on the construction of more facilities to reprocess waste paper and recycle plastics. Businesses have been wary of investing large amounts of

★ *New York Times,* December 11, 1990, p. A7.

FIGURE 14-5 Zabaleen Collecting and Sorting Center on the Outskirts of Cairo. (*Photo:* Lois Jensen/ UNDP)

money in recycling plants. Indications are that the supply of recycled materials will continue to increase, however. In the United States, 27 states passed a total of 65 recycling laws in the first five months of 1990. Many of these laws were prompted by the decreasing availability of landfill space, a problem that is not likely to go away.

Recycling and Developing Countries

In developing countries, recycling has always been a way of life. People produce much less waste because their poverty forces them to reuse and recycle their possessions. Even so, the rapid growth of urban areas has created solid waste problems. Although only 50% to 70% of urban trash is collected, this effort can take up to 50% of a municipal operating budget.

In Cairo an entire class of people, the Zabaleen, make their living by collecting, sorting, and selling recyclable trash (Figure 14-5). Although the government initially attempted to solve Cairo's growing solid waste problem by replacing the Zabaleen collection system with modern trucks and dumpsters, a better plan has been worked out. The Zabaleen have organized into a corporation and have been given loans to buy small trucks to improve their collection efficiency. The sorting and recycling on which the Zabaleen economy is based have thus been integrated into a modern and workable system.

SOURCE REDUCTION AS A SOLUTION

Among the industrialized nations, Japan is the champion recycler. The Japanese recycle 43%–53% of their garbage and incinerate the rest. However, they also produce less waste than U.S. citizens to start with—about 330 kilograms (726 lb) per person per year, compared to 660 kilograms (1,452 lb) for Americans or Canadians. Moreover, Americans produce three times the waste of citizens living in developing countries such as India.

Clearly there is another possible way of reducing solid wastes, one that also saves energy. It is **source reduction**—or not generating the waste in the first place.

A number of countries and some jurisdictions in the United States have passed laws requiring reuse of beverage containers. Numerous studies have shown that it takes much less energy to wash and refill a beverage container than to make a new one from virgin materials, or, for that matter, to melt it down and form a new one. German officials have proposed putting deposits on all liquid containers, not just beverage containers (Figure 14-6).

Laws requiring minimum warranties on products such as small appliances and electronic devices

Box 14-1

Ocean Dumping: Are We Using the Oceans as Garbage Cans?

In the late 1960s the United States was dumping about 60 million tons of wastes into the oceans at over 200 different sites. Most of this material was dredge spoils, which result from the maintenance of navigation channels. Industrial waste and sewage solids made up the bulk of the rest. Municipal solid wastes were not a part of this material; the legal disposal of municipal refuse at sea was ended more than 25 years previously as a result of public disgust with the floating litter that resulted.

Although the term *dredge spoils* sounds innocuous, in fact, many harbor sediments are polluted and thus many harm aquatic life at the site where they are dumped. Sewage solids (see Chapter 18) were barged to the ocean from a number of localities, notably New York City and Philadelphia, until quite recently. Sewage solids can deplete the oxygen in the water into which they are dumped and also may carry dangerous bacteria.

Public reaction against any sort of ocean disposal of wastes stimulated passage of the Ocean Dumping Ban Act in 1988. This public reaction was in part due to litter, including medical wastes, that washed up on beaches in the late 1980s as a result of illegal dumping.

Unfortunately there is still a serious problem with floating litter in marine waters. Most of this litter appears to come from ships. The vessels dump their garbage before entering port rather than complying with strict rules requiring them to steam-sterilize or incinerate solid wastes before unloading them. In some areas there is also a significant contribution from pleasure boats, storm sewers, and wash from landfills.

This trash washes up on shores all over the world, spoiling beaches. Because of prevailing winds and currents, even remote islands are littered. Bermuda and the Bahamas are especially subject to this type of pollution. In addition to despoiling beaches, trash, especially plastics, poses a hazard to marine animals. Many instances have been documented of seals, birds, and turtles strangled by the plastic rings from six-packs of soda or beer. Plastic bags, balloons, and pellets have been recovered from the stomachs of dead fish and sea turtles.

However, cleaner oceans may be on the way. Annex 5 of the 1973 international treaty governing prevention of marine pollution by ships (MARPOL) deals with the issue of garbage from seagoing vessels. This annex came into force on December 1988, when it was finally ratified by countries representing 50% of the world's shipping.

The convention prohibits the dumping of any plastics into the ocean; the dumping of dunnage and packing materials within 25 miles of shore; and the dumping of other garbage, such as food wastes, glass, and rags, within 12 miles of shore.

would encourage more durable goods and result in fewer throwaways.

Major reductions could be achieved by eliminating government subsidies on raw materials. The U.S. government allows tax deductions to mining companies to compensate them for depletion of mineral reserves. Public mineral and timber resources are available to corporations at low or no cost. Many other governments also give subsidies to logging companies. The net result of such subsidies is to reduce the cost of virgin materials compared to recycled ones.

The problem of stimulating recycling and reuse is an economic one. As an example, so long as the price of producing new aluminum ingots from ore is less than the price of collecting and recycling the

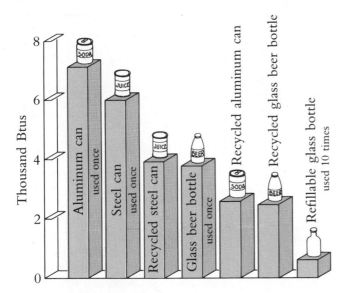

FIGURE 14-6 Comparative Energy Consumption of Beverage Containers. The graph compares the amount of energy consumed, per use, for a 12-ounce beverage container that is made from raw materials, made from recycled materials, or reused. (*Source:* L. L. Gaines, "Energy and Materials Use in the Production and Recycling of Consumer Goods Packaging," Argonne National Laboratory, Argonne, Ill., 1981)

FIGURE 14-7 Collecting paper at a community recycling center. Community recycling programs like the one pictured have proven successful in hundreds of cities and towns across the United States. Their success has been limited, however, by the lack of markets. Recycling is an economic activity. People who work hard to save materials sometimes forget that the recycling loop will not be complete without mills or other markets to buy the materials (for prices that cover at least part of the costs of collection). Many states are now exploring new policies and public-private partnerships to increase demand for materials. In Illinois, for example, state agencies must purchase recycled paper, re-refined motor oil and retreaded tires. (Caption courtesy of Greg Lindsey)

metal from its current uses, recycling/reuse will not occur to a significant extent—unless some outside economic stimulus is applied to the system. Unless economic incentives are used to modify the system, vast quantities of energy will continue to be expended on production of materials from primary sources. And associated mining, health, and atmospheric impacts will continue due to the production and combustion of the fossil fuel. At the same time, landfill space will continue to be consumed by the discarded products containing these resources.

The economic incentives that encourage recycling/reuse can take many forms, but basically a forced, up-front injection of money into the system and a return of that money somewhere in the recycle system seems to have the right properties. The upfront deposit on a bottle or can reminds a consumer that there are resource replacement costs, energy costs, and disposal costs associated with the

bottle or can. The return of the deposit upon return of the container provides incentives for recycling behaviors. A tax on nonrecycled paper or a tax break on recycled materials serves the same purpose in manufacturing.

It was only in the 1960s that America abandoned deposits on beverage bottles. Now the New England states, Oregon and other states, have legislated

Controversy 14-1

Paper or Plastic?

"If you want to cut down on the weight of what you're throwing away, you should be using plastics."

James E. Guillet, professor,
inventor of a degradable plastic

"When you look at purchased energy, it's about the same (for paper or plastic), maybe a hair or two favorable to the paper side."

Paul Carroll, James River Corp.,
paper bag manufacturer

"I think the distinction is throwaway versus nonthrowaway, not paper versus plastic."

Shelley Stewart, U.S. Pulp and
Paper Director, Greenpeace

The checkout person at the supermarket wants to know if you'd like paper or plastic grocery sacks. The server at the college cafeteria asks you to choose a polyfoam plate or a paper one. Granted, there are undoubtedly larger decisions you will have to make in your lifetime, but what *should* you say when faced with one of these plastic versus paper questions?

The necessity for such decisions is the basis for a whole new field of study—determining the life-cycle impact that various consumer products have on the environment. In order to make the best choice from the point of view of the environment, a consumer would need to know the amount of energy used in the manufacture of competing products, whether any special environmental problems result from the gathering of the resources used in their manufacture, and whether those resources are renewable or nonrenewable. Also important would be the amount of air and water pollution generated in the manufacture of the products, what sort of disposal problems they present, and whether the products can be recycled or reused. Unfortunately the answers to such questions may seem to obscure rather than highlight the right choice.

Take paper versus plastic bags, for instance. Plastic bags require 20% to 40% less energy to produce than paper bags; less air and water pollutants are generated per ton of plastics manufactured than are generated per ton of paper manufactured by pulp and paper mills; and because they are lighter in weight than comparable paper bags, the plastic ones take up about 70% less space in landfills.

Paper bag manufacturers counter that they generate 50% of their manufacturing energy from wood by-products, so the need for more energy to manufacture paper than plastic does not translate into a need for more power plants. Furthermore, they point out that the raw materials for making paper bags come from trees, a renewable resource, while the raw material for making plastics is petroleum, which is not renewable. Moreover, they add, paper is biodegradable, while plastics are not.

The plastics manufacturers respond that in today's landfills very little biodegrades, anyway, be it paper or plastic. And it is true that scientists excavating in landfills have found newspapers, buried 40 years ago, that are still readable.

How would you weigh these various factors in deciding on paper versus plastic grocery bags? Which would you choose and why? What is an alternative to either paper or plastic bags?

Sources: Paul Carroll and James Guillet quoted in *Chemecology,* November 1990, p. 4; Shelley Stewart quoted in *Harrowsmith,* July/August 1990, p. 40.

deposits on bottles and cans in order to fight litter and reduce solid waste. Interestingly, the countries of Western Europe never went to throwaways and never ceased to operate their bottle and can deposit systems.

A similar deposit-return system has been proposed for automobiles but never implemented. Instead, penalties in the form of fines for the abandonment of junk cars seem to have been utilized to prevent derelict cars from littering streets and fields. You would think that automobiles would be readily recyclable; so much steel should make the auto hulk valuable. Unfortunately, the design of the automobile makes the recycled product less valuable than it could be. So much copper wiring is intertwined in the auto that separation of the copper from the hulk is difficult; the iron product produced from an auto hulk is contaminated with copper and less useful than a cleaner product. Reinforcing bars for concrete construction is one of the limited uses of this contaminated product.

The example makes a point. Design for recyclability is crucial. Modular snap-out copper wiring in a car would improve its value for recycling. Other metal products, such as stoves and refrigerators, could benefit from designs that enhance the value of the product in the recycling process. Stimulating such design to take place is a challenge for sustainable societies.

Consumer education can also play a role in source reduction. If consumers are made aware of the extra cost they bear in disposing of wasteful packaging, at least some of them will be more likely to choose products that are packaged in recyclable or reusable containers. But the choice may not always be clear and simple. See Controversy 14-1.

How far can recycling and source reduction be pushed? Pilot projects have reached levels of 84% reduction of solid wastes through intensive recycling combined with composting of food and yard wastes. Experts estimate that 85% to 99% of U.S. waste could be recycled through intensive efforts.

A number of localities are beginning to close in on these high estimates. In 1989, Berlin Township in New Jersey recycled 57% of its waste, while the city of Heidelberg, Germany, recycled 37%.

Recycling rates such as these, combined with source reduction measures, promise not only to solve the solid waste problem but also to decrease energy use, increase available resources, and decrease the environmental damage resulting from mining and logging—all goals we must strive for if we are to fashion a sustainable society.

SUMMARY

Americans generate over 180 million tons of municipal solid wastes every year—waste that could be viewed as resources. Methods of disposal include burying the waste in sanitary landfills, incineration, composting, and garbage grinding. Although burial in landfills is the most common method of disposal, the space available in landfills is rapidly being used up.

The category of hazardous waste includes toxic substances, ignitable wastes, corrosive wastes, and radioactive wastes. Such wastes can sometimes be recycled, treated chemically, composted, or incinerated. Most commonly, however, they are buried in landfills. Secure landfills can be designed but must be monitored for long periods of time, possibly forever, to be sure there is no leakage of hazardous chemicals. Recycling, where possible, is a better solution than disposal for hazardous wastes.

A serious problem exists with the hundreds of older dump sites across the United States that are currently leaking waste materials into groundwater. Superfund is a bill designed to provide funds for the cleanup of these old dump sites.

Many municipalities are turning to a combination of recycling and incineration to deal with their solid waste. Some experts feel that recycling and waste-to-energy incineration are compatible, but others point out that the two methods compete for the same resources. In addition, energy-generating incineration captures little of the energy used in producing goods. Recycling captures a much greater portion.

A major problem with successful recycling schemes is that enough facilities do not exist for recycling the collected materials, especially paper.

In developing countries, governments are faced with serious solid waste disposal problems. Nonetheless, the solutions they choose must not displace traditional recycling systems on which whole sectors of society may depend for a living. Developing countries also face the problem of handling hazardous waste shipped from industrialized countries. The Basel Convention is an attempt to regulate such shipments.

An even more environmentally sound solution to the solid waste problem than recycling is source reduction. This promises to solve not only the solid waste problem but also to save energy and resources. Source reduction can be achieved through bottle deposit legislation, minimum warranties on small appliances and electronic devices, elimination of government subsidies on raw materials, and the various economic incentives governments can devise to encourage the use of recycled materials.

Questions

1. What category of waste makes up the largest percentage of municipal solid wastes? Suggest three ways that the amount of waste in this category could be decreased.

2. Much of the material recovered from modern sanitary landfills is still recognizable, decades after it was buried. Why hasn't it decayed?

3. Explain the NIMBY problem in siting sanitary landfills, hazardous waste dumps, and incinerators. Is it a valid objection?

4. Why does environmentalist Barry Commoner say, "The only insurmountable hindrance to recycling is building an incinerator?"★

5. How would you feel if you discovered that your state planned to site a hazardous waste dump on vacant property near your home? What questions would you ask of state authorities? What safeguards would you feel were absolutely necessary to protect yourself and your family?

★ Quoted in J. Young, "Reducing Waste, Saving Materials," in Worldwatch Institute's *State of the World 1991* (New York: Norton, 1991).

Further Reading

Bennett, J. "The Age of Resin," *Harrowsmith,* July/August 1990.

This article and the one following will introduce you to the plastics versus paper debate.

Bloom, G. F. "The Hidden Liability of Hazardous-Waste Cleanup," *Technology Review,* February/March 1986.

The economics of hazardous waste disposal and who eventually pays for it are considered in this article.

Frosch, R., and N. Gallopoulos. "Strategies for Manufacturing," *Scientific American,* September 1989, p. 144.

A closed-cycle system for resources used in manufacturing is appealing. The authors explain how this could work.

Hocking, M. "Paper versus Polystyrene: A Complex Choice," *Science, 251*(1) (February 1991), 504.

Choosing one product over another in terms of its environmental impact is mind-boggling. Try following the arguments presented here. Has the author left anything out?

"Love Canal: A Boyhood Is Poisoned," *New York Times,* June 9, 1980, p. B1.

"Love Canal Residents under Stress," *Science, 208* (June 13, 1980), 1242.

The effects of living near a leaking chemical waste site can be as damaging psychologically as physically. This and similar articles give some idea of the stress Love Canal residents lived with.

Maugh, Thomas H. "Biological Markers for Chemical Exposure," *Science, 215* (February 5, 1982), 643.

Summarizes books and conferences on the problems of monitoring toxic substance escape from dump sites and of determining the effects on neighboring populations.

Porter, J. W. "Setting Up a Solid Waste Recycling Program in Schools," McDonald's Educational Resource Center, (800) 627-7646.

Written by a former Assistant Administrator for Solid Waste at EPA, this manual will help you start a recycling program at your school. Worksheets help you decide what items can best be recycled in your environment and where to send them once they are collected. There is a charge of $14 for the manual.

Ryan, M. "Waste Tires Present Environmental Problem of Increasing Magnitude," *Waste Management Research Report,* (2) (Summer 1990). SUNY College of Environmental Science and Forestry, Syracuse, N.Y. 13210.

Used tires present a special solid waste disposal problem. Many landfills will not accept them. The author looks at the various disposal options.

References

Bartone, C. "Municipal Solid Wastes Management in Third World Cities." Baltimore, Md.: Johns Hopkins University, 1990.

Environmental Equity—Reducing Risks for All Communities. Report to the Administrator from the E.P.A. Environmental Equity Workgroup, 1992.

"Facing America's Trash: What Next for Municipal Solid Waste," Office of Technology Assessment. Washington, D.C.: Congress of the United States, 1989.

Hershkowitz, A., and E. Salerni. "Garbage Management in Japan: Leading the Way," *Civil Engineering,* August 1988.

Morris, D. "As If Materials Mattered," *Amicus Journal, 13*(4) (1991), 17.

"The Ocean and Waste Management," *Oceanus, 33*(2) (Summer 1990).

Richard, J. "Better Homes and Garbage: Seattle, Recycling Capital of the Nation," *Amicus Journal,* Summer 1990, p. 50.

Simons, M. "U.S. Wastepaper Burdening the Dutch," *New York Times,* December 11, 1990, p. A7.

Woods Hole Oceanographic Institution. *Plastics Increasing in the North Atlantic.* Woods Hole, Mass.: Woods Hole Oceanographic Institution, 1987.

Young, J. "Reducing Waste, Saving Materials." In L. Brown (Ed.), *State of the World 1991,* Worldwatch Institute. New York: Norton, 1991.

Part Five

Air and Water Resources

Thai children filling bucket with water. (*Photo:* United Nations/Carl Purcell)

Human survival depends on a number of natural resources. The importance of plants and animals as wildlife resources was discussed in Part III, along with land and food resources. Energy resources were the subject of Part IV. This part is concerned with the resources of air and water.

Part V begins with a chapter on the sources and effects of urban air pollution, including a discussion of the weather patterns that contribute to air pollution episodes. Chapter 16 focuses on acid rain and forest decline. Acid rain is seen to be the result of a misguided strategy to control sulfur oxides and nitrogen oxides. Chapter 17 traces the potential effects on temperature, climate, and sea level of the accumulation of carbon dioxide and other "greenhouse gases" in the upper atmosphere.

When we burn fossil fuels—coal, oil, and gas—we furnish heat for homes, energy for mobility, and power for the production of goods. Fossil fuel energy has become our servant. Our skill at capturing this energy has transformed society from one powered by hand and horse to one of remarkable abundance and comfort. But energy has turned out to be a dangerous servant.

Our misuse of fossil fuels has resulted in air pollution episodes so severe that people have died. In parts of Eastern Europe and the developing world, in cities like Cracow, Poland and Mexico City, people are still dying from air pollution. In the United States, numerous pollutants still contaminate the air we breathe. Our upper atmosphere, the stratosphere that surrounds the entire globe, has been fouled as well.

In the lower atmosphere the contaminants in the air have direct biological effects on humans. Breathing may be impaired; diseases of the heart and lung are made worse. Vegetation is harmed, and construction materials such as mortar and metal are corroded. Near Los Angeles, the most sprawling city in the country and the most dependent upon the automobile, smog is destroying the pine trees in the hills that surround the city. Almost 200 miles away, about the distance between New York and Boston, the desert holly, a plant that grows in the isolation of Death Valley, is threatened by the creeping smog from Los Angeles. The smog results from reactions between hydrocarbons and nitrogen oxides—products of automobile exhausts. In Ankara, Turkey, air pollution episodes as terrible as the famed London fog are still occurring. In Tokyo, oxygen is available on the streets for people overcome by air pollution. Mexico City is choking in the pall of smoke it produces each day.

In the eastern United States, as well as in Europe, Scandinavia, and Japan, acid rain is turning inland lakes acid, destroying fish life, and laying waste to soils and forests. The acidity is caused by the solution in rain of sulfur oxides from the burning of coal. Oxides of nitrogen, principally from combustion occurring at fossil fuel power plants and from the combustion of gasoline in automobiles, also contribute to the nightmare of acid rain.

In the stratosphere, the upper atmosphere shield of the globe, the protective gas ozone is being eaten away. As the ozone concentration falls, cancer-causing UV light penetrates to the surface of the earth more easily. At the same time, carbon dioxide and other greenhouse gases rise, causing further harm by trapping the heat energy that would have escaped from the earth. The heat-trapping capability of these gases threatens the climate of the earth with a rapid warming trend with which we may be unable to cope.

In Chapter 18 we look at the quality and quantity of natural waters, while Chapter 19 examines drinking water issues. Chapter 18 first considers U.S. and world water resources, both above and below ground. Next, the chapter details problems caused by wastewaters.

Wastewaters flow from cities and industries, from mining operations, from farming and rural homes. These wastes are treated in different ways but are generally disposed of in the same way: into the nearest river or lake or into the ocean.

The problem with wastewaters is not just that

they might contaminate our drinking water supplies. Wastewater can be fairly easily chlorinated so that it does not carry large quantities of disease-causing organisms, and the water we drink, even if it comes from a highly polluted source, can be treated until it is not only healthy but pleasant to drink. Thus, our insistence that wastewater be treated before it is released is not focused only on human health problems. We must also consider how the wastewater will affect the natural waters into which it flows.

If organic pollutants are not removed from wastewater, they can set up a chain reaction that robs water of the oxygen normally present. Further, certain chemicals, such as pesticides, may be directly poisonous to aquatic organisms. Fish and other aquatic creatures may not be able to live under these conditions, and other less desirable species may take over. In addition, certain inorganic elements in wastewater, such as phosphorus and nitrogen, cause excessive growths of the microscopic green water plants called algae. These "blooms," as they are called, form unpleasant scums and mats over the surface of lakes.

Water pollution control is the term given to methods of cleaning up wastewaters so that they can be released to natural waters without causing problems. What are these methods? Surprisingly, biological processes are used to purify the water.

Finally, pollution problems of natural salt waters, especially oil pollution from shipping and drilling operations, are noted.

In the final chapter in this part we ask the questions: When is water pure and when is it safe? What are the substances that contaminate water supplies, and how do we remove them?

These questions deal with *the water we drink*. They involve basic facts we should know about the safety and quality of our supply of drinking water.

The impurities that influence the safety of a water supply for drinking fall into three broad classes. *Inorganic chemicals* are one class; included in it are the ions arsenate, nitrate, fluoride (at high levels), and other chemicals that can have adverse effects on our health. *Organic chemicals,* a second category, may also be dissolved in the water; some of these compounds have been linked to cancer. Finally, water may contain *microorganisms* (*microbes*) that cause diseases such as typhoid and cholera. Fortunately, these diseases are only a distant memory to most of us in the United States. Once widespread in this country, they still occur commonly in nations that have not yet treated their water supplies.

This part closes with discussion of a water issue of truly global dimensions: a United Nations initiative to provide safe drinking water to the entire population of the world.

Chapter 15

Urban Air Pollution

AIR POLLUTION ECOLOGY— THE EARTH'S ATMOSPHERE

We usually speak of the material we breathe simply as "air," but it is actually a mixture of substances. Clean, dry air is about 78% nitrogen and 21% oxygen. Other gases are present in minute quantities, including argon, carbon dioxide, and ozone. Water vapor is also an important component of the atmosphere. The amount of water vapor varies from 0% by volume in dry air to about 4% in humid air. Dust particles from both human and natural sources (for example, volcanoes) may also be a significant component in the air, even though present in relatively small quantities.

Origin of the Oxygen in Air

The oxygen in air is essential for respiration by plants and animals, but oxygen has not always been part of the earth's atmosphere. Scientists believe that 4.5–5 billion years ago the earth's atmosphere was similar to the mixture of gases released when volcanoes erupt—primarily water vapor, carbon dioxide, and nitrogen. During the period when the

earth was cooling and becoming more solid, heavy rains washed out most of the carbon dioxide. The oxygen now in the atmosphere appeared later, when life on earth evolved. The oxygen was furnished by green plants carrying on photosynthesis.

The evolution of the earth's atmosphere to its present oxygen-rich composition is the subject of a now famous book by Lovelock (1979), who calls both his concept and his book *Gaia*. The argument of Gaia is that life and the earth's atmosphere evolved together and that the earth's atmosphere is in a homeostatic state. That is, if events were to occur that pushed the atmosphere away from its present composition, "righting" mechanisms would slowly correct the composition back to its present status. Those mechanisms include the natural processes of air, earth, sea, plants, and animals. The mechanisms would operate on a global scale but in geologic time (millions of years) rather than within the human time frame. Gaia is an intriguing concept, but it may also be a dangerous one. Scientists in the pocket of industry may argue that insults to the earth's atmosphere will be corrected naturally, but they may not mention that those corrections will take millions of years. The Gaian hypothesis, elegant though it is, has the potential to

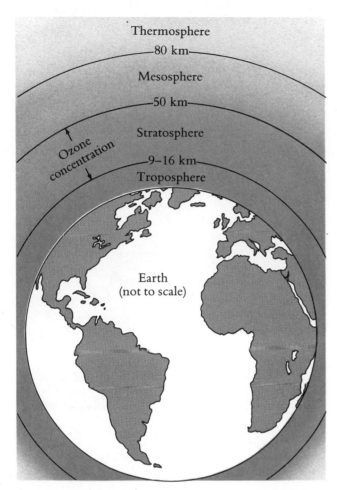

FIGURE 15-1 Atmospheric Layers. Diagram of the earth's atmosphere, divided into layers on the basis of temperature. Heights given are approximate because they vary from place to place around the globe.

be abused. The notion that the earth will survive the worst of human insults is only partly true. Life may survive, but not necessarily in its present form, nor with a human presence.

Zones of the Atmosphere

Like the term *air,* the word *atmosphere* is often used loosely to describe the whole envelope of gases surrounding the earth. Scientists who study the atmosphere recognize several zones at different heights above the earth, depending on their temperature characteristics (Figure 15-1).

The layer closest to earth's surface is called the **troposphere.** In this layer, 5–10 miles (9–16 km) high, most of what we call *weather* occurs. All rainfall, almost all clouds, and most violent storms occur in this layer. The temperature in the troposphere usually decreases as we go up. Above the troposphere from 11 to 30 miles (18–50 km) is the **stratosphere.** Temperatures in this layer first remain constant and then begin to increase with height. Most of the ozone is concentrated in the stratosphere, and it is ozone that is responsible for the temperature increase. Ozone absorbs ultraviolet light from the sun, and the resulting heat causes the stratosphere to increase in temperature. Even higher, above 30 miles (50 km), is the **mesophere,** a zone in which temperatures again fall. Finally, there is the **thermosphere,** which begins about 50 miles (80 km) above the earth's surface. There is no well-defined upper boundary to this layer. In the thermosphere, temperatures again rise with height.

Most of the gases are present in about the same percentages in the troposphere, stratosphere, and mesosphere. However, the density of the atmosphere decreases with height, so that 90% of the weight of the atmosphere is concentrated within 10 miles (16 km) of the earth's surface.

AIR POLLUTION EVENTS: THE AWAKENING

Air Pollution Episodes

Our recognition of the threat of air pollution stems from the occurrence of serious events in the past that sharply focused our attention on the significant hazards of polluted air. The earliest recorded air pollution episode in the United States was in 1948 in the small town of Donora, Pennsylvania, where a zinc smelter was producing enormous quantities of sulfur oxides. Pollutants accumulated in a layer of air trapped over the city in a windless environment. Twenty people died as a result of the three-day fog.

Four years later, in December 1952, an air pollution episode gripped the city of London for five successive days. The fog that blanketed the city was due to particles and sulfer oxides from coal burning for heat. More than 4,000 deaths occurred in that interval as a result of the extensive air pollution. In the years following, episodes occurred again in London, but fortunately, because coal heating was phased out, the tragic extent of the 1952 fog was never repeated.

Episodes occurred in New York City in the 1960s (Figure 15-2), and alerts have been announced in a number of major cities in recent years. When our senses have failed to tell people of the decline in the quality of our air, chemical sensors have detected pollutants. When the effects of health have not been visible to the untrained eye, statisticians have shown deterioration of health at times of high pollution levels.

These episodes are not the result of sudden and vast discharges of pollution from many sources. The pollutants that are present during an episode are typically only a portion of the normal output from domestic, industrial, and transportation activities. Instead, an air pollution episode represents a massive accumulation, a gathering together of these ordinary pollutant discharges on a huge scale. The massive accumulation is the result of weather conditions—specifically, **inversions** that hinder the natural mixing of the atmosphere and prevent the natural scattering of pollutants. Inversions clearly illustrate how human activities can interact with the natural phenomena of weather and climate to cause serious ecological or health disturbances.

Inversions

Pollutants emitted from smokestacks tend naturally to be diluted in air to nonharmful levels. Winds speed this mixing, as do upward air currents, which carry pollutants aloft to mix into the upper atmosphere. A condition can arise, however, in which the air layers are very stable and vertical mixing is halted. The pollutants, instead of mixing into the upper layers of the atmosphere, are restricted to the layer of air close to the ground. There the pollutants accumulate to unhealthy levels. In an inversion, a common occurrence in the autumn, a layer of colder air sits beneath a layer of warmer

FIGURE 15-2 Urban Smog. The buildings in New York City fade into a haze of pollution. In the city itself, respiratory problems are likely to be increasing. (*Photo:* National Archives, Documerica Collection)

air. In this situation, smoke will be quickly cooled and will not rise up to the warmer air layer above it. Pollutants collect below the "lid" of warmer air.

Inversions commonly form during the cold, clear nights of fall (Figure 15-3). During the night the earth radiates stored heat into space. As the earth cools, it chills the layer of air next to the surface. By morning a temperature inversion exists: Cold air lies close to the earth, while the air above is still fairly warm. Once the sun rises, the earth's surface is warmed again, and so the layer of air next to the surface is warmed as well. The inversion then disappears as the day advances. These so-called surface inversions tend to be shallow except where there are valleys. Here, the cold air drains off the uplands during the night, forming deeper inversions that may be slow to disappear.

FIGURE 15-3 Autumn in the Country. The sunny days of fall are beautiful to behold in rural areas. In urban areas, however, these same days can create air pollution episodes. If the air over a city remains windless for too many days, the pollutants from autos, industries, homes, and shops may become dangerously concentrated, to the point at which human health can be harmed. (*Photo:* Wilbrecht, USDA—Fish and Wildlife Services)

Once the inversion is formed, pollutants begin to accumulate in the cooler lower layer. Autos carrying people to work and trucks carrying goods discharge carbon monoxide, nitrogen oxides, and hydrocarbons to the atmosphere. Industrial activities discharge these contaminants plus sulfur oxides and particulate matter. As the sun begins to warm the lower air, vertical thermal currents are set in motion, rising until their temperature has reached that of the surrounding air. However, if the cold layer is thick and extends far above the surface of the earth, the currents may be unable to escape into the upper air. Thus, the concentrations of contaminants increase through the day because little pollution escapes. Sometimes these conditions are repeated for several days, and the level of contaminants becomes increasingly dangerous. Strong winds are needed to break up the cool lower layer. Sometimes they arrive in time; sometimes, as in Donora in October 1948, they do not.

It is important to note that the emissions leading to and continuing during an episode are occurring at no more than the normal rate. Hence, if an episode happens once in a particular city, the potential exists for an episode to happen again when weather conditions that trap pollutants recur. The potential for an episode will decrease only if some positive action is taken to reduce the output of pollutants.

What are the air pollutants that so injure health? Where do they come from? How do they harm people? How can we control them? In the sections that follow we will describe the various air pollutants, their origins, their effects, and the methods to decrease their discharges.

SULFUR DIOXIDE AND PARTICLES

Sulfur Dioxide

Sulfur in coal and oil is oxidized when these fuels are burned; the result is **sulfur oxides.** Coal, by far the greatest source of sulfur oxides, averages about 2.5 pounds of sulfur in every 100 pounds of coal. Oil has far less sulfur, and refining removes most sulfur from gasoline, making the automobile a minor player in sulfur oxide pollution. Burning coal in electric power plants produces about 80%–85% of the annual emissions of sulfur oxides. The smelting of copper, nickel, and lead ores and the refining industries are other large contributors of sulfur oxides.

The oxidation of sulfur produces almost exclusively sulfur dioxide. The solution of sulfur dioxide in water vapor and further oxidation produce sulfurous and sulfuric acids. Oxides of calcium and iron are also formed in coal combustion. The oxides react with the sulfurous and sulfuric acids to produce such acidic particles as calcium sulfite and calcium sulfate.

The acid and acid particles attack marble and mortar and corrode such metals as copper, steel, and aluminum. Needles and leaves of ornamental and agricultural plants are injured by elevated levels of sulfur oxides in the atmosphere. High levels of sulfur oxides have been linked to respiratory illness and to deaths in such cities as New York, Osaka, and London. In the infamous London Fog of 1952, sulfur oxides reached 10 times the U.S. daily standard for the air pollutant. In the 1962 air pollution episode in New York and in Ankara's 1982 air pollution episode, sulfur oxides reached 7 times the standard.

Emissions of sulfur oxides can be reduced by using a low-sulfur coal or by removing sulfur from coal prior to burning. A water washing removes sulfur that is bound to iron in coal, but a chemical washing process is needed to remove the sulfur bound to the carbon in coal. Several chemical processes to remove sulfur and ash from coal are under development and are very promising.

Emissions of sulfur oxides in stack gases can also be reduced by the use of **scrubbers,** processes that use chemical reactions to remove sulfur dioxide from the combustion gases. More than 50 different kinds of scrubbers have been developed, but the process system in use most is the lime-limestone wet scrubber. The lime-limestone scrubber is an accepted technology already in use on several hundred coal-fired power plants in the United States. The scrubber removes the sulfur oxides as a calcium sulfate/calcium sulfite sludge.

New combustion processes—that is, new ways to burn coal—are already being tested on a number of power plants as a means to reduce sulfur dioxide emissions. The most promising of these are sorbent injection and fluidized-bed combustion, both of which remove sulfur oxides as dry particles of calcium sulfate/calcium sulfite. Fluidized-bed combustion of coal proceeds at a lower temperature than conventional coal combustion and, as a consequence, produces lower emissions of nitrogen oxides as well as decreased quantities of sulfur dioxide.

Although total sulfur dioxide emissions have barely declined over the last several decades, most urban areas now meet air quality standards for sulfur dioxide. The improvement in air quality occurred as old power plants in urban areas shut down and were replaced by new coal-fired power plants in rural areas. In addition, the power plants installed tall stacks in order to discharge sulfur oxides high up in the atmosphere, thereby decreasing ground-level concentrations. Simply put, sulfur oxides were being put "somewhere else"—namely mountain lakes and evergreen forests. From ground-level pollution, we created acid rain (Chapter 16).

Particles

Particulate matter, or **particles,** are not of a single chemical type. Instead, numerous solid and liquid compounds are dispersed in the air from transportation, fuel combustion, industrial processes, solid waste disposal, and other activities.

The burning of coal produces solid particles in the air—not only ash particles (calcium silicates) and carbon particles, but also calcium and iron oxides. The sulfuric acid droplets themselves are particles derived from the oxidation of sulfur dioxide and solution in water vapor. Although the quantity of particles derived from coal burning is enormous, a large proportion of the particles is removed from the stack gases and is never emitted. Only a small amount of ash comes from the burning of oil.

The incomplete burning of gasoline and diesel fuel produces liquid hydrocarbon droplets in the air; these are particles. Photochemical, or sunlight-stimulated, reactions between nitrogen oxides and hydrocarbons also produce liquid organic substances that are scattered as tiny droplets in the air. The term *smog* has been coined to describe the resulting fog of photochemical particles evident in such automobile-strangled cities as Los Angeles. The grinding and spraying that accompany construction are also sources of particles. Finally, the incineration of solid wastes may in some cities be a significant source of particles.

Particles may settle on surfaces, leading to a dirty gray appearance. Particles may cause corrosion by acting as the centers from which corrosion spreads. Sulfuric acid droplets may damage plant tissue. Compounds from photochemical reactions produce a burn on the leaves of many vegetables. Particles may also act as nuclei upon which water vapor condenses. As a consequence, prolonged periods of fog may result from high levels of particles in the air.

Particle emissions can be controlled by use of the **electrostatic precipitator.** The device has been employed since the 1920s and is now utilized at nearly 1,000 electric power plants in the United States. The device can attain efficiencies of particle collection up to 99% and can operate with low maintenance while drawing little electric power (Figure 15-4).

An alternative to the electrostatic precipitator is the **baghouse,** which is composed of fabric bags to capture the fly ash. The principle of the baghouse is simple: It is a very large vacuum cleaner. Air is drawn up through the bags, whose fine-weave material traps particles. Only clean air exits. The units have impressive efficiency, over 99%. Utilities are now convinced that the baghouse rivals the electrostatic precipitator in efficiency, reliability, and cost. The baghouse can also be used to capture sulfur oxides. Injection of limestone into the combustion gases can be used to convert gaseous sulfur dioxide to particles, and these particles can be removed cost-effectively by the baghouse.

The Deadly Duo of Particles and Sulfur Oxides

In terms of human health, high levels of both sulfur oxides and particles have been measured during some of the worst air pollution episodes recorded. In the incident in the Meuse Valley of Belgium in 1930, in the tragedy at Donora, Pennsylvania, in 1948, and in the London fog of 1952—in all these events, sulfur oxides and particles were both present

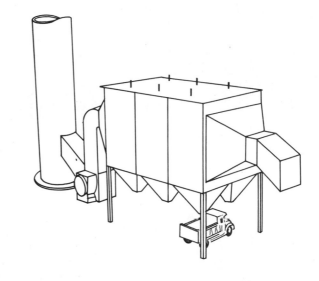

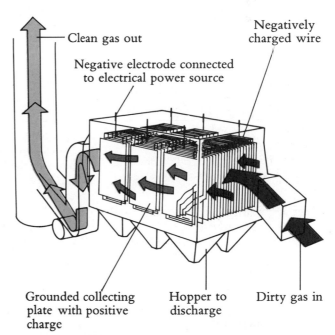

FIGURE 15-4 Electrostatic Precipitator. Dirty air flows between negatively charged wires and grounded metal collecting plates. The particles in the flowing air become charged and are then attracted to the plates, which hold the accumulated dust until it is periodically knocked into hoppers. The clean air is then pumped out through the stack. (*Source:* Adapted from *Controlling Air Pollution*, American Lung Association, 1974)

Controversy 15-1

Should Society Protect the Unhealthy from Air Pollution?

Would it not be better to close the EPA and buy each person sensitive to carbon monoxide a condominimum in Key West?

Paul MacAvoy, professor of economics, Yale University

Should the entire populace assume the burden of preventing aggravation of a disease in a relatively small group of people who unfortunately live in large cities?

R. Jeffrey Smith

In setting standards . . . we must be concerned with the health effects on the most vulnerable in our population rather than upon the healthy groups.

Edmund Muskie, U.S. Senator from Maine

For over a decade, we have sought to protect particularly sensitive citizens, such as children, the aged and asth- *matics, from polluted air. I don't think the American people would stand for abandoning these sensitive populations by misguided use of cost/benefit analyses. . . . It is useless to pretend that some kind of ultilitarian calculus can give us the answers to what are essentially moral and political questions.*

Henry Waxman, U.S. House of Representatives

As originally written, the Clean Air Act required the Environmental Protection Agency to set air-quality standards at levels that would protect the public health "with an adequate margin of safety." The *public health* meant not only the health of the general population but the health of those most susceptible to damage from air pollutants. Those with chronic respiratory disease, such as emphysema and asthma, and those with heart conditions, such as angina, are among the people most susceptible to ill effects from air pollutants. Children, because their rate of breathing is more rapid than that of adults, in some cases show greater susceptibility to air pollutants. The original Clean Air Act assumed that protection of the most sensitive segment of the population was a reasonable proposition, but this assumption has been challenged by industry and economists, who claim some substances are too expensive to control. The National Commission on Air Quality does not agree with industry about costs, but notes that:

at high concentrations. These pollutants appeared together because they had a common source: the burning of coal. Not only is coal burned for electric power generation, but before World War II, it was used widely to heat homes and buildings in the United States.

For a time, we did not understand why the problem in these pollution episodes was always sulfur oxides *plus* particles. We now understand that sulfur dioxide quickly dissolves in the water droplets that have condensed around airborne particles, thereby producing a highly acid, highly corrosive mist. It is this acid mist that is responsible for so much damage to life and health.

This is not to say that particles alone do not have an effect on human health. The frequency of respiratory infections such as colds and bronchitis is seen to increase as particle levels increase. Furthermore, at high concentrations of particles, deaths in excess of the number expected for the time of year have been seen to occur. Both these health effects and deaths fall most heavily on the health-impaired, many of whom are elderly. People in good health experience fewer effects. Controversy

"The costs of meeting primary air-quality standards are best taken into account in determining what control programs should be implemented in specific areas of the country, not in establishing a national air quality standard to protect public health" (*To Breathe Clean Air,* 1981).

Paul MacAvoy (1981) suggests that carbon monoxide control is so costly that the solution is to relocate people sensitive to carbon monoxide. It is now clear that carbon monoxide can aggravate angina pectoris, an extremely common form of heart disease, at levels in the air not far above the air-quality standard. MacAvoy suggests that it costs too much to protect people with angina. His solution is a restatement of the sentiment of conservative economists: "Let them vote with their feet," which translated means "If they can't handle poor air quality from a health standpoint, they should move."

There are two issues here in suggesting that people move if they don't like air quality. The first is the cost of moving. Do all people have the money to move? Are there social costs as well as economic costs involved in moving? What are the social costs? Are the social costs higher to the elderly? The second issue is the choice of where to move. An example of the risks in choosing a destination occurred in a family we know. Because of his heart condition, the father moved to an area noted for clean air. But in 15 years Tucson, Arizona, went from being one of the cleanest cities to one of the most polluted in the nation. If pollution is not controlled everywhere—if the most susceptible are not protected everywhere—there may well be no safe place to move.

Does anyone in your family have angina? Do you think they need to be protected by safe air quality? Would they consider moving? If they would consider it,

is their destination safe both today and in the future?

Two other common diseases that make people susceptible to poor air quality are emphysema and asthma. Sulfur dioxide has a particular impact on people with these lung conditions. Asthma is a disease that often begins in childhood. What bearing does this have on MacAvoy's suggestion that afflicted people move? Do you think we should protect the most vulnerable in our population?

Sources: Paul MacAvoy, quoted in *Science, 212* (June 12, 1981), 1251; R. Jeffrey Smith, quoted in *Science, 212* (June 12, 1981), 1251; Edmund Muskie, "Air Pollution, 1970." Part I, Hearings before the Subcommittee on Air and Water Pollution of the Committee on Public Works, U.S. Senate, March 16, 17, 18, 1970, p. 74; Henry Waxman, Joint Hearing before the U.S. Senate Committee on Environment and Public Works and the U.S. House of Representatives Committee on Energy and Commerce, March 2, 1981, p. 59; and *To Breath Clean Air,* Report of the National Commission on Air Quality, 1981, p. 8.

15-1 examines the question of whether we should control air pollution to protect the portion of the population in poor health.

CARBON MONOXIDE AND PHOTOCHEMICAL AIR POLLUTANTS

Carbon Monoxide

In most cities, autos are responsible for 90% of the carbon monoxide emissions. The carbon monoxide results when the carbon from gasoline is only partly oxidized (Figure 15-5). Cigarette smoke also contains carbon monoxide gas. When the gas is inhaled, no matter the source, it ties up hemoglobin in the bloodstream, decreasing the amount of oxygen that can be carried to the cells. A moderate smoker, based on his or her hemoglobin out of service due to carbon monoxide, is living in the equivalent of an air pollution emergency.

Since 1971, controls on automobiles, especially the catalytic converter, have been decreasing carbon monoxide emissions per vehicle mile. The con-

FIGURE 15-5 What We Are Up Against in Air Pollution Control. Although numerous air pollution control technologies have been added to the auto since 1967, air pollution from cars has not been brought under control. While the technologies have been dramatically effective at reducing pollutants emitted from the individual vehicle, the number of vehicles and the distances they travel have more than doubled since controls were first applied, bringing progress at a painfully slow pace. (*Source:* Graph courtesy of the U.S. Environmental Protection Agency)

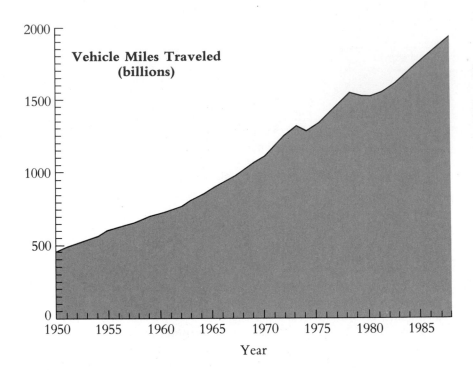

verter oxidizes the carbon monoxide to carbon dioxide. Unfortunately, the increasing number of vehicles in the United States and the increased travel per vehicle have doubled annual vehicle miles in the last two decades, to a large extent undoing the technical progress in control. In 1990 the Environmental Protection Agency (EPA) estimated that a third of the nation's population (78 million people) still lived in areas where the carbon monoxide standard was exceeded. Los Angeles had the worst record, with concentrations violating the carbon monoxide standard on nearly 20% of the days in 1990.

At low levels of carbon monoxide in the air (resulting in 2%–5% of hemoglobin out of service), the perception of light brightness is hampered and the capability to add columns of numbers correctly decreases. With only 3% of their hemoglobin tied up, individuals with angina experienced more rapid onset of heart pain when they exercised.

Nitrogen Oxides and Photochemical Pollutants

Another class of air pollutants, the oxides of nitrogen, also stem from combustion of fossil fuels. Both the nitrogen and oxygen in nitrogen oxides are almost entirely from the air, rather than the fuel. About 40% of annual emissions are from gasoline combustion, and 30% are from fuel combustion at electric power plants (Figure 15-6). Hydrocarbons, another air pollutant, stem principally from automobiles (36%) and from industrial processes (35%). The reactions of nitrogen oxides and hydrocarbons in the presence of sunlight produce the photochemical air pollutants, of which the most prominent is ozone. Ozone is called an *oxidant* because of its strong oxidizing power.

Although most of the nitrogen oxides (90%) are produced as nitric oxide (one nitrogen atom and one oxygen atom), an additional oxidation step quickly yields nitrogen dioxide (one nitrogen and two oxygen atoms). Nitrogen dioxide in the atmosphere at levels above the air-quality standard increases the number of cases of respiratory disease, such as colds and bronchitis, probably by making people more susceptible to the pathogens that cause the disease. People with chronic (continuing) respiratory diseases, such as emphysema and asthma, are more likely to have serious complications (for

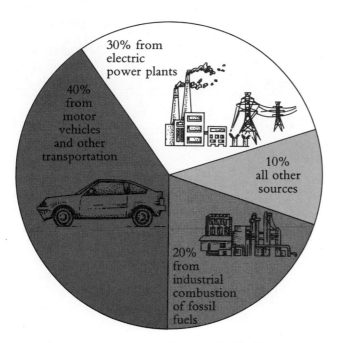

FIGURE 15-6 Sources of Nitrogen Oxide Emissions. (Data from *To Breathe Clean Air,* National Commission on Air Quality, 1981)

30% from electric power plants

40% from motor vehicles and other transportation

10% all other sources

20% from industrial combustion of fossil fuels

example, pneumonia) because of exposure to nitrogen dioxide.

Photochemical pollutants in the air have been found to cause asthmatics to have more frequent attacks—even at ozone levels only 25% above the current air-quality standard. Asthmatics constitute 3%–5% of the nation's population. Ozone damage to both commercial and ornamental plants is extensive (in the billions of dollars); such damage would continue even if ozone levels were brought to the current ozone standards.

Modifications of automobile engines and of exhaust systems have been utilized to reduce emissions of nitrogen oxides and hydrocarbons as well as levels of photochemical oxidants. The catalyst system oxidizes unburned hydrocarbons to carbon dioxide and to water vapor and converts nitrogen oxides back to nitrogen gas, a relatively unreactive form. Changes in industrial combustion such as at coal-fired power plants (for example, decreased air intake) are also being used to decrease nitrogen oxide emissions. Even with these changes that reduce in-

dividual emissions, increases in coal combustion at electric plants and increased vehicle miles have maintained total annual emissions of nitrogen oxides and hydrocarbons at nearly steady levels. As a consequence, cities are having trouble meeting the ozone standards. Eastern cities are having almost as much difficulty meeting the ozone standard as are metropolitan areas in California, the birthplace of photochemical smog. How widespread are violations of the ozone standard? In 1990 the EPA estimated that 133 million people lived in areas where the ozone standard was exceeded. These places ranged from rural counties in Maine to congested major metropolitan areas. The Los Angeles Basin had far and away the worst ozone air quality, violating the standard on nearly one-third of the days in a year (See Table 15-1).

The quest for clean air brought us the catalytic converter, but the converter is poisoned by the lead that has been in gasoline. As a consequence of this effect, lead, an anti-knock additive that has been in gasoline for many years, is finally being removed. All lead will be out of gasoline by 1992. Lead compounds in the air from the combustion of leaded gasoline had been increasing the level of lead in people's bloodstreams. Children are at special risk of elevated lead levels because of greater sensitivity and greater exposure. Prior to 1973, lead had been a major component of paint. Although it is now banned from paint, children living in decaying, inner city neighborhoods are often exposed to peeling paint. Lead poisoning results when small children sample their environment by eating loose chips of paint. Lead in the air increases lead levels in these children, making poisoning more likely. Although lead is no longer in gasoline or paint, the peeling paint remains and the problem of childhood lead poisoning continues.

AIR POLLUTION IN THE WORLD'S CITIES

The United States, Canada, Japan, and many of the nations of Western Europe have brought their air pollution under some control or at least have stabilized it through the application of new fuels or new technology. In contrast, most of the cities in

TABLE 15-1 The Average Number of Days per Year That the Ozone Standard Is Violated, by City (1987–1989)

City Area	Days below Air-Quality Standard	City Area	Days below Air-Quality Standard
Los Angeles–Anaheim–Riverside, Calif.	137.5	Parkerburg-Marietta, W. Va.–Ohio	7.2
Bakersfield, Calif.	44.2	Greensboro–Winston Salem–High Point, N.C.	7.2
Fresno, Calif.	24.3	Pittsburgh, Penn.	7.0
New York, N.Y.–N.J.–Conn.	17.4	Springfield, Mass.	6.7
Sacramento, Calif.	15.8	Providence, R.I.–Mass.	6.4
Chicago, Ill.–Ind.–Wis.	13.0	St. Louis, Mo.–Ill.	6.2
San Diego, Calif.	12.3	Portland, Me.	6.1
Houston–Galveston–Brazoria, Tex.	12.2	Nashville, Tenn.	5.6
Knox County, Me.	11.1	Huntington–Ashland, W. Va.–Ky.–Ohio	5.5
Baltimore, Md.	10.7	Kewaunee County, Wis.	5.5
Boston, Mass.	10.0	Cincinnati, Ohio–Ky.–Ind.	5.4
Milwaukee-Racine, Wis.	9.8	Portsmouth–Dover–Rochester, N.H.–Maine	5.3
Muskegon, Mich.	9.4	Worcester, Mass.	5.2
Atlanta, Ga.	9.3	Cleveland–Akron–Lorain, Ohio	5.2
Sheboygan, Wis.	9.1	Washington, D.C.–Md.–Va.	4.9
Philadelphia, Penn.–N.J.–Del.	8.8		
Hartford, Conn.	7.9		
El Paso, Tex.	7.9		
Modesto, Calif.	7.6		

Source: EPA, 1990.

the rest of the world are reeling from the effects of the smoke and fumes from power plants, factories, vehicles, and even from homes.

In the historic city of Cracow, Poland, air pollution threatens the health of people and the city's historic structures. Respiratory ailments including asthma are tragically common among children because of the presence of high levels of sulfur dioxide in the air. The sulfur oxides are from coal burning at the nearby Lenin Steel Works at Nova Huta and from power plants in Czechoslovakia some 60 miles (100 km) away. The steel works at Nova Huta, built after World War II, was patterned after steel works built in Pittsburgh, Pennsylvania, in the

1930s. Though its model is gone, the Lenin Steel Works continues in operation. The sulfur oxides and particles from the steel works injure not only health but also the architectural treasures of the city. At risk are the royal castle of the King of Poland, which dates from the eleventh century, the university where the astronomer Copernicus studied, the Santa Maria Cathedral and some 70 other churches, and numerous historic buildings. Though the role of the steel works in air pollution is clear, the steel plant employs 30,000 people and cannot quickly be replaced with a more modern plant. Yet 3 million tourists visit historic Cracow each year, many to witness its wonderful history in stone. The

FIGURE 15-7 Cairo Cityscape. Cairo's air pollution problems typify those of cities in developing nations. The city is strangled with traffic and choked with fumes from innumerable old cars and buses. The sun is often not visible through the haze of pollution that envelops the city. (*Photo:* UN/B. Wolff)

dilemma is acute; somehow the city must protect jobs, protect health, and preserve its history, and it must do it all on a shoestring.

Cracow's air pollution resembles that of many other cities of Eastern Europe in that high sulfur coal and/or lignite are the primary sources of its pollution. Cities such as Prague (Czechoslovakia), Budapest (Hungary), Bucharest (Romania), and Warsaw (Poland), are also plagued by severe levels of sulfur dioxide and particulate matter in the air. These are the same pollutants that were responsible for the very first of the recorded air pollution episodes in the cities of North America and in London. Why are sulfur oxides and particle levels so terrible in these Eastern European cities? First, there are the coal-burning power plants, then there are the coal-burning steel plants, and then there are the refineries that coax the sulfur from oil and burn the sulfur. Finally, even the homes burn coal for warmth. Coal, an industrial and domestic necessity of these countries' economies, has a violent effect on their environment.

Athens, Greece, also experiences severe sulfur dioxide pollution. In response to the risk to the historic landmarks of Grecian culture, the government has taken steps to decrease sulfur emissions from industry and from heating.

Ankara, Turkey, is likewise beset by fearsome levels of sulfur dioxide and particulate matter. Its 1982 air pollution episode was nearly as severe as the London Fog that claimed 4,000 lives in 1952. The burning of high-sulfur fuel oil and high-sulfur lignite is the primary cause of Ankara's fierce air pollution burden. Cairo, Egypt, also suffers from a choking level of air pollution from its ancient cars and trucks and its older industries (Figure 15-7).

The great industrial cities of China are enduring the effects of an economy that depends on coal. The Chinese capital of Beijing and the cities of Shenyang and Xian regularly experience some of the world's worst recorded levels of sulfur dioxide. Only Tehran, Iran, and Seoul, South Korea, are known to compare to these cities in the frequency of high levels of sulfur dioxide.

When concentrations of particulate matter are considered, the same Chinese cities again top the list of the world's most polluted cities. Tehran, in addition to its burden of sulfur dioxide, is also one of the world's most polluted cities in terms of particles. The Indian cities of Bombay, Calcutta, and Delhi join the list here, as do Bangkok, Thailand, and Jakarta, Indonesia. The particle levels in Chinese cities may be influenced by windblown dust because parts of China have a fragile soil that the wind erodes easily. However, since both sulfur dioxide and particles stem to a large degree from coal burning and since coal burning in China is extensive, the high levels of sulfur dioxide also noted in these cities suggest that, even if the influence of windblown dust were absent, particle levels would still be very high.

In contrast to the cities of Eastern Europe and China where automobiles have not yet taken over, many of the cities in developing nations suffer from the air pollutants associated with the automobile. In the developing countries of Asia and South America, vehicle ownership has more than doubled since 1979. Mexico City is reputed to be the city with the world's dirtiest air. Its 20 million people drive 3 million cars and work in 36,000 factories. The ozone levels, nitrogen oxide levels, carbon monoxide concentrations, and lead emissions have caused such serious illnesses that new regulations are limiting cars from being driven at least one day of the week. Seven out of 10 infants in Mexico City whose blood lead levels have been examined have lead concentrations exceeding the World Health Organizations' blood lead standards. Birds have been reported to fall dead or dying from the skies of the city.

Although the cities of Western Europe have made significant progress in cleansing the air of sulfur dioxide and particles, they are failing to control the pollutants that contribute to photochemical air pollution—the oxides of nitrogen and hydrocarbons. The reason is that automobile use is growing. London, Frankfurt, Berlin, Copenhagen, Zurich, Vienna, and Brussels are among the cities of Western Europe where levels of nitrogen dioxide, one of the photochemical pollutants, are high. In most of these cities, though, carbon monoxide levels are declining because of some control technology that has been placed on automobiles.

As bad as the air is in the cities of the world, in the huts in the rural areas of the developing world, it is worse. Primitive stick fires in mud huts and in tar-paper shacks produce copious fumes that can keep a family sick and coughing through the winter. Thus, air pollution reaches even into remote areas.

In all, the cities of the world have far to go in controlling air pollution. The United States switched from coal home heating in the late 1940s and began shifting its coal-fired power plants out of cities in the 1960s. Home heating with coal was phased out in England in the 1950s and 1960s—after the disastrous London Fog. A similar pattern was followed in Western Europe. Scrubbers to remove sulfur oxides from the stack gases of coal-fired power plants began to be installed in the late 1970s and early 1980s in the United States and in Japan. Electrostatic precipitators had already been in wide use in the United States since at least the 1950s.

Serious efforts at control of pollution from the automobile began in the 1970s in the United States and Japan and in the late 1980s in Western Europe. Efforts at control are clearly linked to the severity of pollution and to the economic prosperity of the nation in which the pollution occurs. The cities of Eastern Europe and other cities where coal is widely used are facing the problems faced in the industrialized countries 20 or more years ago. Where automobile use grows unchecked and no control devices are on vehicles, such as in Mexico City, levels of photochemical pollutants and carbon monoxide are growing as well. Where control devices are in use, some stabilization in emissions has occurred despite traffic growth. The lesson is that living together creates air pollution problems that

TABLE 15-2 Pollutant Standards Index and Air-Quality Categories

Index Value	Air-Quality Classification	Pollutant Levels					Air Quality Regarded as
		Particulate Matter (24-hour), Micrograms per Cubic Meter	Sulfur Dioxide (24-hour), Micrograms per Cubic Meter	Carbon Monoxide (8-hour), Milligrams per Cubic Meter	Ozone (1-hour), Micrograms per Cubic Meter	Nitrogen Dioxide (1-hour), Micrograms per Cubic Meter	
500	Significant Harm	1000	2620	57.5	1200	3750	
400	Emergency	875	2100	46.0	1000	3000	Hazardous
300	Warning	625	1600	34.0	800	2260	
							Very unhealthful
200	Alert	375	800	17.0	400	1130	
							Unhealthful
100	NAAQS	250	365	10.0	235	No short-term standard for nitrogen dioxide	
							Moderate
50	50% of NAAQS	75[a]	80[a]	5.0	180		
							Good
0		0	0	0	0		

Source: Pilot National Environmental Profile, 1977, U.S. Environmental Protection Agency, October 1980.

[a] Annual primary NAAQS (National Ambient Air Quality Standard).

Note: An Alert, Warning, or Emergency is declared when any one of the pollutants exceeds the appropriate value, but none exceeds the value listed in the next more serious category.

technology can help some, but technology cannot cure these problems when the growth in population, in vehicle numbers, and in industrial activity is rapid.

POLLUTANT STANDARDS INDEX AND SUMMARY OF STANDARDS

The Pollutant Standards Index is a means by which the general public is informed of air quality. A radio or television announcer may say that the state health department has declared air quality is "moderate," or that air quality is "good," or perhaps "unhealth-

ful." *Moderate* air quality means that one or more of the pollutants exceed 50% of its air-quality standard, but no pollutant exceeds 100% of its air-quality standard. *Good* air quality, on the other hand, means that none of the pollutants exceeds 50% of its air-quality standard. The benchmarks for air quality are indicated in the accompanying chart (Table 15-2).

When one or more pollutants exceed 100% of their air-quality standards, but none exceeds the respective alert level, the air is regarded as *unhealthful*. During intervals when the air is unhealthful, persons with existing heart or lung disease should reduce exertion and outdoor activity. Dur-

Towards a Sustainable Society

Fighting "Environmental Racism"
by Richard Moore

Richard Moore is Co-Director and a founding member of SouthWest Organizing Project (SWOP). He has worked for 25 years as a community activist and organizer. Much of his work is devoted to local leadership development.

Race, poverty, and the environment are increasingly recognized as interlocking issues. Low-income communities and especially people of color are inordinately impacted by toxic pollution. Children, the elderly, and women—especially women of color—are paying the highest price from pollution as a result of increased work and health problems and economic devastation.

The military, industry, agribusiness, and government at all levels are the major polluters in poor communities. The harmful social,

economic, and cultural effects include loss of resources such as clean water, land, and air. For indigenous peoples, contamination of traditional holy sites leads to the loss of cultural and religious expression and freedom. Workplace hazards and environmental degradation impact severely on human health, on the job and in the community.

- Navajo teenagers have organ cancer 17 times the national average. Uranium spills from mining activities on Navajo land have contaminated their water, air, and soil. Another indigenous people, the Havasupai of the Grand Canyon, fear the same kind of contamination in their area and have been resisting the permitting of United Nuclear Corp. by the U.S. Forester General to mine uranium on their sacred lands.
- Although the dangers of lead poisoning are well documented, children in older urban areas throughout the United States still live with lead-based paint on their walls. Studies done at the University of Pittsburgh conclude that over 900,000 families live in housing projects with lead-based paint.

This is environmental racism. How can we combat it?

- There is a need for activists and organizations to work together to broaden regional strategies and perspectives on environmental degradation and other social, racial, and economic justice issues.
- We must recognize that a strong and viable regional effort will strengthen the local work of our organizations and further empower us to pursue campaigns of regional and national significance.
- There is a need for people of color to assist one another in, and take the leadership of, efforts addressing the poisoning of communities of color.
- We must work towards training and leadership development efforts relevant to the history and cultures of the Southwest.
- We must recognize the inherent relationship between economic and environmental issues and the need to strengthen work that draws the links in practice between the two.

Now is the time that we must come together to build a truly multi-racial movement that addresses toxic issues as a part of a broad agenda for social and economic justice, one that is fully inclusive of people of color.

TABLE 15-3 Primary (Public Health) Standards for Air Quality (As of 1990)

Pollutant	Time Period of Standard[a]	Maximum Permissible Concentration	Equivalent Nonmetric Concentration[c]
Suspended particles	Annual geometric mean[b]	75 micrograms per cubic meter	—
	Maximum 24-hour concentration	260 micrograms per cubic meter	—
Sulfur oxides	Average annual concentration	80 micrograms per cubic meter	.03 ppm
	Maximum 24-hour concentration	365 micrograms per cubic meter	.14 ppm
Carbon monoxide	Maximum 8-hour concentration	10 milligrams per cubic meter	9.0 ppm
	Maximum 1-hour concentration	40 milligrams per cubic meter	35.0 ppm
Oxidants/ozone	Maximum 1-hour concentration	240 micrograms per cubic meter	0.12 ppm
Nitrogen dioxide	Average annual concentration	100 micrograms per cubic meter	0.053 ppm
Hydrocarbons	Maximum 3-hour concentration	160 micrograms per cubic meter	

Source: U.S. Environmental Protection Agency.

[a] All standards based on concentrations over 24 hours or less are not to be exceeded more than once a year.
[b] The geometric mean is the antilog of x, where x is the sum of the logarithms of the data divided by the number of data points.
[c] ppm = parts per million

ing such a period, even healthy people show evidence of pollutant irritation.

An *alert* is declared when one or more of the five major pollutants exceeds the value listed in Table 15-2 in the row labeled "Alert," but when none exceeds the values in the row labeled "Warning." During an Alert, the air quality is said to be "very unhealthful." Health scientists advise that those with heart and lung disease *and* those who are elderly should stay indoors and reduce exertion.

A *Warning* is declared if the concentration of one or more of the major pollutants exceeds the appropriate value in the row labeled "Warning," but none exceeds the values in the row labeled "Emergency." Now, in addition to the cautions offered during the Alert, *all* the population should reduce outdoor activity.

An *Emergency* occurs when the concentration of one or more of the pollutants exceeds the appropriate value in the row labeled "Emergency," but none yet exceed the values in the row labeled "Significant Harm." In addition to the previous advice, *all* people should now remain indoors and avoid physical exertion.

Finally, when one or more pollutants exceeds the level associated with significant harm, air quality is at its lowest ebb. Vehicle use may be curtailed by closing all but the most vital government offices and by closing banks, schools, food stores, and the like.

The standards for the major air pollutants are summarized in Table 15-3.

NEW STRATEGIES FOR URBAN AIR POLLUTION CONTROL

In the early 1990s, efforts to cure urban air pollution in the United States underwent a transition. In the 1970s and 1980s, emphasis was placed on modifying gasoline-burning engines and automotive equipment to decrease emissions. Attempts to shift people from cars to public transportation did succeed in this period in those situations where cities were wise enough to build subways and upgrade and expand other transit systems. Nonetheless, in most cities a dramatic growth in automobile numbers and use prevented significant reductions in the emissions of air pollutants. Thus, a transition in the form of the control efforts reflected an awareness that new strategies were sorely needed.

The new strategies included such ideas as a per-car parking tax for cars parking in the city. The parking tax is paid by the industries or employers that attract employees and their cars into the city. Another idea was to fine employers if more than a certain percentage of employees drove their cars to work. In California, these steep fines give employers an incentive to encourage their employees to form ride pools and van pools. As an example, a company might provide a van to an employee who regularly carries other employees to work. These creative ideas may, in fact, ultimately provide the means to clean up urban air. But the penalties may also drive industries away from places like Los Angeles to states not now facing severe air pollution problems, thereby clearing the air but also creating unemployment. Such strategies must be delicately employed.

Not all new strategies focus on the driver; some strategies focus on the car and its fuel. The attention to different automotive fuels may have come about because refiners were already tinkering with automotive fuel, causing in the process a deterioration of air quality. The tinkering began when lead was being phased out of gasoline in the 1970s and 1980s. Lead compounds had been utilized in gasoline to increase effective octane levels, and when lead was being phased out, some adjustment in the gasoline formulation was needed to "beef up" the gasoline. Refiners blended benzene and related organic compounds into their mixtures. Unfortunately, these organics, when they were emitted as part of the unburned fuel, proved to be potent smog formers. That is, they readily underwent the sunlight-stimulated reactions that created the urban air pollutant ozone. Pollutant control measures, namely the reduction in hydrocarbon emissions by the catalytic converter, were thus undone to a very large measure because of the changes in gasoline composition. To correct this situation, the Clean Air Act of 1990 calls for a "reformulation" of gasoline for new cars in the nation's smoggiest cities by 1995. The reformulation must reduce the added ozone-forming pollutants by 15%.

Since gasoline is to be reformulated anyway, it makes sense to consider entirely new automotive fuels. A number of new fuels are being touted as virtual replacements for gasoline. Prime among the new fuels is methanol, a fuel that would require very little engine modifications by car makers.

Methanol, a simple alcohol, can be made from coal, wood, natural gas, or biomass such as corn. The Department of Energy has begun in a modest way to place methanol-fueled vehicles into its fleet to examine their characteristics. The advantage of methanol lies in the fact that much of the organic emissions of methanol-fueled vehicles are unburned methanol itself. Methanol does undergo photochemical reactions that produce the air pollutant ozone, just as the organics from a gasoline-fueled vehicle do. Methanol, though, is less reactive than the organic emissions from the gasoline vehicle, producing for every gram of emissions only one-fifth to one-third of the ozone that gasoline vehicles do. Unfortunately, the remainder of the organic emissions of the methanol vehicle are mostly formaldehyde—a compound that produces substantial ozone through extensive photochemical reactions. Formaldehyde is a suspected carcinogen as well.

Although automakers claim that methanol-powered cars will cause less ozone formation, precisely how much less is not yet known. Carbon monoxide and nitrogen oxide emissions, in fact, may not be reduced much at all. Much research is still needed to substantiate claims of methanol's superiority to gasoline with respect to a diminished contribution to air pollution.

Methanol has some severe disadvantages as well. Methanol-fueled cars are hard to start below 50°F. Also, the fuel is a potential hazard to mechanics and to service station attendants, as it causes skin burns on contact. Further, methanol is so poisonous that only an ounce of methanol, when drunk, can cause blindness or death.

As a consequence of methanol's drawbacks, if methanol is adopted as an automobile fuel, it is likely to appear as a blended fuel, perhaps 85% methanol, 15% gasoline. This experimental fuel is widely referred to as "M85." The gasoline fraction helps the engine to start better at cold temperatures and makes a fuel fire more visible. The gasoline also imparts a bad taste to the motor fuel to discourage possible drinking of the liquid.

Finally, the method chosen to manufacture methanol can be a problem. Using wood as the feedstock for production of methanol would cause new stresses on a resource already under pressure. Using coal means more surface mining and extensive carbon dioxide emissions during methanol manufacture. Using corn could push up the price of this basic foodstuff. Methanol is not in any sense the clear fuel of choice.

Nor is ethanol, methanol's chemical cousin, a fuel of choice. It has been more costly than gasoline, until the oil shocks that temporarily accompanied Iraq's invasion of Kuwait. It, too, would put pressure on corn prices since corn has been a favorite starting point in ethanol manufacture. Reports of ethanol's manufacture from solid wastes might, however, offer hope of a lower price. In Brazil, ethanol for use as a motor fuel is produced from sugar cane.

One alternative fuel that may have promise is compressed natural gas. Unfortunately, from a resource point of view, it is not clear that the United States has sufficient reserves to warrant conversion to cars that run on natural gas. Compressed natural gas, which is really methane, burns quite cleanly with respect to organic emissions. This is because the unburned methane fuel that may be emitted is almost completely unreactive with nitrogen oxides. As a result, the photochemical reactions that produce ozone and smog occur to only a minor extent. But the fuel isn't liquid; new types of filling stations would be needed to dispense it. Further, compressed natural gas needs five times the storage volume as gasoline, requiring either a much bigger vehicle to hold the fuel or a much reduced driving distance between refueling stops. Nonetheless, a number of vehicles fueled by compressed natural gas are already on the road. These experimental efforts by states, by Canada, and by private companies are meant to test the fuel in realistic situations.

And, if you like to dream, you could dream about vehicles fueled by **hydrogen.** The vehicles would have no organic emissions, only water vapor and some nitrogen oxides. Unfortunately, the current cheapest source for hydrogen (which is probably four times the cost of gasoline) is natural gas. We have already pointed out that natural gas is unlikely to be in sufficient supply in the United States to heat our homes and factories *and* to power our vast fleet of cars. Someday, electricity generated by photovoltaic panels will be able to produce hydrogen by electrolysis of water, but that day is not near. The possibility, however, speaks to the importance of renewed and expanded funding of research on photovoltaic solar energy.

But what about electric cars, the ones that operate on storage batteries? Sad to say, the electric car, while it could reduce urban air pollution, must get the electric energy in its storage battery from somewhere. That somewhere will be new electric power plants fired most likely by coal or deriving their energy from nuclear fission. The pollution from coal-fired power plants is severe in terms of sulfur oxides and nitrogen oxides. And nuclear power is a problem in terms of waste disposal. Nuclear energy also produces plutonium, which can be used for atomic weapons. Further, its safety seems impossible to guarantee. Thus, the electric car is not the "white knight" of the environment. Behind its clean exterior are potentially all the old pollutants of 50 years ago.

While we wait for reformulated gasolines and alternative fuels, other actions must be taken. Thus, the Clean Air Act of 1990 calls for a new round of reductions of tailpipe emissions. The 1990 limit on nitrogen oxide emissions is 1.0 gram per mile; by 1996 this limit is reduced to 0.4 gram per mile. The limit is further reduced to 0.2 gram per mile by 2003 if urban smog levels are not abated. At the same time, hydrocarbon emission limits are being tightened—from the current bound of 0.41 grams per mile to 0.25 grams per mile by 1996. Again, should urban smog remain unchecked, the hydrocarbon limit is to be ratcheted down once again, to 0.125 grams per mile.

Because of our need to control urban air pollution, we are now being forced to examine a number of changes in how we use our automobiles and in the improvement of public transportation. Changes may also occur in the fuels that power our vehicles. Gasoline may not remain our primary motor fuel. The future of the automobile's power source is now an open question, just as it was in the first decades of the twentieth century when the steam engine vehicle and the electric auto challenged the internal combustion engine. New possibilities could benefit the environment significantly. Nonetheless, the resistance to change because of an existing infrastructure of engine design and fuel delivery is very great.

SUMMARY

The atmosphere is naturally composed of about 78% nitrogen and 21% oxygen, with trace levels of carbon dioxide, ozone, and argon and variable levels of water vapor. Scientists think that the atmosphere of the primordial earth was originally devoid of oxygen and that photosynthesis is responsible for its current high levels. The lowest level of the atmosphere is the troposphere; the layer above it, in which ozone is disappearing and carbon dioxide accumulating, is the stratosphere.

Air pollution episodes in Donora, Pennsylvania, in New York City, and in London, England, focused people's attention on the growing problem of air pollution after World War II. These episodes, which included numerous deaths, were the result of inversions. These are atmospheric events, common in the autumn, in which a layer of cold air sits beneath a layer of warm air. Normal vertical mixing of the atmosphere is blocked by inversion conditions, causing pollutants from industry and autos emitted at ordinary rates to build up to high concentrations.

The air pollutant sulfur dioxide results when the sulfur in fossil fuels, especially in coal, is oxidized during the combustion process. About 80%–85% of the annual U.S. emissions of sulfur dioxide stems from coal burning. Solution of sulfur dioxide in water and further oxidation produces a corrosive mist of sulfurous and sulfuric acids. The sulfur oxide compounds attack stone, mortar, and metal building materials, damage almost all vegetation, and injure human respiratory health as well. Sulfur can be partially removed from coal by a washing process, decreasing formation of sulfur dioxide. Sulfur dioxide can be removed from stack gases by chemical processes referred to as "scrubbers." New ways to burn coal, such as fluidized-bed combustion, decrease both sulfur dioxide and nitrogen oxides emissions. Ejection of sulfur oxides through tall stacks only places the pollution burden elsewhere.

Particles that pollute the air arise from coal burning, from the incomplete combustion of gasoline, and from industrial processes. The electrostatic precipitator is up to 99% effective in removing particles from stack gases at electric power plants. A promising particle removal device is the baghouse. Particles and sulfur dioxides have both been present at major air pollution episodes, causing illness and death.

The air pollutant carbon monoxide comes largely from the incomplete combustion of motor vehicle gasoline. Inhaled carbon monoxide acts by tying up hemoglobin in the blood, decreasing the oxygen that the hemoglobin can carry from the lungs to the tissues—including to the brain. Smoking also introduces carbon monoxide to the blood; a moderate smoker places himself in the equivalent of an air pollution emergency. The effectiveness of the catalytic converter, which oxidizes carbon monoxide exhaust emissions to carbon dioxide, has been largely undone by a doubling of vehicle miles traveled in the last two decades.

Nitrogen oxides air pollutants are formed when nitrogen from the air is oxidized during fossil fuel combustion. Hydrocarbons are emitted when a portion of gasoline is not burned and from industrial processes. Hydrocarbons and nitrogen oxides react in the presence of sunlight to produce ozone and other smog compounds. These resulting photochemical compounds damage plants and human health. People with chronic respiratory problems, such as asthma and emphysema, are most at risk from photochemical air pollutants. Again, the catalytic converter has been used, this time to reduce automotive emissions of nitrogen oxides and hydrocarbons. And, again, progress has been largely undone by increased vehicle miles, and also by nitrogen oxides emissions from an increasing number of coal-fired power plants.

Lead will be entirely out of gasoline by 1992 because it poisons the catalytic converter. This will decrease the risk of lead poisoning in cities but not eliminate it, because lead-based paint is still peeling from decrepit older homes.

Most of the major cities of the world suffer from air pollution. In the cities of Eastern Europe, such as Prague, Cracow, Warsaw, and Budapest, levels of sulfur dioxide and particles are extremely high because of the burning of high-sulfur coal in industry, for electric power, and in the heating of apartment buildings. Ankara, Turkey, and Athens, Greece, are likewise bedeviled by high levels of sulfur dioxide from coal burning, as are the great cities of China, Tehran in Iran, and Seoul in South Korea. Particles in the air beset the cities of China in addition to sulfur oxides; the cities of the Indian subcontinent and of Southeast Asia are also burdened by high levels of particles in the air. In the cities of South and Central America, the automobile is often the culprit. Mexico City, the world's largest city, reels under the impact of three million cars and thousands of factories without pollution controls. Even the cities of Western Europe are having to face up to a second generation of air pollution. Sulfur dioxide and particles from coal burning are largely defeated, but pollution from the automobile threatens their air quality anew.

New strategies are being suggested to control air pollution in U.S. cities largely because little progress in air pollution control has occurred in our auto-choked cities in the past two decades. These strategies involve economic incentives and penalties to shift people over to public transportation and ride sharing. New fuels are also being considered, especially compressed natural gas and a methanol/gasoline (85%/15%) blend known as M85. It is not clear that we have enough natural gas to power the nation's vehicles, and the impact of M85 on photochemical smog is not yet fully understood. M85 could potentially offer little improvement because of tailpipe formaldehyde emissions. Formaldehyde is a potent smog former. Methanol has other disadvantages including sources that include wood, a resource in short supply, and coal, a source that would generate more surface mining and much pollution. Hydrogen-fueled vehicles depend on an in-

expensive source of hydrogen, which is not yet available. Electric cars require a fuel burned somewhere to generate the needed electric power. If coal is that fuel, the pollution impact is large indeed. Finally, new, tighter tailpipe emission standards will be phased in by the Clean Air Act of 1990.

Questions

1. What is an inversion and how does it influence air pollution?

2. Why does the gas sulfur dioxide cause mist to be acid? How can sulfur oxide emissions be decreased? Are tall stacks an answer? Why?

3. What are three categories of chemical categories of air pollutants caused by the automobile? What fourth category results from the chemical reactions of automotive emissions? Which automotive pollutants affect human health?

4. What does the catalytic converter on automobiles accomplish? Why has urban air quality remained poor despite the use of the converter since 1975?

5. Discuss some of the strategies meant to alter people's habits to bring automotive air pollution under control. Is the alternative fuel M85 the answer to air pollution in cities? Why or why not?

Further Reading

"Air Pollution in Donora, PA." Public Health Bulletin No. 306, U.S. Public Health Service, 1949.
Of historical interest.

American Lung Association. "Controlling Air Pollution." Washington, D.C.: American Lung Association, 1974.
Methods to control air pollution from stationary and mobile sources.

Lovelock, J. E. *Gaia*. Oxford and New York: Oxford University Press, 1979.
The theory of Gaia. Some chemistry knowledge would help the reader.

Office of Technology Assessment. *Replacing Gasoline: Alternative Fuels for Light Duty Vehicles*. Washington, D.C.: U.S. Congress, 1990.

Seinfeld, J. H. *Atmospheric Chemistry and Physics of Air Pollution.* New York: Wiley, 1986.

This book requires a strong knowledge of chemistry.

To Breathe Clean Air. Report of the National Commission on Air Quality, March 1981. (Available from the Superintendent of Documents, Washington, D.C., 20402).

A thorough compilation of regulations, recommendations, and data.

Urban Ozone and the Clean Air Act: Problems and Proposals for Change. Washington, D.C.: Office of Technology Assessment, 1988.

Policy options; chemistry and mathematics are not emphasized.

Waldbott, G. *Health Effects of Environmental Pollutants,* 2nd ed. St. Louis, Mo.: Mosby, 1978.

Well-illustrated, clearly written book with a wealth of information.

Chapter 16

Acid Rain

Acid rain is a reincarnation of a problem that we used to know simply as air pollution. The air pollutants are the sulfur oxides and the nitrogen oxides. We were and are concerned about them as air pollutants primarily because of their effects on human health and because of their impacts on materials and vegetation. Our concern about these substances led us to take control actions in the 1960s and into the present, actions that have decreased their concentrations in the local areas in which they were emitted.

We imagined that it was possible to control these pollutants by ejecting them from tall smokestacks that reached far up into the atmosphere. The theory—chiefly promoted by the electric utilities—was that the pollutants would be mixed into the prevailing winds and transported far away. As a consequence, the theory went, the pollutants would do no damage. It was not a very plausible idea.

The tall stacks on coal-fired power plants and at smelters do disperse sulfur oxides and nitrogen oxides across great distances. Reaching the earth as acidic particles or as an acidic rainfall, these pollutants play havoc with the acidity of natural waters, impair forest growth, and decimate populations of fish, wild fowl, and reptiles. **Acid rain** is the name we give to the long-distance transport and deposition of the sulfur oxides and nitrogen

oxides. This is not a new form of pollution; it is simply the result of our badly flawed efforts to control these sulfur and nitrogen oxides.

Acid rain has no respect for boundaries of states or nations; it is an international pollutant. Britain and northern Europe export acid rain to Sweden, Norway, and Finland. Emissions in the United States contribute to acid rain in Canada, and Canada donates emissions that produce acid rain in the United States. Canada and the United States negotiated for much of the 1980s on how each nation would handle its emissions of sulfur oxides and which nation bore the most responsibility for acid rain. The discussions were rancorous at times. It was clear that the United States was the greater producer of sulfur oxides and that prevailing winds blow toward Canada from the eastern United States. The bone of contention was how much of each nation's production crossed the boundary. Similar arguments have occurred regularly among the European nations.

SOURCES OF ACID RAIN

Acid rain was first noted in Norway and Sweden in the late 1960s. At the 1972 United Nations Conference on the Human Environment held in Stockholm, the Norwegians and Swedes documented the acidification of their lakes and streams and the decline of their fish populations.\It was also in 1972 that Likens and his co-workers published an article in *Environment* describing the dramatic increase in the acidity of rainfall in the northeastern United States.᷄ Since that time, scientists have found acid rain not only in the United States and Scandinavia, but also in Canada, Japan, Taiwan, and most of Europe.᷄

᷄ Sulfur oxides, as we have pointed out, are the result of burning fossil fuels that contain sulfur. Coal is the prime source of sulfur among the fuels, oil is second, and natural gas is a distant third. Nitrogen oxides also result from the burning of fossil fuels, but the main source of the nitrogen is likely to be the air itself, since most fossil fuels are relatively low in nitrogen. High-temperature combustion of all three fossil fuels results in significant emissions of nitrogen oxides.

Oxides of sulfur originate largely from coal-fired power plants and smelters. Oxides of nitrogen also stem largely from power plants, but automobiles are another significant source. Since power plant emissions are often from tall stacks, sulfur oxides and nitrogen oxides from these sources are likely to be caught up in high-elevation winds and undergo long-distance transport. In contrast, ground-level emissions, such as occur from the automobile, are less likely to be captured by high-altitude winds and transported the long distances so characteristic of acid rain.

Sulfur dioxide and nitric oxide, the forms in which the pollutants are first emitted, undergo chemical reactions in the atmosphere. Sulfur dioxide is oxidized to sulfur trioxide, which then dissolves in water droplets to form *sulfuric acid*. Nitric oxide is oxidized to nitrogen dioxide, which dissolves in water droplets to form *nitric acid*. These two acids, as well as salts of these acids, are the culprits in the acid rain story. The more of these acids that are present in the atmosphere, the more acidic the rainwater becomes.

The two acids do not contribute equally to acid rain. In the northeastern United States, about 15%–30% of the acidity is due to nitrates (nitric acid); the remainder is attributed to sulfates (sulfuric acid). In California, in contrast, nitrates are the most com-

mon component of acid rain. Measurements of acid rain in Pasadena, California, showed 57% of the acidity was due to nitric acid and the remainder (43%) due to sulfuric acid. The large portion of acidity due to nitric acid is the result of the high tonnage of nitrogen oxide emissions from automobiles in Southern California.

Acid particles are also deposited dry from the atmosphere onto vegetation and soil. These are typically the sulfates of calcium and magnesium. This **dry deposition** component of acid deposition is increasingly thought to be an important mechanism by which acidity is reaching the earth.

The measure of acidity of water is the number of hydrogen ions per liter of water. Water molecules (H_2O) are normally dissociated into hydrogen ions (H^+) and hydroxyl ions (OH^-). In a sample of pure water we would expect to find about 0.0000001 (one ten-millionth) of the water molecules dissociated into hydrogen ions and hydroxyl ions; in pure water the two ions are present in approximately equal numbers. A solution with equal concentrations of hydrogen and hydroxyl ions is called *neutral*. It is neither acidic (having more hydrogen ions) nor basic (having fewer hydrogen ions).

Rainwater is not pure; it comes in contact with and dissolves carbon dioxide, a natural component of the atmosphere. The solution of carbon dioxide in water produces carbonic acid, a weak acid. The concentration of hydrogen ions relative to the number of water molecules in unpolluted rainwater containing dissolved carbon dioxide would be about 0.000001, or one hydrogen ion per million molecules of water. If you count the zeroes after the decimal, you will see that the hydrogen ion concentration has increased by a factor of 10 due to the solution of carbon dioxide. This level of hydrogen ions is presumed to be the natural condition for rainwater.

The rain falling in New England, on the other hand, has about one hydrogen ion per 10,000 water molecules—a 100-fold increase above the expected concentration. New England has acid rain because the region is downwind from coal-fired power plants in the Ohio valley and from the major industrial centers of the Northeast, where sulfur-bearing fossil fuels are burned in enormous quantities.

Acidity is not commonly measured by the ratio

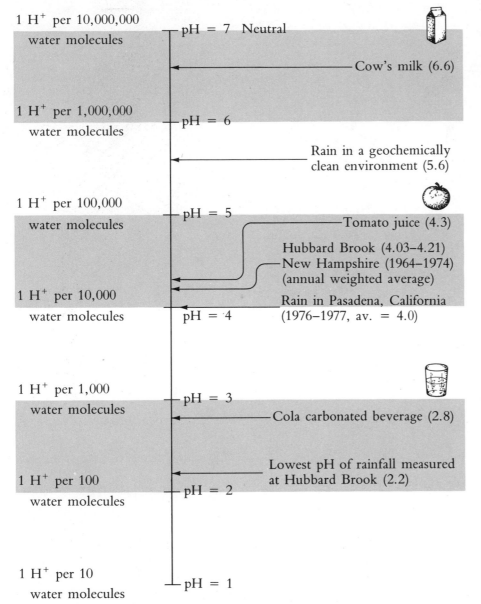

1 H$^+$ per 10,000,000 water molecules — pH = 7 Neutral

Cow's milk (6.6)

1 H$^+$ per 1,000,000 water molecules — pH = 6

Rain in a geochemically clean environment (5.6)

1 H$^+$ per 100,000 water molecules — pH = 5

Tomato juice (4.3)

Hubbard Brook (4.03–4.21)
New Hampshire (1964–1974)
(annual weighted average)

1 H$^+$ per 10,000 water molecules — pH = 4

Rain in Pasadena, California
(1976–1977, av. = 4.0)

1 H$^+$ per 1,000 water molecules — pH = 3

Cola carbonated beverage (2.8)

Lowest pH of rainfall measured at Hubbard Brook (2.2)

1 H$^+$ per 100 water molecules — pH = 2

1 H$^+$ per 10 water molecules — pH = 1

FIGURE 16-1 Relation Between pH and Acidity. The diagram shows the pH levels of some common substances and of rain in different environments. The lower the pH, the more acidic the substance.

of hydrogen ions to water molecules. Instead, it is measured by the negative logarithm of the hydrogen ion concentration, which is called the **pH.** Thus, $-\log_{10} (.0000001) = 7$, and a pH of 7 indicates water that is neither acid nor basic, but neutral. The rain in New England, with about 0.0001 hydrogen ions per molecule of water, has a pH of $-\log_{10} (.0001)$, or 4. In general, the lower the value of pH, the more acidic the water (see Figure 16-1). A pH of 4 for rainwater used to be very unusual.

Now pH values even less than 4 are commonly observed in some areas.

In 1955–56, rainfall in 10 of the eastern states had an average pH value less than a 4.5. In that period, no state had an average pH level less than 4.2. By 1972–73, average pH levels of 4.5 and below were occurring in 19 eastern states, and 3 of these states, New York, Pennsylvania, and Vermont, experienced average rainfall pH levels below 4.2. By 1980, 8 eastern states plus the province of

FIGURE 16-2 Average Rainfall Acidity Levels, United States, 1980. (*Source:* L. Barrie and J. Hales, "The Spatial Distribution of Precipitation Acidity and Major Ion Wet Deposition in North America during 1980." *Tellus, 36B,* 333–335)

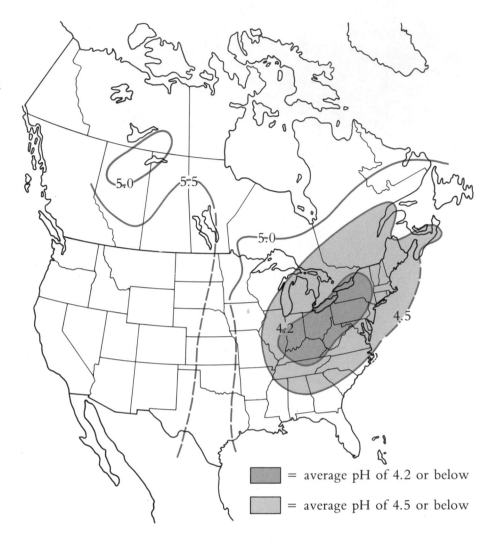

= average pH of 4.2 or below

= average pH of 4.5 or below

Ontario had joined New York, Pennsylvania, and Vermont to make 11 states and 1 province with average pH levels of rainfall below 4.2. Portions of all states east of the Mississippi, with the exception of Florida and Louisiana, are now experiencing pH levels of 4.5 and below (see Figure 16-2).

Europe suffers from the same plague. Extensive coal burning, particularly in the United Kingdom and central Europe, appears to be causing acid rain even more severe than in the United States and Canada. The worst levels of acid rain are occurring in Holland, northern Germany, Denmark, and southern Sweden and southern Norway. Based on the evidence of forest destruction, Poland and Czechoslovakia are devastated by acid rain, but pH levels to prove the connection are not available. Japan, too, is washed by an acid rain (see Figure 16-3).

BIOLOGICAL IMPACTS OF ACID RAIN

Of all the biological impacts of acid rain, the most obvious is the reduction and even elimination of fish populations in lakes that have been made acidic. In Sweden, Norway, and eastern North America,

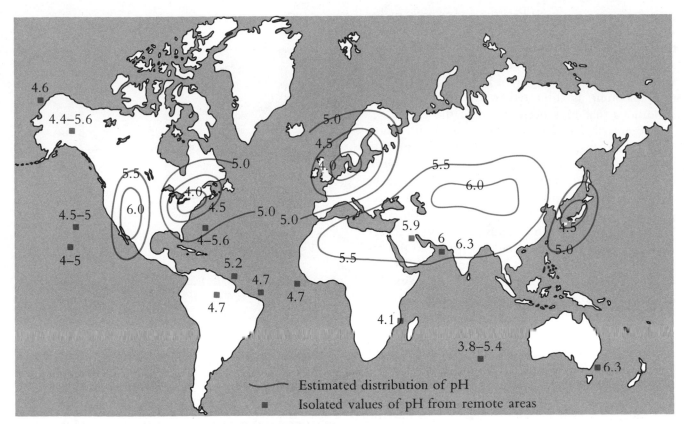

FIGURE 16-3 Geography of Acid Rain in the Early 1980s. (*Source:* Chris Park, "Acid Rain: Trans-Frontier Air Pollution," *Geography Review*, *2*[1] [September 1988])

commercial and sport fishing have suffered as fish populations have declined or disappeared.

In the numerous lakes of the Adirondack Mountains at high elevations (610 m and above), acid waters are now the norm. In 1975, 51% of these lakes had pH values less than 5, and 90% of these low-pH lakes had no fish. In total, 45% of the high-altitude lakes were without fish populations; only 4% of these lakes were without fish in the 1930s. It has also been found that one-third of the more than 2,000 lakes in southern Norway are devoid of fish, a change that has taken place since the 1940s. The Adirondack Lakes Survey Corporation gathered data from 1984–1987 on the acidity of nearly 1,500 lakes and ponds in the Adirondack region; they also noted the presence or absence of fish populations in these same lakes. No fish were

found at 350 of the 1,500 sites surveyed. Of the sites without fish, 75% were found to have pH values less than 5, which is the pH value at which most fish species fail to survive.

It is clear that acid waters have something to do with declining fish populations, but it is generally not the case that mature fish are killed in massive numbers by the acidity in these waters. Instead, it appears that acid waters are preventing fish from reproducing. Female fish may not be able to spawn (release their eggs) in acid waters, and if they are able to do so, eggs and larvae may die at an increased rate. Thus, it is common in lakes that are in the process of becoming more acidic to see no young fish, only mature adults.

Many areas where fish populations have declined due to acid rain have cold winters, with the accumulation of snow. When the snow pack melts, a rush of acid water may enter the lake, turning the lake sharply acid. The melting of the snow pack and the sharp increase in acidity coincide roughly with the spawning activity of fish. Thus, it appears that spawning is subjected to the maximum acid conditions that may occur through the year.

Ocean fish are also affected by acid rain. Biologists are trying to restore the Atlantic salmon to the rivers of eastern North America. These rivers, which empty into the North Atlantic, used to be the spawning grounds of the salmon. With water pollution coming under control, the salmon's restoration seemed possible. Unfortunately, hatchery salmon released in New England rivers do not return in sufficient numbers to their "home" river. As a consequence, the required cycle of spawning, hatching, ocean migration, and return does not occur. Acid runoff in the rivers seems to be the explanation. The characteristic smell of the river seems to be masked by the acid levels, and the salmon return to wrong and perhaps less hospitable streams to spawn.

As fish populations decline, it would be expected that those species that feed on fish, such as the bald eagle, the loon, the osprey, the mink, and the otter, would also see decline.

Acid rain affects other animal species by other routes than through the fish population; the black duck is an example. The black duck is a common bird in the migratory routes of wildfowl over eastern North America, and it has been very popular among hunters. In the past 40 years its population appears to have declined by over 60%. Habitat loss does not explain this dramatic loss adequately, but acid rain does.

Lakes that have gone acid no longer support the species that form the basic diet of the black duck. In acid conditions, aquatic insects such as mayflies and dragonflies die away, as do such gastropods as slugs, snails, and freshwater clams (see Figure 16-4). Eggs of the black duck require calcium from the gastropods; hatchlings need protein from both insects and gastropods. The decline in population has also been seen in mallards, pintails, and canvasback ducks, which, like the black duck, breed in the acidifying waters of eastern North America.

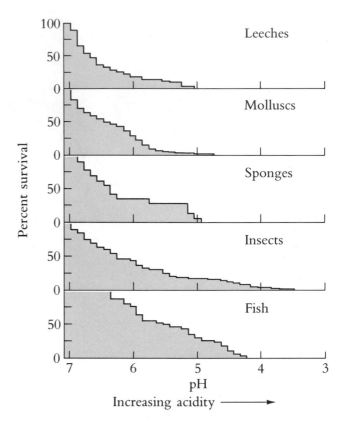

FIGURE 16-4 Decline in Food Organisms of the Wild Duck. (*Source:* J. M. Eilers, G. L. Lien, and R. G. Berg, *Aquatic Organisms in Acidic Environments: A Literature Review*, Technical Bulletin No. 150, Department of Natural Resources, Madison, Wis., 1984)

Scientists predicted that populations of frogs, toads, and salamanders might all be reduced by acid rain. Their prediction was based on the fact that many of these species breed in the temporary pools of water found during spring rains; the pools are likely to be more acid than the lakes because they are supplied only by the acid rainwater. These species were predicted to decline quietly rather than in massive numbers; new young individuals will simply not survive to join the population. Studies of the tiger salamander, which breeds in spring pools in the Rockies, confirm a failure to breed in acid pools. Indeed, biologists have observed a stark decline in frogs, toads, salamanders, and turtles.

Acid rain is thought to have an effect on plants as well as on animals. Changes in plant species where acid rain falls are difficult to detect; long periods of time are thought to be necessary to pick up changes, such as in forest growth. To fill the gap, laboratory experiments were performed in which plants were irrigated by water that had been made acid to the same extent as rainwater in the northeastern United States. The water was sprayed on pine trees and tomato plants to mimic the way rain arrives. Pine needles grew to only half their normal length in these experiments, and fewer tomatoes were produced than normally. The experiments have been prophetic, as you will see when you reach the heading "Forest Decline."

OTHER EFFECTS OF ACID RAIN

Scientists have not yet detected any direct impact of acid rain on human health, but there are clearly possibilities for such effects. All the possibilities revolve around the increased ability of acid water to dissolve or otherwise act on minerals. Mercury in natural waters can be converted to monomethyl mercury under acid conditions. Fish will accumulate monomethyl mercury in their flesh. High mercury concentrations in fish have been found in areas where acid rain is falling and lakes are acidifying. Mercury is a known human poison that has also contaminated fish in the past under other circumstances.

If reservoirs used for drinking water were to become acidic, toxic metals from the watershed could dissolve in water being used for human consumption. In addition, acidic drinking water could dissolve lead from household plumbing systems. Such a case has apparently already occurred in New York State. There, the highly acid water from the Hinckley Reservoir near Amsterdam, New York leached lead from household plumbing, causing concentrations of lead above the drinking water standard. The water had stood in pipes overnight; once this water was run out of the system, lead concentrations returned to their typically low levels.

Acid rain also damages mortar and stone by chemically reacting with the calcium and magnesium in them. Irreplaceable statuary is particularly at risk from such damage (Figure 16-5). In addition, iron products and other metals are very susceptible to corrosion from acid rain. Swedish investigators found a high correlation between acid rain and the corrosion rate of steel.

WHAT MAKES SOME LAKES AND SOILS SENSITIVE TO ACID RAIN?

Some lakes seem not to be subject to becoming acidic; these lakes or their watersheds seem to have the capability of neutralizing acid additions. Other lakes, based on their present conditions, are obviously sensitive to acid rain. Vulnerable lakes typically are fed by a watershed in which the bedrock contains igneous rock (such as granite) or metamorphic rock (such as gneiss). These rock types are resistant to solution; water flowing over them dissolves little in the way of minerals. Hence, the lakes into which they flow have very "soft" waters.

The minerals in sedimentary rock, on the other hand, are more easily dissolved by water flowing over them. Lakes whose watersheds are composed of sedimentary bedrock tend to have "hard" water, water rich in dissolved minerals. If limestone bedrock (a sedimentary rock composed of calcium carbonate) is present in the watershed, the runoff tends to be a hard water. Lakes whose watersheds are composed of sedimentary bedrock tend to resist becoming acidic because the carbonate minerals neutralize acidity.

The Adirondack lakes have watersheds whose bedrock is largely granite. The waters in the lakes are typically soft, low in dissolved minerals. Acid rain makes a big impact on these lakes. Regions of North America whose lakes are thought to be sensitive to the impact of acid rain are shown in Figure 16-6.

The composition of the bedrock is not the only factor in determining whether lakes are sensitive to acid additions. The soil in the region also plays a role. Watershed soils that are rich in soluble minerals, such as calcium or magnesium carbonate, tend to protect lakes because these minerals neutralize acidity. As an example, although granite bedrock is common in areas of Maine, the lakes in these

(a)

(b)

FIGURE 16-5 Effects of Acid Rain. Statue in Germany (*a*) before acid rain and (*b*) after acid rain. (*Photo:* TK)

areas do not seem to have acidified, apparently because of the neutralization of acid rain in the lime-bearing soil—this in the face of rain with an average pH of 4.3. Some lakes in Florida, in contrast, have acidified despite having a watershed in which there was sedimentary bedrock. These lakes apparently did not get much groundwater inflow, and the surface flows drained over soil in which little calcium carbonate was present.

Not only are lakes and their populations sensitive to acid rain, but soils and land-based ecosystems are sensitive as well. Soils have differing sensitivity to acid rain, just as lakes do. Again, soils that are derived from sedimentary materials, such as carbonate materials, or that are rich in organic material tend to neutralize acid rain. Those soils that stem from rocks such as granite and gneiss,

which resist solution, tend to be easily acidified. About 70%–80% of the land in the eastern United States possesses soils sensitive to acidification. Acid rain may leach the already small mineral content and plant nutrients from these soils, decreasing their productivity. It has been hard to demonstrate such effects on productivity except under laboratory conditions, but that such possibilities exist, coupled with the other known effects of acid rain, should be enough to stimulate action.

FOREST DECLINE

The term *forest decline* carries two meanings. It can refer simply to a slowing in the growth of trees, as reflected by a decrease in the thickness of tree

---

Towards a Sustainable Society

Collecting Data for Environmental Decision Making

by Chonghua Zhang

Chonghua Zhang has been Director of Environmental Protection for Shanghai Petrochemicals and worked in China's Environmental Protection Agency. He is currently in the Environment division of the World Bank.

The creation of environmental institutions such as water agencies, air agencies, solid waste authorities, and the like must be accompanied by the collection of data in support of the activities of those institutions. Environmental institutions are designed to make decisions on environmental improvements, to monitor progress in the achievement of those improvements, and ultimately to enforce the rules that they have laid down. Environmental decision making to achieve some goal cannot be fairly accomplished without data to support those decisions. Nor can progress toward that goal be measured without appropriate data.

Enforcement requires data—as the baseline against which to lay down penalties. In addition, the preparation of environmental impact statements and forecasting require such baseline data.

As a consequence, when nations create environmental institutions, they must, at the same time, commit to a vigorous and appropriate program of data collection, a program that coordinates with and supports the decision making that is the institution's mission. Collected data must be made available not only throughout the collecting environmental agency, but also to agencies whose missions are parallel to and coordinate with the

---

rings. The technical description for this slowing in growth is known as "a decline in forest productivity." An individual looking at a forest that has experienced such a decline in productivity would be unable to recognize what has occurred. Biologists, however, can detect the drop in productivity. The other meaning for *forest decline* is actual *damage* to trees, even *tree death*. Such a decline is not hard to observe.

Arthur Johnson at the University of Pennsylvania has studied the thickness of tree rings of both red spruce and pitch pine in order to detect whether a decline in forest productivity has occurred. His

red spruce cores were drawn from a number of stands in the northeastern United States; his pitch pine cores were from southern New Jersey. He found a menacing pattern in 30%–40% of the tree cores. Beginning in the 1960s, the thickness of the rings—the extent of new growth—narrowed substantially, and in many trees the thickness did not recover.

In Tennessee, scientists have found a similar decline not only in red spruce and pitch pine but also in shortleaf pine, hemlock, and Fraser Fir. They have discovered, too, that the decline extends to deciduous trees—hickory and yellow birch. In Ger-

missions of the collecting agency. Errors in the type of data to collect and the amount to collect, especially in the case of developing nations, will be costly to reverse and will render decision making more difficult.

Having worked in developing nations in Asia, I have first-hand experience in the tragedy of mistakes in data collection, of the waste of scarce resources that can occur when data is not made available, even though it exists. The failure to make data available can lead to wasteful duplication of effort, to the repeat collection of the same information that already exists.

I was told by an information officer at a national data center in China that a survey showed that the average use of data is about 0.8 times per item. Judging from this, I concluded that most data must have been inaccessible to the majority of the people. Elsewhere, I also observed how some very important programs ended up achieving only fractions of their intended objectives simply because data were poorly presented, rarely analyzed, and, worst of all, hardly taken account of by the decision-making agency.

Data sets collected by one agency and used by several agencies must be published regularly by the government to prevent duplication of efforts.

Problems with data collection and distribution do not end at the national level. International aid agencies that provide assistance in development have yet to create a long-term strategy to resolve problems in information availability. The emergence of urgent issues of global significance—such as global warming and ozone depletion—also focuses our attention on the lack of available data. Decisions must be taken and burdens and responsibilities must be allocated among the nations of the globe. To do this, the data to support these decisions and allocations must be made available, must be shared, if the right and just approaches are to be taken. In recent years, new tools for both local and global information management have been developed for use by the community of analysts. These include geographic information systems and remote sensing, two powerful tools that gather, store, organize, and retrieve data. These tools should be put to use promptly.

In 1992, we celebrated the 20th anniversary of the UN Conference on the Human Environment. Yet most of the developing countries are still lagging in developing their environmental agendas. When resources are already so limited, the cost/benefit of data and its value in decision making should be evaluated constantly, both domestically and internationally. Data management and development of environmental institutions must form a benign and supportive cycle.

---

many's Black Forest, damage and decline occur among spruce, oaks, beeches, mountain ash, and sycamore. A plant disease that afflicts so many species of trees, deciduous and coniferous, is unheard of. Nor can drought fully explain what is happening to so many trees. Most scientists agree that air pollution and acid rain are the cause, but the evidence is circumstantial. That is, air pollutants and acid rain are present at the scene, but other factors, drought in particular, may be operating.

If a decline in forest productivity were all that had been observed, people might be less concerned, but decline has turned to damage and damage to death. In Germany's Black Forest, one out of every five trees shows moderate damage already; two of every three trees show some symptoms of damage, and diseased trees extend to fully two-thirds of the area of the forest. In 1984 it was estimated that three-quarters of the fir trees in Germany are in some way affected. In Germany the phenomenon is called *Waldsterben* (literally "forest dying" or "forest perishing"), and it has been observed on over 50% of Germany's forested area, some 6.25 million acres (2.5 million hectares). Germany's forests in Bavaria are also severely affected.

In Germany's red spruce, the species that seems

most sensitive to damage, a yellowing and early loss of needles is seen. The dropping of needles begins at the top of the tree (the crown) and proceeds down, and it begins at the outermost tips of branches and moves inward toward the trunk. Roots may deteriorate, boughs sag. Insects and fungus growths invade the bark of the tree. High levels of toxic metals, including aluminum, cadmium, copper, and manganese, may be found in the layer between the rings and the bark.

Germany is not the only European country afflicted with forest decline. In the Erzgebirge mountain range of Czechoslovakia is a scene of devastation. The mountain range is downwind from a region in which a high-sulfur brown coal is burned extensively. Whole forests have been destroyed in this area. A half-million-acre (200,000-hectare) area of damaged trees has been reported. One-fifth of the entire area is said to contain dead trees. Poland, where brown coal is also used, is reputed to be suffering even greater devastation; damaged trees are found on 1.25 million acres (500,000 hectares) of forested land area. Forest death has also been discovered in Austria, Switzerland, Sweden, East Germany, the Netherlands, Romania, the United Kingdom, and Yugoslavia. In southwest Sweden, every tenth tree is damaged or dying. The spruce trees in the Scania section of Sweden hold their needles only a single year (healthy adult trees normally hold their needles for three years). The beech trees in Scania, as in the afflicted areas of western Germany, are losing their leaves in August; the leaves fall while they are still green. The bark of the beeches is swollen and cracked; the trunks of the trees are pitted with craters the size of the palm of a hand.

In the United States, tree damage has now been found in the Adirondack Mountains of New York, the Green Mountains of Vermont, the White Mountains of New Hampshire, and the Great Smoky Mountains of eastern North Carolina. Red spruce, which account for about 25% of the high-elevation trees in these forests, have exhibited dramatic dieback, but the extent has not been estimated as it has in Germany and other European countries.

In Quebec, Canada, sugar maple trees are suffering extensive damage and dieback. Leaves of the sugar maple yellow, shrivel, and fall. On the branches and trunk the bark has loosened; near complete mortality has been projected for some sites. Nor is maple the only tree being damaged in Quebec; yellow birch, red oak, ash, and beech trees are also experiencing dieback. It appears that the low mineral content of the thin, fragile soil in the province is being depleted further by acid rain blowing in from the United States.

It is remotely possible that some new tree disease is at work in the eastern United States and in Europe. Tree diseases, however, are far more specific, most often attacking single species of tree. For instance, the chestnut blight that arrived in the United States in the early 1900s is thought to have destroyed three billion American Chestnut trees. The Chinese Chestnut, a near relative on which the blight arrived, was resistant to the disease. Dutch elm disease is gradually destroying the United States' population of elms and only elms. Clearly such blights are highly specific. The prospect of a tree disease that attacks many species of tree, including both conifer and broadleaf, is without precedent. We need to look elsewhere for the source of the stress on so many species of tree.

In the Adirondack Mountains, in the White Mountains, and in the Green Mountains of the acid-rain-swept northeast United States, dwarf mistletoe, a parasite related to the leafy mistletoe of Christmas, is decimating spruce trees. Forest epidemics of spruce budworm are underway in New Brunswick, Nova Scotia, and Newfoundland, areas that are downwind of major sulfur emissions. The spruce forests are being sprayed with the insecticide dimilin and with a bacterium Bt (*Bacillus thuregensis*) to control the budworm. Although drought has occurred in all these regions, tree growth should recover when normal rainfall patterns return. The failure of tree growth to recover suggests that other agent(s) are operating. Insect pests and fungus diseases have been widespread, but these tree diseases are opportunistic; they invade trees that are already weakened by some other insult.

Damage to vulnerable soils by acid rain could be an explanation for the insect, pest, and fungus invasion. The vulnerable mountain range soils are already low in minerals, and acid rain could deplete further the calcium, magnesium, and sparse organic content of these soils. As a consequence, the soils' ability to support trees and other plants will decrease.

Aluminum, a soil constituent normally bound up in the organic portion of the soil, is made soluble by acid rain. In the soluble form it will be taken up by the roots in place of calcium. Aluminum is toxic to plants, and this plant toxin places stress on the trees. In this new environment, previously harmless needle fungi become pathogens.

In all the instances of forest damage and decline, certain features occur again and again. First, acid deposition afflicts all the regions. Long-distance transport has brought sulfur oxides and nitrogen oxides to the areas, resulting in acid rainfall and dry deposition of metal sulfates. Second, in a number of situations the forests are at relatively high elevations and stand in the cloud cover for a substantial portion of the year. This is true of Germany's Black Forest and of Vermont's Green Mountains, where clouds may surround the trees for a quarter of the year. Since cloud moisture may have a pH as low as 3.5 (even more acid than acid rain), tree damage may be a likely consequence. Third, droughts preceded the intervals in which tree-ring decline began to be noted. If drought were the only culprit, however, recovery in growth would be expected after weather patterns improved. In one study, recovery in tree-ring growth did occur in about 20% of the tree cores examined, but ring growth never recovered in 40% of the samples.

The fourth common characteristic is the status of the soils. Soils in these high-altitude forests are subject to acidification because they are thin and contain relatively little organic material. Essential minerals such as magnesium and calcium may be leached from the soil by the hydrogen ions and lost in runoff, making these minerals unavailable to the growing tree. On the other hand, the acidity of rainfall may cause aluminum, an element toxic to plants that is normally chemically bound in mineral form and unavailable, to be "mobilized" or made chemically available in the soil. It may then enter the tree roots, where it may disrupt normal root function. Fifth, chemical analysis of leaves and needles of declining trees shows about a 10% higher

sulfur content than that found in the foliage of healthy trees, at least in the United States.

Sixth, considering mountain forests, especially in the southern United States and in Europe, relatively high ozone concentrations have been observed in the air—higher than those observed at lower elevations, and even higher than in some cities. Ozone has long been known to damage evergreens, but high ozone concentrations on mountain slope environments is an unusual finding. A possible explanation is the presence of nitrogen oxides in the air. We know that nitrogen dioxide reacts in a complex way with hydrocarbons in the presence of sunlight to produce ozone. But where are the hydrocarbons coming from? They may come from the trees themselves. The Great Smoky Mountains are so named because of the haze of *terpenes,* produced by the trees, that hangs over the forests. Terpenes are highly reactive hydrocarbons produced by the trees of the coniferous forest. The terpenes may be reacting with nitrogen dioxide in the presence of sunlight to produce the ozone.

These are the factors: acid rain, high elevations and cloud cover, drought preceding damage, soil acidification and mineral change, sulfur in needles and leaves, and ozone in the atmosphere. Together they characterize what is becoming a Northern Hemisphere ecological disaster.

CALLS FOR ACTION ON ACID RAIN

Four benchmark scientific reports have pointed to the need for action on acid rain. As early as 1981 a report of a panel of the National Research Council (the research arm of the National Academy of Sciences and the National Academy of Engineering) concluded that a 50% reduction in acidity of rainfall was needed to protect forests and lakes. The report did not say how to accomplish the 50% reduction, only that such a reduction was needed.

In 1983, another acid rain committee of the National Research Council, this one chaired by Jack Calvert of the National Center for Atmospheric Research, concluded that the extent of acid rain in eastern North America "is roughly proportional to sulfur emissions from power plants, industries, and smelters." The link of acid rain to sulfur emissions was thus firmly supported by the committee. The report made clear that a 50% reduction of sulfur oxide emissions would be expected to produce a 50% reduction in acid rain.

A third panel, chaired by William Nierenberg, director of the Scripps Institution of Oceanography, reported in 1984 to the science advisor to the President. The panel recommended "reductions from present levels of emissions of sulfur compounds beginning with those steps that are most cost effective in reducing total (acid) deposition." The panel further concluded that "actions have to be taken despite incomplete knowledge." The report warned: "If we take the conservative point of view, that we must wait until the scientific knowledge is definitive, the accumulated deposition and damage to the environment may reach the point of irreversibility."

In 1984 a fourth report was released, this one from the Office of Technology Assessment (OTA), an arm of Congress. This report estimated that 3,000 lakes and 23,000 miles of streams (about 20% of lakes and stream miles sensitive to acid rain) are at risk of being acidified or are already acidic. The OTA projected that 10 million tons of sulfur oxides (about 50% of the annual emissions) could be removed at a cost of $3 to $4 billion, increasing electric rates by only about 2%–3%. The report indicated that this level of removal is likely to be able to protect all but the most sensitive aquatic areas.

The last policy study was commissioned in the early 1980s and finally issued its report in 1991. Although highly politicized in its early years by the Reagan administration–appointed director, a new director stabilized the program. The National Acid Precipitation Assessment Program (NAPAP) was conducted by an interagency task force that supported millions of dollars of scientific research. The program's conclusions on the effects of acid rain confirmed the research results reported in this chapter, but downplayed several aspects of acid rain's impact. Among other issues, red spruce was identified as the tree species particularly sensitive to acid rain, but the report failed to highlight the domi-

nance of red spruce in high altitude forests. In addition, the report asserted but could not support its contention that emissions trading would not have a significant effect on environmental quality resulting from the control program (emissions trading is discussed on page 366). Publicity from the NAPAP office suggested that acid rain was "not a crisis." Interestingly, the final report was issued over a year after the passage of the 1990 Clean Air Act that mandated controls on sulfur oxides emissions to decrease acid rain.

CONTROL OF ACID RAIN

Ministering to the Patients

Limestone has been applied to the acidified lakes in Sweden and to those in the Adirondack Mountains of New York chiefly on an experimental basis. The limestone, which is mainly calcium carbonate, can be applied in a crushed form or in a water slurry. Liming decreases the acidity of a lake and provides some resistance (a buffering capability) to further acid inputs. If the lake or pond flushes quickly — that is, if its inflow and outflow rates are high — the liming will have to be repeated every one or two years. Because most of the critically acidified lakes in the Adirondacks cannot be reached by road, liming them will require application by helicopter or airplane, increasing the expense. Electric utility spokespeople and coal industry spokespeople were the chief recommenders of this band-aid approach.

Limestone can also be applied to the declining forests. Liming slows the rate at which soil acidifies and raises the pH toward neutral. It is expected, however, that the growth rate in a limed soil will not be optimum. In Germany's Black Forest, foresters have fertilized the soil with a combination of magnesium sulfate (at 700 pounds per acre) and limestone (at 2,000 pounds per acre). Trees not too far injured have recovered under this formula. Foresters guess that this process might buy the trees 5 to 10 years while the air is being cleaned up.

The fact that trees recover under this treatment suggests that the explanations for forest decline are not far off the mark. Magnesium is apparently being leached from the soil, since restoring it helps. Soil acidity is also a causative factor, since decreasing soil acidity also helps. Somehow, though, these seem like heroic measures to keep dying patients alive. The patients will fully recover only if they are given clean air and water.

Recovery, however, is expected to be slow in any event. The lakes will gradually flush, but the soils of their watersheds may have already lost their capacity to neutralize even slightly acid rain. The restoration of these soils, and hence of the water flowing through them, may take decades.

Attacking the Causes of Acid Rain

Technical Control of Emissions. The United States burned about 750 million tons of coal in electric power plants in 1988, in the process creating about 20 million tons of sulfur oxides emissions. Since 80% of the annual use of coal in the United States is consumed in coal-fired power plants, the electric plant must be the prime target for control. Natural sources of sulfur may contribute up to 10% of sulfur dioxide emissions, but these natural background emissions are not producing the levels of acid rain that are occurring. In fact, the increase in the acidity of rainfall in the northeast United States corresponds in time with the increase in the use of coal for power generation. Furthermore, the spatial concentrations of greatest acidity is directly downwind of the major emissions of sulfur oxides and nitrogen oxides.

Control of acid rain and of forest decline is accomplished by limiting emissions of sulfur oxides and nitrogen oxides—principally from power plants since these are the sources that discharge the pollutants to long-distance transport. In turn, controlling emissions from power plants mean focusing on coal.

Coal can be cleansed of a portion of its sulfur so that less sulfur oxides are produced at the power plants. The inorganic sulfur, the sulfur in iron pyrites in coal, can be removed by simple water washing of crushed coal. The organic sulfur, bound to the carbon in coal, is more difficult to remove. Several chemical processes appear to be attractive in removing the organic sulfur. A chemical process developed by the Batelle Memorial Institute produces a coal that is lower in both sulfur and ash, as does a process created by the TRW Corporation. Naturally low-sulfur coal is also available, primarily from the huge coal surface mines in Montana, Colorado, Wyoming, and the Dakotas. The washing processes add to the cost of coal. So also does transportation of the low-sulfur surface-mined coal from the western United States to the eastern United States, but, again, fewer emissions of sulfur oxides result.

In contrast to decreasing the sulfur in coal before oxidation takes place, it is possible to remove the sulfur oxides after their production. **Scrubbers,** sequences of chemical steps, treat the stack gases themselves, removing the sulfur oxides emissions. The technical name for these processes is *flue gas desulfurization,* and more than 50 different scrubber concepts are available. The most reliable scrubber and the one with the longest history of use is the lime-limestone wet scrubber. A sludge mixture of calcium sulfite and calcium sulfate results from this scrubbing process and requires disposal. Another scrubber type produces a saleable product, high-purity sulfur, in the process of removing sulfur oxides. Criticized for 20 years by the foot-dragging electric power industries, scrubbers are now a proven technology that can get the job done.

All these processes—washing of coal, transport of low-sulfur coal, and scrubbing—can be used separately or combined in various ways to decrease sulfur oxides emissions. The combination of these alternatives may prove especially cost-effective.

Two other options reduce the emissions of sulfur oxides. One concept already proving its worth is *fluidized-bed combustion.* This special process "floats" the burning coal in a high-volume stream of combustion air in the presence of granular limestone. As it is produced, the sulfur dioxide reacts with the limestone, producing calcium sulfate particles that are entrained in the stack gases. These particles are removed with the fly ash by the reliable electrostatic precipitator. Fluidized-bed combustion proceeds at a lower temperature than does conventional coal combustion. As a consequence, nitrogen oxides emissions are decreased. The fluidized bed holds great promise as a tool to control the emissions that produce acid rain. Another chemical option is *sorbent injection,* in which a dry chemical is sprayed into the flue gas, causing the quick formation of a dry sulfur compound that is then removed.

The nuclear industry is, of course, promoting new nuclear power plants to meet our needs for electrical energy. Unfortunately, the trade is nuclear wastes for sulfur oxides emissions. It is a bad bargain. Photovoltaic solar electric power and wind electric power, are better possibilities. Wind is ready now; solar will be soon. (See the energy chapters.)

Emissions Policy Choices in Europe and North America.

Beginning in 1982, eight nations in the north Atlantic community pledged a 30% reduction in sulfur discharges from 1980 levels by 1993. Norway, Finland, and Sweden led the way, and Denmark, West Germany, Switzerland, Austria, and Canada followed suit. Great Britain and France declined to make such a pledge. In fact, Canada promised a 50% reduction in sulfur emissions, proceeding at the time without the cooperation of the United States.

Although automobiles are only a minor source of sulfur emissions, they are a major source of nitrogen oxides. To control nitrogen oxides from autos, catalytic converters and engine modifications are used. The United States has applied these controls, but vehicle miles keep climbing, preventing substantial progress in emission reductions.

In 1989 a number of European nations, through the European Commission, proposed meeting auto emissions standards similar to those current in the United States, with a target compliance date of 1993. Less stringent standards are currently being phased in.

The Clean Air Act passed by the U.S. Congress in 1990 calls for the removal of 10 million tons per year of sulfur dioxide from power plants and other sources. This removal level, about one-half of total annual sulfur oxides emissions in the United States, may not have the desired result. Although acid rain should be cut in half, the reversal of the acidification of lakes and streams and the recovery of forests are not likely to occur quickly. The reversal will take decades at the minimum, because the acid-neutral-izing capabilities of the associated soils have already been used up. The threat to forests and to species is likely to continue.

In addition, the Clean Air Act allows *emissions trading,* a regulation that gives polluters the privilege of reducing emissions or buying the rights of others to pollute. If a company reduces its emissions below the emissions standards set by the act, it gains a credit that can be sold. The cost of the control program will be reduced by this emissions trading process, and that is to the good. Nonetheless, emissions trading has a distinct likelihood of allowing emissions reductions to occur in the wrong places, thereby reducing, possibly to a large degree, the impact of the program. Emissions trading is not a bad idea, but the trades need to be limited to transfers within the same state so that the important emissions reductions occur in the correct places and not at some inconsequential, out-of-the-way place.

SUMMARY

Acid rain, the long-distance transport and deposition of sulfur and nitrogen oxides, is primarily the result of using tall smokestacks on coal-fired power plants. The tall stacks were designed to decrease ground-level pollution but instead created a new pollution problem. Acid rain occurs in many of the world's industrial countries.

The sulfur and nitrogen oxides, which are produced during coal combustion, dissolve in water vapor to form sulfurous, sulfuric, and nitric acids. These acids may react with components of coal to produce acidic salts such as calcium and iron sulfates. Both the acids and acidic salts contribute to acidification of the environment. In the eastern United States, sulfur oxides are the primary cause of acid rain (70%–85%), but in California, nitrogen oxides contribute about 60% to the acidity of rainfall.

The measure of acidity, pH, counts from 7 (neutral) down to 1 or less (extremely acid). Rainfall with a pH as low as 2.2 has been noted in New England. Portions of all states east of the Mississippi, except Louisiana and Florida, are experiencing average pH levels of rainfall of 4.2 and below. Portions of Europe and Japan show similar acid concentrations as in the eastern United States.

Hundreds of lakes in the Adirondack Mountains region, in Quebec, and in Norway have acidity levels so high that fish populations have been wiped out. The elimination proceeds quietly; the acid levels cause fish to fail to breed or hatchlings to die off. Birds that feed on fish, such as the eagle and the osprey, are expected to decline, as are such mammals as mink and otter. Populations of wildfowl such as the black duck, which feeds on water insects and freshwater clams, are declining as their food sources decline due to the acidification of lakes and wetlands. In areas of acid rain, frogs, toads, and salamanders, which breed in temporary spring pools, are declining as well—most likely because the pools are highly acid.

Acid rain also releases mercury from sediments and lead from plumbing into drinking water. It corrodes iron and steel, and it damages mortar and stone building products as well as priceless statuary.

Lakes and streams become acidified when they receive acid inputs, but acid rain on a watershed whose *bedrock* is sedimentary rock is likely to be partially neutralized before it reaches a lake or stream. Likewise, acid rain on a *soil* derived from sedimentary rock is likely to be partially neutralized. Carbonate minerals in the sedimentary rock and soil provide the neutralization. Watersheds whose bedrock is granite and with thin soil derived from igneous rock are less capable of neutralizing acid rainfall. About 70%–80% of the land area of the eastern United States has soils that are easily acidified.

Forests are suffering damage due to acid rain. In addition to tree death and damage, in a number of areas, tree growth has been markedly slowed, as seen in the thickness of tree rings. Not only are conifers, such as the red spruce, pines, and hemlock, being damaged, but broadleaf trees like the maple and yellow birch are suffering as well. Tree pathogens are more specific than this, usually targeting a single species at most, so the decline of trees across Europe, eastern Canada, and the eastern United States is an acid-rain problem and not the primary result of an insect or blight. Poland and Czecho-

slovakia appear to be hardest hit in Europe, although Germany and the Scandinavian countries are reporting extensive damage to forests. In North America, Quebec and Ontario provinces in Canada and the mountainous areas of the northeastern United States are affected most acutely. It appears that trees are being weakened by the stress of acid rain, probably by aluminum that is released from the soil by the acid rain, and that insect and other pests such as fungi are stepping in for the kill.

The common characteristics of the high-elevation forests undergoing damage are (1) acid rain, (2) a frequent cloud cover (which is even more acidic than the rain), (3) drought that initiates damage, (4) thin, mineral-poor soils, (5) sulfur in the foliage, and (6) high ozone concentration in the area. The high ozone levels are probably due to photochemical reactions of the oxides of nitrogens. Every major expert panel that reported in the 1980s called for sulfur oxide removal to reverse acid rain, halt lake acidification, and limit forest damage.

Liming of lakes and soils may temporarily restore proper acid balance but will likely require many repetitions. Addition of limestone (calcium carbonate) and magnesium sulfate has helped trees recover in Germany's Black Forest, so the hypothesis that acid rain is acidifying soils appears to be correct. Even after sulfur oxide levels are decreased, as the Clean Air Act of 1990 promises, either by removal of sulfur from coal or sulfur oxides from stack gases, forest and lake recovery will be expected to be very slow—probably decades at the minimum. International agreements are being sought so that one country's emissions do not damage the forests and lakes of another.

Coal can be cleansed of its sulfur by water washing and by chemical steps, the latter more costly than the former. Scrubbers can clean the sulfur oxides from the stack gases. Fluidized-bed combustion and sorbent injection are promising options for removing sulfur dioxide from stack gases. The Clean Air Act of 1990 calls for removal of 10 million tons of sulfur dioxide, about half of the annual emissions in the United States, but recovery of lakes and forests will be slow. The impact of the act will be diluted by the provision that allows polluters to buy emission rights from anywhere in the United

States; the rights to emit sulfur oxides belong to those who have removed more of the pollutant than they were required to remove.

Questions

1. What two gases are primarily responsible for acid rain? What are the principal sources of these gases? Why are emissions in Indiana causing acid rain in New England?
2. Would you expect lakes in the Rocky Mountains to be as sensitive to acid rain as those in the Adirondacks? Why or why not?
3. What evidence, relative to forest decline, can be gained from studying tree rings?
4. Why have tree pests such as insects or fungi been ruled out as the culprits causing forest decline?
5. Name the six factors that seem to be operating in most cases of forest decline.

References/Further Reading

(All references are readable and nontechnical.)

"Is There Scientific Consensus on Acid Rain?" Excerpts from six governmental reports. Ad Hoc Committee on Acid Rain Science and Policy, October 1985, Published by the Institute of Ecosystem Studies, The New York Botanical Garden, Mary Flagler Cary Arboretum, Box AB, Millbrook, N.Y., 12545.

Kiester, E. "A Deathly Spell Is Hovering above the Black Forest," *Smithsonian, 16*(8) (November 1985), 211.

La Bastille, A. "Acid Rain: How Great a Menace?" *National Geographic,* November 1981, p. 657.

Likens, G. "The Not So Gentle Rain." In *Yearbook of Science and the Future, Encyclopedia Britannica,* 1981, pp. 212–227.

Likens, Gene, F. Herbert Bormann, and Noye M. Johnson. "Acid Rain," *Environment,* March 1972, pp. 33–40.

National Research Council. *Acid Deposition: Long Term Trends.* Committee on Monitoring and Assessment of Trends in Acid Deposition. Washington, D.C.: National Academy Press, 1986.

Office of Technology Assessment. "Acid Rain and Transported Air Pollutants: Implications for Public Policy." Washington, D.C.: Congress of the United States, 1984.

Ruben, E., et al. "Controlling Acid Deposition: The Role of FGD," *Environmental Science and Technology, 20*(10) (1986), 960.

Schmandt, Jurgen, and Hilliard Roderick (Eds.). *Acid Rain and Friendly Neighbors,* Durham, N.C.: Duke University Press, 1985. 333 pages.

The policy dispute between the United States and Canada.

U.S. National Acid Precipitation Assessment Program. *Acidic Deposition: State of Science and Technology,* Summary report. Washington, D.C.: U.S. Government Printing Office, September 1991.

Sustainable Cities / Transportation and Air Pollution

Transportation problems plague the world's growing cities. Large numbers of automobiles cause such severe air pollution that some cities in developing nations are on the verge of becoming unlivable.

U.S. Superhighway system girdling a city. In developed countries such as the U.S., the growth in automobile use foils attempts to reduce air pollution, even though the amount of pollutants generated by each individual car has decreased. *(U.S. Department of Energy)*

Bicycle "truck" in Beijing. In some cities in developing countries, transport is still human powered. As these cities transist to automotive transportation, severe air pollution is the result. *(Charles ReVelle)*

Public transport in India. In developing nations, even where public transport is available, it is often unable to keep up with the demands of a rapidly growing population. *(UN Photo)*

The horizon in Mexico City disappears into a haze of air pollution. Mexico City may hold the dubious distinction of having the worst air pollution in the world. *(UN Photo)*

Sustainable Cities / Water and Sanitation

Provision of safe drinking water and safe disposal of wastes for the large and growing populations in cities may turn out to be the greatest environmental challenge faced by city planners. In some areas, such as Tucson, Arizona and Beijing, China, aquifers on which cities depend are being drawn down at alarming rates. In other cities, such as Mexico City, ancient water mains and sewage pipes are crumbling and leaking, allowing sewage to contaminate drinking water. In still other cities, householders must collect their own water from public standpipes every day; these people are calling for pipes to be laid to their homes so they can have running water.

Public standpost on a downtown street in Xi'an, the capital of Shaanxi province in China. Even in large cities, many householders do not yet have water piped into their apartments. *(Daniel Okun)*

Chinese man carrying water home. Unlike men in developing countries in Latin America, Africa, and other parts of Asia, Chinese men commonly share the work of carrying home the daily supply of freshwater from community standpipes. In most other parts of the world women carry home the household water supply, while men carry water only if it is to be sold. *(Beth Okun)*

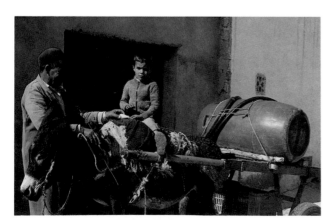

Water seller in Tunis, Tunisia. *(Alex McPhail)*

Sewage floods the streets in Alexandria. Inadequate drains allow sewage from these homes to flood the streets. Cholera and typhoid spread easily in conditions like this. *(Daniel Okun)*

Chapter 17

Carbon Dioxide, Global Climate Change, and Ozone Depletion

The industrial revolution has brought material abundance to the people of many nations. Powered primarily by the burning of fossil fuels, it also brought air pollution on a massive scale and the release of carbon dioxide to the atmosphere at unprecedented rates. We are gradually learning to combat the air pollution, but carbon dioxide is another question. Carbon dioxide is a basic and unalterable result of burning fossil fuels. Our entire strategy of powering society is called into question by the concern that the accumulation of carbon dioxide may alter the earth's climate.

Carbon dioxide in the stratosphere has been increasing steadily for over 100 years. Before the industrial revolution, carbon dioxide was in rough balance in the atmosphere. Natural removal rates were keeping pace with carbon dioxide additions. As the industrial revolution powered up, however, the natural removal processes were overwhelmed. Near the turn of the century the Swedish scientist Arrhenius noted the rapid addition of carbon dioxide to the atmosphere and was concerned about its impact on the temperature of the earth.

Society successfully managed to ignore warnings about the rapid accumulation of carbon dioxide until the middle of the 1980s. That decade had severely hot summers, and new, more detailed computer models suggested that climate changes were in the wind. The computer models do not all agree in their predictions of the impact of the greenhouse effect, and some scientists dissent from predictions of global warming. Nonetheless, a consensus is forming in the scientific community that the greenhouse effect is real and that some actions must be taken. Unfortunately, the uncertainty associated with the issue is stalling meaningful actions—actions that would be in the best interests of the United States and most of the world in any event.

To comprehend the greenhouse arguments we need to understand the role of carbon dioxide in the atmosphere. We also need to know who the other players are among the greenhouse gases and why their concentrations are increasing. We need as well to investigate the impacts of the greenhouse effect and how the effects can be softened. Finally, we need to know the options we have to reverse the accumulation of greenhouse gases.

One group of greenhouse gases, the chlorofluorocarbons, not only contribute to global warming, but are also responsible for a decrease in levels of ozone in the earth's atmosphere. For this reason we discuss in this chapter both the potential for global

FIGURE 17-1 How the Ocean Removes Carbon Dioxide from the Air.

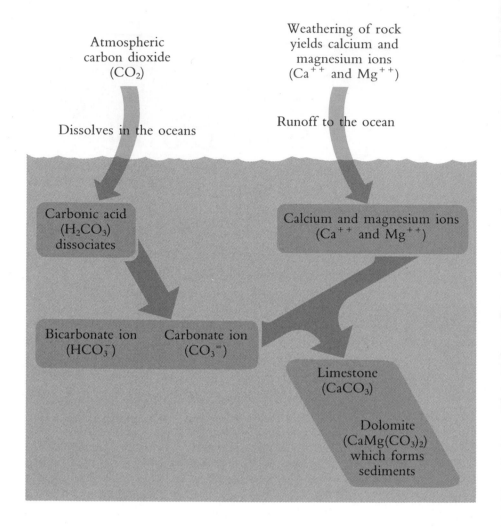

CARBON DIOXIDE IN THE ATMOSPHERE—THE CARBON CYCLE AS MODIFIED BY HUMAN ACTION

warming and also the decline in ozone concentrations in the stratosphere.

CARBON DIOXIDE IN THE ATMOSPHERE—THE CARBON CYCLE AS MODIFIED BY HUMAN ACTION

The burning of fossil fuels produces two oxides of carbon. One, carbon dioxide, is not poisonous, although it could change the earth's climate. The other, carbon monoxide, has known harmful effects on humans.

Both animals and plants produce carbon dioxide as a waste product during the process of respiration,

a process that consumes oxygen. Only plants consume carbon dioxide. Plants use carbon dioxide during the process of photosynthesis, producing oxygen as a by-product. Since carbon dioxide is a product of the respiration process, it is naturally present in the atmosphere in reasonable quantities. A normal sample of air contains about 0.03% carbon dioxide by weight.

Carbon Dioxide Removal Processes

Carbon dioxide is not only consumed in photosynthesis but also dissolves in the water of the great oceans. When carbon dioxide dissolves in ocean waters, carbonic acid is produced *at a very low concentration*. The carbonic acid dissociates in part to bicarbonate and carbonate ions. These ions combine

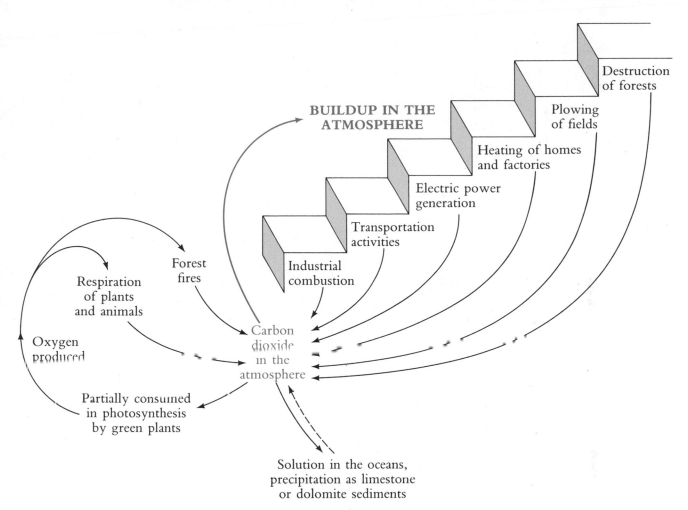

FIGURE 17-2 The Carbon Dioxide Cycle as Modified by Human Activity. If human activities are excluded, carbon dioxide is only added to the atmosphere by the respiration of plants and animals and by forest fires. It is removed from the atmosphere by photosynthesis and by solution in the oceans. The removal and restoration rates were in rough balance before humans began burning fossil fuels. The combustion of fossil fuels has upset the balance and carbon dioxide is now accumulating in the atmosphere.

with dissolved calcium and magnesium that have been carried into the ocean as the result of the natural weathering of rocks. The reaction of the calcium ions with carbonate ions produces calcium carbonate. We know this relatively insoluble substance as limestone. Magnesium and calcium may jointly react with the carbonate ion to produce dolomite. These precipitation reactions remove carbonate from the water, making room for more carbon dioxide to dissolve (see Figure 17-1).

Thus, there are two natural mechanisms for carbon dioxide removal from the atmosphere: (1) solution in the ocean, followed by precipitation as limestone and dolomite, and (2) the utilization of carbon dioxide by green plants in photosynthesis (see Figure 17-2).

Additions of Carbon Dioxide

Carbon dioxide is now being produced in massive quantities from the burning of fossil fuels. In 1990

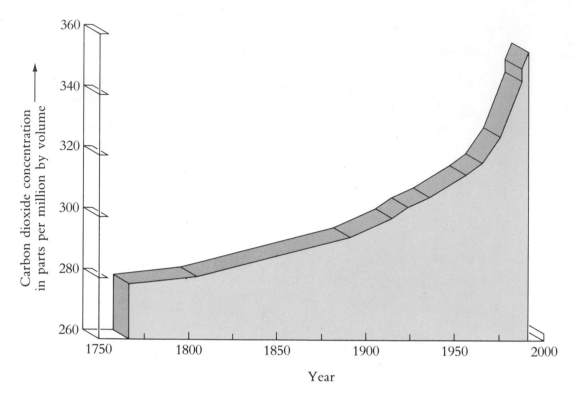

FIGURE 17-3 Carbon Dioxide Concentrations in the Atmosphere Since 1750 A.D. The concentrations since 1957 are based on direct atmospheric measurements at Mauna Loa, Hawaii. Earlier concentrations come from analysis of air trapped in the ice in Antarctica. The rapid increase in concentration since the 1900s reflects increasing combustion of fossil fuels and forest destruction in both temperate and tropical regions.

the United States alone was annually burning about 850 million metric tons of coal in electric power plants. The nation also consumed a comparable tonnage of oil that year. The rest of the world, taken together, consumes about twice the quantity of fossil fuel energy that the United States does, so the worldwide consumption of fossil fuels is enormous. In addition, the process of calcination, a basic step in cement manufacture, converts limestone to lime and carbon dioxide, accounting for 2% of the annual production of the gas from all human activities. The global combustion of fossil fuels is sharply forcing up the rate at which carbon dioxide enters the atmosphere.

Fossil fuel combustion now adds 5%–7% more carbon dioxide each year than is produced annually by animals and green plants. About half this additional quantity is accumulating. That is, it is not being consumed in photosynthesis. Nor is it being dissolved in the ocean. Instead, it is remaining in the atmosphere (see Figure 17-3 indicating the increase in carbon dioxide levels in the air). Unless actions are taken to reverse the trend, the annual amount of carbon dioxide from combustion is expected to grow continuously in lockstep with increasing population and increasing economic activity.

The extent of the increase in fossil fuel combustion will depend on energy conservation measures that may be taken. It will also depend on the extent to which nuclear and solar energy replace coal, oil, and natural gas. Total fossil fuel combustion might be expected to increase by 3%–4% annually through the year 2000. At current rates of combustion, carbon dioxide levels in the atmosphere are increasing at about 0.5% each year. Since combustion rates are increasing, buildup rates will increase as well. Another factor hastening the increase in carbon dioxide levels is the destruction of tropical rain forests for agriculture, as is happening in countries such as Brazil. Northern forests in the United States and Canada are being destroyed as well for wood products and pulp for newsprint. The release of carbon dioxide occurs when the forests are destroyed, because trees hold 10 to 20 times more carbon dioxide per unit of land area than do most agriculture crops.

The processes of removal of carbon dioxide, by photosynthesis and by solution in the oceans, are being overwhelmed by our combustion of coal, oil, and natural gas, by our destruction of forests and by the manufacture of cement. Basically, the carbon stored in fossil fuel materials during the carboniferous era of geologic history is being recycled into the atmosphere in the present. As a consequence, we may be creating climate conditions with which we cannot adequately deal. The new climate conditions could be expected to affect not only humanity, but all life on earth. Our knowledge of future climate is fragmentary and, to a degree, speculative, but if the results turn out to even resemble the scenarios foreseen, we will face enormous risk.

OTHER GREENHOUSE GASES

If carbon dioxide were the only gas in the stratosphere that trapped heat, our concern would not be so urgent. It would be real, but not so urgent. Because of the quantity of carbon dioxide being emitted, it is at the center of our concern, but the other greenhouse gases are coming to occupy more prominent roles in predictions of global warming. The most important other greenhouse gases—that is, gases whose molecules also absorb infrared radiation—are methane and the chlorofluorocarbons (CFCs). Both of these heat-trapping gases are increasing in the atmosphere. Within the next 50 to 60 years, their joint impact on heat trapping is expected to approach that of carbon dioxide alone.

Methane is a natural component of the atmosphere, arising from forest fires and from swamps and other wetlands. The ghostly will-o-wisp that inhabits swamps is nothing but burning methane gas emitted from the swamp. The methane has caught fire and continues to burn as the gas seeps out of the watery ooze. Methane is also released when coal, petroleum, and natural gas are produced (the key component of natural gas *is* methane). And methane seeps out of landfills and rice paddies. The gas is also produced in the guts of the ruminant species we use for food, such as sheep, steers, and water buffalo. Finally, methane may be escaping in quantity from the leaky natural gas pipeline that extends from the Soviet Union to Western Europe. Fortunately, methane molecules survive in the atmosphere only about 10 years, so efforts to control methane emissions would have a near-term payoff.

In contrast to short-lived methane gas, the chlorofluorocarbon molecules remain intact in the atmosphere for up to 120 years. Their ultimate breakdown brings another problem because the chlorine in the CFCs destroys ozone in the stratosphere (see later in this chapter). The long-lived CFC molecules are potent greenhouse gases; that is, they are extremely effective at absorbing infrared radiation that was headed out to space. Thus, their impact is far out of proportion to their low concentration in the stratosphere. Computer models suggest that the CFCs *already* in the atmosphere will be responsible for 25% of the global warming predicted for the next 60 years. Methane's potential contribution may be about half that of the CFCs.

The chlorofluorocarbons are CFC-11, which was once widely used to expand polystyrene, and CFC-12, a refrigerant used in heat pumps, air conditioners, and refrigerators. The former lasts 60 years in the atmosphere; the latter, 120 years. Substitutes for the CFCs are being developed and tested (see later in this chapter); one chemical uses hydrogen in place of chlorine in the chemical structure of the CFC molecule. The new molecule breaks down more quickly, in about 15 years, so that its use in place of the current chemicals would be advantageous.

The global greenhouse then is being fed not only by carbon dioxide but by methane and the CFCs as well. Control of carbon dioxide alone will not limit the greenhouse effect.

THE EFFECTS OF CARBON DIOXIDE AND OTHER GREENHOUSE GASES

The Greenhouse Effect

For about three-quarters of a century, scientists have been aware of the buildup of carbon dioxide. Now it is being carefully watched, as carbon dioxide is joined by serious competitors for heat trapping. The concern is that carbon dioxide, methane, and the CFCs will trap heat in the earth's atmosphere. The effect of these gases has been compared to the effect of the glass panes of greenhouses. The panes let sunlight into the greenhouse, and the greenhouse is warmed by the solar radiation. At night, heat radiates away from the building. However, the glass panes decrease the rate of heat radiation out of the structure.

Carbon dioxide, methane, and the CFCs are expected to act in a similar way. Solar energy would continue to reach the earth without being affected by the gases, and the earth would be warmed. But the radiation of heat away from the earth would be slowed by the greenhouse gases that absorb a portion of the infrared radiation from the earth that is escaping to outer space. The heat absorbed by the gases is then radiated back to earth. As a consequence, the earth would be expected to heat up (Figure 17-4).

From the turn of the century until World War II, a small warming trend was noted. From 1940 to the early 1980s, however, the trend reversed, and the earth's temperature seemed to be stabilizing—in a rough sense perhaps even cooling. In the decade of the '80s, however, a definite warming was noted. Overall, in the last 100 years, the earth seems to have warmed by about 1°F. Are we warming? It depends on where you start to count. It is no wonder there is so much controversy about what may happen. All that we can say is that the evidence so far, as contained in temperature records, is not definitive. Nonetheless, the buildup of carbon dioxide and other greenhouse gases is established fact.

And the mode of action of these gases, namely its absorbing capacity for infrared radiation, is not in doubt. Other factors may be operating, however.

In 1980, Mount St. Helens in the state of Washington spewed forth enormous quantities of volcanic dust. In 1982, El-Chichón, a volcano in Mexico, rocketed even more massive amounts of dust into the stratosphere. A volcano in Indonesia was also releasing volcanic dust into the atmosphere during this period. Such particles, suspended in the atmosphere, reflect sunlight away from the earth, robbing the earth of the heat that the sun's radiation would have provided. Years with extremely cold winters and cold summers followed the massive eruption of Mt. Tambora in Indonesia in 1815. Volcanic activity then with its release of particles to the upper atmosphere may temporarily be producing a countereffect to the greenhouse effect. The massive eruption of Mount Pinatubo in the Philippines in 1991 could influence world weather patterns for several years.

Particles stem not only from volcanic activity but are also discharged in abundance by our industrial society. Combustion produces not just carbon dioxide but also atmospheric particles in tremendous quantities. Observations do show that the fraction of sunlight reaching the earth has been decreasing. Presumably, this has been due to particles suspended in the atmosphere. Particles from combustion and particles from volcanic eruptions may be affording us temporary protection from the initial stages of the earth's warming.

One additional confounding factor may be influencing global temperatures. In 1991, Danish scientists discovered a correlation between temperatures in the northern hemisphere and sun-spot activity over a 130-year period. Their hypothesis is that observed global warming corresponds to increases in the intensity of solar radiation and not to levels of greenhouse gases in the atmosphere. The established correlation of sunspot activity with warming does not prove or disprove the greenhouse effect. Even if the hypothesis of warming due to solar radiation were true, there is no way to separate what portion of the warming is sun-initiated and what portion is due to the accumulation of heat-trapping gases. Critics of the greenhouse model will

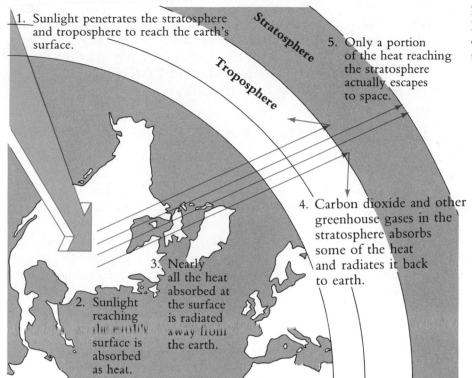

1. Sunlight penetrates the stratosphere and troposphere to reach the earth's surface.

2. Sunlight reaching the earth's surface is absorbed as heat.

3. Nearly all the heat absorbed at the surface is radiated away from the earth.

4. Carbon dioxide and other greenhouse gases in the stratosphere absorbs some of the heat and radiates it back to earth.

5. Only a portion of the heat reaching the stratosphere actually escapes to space.

FIGURE 17-4 Heat Balance. High levels of carbon dioxide and other greenhouse gases influence the heat balance of the earth.

be arguing loudly, however, that there is little cause for concern.

Projections of Global Warming and Rise of Sea Level

People commonly ask, "What are the effects of the buildup of the greenhouse gases?" Predictions about the effects of the buildup require assumptions about the rate of production of carbon dioxide, of methane, and of chlorofluorocarbons. Unfortunately, such predictions are filled with uncertainty because of the assumptions that need to be made about population growth, about economic productivity, and about conservation behavior, to name a few of the many factors that underlie such projections.

To pose the question of effects more precisely, "What would happen if the heat-trapping capacity of the greenhouse gases were to double due to increased concentrations of carbon dioxide, methane, and the CFCs?" If CFCs continue to be emitted at their current rates, that doubling of heat-trapping

capacity could occur by 2050, although it could take until 2100 for carbon dioxide levels alone to double. To predict the temperature, atmospheric scientists trace through a series of interlocking effects that include feedback. A number of teams of scientists are making independent calculations, using these effects, to predict the earth's temperature.

Among the effects are increased evaporation, the melting of snow and ice cover, and an increase in cloudiness. A warmer earth means more evaporation from the great oceans. That evaporation puts more water vapor into the atmosphere. And water vapor is, as you have probably guessed, a heat-trapping greenhouse gas, capable of accelerating the warming. As snow and ice melt, less sunlight is reflected from the earth's surface; that is, more sunlight is absorbed and is translated into heating the surface of the earth. At the same time, moisture in the air will contribute to greater cloudiness. The effect of cloud cover is the largest unknown in predicting global warming. On the one hand, water vapor in the clouds could accelerate warming because water vapor is a greenhouse gas. On the other hand, the cloud cover could reflect significant amounts of sunlight *away* from the earth, softening the warming trend. At the moment, the jury is out on which effect will predominate.

There is no standard set of assumptions that each scientific team makes because none has a crystal ball. The best that exists is informal opinions. As a consequence, predictions differ. An effective doubling of greenhouse gases (which could occur by 2050) could bring a global warming of between 1.5° and 4.5°C (3° to 9°F), depending on which computer model or which expert committee you choose to believe.

Since a rise in temperature causes liquid water to expand, one result of global warming would be a thermal expansion of the oceans. In addition, melting of the Arctic and Antarctic ice sheets should increase the amount and volume of sea water. Glaciers in the Rocky Mountains of Canada, the Swiss Alps, and the Himalayas of Southern Asia would also be expected to contribute meltwaters. Mean sea level would then rise due to the twin effects of thermal expansion and ice melting. The roughly 1°F of warming of the last century has been accompanied by a 4-to-6-inch increase in mean sea level, but whether the observed temperature increase caused the sea level rise is open to debate.

In the warming scenario envisioned, the mean sea level has been predicted to rise because of thermal expansion and the addition of ice sheet and glacier meltwater, but the predictions have varied all the way from 15 inches (.38 meters) to 7 feet (2.1 meters). The flooding of coastal wetlands, critical habitat for migrating birds, would occur to a greater or lesser degree depending on the actual rise. Coastal beaches would be likely to erode; coastal structures from lighthouses to cottages to high-rise hotels would be put at risk. More violent hurricanes and typhoons have been predicted, and the effects of their associated waves would reach further inland as well. Major coastal cities such as New Orleans, Tampa, and Charleston in the United States and Rotterdam and Venice in Europe would be threatened by the upwelling of the seas. Hong Kong on the Pacific rim and Saõ Paulo in South America are also at risk. The Dutch are the masters of sea for-

tifications by necessity, having wrested their nation from the sea by using massive dikes. The government of the Netherlands and the Dutch scientific community take global warming and sea level rise very seriously. Much of Bangladesh could be subject to flooding by the sea.

Climate Changes and Impacts

In the last half dozen years, a number of computer models have been built to predict the climate changes that may be caused by global warming. The models aim to duplicate the natural laws and processes that give us weather and climate. They succeed in creating predictions, but they do not agree with any precision. In general, the models predict that the climate regions of North America will shift northward so that, for instance, Maine's climate will be more like Georgia's climate used to be. As a consequence of the shift in climate, growing regions of important food crops would move quickly northward. It seems unlikely that North American farming practices could adjust quickly enough to continue unimpaired production, unlikely that our farms can continue to be the world's breadbasket.

The polar regions in a number of models seem to experience the largest winter warming and this, in turn, has an impact on the melting of the ice sheets. Melting of the ice caps, in turn, reduces reflectivity and increases absorption of sunlight, leading to greater warming in these regions. In one of the most widely known models, that of Dr. James Hansen of NASA, the interior land masses of Asia, including China, show significant warming as well.

The climate changes will, in turn, have an impact on forests, on other vegetation, and on agriculture. Here we find perhaps the first and only possible benefit of the increasing levels of carbon dioxide: Photosynthesis is stimulated and plants seem to grow better in the presence of higher concentrations of carbon dioxide. For instance, plant scientists predict a 32% increase in soybean yields with a doubling in the carbon dioxide concentration in the atmosphere. This quickened growth would be expected of vegetation growing in regions that have temperature and rainfall for which the plant type is already adapted. The soybean, for instance, would not do well if the region in which it was being grown became quite hot and extremely arid, no matter whether carbon dioxide stimulated its growth or not.

Other vegetation types, including trees, are expected to respond with increased growth to higher carbon dioxide levels where temperature and moisture requirements are also met. On the basis of this phenomenon of carbon dioxide stimulation of plant growth, some agricultural economists are predicting positive benefits for farming, but their models assume that adjustments to new climates are costless. Adjustments may, in fact, be very difficult, costly, and time-consuming. The conclusions of some economists that the greenhouse effect will be good for us should not be believed. At best, such conclusions are narrow lenses on a problem of enormous dimensions.

The northward-shifting band of warmth could be expected to cause the northern forests of North America to grow more rapidly. However, as the warming proceeds, tree species currently adapted to the more southern latitudes could fail to survive in their now warmer home. Georgia could become tropical, Maine like Georgia was, and Newfoundland like Maine had been. The beech, sugar maple, birch, and hemlock could have their ranges shifted 300–600 miles northward. The planting of southern tree species in more northerly locations might become necessary not only to ensure the survival of these tree species but also to provide forests capable of growing in the newly warmed regions. The question is if and when such a process of tree transferal should be begun.

Animal species will be impacted as well. With all regions becoming warmer, many species would probably try to migrate to colder latitudes to find conditions suitable for reproduction and survival. Roads and railroad tracks may hinder their movement. The plant species on which animals depend may become extinct at their current latitude, necessitating movement of the animal species just to follow their needed vegetative support. The interplay of plants and animals, the plants providing food and shelter for the animals, the animals spreading seeds and pollinating flowers, will be complex. Survival of individual species in either the plant or animal kingdom would not be ensured. Ask economists to put values of plant and animal species in their equations on the benefits of global warming. They cannot. Some species already require the support of wildlife refuges, and these refuges could lose their habitability due to temperature and rainfall changes. The species could fail to survive unless new refuge areas were established in areas with appropriate conditions of temperature, moisture, and vegetation.

Many migratory birds will still spend their summers on the now warmer and changed Arctic tundra. On their migratory routes their coastal feeding places, the tidal ocean beaches, may be flooded. We do not know how migratory birds will adapt to these changed conditions. Reptile reproduction is altered by warmer temperatures. Turtles will have more female offspring; alligators more males. The complete list of potential, unknown consequences for plants and animals can hardly be assembled.

Dealing with the Greenhouse Effect

Probably the single most important step we can take, the step that should be taken first, is to eliminate the use of chlorofluorocarbons. This would be accomplished by finding less damaging substitutes. The CFCs are being phased out not only because they contribute significantly to projected global warming but also because they are destroying ozone in the stratosphere.

The CFCs must be phased out quickly because it takes 60 to 120 years for these chemicals to degrade once they reach the atmosphere. The legacy of our current use of CFCs will haunt us for the next century. Development of substitutes should be pushed by government incentives. The hydrohalocarbons may be a good family of compounds to substitute for the time being because they break down in tens of years and absorb only one-fiftieth of the infrared radiation that the CFCs do.

We can also hasten the removal of carbon dioxide from the atmosphere by planting trees, billions of trees, replacing the forests of both North and South America that have been cut or burned. Re-

Towards a Sustainable Society

Preserving a Coastal Ecosystem

by James Titus

Since 1982, Jim Titus has been the U.S. EPA's Project Manager for Sea Level Rise. That small project has been the only federal program dedicated primarily to accelerating the process by which society learns to adapt to global warming, and is generally recognized as having convinced U.S. coastal officials to take global warming seriously, several years before the national environmental groups became interested in the issue. The opinions expressed do not necessarily reflect official policy of the U.S. government.

While avoiding global warming requires a worldwide consensus, preparing for its consequences does not. Because climatologists generally agree that some warming is inevitable, communities will have to adapt to global warming even if drastic policies are enacted in time to avoid a 2–5 degree warming. In the case of rising sea level, some communities are already beginning to take action.

The prospect of rising sea level poses both engineering and environmental problems. The world's coastal engineers have substantial experience in protecting cities like New Orleans, Shanghai, and London from the sea—as well as farmland in Malaysia, Guyana, and the Netherlands. However, this protection has often been at the expense of the coastal environment. The Dutch have eliminated all but one of their estuaries, and the same is happening in Louisiana today. Environmentally benign techniques for holding back the sea

have only proven to be economical along highly valuable sandy resort beaches.

The only way to ensure that we keep the many other ecosystems that depend on natural shorelines—including marshes, mangroves, cypress swamps, and mudflats—is to allow these ecosystems to encroach landward onto areas that are dry today, which will require the United States to abandon about 7,000 square miles (an area the size of Massachusetts) for a one-meter rise in sea level. At first glance, such a proposal sounds prohibitively expensive. But if implemented gradually, the abandonment need not be disruptive, and it certainly would be less disruptive and less costly than the alternative of building elaborate networks of dikes, pumping systems, and artificial beaches.

Should we act now or wait a few decades? If our only choices were to abandon the coast now or do nothing, we would be best ad-

member that much of North America was a deep forest when the first settlers arrived. Trees not only take carbon dioxide out of the air; they prevent erosion, provide food and building materials, stabilize climate through their moisture- and temperature-mediating effects, and shelter wildlife. Not

only do trees need to be planted; the destruction of tropical forests in Central and South America needs to be controlled, as does the cutting of old-growth trees in North America. If tree planting were going to be used as a method to moderate the greenhouse effect, now is the time to begin. Once climate shifts

vised to do nothing: Buying all the coastal property (or prohibiting development) would be far more expensive than establishing an escrow account that could be used to buy the property as it becomes inundated — either way the wetlands are protected, but in the latter case people could benefit from the use of the property for the next several decades. Most economists would agree that under such situations, it would be irrational to prohibit development.

Unfortunately, state and local governments cannot establish escrow accounts to ensure that the developed areas are abandoned. They can, however, modify property ownership in a manner that accomplishes the same thing: Allow new and current development to continue, but on the condition that the land will be abandoned when the sea rises. A convenient feature of this approach is that developers and others who argue that sea level rise is unlikely would have no reason to object, since the policy would only have teeth if and when the sea actually rises.

Because of the public trust doctrine (the public ownership of tidal waters and tidelands), some legal scholars believe that such a policy is already implied by our common law, and we need merely enforce it. The State of Maine's Department of Environment has already implemented issued regulations that apply the public trust doctrine to sea level rise, by explicitly telling property owners they will have to move their buildings as the natural ecosystems migrate inland. Nevertheless, courts and politicians may find it difficult to resist pressures to relax these rules, once compliance actually requires people to tear down buildings.

A more legally binding approach that would also appeal to economists and people who take literally the Bill of Rights prohibition of governmental takings without compensation would be for local governments to purchase coastal property and sell back a lease to inhabit the property until the sea rises enough to inundate it. We can only guess about the net cost of the leasing approach, but it seems likely to be less than 1 percent of the assessed value of most property, because (1) the market probably would not expect most coastal property to be inundated for 100–200 years, and (2) the mar-

ket heavily discounts the future. Unlike most environmental regulations, high interest rates and skepticism about the supposed threat reduce the cost to the government of implementing this market-based scheme.

Best of all, even small companies, local environmental groups, and average citizens can begin to take action. Nonprofit groups that usually sell donated land could add a clause to the deeds indicating that the land must be returned to the public trust when the sea rises enough to inundate it. Individuals can donate to a conservancy the right to take over a coastal property when the sea rises, and attempt to claim a tax deduction. Even if the courts disallow all or part of the deduction, the local environment wins: If the courts rule that the market value of this right is trivial, that must mean that local governments wishing to purchase the right from property owners must only pay a trivial compensation.

The various options for protecting coastal ecosystems in the event of sea level rise are illustrated in Figure A, page 380.

begin, it may be difficult to find the right zone for a tree to thrive.

There is no doubt that we are capable of reducing carbon dioxide emissions. In Chapter 13 we described the many opportunities for energy conservation. In Chapters 12 and 13 we also discussed renewable sources of energy available to humankind, such as solar, wind, and geothermal. A number of the new sources are ready to use now without new technology, without further research and development. Energy conservation and these renewable sources all eliminate carbon dioxide emissions.

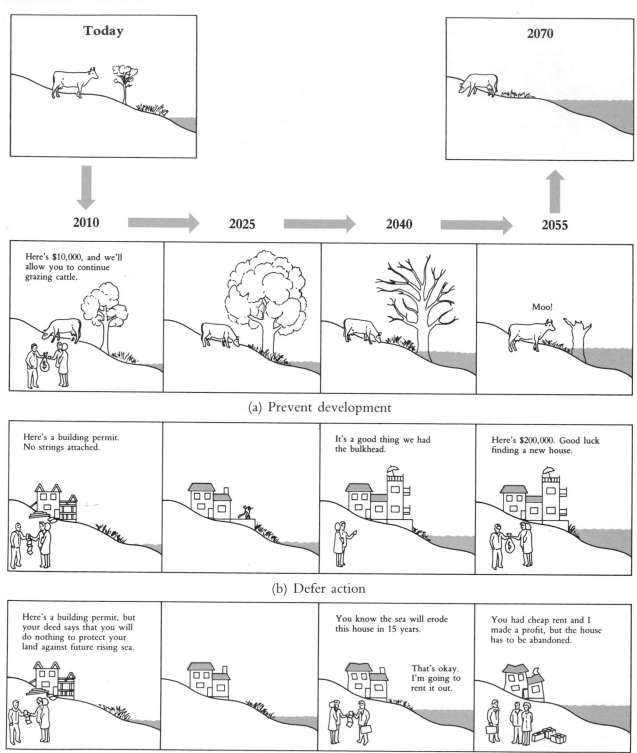

FIGURE A Options for Enabling Wetlands to Migrate Inland. (*a*) Prevent development today, compensating current owners (*b*) Defer action until we see if the sea level rises or not (*c*) Presume mobility—allow development but specify property must be abandoned to allow shoreward migration of coastal ecosystems if the sea level rises. (*Source:* Adapted from James Titus)

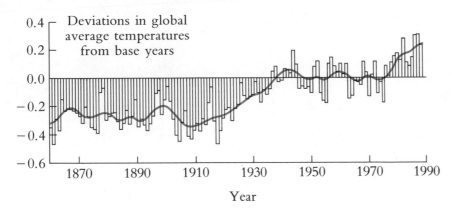

FIGURE 17-5 Change in Global Average Temperatures. The global averages of the temperatures of the air over land and of the sea surface temperatures are subtracted from global averages for the period 1951–1980. The difference indicates that the period before 1951 was much cooler and the period after 1980 much warmer. (*Source:* "Policy Implications of Greenhouse Warming," Washington, D.C., National Academy Press, 1991)

We do not suggest nuclear energy as an alternative here; its many liabilities make it a choice of last resort.

New fuels for automobiles will decrease carbon dioxide production. Methanol has been proposed as such a fuel. Its use would cut carbon dioxide emissions by 80% from autos, and other pollutants would be decreased as well, but it, too, has disadvantages. (See Chapter 15 for a discussion of methanol as an automotive fuel.) Ethanol is already in use in Brazil as the fuel for 25% of that nation's cars. The remaining three-quarters of the vehicles use a gasoline (80%) and ethanol (20%) blend. Ethanol use also reduces carbon dioxide emissions. Canada has an experimental program powering a thousand cars on compressed natural gas, a fuel as low in carbon as methanol.

We can conserve enormous quantities of energy by increasing the fuel efficiency of our cars, by insulating homes, and by switching to fluorescent lighting and to more energy-efficient appliances (see Chapter 13).

All these energy conservation and fuel-switching activities will limit and soften potential global warming. In addition, however, they will also help to make the United States secure from the oil cartel, from embargoes, from price increases, from eco-

nomic blackmail, and from the necessity of going to war to protect sources of supply in other nations.

Should We Act?

When will the carbon dioxide effect be seen as a clear increase in temperature, distinct from other trends? Scientist J. M. Mitchell suggests that by the turn of the century the upward trend of surface temperature will become utterly apparent (see Figure 17-5). He also notes that "By the time the CO_2 disturbance will have run its full course, more than a millennium into the future, temperature levels in the global atmosphere may possibly exceed the highest levels attained in the past million years of the earth's history."

The theory that carbon dioxide and other greenhouse gases would change the climate of the earth has now moved from the desks of scientists onto the desks of politicians around the globe. Concerned atmospheric scientists and their graphic computer models combined with a decade of unusually warm weather to stimulate the shift.

We still do not know all the effects that greenhouse warming could bring. Certainly the impacts could be very large, even devastating, to human, plant, and other animal populations. Basically, we have two alternatives. We can begin limited but

Towards a Sustainable Society

A Carbon Tax

by José Goldemberg

Mr. Goldemberg was Brazil's Secretary of State for Science and Technology when he wrote this essay. He is now Minister for Education.

About 60% of the greenhouse gases entering the atmosphere come from the burning of fossil fuels. Therefore, unless we see startling advances in such alternative sources as nuclear fusion or photovoltaics, any serious proposal to head off global warming must attack the problem of reducing the world's demand for energy.

Yet the less developed countries (LDCs) and, to a lesser extent, the centrally planned economies of the Soviet Union and Eastern Europe will display a steadily increasing energy appetite as they evolve into industrial economies. With more than three times the population of the industrialized world, the LDCs bristle at the idea that they must curtail their energy use. The political leadership and populace of these poorer nations believe they deserve the chance to grow; they are unwilling to forgo development even if development means burning massive amounts of fossil fuels and obliterating more forests.

Thus, although action is urgently needed to halt environmentally destructive practices, the world at large should not—and probably could not—force the LDCs to shoulder the entire burden of solving global warming. Acting both through duty and in their long-term self-interest, the developed nations should help the LDCs onto an environmentally benign path.

Newer, more efficient technologies can lower energy consumption without affecting economic

significant action now to prevent this threat from materializing. Alternatively, we can do nothing now and act only if the threat becomes reality. Then, unfortunately, it may be too late to save what we most want to save, including ourselves. What do you think should be done?

OZONE: AN ESSENTIAL GAS IN DANGER

Besides contributing to the greenhouse effect, CFCs (chlorofluorocarbons) cause another problem—destruction of the stratospheric ozone layer. Ozone is a gas in which each molecule is made up of three atoms of oxygen. Sometimes ozone can be a pollutant. In Chapter 15 we noted how the burning of fossil fuels, especially by automobiles, leads to the production of ozone. This ozone, which ends up in the troposphere, the layer of the atmosphere nearest the earth, causes eye irritation and respiratory distress. In the upper stratosphere, however, this same gas serves an essential function—it absorbs over 99% of the ultraviolet light that comes from the sun. Ultraviolet rays are often welcomed because they cause skin to tan. They can also cause it to burn, and, over long periods of time, ultraviolet rays cause skin cancers.

output. CFC substitutes can provide refrigeration. In fact, an international "carbon tax" of just $1 per barrel of oil, or $6 per ton of coal, would generate $50 billion per year—more than enough revenue to pay for the necessary fuel-saving measures. This tax could result from an international agreement similar to the 1987 Montreal Protocol, which obliges its signatories to cut down on production of CFCs.

The purpose of the carbon tax would not be primarily to discourage energy consumption, any more than a highway toll is intended to discourage automobile travel. Rather, the tax would be a fair and effective way to raise the money needed to fund a transition into an ecologically more benign economy.

The tax would have to be collected at the source, as an increase in the price of oil, coal, and gas. The pool of revenue would be allocated to LDCs by existing United Nations organizations—such as the U.N. Development Program and the U.N. Environment Program—or by the World Bank.

These organizations would, for example, extend preferential financing to projects that are energy-efficient according to standards of industrialized nations. This policy would not only avoid future expensive retrofitting but induce savings in energy consumption.

Suppose a new refrigerator factory is built in Brazil. Banks could offer low-interest loans on the condition that the factory must be tooled to produce models that consume at most 400 kilowatt-hours a year—half the power used by the standard Brazilian refrigerator. If the company sells 1 million units each year, this will represent annual savings of 400 million killowatt-hours. Such a reduction would avoid the need for 35,000 kilowatts of generating capacity—an additional economy of at least $70 mil-

lion. A similar condition could apply to factories that produce automobiles and other products essential for development.

Given the high stakes, an internationally agreed-upon tax is not a very radical step. Cooperation among rich and poor nations will be based not purely on good will and philanthropy but also on enlightened self-interest. The sums of money needed to stabilize the atmosphere are not really that large: $50 billion represents 0.4% of the total gross domestic product of the industrialized world. Spending such a sum to stabilize the atmosphere and avoid environmental catastrophe seems a prudent—and, in the most basic sense, conservative—proposition.

Source: This essay is based on an article that appeared in *Technology Review*, November/December 1990, p. 25.

High concentrations of ultraviolet rays are harmful to many forms of plant and animal life. They are sometimes used to sterilize objects because in high concentrations they kill bacteria. Scientists generally believe that life on land did not develop until the earth's protective ozone layer formed. Because ozone in the stratosphere is essential to life, reports that a number of human activities can destroy ozone are understandably alarming.

Threats to the Ozone Layer

Stratospheric ozone is destroyed by the nitrous oxide produced by supersonic jets in the atmosphere, by chemicals used as agricultural fumigants, and by methylchloroform and carbon tetrachloride from industrial processes. By far the greatest threat to the ozone layer, however, is posed by chlorofluorocarbons. These are chemicals that are both nonflammable and unreactive with most substances. Those properties have made them useful in many industrial and consumer products, for instance as cooling fluids in refrigerators and air conditioners, as propellants in spray cans, as industrial solvent cleaners, and as foaming agents for polystyrene.

CFCs are not broken down in the troposphere. In the early 1970s, James Lovelock measured the atmospheric concentration of one of the early chlorofluorocarbons. By calculating how much had been released, he determined that almost all of it was still around. He called for research into the possible effects such accumulating chemicals might have. What was found was that chlorofluorocarbons rise slowly into the stratosphere, where they are broken down, releasing chlorine that can react with and destroy ozone.

Health Effects of a Decreasing Ozone Layer

A decrease in the ozone layer allows more ultraviolet radiation from the sun to reach the earth. The occurrence of the two most common types of skin cancer, basal cell and squamous cell carcinoma, appears to be strongly related to exposure to sunlight, especially its ultraviolet-B component. (Ultraviolet-B includes the wavelengths from 290 to 320 nm.)

The rate of skin cancer in the United States is reported to be 300,000–400,000 cases of basal cell carcinoma and 100,000 cases of squamous cell carcinoma per year. Each 1% decrease in ozone is believed to cause a 2% increase in ultraviolet radiation and as much as a 2%–5% increase in skin cancer. Proportionately, then, each 1% decrease might cause 10,000–30,000 extra cases of skin cancer each year in the United States. Worldwide, the EPA has estimated that without efforts to protect the ozone layer, some additional 1 to 2 billion cases of skin cancer could occur by 2075.

A related concern is the effect of ultraviolet-B radiation on the immune system of humans and animals. This type of radiation appears to prevent normal immune responses not only in the skin but also in other parts of the body. Scientists speculate that this is how ultraviolet-B radiation causes skin cancers to form.

Plants and animals also show sensitivity to ultraviolet-B rays. An increase in ultraviolet light could be expected to cause the extinction of some microscopic life forms and to damage other species or decrease the living space available to them.

Global Regulation

In the late 1970s the United States was responsible for half the CFCs released in the world. Because of their possible effect on the ozone layer, using CFCs as propellants in spray cans was outlawed in the United States in 1979. CFC production dropped briefly but then began rising again due to increasing use by other countries of CFCs in refrigeration, as cleaning agents, and in foam insulation.

Scientists around the world continued to monitor stratospheric ozone levels both by satellite and by periodic expeditions to the Arctic and the Antarctic; and in the mid 1980s came up with a dramatic finding: During the winter, ozone levels over the Antarctic dropped to near zero. There was a virtual ozone "hole" over the Antarctic. Spurred by this finding, in 1987, 57 countries agreed to a treaty to reduce CFC levels worldwide. The treaty became known as the Montreal Protocol. It required industrialized countries to cut their use of five CFCs by 50% by 1998 and to halt increases in their use of three other ozone-destroying compounds containing bromine that are used in fighting fires.

It became clear, however, that such controls were not going to be enough. Holes continued to show up in the Antarctic ozone layer each winter, while losses of 2%–6% of the ozone layer were recorded over middle latitudes covering most of the United States, the former U.S.S.R., Europe, and China (Figure 17-6). Meanwhile the use of CFCs was increasing in the developing countries, which had not signed the Montreal Protocol. As if that were not bad enough, new evidence showed that chloroform and carbon tetrachloride, cheap and widely used industrial solvents and cleaners, posed a significant threat to the ozone layer, even if the use of CFCs could be controlled.

The result of all this was the 1990 London Ozone Agreement, signed by 93 nations. In this new agreement the signing nations agreed to phase out all use of CFCs by the year 2000 and to limit chloroform and carbon tetrachloride use as well (Figure 17-7).

The agreement would not have achieved a significant degree of protection of the ozone layer, however, if it were not for one other amendment. It was agreed that the developed world would contribute to a fund to help developing countries find alternatives to ozone-destroying chemicals and to retool their industries for use of the substitutes. With this guarantee, China and India agreed to sign the treaty.

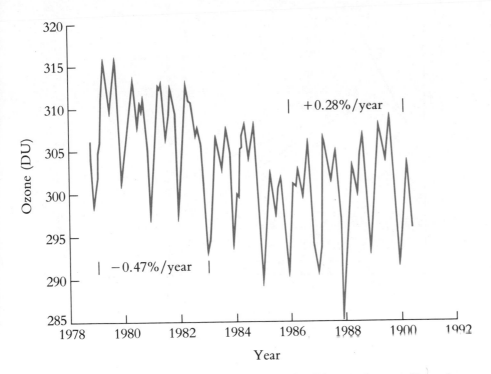

FIGURE 17-6 Interpreting Global Ozone Trends. The Nimbus satellite collects data each day on the amount of ozone over the entire sunlit portion of the globe. Scientists believe that human-caused decreases in ozone are superimposed on a natural variation in ozone concentration that follows an 11-year solar cycle. On the above graph, each point represents a daily global mean concentration of ozone, in Dobson units. Although there is a clear decrease in ozone from 1978 to 1985, there appears to have been a slight increase over the past few years, possibly due to solar cycle effects. After correcting for solar cycle effects, there is still a net ozone loss of 2.22% plus or minus 1.4%, per decade. We will need to collect data for another whole 11-year solar cycle before we can be certain that the downward trend in global ozone is continuing; however, most scientists believe that is what we will see. (*Source:* Graph courtesy of J. Herman, NASA/Goddard Space Flight Center)

What Will We Use Instead?

For the short term, hydrofluorocarbons (HFCs), which contain no chlorine, and hydrochlorofluorocarbons (HCFC), in which some, but not all, of the chlorine is replaced by hydrogen, will probably be the substitutes of choice. Both are largely broken down in the lower atmosphere. Both are expensive, however, and both can still contribute to global warming. Water-based cleaning can be substituted for some CFC uses, and helium may be an attractive substitute in refrigeration systems when some technical problems are solved.

Consumers can help in several ways: (1) Insist that your auto mechanic fix a leaking car air conditioner, not just refill it. In the United States, leaking car air conditioners are now the single largest CFC source. Furthermore, some repair shops recycle CFCs, while others simply vent them to the atmosphere while repairing air conditioners. If your car's air conditioner needs repair or recharging with coolant, make sure the shop doing the work recycles CFCs. (2) Don't buy halon-containing fire extinguishers. (3) Check labels of spray products

FIGURE 17-7 Ozone-Destroying Chlorine Levels in the Stratosphere According to Different Scenarios. If only the 50% decrease in CFCs agreed to in the Montreal Protocol were achieved, chlorine levels would rise according to Line 1. If a complete phaseout of CFCs and carbon tetrachloride is achieved by 2000 and a phaseout of chloroform by 2205, as per the London Agreement, chlorine levels will follow Line 2. In order to return stratospheric chlorine to levels below that at which the antarctic ozone hole appeared, however, it will be necessary to phase out the CFC substitutes, HCFCs, as well (Line 3). (*Source:* U.S. EPA)

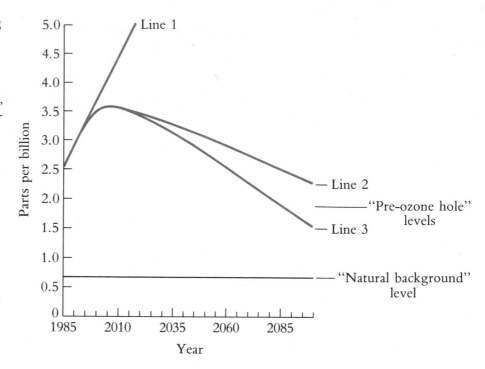

SUMMARY

The production of carbon dioxide from the combustion of coal, oil, and natural gas, from forest fires, and from the respiration of plants and animals exceeds the rate at which carbon dioxide is being removed from the atmosphere. The natural removal mechanisms of photosynthesis and solution in the oceans have simply been overpowered, causing carbon dioxide to build up in the atmosphere. Carbon dioxide reaches the stratosphere, where its chemical structure causes the molecule to absorb infrared radiation that would otherwise escape from the earth to space. Many scientists think this effect of heat trapping will cause the earth to warm.

Carbon dioxide is not the only heat-trapping gas in the atmosphere. The chlorofluorocarbons and methane also trap heat. Together their impact on heat trapping may come to rival that of the far more abundant carbon dioxide. Chlorofluorocarbons

for the presence of HCFCs, or for chloroform, which will be listed as 1,1,1-trichloroethane. Other formulations are available to do the same jobs.

have been used as refrigerants and for foam blowing. Methane, a natural component of the air from swamps and decaying matter, is supplemented by inadvertent release from coal mines and petroleum fields as well as from natural gas fields; it also arises from rice paddies, from the guts of ruminants, and from leaky natural gas pipelines.

Scientists are projecting an effective doubling of heat-trapping capability by the greenhouse gases by the year 2050. Accompanying this increase will be temperature increases estimated to be somewhere between 3° and 9°F (1.5°–4.5°C). The estimates by scientific teams are different because of different assumptions about the natural processes that contribute to global warming. Especially uncertain is the role of cloud cover, which could slow global warming by reflecting sunlight from the earth or hasten it as the water vapor molecules act as greenhouse gases.

With the predicted temperature increase, a rise in mean sea level is expected. The rise would be caused by temperature-induced expansion of the ocean and a melting of the polar ice caps and inland glaciers. Depending on the extent of sea level rise, which is estimated to be between 15 inches (.3 meters) and 7 feet (2.1 meters), coastal cities around the world could be flooded. Wetlands could be destroyed and ocean beaches washed away.

Computer models have been applied to estimate the changes in climate by region of the globe. While the models do not agree in all particulars, they do generally predict that the polar regions appear to warm the most. A movement of elevated temperature regions to higher northern and higher southern latitudes is also a general result. Rainfall as well as temperature patterns appear to shift.

Forests would face a challenge in these climate shifts as the natural range of trees will move to higher latitudes. Some tree species may not survive. The high-latitude forests seem to benefit, but southern forests may suffer. Agriculture is thought to need to shift northward in the Northern Hemisphere. Whether farming practice can adjust quickly enough to the evolution of new growing zones is an open and troubling question. The one positive effect of increased carbon dioxide in the air is a stimulation of photosynthesis and plant growth, but this effect may not bring economic benefits unless farming practices can adjust to the new climate regimes that evolve. Animal species may also need to move to higher northern and southern latitudes to find appropriate temperatures and rainfall as well as to stay with their associated plant species.

The greenhouse effect and global warming can be softened by phasing out the chlorofluorocarbons used in refrigeration and foam blowing. These greenhouse gases, as well as methane, are potent contributors to projected warming. We can plant trees to remove carbon dioxide, and these will be a welcome addition to the planet to replace the forests we have cut down so far; they will provide food and material, erosion control, and shelter for species.

Chlorofluorocarbons (CFCs) not only contribute to predicted global warming. Chlorine-containing chemicals such as CFCs, methylchloroform, and carbon tetrachloride are also responsible for a decrease in stratospheric ozone. Because ozone in the stratosphere absorbs ultraviolet rays from the sun, its destruction threatens an increase in human skin cancer and possible harmful effects on ecosystems. International agreements to limit the use of CFCs, such as the Montreal Protocol and the Lon-

don Agreement, may be successful in limiting ozone-destroying chemicals to approximately 1985 levels. To return to levels that existed before the Antarctic ozone hole appeared, however, CFC substitutes such as HCFCs must be phased out as well.

Solar power, wind power, and geothermal power produce energy without producing carbon dioxide and have the potential to substitute for the energy produced by the fossil fuels. Nuclear power is not a recommended substitute for fossil energy because of its other environmental and social problems.

Low-carbon fuels such as methanol, ethanol, and compressed natural gas can be used to power automobiles rather than carbon-rich gasoline. Energy conservation can reduce carbon dioxide emissions. We can conserve energy by driving more fuel-efficient automobiles, by insulating homes and commercial/industrial buildings more thoroughly, and by using energy-efficient appliances and lighting. All these steps can substantially diminish carbon dioxide emissions to the atmosphere. In addition, energy conservation promotes the economic security of the United States.

The bottom line of the greenhouse effect is how we treat uncertainty. Do we act decisively now at substantial cost in the face of dimly understood but potentially disastrous future conditions? Or do we wait and see how serious the problem turns out to be and, in the process, perhaps foreclose our ability to respond effectively at all?

Questions

1. Draw a diagram of the carbon dioxide cycle, showing natural production of carbon dioxide and routes of carbon dioxide removal from the atmosphere. List the sources of carbon dioxide additions that civilization has introduced from its activities.

2. Name two greenhouse gases in addition to carbon dioxide. One of them is a class of compounds used in refrigerators and air conditioners; the other is a fuel. Which is naturally present in our atmosphere? Which is manmade? Describe the other problem that results from use of the greenhouse gases in refrigerators and air conditioners.

3. How are the greenhouse gases projected to cause warming? That is, what is the mechanism that causes heat to accumulate?

4. The projected warming is expected to cause increased evaporation from the ocean. Will this influence the greenhouse effect? In which direction? Why?

5. What are the two reasons that the mean sea level is expected to rise due to global warming?

6. Describe at least four broad classes of actions that nations can take to reduce the potential for global warming.

Further Reading

Mitchell, John. "The Greenhouse Effect and Climate Change," *Review of Geophysics, 27*(1) (February 1989), 115.

This is a wonderfully written article that reviews the greenhouse gases and their impacts on climate. Technical in spots.

Office of Technology Assessment. *Changing by Degrees: Steps to Reduce Greenhouse Gases,* OTA-482. Washington, D.C.: U.S. Government Printing Office, February 1991.

Absolutely comprehensive, the report begins with an overview, reviews the background, and examines options exhaustively.

Policy Implications of Greenhouse Warming—Synthesis Panel. *Policy Implications of Greenhouse Warming.* Washington, D.C.: National Academies of Science and Engineering, National Academy Press, 1991.

The panel finds that the United States can make significant reductions in its greenhouse emissions quite cheaply and recommends this course as insurance.

Rose, D., M. Miller, and C. Agnew. "Reducing the Problem of Global Warming," *Technology Review,* May–June 1984, p. 49.

A description of policy options for control of carbon dioxide. Emphasis is on energy conservation.

Singer, S. Fred (Ed.). *Global Climate Change,* New York: Paragon House, 1989.

Chapters of interest include: "Carbon Dioxide and Climate Changes," by William Kellog and "Methane in the Atmosphere," by Ralph Cerone.

Smith, Joel, and Dennis Tirpak (Eds.). *The Potential Effects of Global Climate Change on the United States.* New York: Hemisphere (a division of Taylor & Francis), 1990.

This is a voluminous treatment of virtually all impacts by region of the United States and type of impact. Impact discussions on agriculture, forests, sea level rise, biological diversity, air quality, and health are included. The level of discussion is not deeply scientific, although a science background would be helpful.

References

Anderson, J. G., et al. "Free Radicals within the Antarctic Vortex: The Role of CFC's in Antarctic Ozone Loss," *Science 251* (January 4, 1991), 39.

Booth, William. "Johnny Appleseed and the Greenhouse," *Science,* October 7, 1989, p. 10.

Hammond, A., E. Rodenburg, and W. Moomaur. "Calculating National Accountability for Climate Change," *Environment, 33*(1) (January/February, 1991).

Herman, J. R., R. McPeters, and R. Stolarski. "Global Average Ozone Change from November 1978 to May 1990," *Journal of Geophysical Research, 96* (September 1991), 17, 297.

Houghton, S., G. Jenkins, and J. Ephraums (Eds.). *Climate Change—The IPCC Scientific Assessment.* New York: Cambridge University Press, 1990.

Kerr, Richard. "Is There Life after Climate Change?" *Science,* November 18, 1988, p. 1010.

Kerr, Richard. "The Global Warming Is Real," *Science,* February 3, 1989, p. 603.

Kerr, Richard. "EPA's Plan for Cooling the Global Greenhouse," *Science,* March 24, 1989, p. 1544.

Kerr, Richard. "Hansen *vs* the World on the Greenhouse Threat," *Science,* June 2, 1989, p. 127.

Kerr, Richard. "Greenhouse Skeptic Out in the Cold," *Science,* December 1, 1989, p. 118.

Makihijani, A., et al. "Still Working on the Ozone Hole," *Technology Review,* May/June 1990, p. 53.

Nelson, T. P., and S. L. Wevill, "Alternative Formulations to Reduce CFC Use in U.S. Exempted and Excluded Aerosol Products," EPA Project Summary 660/S2-89/061. Washington, D.C.: U.S. Government Printing Office, 1989.

Roberts, Leslie. "How Fast Can Trees Migrate?" *Science,* February 10, 1989, p. 735.

Roberts, Leslie. "Global Warming: Blaming the Sun," *Science,* November 24, 1989, p. 992.

Schneider, Stephen. "The Greenhouse Effect: Science and Policy," *Science,* February 10, 1989, p. 771.

Chapter 18

Water Resources and the Quality of Natural Waters

There are 19 dams on the Columbia and Snake rivers that run through Oregon, Washington, and Idaho. River waters, on their way to the ocean, are captured behind these dams to generate power and to ensure a constant supply of water for the cities and farms along their route. Some nine million salmon once left the ocean and surged up these rivers in search of their ancestral breeding grounds. Today, less than one-third of that number successfully navigate the hazards of the tamed rivers, and four-fifths of those salmon were bred in hatcheries to augment the declining wild population. In 1990 only two sockeye salmon were counted climbing the fish ladder at Lower Granite Dam in Idaho, down from 4,500 in 1950 (Figure 18-1).

Natural waters, both fresh and salt, are a vital resource. Fresh waters are needed for drinking, irrigation of agricultural lands, and industrial processes. Both fresh and salt waters provide habitats for plants and animals, many of which are important food species. Wars are fought for access to salt and freshwater ports essential for transport of goods. But all too often, natural waters are used as sewers for human waste products or toxic industrial discharges. Furthermore, natural waters suffer from unintended inputs of animal wastes, eroded soil, and agricultural and industrial chemicals.

On the eve of a conference on the control of pollution in the Mediterranean Sea, a large number of dead dolphins washed up on Spanish resort beaches. The dolphins, apparently victims of pollutants that injured their immune systems, dramatized the need for measures to control pollutants running into the Mediterranean (Figure 18-2).

In this chapter we discuss the supply and quality of the world's resources of natural fresh and salt waters. For fresh waters, both water supply and water quality are important issues. In comparison, there is no shortage of salt waters on the globe, but human impacts threaten the quality of the marine habitat, especially in coastal areas. In the chapter following this one, we focus on global supplies of drinking water and the effect of hazardous waste disposal practices on drinking water quality.

FIGURE 18-1 Dam on the Columbia River. Conservation groups are pushing to have several salmon runs protected under the Endangered Species Act. If the salmon were listed, their protection would take precedence over economic management considerations, such as storage of water for power generation and allocation of water for irrigation. (*Photo:* Nick Christmas/ Bonneville Power Administration)

FRESH WATER

Sources of Fresh Water

Fresh water is obtained from two sources: wells, which tap underground sources of water called *aquifers,* or from surface flows—lakes, rivers, and reservoirs.

A dam thrown across a river backs up the water flow behind its face, forming a **reservoir.** The dam releases through its gates only enough water to sustain the downstream flow, holding back high flows for gradual release later when low flows occur. Reservoirs increase the amount of water available to communities. Without a reservoir, the largest steady rate of daily water withdrawal from a flowing river can be no greater than the *lowest* daily flow rate occurring in the river during the time of operation. Any larger quantity of water could not be withdrawn steadily day after day. With a reservoir, a city or town can draw water steadily week after week, month after month, without interruption.

The above-ground reservoir is a human invention to steady the flow of fresh water through time, collecting high stream flow from one season to make water available in the low-flow season. The **aquifer,** in contrast, is a natural underground res-

FIGURE 18-2 Garbage Washed up on the Mediterranean Shore near Athens. Seventy coastal cities with populations greater than 100,000 put great pressure on the sea waters. Compacts between the countries surrounding the Mediterranean have been successful in limiting some pollutants. Mercury levels in shellfish are lower than 10 years ago, and the waters at tourist beaches are also improved. However, a number of large cities on the heavily industrialized north shore still do not treat their sewage. (*Photo:* T. Farkas/UNEP)

ervoir, where water temporarily resides on its route to lakes, streams, rivers, or oceans. An above-ground reservoir is a large, empty space when not filled with water, but an aquifer is not necessarily empty. It may consist of free-flowing water, as in an underground cavern or stream, but it may also be water that simply fills the spaces between particles of sand and gravel. Aquifers can be huge, extending for hundreds of miles, and the volumes of water in such aquifers can be enormous. The volume of water stored in the Ogallala Aquifer, in the High Plains states, is probably comparable to the volume of water in Lake Huron.

Aquifers are filled or **recharged** by water that seeps through the ground from rainfall or above-ground sources. About 25% of the yearly precipitation in the United States becomes groundwater. The process is very slow, however. Although world groundwater resources far exceed surface water sources (Table 18-1), this groundwater has collected over hundreds or thousands of years, at relatively slow rates. (Sources of fresh water are summarized in Figure 3-3.)

Uses of Reservoirs

Reservoirs can serve more purposes than simply to provide a community with a constant supply of drinking or irrigation water. Many dams and reservoirs are part of a hydroelectric power-generating system. Reservoirs may also be used for recreational boating or swimming, and in some cases they are meant to provide flood protection. The operation and purpose of a reservoir can affect its impact on the environment—and reservoirs have a strong impact.

As flowing waters slow down, which indeed they must as they are brought to a halt by a reservoir, the sediment suspended in the turbulent waters settles out and drops to the bottom of the reservoir. Downstream from the reservoir, the clear water released into the river erodes earth from the river bank at a faster rate than the free-flowing river would have.

The bottom of the reservoir becomes coated with the sediments transported from upstream areas. This blanket of sediments is exposed to view

TABLE 18-1 Freshwater Resources of the World

Resource	Volume (thousands of km³)
Fresh water in lakes and inland seas	125
Fresh water in streams, rivers, etc. (average)	1.25
Groundwater within 0.8 km of surface	4,200
Groundwater between 0.8 km and 4.0 km depth	4,200
Fresh water in glaciers and ice caps	29,000

Source: Adapted from H. Bouwer, *Groundwater Hydrology* (New York: McGraw-Hill, 1978).

periodically as the level of water in the reservoir rises and falls in response to inflows and releases. The sediments gradually build up and, unless dug out occasionally, begin to consume the storage volume of the reservoir.

Large deposits of sediment in reservoirs can be partially prevented. Although erosion and sediment transport are natural and continuing events, farming, road development, construction of homes, and forest cutting all accelerate erosion processes by exposing fresh and unanchored soil. Careful management of the soil (see Chapter 7) can help reduce the burden of sediment carried by streams and thus help prevent the rapid deposition of sediment in reservoirs.

The unsightly mounds of sediment that become visible during times of low reservoir storage are one reason why many individuals express distaste for dams. Another reason is more basic: Valued lands are lost to view and to use forever. Valued animals and plants are also lost. Not only are land species driven out, but fish that inhabit the stream may also be barred. Where once they swam upstream to spawn, the reservoir wall now blocks their path.

Structures can be added to reservoirs to allow the fish to climb up and over the dam. For instance, *fish ladders* consist of a series of concrete steps filled with water that allow fish to ascend or descend the dam in a series of leaps. This adds time to the journey the fish must make, however, and time is something they do not have. The newly hatched fish must return to the ocean within a certain time, before their metabolism changes, or they will never mature and return to the river to spawn.

The reservoir may flood out valuable farmlands or displace families or Indian tribes from ancestral homes. Graveyards and tribal burial grounds may be forever obliterated. It is not always clear that a just compensation can be found for the people uprooted from such an area, for their loss is more than economic.

Uses of Groundwater

Groundwater serves a more limited set of functions than does surface water. In many cities, groundwater provides community water supplies. Especially in rural areas, where the cost of extending the water distribution system is high, people turn to wells to deliver their water needs. Groundwater is also used for irrigation of crops, a common practice in farming areas that are short of surface water or where the building of irrigation canals is costly. Groundwater provides the household water supply for about half the population in the United States.

Groundwater also serves a relatively unseen and unappreciated function: Its flow contributes to and often sustains the summertime flow of streams and rivers, which themselves may be used for water supply.

Use of groundwater provides a number of advantages to consumers. First, since groundwater may be located near its point of use, savings can be realized in piping and possibly pumping costs. Second, the firm yield can be sustained over a long period through both dry and wet seasons. (This advantage may prove to be illusory, however, if the aquifer is depleted by a consistent *overdraft,* or withdrawal of more than the recharge rate.)

What is the safe yield of an aquifer? As with reservoirs, it depends on the flows that enter the aquifer. No more can be withdrawn year after year than the annual recharge rate of the aquifer—unless the user of the water is willing to see the volume in the aquifer drawn down. In a number of parts of the world, including the United States, withdrawal rates are exceeding recharge rates and the water levels in the aquifers are declining. The fact is that in desert basins, rainfall only rarely recharges an aquifer. During most years, evaporation draws most water up from the surface into the atmosphere. Only during extremely wet years will enough water be present for some of it to recharge the aquifer.

Quality of Reservoir Water versus Groundwater

Water from a surface reservoir and water from an underground aquifer are likely to be quite different in quality. In the surface reservoir, water will contain sediment picked up by the river that fills the reservoir. Some of the sediment particles settle to the bottom, depending on how long the water is detained, but some particles remain.

In surface water, organic matter from both municipal and agricultural sources is likely to be present and can cause the removal of oxygen. Algae often find the reservoir environment inviting, as it offers both the nutrients and sunlight they need for growth. Because reservoirs receive "fresh" sources of pollution, the water, if used as drinking water, needs to be fully treated. Treatment is required to remove undesirable tastes, color, and odors, to make the water clear, to make it free from hazardous chemicals, and to destroy any disease-causing organisms.

Water drawn from aquifers is likely to be far clearer than water taken from surface reservoirs, especially if the aquifer has not been drawn on for long or has not been extensively depleted. Water from an aquifer is also likely to have a higher content of dissolved minerals. Groundwater will not have algae in it, since no sunlight has illuminated the water for many years. Because water reaches the aquifer by filtering through thick layers of soil, its bacterial and viral content is likely to be lower than that in surface reservoir water. However, the odor of hydrogen sulfide is common in groundwater, a result of the bacterial degradation of organic material that takes place in groundwater in the absence of oxygen.

There are exceptions to these generalizations about quality. Groundwater can become polluted by chemicals and by microorganisms. Without sunlight to accelerate their breakdown, chemical pollutants may last longer in groundwater than in surface water. And, once polluted, groundwater may remain polluted through many lifetimes, because aquifers are recharged very slowly, often over hundreds of years. Groundwater supplies are thus extremely fragile resources, in that the entry of pollutants can ruin them for generations.

Global Supplies of Fresh Water

In many parts of the world, limited resources of fresh water limit food production. In the United States, **water tables** (the level of the aquifer closest to the surface) are declining under one-third of the irrigated cropland. Lack of water limits the acreage planted in the former U.S.S.R.'s central Asian republics and southern Kazakhstan. So much water has been diverted from freshwater flows into Soviet central Asia's Aral Sea that the sea has shrunk 30% in the last 30 years and the fishing industry there has collapsed. The North Plain of China, in which one-fourth of that country's crops are grown, is also bumping up against limits on the amount of available water.

Huge water diversion schemes have been planned in the U.S.S.R., where Siberian rivers may be diverted into central Asia, and for China, where waters from the Yangtze will be diverted to the North Plain. Water diversion projects on this scale are both costly and environmentally risky. Wildlife habitat in areas from which water is diverted will suffer during dry years. Lakes and seas whose freshwater inflows are reduced will decrease in area and increase in salinity.

In numerous urban areas, dry years lead to restrictions on water use. As populations continue to grow in developing countries, so will needs for fresh water.

Much can be done in the area of water conservation. In many areas, simply raising the price of water will encourage its conservation, although subsidies may need to be given to poorer sectors of society.

The modern engineering discipline of water resources systems analysis has found methods for taking independent river basins and by means of interconnections managing them in a way that increases the system yield *above* the yield that occurs with independent operation. That is, the component reservoirs of a system can reliably deliver more water when their releases are synchronized and pooled than when each is managed individually. For example, in the metropolitan area of Washington, D.C., 16 new reservoirs had been proposed by the U.S. Army Corps of Engineers to meet the demands of the growing capital district. However, with only one of the proposed reservoirs built, a study of the water supply system showed that the needs of the area could be met to the year 2020 if releases from the existing reservoirs were coordinated properly through the seasons.

Irrigation accounts for 70% of water withdrawals worldwide—as much as 90% in mainly agrarian developing countries. The use of such techniques as buried pipe or drip irrigation can reduce the amount of water used in irrigation by 60%–90% in some countries.

Rising costs for fresh water will make recycling of wastewaters more attractive. In the United States, only 0.2% of water demand is met by recycled water. In Israel, where all available freshwater sources have already been tapped, recycled water supplies 25% of irrigation needs, and by the year 2000 will supply 16% of the country's total water use.

Although we appear to be discussing them separately, the issues of supply and quality are not separate. Water supplies are decreased when aquifers and surface flows are polluted. When water supply engineers and planners ask whether adequate water supplies are available, they really mean, "Do we have available a sufficient quantity of water of the quality that we need?"

THE CONSEQUENCES OF POLLUTING NATURAL WATERS

Types of Pollutants

Pollutants of natural waters can be divided into seven classes:

1. Organic wastes in sewage inflows

2. Plant nutrients, which enter waters either from sewage inflows or as components of urban and agricultural runoff and cause a condition known as *eutrophication*

3. Disease-causing agents from sewage

4. Thermal additions from power plants or industrial processes

5. Oil pollution from drilling for or shipping oil

6. Toxic chemicals from waste flows or leached from landfills (discussed in the following chapter)

7. Soil sediments and other suspended solids (Chapter 7)

These pollutants are sometimes added to natural waters intentionally, for instance when they are part of urban or industrial sewage flows. This is known as **point-source pollution.** However, the water that runs off land into streams, rivers, lakes, and oceans can also carry pollutants, such as lawn fertilizers, animal wastes, and agricultural pesticides. This more diffuse flow of pollutants is called **non-point-source pollution.** For certain types of pollutants (e.g., the plant nutrients that cause eutrophication), non–point-source pollution is a much larger problem than is point-source pollution.

The Effects of Organic Wastes on Dissolved Oxygen

Water pollution means different things to different people. To some, it means the presence of toxic chemicals; to others, it means the presence of disease-causing bacteria. To many engineers and scientists, however, water pollution is indicated by organic wastes. Such wastes can come from industry, from farming, and from cities. These organic wastes are mainly composed of carbon, hydrogen, oxygen, and nitrogen. The reason organic wastes are considered pollutants is that they use up the oxygen dissolved in natural waters.

When water is well mixed in the presence of air, the water dissolves a maximum amount of oxygen, called the **saturation concentration.** This is the number of milligrams of oxygen that can be dissolved in 1 liter of water before the water can hold no more. The saturation concentration achieved by thorough mixing is between 8 and 9 milligrams of oxygen per liter of water, depending on the temperature. In summer, at higher water temperatures, the saturation concentration falls as low as 8 mg/L. In winter, at colder water temperatures, the saturation concentration is nearer 9 mg/L.

When organic substances from the waste outfall of a community or industry enter a river or estuary, the concentration of dissolved oxygen in the receiving waters decreases, due to the oxidation of the organic material by bacteria and protozoa. If the concentration of organic material is sufficiently large, oxidation of the organics by bacteria and protozoa may use up all the oxygen in the sample; that is, the concentration of oxygen in water may be reduced to zero. When there is no oxygen in natural waters, we say the water is in an **anaerobic condition.** Under anaerobic or very low oxygen conditions, normal aquatic life, such as fish species, die.

Natural mixing of the water with the air does tend to replace the removed oxygen, but not immediately. Instead, a competition arises between the oxygen-depleting forces (the oxidation of organic wastes) and the oxygen-restoring forces (the mixing of water with air). This competition produces a typical pattern of oxygen concentrations. Such a pattern in a stream is shown in the top of Figure 18-3. The aquatic organisms found in such a stream will mirror the depletion and reoxygenation of the water. For instance, in the zone of little or no oxygen, the few species that do survive and thrive in any numbers are those especially adapted to these conditions.

In low-oxygen conditions, the normal bacterial population that uses oxygen also dies out. In its

	Origin of pollution		Zones of pollution		
	Clean water	Decline	Damage	Recovery	Clean water
Dissolved oxygen level (9 mg/L to 1 mg/L)	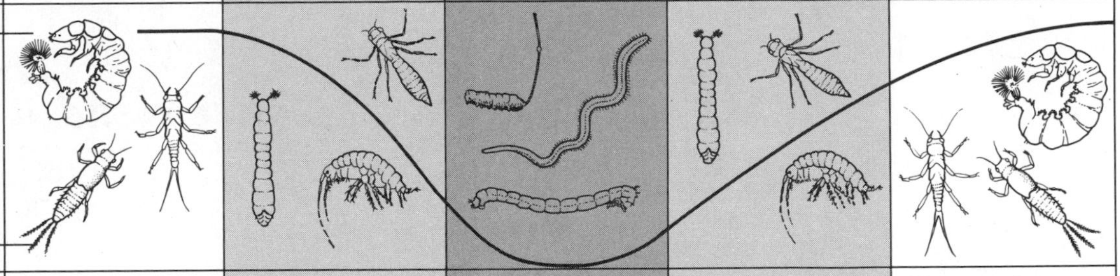				
Physical measure	Clear, no bottom sludge	Floating solids, bottom sludge	Turbid, foul gas, bottom sludge	Turbid, bottom sludge	Clear, no bottom sludge
Fish present	Game, pan, food, and forage fish	Tolerant fish— carp, buffalo, gar	None	Tolerant fish— carp, buffalo, gar	Game, pan, food, and forage fish
Bottom animals present	Caddisfly Mayfly naiads Stonefly Helgrammite Unionid clam	Sowbug Snail Scud Leech	Sludgeworm Rat-tailed maggot Bloodworm	Sowbug Snail Scud Leech	Caddisfly Mayfly naiads Stonefly Helgrammite Unionid clam
Algae and protozoa present	*Dinobryon Cladophora Ulothrix Navicula*	*Paramecium Vorticella Spirogyra Euglena*	*Phormidium Stigeoclonium Oscillatoria*	*Paramecium Euglena Spirogyra Pandorina*	*Dinobryon Cladophora Ulothrix Navicula*

FIGURE 18-3 The Zones in a Polluted Water Course. The graph at the top shows the pattern of oxygen depletion and recovery after polluted water is added to a typical stream. The other boxes show the physical characteristics and some of the organisms found in each zone of the stream: clean, declining in quality, damaged, recovering, and clean again. (*Source*: Adapted from K. Mackenthun, *Toward a Cleaner Aquatic Environment* [Washington, D.C.: U.S. Government Printing Office, 1973])

place, a population of bacteria grows that lives on sulfur instead. The sulfur atom occurs in organic wastes and is structurally similar to oxygen, except that it has one more shell of electrons. Sulfur then takes the place of oxygen in the oxidation reaction, producing, for instance, hydrogen sulfide (H_2S) instead of water (H_2O). The well-known smell of rotten eggs is the smell of hydrogen sulfide.

The quantity of organic material in wastewater is not measured directly. Instead, because the amount of oxygen that would be used up in the receiving waters is the quantity of interest, this is what is measured. The number reported is the **biological oxygen demand**, or **BOD**. This is the amount of oxygen that would be consumed if all the organics in 1 liter of polluted water were oxidized by bacteria and protozoa. It is reported in number of milligrams of oxygen per liter.

Eutrophication

Why Phosphates and Nitrates Are Pollutants. Eutrophication is the process by which bodies of water become enriched with plant nutrients. Carbon, oxygen, hydrogen, nitrogen in nitrates, and phosphorus in the form of phosphates are some of the elements, or "foods," needed by plants for

Towards a Sustainable Society

Reuse of Wastewater Can Extend a Precious Resource

by Daniel A. Okun

Daniel Okun is chairman of the Water Science and Technology Board and professor emeritus in the Department of Environmental Sciences and Engineering at the University of North Carolina. Dr. Okun has been a consultant to many international organizations on water issues.

The reuse of wastewater has been practiced in the United States and abroad for more than a century. The initiatives for this practice arose from two different needs: originally, to provide an economical method for disposing of urban wastewater from the capitals of Europe without polluting rivers and lakes, by using wastewaters for agricultural irrigation; and, more recently, the need for additional water resources in water-short areas. Today, most water reclamation and reuse projects serve both needs, reducing pollution and enhancing water supply resources in urban areas, with the latter becoming increasingly important.

Urban populations are growing, from about 30% in 1950 to almost half the total population at the end of the decade. The number of cities of over one million population will have grown five-fold to about 400 in the same period.

Urban and industrial communities as they grow find themselves having to go longer distances to find additional sources of water. Such distant sources are often not feasible economically or politically. Environmental impacts such as flooding of land by reservoirs or decreasing stream flows are further stumbling blocks to acquiring ad-

growth. Smaller amounts of many other substances, such as iron, calcium, and copper, are also required. Lakes and estuaries with large amounts of these necessary plant nutrients are called *eutrophic* (from the Greek words *eu,* meaning "well," and *trophe,* meaning "nourishment"). Relatively high concentrations of plant nutrients allow huge amounts of aquatic plants, such as algae, to grow. This overpopulation of algae makes water unpleasant to swim in. Some kinds of algae, which grow in long strands, wind themselves around boat propellers, making boating impossible. Eutrophic waters tend to be scummy, cloudy, or even soupy green. A rapidly growing population of algae, called a *bloom,* may wash onto the shores in storms or high winds and die there, its decay producing bad smells.

Some of the worst effects of eutrophication involve changes in the dissolved oxygen content of waters. Sport fish have trouble living where there are blooms because, at night, the algae respire and use up most or all of the oxygen, leaving none for the fish.

Cities or industries that want to use eutrophic

ditional water supplies from surface sources. Reclaimed water serves as a substitute for the limited fresh water supply in uses such as urban irrigation, industrial processing, cooling, cleansing, construction, and toilet-flushing, thereby releasing the existing drinkable water supply to serve larger populations.

Initially, such reuse was dedicated to single large users, such as agriculture or industry. More recently, dual distribution systems are being built with the reclaimed water being used throughout the urban area. In the many instances where distribution systems are being expanded, the additional costs for dual distribution systems have been more than offset by savings. These savings occur because the cost of treatment of wastewater for reuse is generally less than the cost of treatment for disposal to sensitive waters. Such sensitive waters include those that are used for drinking or that would be harmed by the addition of nutrients such as phosphates or nitrates. For most reuse applications, the toxic compounds, particularly chlorine reaction products, are of little significance, and the nutrients are beneficial. The typical reclamation plant involves secondary (biological) treatment followed by conventional filtration and disinfection, so that there is no danger from occasional accidental drinking.

Reuse projects generally originate with single large users, such as for an industrial or agricultural area. Where the prospects are economically attractive, reuse extends to newly developing areas of a city. Retrofitting distribution mains in existing urban areas is more costly than installing them as the areas are developed.

Wastewater reuse has become so much a part of the armamentarium of the engineer that it is increasingly being considered one of the options for additional water supply. Reuse is understandably widely practiced on the West Coast and in the southwestern United States, although the practice is growing rapidly in Florida despite an annual rainfall of 50 to 60 inches.

While the provision of water supply and the control of water pollution have been considered entirely separate enterprises, as demonstrated by the Safe Drinking Water Act and the Clean Water Act, which are not at all related in their administration, reuse will force the integration of these two activities and reinforce the principle that water is part of a continuum and cannot be managed effectively if fragmented.

Reuse of wastewater for drinking is not practiced because of uncertain health consequences and an understandable public reluctance. A principle of water supply is that drinking water should be taken from the purest source available. Reusing wastewater for purposes other than drinking poses few health threats and has received enthusiastic public endorsement wherever introduced.

lake water find they must remove the algae, thus increasing costs. Almost 10,000 public lakes in the United States need treatment for the effects of eutrophication caused by excess plant nutrients.

In eutrophic estuaries, important underwater rooted plants cannot grow, because algae block out the sunlight these plants need for photosynthesis.

An **oligotrophic** lake (from the Greek words *oligo,* meaning "poorly," and *trophe,* meaning "nourishment") is one with low levels of plant nutrients. Such lakes have only small populations of algae and remain sparkling clear. They are enjoyable to swim in or boat on, are delightful to look at, and should provide good drinking water.

Limiting Nutrients. Most experts agree that phosphates and nitrates are responsible for eutrophication. Although there are many other necessary nutrients, these two are noteworthy because, together or singly, they are usually the limiting factors in natural unpolluted waters. A **limiting factor** is the nutrient present in the smallest amount compared to the amount needed for growth; that is, aquatic plants such as algae will grow until all available nitrogen or phosphorus is used up. Unnatural amounts of phosphorus or nitrogen can allow more than the normal amount of algae to grow.

Nitrates and Eutrophication. In most U.S. coastal waters and in lakes fed by steep mountain streams, the concentration of nitrates seems to be the factor that normally limits plant growth. Nitrates can enter natural waters from several sources. City sewage and animal feedlots (where cattle are grouped together in large pens to be fattened for market) are two major sources, since human and animal wastes are about one-half nitrates. Fertilizer, which runs off croplands or suburban lawns during a rainstorm, also contains a large amount of nitrates.

In addition, several natural sources of nitrates exist. Volcanic eruptions and lightning can change nitrogen gas in the air into nitrates. Just as legumes found in land ecosystems can "fix" atmospheric nitrogen into a form usable by other plants, some blue-green algae found in aquatic systems can turn nitrogen from the air into nitrates. This process is called **nitrogen fixation.** Thus, these algae, which are usually considered the worst nuisance plants, do not depend on an outside source of nitrate. (There is evidence that sulfate in seawater hinders nitrogen fixation. This may explain why algal growth in coastal waters is nitrate-limited.) Finally, waterfowl, which feed on the shores of lakes and ponds and then fly over the water, are the source of what one wildlife expert termed "bombed in" nitrates.

Phosphates and Eutrophication. In contrast to nitrogen, phosphorus in the form of phosphates is found naturally in waters in only trace amounts. Most pollutant phosphorus comes from human activities. Phosphate mines pollute certain areas of the country, such as central Florida. Fertilizer runoff contains large amounts of phosphate. Domestic sewage is high in phosphates, too, with one-half coming from human wastes and 20%–30% from detergents. Animal feedlots are sources of both nitrates and phosphates.

Although growth of algae in coastal waters and in some wilderness lakes is limited by low concentrations of nitrates in the water, algal growth in lakes and rivers is believed to be limited by the amount of phosphate present.

How Can Eutrophication Be Controlled?

Detergent Phosphates. Since phosphate is the nutrient that limits plant growth in most U.S. waters, and because detergents are a major source of phosphates, it is natural to ask whether we would not be better off banning the use of phosphates in detergents in an effort to stop eutrophication.

The chemical present in the largest amount in phosphate detergents is the phosphate builder: Dry detergents usually contain sodium tripolyphosphate (STPP) as a builder; liquid detergents may contain sodium or potassium phosphates. Builders are necessary because water often contains calcium and magnesium ions. These ions combine with soap to form a hard precipitate. This precipitate does not make suds and does not dissolve grease or dirt. In a similar fashion, calcium and magnesium ions can tie up the surfactant, or dirt-dissolving, molecules in detergents. Builders "complex," or tie up, these calcium and magnesium ions. Without builders, manufacturers would have to include a great deal of relatively expensive surfactant in their detergents to be sure their product performs well in hard-water areas. In addition, builders help keep dirt from reattaching itself to clothes.

A complete ban on phosphates in detergents would remove about 20%–30% of the phosphates in sewage. In a number of areas, either a ban on or a reduction in the amount of phosphate allowed in detergents has been tried in an attempt to reverse lake eutrophication. Detergent phosphate bans in states such as Maryland and Michigan appear to have significantly reduced phosphate loading to the Chesapeake Bay and the Detroit River, respectively. By 1988, all of the states with major watersheds bordering the Great Lakes had passed statutes limiting detergent phosphate to 0.5%, and Ontario, Canada, had declared a limit of 2.2%.

It is not clear, however, that a detergent phosphate ban alone will make a significant improvement in lake waters that are already eutrophic. If phosphate inputs to a eutrophic lake are not reduced below a certain level (generally by 50% or more), eutrophic growth of aquatic plants seems to continue. Removal of detergent phosphates, by itself, will not usually accomplish such a large reduction because other inputs, such as runoff from agricultural lands, are much greater sources of phosphates.

Tertiary Treatment. Another way to attack the phosphate problem does exist, however. Phosphates can be removed from sewage by **tertiary treatment** of wastewater. In this method, phosphates are precipitated out of sewage before the treated water is released into lakes or rivers. About 80%–90%, or even more, of the phosphates in sewage can be removed, and the cost is not great. Further, phosphates from all sources (for example, human wastes) are removed. Unfortunately, not everyone in this country is served by a sewage treatment plant. Some have septic tanks; others have only treatment ponds. Only 1% of the people in this country are served by sewage treatment plants that have facilities for phosphate removal. This particular solution, then, is tied up in the economics and politics of building and improving sewage treatment plants.

Good Farming Practices. EPA surveys show that agricultural nonpoint sources are the major source of nutrients for eutrophic waters. Nutrients from manure and chemical fertilizers in agricultural runoff can be controlled by good farming practices, such as strip cropping, terracing, and careful timing of fertilizer application so that fertilizer is not immediately washed away by rains. Feedlot operators may need to install sewage treatment equipment to prevent animal wastes from enriching nearby streams.

Low-tillage or no-till farming and vegetated buffer strips along stream banks and farm fields also reduce nutrient runoff. Land management plans can reduce runoff through zoning in which the use of land near water is strictly controlled.

Community Action. The National Clean Lakes Group is a coalition of interested parties that has convinced Congress to allot funds to communities wishing to restore eutrophic lakes. This is basically a continuation of the Clean Lakes Program run by the Environmental Protection Agency from 1976 to 1982. In order to be eligible for a grant, the lake must be available to the public, it must be classed as fresh water, and the applicants must show that their plan for lake restoration is likely to produce long-lasting benefits. Almost 100 lakes were helped under the EPA's Clean Lakes Program between 1976 and 1982. More information can be obtained from EPA regional offices. (See Figure 18-4 for a case in which a lake recovered.)

WATER POLLUTION CONTROL—CONTROLLING POINT-SOURCE POLLUTANTS

Organic wastes, bacterial and viral pollutants, phosphates, and nitrates can all be removed from urban and industrial sewage before they are released to natural waters. This is done at a sewage treatment plant.

Combined Sewer Systems

When wastewater enters a treatment plant (also called a water pollution control plant), it passes through a rack and a coarse screen that together prevent large objects from passing into the plant. The large objects could include such items as boots, cloth, branches, and so forth. Such objects would seem to be unexpected in municipal wastewater, but they are quite common. Their presence is a clue to a large problem that most communities in the United States continue to face: The drain system that carries storm water and the drain system that carries domestic wastewater are combined.

Runoff entering storm drains is simply water that was not absorbed into the ground. The flow of water from storms may be as much as 100 times the rate of domestic wastewater flow, or *dry-weather flow,* which averages 100 gallons per day per person. Sewage treatment plants are designed only for the domestic flow. When a storm occurs, storm water enters the sewers, and the two flows mix. The treatment plant, however, can handle only its usual volume, the dry-weather flow. The remainder must

(a)

(b)

FIGURE 18-4 Recovery of a Lake. The town of Vaxjo, Sweden stopped pouring sewage into overexploited Lake Trummen in 1958. (*a*) By 1969, the unrecovered lake contained no oxygen, no fish, and no underwater vegetation and was of little use to humans. The main problem was the rapidly increasing black muddy sediment caused by decaying plankton. Starting in 1970, the sediment was sucked out and put into settling ponds; runoff water was cleansed of phosphorus and returned to the lake. (*b*) This is how Lake Trummen looks now, a revitalized recreational asset. (*Photos:* S. Bjork)

overflow into the river or the ocean, where it is left untreated.

Storm water carries many contaminants, including substances washed from the streets by rain. Such substances as lead (from gasoline), particles of earth, dog feces, leaf litter, and unburned fuels may be captured in the flow before it enters the sewers. Once the flow enters the sewers, it may scour up organic solids (including bacteria) deposited there by the slower moving dry-weather flow. Thus, storm water is not at all clean; it carries metals, organics, and possibly pathogenic bacteria into the watercourse.

Primary and Secondary Treatment. Figure 18-5 illustrates a complete water pollution control system. There are three parts to the system. In primary treatment, suspended solids are removed. During secondary treatment, microbes are used to remove dissolved organic wastes in either an activated sludge tank or a trickling filter. Both of these pro-

cesses produce a sludge that is further degraded in a tank called a digester.

The disposal of sewage sludge differs across the country. Many cities bury their dried sludge in landfills. Others burn it in a special unit and bury only the ash in landfills. Some communities (such as Salem, Oregon, and Madison, Wisconsin) spread the sludge on cropland, but heavy-metal contaminants in the sludge may make such use unwise. The city of Milwaukee packages its sludge as a commercial fertilizer. Milorganite, as the product is known, might be called "the sludge that made Milwaukee famous."

Primary treatment is common in many communities in the United States. Secondary treatment is coming into much wider use.

Tertiary Treatment. Up to 90% of the organic material in wastewater is removed by primary and secondary treatment. The processes that follow secondary treatment are designed to remove resistant

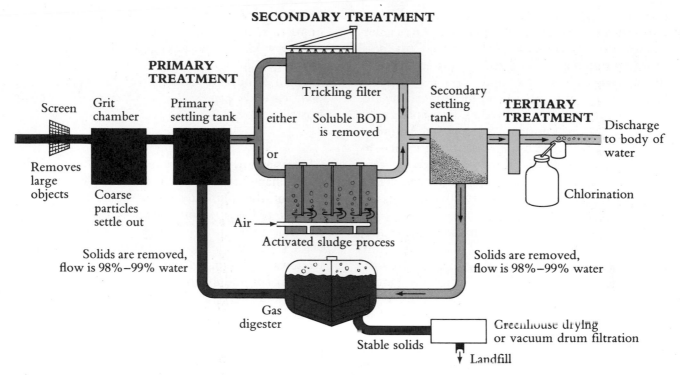

FIGURE 18-5 Water Pollution Control Processes. Three distinct sets of processes are used in sequence. *Primary treatment* removes suspended solids. *Secondary treatment* removes dissolved organics. *Tertiary treatment* is designed to remove phosphorus, nitrogen, and resistant organic compounds. Digestion, not part of any of these three processes, is the means by which organic solids are degraded and stabilized. New schemes are being tried in some cities; see Further Reading.

organics, which remain after secondary treatment, as well as plant nutrients, which are responsible for the eutrophication of lakes and rivers. These processes are known as **tertiary treatment.**

Phosphate removal is accomplished by chemical precipitation and settling. Chemicals such as ferrous and ferric salts, aluminum salts, or lime are added to the waste stream. When one of these chemicals is mixed well with the waste stream flowing from secondary treatment, a precipitate of solid matter forms. For example, the calcium ions from lime (calcium oxide) combine with the phosphate ions in solution to produce solid particles of calcium phosphate. These particles are removed by allowing them to settle out of the waste stream. Engineers have suggested that the addition of chemicals to

"bring down" phosphates could also take place just before the primary settling tank. This would allow the collection of both organic solids and phosphate precipitates to take place at the same time. After the phosphate is precipitated and settled out, any remaining suspended matter may be removed by filtration through beds of sand, crushed coal, garnet, and gravel.

Nitrogen occurs in wastewater in the form of ammonia, nitrate ions, or nitrite ions. Unfortunately, there is no way to remove these nitrogen compounds by precipitation in the treatment plant.

Removing nitrogen that occurs as ammonia (NH_3) is important for a number of reasons. First, ammonia is harmful to fish. Second, ammonia combines with the chlorine that is added to destroy harmful bacteria and viruses. Reactions with ammonia tie up chlorine in substances known as chloramines and hence decrease chlorine's effectiveness. Third, ammonia is oxidized by bacteria in the stream, and this oxidation process may remove large amounts of oxygen from the water. The ammonium ion may be removed as ammonia gas by a physical process known as *gas stripping*. Ammonia may also be removed by biological treatment—by passing the wastewater through an aerated tank with a specialized population of microbes. These microbes convert the nitrogen in both ammonia and nitrites to nitrate ions.

Nitrate ions should be removed because they increase eutrophication, but an even more compelling reason exists for removing nitrate and nitrite ions. If high-nitrate water is used for drinking, a blood disorder in infants, methemoglobinemia, could result. Nitrate removal can be achieved by specialized populations of microbes that convert nitrate to nitrogen gas and water. Methyl alcohol must be present for this reaction, which produces carbon dioxide, water, and nitrogen gas.

A final procedure in tertiary treatment is to pass the waste stream through a tower containing particles of activated carbon. The activated carbon adsorbs dissolved organic substances that were not removed in any previous processes. The organic materials "stick" to the surfaces of the particles. This *carbon polishing* restores the wastewater to such an extent that people have considered reusing this water in public water supplies after it has been filtered and disinfected. In the essay on pages 396–397, Dr. Okun explores this possibility.

In contrast to primary and secondary treatment, tertiary treatment is quite uncommon at present. One of the earliest successful applications of tertiary treatment was at Lake Tahoe, Nevada, in the late 1960s. The clarity of this beautiful lake was threatened by algal growth caused by phosphorus and nitrogen compounds from the community's wastewater. Scientists recognized that the usual primary and secondary treatment steps could not stop the degradation of the lake. Hence, a tertiary treatment plant was opened at Lake Tahoe in 1965. The plant removes the phosphate and the ammonia and "polishes" the water by passing it through carbon columns to remove resistant organics. The wastewater—now clear, colorless, and odorless—is never discharged into the lake. Instead, the water is pumped 27 miles to Indian Creek Reservoir, which was created expressly to receive the plant's wastewater.

Chlorination. Because the bacteria that inhabit the human intestine thrive best in a warm environment, the cold water of sewage treatment plants tends to reduce their numbers. Nonetheless, a considerable population of bacteria still exists in the waste stream even after secondary treatment. Thus, wastewater leaving American sewage treatment plants is commonly chlorinated in order to destroy disease-causing microorganisms.

In contrast to bacteria, viruses from the human intestine die away more slowly in the treatment plant. Primary treatment reduces their numbers little, if at all. Secondary treatment via the trickling filter may reduce viruses by 40%; however, secondary treatment via the activated sludge process can reduce their numbers by up to 98%. The final step of chlorination reduces their numbers again.

The health of people swimming in or boating on the water downstream from a treatment plant is protected by destroying the pathogens in the wastewater. The process of chlorination is inexpensive compared to other methods of disinfecting wastewater. Furthermore, the effectiveness of disinfection is easily monitored by testing for free chlorine in the wastewater.

Several environmental problems do occur as a result of chlorination, however. Chlorine and the compounds it forms with ammonia are toxic to fish. Some fish can be poisoned at concentrations of chlorine as low as 0.002 mg/L (2 parts per billion).

Another problem with chlorinating wastewater is that chlorinated hydrocarbons can form from the reaction of chlorine with hydrocarbons in the water. These persistent and toxic substances, which have been detected in public water supplies, are suspected of being carcinogenic agents.

Once added, chlorine can be removed from

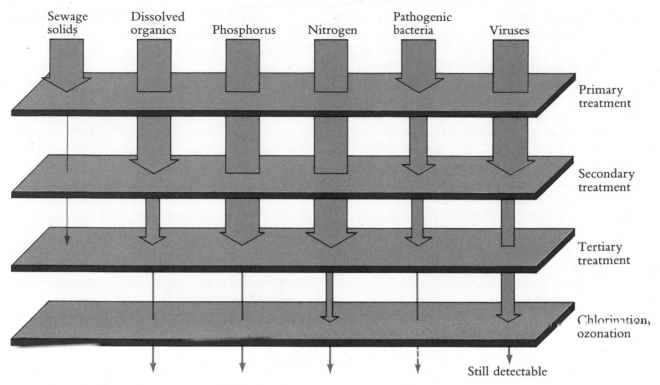

FIGURE 18-6 Removal of Contaminants by Sewage Treatment. The relation between each stage of treatment and the level of removal of contaminants is shown by this diagram. If an arrow meets a treatment plane with an arrowhead and changes thickness in moving through that treatment plane, the level of the contaminant has been reduced by that stage of treatment. The relative reduction in the thickness of the arrow indicates approximately the extent of the reduction. For instance, sewage solids are nearly all removed in primary treatment. Dissolved organics, on the other hand, are not altered by primary treatment but are significantly reduced by secondary treatment. Nitrogen and phosphorus are not generally removed by primary or secondary treatment but are much reduced by tertiary treatment, and so on.

wastewater by contact with sulfur dioxide gas, which leaves sulfate and chloride ions in solution after the process is complete. The sulfur dioxide will even strip chlorine away from the compounds it forms with ammonia, but the sulfur dioxide will not remove any chlorinated hydrocarbons that may have formed.

An alternative to chlorination of municipal wastes is ozonation. Though a powerful disinfectant, ozone disappears quickly in contaminated water and does not seem to form toxic by-products when it reacts with substances in water. Ultraviolet light is also being examined as a possible disinfectant because it would not cause the formation of undesirable by-products. Another alternative is simply not to disinfect wastewater prior to discharge. In Britain, wastewater disinfection is not an element of engineering practice. The removal of contaminants by sewage treatment is summarized in Figure 18-6.

Pollution Control Laws. In the United States, Congress has attempted to control point-source water pollution with a variety of laws, but the most basic rules are found in the Federal Water Pollution Control Act. This law was passed in 1972, further amended in 1977, and brought up for renewal again in 1985. Basically, the law divides pollutants into three classes. For wastes designated as *toxic,* industries must use the *best available technology (BAT)* to treat their wastes before releasing them into natural waters. For pollutants listed as *conventional,* such as municipal wastes, dischargers must use the *best conventional technology (BCT).* Any other pollutants fall into a third class, *unconventional.* These pollutants must meet BAT standards, although waivers are possible.

If even the best available technology would not protect certain waters, stricter standards (for example, no discharge at all) must be imposed. Further, special standards called *pretreatment standards* are imposed for wastes that will pass through sewage treatment plants.

A special permit from the EPA or from the state is required for discharge of any pollutants into navigable waters. This permit would, of course, require that the discharge meet the appropriate toxic, conventional, or unconventional treatment standards.

Control of Water Pollution in Rural Areas and in Developing Countries

Septic Tanks. In rural areas and small subdivisions where there are no wastewater treatment plants, or no sewers to connect to treatment plants, households most often treat their wastes by using **septic tanks.** The septic tank is the successor to the cesspool, which was a structure resembling a well. It was lined with stones or concrete blocks without mortar. Raw, unsettled sewage flowed directly into the cesspool, so groundwater contamination was a distinct possibility.

In contrast, the septic tank is a watertight tank constructed of either metal or concrete (Figure 18-7). Depending on the tank size and the size of the home it serves, the tank may hold sewage flows for anywhere from half a day to three days. During this time, solids settle to the bottom of the tank, where they are degraded by bacterial action.

The overflow from a septic tank is a liquid from which some solids have been removed. The overflow passes to a distribution box that "distributes" the water to a buried **leaching field,** which consists of perforated pipes of clay or plastic pieces. The wastewater seeps into the soil from the joints between the pieces. Microorganisms in the soil decompose the wastes. Lush grass may often be observed above the "arms" of the leaching system. The leaching system helps disperse the wastes and decreases the possibility of groundwater contamination.

If a family uses both a septic system and a well, it is good practice to keep the water supply far away (several hundred feet) and preferably uphill from the waste disposal system.

Developing Countries. In developing countries, appropriate methods of human waste disposal are desperately needed to break the cycle of disease that results from contamination of drinking water with human wastes. In rural areas, construction of ventilated pit latrines for community use can be very effective (Figure 18-7). In cities, where the costs of conventional sewage treatment plants would be prohibitive but where land is available, waste stabilization lagoons or ponds can purify wastewaters. In these ponds, solids settle out as the wastewater flows slowly through the pond. The solids decompose in the absence of oxygen at the bottom of the pond. Near the surface, however, bacteria oxidize organic materials in the presence of oxygen. Weeds and other aquatic plants, including algae, may grow in the pond, making use of nutrients from the wastes. In addition, the algae supply oxygen to the system as a by-product of their photosynthesis. The oxygen helps keep the system operating with minimal odors. Sometimes the lagoon is aerated; that is, air is bubbled into the water, much as in the activated sludge process. The lagoon can thus act as a combination of primary and secondary treatment. In fact, primary treatment is not usually given to the waste entering a lagoon.

Along Peru's coastal areas, where most of the

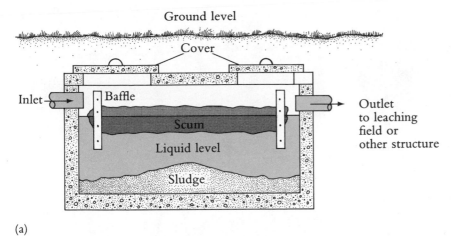

(a)

(b)

FIGURE 18-7 Human Waste Disposal. (*a*) Cross-section of a typical concrete septic tank. The septic tank is the device that replaced the cesspool in rural areas. Closed to the soil by its concrete or metal sides, the device provides a modest amount of treatment to the wastewater from a home. Solids settle out in the tank and are degraded there, while a relatively clear overflow passes out to the leaching field. (*Source:* Adapted from *Cleaning Up the Water*, Maine Department of Environmental Protection, 1974) (*b*) Ventilated open pit latrine. In developing countries, where individual households may have no plumbing, sanitary facilities such as the ventilated open pit latrine provide safe disposal of human wastes without the problems of odors and flies that caused people to reject older designs of latrines. Latrines at school in Zimbabwe. (*Photo:* UNDP/David Kinley)

population lives, fresh water is too scarce to use for agriculture. Wastewater is thus used to irrigate crops. But this has led to high rates of waterborne diseases such as cholera, hepatitis, and typhoid. The United Nations and the World Bank are sponsoring a project designed to purify the wastewater for reuse, at a low cost. Sewage from the town of San Juan de Miraflores is collected and fed through a series of three waste treatment lagoons. By the time it reaches the third lagoon, the water is pure enough to raise fish as well as safe for irrigation of crops.

Mexico and the United States have agreed to share the cost of several sewage treatment plants in areas along their common border. In the past, sewage from Mexican cities has flowed untreated into U.S. rivers and coastal waters because the Mexican government lacks the funds to construct the plants on its own (Figure 18-8).

In other schemes, waste disposal has even been combined with energy production. Gas produced from the digestion of human and animal wastes can be captured and used for cooking (Figure 18-9).

FIGURE 18-8 Sewage and Debris in Tijuana River.
The Rio Grande and Tijuana Rivers carry more than
10 million gallons of raw sewage each day from Mexican cities, past U.S. farmland, and then into the
ocean. Mexico cannot afford the cost of treating the
sewage from its rapidly growing cities. The U.S. government has recently agreed to help pay construction
costs for several sewage treatment plants located along
the border between the two countries. (*Photo:* International Boundary and Water Commission)

FIGURE 18-9 Biogas Plant in an Indian Village. Villagers deliver wastes to the facility and in return receive a share in the gas generated. (*Photo:* UN/
J. K. Isaac)

MARINE WATERS

The world's oceans are the ultimate dump for much
of the air and water pollution produced on land.
Table 18-2 lists the relative contributions of various
sources of pollutants to the marine environment.

The open oceans are still relatively clean, although oil spills and plastic debris in shipping lanes
are common. The situation is otherwise in many
coastal areas, however. Here, runoff from land and
sewage inflows contribute disease-causing microbes, nutrients, and toxic chemicals, while construction projects, plastic litter, and tar balls foul
beaches and destroy wildlife habitat.

Fish kills and die-off of normal vegetation due
to toxic chemicals, oxygen-poor waters and algal
blooms occur in many places, especially in estuaries
and coastal seas, such as the Baltic Sea, which have
limited openings to the oceans.

Consumption of shellfish is hazardous in some
areas of Central and Latin America, Southeast Asia,

and western Africa because of the release of untreated sewage. Bathing on beaches in these areas
is hazardous as well.

Ocean dumping is covered in Chapter 14, and
air pollutants that eventually affect the oceans are
mentioned in chapters 15, 16, and 17. Two other
sources of pollution in the marine environment
remain to be discussed: thermal pollution and oil
pollution resulting from offshore drilling or
shipping.

Thermal Pollution

The generation of electric power produces as a by-
product heat, which must be either used or disposed
of in some way. In the past the most common
means of disposal was to some natural body of
water. Water was drawn from a river or estuary
and cycled through the power plant, where it absorbed the excess heat produced. The heated water
was then dumped back into the body of water from

TABLE 18-2 Sources of Pollution in the Marine Environment

Source	Percent Contribution
Land-Based Discharges and Run-off (disease-causing microbes, plant nutrients, toxic chemicals, organic wastes, thermal pollution, sediments)	44%
Dumping (sewage sludge, garbage, toxic wastes)	10%
Oil Production and Transportation	13%
Atmosphere (dust, soil, chemicals such as pesticides and heavy metals, nitrogen compounds)	33%

which it had been taken. This is called *once-through* or *open-cycle* cooling.

In some areas this method of cooling power plants was eventually found to have a profound effect on the communities of organisms in the receiving waters.

Off Turkey Point on Biscayne Bay, Florida, in the early 1970s, biologists measured an area of almost 75 acres (30 hectares) that was barren of aquatic life. Surrounding this, another 100 acres was only sparsely populated. Yet Biscayne Bay is known to yield over 600,000 pounds per year of marketable seafoods such as spiny lobsters and stone crabs. Sport fish abound in the bay and a valuable bait-shrimp fishery is located there. Many fish and shellfish use the bay as breeding grounds, and a variety of wading birds feed in the shallows. What caused the apparent ecological disaster at Turkey Point, in an area ordinarily teeming with aquatic life? The barren area was centered around an effluent canal from Florida Power and Light's Turkey Point Power Plant. At that time the plant took cool water from the bay and returned heated water through the outflow. It was this heated water that caused a biological desert in the midst of the bay.

As explained in Chapter 1, temperature is an important factor in the well-being of all organisms. For each species, there is a particular temperature range that supports life. Some organisms have adapted to living in the hot springs at Yellowstone National Park, where temperatures may reach 70°C. There are even fish in arctic waters that survive being frozen in ice. But for any particular species, the temperature range necessary for survival is relatively narrow; in some cases, very narrow indeed. For instance, some organisms that build coral reefs in the Caribbean can withstand no more than a few degrees change in temperature.

Most aquatic creatures are not able to maintain a particular body temperature. These creatures must stay the same temperature as the water in which they live. Those that cannot move, such as adult oysters or rooted plants, are at the mercy of water temperatures. Beyond certain limits, they simply cannot survive. Those that can swim, such as fish, move about to find suitable temperatures. This is called behavioral regulation of temperature.

Temperature can affect the whole community structure of an aquatic environment. For instance, different species of freshwater algae compete for light, space, and nutrients. Temperature changes can alter the competitive position of different species, even though the changes are not severe enough to be lethal.

Overall, the effect of heat is to simplify aquatic communities; that is, fewer species are found, although there may be many individuals of each species. One study found that fewer than half as many species were found at 31°C than at 26°C. Another 24% disappeared at a temperature of 34°C.

Many natural waters are subject to seasonal variations in temperature. This variation allows different species to be dominant at different times, and therefore a greater number of species are able to compete for space and nourishment in a given area. A partial explanation for the effect of thermal pollution on communities may be that thermal additions can even out this temperature fluctuation.

FIGURE 18-10 Cooling Tower at the Trojan Nuclear Power Plant on the Columbia River near Prescott, Washington. Note the enormous size of the tower relative to its surroundings.

Cooling towers, cooling ponds, and cooling canals make use of the concept that when water evaporates, a great deal of heat energy is absorbed by the evaporating water molecules. Thus, in evaporative cooling, evaporation of a small amount of water withdraws a large amount of heat from the water that remains behind; this is the source of the cooling effect.

Although new steam electric stations built on inland waters are likely to employ closed-cycle cooling methods, power plants on the ocean or on cold estuaries may escape the requirement, if companies can show their heated discharges will not alter the ecological balance in the receiving waters. Such a demonstration is most likely to succeed on cold natural waters, such as the oceans and bays of the Atlantic Northeast and the Pacific Northwest. (*Photo:* EPA Documerica)

Thus, fewer species are able to coexist in a given area.

A large number of thermal-effect studies have been carried out with respect to the location of power plants. The studies seem to show that obvious harmful effects on ecosystems are more likely to occur from power plants located on naturally warm waters because organisms living in warm regions are often already near their upper thermal limits. The additional heat from the power plant pushes the organisms over their thermal limits.

Closed-Cycle Cooling. The problems that result from thermal pollution are all caused by open-cycle cooling, the use of water to receive waste heat. Technologies have been developed, however, that can transfer much of the waste heat from cooling water to the atmosphere. These technologies are called *closed-cycle cooling* (Figure 18-10).

Oil Pollution of the World's Waters

"Oil pollution." The words bring to mind pictures of wrecked tankers grinding over submerged rocks or of geysers of flaming oil shooting from well blowouts. Yet, historically, such dramatic happenings have accounted for only a small portion of the 2–5 million tons (14–35 million barrels) of oil added each year to the world's waters.

Most of the oil spilled into natural waters has been the result not of accidents but of normal operations. Even in 1979, the worst year on record for accidents, twice as much used motor and industrial oil entered the oceans as was spilled in oil-well or tanker accidents.

Where the Oil Comes From

Used Motor and Industrial Oil. In most years, up to one-half of the oil entering natural waters is used motor and industrial oil from sewer outflows and from runoff. Although anyone found dumping oil into a waterway in the United States is subject to heavy fines, and although waste oil can be collected, refined, and then used again, there are not enough convenient depots for the collection of such wastes as used automobile oil. Thus, much used oil in the United States and the rest of the world finds its way into sewers or garbage dumps. From there it runs into nearby waterways.

Normal Shipping Operations. All ships collect both oil and water in their bilges. The simplest method of disposing of this oily water is to pump it into the ocean.

A further contribution of oil pollution is made by oil tankers. Many tankers pump sea water into empty oil tanks as ballast and use sea water to wash out tanks between cargoes. When such a tanker nears an oil-loading port, it has tanks full of oily water to dispose of. For many years the water was simply pumped back into the ocean. Newer ships are fitted with separate ballast and oil tanks or with slop tanks where oil can be recovered from ballast water. Further, some tankers now wash out tanks with oil rather than with water. As of 1986, ships serving U.S. ports must be fitted with these kinds of oil-pollution prevention equipment.

MARPOL Regulations. On a global basis, the International Convention for the Prevention of Pollution from Ships (MARPOL 73/78) commits all signatory nations to equip their vessels with a specified minimum of oil-pollution prevention equipment. The convention also designates certain areas where discharge of nothing but clean water is allowed (Mediterranean Sea, Black Sea, Baltic Sea, Gulf Area, Red Sea, and Gulf of Aden). Such regulations, along with an actual decrease in the amount of oil transported by sea, have resulted in a reduction over the past 10 years in the amount of oil from normal shipping operations.

A legacy from past practices remains on beaches in many parts of the world, however. When crude oil is spilled on water, the lighter fractions evaporate, leaving floating balls or lumps of tar. These tar balls eventually wash up on beaches. In heavily trafficked areas such as the Red Sea or the Kuwait/Oman area, as much as 1 kilogram of tar per meter of beach can be found. In the Caribbean, another area with a significant production of oil, many beaches have more than 100 grams per square meter. At levels much over 10 grams per meter,

beaches are unsuitable for tourism. In addition to those areas mentioned, tar balls mar the beaches in Indonesia, the Philippines, India's west coast, Pakistan, western Africa, and the Mediterranean. Although the situation appears to be improving, better enforcement of MARPOL regulations is needed.

Tanker Accidents and Offshore Blowouts. Although tanker accidents and offshore oil-well blowouts normally account for only a small percentage of the total amount of oil pollution, they result in most of the visible damage. The reason is that a grounded tanker or an offshore blowout releases an enormous quantity of oil at one time.

Because it is cheaper to ship oil in large quantities, the size of the tankers traveling the oceans is increasing rapidly. The average-size supertanker now in use is as long as three football fields and carries about 250,000 tons.

The Exxon Valdez. Massive spills can result from accidents to tankers of this size. An example occurred in March of 1989, when the Exxon *Valdez* went aground on Bligh Reef in Alaska's Prince William Sound. Nearly 11 million gallons (240,000 barrels) of crude oil, the largest amount ever in U.S. waters, were spilled from the tanker into the pristine waters of the sound. The oil eventually came ashore on 1,355 miles of shoreline, which included three National Park areas (Figure 18-11). The number of tanker collisions has actually decreased since the 1970s in most areas. Nonetheless, between 1980 and 1988, in U.S. waters alone, tankers were involved in 468 groundings, 371 collisions, 97 rammings, and 55 fires and explosions.

Well Blowouts. The largest recorded oil spill was caused by the blowout of the Mexican oil well Ixtoc in the Gulf of Mexico in 1979. It released more than 3 million barrels of oil before being brought under control nine months later. Oil and dead sea birds washed up on the beaches of barrier islands in South Texas, more than 3,600 miles (6,000 km) away.

Such accidents have left a legacy of mistrust about the safety of drilling for oil in marine waters.

Yet the stakes, in terms of energy resources, are high. Some 13.6 billion barrels of oil are believed to lie underground in Britain's North Sea fields, while 12 billion barrels of oil are probably yet to be found offshore under the U.S. continental shelf. Governments want to accelerate the development of these resources, both to decrease reliance on foreign oil and to increase government revenues from the royalty payments oil companies make on the oil they obtain.

Oil Pollution from the Gulf War. Among the environmental consequences of the 1991 war in the Persian Gulf were the series of oil spills into the waters of the Gulf. Two and one-half to 3 million barrels of oil were probably spilled into the Gulf in both accidental and deliberate incidents. About 20,000 birds are known to have been killed by the oil spills, but the effect on other marine life, including fish, sea-grasses, and coral reefs, is unclear. Organisms living in the Gulf were already under stress from various pollutants before the invasion of Kuwait. The waters of the Gulf were, and are, highly polluted by untreated sewage, industrial wastes, discharges from desalinization plants, and oil spills, including about 2 million barrels of oil spilled into the Gulf during the Iran-Iraq War. The newly spilled oil is predicted to flush out of the Gulf in one to four years, but in the process some components of the oil will reach the Arabian Sea and the Indian Ocean.

Effects of Oil on Ecosystems

Some 300,000 barrels of oil are spilled each year in U.S. waters. The oil is spilled in an average of 10,000 separate incidents, and most are not cleaned up. The damage done by this background of spill events is not clear. Some experts dismiss it as trivial; others feel that not enough is known to draw such a conclusion.

There is a salt marsh in Southampton, England, where an oil refinery discharges, each day, 1,500 gallons (5,800 L) of water contaminated with very low levels of oil (10–20 ppm). This chronic pollution has killed off over 90 acres (36 hectares) of

FIGURE 18-11 Oiled Sea Otter at Morgue in Valdez. According to Fish and Wildlife Service counts, about 1,000 sea otters and 34,000 dead birds were recovered after the oil spill in Prince William Sound, but this was probably only 5%–10% of the actual total killed by the oil spill, because most dead birds and marine mammals sink and are not counted.

Otters and birds suffer during an oil spill because the oil soaks into their fur or feathers, ruining the waterproofing and insulating qualities. The animals can no longer keep warm or float. As birds try to preen away the oil, they swallow it and are blinded and poisoned. Oil also contaminates or destroys sea birds' natural foods. Diving birds are especially affected, as they dive through the oil slick again and again in search of food. (*Photo:* John Hyde/Alaska Fish and Game Department)

marsh grasses in the area around the refinery. With the grasses gone, the sandy soil began to erode, so that the affected area is now lower than its surroundings. Birds and other aquatic creatures that once found food in the area have been forced to move elsewhere. Thus, very small amounts of oil can, over a long period of time, have serious effects on an aquatic community.

In areas where many oil spills occur, such as harbors or the Main Pass oil field in the Gulf of Mexico, changes in the kinds of organisms are becoming apparent. For example, one study showed that organisms growing in bottom sediments in Timbalier Bay in the Gulf of Mexico were mainly two hardy species known to take over in polluted areas. The Gulf of Mexico has been contaminated

Controversy 18-1

Are National Interests More Important than Local Concerns?

The Interior Department now appears willing to accept the fact that the people of California want a program . . . that balances the need for oil with the need to protect important fisheries, tourist areas and other environmentally sensitive and economically important areas.

Lisa Speer, Natural Resources Defense Council

This is a classic example of the broad public interest versus narrower local interests, and in this case local concerns do not always reflect national or even regional needs.

James Watt, former Secretary of the Interior

Offshore oil drilling in several areas has been vigorously opposed by many environmental groups and sometimes by the states themselves. Clearly, such development could cause oil pollution due to catastrophic accidents or even just normal operations. For instance,

oil is believed to lie beneath the sediments along two-thirds of the northern California coastline. Wildlife also abounds along the coast, including all of the nation's endangered southern sea otters.

Coastal areas directly opposite proposed drilling sites fear the social and economic upheavals a large influx of workers brings. This was a major concern when Britain started producing North Sea oil. Britain's Orkney Islands were a remote, self-contained, rural area before the huge influx of oil and construction workers arrived, increasing the demand for schools, housing, and other municipal services. Similar upheavals occurred during construction of the Alaskan pipeline. But such concerns are not limited to offshore drilling proposals. Communities and environmental interest groups also protest the siting of nuclear power plants, hazardous waste dumps, and oil refineries. James Watt (see above

quote) appears to feel that national interests must take priority over local concerns.

Do you agree that national priorities (such as a need for oil to reduce dependence on foreign sources or to increase federal revenues) come before the interests of local residents? What efforts can the federal government make to reduce harmful impacts on local residents? Do you feel that the federal government should provide compensation for unavoidable harmful effects? Would this change your opinion about the first question?

What about potential harm to local wildlife or plant populations? Should local feelings about this be taken into account?

Sources: Lisa Speer, quoted in the *New York Times,* June 3, 1981, p. A20; and James Watt, quoted in the *New York Times,* July 17, 1985, p. A14.

with oil for so many years that it is difficult to find an unaffected area to see what the natural communities were like.

In the North Sea, on the other hand, drilling operations began in 1973, and studies have been carried out since then. The studies have found gradual increases in the amount of oil in sediments

around the drill sites. In addition, definite decreases have been seen in the number of species found and in the total number of organisms found. The area in which these decreases are seen becomes larger as time goes on.

Both oil and oil tars contain some cancer-causing substances. Several studies of shellfish grown in polluted waters have shown that they have an abnormally high number of growths similar to human cancer tumors. Oil, which is concentrated by shellfish such as oysters and clams, may be at least a partial cause of these tumors.

Biological Recovery after an Oil Spill. After oil is spilled, recovery time would certainly include the length of time it takes for all traces of oil to disappear. However, it also includes the time necessary for the polluted area to be repopulated with the kinds and sizes of organisms that lived there before the spill. If a spill does not kill all the resident organisms, those left begin to repopulate the area, once poisonous parts of the oil have disappeared. Organisms from other areas also begin to move in, either by swimming and floating (e.g., larvae) or by creeping in from nearby colonies (sea grasses). Competition among species and predation begin to establish a balance between the different groups. But how long does oil persist in the environment after it has been spilled?

When the coastal barge *Florida* ran aground in Buzzards Bay at West Falmouth, Massachusetts, in 1969, there was one positive aspect. Scientists at nearby Woods Hole Oceanographic Institute were well equipped to investigate closely the effects of the spill. They discovered that even though oil may have disappeared from the surface of the water, its effects can still be far-reaching and serious. In Buzzards Bay, heavy seas and onshore winds ensured that the spill of home heating oil was well mixed with the water. In a few days, no oil could be seen floating on the surface. Five years later, however, the oil could still be found in the sediments. Where oil was found, there were fewer organisms than in neighboring regions. The oiled sediments had also eroded away to some degree. This seemed to allow the oil to spread further. The area in which oil was found was much larger than the original spill. Certain of the sea creatures studied, such as fiddler crabs, were still absorbing oil into their bodies. This oil caused them to behave strangely and prevented the population of crabs from increasing to the levels that existed before the spill. Scientists therefore warn that although oil may have only short-term effects in some areas, in others, such as marshes,

the oil becomes mixed into the sediments and lasts for many years.

Recovery after Oil Spill from the Exxon *Valdez*. Although some wildlife populations in Prince William Sound appear to have escaped serious harm, there is evidence that the oil spill from the Exxon *Valdez* may be responsible for some long-term biological effects. Record catches of salmon indicate that the fishery is unharmed, but scientists have found evidence that the fish are ingesting oil. Oil derivatives found in pollock, another ocean fish, also indicate that oil has entered the food chain. One species of bird, murres, that nests in the spill area has failed to reproduce for the two years since the spill.

Furthermore, scientists have called into question a major part of the cleanup effort in which Exxon crews cleaned rocky beaches with hot water to remove the oil. Studies now seem to show that the cleaned beaches are recovering more slowly than comparable areas that were not cleaned because they were less accessible to cleanup crews.

Lessening Oil Pollution and Its Effects

Moderating the Effects of Offshore Drilling. One result of offshore drilling accidents has been an improvement in the safety devices designed to prevent blowouts. Producing oil wells have safety valves designed to close off the wells if storms or earthquakes destroy the platform. Experts believe that these safety devices will work about 96% of the time.

Still, because safety devices are not 100% effective and because there is always room for human error, a high probability exists that some spills and blowouts will accompany any offshore drilling.

Improving Tanker Safety. The U.S. Department of Commerce estimates that as many as 85% of shipping accidents are due to human error. Tanker construction can mitigate or worsen the effects of such error.

As a result of the *Valdez* disaster, the U.S. Congress passed a strong bill designed to decrease oil spills from tanker accidents. All new tankers will be required to have double hulls, so that a rip in the hull caused by grounding or a collision will not necessarily result in spilled oil. Older tankers will have to be rebuilt with double hulls or phased out over the next 20 years. The liability of oil carriers was increased from $150 per gross ton to $1,200. A $1-billion oil spill cleanup fund will be created with a 5-cent-a-barrel tax on both domestic and imported oil. The Coast Guard is directed to set up regional response teams, as well as a national clearing center for oil spill emergency responses.

Cleaning Up Oil Spills. Realistically, however, even well-prepared response teams may be able to do little once oil is spilled. Booms and barriers can sometimes keep oil from coming ashore in sensitive areas, but they do not work in rough waters. Skimmers can remove oil from the surface of the water, but current designs work well only for small to medium spills on calm waters. Once oil is mixed into the water column, recovery is not possible.

New technologies include low-toxicity detergents and bacteria that "eat" oil. Detergents break up oil slicks by mixing the oil into the water. This is helpful if bird populations are threatened but may actually do more harm to fish and bottom dwellers than the oil slick itself.

After the *Valdez* spill, Exxon sprayed beaches with a fertilizer mixture designed to stimulate the growth of organisms that use oil as a food source. In other recent spills, bacteria specially grown for their oil-digesting ability have been sprayed on oil slicks. The final word is not in yet on the success of either of these two new technologies.

Economic and Social Effects of Mixing Oil and Water

People living in coastal areas are understandably uneasy about offshore drilling. While a country as a whole may benefit from the oil, the people living in the coastal states bear all the environmental costs of producing the oil. These include possible oil spills from drilling and transporting the oil, as well as water and air pollution from onshore development of oil-refining facilities. Localized overcrowding may occur as workers stream in to develop the oil fields. In some economically depressed areas, people may welcome the possibility of oil-related jobs.

However, unless there is careful planning by local officials and agreements are drawn up between the oil companies and the towns, few local people may be hired. In such a case, the native population will suffer the inflation, housing shortages, overcrowding of schools, roads, and recreational facilities, and higher taxes that accompany an oil boom, without sharing in any of the money it brings (see Controversy 18-1).

In the United States, vigorous opposition by coastal states to drilling off their coastlines led President Bush to ban offshore drilling through at least the year 2000 along 99% of California's shore, all of Washington and Oregon, all of New England north of Rhode Island, and part of southwestern Florida.

SUMMARY

Fresh water for drinking, crop irrigation, and industrial use is obtained mainly from underground aquifers and from surface waters (in natural rivers, lakes, and streams, or reservoirs built by engineers). In the past, groundwater has been a less polluted water source than surface water. However, hazardous waste disposal practices as well as the use of water from deeper levels of aquifers has led to increasing chemical and salt concentrations in groundwater. Because many aquifers recharge very slowly, pollution of an aquifer can last through many lifetimes. Further, in many areas, groundwaters are being withdrawn at a rate faster than they recharge.

A reservoir may serve many purposes besides water supply, such as flood control, recreation, hydropower, and downstream pollution control. Dams built to create reservoirs may have adverse environmental impacts: loss of wildlife habitat, loss of homesites for area residents, stream erosion below the dam, and interruption of fish migration.

Both reservoirs and natural waters are subject to pollution from organic wastes, phosphates, and nitrates. Organic wastes are oxidized by bacteria and other microorganisms. In the process, these organisms use up the dissolved oxygen in the water. Many desirable water species find it difficult or impossible to survive in the resultant low-oxygen conditions.

When nitrates and phosphates are added to natural waters, they can serve as nutrients for photosynthetic algae, which may then grow into huge, unsightly blooms. This is called eutrophication. At night when the algae in eutrophic waters respire and use oxygen, dissolved oxygen values can plummet, endangering other aquatic creatures.

Nitrates are the limiting nutrient in most coastal waters and steep mountain streams, while phosphates are limiting in most of the rest of U.S. waters. A major source of phosphate additions to natural waters is domestic wastewater that contains phosphates from detergents and from human and animal wastes. Phosphates from these sources can be eliminated by tertiary sewage treatment. An even larger source is the phosphate entering natural waters from nonpoint sources: fertilizer runoff, septic system drainage, and municipal runoff. Nonpoint sources can be controlled by proper land management.

Water pollution control restores the quality of water the consumer has used so that it can be returned to a natural body of water. The three main steps in water pollution control are (1) primary treatment, which removes solids from wastewater by allowing them to settle out; (2) secondary treatment, which removes dissolved organics by allowing microbes to consume the organic materials; and (3) tertiary treatment, which removes nitrogen and phosphorus compounds and some resistant organic materials.

After these three steps, the water is chlorinated to kill any remaining bacteria or viruses and then released. About 63% of Americans are served by a sewage treatment plant with secondary treatment or better. Another 20% have adequate private systems such as septic tanks. About 17% have less than secondary treatment or no treatment at all. In rural areas, septic tanks provide safer treatment for the individual house than the older cesspools. In developing countries, the improved, ventilated pit latrine and waste stabilization lagoons or ponds can provide efficient, low-cost waste treatment.

Major problems that remain in wastewater treatment involve (1) extending sewage treatment to the unserved part of the population; (2) separating the nation's storm sewers from the domestic wastewater sewers so that wastewaters do not bypass the treatment plant during storms; (3) instituting land use practices to control the flow of wastes into natural waters from nonpoint sources; and (4) decreasing the amount of possibly carcinogenic chlorinated hydrocarbons formed during the chlorination of wastewater.

Marine waters are subject to pollution from land-based discharges (disease-causing microbes, plant nutrients, eroded sediments and toxic chemicals), atmospheric pollutants (dust, soil, toxic chemicals, and nitrogen compounds), thermal pollution transportation and offshore production of oil, and ocean dumping of garbage and toxic wastes. Although the open oceans are relatively pollution-free, coastal zones, especially in populated areas, are often seriously polluted.

Oil pollution of the world's waters is primarily due to inputs from land, in both runoff and sewage, and from normal shipping operations. Although tanker accidents and offshore drilling rig accidents contribute only a small portion of the annual total of oil pollution, they cause most of the visible damage due to the large quantity of oil released at one time. Sea birds and marine mammals are often killed in large numbers as a result of these accidents. Of equal importance, however, may be the long-term effects on aquatic communities of small continuous spills, or of the oil buried in the bottom sediments after a large spill disappears from view.

Offshore drilling projects and deep-water ports cause economic and social problems apart from their environmental effects. Opposition by coastal states to offshore oil production has led to a ban until the year 2000 on offshore drilling along a large portion of both U.S. coasts.

Questions

1. Describe the physical and ecological impact of a dam in place across a river.

2. When organic wastes are added to natural waters, they may cause fish to die, even though the wastes themselves are not directly poisonous to fish. How do you explain this?

3. What problems are caused by too much phosphate in natural waters? Would you call phosphorus a poisonous chemical?

4. Why must we be careful about what kinds of chemicals are substituted for phosphates in detergents?

5. How is the sewage from your home treated? Does it go to a sewage treatment plant or into a septic tank or cesspool? If it goes into a septic tank or cesspool, summarize what happens in a few sentences. If it goes to a sewage treatment plant, does the plant give only primary treatment, or does it provide secondary or tertiary treatment?

6. Explain the statement "The world's waters are the ultimate dump for much of the pollution produced on land."

7. Accidents to tankers and offshore drilling rigs are responsible for only a small percentage of the total amount of oil spilled each year. Why are they still of serious concern?

8. Suppose your group decided to start a waste oil recycling project in your community. How would you begin? How would you explain the need for such a project to citizens in your community?

Further Reading

Hagerhall, Bertil. "Saving the Baltic: A Race Against Mankind," *Our Planet, 2* (2) (1990).

A good example of the problems experienced by coastal bodies of water in populated areas.

Joint Group of Experts on the Scientific Aspects of Marine Pollution. *The State of the Marine Environment,* UNEP Regional Seas Reports and Studies #115, United Nations Environment Program. New York: United Nations, 1990.

A comprehensive analysis of the health of the global marine environment.

Kenney, J. "Grave Waters," *National Parks,* July/August 1989.

Good pictures and details on the spill of the Exxon *Valdez* and its effects on parks in the Prince William Sound area.

Kohrl, William. *Water and Power.* Berkeley, Calif.: University of California Press, 1982.

A readable story of the political power struggle in which Los Angeles secured one portion of its water supply from the Owens Valley of California.

Mackenthun, K. *Toward a Cleaner Aquatic Environment.* Washington, D.C.: U.S. Government Printing Office, 1973.

Stock No. 5001-00573. Virtually a textbook on the biology of water pollution. It is interesting, well written, well illustrated, and rarely too technical for the novice to follow. Directions for identifying algae associated with water pollution are provided.

Mydans, S. "U.S. and Mexico Agree on Border Sewage Plant," *New York Times,* August 22, 1990, p. A12.

The United States and Mexico share many environmental problems, among them air and water pollution. This article details sewage treatment problems and solutions along the U.S.–Mexican border.

Sun, M. "Mud-slinging over Sewage Technology," *Science 246,* (October 27, 1989), 440.

The way sewage is treated now may not be the way it is treated in the future. This article details new advanced primary treatment processes, which cost less money and generate less sludge than conventional secondary treatment. Whether they are as safe as conventional treatment is still in question, however.

U.S. Environmental Protection Agency. *Environmental Pollution Control Alternatives: Municipal Wastewater.* Technology Transfer Seminar Publication, EPA-625/5-76-012, Washington, D.C.: U.S. Government Printing Office, 1976.

A profusely illustrated, well-written document that deals with most primary, secondary, and tertiary processes for waste treatment, including European practice and emerging technologies. Since it does not go into process design, the style remains nontechnical at all times.

Wilson, S., and K. Hayden. "Where Oil and Water Mix," *National Geographic,* February 1981, p. 145.

An exploration of the wildlife refuges along the Texas coast, where the protection of whooping cranes and oil production are in a fragile balance.

References

Barnaby, F. "The Environmental Impact of the Gulf War," *The Ecologist, 21*(4) (1991), 166.

Brinkman, D. W. "Used Oil: Resource or Pollutant?" *Technology Review,* July 1985, p. 48.

Commission on Engineering and Technical Systems. *Using Oil Spill Dispersants on the Sea.* Committee on the Effectiveness of Oil Spill Dispersants, Marine Board. Washington, D.C.: National Academy Press, 1988.

Crawdford, M. "Exxon Bets on Bugs in Alaska Cleanup," *Science, 245* (August 18, 1989), 714.

Davis, T. "Managing to Keep Rivers Wild," *Technology Review,* May/June 1986.

The Environmental Program for the Mediterranean, ISBN 0-8213-1382-7. The World Bank, 1990.

Gantenbein, D. "Salmon on the Spot," *Sierra,* January/February 1991.

Guldin, R. *An Analysis of the Water Situation in the United States: 1989–2040.* General Technical Report RM-177. Washington, D.C.: USDA Forest Service, 1989.

Holden, C. "Gulf Slick a Free Lunch for Bacteria," Briefings, *Science, 249* (July 13, 1990), 120.

Lensink, C. "Birds and Sea Otters Killed in the Exxon *Valdez* Oil Spill," *Endangered Species Update,* 7(6) (1990).

Minerals Management Service. *Alaska Update: September 1989–January 1990.* U.S. Department of the Interior, OCS Information Program, #MMS 90-0012. Washington, D.C.: U.S. Government Printing Office, 1990.

Postel, S. *Conserving Water: The Untapped Alternative,* Worldwatch Paper 67. Washington, D.C.: Worldwatch Institute, 1985.

Ryding, S., and W. Rast. *The Control of Eutrophication of Lakes and Reservoirs,* UNESCO Man and the Biosphere Series. N.J.: The Parthenon Publishing Group, 1990.

Sanders, H., et al. "Long-Term Effects of the Barge *Florida* Spill." EPA PB 81 144–792, January 1981.

U.S. Environmental Protection Agency. "Nonpoint Source Pollution in the U.S.: Report to Congress." Washington, D.C.: Office of Water Program Operations, 1984.

Warner, F. "The Environmental Consequences of the Gulf War," *Environment, 33*(5) (1991), 6.

Warren, W. "Long Awaited High Phosphate Detergent Ban Becomes Law in Ohio," *Focus on International Joint Commission Activities, 13*(2) (July/August 1988).

Chapter 19

The Water We Drink

At one time the only water source for the small village of Bolok on Timor Island in Indonesia was a spring in a cave two miles away. But, "the water was salty and brought us disease," says the village's chief, Mr. Lasy. "Our people were very poor and our children never attended school."

In a pioneering program, the United Nations, the World Health Organization, and the Indonesian government helped the villagers build a hand-pumped well. The result has been a resounding success. Over the past 10 years, villagers' income has tripled, cholera and skin diseases have almost disappeared, and the children attend school regularly.

Yet, similar programs in other places have been dismal failures. What was the difference? In the past, governments or international organizations often came in, built a well, and then left it for the villagers to maintain. The rusting remains of broken pumps attest to the failure of such programs.

In Bolok's case, villagers were involved from the beginning in the selection and financing of the pump and in choosing the site for the well. Women, who in Indonesia as in much of the rest of the developing world are responsible for securing water, were not only consulted about the location of the pump, but were also trained in maintaining it and educated about waterborne diseases.

A project like Bolok's holds the key to providing safe water and sanitation for citizens of the developing world. It also, as was seen in Bolok, promises an improvement in other aspects of life. Healthy people are able to work and take advantage of educational opportunities. These factors, along with improved child survival, can provide a climate in which parents begin to see the advantages of smaller families.

In this sense, safe drinking water and sanitation represent more than a phase in third-world rural development. They are key factors in solving the twin problems of poverty and overpopulation.

In this chapter we first discuss drinking water problems that can occur in both developed and undeveloped parts of the world. What do we mean by safe drinking water? How is water treated to make it safe to drink? What are the major sources

FIGURE 19-1 Community Water Pump in a New York City Tenement Courtyard. This pump provided the water supply for a large neighborhood. Sources of contamination of the well water are easy to imagine. (*Source:* The Bettmann Archive, Inc.)

of drinking water contaminants? Then we focus on the ambitious U.N. decision to bring safe drinking water to all people, no matter where they live.

DISEASE-CAUSING ORGANISMS IN DRINKING WATER

The idea that water can carry diseases is not a new one. The ancient Greek physician Hippocrates recommended that water be purified by boiling or filtration before being drunk. But the connection between drinking water and disease was not commonly accepted until the late 1800s in the Western world (Figure 19-1).

Typhoid, cholera, paratyphoid, and amoebic dysentery are all examples of diseases that can be spread by water. Epidemics of these diseases were once common in the United States and Europe because communities disposed of their raw sewage into the same bodies of water from which they drew their drinking water. The situation began to improve once methods were developed for treating drinking water to make it safe.

There is still a need for vigilance, however. Waterborne diseases in epidemic proportions have continued to occur in the United States throughout this century, although with decreasing frequency. The cities struck by these epidemics are typically small and have insufficient treatment of their water supplies. Although such epidemics are becoming infrequent in the United States, they continue to occur where water supplies are not treated, where treatment systems fail, or when water distribution systems become contaminated.

In 1980, just over 20,000 people in the United States were affected in 50 outbreaks of diseases traced to water supplies. In only 22 of the 50 outbreaks was the causative agent identified. In 30% of the cases where the causative agent was identified, the responsible agent was a little-known human parasite, *Giardia lamblia*.

Long thought to be a cause of disease only in hunters, backpackers, and others who drink untreated water, the *Giardia* protozoan is now known as the cause of many waterborne outbreaks in the United States. Symptoms of the disease, giardiasis, include diarrhea, cramps, and weight loss. The disease does not occur until one to eight weeks after infection and may last two to three months. Water supplies that are chlorinated but not filtered (see Figure 19-2) may allow the spread of this disease.

A final word of warning about giardiasis: Hikers in the backcountry can no longer drink from mountain streams without fear. The fact that beavers, muskrats, and other wild animals carry and transmit

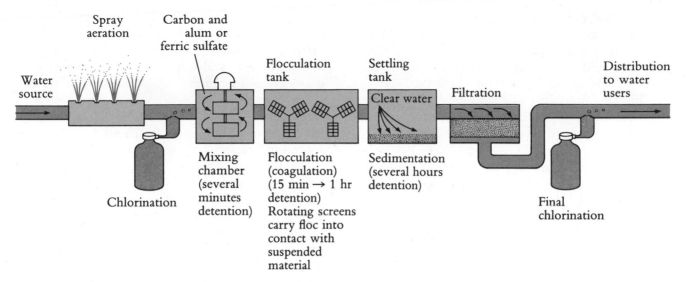

FIGURE 19-2 A Typical Water Treatment Plant Scheme. The first step, aeration, helps to remove dissolved gases such as hydrogen sulfide, which are responsible for bad tastes and odors in water. Next, chlorine gas is added to the water to kill disease causing microbes. Particles that give color and cloudiness to water are removed in the next two steps: coagulation, or formation of a precipitate with alum or ferrous sulfate, and then settling out of the precipitate. Filtration through beds of sand then removes more particles, along with any bacteria and viruses in the water. A final chlorination ensures that any remaining microbes are killed and also provides a little excess chlorine to keep the water safe duing its passage through the distribution system.

A number of European countries, a few U.S. communities, and many bottled water companies use ozone gas rather than chlorine gas to disinfect water. Ozone does not create chlorinated hydrocarbons as chlorine does, and it leaves no taste in the water. On the other hand, ozone leaves no residual in the water to protect against fresh inputs of bacteria and viruses in the distribution system.

the protozoan makes suspect even these once safe sources of water. Numerous cases of giardiasis have already been reported among backpackers. We would not trust any trail method of disinfection other than boiling the water for 15–20 minutes.

How Can We Tell If Water Is Unsafe?

Coliform Bacteria Are Indicators. Three major classes of disease-causing organisms are found in water: bacteria, viruses, and protozoans. The maladies they spread range from severe diseases, such as hepatitis, typhoid, and dysentery, to minor respiratory and skin diseases.

Examining water to isolate all the possible disease-causing organisms in it would be a difficult, costly task. To avoid such exhaustive examination, special tests have been devised. These tests detect a group of bacteria that, if present, are likely to be accompanied by disease-producing microorganisms. If this group of bacteria is absent, or if the level of these bacteria in a water sample is sufficiently small, it is doubtful that the less numerous disease-causing organisms are present.

The bacteria for which scientists test are *non-pathogenic;* that is, with rare exception, they do not cause disease. These bacteria are found naturally in the intestines of warm-blooded animals, including humans, and are known as **coliforms.** Although coliforms rarely cause disease, their presence in water indicates that the water may have been contaminated with raw (untreated) sewage. To drink such water is obviously unwise.

Thus, the procedure of examining water for the presence of disease-causing organisms does not involve looking for the pathogens themselves; it is sufficient to show that water has somehow been contaminated with sewage or not treated enough to kill all the coliform bacteria in it. The coliforms are often called *indicator organisms.*

Testing for Indicator Organisms. The modern method of testing for the presence and number of coliform bacteria is to filter a measured sample of water through a special filter membrane. This paper membrane is made by the Millipore Company and is called a Millipore filter. It is manufactured with pores, or holes, so small that bacteria cannot pass through, although the water can. Thus the bacteria are trapped on the paper filter when a sample of polluted water is poured through it. The filter paper is then placed on a medium containing the special nutrients that coliform bacteria need for growth. On that medium, each coliform bacterium captured on the membrane filter divides and forms a colony. These colonies are visible to the naked eye; they can be identified and counted in order to estimate the number of coliform bacteria in the water.

Determining the presence of viruses in water is not as simple as detecting the presence of bacteria. Most viruses are too small to be trapped by a filter, and they cannot be grown in a simple broth. However, just as water is not routinely examined for the disease-causing bacteria themselves, water is not commonly checked for disease-causing viruses either. Again, the presence of coliform bacteria in a water sample is taken as evidence that disease-causing viruses as well as bacteria are likely to be present in the water.

Water Treatment

Communities treat their water to remove both disease-causing organisms and harmful chemicals. In addition, water purification is designed to make water pleasant to drink. Not all cities purify their water in the same way because of the presence of different substances in their basic supply. Figure 19-2 shows a typical water treatment scheme used in a developed country such as the United States.

The term *water treatment* should be distinguished from the term *water pollution control.* These are very different activities. **Water treatment** is the process that purifies water for the consumer, whether in the home, in business, or in factories. **Water pollution control,** described in Chapter 18, is directed toward restoring the quality of the water that the consumer has used. Organic wastes and bacteria that have been added during use must be removed. Often, nitrates and phosphates need to be removed as well.

CHEMICALS IN DRINKING WATER

Inorganic Chemicals

Cadmium, lead, arsenic, and nitrates are examples of inorganic chemicals that may contaminate water supplies. Table 19-1 notes the sources of inorganic chemicals of concern in drinking water and why they are considered a problem. Between 1991 and 1992, the U.S. Environmental Protection Agency (EPA) reviewed existing drinking water regulations and set new standards. These *maximum contaminant levels,* or *MCLs,* for inorganic chemicals are shown in Table 19-1. Such standards apply to any drinking water supply that regularly serves more than 25 people. States may set standards that are more strict than federal ones, but they may not set less strict standards. Mercury in natural waters can be a problem whether or not the waters are drunk. See Controversy 19-1.

Organic Chemicals

Organic chemical contaminants are found in both surface and groundwater sources for drinking water. There are four main sources of organic chemical contamination: (1) agricultural use of pesticides (discussed in Chapter 8), (2) the treatment process used in water purification and water pol-

TABLE 19-1 Inorganic Chemicals of Concern in Drinking Water

Chemical	Source	Hazard	MCL[a] mg/L
Arsenic	Mining	Cancer-causing	0.05
Asbestos	Mining, asbestos/cement pipes, natural rock	May cause cancers	7 MFL[b]
Barium	Industrial, oil and gas drilling, natural deposits	Affects circulatory system	2
Cadmium	Mining and industrial waste	Kidney disease, high blood pressure	0.005
Chromium	Industrial, natural deposits	Affects liver, kidney, skin, digestive system	0.1
Fluoride	Natural, added to prevent tooth decay	Not clear; see "Further Reading"	1.4–2.4
Lead	Gasoline, old paint	Poisonous to humans, especially children	0.05
Mercury	Industrial and consumer products (thermometers), drugs, dental fillings	Toxic to fish and people biologically magnified	0.002
Nitrates	Fertilizers, feedlots, sewage, mineral deposits	Methemoglobinemia, "blue baby" syndrome	10
Nitrites	Produced biologically from nitrates	Methemoglobinemia, "blue baby" syndrome	1
Silver	Industrial, natural	Bluish discoloration of skin and membranes	0.05
Selenium	Mining, natural deposits	Affects nervous system	0.05
Iron, manganese	Acid mine drainage	Poisonous in high concentrations, destroy aquatic habitat	0.3[c] 0.05[c]
Sodium	Natural, water softeners	May contribute to heart disease	20[d]

[a] Maximum contaminant level, set January 1991 to July 1992
[b] Million fibers per liter, fiber length greater than 10 microns
[c] Secondary standards—not required, but recommended
[d] Recommended level to protect people on low-salt diets

lution control, (3) chemical waste disposal practices, and (4) leaking underground petroleum storage tanks.

More than 700 organic chemicals have been identified in U.S. drinking water sources, most at levels not deemed to be harmful to humans. The EPA has set maximum contaminant levels for 18 pesticides, PCBs (polychlorinated biphenyls), and a variety of volatile organic compounds, most on the basis of their cancer-causing potential. Table 19-2 lists these compounds and their MCLs.

Chlorination and Cancer-Causing Organics. A major concern about organic compounds in

Controversy 19-1

Who Bears the Economic Burden of Pollution?

[Oak Ridge is] a relatively affluent city ... populated by scientists and engineers who have other life pursuits than sports fishing.

Officials at Oak Ridge
Tennessee Plant

This town is structured around the needs of the elite and no one else.

Jimmy Fuzzell II, resident, Oak Ridge, Tennessee

Environmental improvement is sometimes viewed as a concern of relatively wealthy people who don't have to worry about more basic necessities, such as jobs, food, or doctor bills. That this can be a real misreading of where the pollution burden often falls is illustrated by two cases of mercury pollution: the pollution of the Wabigoon–English River system in northwestern Ontario and the Oak Ridge Y-12 plant incident in Tennessee.

A chlorine–caustic soda plant in Dryden, Ontario, discharged 9,000–11,000 kg of mercury into the Wabigoon River from 1962 to 1970. Fish caught in this river system show high mercury levels. Concern has been voiced because two Ojibway reservations are located nearby—the Grassy Narrows and the White Dog Reserves. The Ojibway Indians eat a diet high in fish, and government studies have found that many of them have excessive mercury levels in their blood. In addition, a Japanese group that came to study the Indians found signs of mercury poisoning, such as visual problems and lack of coordination.

Mercury pollution of the food supply was not the only problem the Ojibway Indians had to contend with. In 1963 the Canadian government had begun moving residents from their reservation to a new site to provide electricity, medical care, and schooling for them. For the Indians, separation from their ancestral lands and from their hunting-fishing culture was devastating. Alcoholism became a problem for many who were unable to handle the loss of their former way of life and who were unable to fit into the new lifestyle offered them. Still, sociologists who originally investigated believed the reaction of the Grassy Narrows Indians was extreme compared to similar cases they had studied among other North American Indian groups. It was then discovered that the Indians might be suffering from mercury poisoning. The effect, both of the poison and of experiencing this further loss of control of their environment, seems to have been an almost total disintegration of the social fabric of the community.

In another case of mercury contamination, officials at the Oak Ridge complex in Tennessee were informed that fish caught in the creek near the Y-12 plant had high mercury levels. The officials responded that, since most people in the town were scientists and engineers, they would not be spending a lot of time fishing and eating mercury-contaminated fish. True or not, there was indeed a group of people in town who were not affluent engineers and scientists, who did commonly fish the creek, and who swam in it as well. This group, the black community of Scarboro, consisted of 1,500 people who lived along the East Fork Poplar Creek. High unemployment in the community had encouraged a fair amount of fishing by Scarboro residents before the mercury pollution was discovered.

In these two cases of mercury contamination, what factors led to the unequal burden of pollution, which fell on the poor rather than on the wealthy members of society? Can you think of another case in which this unequal burden is common? Can you think of instances in which the more affluent members of society are at higher risk than the less affluent? Is there a difference between the two types of cases?

Source: A. Shkilnyk, *A Poison Stronger Than Love* (New Haven, Conn.: Yale University Press, 1985).

drinking water involves the chlorination process in water purification and water pollution control. The chloroform and carbon tetrachloride listed in Table 19-2 may of course come from industrial wastes, but they are more likely to have resulted from the chlorination of drinking water to kill disease-causing microorganisms or sewage.

Chlorine, in the form used to disinfect drinking water, can react with natural or pollution-related organic materials to form chlorinated hydrocarbons. Some of these chlorinated hydrocarbons are known to cause cancer.

It is unlikely that we will stop chlorinating drinking water. The immediate risk of incurring epidemics of waterborne bacterial diseases such as typhoid fever and viral diseases such as hepatitis or polio is too great. Instead, the focus has been on removing organic compounds from drinking water. Water treatment methods are being changed as well in an effort to reduce the formation of chlorinated hydrocarbons.

The EPA is now requiring many water suppliers to reduce the level in drinking water of a group of chemicals called *trihalomethanes,* a group that includes chloroform. Trihalomethanes are one class of compound that may be formed when chlorine reacts with hydrocarbons dissolved in water. Reduction of trihalomethane levels can be accomplished in several ways:

- The source of raw water can be changed to a less polluted one, decreasing the amount of organic material able to be chlorinated to trihalomethanes.
- Adjustments can be made in the water treatment scheme, such as changing the point at which chlorine is added.
- Other methods of disinfection, such as the use of ozone, can be tried.

Hazardous Wastes and Groundwater Contamination

The major source of chemicals in groundwater is hazardous waste that has been buried in industrial and municipal waste dumps or collected in waste lagoons and ponds. In fact, of the various possible

TABLE 19-2 Organic Chemicals of Concern in Drinking Water

Chemical	MCL[a] (mg/I)
Pesticides	
Alachlor (Lasso)	0.002
Aldicarb (Temik), A. sulfone, A. sulfoxide	0.003
Atrazine	0.003
Carbofuran	0.04
Chlordane	0.002
DBCP (Nemafume)	0.0002
2,4 D (Formula 40, Weedar 64)	0.07
EDB (Bromofume)	0.00005
Endrin	0.0002
Heptachlor	0.0004
Heptachlor epoxide	0.0002
Lindane	0.0002
Methoxychlor (Marlate)	0.04
PCBs (Arochlor)	0.0005
Pentachlorophenol	0.001
Toxaphene	0.003
2,4,5 T (Silvex)	0.05
Volatile Organics	
O-Dichlorobenzene	0.6
cis-1,2 dichloroethylene	0.07
trans-1,2 dichloroethylene	0.1
1,2 Dichloropropane	0.005
Ethylbenzene	0.7
Monochlorobenzene	0.1
Styrene	0.1
Tetrachloroethylene	0.005
Toluene	1
Total trihalomethanes (e.g., chloroform, carbon-tetrachloride)	0.10
Xylenes	10

[a] Maximum contaminant level, set by EPA 1991–1992

problems resulting from hazardous waste disposal, EPA ranks groundwater contamination as the most serious. When the EPA investigated 929 existing hazardous waste sites in 1982, it found groundwater contamination at 320 sites and evidence that it might exist at 326 other sites. Drinking water had been contaminated at 128 of the sites and was suspected at 213 others.

Cleaning Up Groundwater. An example of the possible extent and cost of groundwater contamination is found at Colorado's Rocky Mountain Arsenal. Waste dumps on the property, which were administered by the U.S. Army Chemical Corps and by Shell Chemical Company, have leaked waste synthetic chemicals into groundwater, contaminating 30 square miles of the aquifer over which the arsenal is sited. Numerous wells in the area have been closed. The Army has spent over $200 million to clean up the aquifer and to prevent further contamination. It is expected that $1.8 billion more will be needed to finish the job.

It first became apparent that groundwater beneath Rocky Mountain Arsenal was contaminated when, in the 1980s, nearby crops irrigated with groundwater were killed. Two attempts to solve the problem failed. Wastes were pumped from unlined surface ponds into asphalt-lined basins; then, when the basins were full, the remaining wastes were injected deep into geologic strata underneath Denver. A series of earthquakes occurred during this injection, however. Some experts believed the waste injection was causing the earthquakes, so deep-well injection was stopped. Meanwhile, the asphalt lining on the new ponds was eaten away by solvents in the waste materials. In 1975, in the face of continued pollution of groundwater, a new strategy was devised. An underground barrier wall was built at one end of the property to prevent the flow of contaminated groundwater. Now, the water that collects behind the wall is pumped out, treated with granulated activated carbon to remove contaminants, and added back on the other side of the wall.

The Rocky Mountain Arsenal case illustrates three of the possible actions when groundwater is contaminated:

1. Containment of the source of contamination with an underground barrier

2. Pumping out already contaminated water

3. Treatment of the groundwater to remove contaminants, after which it is returned to the ground

A fourth possibility is to pump the contaminated water out and dispose of it elsewhere. This is more a displacement of the problem than a solution, however. A fifth option involves pumping water (not necessarily contaminated water) from one place to another in order to charge the underground flow of water and so contain a pollution source or keep it away from wells that are in use.

The Rocky Mountain Arsenal case illustrates one other feature of cleaning up groundwater: the high cost involved. In fact, the most common solution to groundwater contamination involving a drinking water source is to drill a new well somewhere else. This is due, in part, to the high cost and technical difficulty of cleaning up contaminated groundwater. It is also a result of other considerations, however. A new well or a hookup to a noncontaminated source can often be arranged much more quickly than the contaminated groundwater can be cleansed. When an upset and angry public needs to be supplied with safe water, the deciding factor may be time, not cost. In the same way, if certain standards need to be met within a few years, an expensive barrier wall may be built rather than a less expensive pumping system that could take 10 times as long to achieve the same result. One economic fact is clear, however. It is cheaper to prevent groundwater pollution than to clean it up afterward.

At the present time, groundwater protection in the United States is viewed as a state responsibility. A 1984 GAO study found that all states have some sort of program for groundwater protection. The extent of the existing programs varies widely, however. Between 1977 and 1983, Ohio authorities estimated they spent $35,000 on groundwater protection efforts, while California spent $5,160,000 and Texas spent $22,969,700. Provisions in the 1985 reauthorization of the Safe Drinking Water Act require each state to formulate a plan to protect groundwater drinking water sources. A major part

CHAPTER 19 The Water We Drink   425

of such plans will involve mapping aquifers and patterns of land use. This will both identify problems and permit protection of aquifers by zoning regulation.

Underground Gasoline Storage Tanks

Experts estimate that about 50,000 to 100,000 leaky gasoline tanks are buried all over the United States. Most are the legacy of a gasoline-station construction boom in the 1950s and 1960s. When the stainless steel tanks were buried, no one realized they would begin to leak 20 to 30 years later. One gallon of gasoline can make 1 million gallons of water undrinkable.

GLOBAL DRINKING WATER ISSUES

Although they involve serious issues, drinking water problems in the developed world pale before the obstacles to obtaining safe drinking water in developing countries. Fully half of the children in the world who die each year die from diseases carried by water, and 98% of these children are in developing countries. In fact, the lack of a safe water supply and of a safe way to dispose of human wastes is responsible for waterborne diseases that account for 80% of the death and disease in the world today. The suffering and disability caused by the lack of safe drinking water are almost incalculable, as is the economic burden of people too ill to work or care for themselves.

What importance does the World Health Organization (WHO) place on water supply and sanitation for the developing world? Dr. Halfdan Mahler, Director General of WHO, put it this way, "The number of water outlets per thousand inhabitants is, in my opinion, a better health indicator than the number of hospital beds per thousand inhabitants."

Waterborne and Sanitation-Related Diseases

What are the diseases caused by lack of clean water that afflict people in the developing world? They include diseases spread by drinking contaminated

water, by contact with contaminated water, and by lack of washing.

Diseases Spread by Drinking Contaminated Drinking Water. Cholera, typhoid, amoebic dysentery, viral diarrhea, and viral hepatitis are diseases spread through contaminated drinking water that have disappeared almost completely from the industrialized Western world. In the developing world, however, such diseases still strike with discouraging frequency among the poorest people, especially among the children of the poor. The burden of poverty and malnourishment is bad enough, but the burden of ill health to the 500 million to 1 billion children under the age of 5 who experience diarrheal diseases each year is crushing. It is estimated that 5 million children die each year of diarrheal diseases. That is 10 deaths every minute of every year. These diseases are the result of consuming water infected with the disease-causing microorganisms. The water is infected because it has somehow received human wastes, either directly or indirectly.

Another disease that results from drinking contaminated water is dracontiasis, often referred to as Guinea worm disease because of the meter-long worm that causes the disease. The worm's larvae enter the water from feces of infected individuals. The larvae then infect a common algae that enters the human body in contaminated drinking water.

Diseases Spread by Contact with Contaminated Water. It is thought that over 200 million people, 5% of the world's population, are infected with schistosomiasis (bilharzia). The disease organism is a schistosome, a parasitic worm that lives in the veins of infected individuals, causing liver and urinary disease. Eggs of the worm enter the water mainly through the urine or feces of infected individuals. The eggs hatch to larvae, which then reside for several weeks in freshwater snails. Leaving the snails, the larvae enter the human body by penetrating the skin of an individual who comes in contact with the infected water. Such people may be bathing, washing, or simply wading in the water.

Another disease spread by contact with contaminated water is leptospirosis, a disease characterized

---

Towards a Sustainable Society

Grassroots Action Rather Than "Top-Down" Solutions
by Lois Gibbs and Michael Williams

Lois Gibbs is President and founder of Citizens Clearing House for Hazardous Wastes, a citizens' advocacy group for safe disposal of hazardous wastes. She has won numer-

ous community service awards for her activities.

The Citizens Clearinghouse for Hazardous Waste (CCHW) began when Lois Gibbs discovered her community was contaminated by more than 20,000 tons of toxic wastes. Lois helped start a local group, the Love Canal Homeowners Association, which spent two years in a successful fight to relocate the Love Canal residents away from the dangerous chemicals.

During her local fight, it became clear to Lois that no environmental or governmental group existed to deal with and help local commu-

nity fights such as the Love Canal efforts, so she and her colleagues formed the Citizens Clearinghouse for Hazardous Wastes. In the 10 years since, CCHW has provided direct organizing, scientific, and legal help to over 8,000 citizens groups across the continent and the world as these local groups have fought to clean up or protect their own backyards.

One of the lessons CCHW and local citizens groups have learned is that effective local action often translates into larger-scale actions, such as the establishment of the Superfund Act — the federal law that deals with identification and cleanup of severely contaminated

---

by fever, chills, headache, vomiting, and muscular aches. The disease organism is deposited in water through the urine of wild or domestic animals (cattle, dogs, and swine). People who bathe in contaminated water, workers in rice fields and sugar fields, and farmers in general are at greatest risk of contracting the disease in this way. Presumably the organism enters through wounded skin.

Diseases Spread by Lack of Washing. Ascariasis, another worm disease, causes digestive upsets,

abdominal pain, and vomiting. Complications can lead to death. The disease is not spread by drinking water. Nonetheless, hands soiled with human feces will transmit the ascariasis eggs to foods. Sanitary disposal of excreta and washing hands before eating would block transmission of the disease.

Scabies, caused by a mite that burrows under the skin, is characterized by lesions of the skin with intense itching. Yaws is a bacterial disease also characterized by lesions of the skin, but the bacterium is more destructive of tissue and causes bone lesions as well. Yaws is thought to be spread by contact

sites across the nation. The Superfund Act is an example of a series of local environmental justice battles that spurred the larger society into action.

Because of such successes we've come to recognize that the environmental justice movement of the grassroots has grown from the "Not in My Backyard" concept to the "Not in Anyone's Backyard" stage. We believe this model is an important tool for any society that is striving for a permanently sustainable state.

Indeed, in comparing the global versus local movements towards a sustainable society, it is important to note that global efforts at protecting the environment are necessarily fraught with the same problems. For instance, as long as there is an imbalance of power between nations, the more powerful nations will inevitably have controlling interest in any decisions or actions that might lead to, or prevent, sustainability. In other words, the stronger nations have always preyed upon the weaker ones, and we see no evidence that this pattern will change in regard to protecting resources.

CCHW's experience is that even within our own society, decisions/actions concerning the protection or degradation of the environment are most often made with regards to profits for the powerful at the expense of the less powerful. But it is also CCHW's experience that with creative, committed organizing at the local level a more equal balance of power can be achieved. For example, when Lois first began organizing at Love Canal, most people believed there was no hope for a small, working-class community to win justice in a fight against rich, multinational corporations and uncaring governments. The Love Canal Homeowners' Association proved this theory wrong, and thousands of grassroots groups everywhere have continued to disprove the idea that "might makes right."

In short, we believe that any attempt at creating a truly sustainable society must be generated from the grassroots — the people — upwards to the government, rather than from the government/corporations down to the people. We believe that even the global environmental crisis cannot be solved without direct action from local groups.

In essence, all the environmental destruction in the world is taking place in *someone's* backyard, and only by empowering people, through organization and education, will people everywhere be strong enough to protect their own local resources — thereby establishing a strong social base for allowing the world as a whole to achieve a sustainable society.

---

with the "weeping" lesions of infected people; the disease may last for years. The transmission of trachoma, an eye inflammation that can lead to blindness, can often be broken by personal washing. Similarly, the transmission route of typhus, an often fatal disease marked by fever and chills, can often be blocked by frequent bathing and washing clothes.

From simple eye diseases (conjunctivitis), to food poisoning, to typhoid fever, the range of diseases that can occur from lack of washing is enormous. The simple act of washing the body and washing clothes can help to prevent this host of diseases.

Breaking the Cycle of Disease

Motivation and Understanding. It is a simple matter to say, "Provide clean water and educate people to use it," but it is a formidable task to carry out this program. There are problems not only in finding the appropriate technology but in convincing people to use a distant hand pump. The nearness of the pump is a major factor in whether safe water or polluted water will be chosen for use.

We know that groundwater will in general be safer to use than streams, rivers, or springs, but we need to warn people of the hazard of having privies nearby that could contaminate well water. We know, too, that a water supply should be covered to prevent entrance of infectious material.

People, especially children, often need to be convinced to use latrines rather than leaving their feces on the soil. Privacy needs to be provided in the latrines or people will reject their use. The simple act of handwashing after defecation may prevent untold disease, but people must be made aware of the connection between sanitation and lack of disease.

For many people in developing countries today, the notion that human wastes can contaminate water and cause disease is a new one:

In a village in West Nile, Uganda, I was asked by the schoolmaster and school committee to look at the water supply. They were taking water from a seepage—you couldn't call it a spring—on the side of a hill. Just above it were several houses with no latrines. I said I thought there must be contamination, that it was likely to increase, and that they could have an epidemic of diarrhea. One woman did not agree with me. She held up a glass bottle of water and said in Lugbara: "Look, this water is clear, it flows, and it tastes all right. Show me where the disease is in this water." A long discussion followed. It was a crowded meeting, and most of the people there were unconvinced by anything I said. (Scotney, 1984)

The idea that wastes can contaminate water has not long been a part of Western knowledge either—see Figure 19-1.

Training Local People. Besides motivation, a second need is for trained people to ensure that the water system continues to work after it is installed. Many a new well has silted up or its pump has broken down, leading the well to be abandoned because no one knew how to fix it. If hand pumps are provided, someone should be trained to repair them and provision should be made for obtaining

FIGURE 19-3 Pump Operated and Maintained by Local Woman, Madagascar. It is fundamental to the success of a water supply project, that the people who will use the water are involved in planning and designing the system. In this way they will feel they have a stake in maintaining and repairing the system after the experts have gone home. Here, Angèle Ravas stands by the pump she operates and maintains. (*Photo:* Emma Robson/UNDP)

the parts that may be necessary. Manufacture of pumps in the country of use may be needed.

These problems are intertwined with the issues of appropriate technology and respect for peoples' traditional ways of doing things. That is to say, if the people who are to use a well are involved in its design, construction, and location, they are more likely to use it and to help maintain it (Figure 19-3).

FIGURE 19-4 A New Tap in Kobobati, Ethiopia. (*Photo:* Seitz/UNICEF)

FIGURE 19-5 Clean Water in Indonesia. Village chief Lamburthus Lasy demonstrates the new well and hand pump that replaced the old, unsafe water supply for the village of Bolok. (*Photo:* David Kinley/UNDP)

The Drinking Water and Sanitation Decade

In an attempt to alleviate the tragic burden of disease and death, the United Nations instituted its International Drinking Water and Sanitation Decade campaign. The goal was to bring safe drinking water and sanitary waste disposal to all of the world's people by 1990 (Figure 19-4). However, the four-fold increase in monies needed for water supply projects did not materialize in the poor economic climate of the early 1980s, and as a result the United Nations did not meet its stated goal. Nevertheless, on balance, the results of the campaign are positive. Several programs resulted in the design of affordable, easily maintained hand pumps for drinking water supplies, and improved designs

for pit latrines. Much was learned about how to secure safe water supplies. The most successful projects were low-tech, involved community residents in decisions from the very beginning, and paid special attention to involving women (Figure 19-5).

Failed water projects and inoperative pumps taught project directors that simple systems, which rural people could install and maintain themselves, were the best. During the decade the number of people in the world without safe drinking water decreased by 624 million and the number of people without adequate sanitation decreased by 79 million.

But the sobering fact is that much of the real progress of the campaign was eaten up by population growth. In urban Africa south of the Sahara, although the *number* of people provided with safe water and adequate sewage disposal doubled, the *percentage* of people without safe water actually in-

FIGURE 19-6 Street Scene in Mali. Most people in Mali still lack safe water and adequate sanitation. Because of urban growth of about 80% between 1980 and 1990, urban water systems in Africa as a whole actually served 5% fewer people at the end of the decade than at the beginning of it. (*Photo:* Kurt Carnemark/UNDP)

creased by 29% and the number without adequate sewage disposal increased by 31%. The population of developing countries increased by 754 million during the Decade of Safe Water, and even unprecedented efforts during the decade were not enough to provide all of them with safe water and sewage disposal (Figure 19-6). The campaign will continue, although goals set for the turn of the century are stated less in terms of achieving complete world coverage in safe water and sanitation than in increasing the amount of funds available for such projects.

SUMMARY

It was in the middle to late 1800s that people discovered that their drinking water could carry diseases such as typhoid and cholera. Two processes, still in use today, proved effective in removing the bacteria that cause these diseases. These are filtration

of water through beds of sand, and chlorination—the addition to water of chlorine at low levels. Filtration removes microorganisms; chlorination kills them. Waterborne disease-causing viruses, such as the hepatitis virus, are eliminated by these processes as well. It has recently become apparent that a protozoan, *Giardia lamblia,* poses a new threat to safe drinking water. Because it is carried by species other than humans, such as beavers, even waters that are free of human contamination must now be considered potentially unsafe. Filtration is effective in the removal of the *Giardia* cyst.

The safety of water supplies (from diseases other than giardiasis) is determined by testing the water for the presence of indicator bacteria called coliforms. These bacteria, not usually the cause of disease themselves, are normal inhabitants of the human gut and indicate the presence of fecal contamination of the water.

Water supplies are treated to remove contaminants that make the water either unpalatable or unsafe. The important steps and their functions are as follows:

1. Copper sulfate addition and aeration for taste and odor removal
2. First chlorination for destroying microbes
3. Coagulation/settling for removal of large particles
4. Filtration for removal of disease-causing microorganisms
5. Final chlorination for a parting shot at killing microorganisms

A small residual of chlorine is purposely left in the water after treatment is complete; the residual is intended to act against any new sources of contamination between treatment plant and final use; however, chlorination may also produce low levels of chlorinated hydrocarbons in the water, some of which have been found to be carcinogens.

Ozonation, the treatment of water with ozone gas, is an alternative method to disinfect water supplies. This process, widely used in Europe in place of chlorination, creates no chlorinated hydrocarbons but leaves no residual to act against new contamination.

Toxic inorganic chemicals that can contaminate drinking water include cadmium, arsenic, lead, nitrates, and mercury. Concern is also expressed over inorganic chemicals that may be involved in the cause or prevention of cardiovascular disease: sodium, calcium, and magnesium. Hazardous organic chemicals appear in drinking water from four main sources: use of agricultural pesticides, chemical waste disposal of such materials as PCBs, the treatment of water with chlorine, and leaking underground gasoline storage tanks.

Groundwater drinking water sources, on which 50% of Americans rely, are in danger of pollution from toxic chemicals buried in hazardous waste dumps and municipal or industrial landfills. Groundwater pollution, especially by organic chemicals, is the major problem resulting from hazardous waste disposal in the United States today.

An equally serious problem is groundwater contamination by petroleum from underground storage tanks. These were buried in the 1950s and are now starting to corrode and leak. In certain sections of the country, groundwater contamination by agricultural pesticides, road salt, or oil drilling brines is a serious problem.

The high cost of cleaning up contaminated groundwater sources and the slow, natural renewal of such sources makes prevention of pollution a necessity. Most states are currently mapping aquifers and devising land-use plans to protect them.

Even more serious than drinking water problems in developed countries are the problems associated with obtaining safe drinking water in developing countries. Many waterborne or water-related diseases are common in these countries. Programs must address the problem of convincing people that water can carry disease. The U.N. Safe Drinking Water Decade was intended to bring safe water and sanitation to people all over the earth. Two factors prevented this goal from being reached: economic constraints, and population growth, which ate up almost all progress. Nonetheless, a great deal of experience was gained in predicting what kind of program was most likely to be successful: one involving simple hand pumps and involving the people who would eventually use the pump in its design, construction, and maintenance.

Questions

1. The spread of certain diseases to epidemic levels can be described in terms of a cycle. Describe the role of water in the spread of such diseases as typhoid and cholera. The engineering solution to the spread of infectious disease has been to break this cycle. List several ways in which this can be accomplished.
2. Describe briefly the method used in testing a water sample for the presence of coliform indicator organisms. Is this method suitable for detecting virus contamination? Explain your answer.
3. Suppose you are a public health official in charge of deciding whether to allow a manufacturer to sell a new chemical that is supposed to kill nuisance plants in lakes. List three questions you

would want answered before you decide whether the chemical seemed safe to add to the water environment.

4. Not all trace minerals are undesirable. Some give water the flavor to which we are accustomed. Try the taste of distilled water, which has none of these minerals: Catch the steam from a tea-kettle on a piece of aluminum foil (be careful— steam burns are painful) and let the drops run into a glass. Compare the taste to that of water straight from the tap.

5. Should industries be responsible for cleaning up environmental pollution caused by illegal discharges? by accidents? by employee negligence? by "acts of God"? Oil companies are legally obligated to clean up oil spills that occur during drilling off the coast, whatever the cause of the spill. Is this an acceptable burden on a particular industry? Are there other ways to achieve the cleanup?

6. Explain the importance of safe water supplies to overall development in third-world countries.

Further Reading

Borelli, Peter. "To Dredge or Not to Dredge," *Amicus Journal,* Spring 1985, p. 18.

A well-written summary of the Hudson River's PCB problem.

Evans, R. J., J. D. Bails, and F. M. D'Itu. "Mercury Levels in Muscle Tissues of Preserved Museum Fish," *Environmental Science and Technology,* 6(10) (1972), 901.

One of the unusual aspects of environmental mercury contamination is that fish near the top of saltwater food chains, such as tuna or swordfish, seem to have dangerous levels of mercury even in areas where no human sources of that element are found. This paper gives an introduction to the literature on the subject of mercury in food fish.

Giam, C. S., et al. "Phthalate Ester Plasticizers: A New Class of Marine Pollutant," *Science, 199* (January 27, 1978), 419.

Phthalates are chemicals used in the manufacture of polyvinyl chloride plastics. Because of the widespread use of these plastics, they have become an environmental pollutant. Is this a problem? The evidence is not in yet.

Kinley, D. "Indonesia's Inspiring Water Message," *World Development,* March 1989, p. 9.

"Roundtable: Waterborne Giardia: It's Enough to Make You Sick," *Journal of the American Water Works Association,* February 1985, p. 14.

An informal exchange by experts on the subject of giardiasis; nontechnical.

Sedgwick's Principles of Sanitary Science and Public Health. Rewritten and enlarged by S. Prescott and M. Horwood. New York: Macmillan, 1948.

This classic public health text is easy reading and especially absorbing for those interested in the historical roots of the environmental/public health movement.

Wolman, A. "Reaching the Goals of the International Drinking Water Decade," *Journal of the American Water Works Association,* 77 (1985), 12.

Relatively nontechnical and easy to read, this article is written by Abel Wolman, the individual who suggested at the founding meetings of the World Health Organization in the 1940s that one of the organization's goals must be safe drinking water and environmental sanitation.

Zeighami, Elain. "Drinking Water and Cardiovascular Disease," *Oak Ridge National Laboratory Review, 4,* 1984.

A good discussion of how substances in drinking water may contribute to or protect people from heart attacks and strokes.

References

American Association for the Advancement of Science. "Groundwater Pollution: Environmental and Legal Problems," 1984.

Appleton, B. "Seven out of Ten for Effort," *World Health,* June 1988.

Bates, T. "Rural Water Supply Improvements: Lessons Learned from the Water Decade," *Journal of the American Water Works Association,* June 1988.

Bouwer, H. "Agriculture and Groundwater Quality," *Civil Engineering,* July 1989, p. 60.

Dallaire, G. "U.N. Launches International Water Decade; U.S. Role Uncertain," *Civil Engineering—ASCE,* March 1981, p. 59.

"Federal and State Efforts to Protect Groundwater." Report to the Chairman, Subcommittee on Commerce, Transportation and Tourism, Committee on Energy and Commerce, House of Representatives. Washington, D.C.: U.S. Government Printing Office, 1984.

First Annual Report, State Board of Health and Vital Statistics of Pennsylvania, 1866.

Waiting for water in Bangkok. In some places, even though there is a piped water supply, the water only flows for a short period of time each day. Here, it comes on about 2AM and must be stored for use at other times. Water that does not flow 24 hours a day, however, is rarely safe to drink, because impure water can be sucked into the pipes during the time when water from the treatment plant is not flowing in them. *(Daniel Okun)*

Villagers wait on line for water at a new pump, Zambia. Water-borne diseases can take a terrible toll of life and of health. Pure water from a new well promises a chance for people to be able to work and learn, and to be confident that their children will survive. *(World Bank: David Kinley)*

Water vendors filling their jerry cans from polluted stream in Kisii, Kenya. *(Daniel Okun)*

Waiting to buy water from a truck in Cali, Columbia. In some areas, especially in cities of the developing world, people must use as much as 30 to 40 percent of their income to buy water. Building safe public water supplies is not only important to stop the spread of disease—it makes economic sense, as well. *(Daniel Okun)*

Building a latrine in Zambia. Safe disposal of wastes is the other side of the coin of providing safe drinking water. Drinking water sources must be protected from contamination with human wastes. *(World Bank: David Kinley)*

United States. *(Charles ReVelle)*

India. *(UN: Sudhakoran)*

Mali. *(UN Photo)*

South Africa. *(UN Photo)*

China. *(UN: John Isaac)*

Bolivia. *(UN Photo)*

Global Consultation on Safe Water and Sanitation for the 1990s, Background Paper, Secretariat for Global Consultation, New Delhi, India, 1990.

"Groundwater Contamination by Toxic Substances: A Digest of Reports." Committee on Environment and Public Works, U.S. Senate. Washington, D.C.: U.S. Government Printing Office, November 1983.

Lin, Shen Dar. *"Giardia lamblia* and Water Supply," *Journal of the American Water Works Association,* February 1985, p. 40.

Morse, D. "Lead: Taking It from the Tap," *Civil Engineering,* February 1988, p. 71.

Report on the Cholera Outbreak in the Parish of St. James, Westminster, During the Autumn of 1854. Presented to the Vestry by the Cholera Inquiry Committee, July 1855. London: J. Churchill, 1855.

"Research Needs for Evaluation of Health Effects of Toxic Chemical Waste Dumps." Proceedings of a Symposium, Environmental Health Perspectives, December 1982.

Sayre, I. "International Standards for Drinking Water," *Journal of the American Water Works Association,* January 1988, p. 53.

Scotney, N. "Water and the Community," *World Health Forum, 5* (1984), 234.

U.S. Environmental Protection Agency. *Environmental Pollution Control Alternatives: Drinking Water Treatment for Small Communities,* EPA/635/5-90/025. Washington, D.C.: U.S. EPA, April 1990.

U.S. Environmental Protection Agency. *Reducing Risk: Setting Priorities and Strategies for Environmental Protection,* Science Advisory Board, SAB-EC-90-021. Washington, D.C.: U.S. EPA, September 1990.

U.S. Environmental Protection Agency. *First National Survey of Pesticides in Drinking Water Wells.* Washington, D.C.: U.S. EPA, November 1990.

U.S. Environmental Protection Agency. *Phase II National Primary Drinking Water Regulations.* Washington, D.C.: U.S. EPA, January 1991.

Part Six

Sustainable Global Societies

Photovoltaic-powered Remote Lighting. Solar power offers not only an unlimited source of energy to replace nonrenewable sources such as coal and oil, but also promises power for peoples and places that cannot be easily served by conventional power plants. Here a solar light powered by photovoltaics lights a remote area in the United States. In rural parts of developing countries, solar units such as this can illuminate streets and light rooms for study during the evening hours. Other solar units can cook food, purify water, and provide nonpolluting energy for development. (*Photo:* Courtesy of Electric Power Research Institute.)

The field of environmental studies has evolved from a number of other disciplines. Forestry, soil science, marine science, fisheries and game management, public health, water resources, geography, economics, sociology, and, of course, ecology have all contributed to the discipline that is variously called *environmental science* or *environmental studies*. The field itself has evolved from considering environmental problems as individual issues, each needing a separate solution, to a realization that environmental problems are linked— air pollution cannot be considered separately from water pollution because air pollutants wash out of the air in rainfall, polluting water. Energy issues are inextricably tied to air pollution because fossil fuel use produces the carbon dioxide implicated in global warming— and a host of other atmospheric pollutants.

From an understanding of the interrelationship of environmental problems has come also the realization that environmental problems are often global in nature. These global environmental problems not only impact many nations, but require international cooperation to resolve. Acid rain originates in industrial countries that burn coal, but the rain may fall hundreds of miles away from its source, in other countries. Disputes over water from rivers that run through more than one country occur in Europe, Asia, South America—all over the world. Global warming and ozone depletion are the archetypes of global problems, touching potentially all peoples and nations. The loss of medically useful plants and animals when rain forests are cut down is likewise a loss for the entire human race.

A second perception has also come from the awareness that environmental problems are interrelated. This is the realization that human societies have a severe and pervasive effect on their environment, and they must, if they are to avoid catastrophe, learn how to operate in a manner that their environment can sustain. The term *sustainable society* has been coined to describe a society that "lives within its means," a society that doesn't use up essential parts of its environment that cannot be regenerated.

Throughout this book we have emphasized two themes. First, many of the environmental problems that must be solved today are global in nature. That is, they concern the environment and the peoples of many nations. Second, we should be working towards the establishment of sustainable societies.

The first chapter in this last part of the book proposes a set of principles by which sustainable societies should operate. These principles are based on our thoughts, as well as those of other environmentalists and also on the examination of environmental issues and their solutions that constitutes the main part of this book.

No one set of people, however, will be able to synthesize sustainable societies. The problems and issues are global, and so must be the thinking that goes towards their solution. For this reason we asked people from many countries, from different areas of expertise and from different walks of life, to share with you their best ideas for building sustainable societies. These thoughtful remarks are distributed throughout the book. The concluding section of the book summarizes the ideas of these environmental statespeople.

Chapter 20

Principles for a Sustainable Society

WHAT IS A SUSTAINABLE SOCIETY—ARE WE ONE?

A sustainable human society is a concept that is not hard to articulate in an abstract way. It is a society that interacts with its environment in ways that leave the environment free to be used again and again, in ways that maintain the integrity and interactions of the biosphere, with little other than short-term change. A sustainable society draws on the resilience of the earth's biological and chemical systems, allowing only those alterations of the environment from which relatively rapid recovery is possible. By relatively rapid recovery we do not mean recovery over geologic time but over human time.

How do present human societies measure up against this definition of sustainability? In the developed areas of the world, where labor, resources, technology, and trade have led to material wealth for many, people are seeking to perpetuate and expand that abundance; they purchase new cars and new homes. The homes spread into the farming regions that once supplied the cities' food. They spread also into the forests and deserts surrounding the cities. The suburbs expand; wilderness becomes asphalt; the trip to work lengthens and more gasoline is consumed. Power plants are built to supply the increasing demand for electricity. Dams are thrown across rivers to store more water to sprinkle on more lawns and to irrigate crops grown in arid regions. Forests are cut to supply lumber for the homes.

And in the developing countries of the world, and in parts of the developed world as well, poorer men and women are seeking material security. They are seeking lives in which food and shelter are more certain and in which their children can survive. They often migrate to the cities, looking for this better life. They may leave farming regions whose land is concentrated in the hands of the wealthy or where their land has played out. They leave when mechanization decreases the number of rural jobs or when the city offers better-paying jobs even when jobs in rural areas are still available. The migrants may settle on the fringes of the nearest cities, in shanty towns in Africa, in Asia, and in South America. With luck their squatter settlements are gradually transformed from tar-paper shacks without water and electricity to more secure dwellings.

Drinking water may come first at public standpipes, then at taps in the home; electricity at the house may follow; finally, sewers may be built to carry off wastes.

Around the world, cities are growing rapidly. Twenty-two cities of more than 10 million people are predicted by the year 2000, 18 of them in developing nations. The growth of these cities has profound effects on the environment. Canals divert water from distant rivers to the growing cities. Hydropower dams are built to supply the cities with electricity, and land is drowned, sometimes displacing primitive peoples from ancestral lands. In other cases the dams rob lowlands of their yearly deposits of rich silt, now trapped within the reservoirs. Autos and trucks pollute the air with their exhausts. Rivers become polluted with human wastes. Migrants who do not head for cities strike off into the wilderness to carve out a new life on new soil—as the American pioneers once did.

Growth and development are facts of life in the developing and developed world. And growth and development have serious consequences for the environment, both locally and globally. Are we a sustainable society? Clearly we are not. Thoughtful people have observed the effects of the growth and development of human societies and have sought to alter the cascade of environmentally harmful activities with varying degrees of success. The history with which this book opened, of actions taken to protect the environment in the United States and worldwide, describes the stimulus to action and the results achieved by attacking each problem as it came along.

Now in the 1990s a new idea is being born—in the United States and across the globe. It is only being born, but hope attends the birthing process. The idea is expressed in several ways—as sustainability, as a sustainable society, and as sustainable development. The words have subtle differences. *Sustainability* is a concept; it is the quality of being capable of continuation, virtually forever. The second term, a *sustainable society,* is a goal for today's civilization. Native Americans had achieved a measure of sustainability with their pre-Columbian agriculture and hunting societies. Their numbers and practices were such that the ecosystems and re-

sources on which they depended were in no danger of running out. The essays in this book by environmental statespeople from around the world all deal with ways to achieve a sustainable society in the modern context, using available and soon-to-be available technology, using well-known practices and emerging ideas.

The last term, *sustainable development,* is a term coming into wide use in the United Nations Development Program and at The World Bank to describe the aspirations of these organizations for the development process. The *development process* refers to such activities as the building of roads and dwellings, the irrigation and farming of formerly wild lands, the provision of safe drinking water, the collection and treatment of wastewater, the removal of solid wastes, and the provision of electricity and fuels. The term *sustainable development* is both hopeful and misleading, hopeful because it suggests that development can be sustainable, misleading because development often falls so very wide of the mark. That is because there are two forces driving development. One is the need to improve the lives and health of people all around the globe, and the other is population growth.

New population requires new space, new water supplies, new energy sources. New population must take some toll of the environment. At the same time, that toll can be reduced. Perhaps a better term for what people are calling sustainable development is *reduced impact development.* This is within the realm of possibility. It can be accomplished by setting aside sufficient land area to preserve ecosystems and by using farming practices that do not lead to rapid soil erosion, irrigation that does not lace the soil with salts, and windpower as opposed to the use of electricity from a coal-fired power plant, and by other means. But the impact of development cannot be reduced to zero.

COMPONENTS OF A SUSTAINABLE SOCIETY

The important term, the term on which we will focus, is *sustainable society.* We focus on this term because it is clear that it is a goal to be achieved

TABLE 20-1 The Roots of Non-sustainable Development

Non-sustainable Development Occurs	Example
When rates of critical processes are unknown	Global warming may result from overloading the atmosphere with certain gases
When interactions are not understood	Passenger pigeons became extinct once flocks fell below a certain size, despite preservation efforts
When time frames are too short	Water allocations from aquifers rarely take into account the time needed to recharge the aquifer
When spatial frames are too small	Land management areas may not correspond to wildlife habitat needs so decisions can adversely affect species
When economic incentives for overuse exist	Poaching of elephants for ivory
When externalities aren't taken into account	Non-recyclable containers are cheaper than refillable ones because disposal costs are ignored
When the carrying capacity of a given environment is exceeded	Human population growth

Source: Excerpted in part from Orians (1990).

and has not yet been achieved (Table 20-1). A sustainable society is a goal for both the developing and the developed world.

A sustainable society has a number of readily identifiable components. We propose here eight components: (1) sustainable use of energy, (2) sustainable use of the atmosphere, (3) maintenance of soil fertility and food supplies, (4) sustainable use of water, (5) sustainable use of nonfuel mineral resources, (6) maintenance of biodiversity, (7) sustainable use of biological resources, and (8) limitation of population to the carrying capacity of the environment. Each is achieved differently, but there are strong connections, as will be seen.

Sustainable Energy Use

A sustainable society uses renewable energy resources. Sustainable use of energy resources cannot be achieved with the fossil-origin fuels (coal, oil, and natural gas) because the resources of these fuels are finite. In addition, all these fuels pollute the atmosphere both with short- and long-term pollutants. The short-term air pollutants that injure human health are sulfur oxides, nitrogen oxides, particulate matter, carbon monoxide, and photochemical air pollutants. The same pollutants affect animals as well as vegetation from forest trees to food crops. In this sense the fossil fuels also impact ecosystem stability of both plants and animals. The best we can hope to do, if fossil fuels are used, is to prevent some of these emissions by modifying combustion processes or by practicing end-of-pipe removal by such devices as the catalytic converter on automobiles and scrubbers on power plants.

The long-term air pollutants from the fossil fuels are acid rain and carbon dioxide. Acid rain acidifies both lakes and soils, damaging especially the land and water communities of mountain ecosystems. Carbon dioxide in modest amounts is no problem at all, but in the massive amounts currently being emitted it overwhelms the natural carbon dioxide cycle and accumulates in the atmosphere. Many scientists expect this accumulation to lead to a warming of the globe because of carbon dioxide's capacity to trap long-wave radiation that would have escaped from the earth. The consequences of that warming—in all its dimensions, including changes in rainfall as well as temperature—could include effects on food supplies, water supplies, soil, and the survival of plant and animal species. In short, virtually all of the components of sustainability could be affected. Clearly the fossil fuels, when used in the quantities demanded by a society of 5 to 10 billion people, cannot be the fuels that power a sustainable society.

We must ask then, since the fossil fuels are obviously finite and in other ways inappropriate, why haven't we changed the fuels we choose to use? First, a shift in fuels is a slow process. New technology needs to become generally available, and people to service that new technology are needed. Second, the prices of the finite resources are still so low that people are not choosing to use the renewable and low environmental impact energy sources. The cartel that controls much of the world's oil supply is purposely keeping the price of oil low by high levels of production so that the industrialized countries will not have a sufficient incentive to shift to renewables and other energy sources or to conserve energy in a serious way.

How can society cause a shift to renewables if it does not make immediate economic sense to do so even if it makes long-run environmental and long-run economic sense? How can future effects be made a part of today's decisions? It takes courage to place taxes on the fossil fuels, but if done properly we can induce the shift and not hurt any segment of society. Gasoline taxes can be increased to the levels in Europe, and though this may seem painful, income taxes could be cut so that consumers have as much untaxed income as before. Only their decisions about how to spend that untaxed income would be changed.

Is nuclear energy sustainable in the long run? Resources of the fissionable form of uranium, namely uranium-235, are finite, so light water reactors are not a sustainable energy source. Resources of nonfissionable uranium-238 from which the fissionable plutonium-239 can be bred are much larger. As a power source the breeder reactor, which uses plutonium-239, could last centuries. Nonetheless, the safety issues, the issues of waste disposal and of the spread of nuclear weapons, are all so serious that nuclear energy might make sense only as a temporary solution to the problem of fossil energy consumption. In the long run, only renewable energy resources—wind, solar, and possibly geothermal—are sustainable without serious environmental impact.

Sustainable Use of the Atmosphere

A sustainable society emits to the atmosphere only those substances that will be diluted and consumed in natural biogeochemical cycles without alteration of other chemical constituents, such as ozone. It is well known that the atmosphere of the earth evolved over billions of years from an early oxygen-poor condition to its current oxygen-rich condition. This evolution has been a co-evolution of both the atmosphere and the plant and animal life on earth. The processes that brought about the evolution are still in place, so we can expect that the changes in the composition of the atmosphere that we are causing will be corrected. Unfortunately, the time scale of the evolutionary processes is enormous relative to a human life. As a consequence, though righting mechanisms exist, they cannot be expected to respond quickly enough to the insults we are offering to the atmosphere.

The primary changes we are presently causing in the atmosphere are the introduction of trace gases and carbon dioxide—at rates far faster than natural processes can remove them. The trace gases are the chlorine-containing gases (methylchloroform, carbon tetrachloride, chlorofluorocarbons [CFCs]) and methane. All these gases trap heat that would otherwise be radiated away from the earth. Thus, all are expected to contribute to the potential for global warming. The CFCs have an additional effect: they deplete ozone from the stratosphere, thereby allowing more ultraviolet (UV) radiation to penetrate to the earth. The UV radiation is implicated in human skin cancers and cataracts.

Carbon dioxide, emitted in overwhelming quantities mainly from combustion processes and also from forest destruction, is also a heat-trapping gas. Because of its awesome rate of emission, carbon dioxide accounts for over 50% of the potential warming predicted in a number of scientific calculations by the middle of the twenty-first century.

Atmosphere and climate sustainability appears unlikely with the present set of fuels, the fossil fuels, and the present state of use of chlorine-containing gases. Fortunately, the currently used CFCs are being phased out of production by the year 2000 and will be replaced by more ozone-friendly and greenhouse-friendly materials, but our use of fossil fuels only grows with time. Replacing such fuels by renewables and the replacement of use by energy conservation are the approaches needed to achieve atmospheric and climatic stability.

Maintenance of Soil Fertility and Food Supplies

A sustainable society builds rather than depletes its soil base so that adequate food supplies can be ensured. These critical components, food and soil, of a sustainable society are inextricably linked, for failure of the soil due to erosion or contamination or loss of soil nutrients leads to a loss of food-production capacity. At the same time, food supply is tightly linked to climatic stability because a loss of rainfall due to climate change or a shift in temperature regions of the earth may cause areas of the globe once hospitable to certain food crops to become harsh environments for those crops. Hence, the components of a sustainable supply of food, though tied closely to maintenance of soil fertility, have other dimensions as well.

What factors threaten soil? Soils that are forced to grow only a single crop may be robbed of their nutrients by that crop, eventually failing to support that food plant. That is why farmers are urged to rotate crops and to plant legumes periodically to restore nitrogen to the soil. Water erosion of soils left unprotected by shelterbelts or by terracing or by contour plowing can remove massive amounts of top soil. Not only is fertility lost when the organic layer of the soil is washed away, but the

fragile mineral soil exposed is subject to further erosion by wind. The wind erosion of the Dust Bowl era is a vivid reminder of how delicate the balance of soil and water is.

Erosion is not the only factor that threatens soil. Irrigation of the soil with salt-laden water can load the soil with damaging minerals. The Fertile Crescent, the region surrounding the Tigris and Euphrates River in Syria and Iraq, was once the breadbasket of the Middle Eastern world (circa 2300 BC). Irrigation with the waters of these rivers left the soil so saline that this portion of the world is now a net importer of grains. The same phenomenon of salt accumulation is at work today in the Ganges basin of the Punjab in India and in the basin of the Indus River in Pakistan. And early evidence suggests the same process may be at work in the heavily irrigated soils of California. Techniques to flood the soils with excess water to dissolve the accumulated salts can prevent the buildup, but irrigators must know how to arrange adequate drainage of this water from the soil.

Soils are also in danger in the regions of the great tropical forests where cutting exposes a nutrient-poor soil that can be used for food crops for a few years or to graze cattle for a few years before the nutrients are used up. Then the soil is left barren, supporting only scrub growth. Recovery of such soil may take centuries.

Soils need not support food crops to be valuable. Soils that support trees for timber are also valuable to humankind and to ecosystems as a whole. Mountain range soils, already low in the organic content that resists acidity, are susceptible to mineral leaching by acid rain. Such soils are threatened in eastern North America and in much of Europe by the acid rain that stems from sulfur and nitrogen oxide emissions from fossil fuel combustion. The timber productivity of soils in these regions has already been damaged. The recovery of these soils and their forests, even in the presence of diminished acid rain, is likely to be agonizingly slow.

Sustainable Use of Water

A sustainable society collects and treats its wastewater and treats its drinking water,

Towards a Sustainable Society

Sustainable Development

by V. Rajagopalan

V. Rajagopalan is Vice-President, Sector Policy and Research, at the World Bank. He is trained as a civil and sanitary engineer and graduated from Johns Hopkins University.

Two of the greatest challenges facing the world are environmental protection and promoting development. Since 1950 the world population has doubled to more than 5 billion and the world economy has quadrupled. Global fossil fuel use has increased 10-fold in this century, and yet an estimated 2 billion people, about half the population of the developing world, continue to be without adequate energy supplies for their basic human needs as well as for economic growth. Human demands on biological systems have increased to the point that, according to the World Resources Institute (WRI), the world today consumes an estimated 40% of its terrestrial photosynthetic productivity each year, and much of this is occurring in a way that is not biologically sustainable. In far too many countries the air is polluted, the rivers are poisoned, the land degraded, the forests destroyed, and the pressure of expanding population is relentless. Despite impressive progress in promoting development and reducing poverty, more than a billion people in the world live on less than a dollar a day.

The challenges are global. The stakes are high for industrial countries as well as for developing countries. The challenges are also formidable, but we *can* meet them. Experience has yielded an invaluable lesson: that poverty and environmental degradation fuse together in a vicious circle. In sub-Saharan Africa an ever growing number of people practicing marginal agriculture is degrading huge areas. In Mexico City the health of millions is endangered by the toxic cloud that sometimes turns daylight into twilight. In Asia inadequate treatment of industrial and human effluent threatens water supplies, human health, fisheries, and farming. We cannot protect the environment and reduce poverty in isolation from each other.

If this is so, why is environmental degradation virtually ubiquitous, casting its shadow over countries rich and poor? The fundamental economic answer is that the cost of environmental damage is lower for the polluter than for society as a whole. Individual polluters have insufficient incentive to stop harming the environment. Thus, market failure produces externalities. The fertilizers and irrigation that raise crop yields for one farmer can pollute a village's water and increase soil salinity for other farmers.

Historically, economic growth has been regarded as the antidote to poverty. Growth is certainly indispensable to reducing global poverty in the long term. Growth also tends to raise environmental expectations and to generate resources for investment.

But there is now much more doubt about the ability of growth alone to resolve these problems. For a very long time, economics has generally taken nature for granted and has even been an instrument of human dominion over nature. More recently, that view has been tempered by the recognition that ecological systems have their own logic. Thus, market forces might eventually increase costs sufficiently to deter further pollution. But nature and the market do not necessarily work at the same pace. Irreversible damage can be inflicted in the meantime, as we see when biodiversity is lost where forests are felled. The costs of remedial action can be far higher than the cost of preventive action, as we see may be possible with global warming.

Successful development must be sustainable development, i.e., development that raises the quality of life for the great majority of the world's population without inflicting unacceptable environmental costs on future generations. Development must respect the capacity of Planet Earth to provide raw materials and absorb wastes. Our modest understanding of the planet's capacity dictates caution. How can development be sustainable? Externalities make a very strong case for intervention to protect the environment. But interventions must be soundly based. Market failure may be supplanted by policy failure. Prices should encourage more efficient resource use. Macroeconomic policy that keeps prices as undistorted as possible is fundamental to good environment policy. Using the market also has the great advantage of minimizing administrative costs and reducing the opportunities for corruption and favor-seeking that can bedevil regulation.

Nevertheless, regulation or government intervention is also necessary. Regulation can set standards for the public good that the price mechanism cannot. Higher prices may reduce the *volume* of exhaust emissions, but regulation can improve emission *standards* irrespective of volume and price. Both are needed to cut harmful atmospheric emissions by as much as possible. Regulation can also preserve natural resources that might otherwise be irreversibly lost: Manmade capital cannot replace natural capital such as the soils that nurture our crops or the variety of fish in our rivers and oceans. Regulation can ensure that the polluter pays. Bearing in mind that the mix of market forces and government intervention will vary with circumstances, we can sum up these elements of an effective environmental strategy in the modern Chinese principle: "Prevention first, who develops must protect, who uses must conserve, and who damages must pay."

However, the list is not quite complete. Market forces and government intervention are likely to be most effective when the people affected can participate in decisions—for example, through community and nongovernmental organizations. Environmental questions frequently excite widely varying and passionate views; usually there are losers, at least in the short term, as well as winners. Such views should be reconciled

openly, freely, and peacefully. Experience strongly suggests that popular participation is important for environmental protection and poverty reduction. Cooperation helps us find the most efficient solutions to environmental problems. At the international level this means cooperation between sovereign nations. The benefits are many. First, we have common problems such as depletion of the ozone layer, global warming, and draining the gene pool of biodiversity, which is evolution's raw material. Second, environmental problems are very complex. No single group is likely to accumulate sufficient knowledge to tackle its environmental difficulties alone. Cooperation helps to transfer knowledge and technology, accelerate learning, and integrate companies more into world markets. Third, environmental problems are rarely purely local; destroying tree cover on a watershed readily becomes a regional or even international issue. Fourth, it is logical to extend the multilateralism that has characterized development to the environment.

Multilateralism has served the world well. But international cooperation, although indispensable, does not guarantee effective action. Different countries have different capacities and objectives. What makes an agreement on international cooperation successful? For the answer, one can draw on scores of international agreements, from

(Continues)

Towards a Sustainable Society (continued)

protection of individual species such as whales or elephants, through trans-boundary issues such as protection of the Rhine and the Mediterranean, to global problems such as the ozone layer protection that was the subject of the Montreal Protocol. There are many lessons to be learned from past international agreements, and a crucial one is cooperation among countries. Cooperation is a two-way street. For example, developing countries certainly need better technology for environmental protection. But technology is essentially embodied and transferred in equipment. Industrial countries will therefore more readily transfer technology if they have more free-dom to invest in developing countries.

Indeed, the evidence is overwhelming that sound environmental protection is an investment, not a cost. As the debate shifts from unreasonably allocating blame to reasonably allocating cost, we should all be aware that the price of procrastination may be paid not only by posterity but also by the present generation. The issue is more than saving whales or forests—although they have intrinsic merit. The issue is whether our children and their children will inhabit a planet whose environment can support rising living standards and a rising population.

Big changes will be necessary, not least in attitudes. Industrial countries need to modify their claims on the world's resources and to abandon the assumption that conventionally defined living standards can rise without limit. Developing countries can no longer afford to dismiss environmental concern as a luxury. Despite the many competing demands on finance, new, concessional, and additional assistance will be required if sustainable development is to take hold. Our best efforts are needed to secure for generations to come the world we would want. Sustainable development is within our grasp, if only we are willing to grasp it.

pricing the water at the cost of obtaining new supplies. It also considers the environmental costs of obtaining new supplies. Water is as important to civilization as blood is to the human body. Without water of adequate quality and quantity, civilization can be brought low. With adequate water, civilizations flourish. Water makes possible not only adequate food supplies, but it is also a necessity for drinking, washing, and in most places for human waste disposal. Sustainable use of water is linked to climate stability. The global circulation models used to predict the impact of the greenhouse gases on climate generally indicate a warming and drying of the interior land masses of the continents. If the predicted lack of rainfall does occur, today's areas of agricultural productivity may be lost; new areas would then be required to sustain an adequate food supply. Again, this change follows from the burning of the finite fossil fuels and the production of carbon dioxide. Thus, sustainable use of water may be thwarted if climate stability is damaged.

A sustainable society might get by with water polluted by human fecal bacteria and protozoa, but it would not be a healthy society. It would be racked by cholera, typhoid, and other lesser diarrheal diseases. Drinking water of adequate quality requires not only water treatment processes like sand filtration and chlorination, but relatively clean water to begin with. It is difficult, expensive, and chancy to attempt to "polish" a city's sewage back to drinking-water quality. Wastewater (sewage) can be partially cleaned to a condition where it can be used for crop irrigation, golf course and lawn watering, and toilet flushing, but uses beyond these are not recommended.

Drinking water for a city requires a large, relatively unpolluted water source—a river or a lake. Drinking water for rural areas is often drawn from wells, and, in this case, it is essential that ground water remains unpolluted.

Water carriage of wastes is a practice that has evolved over the last several centuries. It is not a foolproof method of human waste disposal because receiving bodies of water may become polluted by disease-causing microorganisms, but it is better than human wastes in the street, a condition of nineteenth-century Europe. Water carriage of wastes demands wastewater treatment (sewage treatment) at the end of the pipe prior to disposal to the receiving body. If sanitary sewers carry off the wastes from a city and no operating treatment plant is at the end of the pipe, the stage is set for the spread of water-borne diseases.

Regions of many nations seem to need more water than is available nearby. Los Angeles imports water from the Colorado and from distant Northern California rivers. Beijing, China, is considering importation of water from the distant Yellow River. Such needs stem from population and agricultural growth that does not recognize the regional water resource base and hence prices water too cheaply. Importing water from water-rich regions to high water demand regions is a short-term solution unless new water prices reflect the cost of importation. Additionally, river flow regimes and riverine ecology are altered when a new river is exploited for a water supply. If water is priced properly, an appropriate conservation occurs and uneconomic uses are diminished.

Sustainable Use of Nonfuel Mineral Resources

A sustainable society recycles scarce mineral resources for reuse. The earth's supply of a number of mineral resources appears to be finite. If developing countries were to use minerals such as copper and nickel at the rates currently used by developed countries, serious shortages of these minerals would occur. Although classic economic theory tells us that when resources become scarce, higher prices force a shift to new resources or new technologies, it is not at all certain that the huge future demands projected for many minerals could

be satisfied by other resources or by other technologies.

Those minerals whose quantities are not limited at current levels of use are often maldistributed relative to the location of current needs. Furthermore, even where such mineral resources are not maldistributed, the extraction/purification processes are often so energy-intensive or so damaging to the environment as to demand recycle and reuse.

Indeed, a number of mineral production processes are energy-intensive, especially aluminum and steel making. When the energy is drawn from the combustion of fossil fuel resources, which themselves are limited, the atmosphere is affected by the emission of nitrogen oxides and sulfur oxides (contributors to acid rain) and carbon dioxide (the prime contributor to greenhouse warming). Nitrogen oxides and sulfur oxides can impact soils. Greenhouse warming implies climate change.

Recycling thus fulfills two goals of sustainable societies: conservation of scarce mineral resources and wise energy use. In addition, of course, recycling reduces the amount of solid or hazardous waste needing disposal.

The problem of stimulating recycling and reuse is an economic one. As an example, so long as the price of producing new aluminum ingots from ore is less than the price of collecting and recycling the metal from its current uses, recycling/reuse will not occur to a significant extent—unless some outside economic stimulus is applied to the system. Unless economic incentives are used to modify the system, vast quantities of energy will continue to be expended on production of materials from primary sources. And associated mining, health, and atmospheric impacts will continue due to the production and combustion of the fossil fuel. At the same time, landfill space will continue to be consumed by the discarded products containing these resources.

The economic incentives that encourage recycling can take many forms, but basically a forced, upfront injection of money into the system and a return of that money somewhere in the recycle system seems to have the right properties. The upfront deposit on a bottle or can reminds a consumer that there are resource replacement costs, energy costs, and disposal costs associated with the bottle or can. The return of the deposit upon return of the container provides incentives for recycling behaviors. A tax on nonrecycled paper or a tax break on recycled materials serves the same purpose in manufacturing.

It was only in the 1960s that America abandoned deposits on beverage bottles. Now the New England states, Oregon, and other states, to fight litter and reduce solid waste, have legislated deposits on bottles and cans. Interestingly, the countries of Western Europe never went to throwaways and never ceased to operate their bottle and can deposit systems.

A similar deposit-return system has been proposed for automobiles, but never implemented. Instead, penalties in the form of fines for the abandonment of junk cars seems to have been utilized to prevent derelict cars from littering streets and fields. You would think that automobiles would be readily recyclable; so much steel should make the auto hulk valuable. Unfortunately, the design of the automobile makes the recycled product less valuable than it could be. So much copper wiring is intertwined in the auto that separation of the copper from the hulk is difficult; the iron product produced from an auto hulk is contaminated with copper and less useful than a cleaner product. Reinforcing bars in concrete construction is one of the limited uses of this contaminated product.

The example makes a point. Design for recyclability is crucial. Modular snap-out copper wiring in a car would improve its value for recycling. Other metal products, such as stoves and refrigerators, could benefit from designs that enhance the value of the product in the recycling process. Stimulating such design to take place is a challenge for sustainable societies.

Recycling of scarce mineral resources is only one facet of another goal for sustainable societies: closed-cycle industrial systems. Such systems would generate little or no waste or, alternatively, generate waste that is usable as raw material in other industrial processes. Some pressure for waste reduction and recycling is already present in the form of high costs for scarce metals, end-of-pipe pollu-

tion control regulations, and high costs for disposal of wastes in landfills. Nonetheless, government intervention with incentives for recycling and waste reduction could encourage more recycling and reuse. In addition, ways need to be found to incorporate the environmental costs of raw material into the costs of products.

Maintenance of Biodiversity

A sustainable society maintains the richness and diversity of species in its environment. The number and variety of species in an ecosystem are important components of the environment that supports a sustainable society.

Clearly, certain species are very important to any human society. We depend on particular species for food, for fuel, as sources of medicines or building materials. We depend on certain functioning ecosystem units for "ecosystem services": purification, or regeneration of water, soil, and air, flood control, and moderation of climate. A diversity of species, however, is important for other reasons as well. We value a diverse biota first of all because it represents future options. A variety of species ensures that we will have the materials we will require to meet future needs and to solve future problems. Secondly, we value species richness in and of itself. Birdwatchers, visitors to parks, wildlife refuges, and zoos recognize such value instinctively. This is sometimes classed as an aesthetic appreciation of species, but such a designation may not recognize the full value of biological diversity. Humans, having evolved with a rich biota, may actually need this richness in order to function properly and find satisfaction in life.

Finally, we value a diverse biota as something we can pass on to our descendants. This inheritance value stems from the desire of many people to provide for their children at least as much material and spiritual sustenance as they themselves have had.

Maintenance of the resource of biodiversity differs in certain essential ways from the maintenance of nonbiological resources such as minerals. Each species represents a unique whole made up of a specific combination of traits. Loss of all the members of a species—extinction—means the loss of that unique whole. We have no way at present, or in the foreseeable future, to synthesize a species once it is gone.

On the other hand, members of a species do reproduce. Thus, unlike mineral resources, which have finite limits, species can be cropped, and, under the right circumstances, the resource can renew itself. The first question that sustainable societies must answer is: How much of a given species or ecosystem can be harvested without damaging the ability of the species or ecosystem to renew itself?

Members of a particular species may be intentionally harvested for a variety of reasons—food, fuel, medical, or industrial use—but they are also lost incidentally to other human activities. An example is the killing of porpoises in the nets used to catch tuna. Another example is the loss of both animal and plant species when tropical forests are cut down to provide pastures for cattle grazing or land for farming. A second question sustainable societies must answer is: what is the effect of a particular action on plants, animals, and ecosystems?

Unfortunately, we do not have enough information about how species interact within ecosystems to answer these questions with certainty for more than a few species. The information we do have has, by and large, been gained empirically—by seeing what does and does not work. Furthermore, in the process of gaining this information we have already lost or endangered a number of species through overharvesting, through a lack of understanding of the interrelationships among species, and by a failure to take into account the relationship between species richness and the size of a given piece of habitat.

We have endangered many species by not understanding the obligatory interrelationships among species. For example, a number of tropical tree species are endangered because their seeds are dispersed by animals or must even pass through the gut of certain birds before they will germinate. As the number of these animals decreases due to hunting and collecting, reproduction of the trees decreases or ends. In a similar way, spotted owls are endangered because they require the ancient trees found in old-growth forest for nesting and they require the species living in the old-growth forest for food.

As more and more old-growth forest is logged, the survival of the owl becomes less likely.

As a further example, the Everglades kite is endangered because it eats only apple snails. These snails are in short supply because their habitat is decreasing as water from sources supplying the Everglades is diverted for the purpose of crop irrigation. Even the apparent inability of certain populations of marine species to regenerate after intensive harvesting may be due to a poorly understood interaction of species. Certain species of whales have not increased in number after hunting of these species was banned. It is speculated that interactions among species have stabilized at new, lower states for these organisms.

The third reason why species are sometimes unexpectedly lost or endangered involves the fragmentation of habitats. Studies on islands have shown that an island twice as big as another does not have twice the number of species. Rather, an island 10 times as large is needed before twice as many species are found. There is evidence that this type of phenomenon also pertains to tropical forests. Thus, loss of 90% of forest habitat may result in a loss of half of the species found in the remaining 10% of the forest. In addition, if the patches of forest left are widely separated from each other, recolonization from one patch to another when species are lost becomes impossible.

A major task involved in developing sustainable societies thus involves learning more about both individual species and how species interact in ecosystems, so that wise decisions can be made about the use of biological resources and protection of biological diversity.

Sustainable Use of Biological Resources

A sustainable society protects biological resources of food and materials. In addition to the resource of biodiversity, there are a few natural biological resources that human societies depend upon so heavily they need to be discussed separately. Timber is one such resource; seafood is another. People have long recognized the importance of wild biological resources that are utilized for food and materials. The notion of sustained yield of timber comes out of nineteenth-century forest management in Germany. The ideas of fishery management have likewise been with us for many years. Yet, as knowledgeable as we appear to be in books, we have not yet achieved sustainability in managing our timber supplies or our fisheries.

National forests in the United States are supposed to be harvested on a sustained-yield basis, that is, with a cut no larger than anticipated growth. Yet the cut consistently exceeds new growth. In Canada, cutting of the forests proceeds rapidly. In South America and Southeast Asia the trees of the tropical forests are being lost at alarming rates—felled for timber and burned to clear land for farming or ranching.

In addition to destruction of the resource itself, which is of course not sustainable use, immense quantities of carbon that are tied up in the forests are released as carbon dioxide when the trees are burned, hastening the accumulation of carbon dioxide and increasing the threat of global warming.

Our success in managing ocean fisheries has been similarly dismal. Indiscriminate whaling has already decimated many species of whales. A number of fisheries have failed or appear to be failing due to overharvesting. Examples include the California sardine fishery, the North Sea herring industry, the West Africa/Namibia pilchard fishery, and the Chesapeake oyster industry.

A particular example of unsustainable mining of fishery resources is the use of drift nets by factory ships from Taiwan, Japan, and South Korea. These drift nets, which may extend up to 40 miles in length, literally rake the ocean, capturing and killing all fish indiscriminately. Drift net fishing for salmon in the Pacific has already led to a sharp decline in salmon returning to spawn on West Coast rivers. The drift net ships have also been operating in the Atlantic.

A U.N. resolution signed in early 1990 bans drift net fishing on the high seas after June 1992, but without enforcement the "pirate fleet" is likely to stay in business. The protection of the biological resources of timber and of ocean fish is an old concept, but the idea remains empty without the will to enforce appropriate levels of harvesting.

The United Nations Environment Programme, in a report published jointly with two conservation organizations (see References) recommends an international watchdog organization to investigate abuses of the world's environment. If equipped with enforcement powers, such an organization could promote more sustainable uses of the earth's common biological resources.

Limitation of Population Size

A sustainable society aims to limit its population to a size that can be supported indefinitely by its environment. This final component of sustainable societies, the ability to limit their own populations, is probably the most difficult to secure. Population limitation runs directly counter to one of the major biological imperatives—reproduction. For humans, this basic biological imperative to reproduce is overlaid by a thicket of societal expectations, individual goals, and philosophical choices.

Under certain circumstances the net result of all these factors appears to be a stable population size. In the developed countries, personal choices exist about the type of work a person will do or how the income from that work will be spent. Limiting family size is a result of decisions taken by parents to secure economic well-being and personal satisfaction for themselves and for their children. Several countries are currently experiencing zero population growth (Denmark, West Germany), and many others are near that point.

In developing countries and for some people in developed countries, however, these choices may not exist. In such circumstances, as detailed in chapters 5 and 6, children often represent a form of wealth, and the populations of such peoples are consequently growing rapidly. Even in countries where some choice about economic alternatives exists, societal expectations may favor large families or the use of birth control may be frowned upon, thus favoring increased population sizes.

As we mentioned in the beginning of this chapter, development has two driving forces. One is the desire to improve living conditions for the size population that already exists. The other driving force is to provide water, food sanitation, energy, and material wealth for the incremental numbers of people born each year.

While it is easily understood that no environment could provide for an unlimited number of people indefinitely, humans are still unwilling to grapple with the notion that they live in a finite world, capable of supporting only a specific number of people. We appear to be waiting and hoping for a technological rescue that will provide us with food, water, energy, and living space until such a time as development reaches all countries and populations naturally stabilize at some sustainable level.

It is not clear, however, that such development can occur at present rates of population growth. It appears less and less likely that technological innovation will sustain us until populations stabilize. Indeed, we may already have surpassed the population size that is sustainable by this earth if all peoples achieve the American standard of living. We don't know if this is the case. We're not talking about it.

Discussions of population limitation inevitably get hung up on questions of how we could accomplish such limitation. Who will decide who has the children and who does not? These are not trivial questions. They have serious implications for freedom of individual choice, racial justice, and economic and social equity for all the nations of the world. But neither are they inherently unanswerable questions. The first step to answering them, however, must be an acceptance that there is a population problem that we should solve before natural processes such as disease, starvation, global warming, or the physical and societal effects of overcrowding solve it for us.

It is likely that there is a size range for the human population that can be sustained indefinitely by the earth's resources and ecosystems. Determining that size range would involve all of the factors we have just discussed: sustainable use of energy, sustainable use of mineral and biological resources, sustainable use of soil, water, and air. Because many of these factors involve global resources and effects, no country can make a determination of its sustainable population size without taking into account the populations of other countries. If we would, all of us together, work to determine the appropriate size range for the human population, then we could, and would, begin to solve all of the other issues inherent in limiting human populations. Until we make the effort to determine that size range, however, we will find it possible to drift along towards an era of almost certain catastrophes.

Social Characteristics of Sustainable Societies

The preceding discussion has focused mainly on the relationship between human societies and their environment. Truly sustainable societies, of course, also depend upon equitable relationships between people. Racial and economic justice, peace among nations—these are also components of sustainable societies. Although these topics are somewhat beyond the scope of this book, neither can they be truly separated from the discussion of environmental issues. Some of our essay writers have touched upon these subjects, notably Richard Moore in his discussion of the unequal burden racial minorities bear and Prime Minister Brundtland in her call for economic justice. Finally, in the next chapter, Paul Raskin urges that the social justice and environmental movements work together for common goals.

Questions

1. Can you modify or add to the components of a sustainable society that are discussed in this chapter?

2. The components described in this chapter are strategies for a society to follow. Is there a comparable set of strategies or actions for individuals to follow that would help to achieve a sustainable society?

References

Clark, W., "Managing Planet Earth," *Scientific American,* September, 1989, p. 46.

Crosson, P., and N. Rosenberg. "Strategies for Agriculture," *Scientific American,* September, 1989, p. 128.

Fri, R. "Sustainable Development: Principles into Practice," *Resources,* Resources for the Future, Winter, 1991, p. 1.

Frosch, R., and N. Gallopoulos. "Strategies for Manufacturing," *Scientific American,* September, 1989, p. 144.

Orians, G. "Ecological Concepts of Sustainability," *Environment,* November, 1990, p. 10.

United Nations Environment Programme. *Caring for the Earth—A Strategy for Sustainable Living,* United Nations, London, 1990.

Conclusion

Towards a Sustainable Society

Moving human societies in the direction of sustainability is both a necessary and a truly massive undertaking. Because the issues are global in nature and involve expertise in many areas, both scientific and nonscientific, many people must take part in finding the solution to the problems inherent in achieving sustainability. For this reason we have enlisted the help of a number of environmentally concerned citizens of the world. You have already encountered their thoughts in the viewpoints distributed throughout the text. Here we give a synthesis of their ideas and suggestions—a summary of the way to begin to establish sustainable societies. In order to understand their points of view, we first need to ask how humans see themselves in relation to the environment.

A concern for the rights of future generations and an acknowledgment that we do not own the earth, as we might own an object such as a book, is found in many cultures. The idea that we have only the use of the earth during our lifetimes has been expressed in many ways.

The American Joseph Wood Krutch wrote about wilderness:

These are the things which other nations can never recover. Should we lose them, we could not recover them either. The generation now living may very well be that which will make the irrevocable decision whether or not America will continue to be for centuries to come the one great nation which had the foresight to preserve an important part of its heritage. If we do not preserve it, then we shall have diminished by just that much the unique privilege of being an American.

No less eloquently, Renatas, a young Tanzanian park ranger, said:

After I be dead, others will follow. If people be killing, killing, there will be no more buffalo, no rhino. If they be cutting, cutting, there will be no more trees, no oxygen, no rain. Like a desert. What will my daughters think? They will come and there will be nothing. "Our father was stupid," they will say.[1]

In 1854, Chief Seattle of the Dwamish declared: "This we know. The earth does not belong to man: man belongs to the earth." And we hear an echo of his words in this quote from a Nigerian chief: "I conceived that the land belongs to a vast family. Of this family, many are dead, few are living, and countless members are still unborn."[2]

1. Quoted in B. McBride, *Sierra*, March/April 1985, p. 67.
2. Quoted in Virginia Curtis (Ed.), *Land Use and the Environment*, Environmental Protection Agency, Office of Research and Monitoring, Environmental Studies Division (Washington, D.C.: U.S. Government Printing Office, 1973).

Towards a Sustainable Society

Ecological Problems of Sustainable Development of the Former USSR

by Nikita Glazovsky

Nikita Fedorovich Glazovsky is Deputy Minister of Ecology and Natural Resources in the Russian Republic. He is a specialist in the field of geochemistry of land-scapes, in the use of natural resources, and protection of the environment.

An analysis of ecological problems in the territory of the former USSR is interesting not only for the republics comprising the USSR but for the whole world as well since the USSR occupies 1/6 of the land surface of the globe and the problems arising in this region may strongly affect the ecological and socio-economic situation of many regions of the Earth.

The Present Ecological Situation

According to data of the Institute of Geography (Kochurov et al.), regions with a compromised or damaged ecological/environmental situation occupy about 20% of the country. The population inhabiting this territory is about 40% of the total population of the nation. In some regions up to 5–6% of the population live in unfavourable environmental conditions caused by anthropogenic pollution.

Data of the State Committee of Hydrometeorology indicate that in all 570 cities where air pollution monitoring is carried out, some maximal permissible concentrations (MPCs) of air pollutants are exceeded. In 100% of the surveyed cities the MPCs for phenols, carbon-bisulfide, benzopyrene, and ammonia were exceeded. Oxides of nitrogen were exceeded in 90% of cities, and carbon monoxide and dust MPCs were exceeded in 77–78% of cities. In 19 populated areas with a total of 5.5 million people extremely high air pollution is observed with exceedances of MPCs more than 50 times in a year.

Moreover, water pollution is widespread as is soil contamination. Typhoid has been on the increase for the past fifteen years in Kazakhstan and other central Asian republics. The banned pesticide D.D.T. showed up in the soil in 16% of the area surveyed for contamination. It is estimated that 20–50% of foods contain chemical weed killers, or heavy metals or other dangerous pollutants. In some places, infant mortality exceeds 100 deaths for every 1,000 newborn.

Natural resources are inefficiently used as well. Soil erosion is taking place over an area of 300–400,000 km^2 (120–160,000 miles^2). Forest damage due to contamination and excess cutting extends over some 500,000 km^2 (200,000 miles^2). Mining has disturbed 162,000 km^2 (64,000 miles^2) of land. The mining of rocks produces excessive waste, and oil extraction is very inefficient. The rate of use of water resources per unit of gross national product is probably five times that in the United States and ten times that of Japan, Great Britain, or France. From existing estimates 15–20% of the gross national product in the USSR is lost due to ineffective use of natural resources.

Origin of Environmental and Ecological Problems and Pathways to Sustainable Development

1. Absence of clear priorities in the development of society. Estimates of possible influences of various activities upon the environment are lacking as is a plan for the use of natural resources. As a consequence, it is essential that we define social and ecological priorities for development as well as ecological "growth limits" based on achieving sustainability of the biosphere. To my mind, such a plan is required not only for the USSR but for the whole of humankind.

2. An erroneous strategy of economic development with regard to the use of natural resources. More efficient extraction and more efficient production of final goods are necessary.

3. The hypertrophic development of the military-industrial complex (MIC). By recent estimates, real military expenditures of the USSR amounted to 40–50% of the gross national product. Such development caused not only direct damage to nature in the form of environmental contamination and land degradation. It also caused a rise in consumption of useful minerals and other natural resources. As a result of the reduction of military opposition, we may expect some decrease of the MIC participation in the economy and some decrease in its influence on the environment.

4. A bureaucratic departmental system of economic management. Until recently, more than 250 ministries governed the economic activities of the USSR, each ministry was interested in expansion of its own activity, and was unregulated by market forces. As examples, the Ministry of Power Engineering sought the construction of numerous hydropower stations, while the Ministry of Reclamation and Water Management sought to build gigantic irrigation systems as well as channels for river reversal, etc. In the transition to a market economy, many of the ministries have been liquidated (only 25 ministries remain), and it is hoped that this decrease in bureaucracy and increase in responsiveness will improve the efficiency of the use of natural resources.

5. In addition to the above steps and effort, we also need to expand ecological and science education and improve the technologies that are used to protect the environment.

Possible Future Problems

We may hope that the political changes taking place in the former USSR will make it possible to achieve improvement in the quality of the environment. At the same time, however, new problems may occur. Let us mention only some of them.

Parliaments of Russia and other republics will adopt a great number of new legislative statements. These statements, although positive on the whole, will not always take into account ecological needs, but they should.

Another problem is connected with interregional interactions or transboundary pollution between the USSR and its former European territories. One example is the exchange of sulfur oxides (the principle cause of acid rain) between the territories and the USSR. Sulfur oxides flow both into and out of the USSR and the flows are extensive. Another example is the river exchanges from the territories and from other regions. Such flows both originate in the USSR and flow elsewhere and originate elsewhere and flow into the USSR. Quality may be degraded in these flows and quantities diminished by prior use.

In a number of regions of the country, especially in Central Asia, many ecological problems are associated with uncontrolled growth of population. Unfortunately, until recently, even a discussion of this problem caused sharp resistance on the part of local leaders. In the future, this problem may be aggravated. Still another unfavourable phenomenon may impact the ecological situation of the USSR.

(Continues)

Towards a Sustainable Society (continued)

Transnational corporations may try to transfer their production to the developing countries to take advantage of cheap labour and reduced expenditures for environmental protection. We need to prevent foreign expansion of harmful and "dirty" production to our country. Therefore, an effective control of the activity of not only domestic but of joint and foreign ventures is needed as well.

Conclusion

At present, a conception of ecological security of the USSR has been created. It is aimed at ensuring the fundamental human right to live in a clean environment; it includes economic and legal mechanisms to ensure the quality of the human and natural environment.

In the first instance, it is necessary to introduce prices to be paid for the use of natural resources. Also, it is necessary to define limits for environment pollution as well as to establish fees for emissions beyond the permissible levels. Resource conservation and energy conservation and use of secondary resources need to be stimulated. New environment protection technologies are needed. Finally, the conversion of the military-industrial complex to more productive and benign activities is necessary.

In conclusion let us note that the most rational and economical processes for using natural and social resources will be the ones that ensure sustainable development as well as preservation of the biosphere. We must draw from our system of knowledge and ingenuity those technological and social approaches that will guarantee the maximal satisfaction of spiritual and material requirements for both present and future generations and will conserve, at the same time, the fundamental functions of the biosphere.

To native peoples living in societies that meet the criteria for sustainability, the actions of people from more developed societies manifest a basic lack of logic. As a leader of Panama's Kuna Indians said to then-President Omar Torrijos:

If I go to Panama City and stand in front of a pharmacy and, because I need medicine, pick up a rock and break the window, you would take me away and put me in jail. For me, the forest is my pharmacy. If I have sores on my legs, I go to the forest and get the medicine I need to cure them. The forest is also a great refrigerator. It keeps the food I need fresh. . . . So we Kuna need the forest, and we use it and we take much from it. But we can take what we need without having to destroy everything, as your people do.[3]

And it is not only the useful and practical parts of the environment that a nonsustainable society may deny its descendants. As Chief Seattle noted sorrowfully in his speech to President Franklin Pierce in 1885:

When the buffalo are all slaughtered, the wild horses all tamed, the secret corners of the forest heavy with the scent of many men, and the view of the ripe hills blotted by talking wires, where is the thicket? Gone. Where is the Eagle? Gone. And what is it to say goodbye to the swift and the hunt, the end of living and the beginning of survival?[4]

If we feel a responsibility to those who will come after us, to our children, it is critical that we in the developed world look more closely at our type of

---

3. Quoted by A. Durning in "Environmentalism South," *The Amicus Journal*, Summer 1990, p. 15.

4. Quoted in C. Master, "Chief Seattle and the Long View," *Journal of Pesticide Reform*, 8 (1) (Spring 1988).

society, to determine which of our actions are environmentally sustainable and which must be changed to achieve a sustainable society.

AN ENVIRONMENTAL SUMMIT

We have convened in this book the equivalent of an environmental summit, a conference of wise people who have given thought and effort to the needs of the common future. Some of our conferees are famous people on the world stage; some labor quietly and more locally but still as effectively. Their voices are from many lands; their perspectives are different, but their concern is genuine and deeply felt. Most of our conferees have never met; yet their opinions are in surprising accord. They all see ways out of the mess that humans have gotten themselves into; they all are hopeful, as we are, that the best parts of the society we have today can be preserved and that the mistakes of the past can be corrected.

An Environmental Agenda

The ideas put forth by the essay writers fall into three broad categories. In the first place, say several writers, we need a clear understanding of what we value in our environment, and we need a set of goals to preserve or achieve these things—we need an environmental agenda. "Two central questions must be addressed: What kind of planet do we want? What kind of planet can we get? . . . Discussions of what is desirable and what is feasible must finally lead to agendas for action" (Clark).

Surely there is compelling logic to this idea of setting broad environmental goals for ourselves, so that we are not always merely fixing things that have gone wrong—so that we do not find someday that we have been, in effect, "rearranging the deck chairs on the Titanic." Yet at this moment in the United States, we lack not only an "environmental agenda"; we do not even have a forum for developing such an agenda.

There is clear agreement among the essay writers about many of the items that would go on the agenda. One is a commitment to limit the growth of the human population to levels the earth's environment can sustain without disruption. Another item for the agenda is an energy and resources policy that stresses energy efficiency, recycling, and renewable sources of energy, such as solar power. In addition, our writers suggest a closer and more critical look at modern technology, which should serve us, but which can do great harm if it is used without forethought. They also advocate protection of the resource of biodiversity, preserving species both for the future use of the human population and because we value a diverse plant and animal kingdom, in and of itself. Finally, and perhaps most difficult of all to achieve, they see a crucial need for a more equitable distribution of technology and wealth among the nations and peoples of the world. They call for economic equality so that no group needs to "mine" the environment in order to survive. "It is both futile and an insult to the poor to tell them that they must remain in poverty to 'protect the environment.' What is needed is a new era of economic growth—growth that enhances the resource base rather than degrades it" (Brundtland).

Some countries have already attempted to set an environmental agenda. Canada has released a five-year environmental action plan known as the Green Plan; it sets targets and goals for environmental protection and improvement. More than 10,000 Canadians attended information seminars on the plan and submitted comments before it was finalized in 1990. A mechanism was also included for reviewing and updating the plan annually. Probably the first comprehensive environmental agenda was adopted by the people of The Netherlands in 1989. The plan has both long- and short-term goals. It addresses pollution reduction, energy conservation, materials conservation, and integration of environmental costs into product prices. The United Nations Environment Programme report, *Caring for the Earth*, calls for 50% of all countries to have such a plan in place by the year 2000. The agenda for developed countries such as the United States will differ from those of developing countries, who must balance short-term goals of economic development with long-term goals of environmental protection.

There is no shortage of people in the United States willing to work on such a plan. A coalition of 18 environmental action groups presented Pres-

Towards a Sustainable Society

Sustainability and Equity

by Paul D. Raskin

Paul Raskin is President of the Tellus Institute and Director of the Boston Center of Stockholm Environment Institute. The Tellus Institute performs policy-oriented research on environment and resources. The Stockholm Institute conducts an international program on the climate change problem, energy and water planning, and sustainable development.

For more than two centuries, industrial society has revolutionized people's lives, expectations, and values. As a chorus of political leaders, social analysts, and popular opinion has celebrated industrial progress, two oppositional voices — one environmental and one social — have called for the control, reformation, and transformation of the socio-economic system.

Environmentalism has concerned itself with preserving wild places and limiting the damage caused by industrial expansion to ecosystems and human health. Social justice movements have advocated a fairer distribution of wealth and power to the disenfranchised within countries, and between rich and poor countries. Broadly, environmental movements concentrate on the relationship between humanity and nature, while social movements focus on the relationship of humanity to itself.

Although both criticize the dominant system, these two movements have tended historically to be mutually suspicious, insofar as they heeded one another at all. Social justice proponents have viewed environmentalism as the domain of the privileged and elite, concerned about the suffering of animals rather than of people. On their side, environmentalists have found wanting social reformers who would distribute the fruits of industrialism more fairly without questioning its technological culture and environmental insensitivities.

The concept of sustainable development challenges the tension between these two forms of radicalism. Sustainable development holds that the goals of economic development and environmental stewardship are interdependent. Further, I would argue that development must be based on equity to be compatible with sustainability principles. This formulation suggests that poverty, underdevelopment, and political disenfranchisement are both the cause and

ident Bush with a "Blueprint for the Environment" on the occasion of his inauguration. In the light of the Gulf War, many citizens agreed that a new energy policy was needed. William K. Reilly, Administrator of the U.S. Environmental Protection Agency, in a 1991 speech to the Organization for Economic Cooperation and Development, in Paris, suggested items for both a national and an international agenda. Nationally, he suggested we adopt an approach to resource use that emphasizes efficient technologies, waste reduction, and recycling. He also suggested that pollution prevention, rather

effect of environmental degradation. The connection between distributional equity and environmental sustainability can be illustrated in four contexts: within developing countries, within industrialized countries, among countries, and between generations.

A web of interrelated, reinforcing factors maintains rural poverty in developing countries: population growth, over-intensive farming, degradation of land, expansion of farming onto marginal lands, deforestation, fuel wood shortages, erosion, and water pollution. Desperate people mine resources for survival; they do not husband them for the long term. The resulting poverty maintains high birth rates and continued population growth, thereby renewing the cycle of environmental degradation.

In industrial countries, also, poverty is implicated in environmental deterioration. The environmental consequences of the emergence of an underclass in U.S. cities exemplifies the connection. Inner city decay is closely linked to the growing suburban and exurban sprawl, as those with the wherewithal leave. Disbursed settlement patterns expand the automobile culture with its profligate use of fuels, land, and materials. The consequences are measured in air pollution, the greenhouse effect, the loss of a sense of community and place, and congested roadways and aggravated commuters. These patterns extended to a world of 10 billion people in the next century would be profoundly unsustainable. Creating alternative dynamics will require new kinds of communities that are safe and livable, provide livelihoods, and blend with their local environment — and that will tolerate far less poverty.

We live in a world of rich countries and poor countries. Poor countries are under heavy pressure to export commodities in order to meet the basic needs of their people, to purchase vital imports, and to pay international debts. Often, this means exploiting natural land and mineral resources with little regard for the long-term costs in resource depletion and environmental deterioration. If developing countries are to make the transition to globally sustainable practices, affluent countries will need to transfer appropriate technologies, forgive debts, and promote development that meets needs and aspirations while preserving environments. This requires an international redistribution of wealth and greatly improved equity among nations.

At the foundation of the sustainable development paradigm is the idea of the rights of future generations to inherit a planet in which their well-being is not jeopardized. This notion challenges a basic tenet of conventional economics that holds that rational individuals in pursuit of their own interests will achieve socially optimal objectives. But the unborn cannot cast votes on today's resource allocations. Intergenerational equity requires that we adopt, as an ethical matter, technologies and development paths that preserve natural stocks and ecosystems.

I have suggested ways in which a more sustainable society requires more equitable distributions of rights and benefits. If so, then the continued separation of environmental and social justice movements is not valid. Rather, environmental preservation and social equity are complementary aspects of the transition to a sustainable future.

than after-the-fact cleanup, should become the standard in the United States, a suggestion also made by Gustave Speth, of the World Resources Institute, in his essay.

What we lack in the United States is support at the highest levels for the development of an environmental agenda and for an ongoing mechanism for the nation's people to make their choices clearly known. Faith Campbell in her essay in Chapter 10 gives a short, punchy list of the items she would put on such an agenda. You might want to compare this to the list you would make yourself.

Practical Suggestions

The writers of the essays do not stop with suggestions for an environmental agenda. They give clear, practical suggestions on how to go about achieving a sustainable society: A way for us to become less of a "throw-away" society (Hansen); a carbon tax to finance energy-efficient technologies for developing nations (Goldemberg); an innovative debt-for-nature swap concept that is helping to save tropical forest areas (Lovejoy). James Titus makes an equally innovative suggestion about how to save coastal ecosystems—at no cost—in the event that global warming causes a serious rise in sea level. Another essay, which should make us all stop and think about where we are heading, suggests how wastewater can be treated and reused as a means to extend precious water resources (Okun).

Several people deal with the need for more sustainable agricultural practices. We have included an essay that is an excerpt from J. Russell Smith's visionary book *Tree Crops*, in which he points out that trees are a sustainable form of agriculture on sloping lands. Other writers list the advances modern agriculture has developed or adopted that are leading towards a sustainable agriculture (Uphof), describe how we can make the use of pesticides a safer, more sustainable procedure for people in developing countries (Cole), or give clear, useful advice on how to decrease or eliminate the use of pesticides in a home garden (Balge). One contributor also cautions against belief in the "miracle" of chemical pesticides and suggests instead the use of environmentally benign methods of integrated pest management (Odhiambo). Finally, another writer makes the very practical suggestion that we do a better job of collecting environment-related data and making it available for use—in order to know where we are, where we are going, and how we can use our limited financial resources most efficiently (Zhang).

The limitation of human population growth is a necessary component of sustainable societies. Ways to achieve stable population size are detailed by Kalish and Qu.

The prices of goods we consume and the activities we carry out rarely take into account or "internalize" the environmental costs associated with them (Rajagopalan). Prices should reflect the true cost to society of those goods and activities, but the transition to such prices is slow to occur. A series of suggestions to internalize environmental costs is found in the essay by Schmidheiny and also in such books as Tietenberg's *Environmental and Natural Resource Economics* or Daly and Cobb's, *For the Common Good*. N. Choucri (1991) notes that multinational companies can preempt attempts to regulate them by adopting environmental protection strategies—and that only companies that do so will flourish. "While moral suasion is hardly a serious consideration in business decisions, it can be poor practice to ignore sentiments that define what is legitimate. As the Valdez incident has shown, no company can brush aside outrage."

A Change of Attitudes

There is a third kind of suggestion presented by some environmentalists—that a truly sustainable society will not be achieved without some changes of attitude. We may need an entirely new way of viewing the earth and its ecosystems. The Gaia hypothesis represents such a view (Margulis). There should be more citizen participation in the environmental protection movement, because the kind of initiatives needed for sustainable societies may need to come from the grassroots up rather than down from corporations and politicians (Gibbs and Williams). Poor people and minorities suffer more than their fair share of environmental degradation. Ways must be found to empower these groups to improve their environment (Moore).

Finally, Jacques-Yves Cousteau calls for a declaration of the rights of future generations—a formal recognition of our obligation to those who inherit the earth from us. Russell Peterson refers to this recognition as "inter-generational equity." Cousteau writes:

> . . . We demand that the rights of future generations be solemnly declared so that all human beings may inherit an undamaged and uncontaminated planet. The petition we propose for signature by millions of fathers and mothers worldwide is, in fact, the most reasonable of Utopias.

A sustainable world requires another feature of utopias—that we work together for common goals. The last essay calls eloquently for a union of the environmental and the social justice movements, so that a truly sustainable society can be created (Raskin).

A CONCLUDING CHALLENGE

Clearly the world needs work, your work. Clearly the world needs healing, and it needs your hands for healing. The challenge you face is to create a stable, fruitful, peaceful life on earth, a society that exists in harmony with nature, a sustainable society.

The magnificent cathedrals of Europe were rarely built in a single generation. Often three generations of artisans would labor on an edifice, would carve its railings and raise lofty spires. The tools of the parent were handed to the next generation and to the generation that followed before it was complete.

Our challenge is to begin to erect the structure that preserves the earth we inherited, to begin to secure the global future.

References

Abelson, P. H. "National Energy Strategy," *Science, 251,* (March 22, 1991).

Bennett, G. "The History of the Dutch National Environmental Plan," *Environment, 33*(7) (1991), 6.

Blueprint for the Environment: Advice to the President-Elect from America's Environmental Community. Salt Lake City, Utah: Howe Brothers, 1988.

"Canada's Green Plan for a Healthy Environment." Hull, Quebec: Environment Canada, 1991.

Choucri, Nazi. "The Global Environment and Multinational Corporations," *Technology Review*, April 1991, p. 52.

Daly, H., and J. Cobb, Jr. *For the Common Good*. Boston: Beacon Press, 1989.

Energy Use and the U.S. Economy. Congress of the United States, Office of Technology Assessment. Washington, D.C. U.S. Government Printing Office, 1990.

"1991 Directory to Environmental Organizations," *Buzzworm: The Environmental Journal, 3*(3) (May/June 1991).

Reilly, W. K. "Environmental Strategy for the 1990's," Remarks to the OECD, January 31, 1991, Paris, France.

Tietenberg, T. *Environmental and Natural Resource Economics*, 2nd ed. Glenview, Ill.: Scott, Foresman, 1988.

United Nations Environment Programme. *Caring for the Earth*. London: The World Conservation Union and the World Wide Fund for Nature, 1991.

White, A. L. "Venezuela's Organic Law," *Environment, 33*(7) (1991), 16.

Glossary

abiotic Nonliving; referring to the nonliving components of ecosystems (water, light, etc.).

acclimation The biochemical changes that enable an organism to withstand changed temperatures (either higher or lower).

acid mine drainage Water that has dissolved iron pyrites (ferrous sulfide), which were left behind from coal-mining operations. The water becomes acidic and deposits ferric hydroxide (yellow boy) on stream bottoms. The acid makes the water undrinkable and is harmful to aquatic life. The acid waters are also low in dissolved oxygen, a substance needed by aquatic life for survival.

acid rain Rainfall with a high acid content falling downwind of major fuel-burning areas. Sulfur oxides and nitrogen oxides from the burning of fossil fuels are the culprit. Acid rain may stunt the growth of plants and turn lakes and streams acidic, driving out the normal aquatic species.

activated sludge plant A device for removing dissolved organics from wastewater. The plant is a well-aerated tank in which microbes using oxygen convert the dissolved organics to simpler substances.

adaptation A characteristic that helps an organism survive in a particular environment.

aerobic Refers to an environment in which oxygen is present.

agroforestry The interplanting of trees and row crops. The trees help stabilize soil, absorb moisture from deeper soil levels, provide shade for cattle during hot seasons, and usually produce a crop as well.

AIDS (auto-immune deficiency syndrome) A disease spread by sexual contact or contact with human blood, that results in loss of the immune system's ability to fight infection.

algae Simple, often microscopic, plants that live in water or very moist land environments.

anaerobic Referring to lack of oxygen. In the context of water pollution, a condition of water in which all the dissolved oxygen has been used up or removed. Only a few specially adapted species can survive in anaerobic (oxygen-depleted) waters.

appropriate technology Technology which takes into account the needs, wishes, and traditional methods of a people. For instance, in a developing country where labor is cheap, but fuel and credit are largely unavailable, people might benefit more by the invention of an inexpensive, human-powered mechanical thresher, than a machine that operates on electricity or fossil fuels.

aquaculture The farming of fish or other aquatic creatures, either in enclosures in coastal waters or in natural or artificial ponds.

aquifer An underground body of water whose precise dimensions are unknown.

arable Able to be farmed.

area mining of coal A surface-mining method in which the overburden is removed and laid up in successive parallel rows; the technique is used on relatively flat lands.

bacteria Single-celled organisms visible with a microscope. Some bacteria are harmful and cause plant and animal diseases. Many more are harmless or even useful. Bacteria aid in the decay and recycling of organic matter and are used industrially (e.g., to produce drugs or ferment dairy products).

ballast Weight used in ships in certain areas of their cargo space to make them stable and easy to steer. Oil tankers use as ballast either the oil they carry or seawater.

barrel of oil One barrel of oil equals about 43 gallons. A ton of oil varies in volume according to what kind of oil it is (e.g., gasolines are lighter than diesel oils), but as a general statement, one ton of oil is about seven barrels or 300 gallons.

biochemical oxygen demand (BOD) The amount of oxygen that would be consumed if all the organics in one liter of polluted water were oxidized by bacteria and protozoa; it is reported in milligrams per liter. The BOD number is useful in predicting how low the levels of oxygen in a stream or river may be forced to go when organic wastes are oxidized by species in the stream.

biodegradable Able to be broken down by living organisms.

biodiversity The variety of species of living organisms and also the genetic variation among different organisms in a species.

biological controls Pest-control methods that use natural predators, parasites, or diseases or that rely on the use of naturally produced chemicals such as insect pheromones.

biological magnification The process by which certain, often toxic, materials become more concentrated as they move up food chains. That is, organisms at the top of the food chain contain more of the substance than do organisms on the bottom of the food chain, or than does the environment itself.

biomass The weight of the living creatures in a given area.

biomass energy Energy derived from crops (trees, sugar cane, corn, etc.) by either direct burning or by conversion to an intermediate fuel such as alcohol.

biomes Climax communities characteristic of given regions of the world.

biota The living organisms, plant and animal, in a region.

birth rate The number of individuals born in a population over a given time period, divided by the number of individuals already in the population. For humans: the number of babies born each year per thousand people in a population.

bituminous coal The most plentiful form of coal in the United States. Its high heating value and abundance also make it the most widely used coal. Its principal use is in steam electric power plants.

black lung disease A condition in which the elasticity of the lung is destroyed, caused by the inhalation of coal dust over a relatively long period. Many coal miners are permanently disabled by the disease.

bloom A rapid overgrowth of algae.

blowdown The water removed from that circulating in a cooling tower to prevent solids from building up in the tower water. This water is replaced by fresh water called "makeup."

blowout Explosive release of gas and/or oil from an oil well.

BOD See biochemical oxygen demand.

boiling-water reactor (BWR) A nuclear reactor in which the water passing through the core is heated by the fission process and is converted directly to steam, which turns a turbine. The BWR is one of the two major types of nuclear reactors used for electric production. *See also* pressurized water reactor.

breeder reactor A nuclear reactor in which the coolant and heat-transfer medium is molten sodium. The fuel is plutonium-239, which is continuously bred from uranium-238.

Btu The British thermal unit, the quantity of heat needed to raise the temperature of 1 pound of water by 1°F. One Btu is equivalent to 1.054 kilojoules (a common metric energy unit).

bulb turbine A turbine whose blade face is oriented perpendicular to the direction of water flow. In contrast to the Peyton, Francis, and Kaplan wheels, which require water elevations of 100 feet or more, the bulb turbine can generate electricity from only rapidly moving water. It thereby makes possible both tidal power and hydro development at many sites not previously feasible.

Bureau of Land Management The managing agency of the National Resource Lands. The Bureau is within the Department of Interior.

BWR See boiling-water reactor.

calorie A measure of the heat or energy content in food. Human food requirements are usually measured in kilocalories (the amount of heat needed to raise the temperature of 1,000 grams of water by 1°C), and the term is written with a capital c, "Calorie."

carbon cycle The cycling of carbon in nature. Carbon dioxide is produced when plants and animals respire and is consumed by green plants during photosynthesis. Carbon dioxide also dissolves in the oceans and precipitates as limestone or dolomite.

carbon dioxide A colorless, odorless gas at normal temperatures, composed of one atom of carbon and two of oxygen. It makes up about 0.03% of the atmosphere by weight. Carbon dioxide is consumed in photosynthesis by green plants and produced by the respiration of plants and animals and the burning of fossil fuel.

carbon monoxide A gas consisting of one atom of carbon bonded to one of oxygen. Its action on human health is a result of its "tying up" of hemoglobin, the protein that carries oxygen to the cells. The principal source of this major air pollutant, formed from the incomplete combustion of carbon, is the automobile.

carboxyhemoglobin Carbon monoxide combines with the oxygen-carrying blood protein hemoglobin to form carboxyhemoglobin. This combined form cannot transport oxygen in the bloodstream.

carcinogen Anything that causes cancer.

carnivores Meat-eaters.

carrying capacity The largest population a particular environment can support indefinitely

catalytic converter The device used on automobile exhaust gases to convert carbon monoxide to carbon dioxide and hydrocarbons to carbon dioxide and water. An additional converter may be used to convert oxides of nitrogen back to oxygen and nitrogen.

CFCs Chlorofluorocarbon gases (*see below*).

chlorinated hydrocarbons Chemicals composed mainly of carbon and hydrogen plus one or more atoms of chlorine. Examples are the pesticides DDT, aldrin, dieldrin, chlordane, and heptachlor.

chlorinated organics Chemical compounds composed of carbon, hydrogen, oxygen, and one or more atoms of chlorine. These chemicals can be formed in drinking water by the action of the disinfectant chlorine on organic chemicals found in some water supplies.

chlorination The controlled addition of chlorine to water destined for drinking and to wastewaters being discharged into receiving bodies. Chlorine kills bacteria and viruses and so renders the water safe for human consumption and use. The process is also known as disinfection.

cholera An intestinal disease caused by specific bacteria. The disease can be spread by water polluted by human wastes.

chlorofluorocarbons (CFCs) These are gases whose molecules contain chlorine, fluorine, and carbon. They have been used as propellants in spray cans and as foaming agents for polystyrene, and are still widely used in refrigerators and air conditioners. They are implicated in both ozone destruction and global warming.

clear-cutting The practice of cutting all trees in an area, regardless of size, quality, or age. The practice hastens erosion, is visually displeasing, and leads to a loss of species habitat. Better practices are selection cutting, seed-tree cutting, and shelterwood cutting.

climate A complex of factors affecting the environment. Climate includes temperature, humidity, amount of precipitation, rate of evaporation, amount of sunlight, and winds.

climax community The characteristic and relatively stable community for a particular area.

coagulation A process for the removal of suspended material from drinking water. A "floc" of insoluble material is created by the addition of alum or ferrous sulfate. When the floc settles in a detention basin, suspended material is captured in the floc and is settled out as well.

coal cleaning The removal of sulfur from coal by washing and chemical steps. Cleaned coal is less likely to require "scrubbers" to remove sulfur oxides from the stack gases.

coal gasification The conversion of the carbon in coal to a gas that can burn. Coal is burned in the presence of oxygen and steam to produce carbon monoxide and hydrogen gases. This low-Btu gas can be burned directly or can be converted to a high-quality methane by the addition of hydrogen in further reactions. The latter product can be substituted for natural gas.

coal liquefaction The conversion of coal to a hydrocarbon liquid. Pyrolysis is one method for this conversion. A modification of coal gasification will also produce a hydrocarbon liquid. Solvent refining of coal is a third possible process.

coal-slurry pipeline A technology in which coal is transported via pipeline as a mixture (about 50/50) of coal particles and water.

cocarginogen A substance that does not, by itself, cause cancer but that can cause cancer in combination with some other substance.

coliform bacteria A category of bacteria largely derived from fecal wastes. The presence of these bacteria in a river or stream is taken as evidence of fecal pollution and indicates the possibility that pathogenic (disease-causing) bacteria may be present.

combined cycle power plant A power plant in which oil or gas is first burned in a turbine (jet) engine, generating turning power in the engine for electric generation. The hot gases are then used to boil water to steam to turn a conventional turbine for power generation. The efficiency of conversion of heat to electricity is increased by this two-stage process.

combined sewers A sewer system that carries both domestic wastewater and the water from rainstorms. During storms, the total of the flows is too large to be treated and hence sewage enters the water body virtually without treatment.

community All of the living creatures, plant and animal, interacting in a particular environment.

competition In ecological terms, the struggle between individuals or populations for a limited resource.

condense To change from a gas to a liquid, as when steam is condensed to water in a power plant condenser.

consumers Organisms who eat other organisms. Primary consumers eat producers, secondary consumers eat primary consumers, and so on.

contour mining of coal A surface-mining method in which L-shaped cuts are made into the hillside in long curving arcs that follow the contour of the hill.

contraceptive A device, chemical, or action that prevents pregnancy.

cooling tower A structure designed to cool the water that was used to condense steam at a power plant.

core (of a nuclear reactor) The concrete and metal shielded structure that houses the nuclear fuel in a reactor; the place where the fission process and heat production take place.

crude oil Oil as it comes from the ground, in its natural state. Crude oil is a mixture of many chemical compounds.

DDT A member of the chlorinated hydrocarbon family of pesticides. DDT was banned in the United States in 1972 because it was interfering with reproduction in certain bird species.

death rate The number of individuals in a population who die over a given time period, divided by the number of individuals in the population. For humans: the number of deaths each year per thousand people in a population.

deciduous forest biome A biome characterized by trees that lose their leaves each fall.

decomposers Organisms that take part in the decay of organic materials to simple compounds (e.g., bacteria and fungi).

Delaney clause Amendment to the Federal Food Drug and Cosmetics Act that directs that no chemical known to cause cancer in humans or animals may be added to food.

demographic transition Pattern of change in which birth rates fall as, or after, death rates fall. After the transition, a country's birth rate is closer to its death rate and the population does not grow rapidly.

demography The study of populations.

desertification The severe degradation of a land environment to the point where it resembles a desert.

detritus Dead organic matter, composed of plant and animal remains.

developing nation A term applied to countries that have little or no technological development.

development rights The rights, most often accompanying ownership of the land, that enable the owner to construct buildings, build roads and sewers, and otherwise alter the land. Such rights can be sold or transferred to other parties, separating the rights from the land itself.

digester A water pollution control device used to further degrade and stabilize the organic solids that arise from primary and secondary wastewater treatment.

dissolved oxygen The amount of oxygen dissolved in water, reported in milligrams per liter. Levels of 5 mg/l or above indicate a relatively healthy stream. The maximum level of dissolved oxygen is ordinarily 8–9 mg/l, depending on the water temperature.

district heating System by which the spent steam from a steam-electric power plant is carried in underground pipes to homes, offices, factories, and so on for heating during the winter months.

diversity A measure of the number of species in a given area. The more species per square meter, the higher the diversity.

DNA (deoxyribonucleic acid) The hereditary material contained within cells that determines the characteristics of an organism.

drift Particles of liquid water that escape from cooling towers and cause corrosion or other environmental problems.

ecology The study of the interaction between organisms and their environment.

ecosystem All of the living organisms in a particular environment plus the nonliving factors in that environment. The nonliving factors include such things as soil type, rainfall, and the amount of sunlight.

effluent A liquid or gaseous waste material produced from a physical or chemical process.

electric power plant (thermal) Power plant in which the heat (hence the word "thermal") from a burning fossil fuel or from the fissioning of uranium is used to boil water to steam and the steam is then used to turn a turbine, generating electricity.

electrostatic precipitator A device that removes particulate matter from stack gases; the particles are given an electric charge and then attracted to a collecting electrode. The precipitator is highly efficient and is widely used on electric power plants.

emergency core cooling system A spray system designed to inject water rapidly into the core of a nuclear reactor that has experienced a loss-of-coolant accident.

emigration The movement of organisms out of a population.

endangered species A species with so few living members that it will soon become extinct unless measures are begun to slow its loss.

enrichment The process of converting uranium from 0.7% uranium-235 to 3% uranium-235. The higher concentration is needed for the fuel rods of the reactor of a nuclear electric power plant.

entrainment Entrapment of organisms in the condenser water pipes of a power plant.

epidemiology The study of disease in groups of people or populations.

erosion The loss of soil due to wind or as a result of washing away by water.

estuary A coastal body of water partly surrounded by land but having a free connection with the ocean where fresh water from a river mixes with salt water.

eutrophic Water that has a high concentration of plant nutrients.

evolution Change in the frequency of occurrence of various genes in a population over a period of time.

fauna The animal life of a particular region.

fertility rate The total number of live births a woman in a particular country is expected to have during her reproductive years. (Also called total fertility rate.)

fertilizer A material that promotes the growth of plants. It can be natural or artificial.

filtration In the context of water supply, the practice of forcing water through beds of sand to trap the bacteria that cause disease and thereby prevent their presence in drinking water.

first law of thermodynamics Law stating that energy can be changed from one form to another, but it cannot be created and it cannot be destroyed.

fission Process that occurs when the nucleus of certain heavy atoms is struck by neutrons, breaking into two or more fragments (fission products) with the production of heat and more neutrons; fission means "breaking apart."

food chain A picture of the relationship between the predators in an area and their prey (i.e., who is eating whom). This term is applied when the relationships are simple and few creatures are involved.

food web Interconnected food chains made up of many organisms, with many interrelationships.

fossil fuels Fuels like coal, oil, and natural gas, derived from the remains of organic matter deposited long ago.

fuel cell A device in which oxygen combines with hydrogen or carbon monoxide, producing direct current electricity. Fuel cells are expected to be relatively clean producers of electricity, unless coal is burned to provide the carbon monoxide.

fuel reprocessing Process in which spent nuclear fuel rods are broken apart, and the highly radioactive fission products are separated and uranium and plutonium are recovered to be reused.

fusion The combination of the deuterium atom (a form of hydrogen) with either another deuterium atom or a tritium atom (still another hydrogen form). The combination releases enormous heat, which scientists hope some day to capture to produce electrical energy. Fusion is also the basis for the hydrogen bomb.

gamma ray A highly penetrating form of ionizing electromagnetic radiation that is produced by one type of radioactive decay.

genetic bottleneck A time period in the evolution of a species when there were relatively few members of the species, from whom all current members of the species are descended. Such a bottleneck can result in genetic uniformity among members of the species now living.

genetic engineering Changing the genetic makeup of organisms by techniques such as inserting genes from one species into another.

geopressured methane Natural gas known to be dissolved in salt water in deep caverns at extremely high pressures and temperatures. It is not known whether geopressured methane can be recovered profitably.

geothermal heat Heat from the earth's interior carried to the surface as hot water or steam. The steam and hot water can be used to heat homes, offices, and factories or can be used to generate electricity.

geothermal power plant An electric generating station that uses hot water or steam from the earth's interior as the energy source. Releases of steam from the earth can be used directly to turn a turbine. Alternatively, hot water releases can be "flashed" to steam for such uses. Or hot water can be used to vaporize a fluid such as isobutane, which will then be used to turn a turbine.

greenhouse effect Atmospheric heating that occurs when outward heat radiation is blocked by carbon dioxide and other greenhouse gases that absorb the energy. The greenhouse effect suggests the earth will undergo a warming trend as carbon dioxide from fossil fuel combustion and other heat-trapping gases accumulate in the atmosphere.

greenhouse gases Gases whose molecules absorb heat radiation from the earth bound for space. These heat trapping gases include carbon dioxide, chlorofluorocarbons (CFCs), methane, water vapor, and others.

green revolution The term given to the new developments in farming, including the use of high-yielding grains, that promise to enable farmers to grow much more food on the same number of acres than with conventional techniques and older crop varieties.

Green Revolution II Green Revolution II refers to the techniques of selection and gene transfer involved in breeding high yield crops, or crops that grow well under adverse environmental conditions such as high salinity or high aluminum content in the soil.

groundwater Water beneath the earth's surface.

growth promoter A substance that makes an animal grow better or more quickly.

habitat The physical surroundings in which an organism lives.

half-life The time required for one-half of a given quantity of a chemical to disappear from the environment (or to be excreted by the body, if it is a chemical absorbed by a living organism).

hazardous wastes Any waste materials that could be a serious threat to human health or the environment when disposed of, transported, treated, or stored.

HCFCs, HFCs These groups of chemicals are both replacements for CFCs, or chlorofluorocarbons. HFCs stands for hydrofluorocarbons. Chemicals in this group contain no chlorine. HCFCs, or hydrochlorofluorocarbons contain some chlorine but less than CFCs. Both HCFCs and HFCs are "ozone-friendly" but they can still contribute to global warming.

heat pump A device that draws in cold air and exhausts this air at an even colder temperature. The heat captured is transferred via a refrigerant liquid to the indoor air. The heat pump has the potential to cut in half electric requirements for home or hot-water heating.

hectare A metric unit of area. One hectare is 100 meters by 100 meters and equals 2.47 acres.

hepatitis A viral disease in which the liver becomes inflamed. Epidemics of hepatitis have been traced to contaminated water supplies.

herbicides Chemicals used to kill weeds.

herbivores Plant-eaters.

highwall The wall of overburden and coal left behind after contour mining of hillsides.

high-yielding grains New varieties of corn, wheat, and rice developed by agricultural research. These varieties produce much more grain per acre than older varieties. They also require more water, pesticides, and fertilizers.

humus Large, stable organic molecules formed in the soil from the breakdown of organic waste materials. Humus contributes to soil fertility by helping to retain water and keeping the soil loose.

hydrocarbons A class of air pollutants derived principally from the operation of internal combustion engines of motor vehicles. These pollutants contribute to photochemical pollution by the reactions they undergo.

hydroelectric energy Electric energy derived from falling or moving water. The water is commonly stored behind a dam and released through penstocks to turn a turbine and generate electricity.

hydrogen economy An energy system that uses hydrogen to store and produce energy. Hydrogen from chemical processing of fossil fuels or from the electrolysis of seawater is used in fuel cells, which in turn generate electricity by combining the hydrogen with oxygen or carbon monoxide.

hydrologic cycle The cycling of water in the environment, from rainfall to runoff to evaporation and back again.

immigration The movement of individuals into a population.

incineration A method of waste disposal in which the waste is burned, sometimes at very high temperatures.

indicated and inferred reserves (of oil or gas) Oil or gas known to exist and likely to be recoverable with the application of additional technology (indicated) and oil or gas for which we already have some limited evidence of existence (inferred). *See also* proved reserves.

inversion A weather phenomenon in which cold air lies close to the earth's surface, trapped by a warm air mass above it. This is the inverse of the normal situation in which temperature decreases with increasing distance from earth.

ionizing radiation Rays or particles that possess enough energy to separate an electron from its atom. Some ionizing radiation is electromagnetic, for instance, x-rays and gamma rays. Other forms are particles such as electrons (beta radiation), neutrons, and the nuclei of helium atoms (alpha radiation).

IPM Integrated pest management, a combination of techniques designed to control pests using a minimum of chemical sprays.

irrigation scheme To supply water, other than natural rainfall, to farmland.

kilowatt A rate of providing electrical energy; equal to 1,000 watts.

kwashiorkor A children's disease caused by protein deficiency.

laeterization The process by which certain tropical soils containing iron harden into a material called laterite when vegetative cover is removed. The resulting soil is hard enough to cut into blocks for building and is no longer suitable for plant growth.

land application of wastewater A set of three different processes (overland flow, spray irrigation, and infiltration-percolation) in which wastewater is applied to the land as a means of treatment. The wastewater should previously have undergone primary treatment.

leaching The movement of a chemical through the soil.

leaching field A system of underground tiles designed to channel the flow from a septic tank into porous soil.

lead A cumulative poison that can cause brain damage and death; it is present in air (from the lead in gasoline), food, and water. It was once in paint as well, and the eating of paint chips by children is a frequent cause of lead poisoning.

lignite A lower form of coal with a little over half the heating value of bituminous or anthracite coal; it constitutes about 4 percent of the U.S. coal energy resource.

limiting factor Whatever nutrient is in shortest supply compared to the amount needed for growth. This factor limits the growth of plants in a particular environment.

liquefied natural gas (LNG) Natural gas made liquid at very low temperatures ($-162°C$) in order to transport it economically via special tankers.

liquid metal fast breeder reactor (LMFBR) A nuclear reactor in which a liquid metal (sodium) circulates through the core, removing the heat from the fission of plutonium. The heat in the liquid metal is eventually used to boil water to steam to turn a turbine. The fuel is plutonium-239 created by neutrons striking the nucleus of uranium-238. The scheme is designed to use uranium-238 rather than uranium-235 because uranium-238 is so much more abundant.

LISA Low Impact Sustainable Agriculture. In this type of agriculture, a farmer chooses agricultural methods, such as integrated pest management, that cause the least immediate harm to the environment. In addition, the long-term effects of farming on the environment, such as erosion and off-farm pollution, are considered. Attempts are made to keep these effects as small as possible, as well.

longwall mining A relatively new method of mining coal underground. The mine roof is allowed to collapse in a controlled way as the mine "room" moves across the coal seam. Greater coal removal and prevention of acid mine drainage are claimed advantages.

loss-of-coolant accident What would happen in a nuclear reactor if the water in the core were lost because of a pipe break. The temperature in the core would rise rapidly as the heat from fission builds up. The fuel rods could melt and radioactive substances would be released through the pipe break if the core were not cooled quickly by the emergency core cooling system.

low-head hydropower Energy generated using water elevations of fifty feet or less. The bulb turbine, a new technology, makes possible relatively efficient capture of energy from low-head dam sites not currently in use for electric generation.

M85 An experimental fuel for automobiles that consists of 85% methanol and 15% gasoline. The gasoline promotes low temperature starting, makes the fuel taste bad, and causes the flame from a fuel fire to be more visible.

magnetohydrodynamics (MHD) Process in which hot gases from the burning of a fossil fuel are seeded with potassium, which then ionizes. Electric current is extracted from the hot gases, which are then used to boil water to steam for conventional electric generation.

malnourished Referring to someone who does not get enough of the various nutrients needed for good health.

marasmus A form of malnutrition caused by feeding infants overdiluted formula using unsterile water.

mariculture The "farming" of marine organisms. This may be done in pens or rafts in coastal waters or in artificially maintained salt-water environments.

marine Having to do with the oceans or salt waters of the earth.

megawatt A term describing the rate at which electricity can be generated by a power plant. One megawatt is 1,000 kilowatts.

metabolism The chemical reactions that take place within a living organism or cell. These reactions include those yielding energy for life processes and those synthesizing new biological materials.

methanol A simple alcohol that is being suggested as an automotive fuel. Although little engine modification would be required, the fuel causes dangerous burns, is poisonous, and might not reduce air pollution much. See M85, above.

methemoglobin A form of hemoglobin in which the iron is oxidized. Methemoglobin is not able to carry oxygen in the bloodstream.

metric ton (or long ton) 1,000 kilograms or about 2,200 pounds, 10% larger than the (short) ton of English measure.

MHD *See* magnetohydrodynamics.

middle distillates That portion of crude oil refined to diesel fuel, kerosene (jet fuel), and home heating oil.

migration The periodic movement of organisms into or out of an area.

mineral resource Chemical element or compound or mixture of compounds extracted in pure form or as an ore from the ground.

monoculture The cultivation of a single species of plant as opposed to mixtures of species, as is usually found in nature.

multiple-use The concept applied to the management of lands in the national forests. The concept allows timbering, mining, recreation, grazing, watershed protection, fishing, wildlife protection, and wilderness as legitimate uses of the same land. The official designation of wilderness, however, most often excludes timbering, mining, and grazing.

mutagen Substance that causes an inheritable change in a cell's genetic material.

mutation An inheritable change in the genetic material of an organism.

National Park Service The managing agency of the National Park System. The National Park Service is within the Department of Interior.

natural gas A gas consisting mainly of methane, a simple hydrocarbon gas. It is derived from chemical and physical processes operating on buried ocean plankton. Nitrogen may be present in the gas as well.

natural selection A difference in reproduction whereby organisms having more advantageous genetic characteristics reproduce more successfully than other organisms. This leads to an increased frequency of those favorable genes or gene combinations in the population.

NEPA National Environmental Policy Act. One of the most important parts of this act is that it requires environmental impact statements. These statements are reports based on studies of how a proposed government project will affect the environment.

neutron A fundamental particle, without any charge, found in the nucleus of an atom. In the fission process, neutrons are unleashed. They strike the nuclei of atoms of uranium-235 and cause these atoms to break apart.

niche Where an organism lives and how it functions in this environment (i.e., what it eats, who its predators are, what activities it carries out).

nitrate (NO_3^-) A salt of nitric acid. Nitrate is a major nutrient for higher plants and also a food additive and water pollutant.

nitrite (NO_2^-) A salt of nitrous acid. Nitrite is a food additive but is very toxic above certain concentrations.

nitrogen oxides (NO_x) A contributor to photochemical air pollution. Nitrogen oxides are produced during high-temperature combustion of fossil fuels. Oxygen and nitrogen from the air produce the pollutant gas. The oxides of nitrogen (nitric oxide and nitrogen dioxide) are both air pollutants, and nitrogen dioxide has been linked to an increase in respiratory illnesses.

non-fuel mineral resources Mineral resources other than coal or oil. Examples include metallic resources such as platinum or aluminum or nonmetallic resources such as sand and salt.

non-point-source water pollution Polluted water, arising typically from rural areas, that enters a receiving body from many small widely scattered sources.

nucleic acids Chemical compounds from which important biological materials (such as the hereditary materials DNA and RNA) are made.

ocean thermal energy conversion (OTEC) A concept now being tested on a pilot scale to use the temperature difference between the warm surface waters of the ocean and the cold deeper waters to produce electrical energy. The warmer waters would boil a working fluid to a "steam," which would turn a turbine. The colder water would condense the vapor for reuse.

old growth forest Virgin forest that has never been cut. Forests of this type contain trees that are hundreds of years old.

oil A substance derived from chemical and physical processes operating on buried ocean plankton. It consists mainly of liquid hydrocarbons (compounds of hydrogen and carbon). Nitrogen and sulfur are other elements that may be present.

oil shale Shale rock containing oil; *see* shale oil.

oligotrophic Referring to water that has low concentrations of plant nutrients.

organic chemical A chemical composed mainly of carbon, hydrogen, and oxygen.

organic wastes A class of water pollutants composed of organic substances. When these substances are oxidized by bacteria and other species, oxygen is removed from the water. When high concentrations of organic wastes are present, aquatic species may be deprived of the oxygen necessary for survival.

organophosphates A major group of synthetic pesticides consisting of organic molecules containing the element phosphorus. A number of them are extremely toxic to humans; however, they do not persist in the environment for long periods of time.

oxidant A chemical compound that can oxidize substances that oxygen in the air cannot. Ozone, a prominent photochemical air pollutant, is an oxidant, as are nitrogen dioxide, PAN compounds, and aldehydes. Levels of photochemical pollution are often reported as oxidant levels.

ozonation The process of treating water intended for drinking with ozone gas in order to kill microorganisms. Although this process is used widely in Europe, most water engineers in the United States prefer chlorination because of the simple test for free chlorine.

ozone A compound made up of three atoms of oxygen (O_3). The oxygen we need to breathe is O_2. In the lower atmosphere ozone is an air pollutant. In the stratosphere, ozone is necessary to block damaging ultraviolet rays from the sun.

particulate matter A class of air pollutants consisting of solid particles and liquid droplets of many different chemical types. Examples are fly ash, compounds from photochemical reactions, metal sulfates, sulfuric acid droplets, and lead oxides. Particles will soil and corrode materials; they may also soil and react chemically with the leaves of plants. Particles are linked firmly to increases in human respiratory illnesses, and some particle types are suspected of causing human cancer.

pathogens Disease-producing microorganisms, including bacteria, viruses, and protozoa.

PCBs Polychlorinated biphenyls; a family of chemicals similar in structure to the pesticide DDT and having a variable number of chlorine atoms attached to a double ring structure.

peak-load pricing The practice of raising the price of electricity during the hours (or season) of peak demand and lowering the price during times of slack demand. The goal is to level the rate of electric usage through time and decrease the need for bringing into service new electrical-generating capacity to meet peak demands.

peat A low-heating-value fossil fuel derived from wood that decayed while immersed in water.

permafrost Frozen layer of soil underlying the arctic tundra.

persistence The length of time a pesticide remains in the soil or on crops after it is applied.

pesticide A substance that kills pests such as insects or rats.

petroleum A mixture of organic compounds formed from the bodies of organisms that died in prehistoric times. This complex mixture is separated into less complex fractions, such as gasoline, heating oil, asphalt, and so on.

pH A measure of the acidity or alkalinity of solutions. Solutions with a pH of 8 or above are alkaline or basic; solutions with a pH of 6 or below are acidic.

photochemical air pollution Air pollutants such as nitrogen dioxide, ozone, aldehydes, and PAN compounds produced as a consequence of sunlight-stimulated reactions involving nitrogen oxides and hydrocarbons. The various compounds have differing effects, but plants are damaged by ozone and PAN compounds. Eye and throat irritation and respiratory illness are common effects of these substances on people.

photosynthesis The process by which green plants use carbon dioxide, water, and the energy in sunlight to synthesize organic materials.

photovoltaic conversion A process in which silicon cells are used to convert sunlight directly to electricity. Although costs of cells are high, attempts to make photovoltaic conversion economical are underway.

phthalates Chemical compounds that are esters of phthalic acid and various alcohols; for example, diethyl phthalate.

physical-chemical wastewater treatment A relatively new set of methods aimed at replacing conventional primary and secondary wastewater treatment processes. Physical-chemical treatment is designed to remove phosphorus by precipitation and settling and to remove dissolved organics by adsorption on carbon particles.

phytoplankton Microscopic, drifting plant species.

pica The habit of eating nonfood items; it occurs among about 50% of all children, independent of social or economic class, beginning at about one year of age. Such items as paper, string, dirt, and paint chips may be eaten.

plankton Microscopic plants and animals that drift in water, mostly at the mercy of currents and tides.

plutonium A radioactive element of high atomic weight, produced in nuclear reactors. Plutonium can be used to make atomic weapons or as fuel for nuclear reactors.

point-source water pollution Water pollutants that arise in urban areas or from industries and that enter a receiving body from a single pipe.

polyculture Growing several crops together or one right after another.

population (natural) The members of a species living together in a particular locality.

population profile A bar graph showing the number of people in each age group in a population.

power tower A method to generate central station electricity using the sun as the energy source. The sun's rays are focused by banks of mirrors on a tower to provide the heat to boil water to steam. The steam turns a turbine for conventional electric generation.

precipitation In ecological terms, the amount of water that falls as rain or snow on a given area.

predator A creature that eats another.

pressurized-water reactor (PWR) A reactor in which the water passing through the core is heated by the fission process but does not boil because it is under great pressure. This extremely hot water is used to boil to steam a parallel but separate stream of water in a steam generator. The steam in this second loop is used to turn a turbine for electric generation. *See also* boiling water reactor.

prey A creature that is eaten by another.

primary production The energy captured by plants in photosynthesis. Gross primary production measures the amount of energy stored as organic materials, as well as that used in respiration by the plant. Net production includes only the amount stored.

primary recovery The quantity of oil that flows out of a well by natural pressure alone; it averages about 20% of the oil in place.

primary treatment of wastewater The first major wastewater treatment process in the typical set of processes used in American cities. Primary treatment consists of allowing the organic particles that were in suspension to settle out of the flowing water.

producers Organisms who produce organic materials by photosynthesis.

productivity Amount of living tissue (plant or animal) produced by a population in a given period of time.

promoter A substance that does not cause cancer itself but that can act to cause another material to be carcinogenic.

pronatalist program A government program that encourages families to have more children.

protein A class of chemicals found in food and required by humans for growth and normal functioning.

proved reserves (of oil or gas) Oil or gas *known* to be contained in the portions of fields that have already been drilled and which is profitable to recover.

pumped storage The pumping of water to a high elevation at times when spare electric capacity is available. The water can then be released from its high pool through the turbine pump that raised it in order to generate electricity. Such releases are made when the existing basic generating capacity is insufficient to meet electrical demand.

PWR *See* pressurized-water reactor.

quad One quadrillion (a million billion) Btu. The annual energy use of an entire nation is often given in quads.

radioactivity Particles or rays emitted by the decay of unstable elements. Examples are alpha, beta, and gamma radiation (*see also* ionizing radiation).

radioactive waste Waste containing radioactive materials, that is, materials that break down spontaneously with release of particles or rays.

rate of growth A country's growth rate is the rate of increase (birth rate minus death rate) plus the rates of change due to immigration (people arriving) and emigration (people leaving).

rate of natural increase The birth rate minus the death rate of a population.

recharge Applied to groundwater, the replacement of water that has been withdrawn from the ground. The replacement can occur from surface or other underground sources.

reclamation of surface-mined land In the mining of coal, the replacement of overburden and topsoil and revegetation of the land.

refining (oil) Separation of crude oil into less complex mixtures of substances (i.e., gasolines, kerosenes, heating oils, waxes, tars, asphalts).

refuse banks (or "gob" piles) The wastes from a coal preparation plant, which washes and grades coal. The wastes include low-grade coal, shale, slate, and coal dust.

reservoir The body of water backed up behind a dam; also refers to an accumulation of underground water.

residue The amount of a chemical left in a food by the time it reaches the consumer.

resistance Condition that occurs when a particular germ or pest is no longer killed by a drug or pesticide.

room-and-pillar coal mining A method of underground coal mining in which pillars are left in the mine in a regular pattern in order to support the mine roof while the coal mining is going on.

runoff Water that comes to the earth as rain and runs off the land into lakes, rivers, and oceans.

salinity Salt content.

salinization The accumulation of salts in soil. Eventually, the salt buildup prevents plant growth.

sand filtration *See* filtration.

satellite solar power station The idea of installing photovoltaic cells in a satellite orbiting earth. Electricity generated by the cells would be beamed to earth via microwave. The system would be enormously costly if ever undertaken.

scrubbers A class of devices (differing widely in their chemical process steps) that remove sulfur oxides from the stack gases of coal-burning power plants.

secondary recovery Techniques such as gas injection or water injection to place increased pressure on oil in a deep reservoir and thus force more of it to the surface.

secondary treatment of wastewater The second major wastewater treatment process in the typical series of processes used in American cities. Two processes, the trickling filter and the activated sludge plant, are used to remove dissolved organic material from wastewater.

second law of thermodynamics Law stating that when energy is changed from one form into another, some energy is always unavailable or lost as heat. Another way of stating this explains the inefficiency of electric power generation—namely, that a natural limit exists on the extent to which heat can be converted to work and hence to electricity. The limit in the conversion of heat to work is about 45%–50% conversion.

sediment The fine particles of soil washed off land by the erosion of water. These are the particles that become suspended in flowing water and ultimately settle to stream or lake bottoms or form river deltas.

seed-tree cutting A logging practice that leaves behind trees to seed the area for regrowth.

selection cutting Cutting only mature timber from an area.

septic tank A device used in rural areas for partial treatment of wastewater. The device is a concrete or metal tank that detains wastes from a home for up to 3 days, providing settling of solids and partial treatment of dissolved organics.

shale oil A hydrocarbon liquid derived by retorting (cooking) crushed oil-bearing rock. The hydrocarbon liquid is known as kerogen. The United States may have the equivalent of 600 billion barrels of oil in the shale rock of Colorado and neighboring states.

shelterwood cutting A three-stage cutting plan in which (1) defective trees are first removed; (2) the stand is "opened" by further cutting 10–15 years later; and (3) the mature trees are cut after seedlings are well established.

siltation The dropping or settling of sediments to the bottom of a body of water. Water brought to a halt behind a dam drops much of its load of sediment into the reservoir; the effectiveness of the reservoir for water storage is thus decreased.

smog The term originally coined to describe the "fog" of photochemical air pollution.

solvent-refined coal *See* coal liquefaction.

species All those individuals that are able to interbreed successfully (if they are given the opportunity to do so), that share ties of common parentage, and that share a common pool of hereditary material.

stratification (of water) Situation that occurs when the water at different levels of a lake or reservoir is at different temperatures and little mixing occurs between layers.

stratosphere The layer of the earth's atmosphere directly above the troposphere, which is the lowest layer. Scientists are concerned because ozone levels in the stratosphere are declining and carbon dioxide levels are increasing.

subsidence Collapse of land as a result of the empty spaces left underground by coal mining. Roads may buckle and sewer lines and gas mains may crack as a result of severe subsidence if it occurs in developed areas.

succession A natural process in which the species found in a given area change conditions to make the area less suitable for themselves and more suitable for other species. This continues until the climax vegetation for the area grows up.

sulfur oxides A class of air pollutants from the burning of fossil fuels (mainly coal and oil) containing sulfur. The sulfur is oxidized to sulfur dioxide and sulfur trioxide when the fuel is burned. The oxides and the acids they form with water vapor will damage building materials like marble, mortar, and metals and they damage plants and the health of people. Respiratory illnesses are increased during times when the levels of sulfur oxides are elevated.

surface mining (or strip mining) The practice of removing coal by excavation of the surface without an underground mine. Area strip mining is practiced on flat lands. Contour strip mining is used on hillsides.

sustainable development Development that attempts to cause the least possible permanent, harmful impact on the environment.

sustainable society Sustainable societies are those that can be sustained indefinitely by their environment. They are, in other words, societies that do not use up essential parts of their environment that cannot be regenerated.

sustained yield A quantity of timber less than or equal to the natural increase in that area occurring over the past time period. Increase is measured in volume units, such as cubic feet.

synthetic pesticide A pesticide that was invented in a laboratory and not produced by any natural system.

taiga Northern coniferous forest biome, characterized by spruce and other coniferous trees.

tailings The remaining waste materials after a substance such as uranium or iron has been extracted from ore.

tar sand A sand coated with bitumen, an oily black hydrocarbon liquid. Extensive tar sand deposits exist in Alberta, Canada, and smaller deposits are in Utah. In the Alberta sands, about two barrels of hydrocarbon liquid can be recovered from three tons of sand; the liquid can be refined to all grades of petroleum.

teratogen A substance that causes a defect during prenatal development.

tertiary treatment of wastewater The third major component of wastewater treatment plants. In tertiary treatment, which consists of a number of processes, nitrogen in its various chemical forms is removed; phosphorus is removed by precipitation and settling; and resistant organics are re-moved by passage through towers containing activated carbon.

tetraethyl lead An organic lead compound that has been added to gasoline to increase octane and decrease "engine knocking."

thermal pollution Pollution of the environment with heat.

threatened species A species that is not yet endangered but whose populations are heading in that direction.

threshold The level or concentration at which an effect can be detected.

tidal power The capturing of the energy of the tides as electrical energy by the use of dams and a turbine/generator unit. Both the receding and arriving tides can be channeled through the bulb turbine to generate electricity.

tolerance The amount or residue of a pesticide or drug legally allowed in food.

topsoil The top few inches of soil, which are rich in organic matter and plant nutrients.

toxic substance A material harmful to life.

toxin A naturally produced poisonous material secreted by certain organisms.

trickling filter A device for removing dissolved organics from wastewater. In the device, the wastewater is distributed across a bed of stones on which a microbial slime is growing. The microbes remove the dissolved organics by converting them to simpler substances.

trophic structure How the various organisms in a community obtain their nourishment.

tropical forest A biome characterized by high rainfall levels, even warm temperatures, and vegetation that grows in three levels: an overarching canopy of trees, a few trees that break through the canopy, and an understory of shrubs and vines.

tundra Arctic biome characterized by a permanently frozen subsoil and low-growing plants such as mosses and lichens.

turbidity A measure of how clear water is. It depends on the amount of suspended solid materials or organisms in the water.

typhoid An intestinal disease caused by specific bacteria. The disease can be spread by water polluted by human wastes.

ultraviolet light A part of the electromagnetic spectrum comprising light waves that are shorter than visible violet light rays but longer than x-rays. These light rays can contribute to the development of skin cancer but are normally absorbed in the upper atmosphere by ozone.

undernourished Referring to a person who does not get enough Calories to maintain body weight with normal activity.

undeveloped nation A country with little technological development.

undiscovered resources (of oil and gas) Oil or gas not yet discovered by drilling but that, on the basis of geological and statistical evidence, is expected to be found eventually.

upwelling A result of offshore winds that "push" surface waters away from shore and allow nutrient-rich bottom waters to rise from the deeper oceans.

uranium-235 An isotope of uranium normally found in a mixture with uranium-238. Uranium-235 serves as the fuel for light-water nuclear reactors. It can also be used for making atomic bombs.

urbanization The change of the habitat of humans from primarily rural to mainly cities.

U.S. Fish and Wildlife Service The managing agency of the National Wildlife Refuge System. The service is within the Department of Interior.

U.S. Forest Service The managing agency of the National Forests. The Forest Service is in the Department of Agriculture.

waste stabilization lagoon A large shallow pond into which wastewater is discharged for biological treatment. Solids settle out, and dissolved organics are removed by microbes in the pond. The device is used primarily where waste loads are small and when land with no conflicting uses is available inexpensively.

watershed The land area that drains into a particular river, lake, or reservoir.

weather The day-to-day variation in temperature, humidity, air pressure, cloudiness, and amount of precipitation. Thus, weather describes the state of the atmosphere at a certain moment.

wetland Land that is flooded during all or part of the year by water. Examples include marshes, bogs, and swamps.

windmill or wind turbine A machine whose blades are rotated by the wind and that converts the wind energy into electricity or work (for example, pumping water).

zero population growth (ZPG) The situation in which birth rates equal death rates. Assuming immigration and emigration are not significant, the population does not grow.

zoning The practice by which local governments designate the allowable uses of a tract or tracts of land as a means of preventing incompatible land uses. Typical zoning classifications are single-family residential, multifamily residential, commercial, and industrial.

zooplankton Microscopic forms of animal life that drift about in water, moving mainly with the currents.

Index

How Much Is a Part per Billion?

A number of environmental problems are defined in terms of parts per million, parts per billion, or even parts per trillion of pollutant chemicals or particles in a given quantity of the resource. These are very small numbers, indeed. But are the numbers so small they can be safely ignored? This, of course, depends on the frame of reference.

The December 1976 issue of *ChemEcology* carried a table compiled by Dr. Warren B. Crumett of the Dow Chemical Company that was designed to show just how small trace concentrations are (Table 1).

Table 1 Trace Concentration Units

Unit	1 part per million (ppm)	1 part per billion (ppb)	1 part per trillion (ppt)
Length	1 inch/16 miles	1 inch/16,000 miles	1 inch/16,000,000 miles (A 6-inch leap on a journey to the sun)
Time	1 minute/2 years	1 second/32 years	1 second/320 centuries
Money	1¢/$10,000	1¢/$10,000,000	1¢/$10,000,000,000
Weight	1 oz salt/32 tons potato chips	1 pinch salt/10 tons potato chips	1 pinch salt/10,000 tons potato chips
Volume	1 drop vermouth/80 fifths of gin	1 drop vermouth/500 barrels of gin	1 drop vermouth/25,000 hogsheads of gin
Area	1 sq ft/23 acres	1 sq ft/36 sq miles	1 sq in./250 sq miles
Quality	1 bad apple/2,000 barrels	1 bad apple/2,000,000 barrels	1 bad apple/2,000,000,000 barrels